Lecture Notes in Computer Science 14621

The series Lecture Notes in Computer Science (LNCS), including its subseries Lecture Notes in Artificial Intelligence (LNAI) and Lecture Notes in Bioinformatics (LNBI), has established itself as a medium for the publication of new developments in computer science and information technology research, teaching, and education.

LNCS enjoys close cooperation with the computer science R & D community, the series counts many renowned academics among its volume editors and paper authors, and collaborates with prestigious societies. Its mission is to serve this international community by providing an invaluable service, mainly focused on the publication of conference and workshop proceedings and postproceedings. LNCS commenced publication in 1973.

Munir Mandviwalla · Matthias Söllner ·
Tuure Tuunanen
Editors

Design Science Research for a Resilient Future

19th International Conference on Design Science Research
in Information Systems and Technology, DESRIST 2024
Trollhättan, Sweden, June 3–5, 2024
Proceedings

 Springer

Editors
Munir Mandviwalla [iD]
Temple University
Philadelphia, PA, USA

Matthias Söllner [iD]
University of Kassel
Kassel, Germany

Tuure Tuunanen [iD]
University of Jyväskylä
Jyväskylä, Finland

ISSN 0302-9743   ISSN 1611-3349 (electronic)
Lecture Notes in Computer Science
ISBN 978-3-031-61174-2   ISBN 978-3-031-61175-9 (eBook)
https://doi.org/10.1007/978-3-031-61175-9

This Springer imprint is published by the registered company Springer Nature Switzerland AG
The registered company address is: Gewerbestrasse 11, 6330 Cham, Switzerland

If disposing of this product, please recycle the paper.

Preface

This volume of Springer LNCS (LNCS 14621) contains the accepted research papers of DESRIST 2024, the 19th International Conference on Design Science Research in Information Systems and Technology. DESRIST 2024 was held from June 3–5, 2024 at the University West in Trollhättan, Sweden. The theme of the conference was Design Science Research for a Resilient Future.

The world of humans has undergone rapid developments of technological innovation during the recent few decades. Consensus exists around the very fact that our modern ways of living and interacting with humans, organizations, and society is heavily influenced by the implications of digital technologies. At the same time, the challenges of coping with the increasing effect of digital technologies creates incentives for humans, organizations, and society to develop knowledge and skills that make them resilient towards emerging relationships with future digital technologies.

The notion of being 'resilient' is defined differently depending on the research context. In general, resilient people demonstrate flexibility, durability, and attitude of optimism, and openness to learning. Resilience on system and society level is becoming critical, as we face environmental challenges and geopolitical tensions, both of which make the digital systems and communication networks at the same time very important and vulnerable. As such, for this conference, we position the notion of a resilient future as a future where humans might have to develop flexible abilities for adapting, recovering, and sensing change.

One thought that arises as we move into the future is: how can the development of knowledge and innovative digital technology help us to develop abilities and skills for a resilient future? Design Science Research (DSR) aims to bridge the development of technologies that are useful for humans, organizations, and society, with the development of research knowledge that contributes to a scientific discourse of methodological and conceptual/theoretical foundations for doing IS-research.

DESRIST 2024 submissions show that the scope and influence of DSR is broadening and increasingly influencing other disciplines. For example, the research track on DSR as a tool and form of entrepreneurship. This shows that the DSR ethos—broad problematization and design of solutions that provide demonstrable utility—resonates well with researchers in different disciplines. It is therefore not surprising that many of the papers presented at DESRIST 2024 and published in the proceedings focus on leveraging DSR to design solutions for problems in an ever-expanding set of domains. The domains range from decentralized finance to sustainability, from group decision making to urban planning, and from learning to research on cancer. The broad range of topics showcase the transdisciplinary nature and value of DSR.

A parallel stream of research extensively discussed at DESRIST 2024 and in the proceedings is improving the methodological and theoretical foundations of DSR. There is an established body of work that guides rigorous and relevant DSR research. However, it is very healthy to see that the theoretical and methodological frontiers of DSR are continuously expanding. The theoretical and methodological advances and the ongoing, ever-expanding application of DSR to problematize and design innovative solutions across domains illustrates the significant contribution DSR can make to designing a resilient future.

This book contains 30 full research papers organized into research tracks included for presentation in the program of DESRIST 2024. With 69 submissions, the acceptance rate for full research papers was less than 45%. The review process was rigorous with every paper receiving on average three substantive double-blind reviews from expert DSR researchers from around the globe. A distinguished group of research track chairs managed the review process and supported the author teams to revise their papers for inclusion in these proceedings. DESRIST 2024 also made significant efforts to expand the DSR community by including an emerging topics track, and accepting 8 research-in-progress papers, 9 prototype demonstrations, and 6 panels, tutorials, and workshops to discuss timely DSR topics. The DESRIST doctoral consortium provided doctoral students with the opportunity to discuss their research with senior faculty.

We send our deepest gratitude to these outstanding track chairs and reviewers for their hard work and dedication on very aggressive time schedules. Thank you to the authors of all the submitted papers for sharing their exciting design science research projects. We hope the opportunity to participate in DESRIST 2024 will have a lasting impact on the quality and productivity of your future research as well as on the future growth and impact of the DESRIST community.

We also acknowledge the enthusiasm and outstanding contributions of the organizers of DESRIST 2024. All chairs and reviewers who contributed to organizing DESRIST 2024 are listed on the following pages, and we would also like express our gratitude to the administration, faculty and staff of University West. Thank you to everyone who contributed to the success of DESRIST 2024.

June 2024

Munir Mandviwalla
Matthias Söllner
Tuure Tuunanen

Organization

Conference Chairs

Amir Haj-Bolouri   University West, Sweden
Matti Rossi   Aalto University, Finland

Program Chairs

Munir Mandviwalla   Temple University, USA
Matthias Söllner   University of Kassel, Germany
Tuure Tuunanen   University of Jyväskylä, Finland

Doctoral Consortium Chairs

Leona Chandra Kruse   University of Agder, Norway
John Venable   Curtin University, Australia

Prototype Chairs

Frederik Möller   Technische Universität Braunschweig, Germany
Thorsten Schoormann   Technische Universität Braunschweig, Germany

Panel and Workshop Chairs

Kieran Conboy   University of Galway, Ireland
Jan Ljungberg   Gothenburg University, Sweden

Local Chair

Gunnar Peterson   University West, Sweden

Website Chair

Anna Hallberg   University West, Sweden

General Chairs

Aalta Van Der Merwe   University of Pretoria, South Africa
Robert Winter   University of St. Gallen, Switzerland

Track Chairs

DSR for a Resilient World (Theme Track)

Abayomi Baiyere   Copenhagen Business School, Denmark
Daniel Beverungen   University of Paderborn, Germany
Netta Iivari   University of Oulu, Finland

General Track

Stefan Morana   Saarland University, Germany
Matthew Mullarkey   University of South Florida, USA
Monica C. Trembley   William & Mary, USA

DSR Methods and Education

Andreas Janson   University of St. Gallen, Switzerland
Alexander Mädche   Karlsruhe Institute of Technology, Germany
Samuli Pekkola   University of Jyväskylä, Finland

DSR in Practice

Jan vom Brocke   University of Münster, Germany
Jan Marco Leimeister   University of St. Gallen, Switzerland
Ali Sunyaev   Karlsruhe Institute of Technology, Germany

Emerging Topics in DSR

Brian Donnellan   Maynooth University, Ireland
Juho Lindman   University of Gothenburg, Sweden
Sarah Hönigsberg   ICN Business School, France

Reviewers

Thomas Auer
Xavier Babu
Christian Bartelheimer
Vincent Beermann
Dennis Benner
Marten Borchers
Lina Bouayad
Julia Bräker
Micha Brugger
Alice Cai
Lu Cao
Noel Carroll
Arturo Castellanos
Friedrich Chasin
Samir Chatterjee
Gabriela Ciolacu
Raffaele Ciriello
Isabelle Comyn-Wattiau
Niall Connolly
William Cook
Dalton Crabtree
Daniel Curto-Millet
Izabel Cvetkovic
Christian Daase
Johannes Damarowsky
Clinton Daniel
Malshika Dias
Ernestine Dickhaut
Till Diesterhöft
Barbara Dinter
Andreas Drechsler
Jana Driller
Philipp Ebel
Paula Elsensohn
Cecilie Falch
Amjad Fayoumi
Andreas Fink
Leonie Rebecca Freise
Michael Gau
Leonhard Gebhardt
Mona Ghazi
Maren Gierlich-Joas
Erica Giuliani

Philipp Gordetzki
Ewa Grabska
Maximilian Greiner
Kirsten Greiner
Linda Grogorick
Jonas Gunklach
Richard Guse
Philipp Hagenhoff
Veikko Halttunen
M. Redwan Hasan
Marie Hattingh
Daniel Heinz
Markus Helfert
Simon Hemmrich
Martin Henkel
Pascal Henninger
Savindu Herath
Alexander Herwix
Alan Hevner
Sara Hofmann
Jan Holmström
Simo Hosio
Razvan Hrestic
Shanshan Hu
Jukka Huhtamäki
Sami Hyrynsalmi
Ulvi Ibrahimli
Najmul Islam
Anna Sigridur Islind
Jenny Jakobs
Sabine Janzen
Alireza Jaribion
William Jobe
Tobias Käfer
Frank Kammer
Bijan Khosrawi-Rad
Padmashcela Kiiskilä
Gregor Kipping
Lisa Kolb
Niklas Kuehl
Arto Lanamäki
Ulrike Lechner
Hippolyte Lefebvre

Dirk Leffrang
Christiane Lehrer
Florian Leiser
Mahei Manhai Li
Sascha Lichtenberg
Shi Liu
Benedict Lösser
Leonie Manzke
Robert Marohn
Agnieszka Mars
Martin Matzner
Quintin McGrath
Alexander Meier
Rahul Mohanani
Frederik Möller
Devid Montecchiari
Jan Muntermann
Tapera Musungwa
Vasiliki Mylonopoulou
Sanaz Nabavian
Nicole Namyslo
Jarkko Nurmi
Monelo Nxozi
Celine Offerman
Tero Päivärinta
Erik Perjons
Nargis Pervin
Jose Pineda
Itilekha Podder
Zohreh Pourzolfaghar
Joann Quinn
Joni Rajala
Jolita Ralyté
Sascha Rank
Philipp Reinhard
Konstantin Remke
Melanie Reuter-Oppermann
Annamina Rieder
Lara Riefle
Dennis Riehle
Roman Rietsche
Susanne Robra-Bissantz
Chrissann Ruehle
Markus Salo

Nada Sanad
Gerhard Satzger
Till Carlo Schelhorn
Anna Maria Schleimer
Ricarda Schlimbach
Johannes Schneider
Sofia Schöbel
Thorsten Schoormann
Christoph Seckler
Karl Seidenfad
Julia Seitz
Abhishek Sharma
Sumita Sharma
Dominik Siemon
Markus Siepermann
Jonas Sjöström
Grażyna Ślusarczyk
Tom Stablein
Dario Staehelin
Lisa Straub
Gero Strobel
Barbara Strug
Kari Systä
Frank Teuteberg
Marian Thiel de Gafenco
Christoph Tomitza
Simon Trang
Srikar Velichety
Leena Ventä-Olkkonen
Hendrik Wache
Thiemo Wambsganss
Sofie Wass
Laura Watkowski
Pauline Weritz
Lauri Wessel
Mathias Willnat
Axel Winkelmann
Dennis Wischer
Antonia Wurzer
Maija Ylinen
Eva-Maria Zahn
Christian Zeiß
Shiyan Zhang
Philipp Zur Heiden

Contents

DSR Methods and Education

DSR in Practice

Emerging Topics in DSR

DSR for a Resilient World (Theme Track)

Disentangling the Problem Space: A Validated Problem Statement for Sustainability Support Systems

Vincent Beermann[1](✉), Annamina Rieder[2], Falk Uebernickel[1], and Jan vom Brocke[3,4]

[1] Hasso Plattner Institute, University of Potsdam, Potsdam, Germany
{vincent.beermann,falk.uebernickel}@hpi.de
[2] Beedie School of Business, Simon Fraser University, Burnaby, Canada
annamina_rieder@sfu.ca
[3] University of Münster, Münster, Germany
jan.vom.brocke@uni-muenster.de
[4] ERCIS - European Research Center for Information Systems, Münster, Germany
jan.vom.brocke@ercis.org

Abstract. The literature on information systems (IS) has produced empirical evidence that IS can support behavior changes toward sustainability. Leveraging design science research (DSR) methodologies, this paper concentrates on the problem analysis around designing for sustainable behavior, especially by investigating the challenges and potential solutions to resource conservation of energy and water in residential environments. Collaborating with a real estate management firm, we employ the echeloned DSR (eDSR) approach in a field setting, focusing on the problem analysis echelon to refine the problem of encouraging sustainable behaviors among residents. We contribute to the DSR body of knowledge by demonstrating the utility of the eDSR methodology in navigating complex problem spaces, particularly those related to sustainability in IS. We provide a detailed account of our problem-analysis process and offer insights into the role of continuous problem refinement in DSR.

Keywords: Design Science Research · Pro-Environmental Behavior · Decision-Making · Behavior Change

1 Introduction

Implementing sustainable practices is essential to countering the widespread overuse of natural resources. In the evolving landscape of information systems (IS) research, there is a growing recognition of technology's critical role in promoting pro-environmental (i.e., sustainable) behaviors, particularly in conserving resources like energy and water [1]. This paper investigates the challenges and potential solutions for facilitating sustainable behaviors in pursuit of resource conservation, which is defined as the efficient use of resources. In this context, previous studies have shown how technology can lead individuals to reduce their energy and water use [2, 3], successes that set the stage for further exploration of resource conservation.

© The Author(s), under exclusive license to Springer Nature Switzerland AG 2024
M. Mandviwalla et al. (Eds.): DESRIST 2024, LNCS 14621, pp. 3–17, 2024.
https://doi.org/10.1007/978-3-031-61175-9_1

At the same time, design science research (DSR) has emerged as an essential approach to designing IS that addresses such complex challenges as facilitating sustainable behavior. The DSR paradigm traditionally uses IS to solve organizational problems [4]. However, before focusing solely on the solution, the researchers must understand and define the problem [5]. Still, DSR projects are often guided by practice-inspired challenges without a clear understanding or definition of the problem and how to address it [6]. In this situation, DSR researchers must turn an initially ill-defined challenge into a well-defined problem statement to guide the project forward. To manage the complexity of our project, we turned to the echeloned DSR (eDSR) approach [7], focusing on the problem analysis echelon, in which we break down our knowledge path toward a validated problem statement. This paper is characterized by multiple rounds of knowledge increments and continuous refinements of the problems we encountered and includes an assessment of the solvability of our design challenge.

Our project is an ongoing collaboration, initiated in early 2022, with a real estate management firm set in two residential buildings that contain over 1,000 apartments, each equipped with smart metering technology. Central to the project is the design challenge to encourage sustainable behavior through resource conservation among the tenants. Throughout the project, we conducted multiple rounds of qualitative interviews with tenants, held regular meetings with the real estate management firm, held workshops with the property owners, conducted quantitative analyses on consumption patterns, and designed field experiments to test behavioral interventions. However, this paper focuses on communicating the knowledge increments toward a validated problem statement as suggested in the problem analysis echelon of the eDSR framework [7].

With the present paper, we aim to uncover the problems underlying our design challenge and the exploration of its solvability. Our project led us to investigate how the various challenges of encouraging sustainable behavior, such as that the outcomes lie far in the future, that sustainability is fuzzy and abstract, and that the success of sustainable behavior depends on collective action, can be overcome by steering behavior toward optimizing the use of resources through behavioral interventions using sensemaking and habit formation mechanisms.

2 Background

Sustainability has emerged as an essential research stream for the IS community, with the subfield of Green IS gaining increasing prominence [8]. This stream of research explores various strategies for enhancing sustainability and emphasizes the significance of encouraging sustainable behaviors to minimize negative impacts on the environment. A key focus in this area is behavior change, which can be achieved by introducing new sustainable practices or modifying existing ones to make them more eco-friendly. Various strategies can facilitate this change, including implementing mandates and regulations, providing subsidies and price incentives, and applying interventions that do not involve price mechanisms. Central to the effort to change behavior through IS are persuasive systems [9], decision support systems [10], and digital nudging [11], all of which have been shown to be effective in steering behavior toward sustainability.

As the applied Green IS stream is primarily interested in the design, implementation, and evaluation of interventions to reduce carbon emissions, studies in the field investigate the effectiveness of such interventions, especially non-price interventions, which are increasingly appealing to researchers, organizations, and governments because of their subtle, yet effective, methods of influencing behavior. A nudge "is any aspect of the choice architecture that alters people's behavior predictably without forbidding any options or significantly changing their economic incentives" [12, p. 8]. Translated to digital environments, nudges refer to "the use of user-interface design elements to guide people's behavior in digital choice environments" [11, p. 433]. Nudges shape decision-making by leveraging the intuitive (System 1) and reflective (System 2) thinking processes. System 1 is quick, unconscious, and prone to biases, whereas System 2 is deliberate and analytical [13]. Initially, nudges mainly altered the decision environment to exploit System 1 thinking. Still, they also include strategies that engage System 2 thinking, such as providing feedback and setting goals to guide behavior toward a desired outcome [14].

The increase in data availability led engineers and designers to create more personalized and contextualized user experiences, also known as "smart nudges" [15]. These smart nudges leverage the advanced capabilities of artificial intelligence and big data analytics to offer experiences that are interactive, engaging, and tailored to individual preferences [16]. Personalized interventions are more effective in encouraging environmental sustainability than generic strategies are [17]. For example, providing real-time feedback on personal water and energy consumption during showering resulted in a s 22% in resource use [2]. However, the process of changing behavior is complex, and behavior changes, once achieved, can be ephemeral, suggesting that the stability of such effects necessitates further investigation [18].

3   Research Design

To design and implement IS with long-term impact, a good understanding of the problem is crucial. In the DSR literature, the eDSR methodology emerged recently to tackle complex socio-technical challenges in DSR projects [7]. eDSR introduces the concept of "echelons" by dividing DSR projects into smaller, self-contained segments to improve projects' structure, management, and communication. We emphasize eDSR's iterative nature and recognize that a complex project evolves through non-linear cycles. In eDSR, knowledge is shared dynamically without following a strict chronological order. As a result, eDSR is agile and responsive and allows for more precise and adaptable outcomes than traditional approaches, providing an ideal fit for our context.

The eDSR methodology encompasses five stages: (i) problem analysis, (ii) definition of objectives and requirements, (iii) design and development, (iv) demonstration, and (v) evaluation, each contributing to the design knowledge through systematic validation. Perhaps because of eDSR's novelty, it lacks extensive guidelines for communication in each echelon. Hence, our paper proposes knowledge communication within eDSR, focusing on the **problem analysis echelon**.

4 The Problem Analysis Echelon

In the eDSR methodology [7], the problem analysis echelon provides a problem state-ment [19], which is validated based on the degree to which the problem was solved previously and the solvability of the problem, expressed in terms of a continuum, judg-ing the degree to which it may be solved [7]. For validation techniques, we analyzed the literature on intervening toward sustainable behavior, especially resource conservation, and the limitations of existing research. We continuously validated our findings with internal (i.e., tenants, real estate managers, property owners) and external (i.e., experts) stakeholders in workshops, interviews, and regular meetings.

The following sub-sections describe our learning journey through the problem anal-ysis echelon. After understanding the project partner's problem (Sect. 4.1), we focus on the scholarly literature on the problem class of sustainable behavior (Sect. 4.2). Then, we define our problem situation (Sect. 4.3), examine the barriers to sustainable behavior (Sect. 4.4), and check the challenges and solvability in the field (Sect. 4.5). Then, we turn to solvability and analyze behavioral interventions for sustainability (Sect. 4.6). Next, we explore the implementation challenges of these interventions (Sect. 4.7) and investigate the mechanisms to support solving the addressed problems (Sect. 4.8). Our process leads us to a well-defined and validated problem statement that incorporates feedback from stakeholders and experts (Sect. 4.9).

4.1 Understanding the Practitioner's Problem

Our collaboration with the real estate management firm was initiated in light of a mutual interest in promoting sustainable practices by leveraging available technolog-ical advancements; two buildings providing housing for international students in Berlin, Germany, are under the firm's management and were equipped with smart metering devices for monitoring daily electricity, heat, and water consumption.

A kick-off workshop that marked the formal commencement of our project included executing necessary agreements. The management firm's objective was to emerge as a leader in environmental, social, and governance (ESG) initiatives while reducing opera-tional costs. We identified the stakeholders as international student tenants, researchers, the real estate management firm, and property owners interested in cost-effective ESG achievements. One unique context factor emerged as tenants pay an *all-inclusive rent*, diminishing tenants' incentives to conserve resources by adopting sustainable prac-tices despite the broader social benefits. However, an initial survey ($N = 205$) revealed that most tenants (89%) were interested in receiving more insights into their resource consumption.

4.2 Abstracting Sustainable Behavior

With a foundational understanding of the practitioner's problem, we abstract the spe-cific issues into a broader problem class that was identifiable in the existing scholarly literature. We pinpointed sustainable behavior as the category most relevant to our inves-tigation into resource conservation [20]. Sustainable behavior is a class of behavior that seeks to minimize actions' environmental impacts [20]. This concept resonates with the definition of sustainable development, which emphasizes meeting current needs without compromising future generations' ability to meet theirs [23]. Exploring the pro-social aspect of sustainable behavior revealed that sustainable practices often yield widespread social benefits but lack immediate personal gain.

As our context required a specific focus, we investigated behaviors such as conserving electricity, heating energy, or water. Resource conservation is a facet of sustainable behavior, defined as using resources efficiently in everyday activities, including showering, use of electronics, and heating. This notion aligns with the eco-efficiency paradigm of minimizing waste and environmental impact through the prudent use of resources [22]. The objective of eco-efficiency is to improve practices and behaviors to create value while reducing adverse environmental impacts [23].

4.3 Defining Our Problem Situation

Interviews with 22 tenants revealed varied attitudes and motivations behind their consumption patterns. Their environmental attitudes varied significantly from very environmentally conscious ("Every time I can, I care for the environment and use the option that's better for the environment") to not very ecologically conscious ("I don't think I am an environmentally conscious person"). The interviewees also mentioned that external motivators affected their considerations about adapting their behavior ("If our rent depended on our consumption, then I think people would pay more attention"). In addition to the interviews, we analyzed consumption data quantitively to reveal potential avenues for savings, especially for high consumers, as we found a right-skewed distribution of all three types of consumption.

Definition of the Problem Situation: Our problem situation is characterized by the inefficient use of resources in the context of all-inclusive rental agreements, compounded by the tenants' diverse environmental attitudes and motivations. Addressing this problem requires a nuanced understanding of these motivations and the development of strategies that can cater to the needs and motivations of this diverse tenant base.

4.4 Analyzing the Challenges Around Sustainable Behavior

We investigated the literature to understand the challenges of encouraging and enacting sustainable behavior. We identified relevant papers encapsulating the facilitators and barriers to sustainable behavior. Many everyday behaviors have environmental effects—showering uses water and energy—but transitioning to environmentally friendly behaviors entails overcoming significant obstacles, such as disrupting ingrained habits and dealing with inconvenience (e.g., taking shorter showers). In their literature review, White et al. [24] synthesized unique challenges to sustainable behaviors that were central to advancing our understanding of the topic:

The **first challenge** highlights the *long-term horizon* of sustainable actions [24], where tangible benefits are realized only in the distant future, making it difficult for individuals to commit to these behaviors because they prefer immediate rewards [25]. The delayed gratification that characterizes sustainable behavior contrasts sharply with the immediate pleasures of conventional consumption. The **second challenge** focuses on the necessity for *collective action* to achieve social goals [24], which requires widespread community engagement [26], as a single individual's decision to participate alone is likely to have no effect. The need for collective action differentiates the promotion of sustainable behavior from actions like health promotion, which yield individual results. The **third challenge** deals with the *abstract* nature of sustainable behaviors [24] because of their often intangible or uncertain outcomes, unlike the more immediate and tangible results of more traditional behaviors [27]. The abstract nature of sustainable behavior complicates efforts to motivate individuals to engage in sustainability. The **fourth challenge** concerns the *self-other trade-off* [24], where sustainable actions' environmental and social benefits entail individual costs like effort, expense, or compromises on quality [28]. This conflict between personal ease and the greater good is a significant obstacle to sustainable behavior. The **fifth challenge** describes the shift from *automatic to controlled processes* in adopting sustainable behaviors [24]. This shift necessitates conscious effort, such as remembering to bring a reusable shopping bag. Leveraging life changes or adopting a "fresh start" mindset could facilitate new, sustainable habit formation, suggesting the power of viewing sustainability as an opportunity for a new beginning [29].

4.5 Field Check on Challenges and Solvability of Resource Conservation

Armed with a thorough understanding of sustainable behaviors and their challenges, we conducted workshops and meetings with our project partners and stakeholders to discuss the problem understanding and initiate a first exploration of the solvability of our design challenge [7]. We identified two opportunities for intervention: The first is a structural intervention to entice tenants financially by changing the contract agreement from an *all-inclusive* to a *pay-by-use* model, and the second is designing a behavioral intervention using psychological mechanisms to change behavior. Hence, we developed an initial set of solutions that would address the specific contextual factors of our project (i.e., daily measurements of energy and water) and build prototypes to counter the challenges (e.g., focus on the present, including the collective, and make consumption concrete).

We did field checks with the same cohort of tenants as before (see Sect. 4.3) to investigate the challenges and their solvability using prototype artifacts. The interviewees mentioned that a *pay-by-use* model would increase the importance of resource conservation ("[…] Because if I would have to pay for each lamp that I have on, then I wouldn't use every lamp right now"). However, the helpfulness of feedback on consumption, including social references, was appreciated despite not being economically incentivized to save resources ("I think it is nicer to have a comparison between the optimal consumption or, actually, the average level you should maintain", "That is one of my reasons for saying we should be told how much we can consume so that we can monitor against it"). We discussed both opportunity areas with the management firm and the property owner, and it was decided to explore further saving potential under the all-inclusive model.

4.6   Facilitating Sustainable Behavior with Behavioral Interventions

Against this backdrop, we extensively reviewed the literature on behavioral interventions toward sustainability, after which we identified helpful theories and concepts to assess solvability better. Most interventions that foster efficient use of resources center on decision information and assistance. The literature on decision information, such as feedback interventions—often in companion with social norms—has become the most significant stream of literature on reducing resource use. For example, Tiefenbeck et al. [2] use devices to show real-time feedback on water consumption while a user showers. In addition to its 22% reduction in energy and water in private households, the intervention achieved a conservation effect of 11.4% when it was tested in hotels (excluding monetary incentives) [30]. Decision assistance through commitments, goal setting and reminders can also be combined with feedback. For example, Loock et al. [3] show that setting specific energy-reduction goals via a web portal can decrease resource use by 4.18%. However, overly ambitious goals can be counterproductive, as they might be perceived as unattainable, reducing the motivation to pursue them. Interventions that use decision information and assistance overlap with sensemaking. Sensemaking involves an individual's ability to understand, interpret, and give meaning to information, an essential process for breaking unconscious habits and making informed decisions [31]. Including sensemaking functionalities for monitoring, analyzing, and displaying data prompts individuals to reassess their behaviors.

Moreover, including features that enhance interactivity and access to information empowers individuals to participate more thoroughly in understanding and interpreting their environments and carrying out eco-friendly practices [32]. In this context, Seidel et al. [33] outline critical principles, including the presentation of diverse environmental information to raise users' awareness, functionalities for organizing and storing ideas for efficient information management, interactive features like commenting and forums to encourage collaborative approaches and tools for action-planning and feedback to evaluate and guide sustainable actions. By presenting feedback and encouraging commitments, these studies use sensemaking to foster awareness and deliberate action in the efficient and sustainable use of resources. Table 1 gives examples of characteristics of behavioral interventions toward resource conservation found in the literature.

The literature mainly focuses on short-term behavioral interventions, with most studies (67.4%) examining periods shorter than one month [34]. This approach is at odds with the established understanding that forming stable, long-term habits typically requires an average of 66 days [35]. The research's comparative neglect of studies on sustaining habits is a significant oversight, as the durability of behavior is critical for long-term conservation outcomes in repeated activities that consume resources [36]. While behavioral interventions are cost-effective, they are criticized for being "transitory" [18, p. 60], so their long-run effects should be explored. Research on sustainable habits also provides insights into the influence of automatic processes on daily activities, the role of boundaries and context in shaping behavior, and how habits inform our values and perceptions [36]. The complexity of behavior and the time needed to form a habit [37] suggests that simple actions, when aggregated, form a complex behavioral ecosystem.

Table 1. Characteristics of Interventions for Resource Conservation.

Attribute	Characteristic	Example	Implication (see Sect. 4.8)
Type of resource	Electricity, heating, water	[2, 3]	Sensemaking and habit formation are relevant to these types of behaviors
Timing of data provision	Real-time, near-time, batch	[2, 38]	The more immediate the feedback, the better the sensemaking. Repeated feedback is central to habit formation
Medium	Mobile application, web portal, e-mail	[3, 39]	The medium should be closely tied to the target behavior in space and time, facilitating sensemaking and habit formation
Display format	Numeric, symbolic, graphic	[38]	Various formats can prompt reflective thinking and are relevant to sensemaking
Intervention mechanisms	Feedback, social norms, goal setting	[2, 3]	Prompting reflection is relevant to sensemaking, and prompting automatic behavior is crucial for forming habits

4.7 Analyzing the Challenges in the Behavioral Intervention Literature

The literature has presented interventions to overcome the challenges above. Research on nudge interventions, including those that seek to promote sustainable behaviors, were extensively analyzed in meta-analyses like [33, 40, 41], which identify common limitations in the field. Most behavioral intervention studies have a short-term focus, so they do not explore the long-term effects of behavior change. As forming a habit can take months [35, 37], future research needs to consider how sustainable behaviors are maintained over time. We address as our **sixth challenge** that sustainable behaviors must *be maintained over time* to be effective.

Furthermore, the effectiveness of behavioral interventions like nudges varies widely. Sunstein suggests personalized interventions as a solution, highlighting the need to consider individual differences and contextual factors [42]. He advocates targeted nudging, which can be more beneficial and equitable than generic approaches. Research in residential electricity conservation supports this notion by showing that real-time feedback and personalized electricity-saving tips are more effective than general advice or cost feedback, which can, paradoxically, increase consumption [17]. Hence, our **seventh challenge** is ensuring a *loose coupling between the intervention, the decision-maker, and the target behaviors.*

4.8   The Mechanisms for Encouraging Sustainable Behavior

Therefore, two pivotal challenges in influencing sustainable behavior concern how we motivate individuals to initiate sustainable behaviors and, once these behaviors are initiated, how we ensure their maintenance and longevity. Addressing these challenges is central to translating short-term behavioral changes into sustained habits that contribute to long-term resource conservation. We draw on *sensemaking* and *habit formation* to address both challenges. Sensemaking, which refers to how individuals comprehend, interpret, and ascribe meaning to information [43], is a helpful mechanism for transforming unsustainable behaviors into sustainable ones [32]. It encompasses the reflective processing of information that leads (or does not) to behavior. For example, a sensemaking intervention involved a reflective comparison of personal paper use against past consumption and others in an organizational context [31]. Habit formation describes how actions become automatic responses to specific situations through repetition and reinforcement over time [44]. This concept is central to understanding how sustainable behaviors evolve from conscious efforts to routine practices. Habit formation involves repetition of the behavior's context and the rewards that reinforce it [45, 46], which inform us of how eco-friendly actions can be sustained.

4.9   Validated Problem Statement as Design Knowledge

Table 2 summarizes the pieces of the problem. From the problem elements, we have crafted the problem statement, which we validated with the stakeholders of our project: *Facilitating sustainable behaviors involves facing several challenges: the delayed and abstract nature of their outcomes, which are often realized through collective action rather than individual efforts; the perceived and actual costs that are associated with adopting these behaviors; the need to replace unsustainable habits with sustainable ones; the requirement of sustained commitment over time; and the need for interventions to be directly and immediately relevant to the behaviors they encourage.*

Table 2. Problem Elements Derived from the Problem Analysis Echelon.

Problem Element
1. The outcomes of sustainable behaviors will be realized in the future
2. The outcomes of sustainable behaviors are realized through collective action
3. The outcomes of sustainable behaviors are abstract
4. Sustainable behaviors are associated with actual and perceived costs
5. Unsustainable behaviors need to be replaced with sustainable behaviors
6. Sustainable behaviors need to be maintained over time
7. Interventions need to be closely tied to sustainable behaviors in space and time

Solvability Assessment: Besides providing the validated problem statement as design knowledge, the eDSR methodology proposes an assessment of the problem's solvability.

Considering the context's supportive factors (i.e., smart metering technology, budget for technological solution) and the context's challenging factors (e.g., all-in-rent, three target variables of electricity, water, and fuel consumption) and the knowledge we gained from the literature, we consider this problem as challenging to solve yet solvable, requiring multiple iterations of artifact design and evaluation. We rate this problem as a six on a scale from zero (unsolvable) to ten (easily solvable).

5   Discussion

Our problem analysis echelon reveals several key findings. The dynamic nature of sustainability challenges necessitates a continuous and adaptive approach to problem understanding. This approach contrasts with traditional models that often view understanding the problem as a static initial phase of a DSR project. By continuously refining the knowledge of the problem space, we adapted our strategies to emerging insights, which enhanced our solution's relevance and impact. The problem analysis echelon was guided by an iterative approach of using a micro-cycle to create new knowledge through problem analysis and solvability assessment. The cycle included the phases of (i) exploration and understanding, (ii) forming assumptions about the problem/solvability, (iii) testing them in the field, and evaluating and updating our knowledge.

We conceptualized our journey through the problem space in Fig. 1 by illustrating the dialectic approach to defining the problem. We navigated between theory and practice, that is, between abstract concepts and concrete realities, to achieve a balanced definition. This equilibrium ensured the problem space is sufficiently concrete to address fundamental issues—our industry partner's goal—while maintaining a level of generality that enriches theoretical understanding. Figure 1 also introduces the concept of "projectability," which indicates the extent to which the research's context and goals align with existing knowledge, as such alignment affects the project's applicability to other projects [47, 48]. A high level of projectability uses theoretical or scientific insights, whereas a low level relies more on empirical evidence from the field. This process, characterized as a dialectical exchange between generalization and specificity, leads to increments in knowledge over time (dashed circles in Fig. 1) and a validated problem statement that encapsulates our synthesis of the problem (full circle).

Particularly during problem analysis, DSR projects use **problem analysis movements** based on established problem-solving strategies (marked by the arrows with dashed squares in Fig. 1), which offer a structured approach to identifying and understanding problems. These movements guide us through critical initial stages, from understanding the problem's fundamentals to developing and testing theoretical solutions. Our project highlights two main types of movements. The first type progresses *from low to high projectability*, starting with immersing ourselves in the problem by abstracting, conducting root cause analysis, performing morphological analysis, and, finally, theorizing. This process resembles moving from laying the groundwork to testing hypotheses in a lab setting. The second type of movement moves *from high to low projectability*, beginning with defining a clear problem statement and concluding with a field check to assess a solution's feasibility and practicality. This back-and-forth movement ensures a

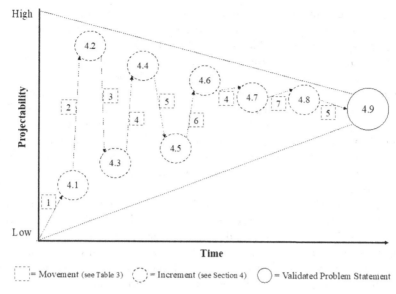

Fig. 1. Conceptual Framework of Problem Space Exploration in eDSR Methodology

comprehensive approach to problem-solving in DSR by balancing theoretical abstraction with practical implementation to find innovative solutions applicable in the real world (Table 3).

Table 3. Problem Analysis Movements in the Problem Analysis Echelon.

Movement	Description
1. Understanding	Grasping the problem's fundamental nature and implications
2. Abstracting	Problem-solving from a theoretical perspective
3. Defining	Clearly articulating and outlining the problem's boundaries
4. Root Cause Analysis	Identifying the problem's underlying cause to address it effectively
5. Field Check	Assessing theoretical concepts' feasibility and realism
6. Morphological Analysis	Examining the output and interactions of various components in a system to understand the whole system
7. Theorizing	Developing theoretical models to explain and solve the problem

Our study contributes to the behavioral literature on nudging and sustainable behavior in several ways. First, our research underscores the importance of context in designing interventions for sustainable behavior. The effectiveness of these interventions is a function of not only their design but also how well they align with the target population's needs, values, and behaviors. Addressing behavior with a "mass" approach leads to high heterogeneity in outcomes and may leave considerable room for improvement [34, 40, 42]. This finding resonates with the growing emphasis on personalized and context-aware approaches to problem-solving [15, 49]. Second, our study contributes to what we know about long-term behavior changes. Unlike most research focusing on short-term interventions [34], our work highlights the need for strategies promoting sustained behavioral change. This long-term perspective is central to addressing sustainability challenges requiring ongoing commitment and adoption [36, 50]. Third, our study highlights the importance of analyzing what motivates individuals to engage in sustainable behavior. Few studies investigate resource conservation practices without monetary motive [30]. While, for example, private households have a personal economic interest in saving resources, our study addresses sustainability as an entirely pro-social activity, not monetary [21].

Our study also makes two methodological contributions. First, we demonstrate the applicability and effectiveness of the eDSR methodology in managing the complexities of DSR projects [7]. With its structured yet flexible approach, the eDSR methodology proved instrumental in our ability to navigate the evolving problem space of our sustainability project. It allowed us to break the research process into manageable segments, each with its specific focus and validation criteria, ensuring that each research phase was responsive to the current understanding of the problem space. Second, our study contributes to the discourse on understanding problems in DSR [5], a continuous, integral aspect of the research process. This perspective is particularly pertinent in complex and dynamic problem spaces like sustainability, where new challenges and opportunities continually emerge and need time and space to be found and addressed. In this context, we identified the need to continuously update our knowledge of the problem and the solvability of the design challenge through multiple increments.

The findings of our study have implications for both researchers and practitioners in the fields of IS and DSR. For researchers, our study highlights the need for flexible and adaptive methodologies to accommodate the evolving nature of complex problem spaces. For practitioners, particularly those in the sustainability domain, our study underscores the importance of continual engagement with the problem space to develop effective and contextually relevant interventions. Future research could explore the application of the eDSR methodology in other complex problem spaces. Further investigation into the long-term effectiveness of the interventions designed using this methodology, particularly in the context of sustainable behavior changes, is also needed.

Acknowledgments. We thank our project partner, *Cresco Immobilien Verwaltungs GmbH*, whose expertise and insights were invaluable in completing this work.

Disclosure of Interests. The authors have no competing interests to declare regarding this article.

References

1. Beermann, V., Rieder, A., Uebernickel, F.: Green nudges: how to induce pro-environmental behavior using technology. International Conference on Information Systems Proceedings (2022). https://aisel.aisnet.org/icis2022/hci_robot/hci_robot/15

2. Tiefenbeck, V., et al.: Overcoming salience bias: how real-time feedback fosters resource conservation. Manag. Sci. **64**(3), 1458–1476 (2018). https://doi.org/10.1287/mnsc.2016.2646
3. Loock, C.-M., Staake, T., Thiesse, F.: Motivating energy-efficient behavior with green IS: an investigation of goal setting and the role of defaults. MIS Q. 1313–1332 (2013)
4. Gregor, S., Hevner, A.R.: Positioning and presenting design science research for maximum impact. MIS Q. **37**(2), 337–355 (2013). https://doi.org/10.25300/MISQ/2013/37.2.01
5. Maedche, A., Gregor, S., Morana, S., Feine, J.: Conceptualization of the problem space in design science research. In: Tulu, B., Djamasbi, S., Leroy, G. (eds.) DESRIST 2019. LNCS, vol. 11491, pp. 18–31. Springer, Cham (2019). https://doi.org/10.1007/978-3-030-19504-5_2
6. Sein, M.K., Henfridsson, O., Purao, S., Rossi, M., Lindgren, R.: Action design research. MIS Q. **35**(1), 37 (2011). https://doi.org/10.2307/23043488
7. Tuunanen, T., Winter, R., Vom Brocke, J.: Dealing with complexity in design science research - a methodology using design echelons. MIS Q. (2023)
8. Melville, N.P.: Information systems innovation for environmental sustainability. MIS Q. **34**(1), 1 (2010). https://doi.org/10.2307/20721412
9. Shevchuk, N., Oinas-Kukkonen, H.: Exploring green information systems and technologies as persuasive systems: a systematic review of applications in published research (2016)
10. Seok, H., Nof, S.Y., Filip, F.G.: Sustainability decision support system based on collaborative control theory. Annu. Rev. Control. **36**(1), 85–100 (2012). https://doi.org/10.1016/j.arcontrol.2012.03.007
11. Weinmann, M., Schneider, C., vom Brocke, J.: Digital nudging. Bus. Inf. Syst. Eng. **58**(6), 433–436 (2016). https://doi.org/10.1007/s12599-016-0453-1
12. Thaler, R.H., Sunstein, C.R.: Nudge: improving decisions about health, wealth, and happiness. In: Nudge: Improving Decisions About Health, Wealth, and Happiness, pp. x, 293. Yale University Press, New Haven (2008)
13. Kahneman, D.: Thinking, Fast and Slow, 1st edn. Farrar, Straus and Giroux, New York (2013)
14. Münscher, R., Vetter, M., Scheuerle, T.: A review and taxonomy of choice architecture techniques: choice architecture techniques. J. Behav. Decis. Mak. **29**(5), 511–524 (2016). https://doi.org/10.1002/bdm.1897
15. Mele, C., Russo Spena, T., Kaartemo, V., Marzullo, M.L.: Smart nudging: how cognitive technologies enable choice architectures for value co-creation. J. Bus. Res. **129**, 949–960 (2021). https://doi.org/10.1016/j.jbusres.2020.09.004
16. Schuetz, S., Venkatesh, V.: Research perspectives: the rise of human machines: how cognitive computing systems challenge assumptions of user-system interaction. J. Assoc. Inf. Syst 460–482 (2020). https://doi.org/10.17705/1jais.00608
17. Buckley, P.: Prices, information and nudges for residential electricity conservation: a meta-analysis. Ecol. Econ. **172**, 106635 (2020). https://doi.org/10.1016/j.ecolecon.2020.106635
18. Gillingham, K., Stock, J.H.: The cost of reducing greenhouse gas emissions. J. Econ. Perspect. **32**(4), 53–72 (2018)
19. Mullarkey, M.T., Hevner, A.R.: An elaborated action design research process model. Eur. J. Inf. Syst. **28**(1), 6–20 (2019). https://doi.org/10.1080/0960085X.2018.1451811
20. Steg, L., Vlek, C.: Encouraging pro-environmental behaviour: an integrative review and research agenda. J. Environ. Psychol. **29**(3), 309–317 (2009). https://doi.org/10.1016/j.jenvp.2008.10.004
21. Wced, S.W.S.: World commission on environment and development. Our Common Future **17**(1), 1–91 (1987)
22. Hauschild, M.Z.: Better – but is it good enough? On the need to consider both eco-efficiency and eco-effectiveness to gauge industrial sustainability. Procedia CIRP **29**, 1–7 (2015). https://doi.org/10.1016/j.procir.2015.02.126
23. Huppes, G., Ishikawa, M.: Eco-efficiency and its xsTerminology. J. Ind. Ecol. **9**(4), 43–46 (2005). https://doi.org/10.1162/108819805775247891

24. White, K., Habib, R., Hardisty, D.J.: How to SHIFT consumer behaviors to be more sustainable: a literature review and guiding framework. J. Mark. **83**(3), 22–49 (2019). https://doi.org/10.1177/0022242919825649
25. Hardisty, D.J., Weber, E.U.: Discounting future green: money versus the environment. J. Exp. Psychol. Gen. **138**(3), 329–340 (2009). https://doi.org/10.1037/a0016433
26. Bamberg, S., Rees, J., Seebauer, S.: Collective climate action: determinants of participation intention in community-based pro-environmental initiatives. J. Environ. Psychol. **43**, 155–165 (2015). https://doi.org/10.1016/j.jenvp.2015.06.006
27. Reczek, R.W., Trudel, R., White, K.: Focusing on the forest or the trees: how abstract versus concrete construal level predicts responses to eco-friendly products. J. Environ. Psychol. **57**, 87–98 (2018). https://doi.org/10.1016/j.jenvp.2018.06.003
28. Luchs, M.G., Kumar, M.: 'Yes, but this other one looks better/works better': how do consumers respond to trade-offs between sustainability and other valued attributes? J. Bus. Ethics **140**(3), 567–584 (2017). https://doi.org/10.1007/s10551-015-2695-0
29. Price, L.L., Coulter, R.A., Strizhakova, Y., Schultz, A.E.: The fresh start mindset: transforming consumers' lives. J. Consum. Res. **45**(1), 21–48 (2018). https://doi.org/10.1093/jcr/ucx115
30. Tiefenbeck, V., Wörner, A., Schöb, S., Fleisch, E., Staake, T.: Real-time feedback promotes energy conservation in the absence of volunteer selection bias and monetary incentives. Nat. Energy **4**(1), 35–41 (2019). https://doi.org/10.1038/s41560-018-0282-1
31. Degirmenci, K., Recker, J.: Breaking bad habits: a field experiment about how routinized work practices can be made more eco-efficient through IS for sensemaking. Inf. Manage. **60**(4), 103778 (2023). https://doi.org/10.1016/j.im.2023.103778
32. Seidel, S., Recker, J., vom Brocke, J.: Sensemaking and sustainable practicing: functional affordances of information systems in green transformations. MIS Q. **37**(4), 1275–1299 (2013). https://doi.org/10.25300/MISQ/2013/37.4.13
33. Seidel, S., Chandra Kruse, L., Székely, N., Gau, M., Stieger, D.: Design principles for sensemaking support systems in environmental sustainability transformations. Eur. J. Inf. Syst. **27**(2), 221–247 (2018). https://doi.org/10.1057/s41303-017-0039-0
34. Nisa, C.F., Bélanger, J.J., Schumpe, B.M., Faller, D.G.: Meta-analysis of randomised controlled trials testing behavioural interventions to promote household action on climate change. Nat. Commun. **10**(1), 4545 (2019). https://doi.org/10.1038/s41467-019-12457-2
35. Lally, P., van Jaarsveld, C.H.M., Potts, H.W.W., Wardle, J.: How are habits formed: modelling habit formation in the real world. Eur. J. Soc. Psychol. **40**(6), 998–1009 (2010). https://doi.org/10.1002/ejsp.674
36. Linder, N., Giusti, M., Samuelsson, K., Barthel, S.: Pro-environmental habits: an underexplored research agenda in sustainability science. Ambio **51**(3), 546–556 (2022). https://doi.org/10.1007/s13280-021-01619-6
37. Buyalskaya, A., Ho, H., Milkman, K.L., Li, X., Duckworth, A.L., Camerer, C.: What can machine learning teach us about habit formation? Evidence from exercise and hygiene. Proc. Natl. Acad. Sci. **120**(17), e2216115120 (2023). https://doi.org/10.1073/pnas.2216115120
38. Allcott, H.: Social norms and energy conservation. J. Public Econ. **95**(9–10), 1082–1095 (2011). https://doi.org/10.1016/j.jpubeco.2011.03.003
39. Schultz, P.W., Messina, A., Tronu, G., Limas, E.F., Gupta, R., Estrada, M.: Personalized normative feedback and the moderating role of personal norms: a field experiment to reduce residential water consumption. Environ. Behav. **48**(5), 686–710 (2014). https://doi.org/10.1177/0013916514553835
40. Mertens, S., Herberz, M., Hahnel, U.J.J., Brosch, T.: The effectiveness of nudging: a meta-analysis of choice architecture interventions across behavioral domains. Proc. Natl. Acad. Sci. **119**(1), e2107346118 (2022). https://doi.org/10.1073/pnas.2107346118
41. Beshears, J., Kosowsky, H.: Nudging: progress to date and future directions. Organ. Behav. Hum. Decis. Process. **161**, 3–19 (2020). https://doi.org/10.1016/j.obhdp.2020.09.001

42. Sunstein, C.R.: The distributional effects of nudges. Nat. Hum. Behav. **6**(1), 9–10 (2021). https://doi.org/10.1038/s41562-021-01236-z

43. Weick, K.E.: Sensemaking in organizations. In: Foundations for Organizational Science. Sage Publications, Thousand Oaks (1995)

44. Wood, W., Rünger, D.: Psychology of Habit. Annu. Rev. Psychol. **67**(1), 289–314 (2016). https://doi.org/10.1146/annurev-psych-122414-033417

45. Neal, D.T., Wood, W., Quinn, J.M.: Habits—a repeat performance. Curr. Dir. Psychol. Sci. **15**(4), 198–202 (2006). https://doi.org/10.1111/j.1467-8721.2006.00435.x

46. Schultz, W.: Behavioral theories and the neurophysiology of reward. Annu. Rev. Psychol. **57**, 87–115 (2006)

47. Baskerville, R., Pries-Heje, J.: Projectability in design science research. J. Inf. Technol. Theory Appl. **20**(1) (2019)

48. Vom Brocke, J., Winter, R., Hevner, A., Maedche, A.: Special issue editorial–accumulation and evolution of design knowledge in design science research: a journey through time and space. J. Assoc. Inf. Syst. **21**(3), 520–544 (2020). https://doi.org/10.17705/1jais.00611

49. Mills, S.: Finding the 'nudge' in hypernudge. Technol. Soc. **71**, 102117 (2022). https://doi.org/10.1016/j.techsoc.2022.102117

50. Stern, P.C.: A reexamination on how behavioral interventions can promote household action to limit climate change. Nat. Commun.Commun. **11**(1), 918 (2020). https://doi.org/10.1038/s41467-020-14653-x

Let Citizens Speak Up: Designing Intelligent Online Participation for Urban Planning

Marten Borchers[1]([✉]) [ID], Maren Gierlich-Joas[2] [ID], Navid Tavanapour[1] [ID],
and Eva Bittner[1] [ID]

[1] University of Hamburg, Hamburg, Germany
{marten.borchers,navid.tavanapour,eva.bittner}@uni-hamburg.de
[2] Copenhagen Business School, Copenhagen, Denmark
mg.digi@cbs.dk

Abstract. Urbanization and the transformation toward sustainability pose new challenges to governments, leading to an increase in citizen participation in urban planning. Due to the demand for scalability, urban participation is often conducted online. However, past projects showed that the asynchronous and impersonal exchange reduces the value of citizens' submissions as inquiries are omitted. Thus, this study investigates how to design an IT artifact to support citizens in contributing to online participation in urban planning projects. To do so, we initiated a design science research project. We analyzed the literature to define issues, formulate meta-requirements, and derive design principles to develop and qualitatively evaluate an AI-based prototype that enables immediate responses to citizens considering their contributions. This study contributes to the field of information systems with prescriptive knowledge. Furthermore, this study can guide practitioners in citizen participation in urban planning in building and utilizing digital tools to support citizens in contributing to subsequent processes.

Keywords: Online Citizen Participation · Urban Planning · Artificial Intelligence · Design Science Research

1 Introduction

Governments are confronted with enormous challenges like urbanization [62] and the transformation toward sustainability due to climate change [42], which are affecting the way how we build and live [56]. As many authors describe, acceptable and feasible solutions that provide public value are required [48]. To achieve that, many scientists, governments, and citizens argue to include citizens' opinions through participation [56], which led to an increase in online participation during the last decade [1] for urban planning. This and the demand scalability led to the development of urban participation platforms, like Decidim Madrid [52] and CONSUL [55]. Besides the many advantages, online participation is not comparable to on-site face-to-face participation [43, 64]. Due to asynchronous communication, citizens can participate over several weeks, which reduces interactions due to a lack of immediate response and exchange [54, 57], resulting

M. Mandviwalla et al. (Eds.): DESRIST 2024, LNCS 14621, pp. 18–32, 2024.
https://doi.org/10.1007/978-3-031-61175-9_2

in insufficient and vague contributions [50]. This aggravates public value creation in decision-making processes for urban planners and public authorities if citizens' needs and requirements are difficult to understand and can be misinterpreted [56]. The financial and political consequences of this are high and can result in a loss of trust [33]. Therefore, comprehensive information about the needs and requirements of citizens is crucial for urban planning projects. Few prior works have considered interactive approaches, like conversational agents and recommendation systems based on artificial intelligence (AI) in urban planning [40, 51]. However, the existing solutions do not overcome the described issues, which is why we propose the following research question (RQ).

RQ: How to design IT artifacts to support citizens in contributing in online participation projects in urban planning?

To address the RQ, we initiated a design science research (DSR) project following the framework by Kuechler and Vaishnavi [36] and described the findings of the first cycle in this paper. The related work section describes the state-of-the-art in citizen participation in urban planning, including the use of AI (cf. Sect. 2). Next, we emphasize our research approach and specify the first DSR cycle (cf. Sect. 3). In awareness of the problem, we describe the identified issues (cf. Sect. 4) followed by the section suggestions, in which we condense the issues into meta-requirements and derive design principles (cf. Sect. 5). The instantiation of the design principles in a feasible prototype is described in Sect. 6 and evaluated as described in Sect. 7. Afterward, the findings are discussed, considering the theoretical and practical contributions (cf. Sect. 9) and finally summarized (cf. Sect. 10).

2 Related Work

2.1 Online Participation in Urban Planning

Urban planning has historically been a non-participatory process. However, as cities grow in size and complexity, so does the need for participation. Citizen participation in urban planning aims to enable citizens to contribute to urban projects with their opinions, requirements, and ideas [58], further referred to as contributions [12], to develop and shape urban project's visions and subsequent decision-making processes [11]. The approach, strategy, and participation plan depend on the responsible parties, e.g., governments, institutional investors, or private individuals. The impact of citizens on the project varies [7] and often follows predefined objectives [56]. These do not necessarily originate from social responsibility or grassroots democratic ethos and can merely follow economic interests [11], as public or political resistance can delay or prevent urban projects, reducing the return on investment [56]. At the same time, citizen participation can increase the project's value and real-world benefits for locals and whole cities, improving its overall acceptance and reducing risks [9]. Citizen participation can be conducted in analog, digital, or hybrid forms [57]. The last two correspond to electronic participation (e-participation), which the United Nations defines as" the process of engaging citizens through ICTs in policy, decision-making, and service design and delivery to make it participatory, inclusive, and deliberative" [62]. Thus, e-participation can also occur on-site with workshops or town hall meetings if they are enabled and supported with digital tools such as touch tables [40] and virtual or augmented environments [45]. Online participation, on which we focus in this work, is a subset of e-participation, where participation is mediated via the internet [57]. It is often achieved with websites and urban participation platforms [21], especially in the case of extensive citizen participation initiatives with several thousand participants, as described by Royo et al. [52].

2.2 Online Participation in Urban Planning

Online participation omits face-to-face interactions, relies on asynchronous communication, and usually does not have ubiquitous moderators and urban experts [52, 57]. This often reduces the submission of comprehensive and understandable citizen contributions. One approach to address this is to increase information exchange and the elaboration on contributions comparable to human-to-human interaction by utilizing AI [51], by providing immediate responses [13, 51]. Interactive systems and conversational agents like chatbots [68] can replace humans under certain conditions [66]. They must be able to accept inputs and should respond to support interaction and the exchange of content [12]. This requires a procedure for analyzing content and deciding on appropriate responses like questions or hints [60]. Besides this, recent projects have examined how AI can support online discussions in urban planning via content analysis to identify hate speech and conduct fact-checking [30]. This also applies to the possibilities of summaries of citizens' contributions for subsequent processes of urban experts by automatically linking and merging similar content [44]. Bachiller et al. [8] focused on visualization and used clustering to identify citizens' interests connected to specific districts to highlight differences. In Spain, a study has examined the participants' interest in urban projects with AI on the participation platform DECIDIM Madrid to recommend and advertise further projects to increase online participation [22]. Also, chatbot systems were examined to support citizens via dialog flows [68]. Most examples have focused on approaches to automatically analyze citizens' contributions concerning their content to identify specifics, visualize patterns, and support moderators and subsequent processes. However, they do not address the challenge of supporting citizens during their participation and the process of contributing to urban planning projects.

3 Research Approach

To answer the RQ, we conducted a DSR project according to Kuechler and Vaishnavi [36], as illustrated in Fig. 1. For the step awareness of the problems, a structured literature review following the approach by Kitchenham, including the steps of identification of research, study selection, quality assessment, data extraction, and data synthesis [34], was conducted to identify issues, formulate meta-requirements, and derive design principles [35]. We used these to develop a web-based prototype, which we evaluated qualitatively by conducting two focus groups, including guiding questions and a SWOT analysis to identify strengths and weaknesses of the instantiated prototype and the potential and risks of its usage in online citizen participation in urban planning.

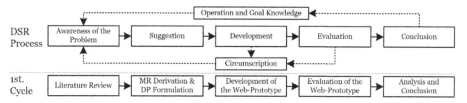

Fig. 1. General and conducted Design Science Research Process.

4   Awareness of the Problem

In the systematic literature review, we focus on the libraries of Springer Link, the Association of Information Systems (AIS), ScienceDirect, and the Association for Computing Machinery (ACM) to consider information systems, computer science, and economics findings. The applied search string is ("challenges") AND ("online citizen participation") AND ("urban planning participation"), and we focused on the recent findings of the last three years [34]. The search provided 410 results, of which 290 originated from Springer Link, 113 from AIS, five from Science Direct, and two from the ACM library. We excluded all publications that were not accessible, duplicates, and unrelated to the RQ. The remaining 35 publications were analyzed to identify issues (ISS), which we inductively clustered as shown in Fig. 2). The cluster citizen's situation shows that many citizens lack the time (ISS1) to be informed and participate [9, 31, 41], even if they are aware of the project and their influence [20]. Another challenge is the lack of expertise and knowledge, as more time would allow participants to inform themselves better and can prevent citizens from participating as they do not feel comfortable submitting meaningful contributions [4, 49]. Therefore, citizens should be informed during the participation about their possibilities and the project to overcome the lack of knowledge (ISS2) [9, 16, 33, 39, 49, 70]. This also affects advertising campaigns before and during the participation, which is attributable to a lack of acceptance of urban projects (ISS3) [9, 24, 28, 33, 43, 49, 69], as citizens are often unaware of their impact and the chance of co-developing their living environment. This is enhanced if the participation objective is unclear or irrelevant for them or if citizens mistrust the initiator due to intransparent processes, which can create the impression that their contributions do not have any influence [6]. The literature describes a lack of immediate responses for the cluster interaction process, as online surveys do not provide any human-to-human interaction. This also applies to participation platforms and is argued with the absence of moderators due to the costs and the not bearable workload in large participation [40] and present participants because of the asynchronous communication and duration of several weeks, which increases waiting times for feedback and comments (ISS4) [3, 10, 12, 20, 23, 25, 64, 67]. This is also affected by the number of participants, which can vary from less than a hundred to thousands and approximates to a lack of scalable interaction (ISS5) [14, 32, 46, 70].

Another challenge is the reflection on and elaboration of citizens on their contributions. In on-site participation, moderators and immediate exchange support the reflection of needs and understanding, which enables compromises. In online participation, responses, if available, often lack this (ISS6) [1, 4, 14, 15, 17, 18, 41, 42, 48], but is highly

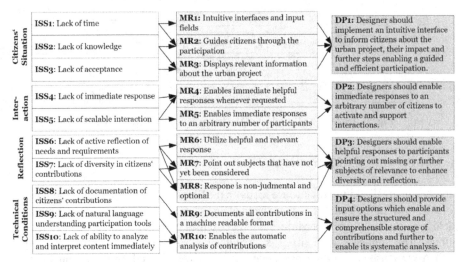

Fig. 2. Issues (ISS), Meta-Requirement (MR), and Design Principles (DP).

relevant in one-sided discussions in which a popular opinion is shared without critical questioning and reflecting needs and individual situation (e. g. age, gender, wealth), which can be exhausting and time-consuming. If this is not noticed, discussion and whole participation can lack diversity in opinions and contributions (ISS7) [2, 39, 53], described by the cluster reflection. Considering the technical conditions of participation, the literature states that the lack of documenting citizens' contributions (ISS8) needs to be overcome [3, 19, 47]. However, this mainly applies to on-site participation, in which oral communication dominates. Due to the amount of data, digital participation is often grounded on scale-based queries and yes and no questions. However, to enable auto-mated responses and in-depth text-based exchange to support interaction and reflection, online participation tools have to overcome the lack of natural language understanding (ISS9) [22, 63]. This also is a prerequisite to overcome the lack of analyzing and inter-preting content (ISS10) [5, 37] to enable content-based responses, as highlighted in the literature by Romberg et al. [51] and Cai et al. [13].

5   Suggestion

All issues were discussed to formulate meta-requirement (MR) and derive design prin-ciples (DP) [27], as shown in Fig. 2. Together, they initially describe the design of IT artifacts responding to the RQ. ISS1, lack of time, affects information and participation itself. Therefore, digital participation should be intuitive (MR1), removing settling-in and long reading times. This should be supported with guidance (MR2) and precise, relevant information (MR3). MR1, MR2, and MR3 consider citizens' situation and are reflected in DP1: "Designer should implement an intuitive interface to inform citizens about the urban project, their impact, and further steps enabling a guided and efficient participation". ISS4 and ISS5 address the lack of immediate responses and scalability, which led to MR4, which demands that responses be provided whenever requested to increase interactions. MR5 addresses the scalability of this approach, as this should be applicable to an arbitrary number of participants simultaneously, which led to DP2: "Designers should enable immediate responses by the IT artifact to an arbitrary number of citizens to activate and support interactions". ISS6 and ISS7 address citizens reflecting and elaborating on their contributions, which led to MR6, MR7, and MR8. MR6 specifies that the response should be helpful and is based on ISS6 and ISS7. MR7 specifies that missing subjects of the urban project should be pointed out to support diversity and reflection. Both should be non-judgmental and optional (MR8) to not discourage participants, which leads to DP3: "Designers should enable helpful responses to participants pointing out missing or further subjects of relevance to enhance diversity and reflection". ISS8, ISS9, and ISS10 address technical lacks, leading to MR9 and MR10. MR9 describes that all contributions must be stored in a machine-readable format, which is crucial to enabling scalable and immediate responses (MR10). This leads to DP4: "Designers should provide input options, which enable and ensure the structured and comprehensible storage of contributions and further enable its systematic analysis".

6 Development

Figure 3 shows the interface of the developed prototype. It combines the design of existing urban participation platforms [52] and the idea of conversational agents to provide immediate responses to citizens whenever required while creating their contributions [40]. DP1 is instantiated with a simple and clear interface structure. It provides information about the urban project, which can be extended depending on the user's needs and the objective of the urban participation. However, the length of the description should not be too extensive, as a time-consuming familiarization with the project can be discouraging. DP2 is instantiated with the "Get Feedback" button, which participants can use to receive a response [23] (cf. Fig. 3). DP3 specifies the subjects of the response by always asking one question that addresses a topic not yet considered. The text field, which can be changed in size, ensures that all data is stored (DP4). To enable content-based responses, as stated by DP2 and DP3, a systematic AI-based analysis and decision-algorithm is required. Considering existing approaches in this domain as described in Sect. 2.2, we decided to merge urban participation platforms and conversational agents. Urban participations are aligned with the overall project and usually focus on specific topics. Therefore, the responses should do the same and, e.g., not ask questions about culture if the focus is on mobility. To ensure that and to enable the evaluation, we developed an AI-based prototype that analyses citizens' contributions to identify non-addressed topics to choose responding questions flexibly. To realize this, we used machine learning (ML) algorithms. ML is an AI subcategory that focuses on training models on data to enable predictions and decisions [13]. For our prototype, we used data from an existing urban planning project of a large city with a total of 2006 citizen contributions. The dataset was analyzed to define classes that apply to urban projects, which are public spaces and culture, economy and social affairs, environment and green spaces, and mobility.

The categories define possible and anticipated content and were labeled by the authors. For the training, we removed meaningless contributions and stopwords and

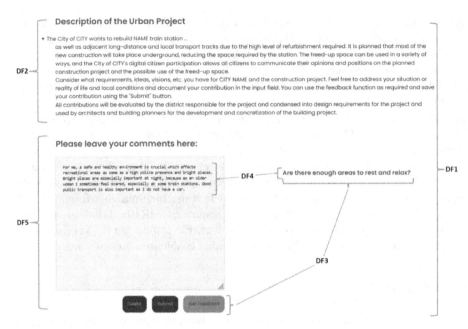

Fig. 3. Design of the Prototype.

converted these to word embeddings using the natural language processing framework spaCy [26]. For the training, we used 80% of the data and 20% for evaluating [38] and tried different ML algorithms. We reached the highest accuracy of 63% with a long short-term memory (LSTM) neural network. The reliability of the ML model is expandable, but considering the limited number of training data and the purpose of evaluating the prototype's interface, this is sufficient [29]. The ML Model classifies citizens' contributions and stores all results in a class table to determine the response. An algorithm then decides which question from a predefined catalog is chosen as the response. If two categories are equally often considered, the decision is made by chance. In addition, all questions asked are marked to prevent them from being asked more than once, as this would contradict DP3. For the prototype, we defined 24 questions, three for each class, and the prototype asked a maximum of 10 to convey a feeling of completion. If the delete button is pressed (cf. Fig. 3), all background savings are deleted, and the participation restarts.

7 Evaluation

Following Venable et al.'s guidelines for DSR evaluation [65], the prototype evaluation was conducted qualitatively, including a pretest, to test the functionality of the AI-based response beforehand, as shown in Table 1. The participants were advertised and acquired through the university. They were citizens of an urban region and possessed media competence computers to prevent errors due to a lack of skill. No further capabilities were required as digital citizen participation is usually open to all citizens.

Table 1. Overview of the Evaluation.

Procedure/Group	Participants	Male	Female	Minutes
Pretest	5	5	-	28
Focus Group (FGI)	6	3	3	56
Focus Group (FGI)	9	5	4	48
Total without Pretest	15	8	7	104

We facilitated and moderated the focus groups in our media lab [61]. Every participant received a convertible laptop to explore and use the prototype, for which we provided a fictive scenario in which all participants lived close to the urban projects' area, which also applies to a third of the participants. The scenario describes that the city is rebuilding a central overground train station underground and conducts participation to elicit requirements and ideas of how to use the new vacant area above in the future. Further details about the urban planning project were provided to specify the area in and around the train station. The guided evaluation began with the elicitation of participant data, the agreement to record the audio, and the assessment of whether all participants could operate the provided devices. All participants had 15 min to use the prototype, and afterward, we discussed their experiences using guiding questions that leaned toward the design principles and the SWOT analysis (cf. Sect. 3).

8   Findings

We identified seven strengths (S), five weaknesses (W), four opportunities (O), and four threats (T), each with a different degree of approval, which can reach a maximum of 15 (n) (cf. Table 1). The focus groups revealed that feedback in the form of questions is perceived to enhance interactions and diversity of contributions by pointing out further subjects (S1, S2, S3, and S4). The participants also highlighted that open questions are preferred over closed questions (W3), as the prototype contained both. In addition, the participants emphasized that" the questions are helpful, but [they] are no feedback" (FGII), which supports misleading expectations and should be changed (W2). Besides that, it is still possible that participants' contributions are contrary to others, and citizens have no impression at all whether the requirements and ideas are feasible or floating in the air" (FGII).

Furthermore, participants want to have the "possibility to show past questions and suggested that it could be helpful always to provide a cluster of questions" (FGI), but "it should be possible to reach a natural ending of the interaction considering the number of questions" (FGI) not to frustrate participants to conclude. In addition, further information and functions such as a map, images of the project, and more textual descriptions should be provided (W1) to reduce the effort for further research and could also reduce W4.

Table 2. Strength (S), Weaknesses (W), Opportunities (O) and Threats (T).

No		n
S1	Questions support the diversity of topics in citizens' contributions	9
S2	Immediate responses support the interaction with the IT artifact	7
S3	Questions point out unconsidered topics in citizens' contributions	7
S4	Questions always change and are never asked twice	6
S5	Large input field for the participant's contribution	4
S6	Responses can be ignored, and it is optional to use them	3
S7	Questions do not determine a specific direction	3
W1	The scenario description does not provide enough information	9
W2	The word"feedback" is misleading, as an assessment is expected	7
W3	The prototype asked some closed questions as a response	5
W4	Lack of motivational functions (gamification)	3
W5	The response button is not highlighted enough in the front-end	2
O1	More comprehensible and diverse ideas are submitted	7
O2	Citizens can contribute time- and location-independent	4
O3	Participation is scalable for an arbitrary number of participants	4
O4	AI analysis enables immediate and arbitrary responses	1
T1	Citizens' demands and ideas might not be feasible	3
T2	Citizens' demands and ideas can converse with each other	2
T3	Responses/questions can be used to influence participants	2
T4	Risk of misinterpretation of keyword-based contributions	2

9 Discussion

In the discussion, we first reflect on the evaluation's findings and then embed them in the literature on AI's role in online citizen participation in urban planning. The results of the focus group, and in particular, the strengths, confirm and emphasize the derived design principles. DP1 is supported by S3, S4, and S5, highlighting the interaction and guidance created by the questions. However, its implementation was also criticized by W1 and W5 as the usability should be considered more extensively to increase the participant's experience, as indicated by W4 (cf. Table 2). The advantages of an increased interaction by an immediate response (DP2) are approved by S2, O1, and O2, which also emphasizes the potential for large-scale participation, which is of particular relevance for larger cities considering moderation cost as described in Sects. 2.1 and 4. DP3 addresses the helpfulness of the responses and that they point out unconsidered topics, which S1, S3, S4, S6, and S7 approve. S1 and S3 address the content of citizens' contributions, which also corresponds to S4, as they always have to differ. S6 and S7 are of minor approval, but considering existing participation platforms and the user experience, are highly relevant, as participation should be perceived as a chance to co-design their living environment in an open discourse without mandating or influencing participants' contributions to a desired direction, as described as non-participation and manipulation by Sherry Arnstein [7]. DP4 addressed the technical condition of the prototype, and its implementation confirmed it. However, alternative and additional approaches to receiving citizen contributions exist and can include pictures and audio, which would aggravate the ML-based analysis (ISS10). The discussions in the focus groups around O4 highlighted the potential for further AI models to support more complex interactions and exchanges between citizens and machines by generating individual questions, including location data and demographics if elicitated. W1 and W4 describe a major point of criticism as the information provided about participation is insufficient and should be more comprehensive, affecting DP3. Whether this also applies outside of experimental settings, where less time is available, cannot be determined conclusively. In addition, four threats were described (cf. Table 2), of which T1 and T2 highlight a fundamental challenge of online participation. Stelzle et al. [59] describe that the feasibility of contributions is challenging to assess at an early stage of urban projects. Furthermore, citizens' requirements can be considered differently by governments and public authorities, and contradicting demands correlate with the diversity of participants depending on different life situations and visions [2, 53]. Contradictions and diversity are acceptable, and their elicitation is part of participation, including the analysis and development of beneficial compromises to create public value for all. Nevertheless, W3 and T1 should be considered and solved with supplemental questions (DP3). Besides the existing design principles, the focus groups revealed the desire for more control, structure, and an overview of the questions, which results in DP5: "Designers should provide an overview of questions to support participants' control and expectation through the participation." In addition, as a result of W1 and W4, DP6 states, "Designers should provide an interactive map about the location of the urban project to enable additional interaction and provide further information to citizens supporting local references" [64]. This also includes further information about building plans, if already available. The described strengths and weaknesses are inherent to the IT artifact and reflect the users' evaluation of the design principles. Overall, the evaluation was positive. The weaknesses defined further adjustments and will be of special interest in the upcoming design cycle, together with the two new design principles that require further evaluation and validation. Moreover, how the concerns about manipulation (T3) can be reduced needs to be investigated, which affects the IT artifact and the implementation of whole citizen participation projects [25, 39]. Citizen trust in participatory urban planning processes, quite often governmental processes, should be supported, for example, with additional information and transparent subsequent decision-making processes [56]. In addition, further and broader ML models with more categories and higher accuracy should be examined to increase reliability and responses that enable citizens to elaborate on their contributions in depth. Also, further clarification about the possibilities and use of generative AI is of interest to clarify to which degree it could support citizens [13] and if black box models are beneficial as the responses would hardly be comparable and maybe also contradictory, affecting ethical and data privacy aspects. Lastly, it should also be examined whether our findings can be transferred to hybrid and on-site participation to address further citizens and to support moderators [48, 54]. Taking the discussion a step ahead, we want to embed our findings in prior work, as many studies have highlighted the need for e-participation and AI for urban planning in the digital age [9]. They have also investigated the challenges of e-participation that are situated in a lack of interaction, moderation, and data processing [52]. We find fragmented solutions to overcome these burdens, for example, using visualization techniques and clustering [8] and recommender systems for e-participation platforms [48]. Thus, our study builds on prior works that have elaborated on the potential to use AI in e-participation but rarely implemented it. Therefore, we extend the state of literature, as our solution supports the participation phase following an explorative but structured approach. Thus, our study and the prior findings has to be interpreted in the context of interactive support systems [8, 12, 44, 52]. Looking ahead, our design principles should be considered as input knowledge for future design cycles, and we want to encourage the realization of additional and alternative IT artifacts to exploit the described strengths and opportunities and to reduce and avoid the weaknesses and threats (cf. Table 2). Further implementation, extension, and validation of the design principles are necessary to increase validity with qualitative and quantitative research, including the application in real-world projects. However, following the path of developing a novel design theory and a new class of AI-based interaction systems for online citizen participation in urban planning, this paper provides prescriptive knowledge regarding the problem space and a novel prototype that merges the characteristics of online participation platforms and conversational agents contributing to the solution space. We encourage fellow researchers to use and continue with our findings with quantitative evaluation in the context of a real urban participation project, as they can provide additional insights.

10 Conclusion

In this paper, we *investigated how to design IT artifacts to support citizens in contributing to online participation projects in urban planning*, by applying the DSR methodology [36]. To do so, we conducted a structured literature review that resulted in eleven issues, ten meta-requirements, and four design principles. We used the design principles to develop an AI-based web prototype and qualitatively evaluated it with urban citizens to approve, disprove, and extend them. The evaluation highlighted the strength of our prototype but also underlined the demand for adjustments. This led to adaptions and two new design principles, which state that designers should add further information about the number of questions and the possibility of showing the already received ones, as well as an interactive map to support spatial thinking and the exploration of the area of interest.

The prescriptive knowledge of this paper and novel IT artifact, which combines classical characteristics of online participation in urban planning and conversational agents, contribute to the theory and practice of e-participation and the subfield of online participation in urban planning. The design principles describe a new approach to how citizens can be supported in online participation to increase interactions and content of submitted contributions to support subsequent processes. In addition, the results show that AI can support citizens in documenting and elaborating on their contributions in a scalable and efficient way. The developed design principles guide designers and urban experts in extending online participation and the existing knowledge base [13, 51].

References

1. Abel, P., Miether, D., Pl¨otzky, F., Robra-Bissantz, S.: The Shape of Bottom-Up Urbanism participatory Platforms: A Conceptualisation and empirical Study. BLED (2021)
2. Abel, P., Schlimbach, R., Glimmann, V., Schwarz, J., Simon, M., Robo-Bissantz, S.: Designing Urban Participation Platforms Model for Goal-oriented, Classification of Participation Mechanisms. In: 35th BLED eConference (2022)
3. Akasaka, F., Nakatani, M.: Citizen involvement in service co-creation in urban living labs. In: Proceedings of the 54th HICSS (2021)
4. Alexopoulos, Ch., Keramidis, P., Viale Pereira, G., Charalabidis, Y.: Towards smart cities 4.0: digital participation in smart cities solutions and the use of disruptive technologies. In: Themistocleous, M., Papadaki, M. (eds.) EMCIS 2021. LNBIP, vol. 437, pp. 258–273. Springer, Cham (2022). https://doi.org/10.1007/978-3-030-95947-0_18
5. Altafini, D., Mara, F., Cutini, V.: A data-driven approach for a city-university mobility plan: the case of the University of Pisa. In: ICCSA, pp. 401–417 (2023)
6. Amard, A., Hoess, A., Roth, T., Fridgen, G., Rieger, A.: Guiding refugees through european bureaucracy: designing a trustworthy mobile app for document management. In: Drechsler, A., Gerber, A., Hevner, A. (eds.) DESRIST 2022. LNCS, vol. 13229, pp. 171–182. Springer, Cham (2022). https://doi.org/10.1007/978-3-031-06516-3_13
7. Arnstein, S.R.: A ladder of citizen participation. J. Am. Inst. Plann. **35**(4), 216–224 (1969)
8. Bachiller, S., Quijano-S´anchez, L., Cantador, I.: A flexible and lightweight interactive data mining tool to visualize and analyze digital citizen participation content. In: 36th Annual ACM SAC, pp. 413–416 (2021)
9. Becker, F., Siemon, D., Robra-Bissantz, S.: Smart participation design: prescriptive knowledge for bottom-up participation. CAIS **51**(1) (2022)
10. Birghan, F., Hettenhausen, R., Meschede, Ch.: Challenges, barriers, and approaches for providing digital citizen information. A case-study in North Rhine-Westphalia, Germany. In: 54th HICSS (2021)
11. Bjørgen, A., Fossheim, K., Macharis, C.: How to build stakeholder participation in collaborative urban freight planning. Cities **112** (2021)
12. Borchers, M., Tavanapour, N., Bittner, E.: Toward intelligent platforms to support citizen participation in urban planning. PACIS (2022)
13. Cai, M.: Natural language processing for urban research: a systematic review. Heliyon **7**(3) (2021)
14. Cantador, I., Bellogín, A., Cortés-Cediel, M.E., Gil, O.: Exploiting open data to analyze discussion and controversy in online citizen participation. IP&M (2020)
15. Cerreta, M., Liccardi, L., Reitano, M.: A citizen-led spatial information system for collaborative (post-)pandemic urban strategies: the ponticelli experience, naples. In: Gervasi, O., et al. (eds.) ICCSA 2021. LNCS, vol. 12954, pp. 293–306. Springer, Cham (2021). https://doi.org/10.1007/978-3-030-86979-3_22
16. Chiordi, S., Desogus, G., Garau, Ch., Nesi, P., Zamperlin, P.: A preliminary survey on smart specialization platforms: evaluation of european best practices. In: ICCSA, pp. 67–84 (2022)
17. Cifolelli, S., Zirulo, A., Berardi, M.: Exploring the interceptions between smart cities and digitalization for urban development - a systematic literature review and future research agenda. ITAIS (2022)

18. Coenen, J., Biedermann, P., Claes, S., Moere, A.V.: The stakeholder perspective on using public polling displays for civic engagement. C&T 61–74 (2021)
19. Correia, D., Feio, J.E., Marques, J., Teixeira, L.: Participatory methodology guidelines to promote citizens' participation in decision-making: evidence based on a Portuguese case study. Cities **135**, 104213 (2023)
20. Sofia Dastoli, P., Pontrandolfi, P.: Methods and tools for a participatory local development strategy. In: Calabrò, F., Della Spina, L., Piñeira Mantiñán, M.J. (eds.) NMP 2022. LNNS, vol. 482, pp. 2112–2121. Springer, Cham (2022). https://doi.org/10.1007/978-3-031-06825-6_203
21. Diop, E.B., Chenal, J., Tekouabou, S.C.K., Azmi, R.: Crowdsourcing public engagement for urban planning in the global south: methods, challenges and suggestions for future research. Sustainability **14**(18), Article 18 (2022)
22. Dominiković, I., Ćukušić, M., Jadrić, M.: The role of artificial intelligence in smart cities: systematic literature review. In: Bisset Álvarez, E. (eds.) DIONE 2021, pp. 64–80. Springer, Cham (2021). https://doi.org/10.1007/978-3-030-77417-2_5
23. Graf-Drasch, V., Keller, R., Meindl, O., Röhrich, F.: The design of citizen-centric green is in sustainable smart districts. Bus. Inf. Syst. Eng. **65**(5), 521–538 (2023)
24. Flores, C.C., Rezende Alicides, D.: Crowdsourcing framework applied to strategic digital city projects. J. Urban Manag. 12 (2022)
25. Fürstenau, D., Morelli, F., Meindl, K., Schulte-Althoff, M., Rabe, J.: A social citizen dashboard for participatory urban planning in berlin: prototype and evaluation. In: 54th HICSS (2021)
26. Göritz, L., Stattkus, D., Beinke, J.H., Thomas, O.: To reduce bias, you must identify it first! Towards automated gender bias detection. In: ICIS (2022)
27. Gregor, S., Chandra Kruse, L., Seidel, S.: The anatomy of a design principle. JAIS **21**, 1622–1652 (2020)
28. Hölzer, S., Honner, L., Preßler, W., Schulz, A., Erfurth, Ch.: Towards designing a user-centered local community platform to foster social cohesion in a multi-generational smart community. In: I4CS 2023. CCIS, vol. 1876, pp. 277–291. Springer, Cham (2023). https://doi.org/10.1007/978-3-031-40852-6_15
29. Huang, H., Xu, H., Wang, X., Silamu, W.: Maximum F1-score discriminative training criterion for automatic mispronunciation detection. TASLP **23**(4), 787–797 (2015)
30. Jiang, A., Zubiaga, A.: Cross-lingual capsule network for hate speech detection in social media. In: 32st ACM Conference HT, pp. 217–223 (2021)
31. Karadimitriou, N., Magnani, G., Timmerman, R., Marshall, S., Hudson-Smith, A.: Designing an incubator of public spaces platform: applying cybernetic principles to the co-creation of spaces. Land Use Policy **119**, 106187 (2022)
32. Katmada, A., Komninos, N., Kakderi, Ch.: The landscape of digital platforms for bottom-up collaboration, creativity, and innovation creation. In: Streitz, N.A., Konomi, S. (eds.) HCII 2022, pp. 28–42. Springer, Cham (2022). https://doi.org/10.1007/978-3-031-05463-1_3
33. Katzef, A., Gcora Vumazonke, N., Chigona, W., Tonateni Tuyeni, T., Queen Mtegha, Ch.: Factors affecting citizens' use of e-participation platforms: a case of GovChat platform in cape town municipality. In: IFIP, vol. 657, pp. 69–88 (2022)
34. Kitchenham, B.A.: Procedures for Performing Systematic Reviews, vol. 33 (2004)
35. Kuechler, B., Vaishnavi, V.: On theory development in design science research: anatomy of a research project. ECIS **17**(5), 489–504 (2008)
36. Kuechler, B., Vaishnavi, V.: A framework for theory development in design science research: multiple perspectives. JAIS **13**(6) (2012)
37. Küstermann, G.C., Bittner, E.A.C.: Leveraging human and machine capabilities for analyzing citizen contributions in participatory urban planning and development: a design-oriented

approach. In: Fui-Hoon Nah, F., Siau, K. (eds.) HCII 2022. LNCS, vol. 13327, pp. 56–72. Springer, Cham (2022). https://doi.org/10.1007/978-3-031-05544-7_5

38. Kulunchakov, A., Mairal, J.: Estimate sequences for stochastic composite optimization: variance reduction, acceleration, and robustness to noise. JMLR (2022)
39. Leible, S., Ludzay, M., Götz, S., Kaufmann, T., Meyer-Lüters, K., Tran, M.N.: ICT application types and equality of e-participation—a systematic literature review. PACIS (2022)
40. Lieven, C., Lüders, B., Kulus, D., Thoneick, R.: Enabling digital co-creation in urban planning and development. In: Zimmermann, A., Howlett, R.J., Jain, L.C. (eds.) Human Centred Intelligent Systems. SIST, vol. 189, pp. 415–430. Springer, Singapore (2021). https://doi.org/10.1007/978-981-15-5784-2_34
41. Lin, Y.: Social media for collaborative planning: a typology of support functions and challenges. Cities **125**, 103641 (2022)
42. Lòopez-de-Ipina, D., et al.: A collaborative environment for co-delivering citizen science campaigns. In: UCAmI, pp. 322–333 (2023)
43. Maaroufi, M.M., Stour, L., Agoumi, A.: Contribution of digital collaboration and e-learning to the implementation of smart mobility in Morocco. In: Motahhir, S., Bossoufi, B. (eds.) ICDTA 2021. LNNS, vol. 211, pp. 609–619. Springer, Cham (2021). https://doi.org/10.1007/978-3-030-73882-2_55
44. Nicolas, C., Kim, J., Chi, S.: NLP-based characterization of top-down communication in smart cities for enhancing citizen alignment. SCS **66** (2021)
45. Pantić, M., et al.: Challenges and opportunities for public participation in urban and regional planning during the COVID-19 pandemic—lessons learned for the future. Land Article 12 (2021)
46. Dinh Phuoc, L., Giang Son, N.: E-planning and its potential development in Vietnam's urban planning. In: CIGOS 2021, CIGOS (2023)
47. Witt, A.S., da Silva, F.C.C.: Overview of citizen science projects contemplated in the civis platform. In: Pinto, A.L., Arencibia-Jorge, R. (eds.) DIONE 2022. LNICST, vol. 452, pp. 16–28. Springer, Cham (2022). https://doi.org/10.1007/978-3-031-22324-2_2
48. Pristl, A.-C., Billert, M.: Citizen Participation in increasingly digitalized governmental Environments - A structured Literature Review. ECIS (2022)
49. López Reyes, M.E., Magnussen, R.: The use of open government data to create social value. In: Janssen, M., et al. (eds.) EGOV 2022. LNCS, vol. 13391, pp. 244–257. Springer, Cham (2022). https://doi.org/10.1007/978-3-031-15086-9_16
50. Roman, M., Fellnhofer, K.: Facilitating the participation of civil society in regional planning: implementing quadruple helix model in Finnish regions. LUP 1–12 (2022)
51. Romberg, J., Escher, T.: Making sense of citizens' input through artificial intelligence: a review of methods for computational text analysis to support the evaluation of contributions in public participation. DGOV (2023)
52. Royo, S., Pina, V., Garcia-Rayado, J.: Decide madrid: a critical analysis of an award-winning e-participation initiative. Sustainability **12**(4), Article 4 (2020)
53. Sanabria-Z, J., Molina-Espinosa, J., Artemova, I., Alfaro-Ponce, B.: Mobile app prototype for citizen science: toward the development of complex thinking, perspectives and trends in education and technology. In: Mesquita, A., Abreu, A., Carvalho, J.V., Santana, C., de Mello, C.H.P. (eds.) ICITED 2023. SIST, vol. 366, pp. 657–666. Springer, Singapore (2023). https://doi.org/10.1007/978-981-99-5414-8_60
54. Schrammeijer, E.A., van Zanten, B.T., Davis, J., Verburg, P.H.: The advantage of mobile technologies in crowdsourcing landscape preferences: testing a mobile app to inform planning decisions. Urban Forestry Urban Greening (2022)
55. Secinaro, S., Brescia, V., Iannaci, D., Jonathan, G.M.: Does citizen involvement feed on digital platforms? IJPA **45**(9), 708–725 (2022)

56. Stelzle, B., Jannack, A., Noennig, J.R.: Co-design and co-decision: decision making on collaborative design platforms. PCS 2435–2444 (2017)
57. Stelzle, B., Noennig, J.R.: A database for participation methods in urban development. PCS 2416–2425 (2017)
58. Stelzle, B., Noennig, J.R.: A method for the assessment of public participation in urban development. UDI (2019)
59. Stelzle, B.: Influencing factors on citizen participation in urban development. In: 2019 IEEE 2nd UKRCON, pp. 1278–1281 (2019)
60. Svikhnushina, E., Pu, P.: Key qualities of conversational chatbots – the PEACE model. In: 26th IUI, pp. 520–530 (2021)
61. Tremblay, M., Hevner, A., Berndt, D., Chatterjee, S.: The use of focus groups in design science research. DR IS **22**, 121–143 (2010)
62. United Nations, Department of Economic and Social Affairs, Population Division. World urbanization prospects: The 2018 revision (2018)
63. Vagena, F., Sneiders, E.: Communication between citizens and public organizations as a means of public value co-creation. In: The 23rd DGS, pp. 1–12 (2022)
64. Velhinho, A., Almeida, P.: POLARISCOPE – a platform for the co-creation and visualization of collective memories. In: Marcus, A., Rosenzweig, E., Soares, M.M. (eds.) HCII 2023. LNCS, vol. 14031, pp. 273–285. Springer, Cham (2023). https://doi.org/10.1007/978-3-031-35696-4_20
65. Venable, J., Pries-Heje, J., Baskerville, R.: FEDS: a framework for evaluation in design science research. EJIS **25**(1), 77–89 (2016)
66. Verne, G., Steinstø, T., Simonsen, L., Bratteteig, T.: How can i help you? A chatbot's answers to citizens' information needs. SJIS **34**(2) (2022)
67. de Vreede, T., de Vreede, G., Alawi, N.: Achieving success in community crowdsourcing lessons from the field. In: 54th HICSS (2021)
68. Wiethof, C., Bittner, E.: Toward a hybrid intelligence system in customer service: collaborative learning of human and AI. ECIS (2022)
69. Zambon, Z., Bassetti, Ch., Prandi, C.: A close look at citizen science through the HCI lens: a systematic literature review. INTERACT, pp. 414–435 (2023)
70. Živković, L.: Project e-space: building a digital platform for spatial and urban planning and development in Serbia. In: ICCSA, pp. 503–518 (2021)

Overcoming Rebound Effects: A Process Blueprint for Circular Systems Design

Konstantin Remke[1]([✉]) [iD] and Henry Willem Müller[2] [iD]

[1] ESCP Business School, Berlin, Germany
kremke@escp.eu
[2] University of St. Gallen, St. Gallen, Switzerland
henrywillem.mueller@unisg.ch

Abstract. In this study, we develop a process blueprint for circular systems design. While existing tools and frameworks abound for circular product and business model design, a notable gap exists in integrating these two domains. A more systemic view is highly relevant because the mismatched design of products and business models leads to ecologically harmful rebound effects. We employ design science methodology involving 31 expert interviews and a workshop with a design academy. We advance theory by championing circular systems design, providing a process blueprint, and addressing the critical issue of circular economy rebound. This contribution marks a substantive step forward in accelerating the implementation of circular strategies and addressing a fundamental theoretical concern related to the circular economy.

Keywords: Circular Economy · Systems · Design · Process · Rebound Effects

1 Introduction

The Circular Economy (CE) is increasingly advocated as an alternative economic paradigm to tackle global environmental challenges [1, 2]. Despite its commendable goals of preservation and resource efficiency, the CE has encountered recent criticism [3]. Among these concerns is the apparent dearth of empirical evidence substantiating the proclaimed environmental and social benefits [4, 5] as well as rebound effects wherein circular practices inadvertently result in heightened resource consumption [6]. Further critiques address the limited conceptual grounding of the CE [7], overlooked real-world limitations such as spatial and temporal system boundaries [8, 9] as well as various organizational barriers [10, 11]. With the CE gaining prominence, it becomes essential to examine and address these shortcomings and ensure that the envisioned circular transition aligns with the overarching goals of sustainability.

Acknowledging that the identified limitations may partly stem from insufficiently holistic frameworks, scholars and practitioners have advocated for more systems-oriented approaches in sustainable design [12–14]. This paradigm shift is not merely a theoretical abstraction but holds practical implications for the effective implementation of circular strategies, ensuring that they contribute to sustainability objectives while

M. Mandviwalla et al. (Eds.): DESRIST 2024, LNCS 14621, pp. 33–47, 2024.
https://doi.org/10.1007/978-3-031-61175-9_3

minimizing unintended adverse impacts. To exemplify this perspective, consider the case of eScooters. Despite their intended role as a sustainable alternative for car trips, they often succumb to breakdowns because they were not designed for heavy use by inexperienced riders. They further contribute to street congestion due to inadequate partnerships for recharging and missing parking zones, rendering them an unsustainable nuisance [15]. A ban resulting from a public referendum in Paris underscores the consequences of disjointed circular strategies, where product design proves incompatible with a sharing business model, which in turn lacks the necessary support from collaborators [16]. Consequently, we aim to answer the following research question: *How to blend product, service, business model, and collaboration design for more harmonious and systemic design decisions?*

We employ design science research methodology [17, 18] to meticulously craft a process blueprint that empowers businesses to design circular systems holistically. In this paper, systems design encompasses the concurrent design of products, services, business models, and stakeholder collaborations [19]. Drawing on existing literature and frameworks, we have conducted 31 semi-structured interviews with circular design experts and entrepreneurs. This study makes several contributions. First, we significantly enrich the discourse on circular systems design [20, 21]. Our theoretical advancements address crucial gaps in the existing literature, specifically concerning circular economy rebound [6, 22, 23] and organizational barriers encompassing knowledge and implementation [10, 11]. Second, our study contributes to the ongoing discourse surrounding circular product design [24, 25], sustainable product-service systems [26, 27], and circular business models [28, 29]. This multidimensional contribution not only augments existing frameworks but synthesizes diverse perspectives, fostering a more comprehensive and systemic understanding of circular innovation [19]. Third, our study makes a substantial methodological contribution by integrating design science methodology into the CE domain, showcasing its value in advancing this field [18, 30].

In alignment with Peffers et al. [17], the subsequent section of this research paper will delve into a systematic examination of the research problem and its theoretical underpinnings. Section 3 will elucidate the objectives of the solution artifact and expound upon the employed method. In Sect. 4, we develop and demonstrate the artifact, complemented by expert evaluations. Section 5 will discuss the disciplinary knowledge derived from the artifact. Finally, Sect. 6 synthesizes the key findings, reaffirms the contributions, and highlights avenues for further research.

2 Theoretical Background

2.1 Circular Design Strategies

The role of design is paramount in operationalizing the CE as it profoundly shapes subsequent product life cycles, economic and ecological benefits, and consumer behavior [31, 32]. Circular design can be categorized into four nested levels [19]: (1) circular product design as an integral part of (2) product-service system design, supported by the adaptation of (3) circular business models and organizational capabilities, which interact with stakeholders in the surrounding (4) collaborative ecosystem to realize circular value creation. While numerous frameworks and tools have been developed for the first three levels, these resources often lack adequate structure, fail to delineate a clear implementation process, or do not elucidate the intricate interactions and trade-offs between circular design strategies [13, 32–34]. Integrating product, service, business model, and collaboration design is deemed indispensable not only for practical implementation but also for advancing sustainable design theory [19, 24, 35, 36]. Due to their substantial overlap, we examine product-service systems and business models together.

Circular Product Design. Circular Product Design involves strategies that preserve functionality and physical integrity, utilize materials and components throughout multiple lifecycles, and maintain a product's value [32, 35, 37, 38]. The existing body of research predominantly revolves around "Design for X" guidelines, where the "X" represents a specific property such as repairability or recyclability [34, 39–41]. Den Hollander, Bakker and Hultink [24] put an emphasis on product integrity by preserving the value of products for as long as possible, preventing obsolescence, and ensuring effective recovery. Mesa, Esparragoza and Maury [42] advocate for an open product architecture, emphasizing modularity, standardization, and reconfiguration. Product designers should further distinguish between biological and technical materials [43–45]. Additional considerations include design for disassembly [46] and emotional obsolescence [47]. Accordingly, circular product design also requires considering non-technical factors like aesthetics and emotional attachment [48].

Product-Service System and Circular Business Model Design. Implementing circular products necessitates the exploration of innovative product-service combinations and novel business models to seamlessly facilitate their delivery [49, 50]. This paradigm shift underscores a profound evolution in the conceptualization of sustainable products, transitioning from mere physical entities to intricate value-delivery systems [32, 51]. In essence, product-service systems demand that firms shoulder comprehensive responsibilities, extending product delivery to repair, maintenance, upgrades, take-back, and recycling [26]. Circular business models extend product-service systems by combining value creation and delivery with value capture, making sense of the new activities and their long-term returns [29].

Collaborative Ecosystem Design. The successful implementation of circular business models hinges profoundly on collaboration among diverse organizations to enable multiple life cycles [52, 53]. The scope of circular value creation extends beyond traditional supply chains, encompassing a broader spectrum of actors from civil, industrial, and public spheres [32]. Collaboration and experimentation emerge as pivotal for the success of circular business models at the system level [54]. In the context of the CE, designers need to possess extensive knowledge spanning materials, supply chain, ecology, stakeholder management, and economics [55, 56], highlighting the need for multidisciplinary teams [45, 54, 57].

Systems Design. While the imperative for systemic approaches has been reiterated consistently, a notable dearth of consensus persists regarding the constituents of circular systems design (CSD) [58]. We conceptualize CSD as the holistic integration of circular product, service, business model, and ecosystem design into a cohesive, goal-seeking system reminiscent of interlocking cogs [59]. This conceptualization envisions an intricate alignment of these elements, functioning simultaneously to achieve a harmonious and purposeful synergy within the broader socio-technical system [58, 60].

2.2 Rebound Effects

The potential of CSD lies in its ability to substantially reduce negative externalities such as rebound effects [23]. While initially described for energy economics [61], scholars have asserted that rebound effects also subside circular practices [6, 22]. Circular Economy Rebound (CER) manifests when positive environmental impact achieved through sustainable production and consumption is negated by a simultaneous increase in production and consumption levels [6]. For example, the positive perception of recycled coffee cups might encourage consumers to use them more frequently, inadvertently diminishing the initial environmental benefits. Moreover, when circular products fail to compete with linear products in price and quality, they only address environmentally conscious niche markets, leading to additional production and consumption instead of substitution [6]. Castro, Trevisan, Pigosso and Mascarenhas [23] further argue that circular activities often require novel infrastructure and substantial energy (e.g., recycling), which may offset initial benefits. The challenge is that rebound effects are usually identified retrospectively, missing consideration in the design phase [62]. Metic and Pigosso [22] categorize rebound effect estimation into ex-ante and ex-post methods, highlighting a gap for ex-ante tools at the meso and macro levels. Besides early detection through systems design, CER can be mitigated by educating and empowering the population, gamification and penalization for social and environmental causes, environmental policy, and price control [23, 62, 63].

3   Method

We employ design science methodology to create a useful artifact for CSD that proactively mitigates CER [17, 18, 23]. Given the emerging nature of this field, our study positions itself as an exploration [30, 64]. For the development of our design artifact, we follow the research steps outlined by Peffers et al. [17].

3.1   Problem Definition

We have identified problems in both theory and practice. While CSD is insufficiently explored in the literature, practitioners encounter a messy landscape of tools and lack guidance for a holistic implementation of circular strategies [65, 66]. Consequently, our investigation focuses on supporting entrepreneurial actors in designing circular systems. We have developed a semi-structured questionnaire based on scientific knowledge, existing design principles, frameworks, and tools. In total, we have conducted 31 interviews with an average duration of 60 min. Interviewees were selected based on their expertise in circular design, representing a range of professional and geographic backgrounds. We used 'Zoom' to conduct and record the interviews upon the participants' consent. The primary objective of the interviews was to collect hands-on information from designers and entrepreneurs actively involved in circular design. This allowed us to collect unique design knowledge concerning the design process, design considerations, as well as trade-offs and dependencies between elements. We also took inspiration from several frameworks surrounding circular product and business model design to develop our tool [24, 29, 32, 34, 38, 67–69].

3.2 Design Creation and Evaluation

To develop the solution, we have analyzed existing circular design tools alongside empirical data to create the artifact (see Sect. 4). Both authors were involved in the data analysis to improve the robustness of the findings [70]. In case of disagreements, codes were discussed bilaterally to achieve inter-coder agreement [71]. The data analysis revealed more than 1200 first-order codes and 44 s-order themes [72]. These second-order themes were instrumental in crafting a blueprint that mirrors the design process of circular systems. The development of the process blueprint went through several internal iterations to condense the codes and structure the design process appropriately[1].

To demonstrate and evaluate the effectiveness of the conceived CSD process, we organized an online workshop via "Zoom" to enable participants to interact with the process blueprint on the web application "Miro." We invited two managing directors of an established international design academy. During the workshop, we presented the blueprint via screen-sharing on Miro and walked the participants through the process. We purposefully made breaks and left room for questions and comments throughout the workshop. We noted down all the feedback we received from the participants using sticky notes inside the Miro interface. The workshop lasted one and a half hours and was recorded upon consent of all participants. The comments were used to improve the correctness, usefulness, and intuitiveness of the process.

4 Results

4.1 Problem Identification and Objective Definition

To develop the process blueprint, we have reviewed extant generative circular design tools [73]. Our review encompassed 85 generative circular design tools[2] sourced through a systematic keyword search on Web of Science, Google Scholar, and Google, using terms such as 'circular,' 'design,' 'tool,' 'model,' 'framework,' 'product,' 'system,' and 'business model,' which led to the identification of 28 tools from academic research and 57 tools from practice. First, we categorized the tools into seven types. Second, we examined the identified tools based on their alignment with the design levels [19, 58]. Third, we considered additional aspects, such as the outline of the design process and any specific industry focus (Table 1).

To streamline our analysis, we excluded industry-specific tools, resulting in 65 tools. This approach ensures a more cohesive and universally applicable framework that can

---

[1] Due to the large volume of codes, we did not include a coding tree (available on request).

[2] Due to the large number of tools, we only provide an overview (available on request).

Table 1. Tool Landscape

Type of Tool	Principles/Guideline	Framework	Method/Toolkit	Workshop	Canvas	Software/Database	Game/Cards	System Focus	Design Process
Theory Tools	9.09%	54.54%	13.63%	9.09%	18.18%	9.09%	-	0%	13.63%
Practice Tools	27.91%	6.97%	32.56%	-	-	27.91%	4.65%	0%	34.88%
Overall	21.54%	23.08%	26.15%	3.08%	6.15%	21.54%	3.08%	0%	27.69%

be adapted to specific contexts. In addition, our review highlights a significant gap, as evidenced by the absence of tools addressing a systemic approach connecting three or more design levels (0%) and offering a clear design process (27.69%). Although numerous tools excel in ideation, they frequently fall short in facilitating the complex implementation phase. Circular design demands iterative testing with stakeholders under real-world conditions, a requirement not fully addressed by contemporary tools. Refining our tool analysis, we identified 16 practical and 9 theoretical tools that met our criteria satisfactorily. Recognizing the utility of these tools at the different circular design levels, our objective is to integrate these perspectives by developing a comprehensive CSD process that harmonizes design decisions across them. This integrated approach acknowledges and builds upon prior research while creating new synergies, contributing to both theoretical understanding and practical application in the field of circular innovation [64].

4.2 Artifact Development

Leveraging empirical data, we have constructed a comprehensive process blueprint using the second-order themes. Following the coding procedure outlined by Gioia, Corley and Hamilton [72], we discover five aggregate dimensions or "stages" along the CSD process (Fig. 1), namely (1) System Research, (2) Life Cycle Thinking, (3) System Creation, (4) System Fit, and (5) System Evaluation.

Commencing with 'System Research,' entrepreneurial actors immerse themselves in systems thinking and mapping [58, 74], analyze the competitive landscape [75], explore technological enablers [76], understand and anticipate legislation [77], conduct consumer ethnography [78], and delve into waste stream analysis [79, 80], circular supply chains [81], and the (recycling) infrastructure [82]. Potential outcomes of the system research phase are opportunities for circular value creation, such as harmful waste streams, inefficient supply chains, or similar. Building on these system inputs, the subsequent step is 'Life Cycle Thinking' [44]. This involves the selection of an appropriate circular business model archetype for each life cycle of the underlying service, product, component, or resource [69]. Archetypes relate to the inertia principle ranging from high-value retention to low-value retention [24, 83], clustered by circular strategies corresponding to 'narrowing,' 'slowing,' and 'closing' resource loops [67, 68]. With an increasing number of life cycles, users typically relegate to archetypes that relate to low-value retention, such as recycling and recovering [84].

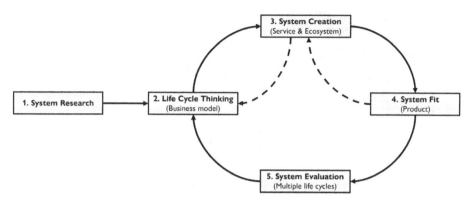

Fig. 1. Circular Systems Design Process

The process then shifts to 'System Creation' involving service and experience design, where the user must think about ownership and take-back strategies. This is followed by ecosystem design, where the user outlines the necessary stakeholder collaborations to realize their respective circular business model archetype while harmonizing the incentive system for each relevant stakeholder with the system's economic viability. The final step involves testing the chosen circular business model with all relevant stakeholders, including the end consumer [85].

During the following 'System Fit' stage, the emphasis is on designing the circular product to align with the outlined system. This involves optimizing material selection for the desired circular strategies [86], including the quality and source of materials, local production capabilities, modularity, biodegradability, recyclability, and more. Depending on their choices, users must balance certain trade-offs between product performance and sustainability [38] while also reducing CER through purposeful design considerations and mitigation mechanisms [6, 23]. The final stage, 'System Evaluation,' foresees using life cycle assessment (LCA) methods [87]. Businesses are further encouraged to formulate a data strategy for continuous improvement and employ product metrics such as circularity, durability, and utilization [88].

An essential facet of this process is its iterative nature. Users must continually test and refine their hypotheses about the business model, service and product design, and how they embed into the system. This iterative approach involves probing with real customers, gathering usage data, and incorporating valuable stakeholder feedback to enhance the efficacy of the CSD.

Upon completing the design for the first life cycle, the process foresees imagining potential scenarios for the product's end-of-life. Users then restart the process by selecting another suitable business model archetype [84]. After designing multiple life cycles, businesses eventually choose a 'closing the loop' business model archetype, such as 'recycling' or 'organic feedstock,' to finalize the CSD. Thus, the iterative process covers the entire life cycle of a product.

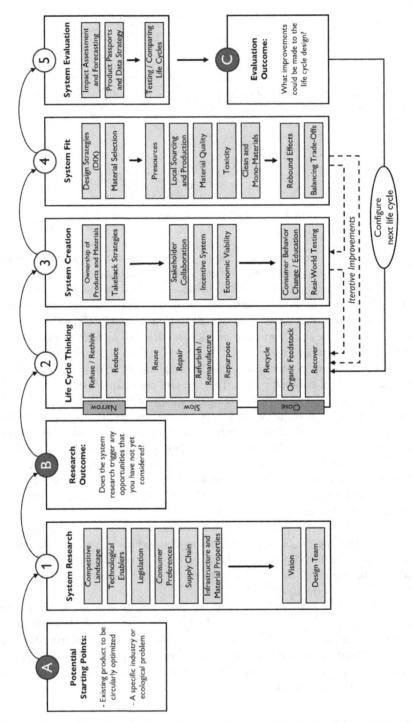

Fig. 2. Process Blueprint for Circular Systems Design (detailed schematic representation)

4.3 Artifact Demonstration and Evaluation

The artifact demonstration and evaluation were held in December 2023. We developed the first "prototype" of the process blueprint using the web application "Miro" (Fig. 2). The demonstration took the form of a workshop with the managing directors of an international design academy. It involved walking through the process blueprint, explaining the interactions, and addressing any arising questions or comments. The entire demonstration session was recorded, and feedback was documented. The overall evaluation feedback was highly positive. The sequencing of the process blueprint was appreciated, finding it logical and well-structured. They also commended the 'look and feel' of the prototype, describing it as straightforward and intuitive. The iterative nature of the tool received particular praise. Naturally, several points for improvement were identified. These included clarifying the exact starting point of the process, allowing for the generation of novel ideas during the System Research and Life Cycle Thinking phase, providing flexibility for creating novel and innovative business models, and incorporating regenerative approaches next to high and low-value retention strategies.

4.4 Adaptation of the Design Tool

Following the initial demonstration, we refined the process blueprint. First, we introduced a clearly defined starting point with two choices – product or industry. The design process starts by selecting a specific product/service for circular optimization or, more broadly, a particular industry or ecological problem. This modification enhances the clarity and specificity of the tool's starting point. Second, we incorporated an unspecified business model archetype for each circular design strategy. This addition aims to provide users with more flexibility and freedom during the "Life Cycle Thinking" stage, enabling the generation of new business models and products. Regenerative business models were not directly included, as they do not align with the categorization of narrowing, slowing, and closing resource loops. Instead, we added a note with regenerative practices to serve as inspiration. Lastly, improvements were made to the blueprint's visual aesthetic.

5 Discussion

Throughout this study, we have developed a process blueprint for CSD. The objectives of the present study were driven by a combination of prevalent insufficiencies. First, extant literature does not align with the complex reality of circular systems. Second, practitioners face a confusing landscape of tools and methods that are limited in scope and prescriptive power. Third, empirical insights and theory suggest that some of the underlying assumptions of CER can be circumvented through informed and holistic CSD [6, 23]. We contribute to theory by establishing CSD as a valuable framework for addressing CER [6]. We define CSD as the holistic integration of circular product, service, business model, and ecosystem design into a cohesive, goal-seeking system that operates within the broader socio-technical system [59, 60]. CSD circumvents rebound effects by prioritizing system functionality, pushing customer convenience, reduction advocacy, and maintaining cost-efficiency through choosing suitable materials and components with mass market quality. Moreover, educating consumers about the lower total cost of ownership can justify higher initial prices, while long-term product recovery strategies enable cost reduction over time, contributing to the avoidance of rebound effects. Balancing trade-offs proved paramount in CSD, encompassing considerations such as product performance versus environmental impact or additional logistics against profitability. It's crucial to navigate these tensions effectively to ensure the sustainability and economic viability of the system.

We, therefore, introduce the first process blueprint for CSD. This artifact outlines how successful circular designers and entrepreneurs go about the complex design process to create a well-informed circular system encompassing product, service, business model, and collaborative partnerships in the ecosystem. It addresses CER comprehensively by aiding in the design of circular systems that match linear product quality and price and target mainstream markets [6]. At the same time, this process blueprint achieves the cohesive design of multiple layers extending the model brought forth by Iacovidou, Hahladakis and Purnell [58]. We outline how the design layers are related and designed iteratively in the context of CSD.

In addition, we bridge the gap between theory and practice by offering practical guidance to businesses grounded in rigorous scientific methods, constituting a strong practical contribution [89]. We thereby contribute proof of concept for the method's value in advancing sustainability research and overcoming the three-body problem by integrating theory, practice, and design [90]. We also add an in-depth review of extant circular design tools that can be used to complement the design process [19].

6 Conclusions, Limitations and Future Research

Our study makes a significant theoretical contribution by introducing and championing the concept of CSD to address the critical issue of CER, as highlighted by Zink and Geyer [6]. This contribution marks a substantive step forward in addressing a fundamental theoretical concern within the broader context of the CE [3]. Moreover, our paper provides a profound practical contribution by creating valuable design knowledge embodied in the CSD process blueprint. Finally, we advocate for the increased integration of design science methodology into CE research to generate practically relevant knowledge that aligns with the sustainability transition.

A second round of demonstration and evaluation should encompass real-world testing, stakeholder feedback, and performance metrics to substantiate the anticipated benefits. It is essential to note that the avoidance of CER can only be assessed qualitatively since these effects come to surface when already operating. Further rounds of testing and stakeholder input will contribute to a comprehensive understanding of the tool's effectiveness in mitigating CER. Additionally, the extensive scientific knowledge on the individual design levels (product, service, and business model) has guided the focus toward the most appropriate industry and role-agnostic tools and frameworks. While this approach suits the current context, further development by other researchers is encouraged. The process blueprint could be customized for specific industries and regional contexts, considering factors such as supply chain characteristics, infrastructure properties and the availability of local materials.

Acknowledgments. We would like to thank our collaborators from the design academy for allowing us to improve and validate our tool with professional designers.

Disclosure of Interests. The authors have no competing interests to declare that are relevant to the content of this article.

References

1. Ghisellini, P., Cialani, C., Ulgiati, S.: A review on circular economy: the expected transition to a balanced interplay of environmental and economic systems. J. Clean. Prod. **114**, 11–32 (2016)
2. Hartley, K., van Santen, R., Kirchherr, J.: Policies for transitioning towards a circular economy: expectations from the European Union (EU). Resour. Conserv. Recycl. **155**, 104634 (2020)
3. Corvellec, H., Stowell, A.F., Johansson, N.: Critiques of the circular economy. J. Ind. Ecol. **26**, 421–432 (2022)
4. Bianchi, M., Cordella, M.: Does circular economy mitigate the extraction of natural resources? Empirical evidence based on analysis of 28 European economies over the past decade. Ecol. Econ. **203**, 107607 (2023)
5. Parrique, T., Barth, J., Briens, F., Kerschner, C., Kraus-Polk, A., Kuokkanen, A., Spangenberg, J.H.: Decoupling debunked. Evidence and arguments against green growth as a sole strategy for sustainability. A study edited by the European Environment Bureau EEB (2019)
6. Zink, T., Geyer, R.: Circular economy rebound. J. Ind. Ecol. **21**, 593–602 (2017)
7. Korhonen, J., Nuur, C., Feldmann, A., Birkie, S.E.: Circular economy as an essentially contested concept. J. Clean. Prod. **175**, 544–552 (2018)
8. Korhonen, J., Honkasalo, A., Seppälä, J.: Circular economy: the concept and its limitations. Ecol. Econ. **143**, 37–46 (2018)
9. Mayer, A.L., Kauppi, P.E., Angelstam, P.K., Zhang, Y., Tikka, P.M.: Importing timber, exporting ecological impact. vol. 308, pp. 359–360. American Association for the Advancement of Science (2005)
10. Kirchherr, J., et al.: Barriers to the circular economy: evidence from the European Union (EU). Ecol. Econ. **150**, 264–272 (2018)
11. Takacs, F., Brunner, D., Frankenberger, K.: Barriers to a circular economy in small- and medium-sized enterprises and their integration in a sustainable strategic management framework. J. Clean. Prod. **362**, 132227 (2022)
12. Bolton, R., Hannon, M.: Governing sustainability transitions through business model innovation: towards a systems understanding. Res. Policy **45**, 1731–1742 (2016)
13. Ceschin, F., Gaziulusoy, I.: Evolution of design for sustainability: from product design to design for system innovations and transitions. Design Stud. **47**, 118–163 (2016)
14. Scoones, I., et al.: Transformations to sustainability: combining structural, systemic and enabling approaches. Curr. Opinion Environ. Sustain. **42**, 65–75 (2020)
15. Schellong, D., Sadek, P., Schaetzberger, C., Barrack, T.: The promise and pitfalls of e-scooter sharing. Europe **12**, 15 (2019)
16. Nouvian, T.: Green Savior or Deadly Menace? Paris Votes on E-Scooter Ban. The New York Times (2023)
17. Peffers, K., Tuunanen, T., Rothenberger, M.A., Chatterjee, S.: A design science research methodology for information systems research. J. Manag. Inf. Syst. **24**, 45–77 (2007)
18. Dimov, D., Maula, M., Romme, A.G.L.: Crafting and assessing design science research for entrepreneurship, vol. 47, pp. 1543–1567. SAGE Publications Sage, Los Angeles (2023)

19. Baldassarre, B., Keskin, D., Diehl, J.C., Bocken, N., Calabretta, G.: Implementing sustainable design theory in business practice: a call to action. J. Clean. Prod. **273**, 17 (2020)

20. Wiprachtiger, M., Haupt, M., Heeren, N., Waser, E., Hellweg, S.: A framework for sustainable and circular system design: development and application on thermal insulation materials. Resour. Conserv. Recycl. **154**, 11 (2020)

21. Velenturf, A.P.M., Purnell, P.: Principles for a sustainable circular economy. Sustain. Prod. Consump. **27**, 1437–1457 (2021)

22. Metic, J., Pigosso, D.C.: Research avenues for uncovering the rebound effects of the circular economy: a systematic literature review. J. Clean Prod. 133133 (2022)

23. Castro, C.G., Trevisan, A.H., Pigosso, D.C., Mascarenhas, J.: The rebound effect of circular economy: definitions, mechanisms and a research agenda. J. Clean. Prod. **345**, 131136 (2022)

24. den Hollander, M.C., Bakker, C.A., Hultink, E.J.: Product design in a circular economy development of a typology of key concepts and terms. J. Ind. Ecol. **21**, 517–525 (2017)

25. Hapuwatte, B.M., Jawahir, I.S.: Closed-loop sustainable product design for circular economy. J. Ind. Ecol. **25**, 1430–1446 (2021)

26. Tukker, A.: Product services for a resource-efficient and circular economy–a review. J. Clean. Prod. **97**, 76–91 (2015)

27. Vezzoli, C., Ceschin, F., Diehl, J.C., Kohtala, C.: New design challenges to widely implement 'sustainable product-service systems.' J. Clean. Prod. **97**, 1–12 (2015)

28. Palmie, M., Boehm, J., Lekkas, C.K., Parida, V., Wincent, J., Gassmann, O.: Circular business model implementation: design choices, orchestration strategies, and transition pathways for resource-sharing solutions. J. Clean. Prod. **280**, 12 (2021)

29. Geissdoerfer, M., Pieroni, M.P., Pigosso, D.C., Soufani, K.: Circular business models: a review. J. Clean. Prod. **277**, 123741 (2020)

30. Seckler, C., Mauer, R., vom Brocke, J.: Design science in entrepreneurship: conceptual foundations and guiding principles. J. Bus. Ventur. Des. **1**, 100004 (2021)

31. Wastling, T., Charnley, F., Moreno, M.: Design for circular behaviour: considering users in a circular economy. Sustainability **10**, 22 (2018)

32. Diaz, A., Reyes, T., Baumgartner, R.J.: Implementing circular economy strategies during product development. Resour. Conserv. Recycl. **184**, 18 (2022)

33. Hofmann, F., Jaeger-Erben, M.: Organizational transition management of circular business model innovations. Bus. Strateg. Environ. **29**, 2770–2788 (2020)

34. Franconi, A., Ceschin, F., Peck, D.: Structuring circular objectives and design strategies for the circular economy: a multi-hierarchical theoretical framework. Sustainability **14**, 9298 (2022)

35. Moreno, M., De los Rios, C., Rowe, Z., Charnley, F.: A conceptual framework for circular design. Sustainability **8**, 15 (2016)

36. Blomsma, F., et al.: Developing a circular strategies framework for manufacturing companies to support circular economy-oriented innovation. J. Clean. Prod. **241**, 17 (2019)

37. Shahbazi, S., Jonbrink, A.K.: Design guidelines to develop circular products: action research on nordic industry. Sustainability **12**, 14 (2020)

38. Luttropp, C., Lagerstedt, J.: EcoDesign and the ten golden rules: generic advice for merging environmental aspects into product development. J. Clean. Prod. **14**, 1396–1408 (2006)

39. Sassanelli, C., Urbinati, A., Rosa, P., Chiaroni, D., Terzi, S.: Addressing circular economy through design for X approaches: a systematic literature review. Comput. Ind. **120**, 23 (2020)

40. Bhamra, T., Lilley, D., Tang, T.: Design for sustainable behaviour: using products to change consumer behaviour. Des. J. **14**, 427–445 (2011)

41. Lofthouse, V., Trimingham, R., Bhamra, T.: Reinventing refills: guidelines for design. Packag. Technol. Sci. **30**, 809–818 (2017)

42. Mesa, J.A., Esparragoza, I., Maury, H.: Trends and perspectives of sustainable product design for open architecture products: facing the circular economy model. Int. J. Precis Eng. Manuf.-Green Technol. **6**, 377–391 (2019)

43. McDonough, W., Braungart, M.: Cradle to Cradle: Remaking the Way We Make Things. North Point Press (2010)

44. Mestre, A., Cooper, T.: Circular product design. A multiple loops life cycle design approach for the circular economy. Des. J. **20**, S1620–S1635 (2017)

45. Wang, J.X., Burke, H., Zhang, A.: Overcoming barriers to circular product design*. Int. J. Prod. Econ. **243**, 16 (2022)

46. Van den Berg, M., Bakker, C.: A product design framework for a circular economy. Product Lifetimes and the Environment, pp. 365–379 (2015)

47. Chapman, J.: Design for (emotional) durability. Des. Issues **25**, 29–35 (2009)

48. Ljungberg, L.Y.: Materials selection and design for development of sustainable products. Mater. Des. **28**, 466–479 (2007)

49. Moro, S.R., Cauchick-Miguel, P.A., de Mendes, G.H.S.: Adding sustainable value in product-service systems business models design: a conceptual review towards a framework proposal. Sustain. Prod. Consum. **32**, 492–504 (2022)

50. Franco, M.A.: A system dynamics approach to product design and business model strategies for the circular economy. J. Clean. Prod. **241**, 16 (2019)

51. Vezzoli, C., et al.: Product-service system design for sustainability. Routledge (2017)

52. Konietzko, J., Bocken, N., Hultink, E.J.: Circular ecosystem innovation: an initial set of principles. J. Clean. Prod. **253**, 119942 (2020)

53. Pieroni, M.P., McAloone, T.C., Pigosso, D.C.: Business model innovation for circular economy and sustainability: a review of approaches. J. Clean. Prod. **215**, 198–216 (2019)

54. Brown, P., Baldassarre, B., Konietzko, J., Bocken, N., Balkenende, R.: A tool for collaborative circular proposition design. J. Clean. Prod. **297**, 15 (2021)

55. Dokter, G., Thuvander, L., Rahe, U.: How circular is current design practice? Investigating perspectives across industrial design and architecture in the transition towards a circular economy. Sustain. Prod. Consum. **26**, 692–708 (2021)

56. Borms, L., Van Opstal, W., Brusselaers, J., Van Passel, S.: The working future: an analysis of skills needed by circular startups. J. Clean. Prod. **409**, 137261 (2023)

57. Cuomo, F.: Urban living lab: an experimental co-production tool to foster the circular economy. Soc. Sci. **11**, 22 (2022)

58. Iacovidou, E., Hahladakis, J.N., Purnell, P.: A systems thinking approach to understanding the challenges of achieving the circular economy. Environ. Sci. Pollut. Res. **28**, 24785–24806 (2021)

59. Ackoff, R.L.: Towards a system of systems concepts. Manage. Sci. **17**, 661–671 (1971)

60. Geels, F.W.: Technological transitions as evolutionary reconfiguration processes: a multi-level perspective and a case-study. Res. Policy **31**, 1257–1274 (2002)

61. Greening, L.A., Greene, D.L., Difiglio, C.: Energy efficiency and consumption—the rebound effect—a survey. Energy Policy **28**, 389–401 (2000)

62. Das, A., Konietzko, J., Bocken, N., Dijk, M.: The Circular rebound tool: a tool to move companies towards more sustainable circular business models. Resour. Conserv. Recycl. Adv. **20**, 200185 (2023)

63. Zerbino, P.: How to manage the circular economy rebound effect: a proposal for contingency-based guidelines. J. Clean. Prod. **378**, 134584 (2022)

64. Gregor, S., Hevner, A.R.: Positioning and presenting design science research for maximum impact. MIS Q. **37**, 337 (2013)

65. Royo, M., Chulvi, V., Mulet, E., Ruiz-Pastor, L.: Analysis of parameters about useful life extension in 70 tools and methods related to eco-design and circular economy. J. Ind. Ecol. **27**, 562–586 (2023)

66. Kalmykova, Y., Sadagopan, M., Rosado, L.: Circular economy - from review of theories and practices to development of implementation tools. Resour. Conserv. Recycl. **135**, 190–201 (2018)

67. Bocken, N.M., De Pauw, I., Bakker, C., Van Der Grinten, B.: Product design and business model strategies for a circular economy. J. Ind. Prod. Eng. **33**, 308–320 (2016)

68. Lüdeke-Freund, F., Gold, S., Bocken, N.M.: A review and typology of circular economy business model patterns. J. Ind. Ecol. **23**, 36–61 (2019)

69. Pieroni, M.P., McAloone, T.C., Pigosso, D.C.: From theory to practice: systematising and testing business model archetypes for circular economy. Resour. Conserv. Recycl. **162**, 105029 (2020)

70. Denzin, N.K.: The research act: A theoretical introduction to sociological methods. Transaction Publishers (2017)

71. Campbell, J.L., Quincy, C., Osserman, J., Pedersen, O.K.: Coding in-depth semistructured interviews: problems of unitization and intercoder reliability and agreement. Sociol. Methods Res. **42**, 294–320 (2013)

72. Gioia, D.A., Corley, K.G., Hamilton, A.L.: Seeking qualitative rigor in inductive research: notes on the Gioia methodology. Organ. Res. Methods **16**, 15–31 (2013)

73. de Koeijer, B., Wever, R., Henseler, J.: Realizing product-packaging combinations in circular systems: shaping the research agenda. Packag. Technol. Sci. **30**, 443–460 (2017)

74. Sumter, D., de Koning, J., Bakker, C., Balkenende, R.: Key competencies for design in a circular economy: exploring gaps in design knowledge and skills for a circular economy. Sustainability **13**, 15 (2021)

75. D'Aveni, R.A.: Mapping your competitive position. Harvard Bus. Rev. **85**, 110–120, 154 (2007)

76. von Briel, F., Davidsson, P., Recker, J.: Digital technologies as external enablers of new venture creation in the IT hardware sector. Entrep. Theory Pract. **42**, 47–69 (2018)

77. Davidsson, P., Recker, J., Von Briel, F.: External enablement of new venture creation: a framework. Acad. Manag. Perspect. **34**, 311–332 (2020)

78. Baskerville, R.L., Myers, M.D.: Design ethnography in information systems. Inf. Syst. J. **25**, 23–46 (2015)

79. Hines, P., Rich, N.: The seven value stream mapping tools. Int. J. Oper. Prod. Manag. **17**, 46–64 (1997)

80. Geissdoerfer, M., Morioka, S.N., de Carvalho, M.M., Evans, S.: Business models and supply chains for the circular economy. J. Clean. Prod. **190**, 712–721 (2018)

81. Burke, H., Zhang, A.B., Wang, J.X.: Integrating product design and supply chain management for a circular economy. Prod. Plan. Control **17** (2021)

82. Ribes, D., Finholt, T.A.: The long now of infrastructure: articulating tensions in development (2009)

83. Achterberg, E., Hinfelaar, J., Bocken, N.: Master circular business with the value hill. Circle Economy (2016)

84. Stumpf, L., Schöggl, J.-P., Baumgartner, R.J.: Climbing up the circularity ladder?–a mixed-methods analysis of circular economy in business practice. J. Clean. Prod. **316**, 128158 (2021)

85. Baldassarre, B., et al.: Addressing the design-implementation gap of sustainable business models by prototyping: a tool for planning and executing small-scale pilots. J. Clean. Prod. **255**, 15 (2020)

86. Mesa, J., González-Quiroga, A., Maury, H.: Developing an indicator for material selection based on durability and environmental footprint: a circular economy perspective. Resour. Conserv. Recycl. **160**, 104887 (2020)

87. Scheepens, A.E., Vogtlander, J.G., Brezet, J.C.: Two life cycle assessment (LCA) based methods to analyse and design complex (regional) circular economy systems. Case: making water tourism more sustainable. J. Clean Prod. **114**, 257–268 (2016)

88. Boyer, R.H., et al.: Three-dimensional product circularity. J. Ind. Ecol. **25**, 824–833 (2021)
89. Baskerville, R., Baiyere, A., Gregor, S., Hevner, A., Rossi, M.: Design science research contributions: Finding a balance between artifact and theory. J. Assoc. Inf. Syst. **19**, 3 (2018)
90. Berglund, H., Dimov, D., Wennberg, K.: Beyond bridging rigor and relevance: the three-body problem in entrepreneurship, vol. 9, pp. 87–91. Elsevier (2018)

General Track

Conceptualizing Multi-party AI Reliance for Design Research

Sven Eckhardt[1]([✉]) [iD], Mateusz Dolata[1] [iD], Ingrid Bauer-Hänsel[2] [iD],
and Gerhard Schwabe[1] [iD]

[1] University of Zurich, Binzmuehlestrasse 14, 8050 Zurich, Switzerland
{eckhardt,dolata,schwabe}@ifi.uzh.ch
[2] University of St. Gallen (HSG), Müller-Friedberg-Strasse 8, 9000 St. Gallen, Switzerland
ingrid.bauer-haensel@unisg.ch

Abstract. Appropriate reliance on artificial intelligence (AI)-based systems is paramount to leverage increasing AI performance. However, multi-party settings, where multiple parties with diverging interests interact with the support of AI systems, are currently neglected. In this study, we use Heider's balance theory to derive a framework that allows us to conceptualize and analyze reliance on AI in multi-party settings. We then use this framework to analyze two large design science research projects. First, we analyze financial advisory service encounters, where the role inequality of advisor and client can lead to a dominance of the advisor. Second, we analyze used car market negotiations, where the problem of *partial reliance* on AI systems creates a misalignment between the two parties, ultimately failing the negotiations. Finally, we discuss implications and future research on AI reliance in multi-party settings and highlight that this study should serve as a starting point in investigating AI reliance in multi-party settings.

Keywords: Artificial Intelligence · Reliance · Multi-Party · Framework

1 Introduction

Artificial intelligence (AI), in the form of machine learning-based systems, is ubiquitous. From chatbots, such as ChatGPT [1], to autonomous cars [2] or medical systems detecting diseases [3], all humans are confronted with AI. The performance of these AI systems is steadily increasing. However, humans play a crucial role in using AI systems in practice, not the least because of regulatory requirements, such as the EU regulations [4], that require human oversight of these AI systems. Therefore, like many IT artifacts, AI systems are sociotechnical [5].

The reliance of users on AI systems is of utmost importance in realizing the potential of increasing AI performance in real-life settings. Reliance can be defined as *"the user's incorporation of the intelligent system's processes and outputs when formulating their own decision"* [6]. For AI systems, reliance can be seen, in short, as *following AI advice* [7, 8]. Only with reliance can the potential of AI be realized. However, always relying on AI systems is also undesirable as it leads to overreliance, i.e., following incorrect AI advice [9]. Therefore, research has pushed the notion of *appropriate reliance*, where a user should follow AI if the advice is correct but not follow if the AI advice is incorrect [7, 10]. Nowadays, much research is concerned with designing systems for *appropriate reliance* in human-AI interactions with a single human decision-maker [11, 12].

However, real-life settings are more complex than single-user human-AI interactions. For example, in a doctor-patient setting, the doctor needs to rely on an AI diagnosis, and the patient also needs to rely on the AI to accept the diagnosis. Further, the patient must also appropriately rely on the doctor, who bases their diagnosis on the AI. This example illustrates that AI reliance becomes more complex in real life than currently considered in the existing literature.

Additionally, when multiple users are present, they often have individual and sometimes diverging interests. This phenomenon is known as the principal-agent problem [13]. For example, a doctor has their own financial interests [14], financial advisors often must meet the bank's interests in selling certain products [15], or in market negotiations, a buyer wants a low price and a seller a high price [16]. We call these settings with multiple users having diverging interests *multi-party settings*. While there are some studies on AI reliance with more than one user, e.g., in groups [17], current research on AI reliance does not satisfactorily cover reliance on AI in multi-party settings, which we denote as *multi-party AI reliance (MPAIR)* and ask:

RQ *How can we conceptualize multi-party AI reliance for design research?*

In the subsequent sections, we engage in the following steps to answer this **RQ**. First, we conceptualize MPAIR based on Heider's balance theory [18]. Heider's balance theory is one of the few theories for triads and, thus, adequate to describe the setting of two parties and one AI system. Second, using this conceptualization, we develop an analytical framework to investigate multi-party situations. This framework stresses the distinction between the behavior of humans in a single-user setting and in multi-party settings, thus allowing for more sound insights into multi-party settings. Lastly, we use this novel conceptualization to present a framework to analyze multi-party situations. We then use this framework to analyze two large design science research (DSR) projects we have previously studied with the lens of MPAIR. Both projects have unique characteristics, allowing us to gain complementary insights into the applicability and relevance of our framework.

2 Background

2.1 AI Reliance

While the performance of modern AI is growing exponentially, in practical settings, humans are still crucial for many AI applications. Revisiting the above example, a doctor needs to rely on the decision of an AI system detecting illnesses and come up with the final decision, as the system does not make the final decision by itself. However, the doctor should only rely on this AI whenever it is correct. When the model is incorrect, ideally, the doctor would not rely on the model but instead on themselves.

Therefore, much research has been conducted on underreliance or overreliance on AI systems [19, 20]. Underreliance is the disuse of the AI system, which means the user does not follow the AI advice, even when it presents the correct output. Overreliance is a misuse of the system, which means the user follows the AI's advice even when it presents incorrect output. Consequently, the remaining option is appropriate reliance, where a user should follow AI if the advice is correct but not follow if the AI advice is incorrect [7, 10]. However, many factors can influence the appropriateness of reliance, such as statistical literacy [21], task experience [6], or malfunctions [22]. Further, mental models are often considered for AI systems and have been shown to influence reliance: a positive mental model increases the reliance on an AI system, while a negative mental model hinders reliance [23].

Often, research requires an initial human decision to measure *appropriate reliance* on AI advice [8, 24]. The initial human decision is defined as the human decision without being exposed to AI advice. This initial human decision enables a more nuanced view of AI reliance [8]: If the initial human decision coincides with the AI advice, we cannot measure the reliance of the human. However, if these two differ and the final decision is correct, we achieve *appropriate reliance* either through correct AI reliance or correct self-reliance. If the final decision is incorrect, we have underreliance (if the AI advice was correct) or overreliance (if the AI advice was incorrect).

One common way to achieve *appropriate reliance* on AI systems is by using explanations [11, 12]. Research on AI systems indicates that reliance cannot only be expressed towards the AI's advice and assisting tasks, such as providing explanations [25]. Overall, research on reliance on AI focuses on single-user human-AI interactions. Recently, there has been some research on group settings [17]. However, real-world multi-party settings, where users have diverging interests, are underexplored in research.

2.2 (Cognitive) Balance Theory

Many real-world decisions involve multiple parties with diverging interests. This can be summarized as the principle-agent problem, which points out conflicting interests and information asymmetries between two parties [13]. While defined for two human parties, research on the principal-agent setting is also transferred to human-AI interaction, where information asymmetries between humans and AI exist [26, 27]. However, such considerations of the principal-agent problem replace one human actor with an artificial one. Instead, we are interested in settings where two human actors are confronted with an additional artificial party participating in the interaction. Examples include market negotiations, advisory service encounters, or doctor-patient encounters supported by AI systems.

Further, the setting of two human actors and one possible inanimate involves more complicated issues covered in the so-called balance theory accredited to Heider [18, 28]. In Heider's balance theory, the triad consists of one person (P) who either has a *positive relation* or a *negative relation* to another Person (O). The positive and negative relations can translate to various meanings, such as *like* and not *like*, or *value* or not *value*. Note that, for example, the negative relation of *like*, i.e., not *like*, does not necessarily translate to disliking but rather being neutral towards another person. This relationship is extended towards an object or a third person (X), to which P and O can have a positive or a negative relation. This results in a total of three binary relationships within the triad and, thus, a total of eight possible configurations between positive and negative relations towards each other. These configurations are presented in Fig. 1. Heider's balance theory explains that there are balanced and unbalanced states. While balanced states are stable and can exist straightforwardly, unbalanced states are more problematic. Ultimately, all unbalanced states must resolve in a balanced one.

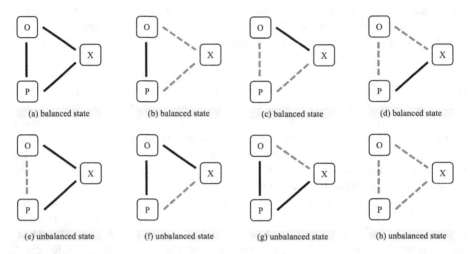

Fig. 1. There are eight possible configurations for (cognitive) balance between a person (P), another (O) person, and an object or a third person (X). The black solid line indicates a positive (+) relationship, and the grey dashed line indicates a negative (−) relationship.

In unbalanced states, the problem of cognitive dissonance between P and O arises [29]. For example, considering state (f) in Fig. 1: While P has a positive relation to O and O has a positive relation towards X, P has a negative relation towards X. This creates cognitive dissonance for X, which can change their relation towards O to a negative one (resulting in state (c)) or change their relation towards X to a positive on (resulting in state (a)). The relation can, for example, be translated to the attitude of liking as follows: If Alice likes Bob and Bob likes Charlie, but Alice does not like Charlie, this is an unbalanced state that can either be resolved by Alice liking Charlie or Alice not liking Bob. Heider's balance theory states that unbalanced states will resolve into balanced ones. While Heider's balance theory is defined for triadic relationships, extensions exist to larger networks, such as the structural balance theory [30].

Balance theory and its extension of structural balance theory have many applications. For example, in marketing, balance theory determines how celebrity endorsements affect customers' attitudes toward products [31]. Another example is athletes' off-field behavior and team identification by fans [32]. Not only attitude but also the buying behavior of consumers is investigated using the balance theory [33], which already shows empirical indications that balance theory is not solely directed towards people's attitudes. Further, structural balance theory is used in machine learning algorithms for recommender systems. For example, Qi et al. [34] developed an algorithm that identifies the target user's "enemies" and "friends" and uses this to recommend certain products. Finally, balance theory was also researched in the early days of software agents, where conversational agents could influence the relationship between two humans [35]. Overall, the application of balance theory is manifold. In the following, we use the balance theory to conceptualize MPAIR.

3 Conceptualization of MPAIR

In this section, we answer the **RQ** by conceptualizing MPAIR based on current definitions of appropriate reliance. We use a binary discrete decision case to develop the theory. In subsequent chapters, we discuss the generalization of this theory towards a broader class of problems. First, we transfer Heider's balance theory [18] to AI reliance. After that, we use this insight to derive a conceptualization of MPAIR and a framework to analyze multi-party settings. Given that this conceptualization entails many constructs, we summarize them and their notations in Table 1.

Table 1. Glossary for the needed terms and constructs

Term	Definition
Reliance	The behavior of following (AI) advice [8]
Appropriate Reliance	The behavior of following correct and not following incorrect (AI) advice [8]
Initial single-user reliance (ISUR)	The reliance a user would have on the AI in a single-user setting without the other party involved. It can be called appropriate ISUR or inappropriate ISUR (see Sect. 3.1)
(Un)balanced states	Configurations in the triadic relationship between two parties and an AI system (see Fig. 1)
(Un)desired cases	Balanced states of the configurations in the triadic relationship between two parties and an AI that are desired to achieve (see Fig. 4)

3.1 Reliance Balance

The naïve way to transfer findings on *appropriate reliance* on AI from the single-user setting into multi-party settings is to define the multi-party setting as the sum of two individual human-AI interactions. Then, reliance in multi-party settings is defined as the sum of two independent reliance behaviors. However, this view is too naïve for various reasons. For one, it neglects the interaction and dynamics between the parties. For the other, this view does not account for varying levels of reliance. For example, if one party has *appropriate reliance* while the other does not, some conflicts might arise between the two parties. Therefore, we need a more nuanced view.

We give a short motivating example of what that entails for the relation of reliance. This example is illustrated in Fig. 2. First, (i) in a patient-doctor dyad, a patient might rely on a doctor's diagnosis. Further, (ii) in a doctor-AI dyad, a doctor might rely on the AI's advice. However, (iii) in the patient-AI dyad, a patient might not rely on the AI's advice. This presents an unbalanced state (cf. state (f) in Fig. 1). Now, in the triadic setting of patient-doctor-AI (iv), the not rely-relation between the patient and AI might change to a rely-relation as the patient interacts with the doctor. This creates a balanced state (cf. state (a) in Fig. 1). However, Heider's balance theory [18] states that unbalanced states must resolve into balanced ones.

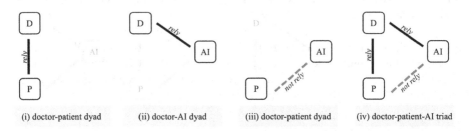

Fig. 2. Motivating example for a doctor-patient-AI triad, where D stands for doctor and P for patient. The black lines indicate reliance, and the grey dashed lines indicate no reliance.

The above example also motivates another aspect. For the concept of appropriate reliance, we assume an initial human decision. Analogously, we define the notion of an *initial single-user reliance (ISUR)*. ISUR denotes a user's reliance behavior in a single-user setting without the other party involved. In the example above, that would be the not rely-relation in the patient-AI setting and the rely-relation in the doctor-AI setting. We note that ISUR can either be *appropriate reliance* (appropriate ISUR) or not *appropriate reliance* (inappropriate ISUR). In the following, we abbreviate the two parties with X_i and X_j ($i, j \in \{1, 2\}$) to stress the symmetry of the two parties.

Further, the doctor-patient-AI example from above also highlights another relation. We also have an initial relation between the two parties (X_i and X_j), which can either be positive (rely) or negative (not rely). We quickly see that this relation is positive if both parties have the same ISUR and negative if both parties have different ISURs. This observation will be important later on.

For now, we are interested in how the ISUR of one party changes after being confronted with the ISUR of another party. Figure 3 is inspired by the current definitions of single-user AI reliance [8] and presents a first approximation and initial notations for MPAIR. One party, X_i, can have appropriate ISUR (blue checkmark) or inappropriate ISUR (grey cross). The same holds for the other party X_j. If X_i is confronted with the ISUR of X_j, they can either change their ISUR or remain constant. Not much will change if both X_i and X_j have the same ISUR. Therefore, these cases are omitted from the figure. While this consideration is helpful and required as a first step towards MPAIR theory, this view is one-sided as X_j does not change their ISUR. Further, Fig. 3 presents a sequential view of that issue, while in practice, these changes in behavior are often more complex and parallel. However, this first approximation helps us to derive the conceptualization of MPAIR in the subsequent section.

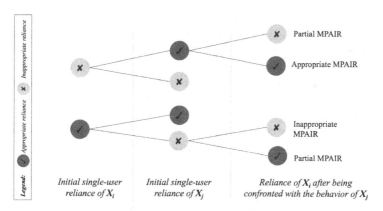

Fig. 3. MPAIR for the two parties X_i and X_j. This representation is a first approximation, where only X_i adapts their ISUR in the multi-party settings.

3.2 Multi-party AI Reliance

Considering all combinatorics of the ISUR of X_i and X_j, we arrive at 16 cases. However, not all cases are reasonable. For example, assuming that one party might switch is unreasonable in a setting with the same ISUR of both participants. Or, to put it more formally with the language of Heider's balance theory, if the ISURs already entail a balanced state, they won't change in the multi-party setting. Therefore, we present the following axiom:

Axiom 1: *If both parties have the same ISUR, they will not deviate from that in the multi-party case.*

Further, while hypothetically possible, it does not make sense that both parties change their ISUR simultaneously, as one change already creates a balanced state. Therefore, we present the following axiom:

Axiom 2: *Only one party will change their ISUR in the multi-party case.*

These two axioms reduce the number of feasible cases and leave us with the cases presented in Fig. 4. Figure 4 presents a framework to analyze MPAIR and consists of five possible cases of MPAIR. Note that all these cases are balanced according to Heider's balance theory. We also observe that both parties have *appropriate reliance* on the AI in two of these cases. We call these the desired cases. In three cases, at least one party does not have appropriate reliance, which we call the undesired cases. Further, the case of partial MPAIR is peculiar. Given that this state must be balanced, this is the only case where the two parties are not aligned in their resulting reliance. This negative relationship between the two parties creates tensions. We analyze these cases in more detail in the following.

All cases have unique characteristics, which are explained in the following. First, in **Case 1**, we have what we propose to call *trivial appropriate MPAIR*. If both parties share the same appropriate ISUR, they are aligned in their behavior. If these parties interact in the multi-party setting, their reliance behavior will not change. Therefore, this setting poses a *trivial appropriate MPAIR*. Second, in **Case 2**, we have a non-trivial form of *appropriate MPAIR*. In this case, the two parties have different ISURs. Therefore, this case presents inherent misalignment and conflict between the two parties. However, when both parties interact in a multi-party setting, their reliance achieves an *appropriate MPAIR*, i.e., both rely appropriately on the AI and, thus, are aligned. Therefore, this case is the desired state for multi-party settings and highlights the potential in these settings: while in the individual case, one party would have relied inappropriately, in the multi-party setting, both parties rely appropriately on the AI. Third, in **Case 3**, we have what we propose to call *partial MPAIR*. In this case, the two parties again have different ISURs. However, contrary to *Case 2,* this misalignment is unresolved in the multi-party setting. While one party remains at their *appropriate reliance* on the AI, the other remains at their *inappropriate reliance*. Following Heider's balance theory, the triad is only balanced if both parties are misaligned, i.e., have a negative relation. This has the potential to induce conflicts and disagreements. Therefore, this state is an undesired state. Fourth, in **Case 4**, we have a non-trivial form of *inappropriate MPAIR*. In this case, the two parties again have different ISURs. However, contrary to *Case 2* or *Case 3*, both parties resolve to rely inappropriately on the AI. While both parties are aligned, i.e., have a positive relation, this case is undesirable, as it presents missed potential compared to *Case 2*. Finally, in **Case 5**, we have what we propose to call *trivial inappropriate MPAIR*. Analogously to Case 1, if both parties share the same inappropriate ISUR, they are aligned in their behavior. However, in this case, both parties have inappropriate ISUR. Therefore, both ISURs are aligned in the multi-party setting, leading to an *inappropriate MPAIR*. This case is trivial for multi-party settings, as it cannot be counteracted through multi-party dynamics. This case is undesirable, as it presents missed potential of *appropriate reliance*.

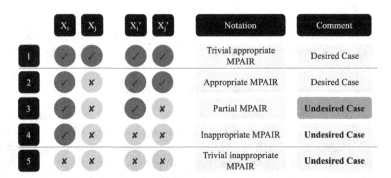

Fig. 4. *MPAIR Framework.* X_i and X_j are the ISUR of the two parties and X_i' and X_j' are the behavior in the multi-party settings of both parties. A blue checkmark indicates *appropriate reliance* of the respective individual, and a grey cross indicates inappropriate reliance. The case of *partial MPAIR* is the only case where the two parties are not aligned.

Utilizing balance theory, we can conceptualize the phenomenon of MPAIR and present a framework to analyze multi-party settings. The goal for multi-party settings should be to aim for the desired cases. MPAIR and its framework contribute to gaining deeper insights into AI reliance in multi-party settings. In the following section, we analyze two large DSR projects that we studied in the past.

4 MPAIR in Practice

In this section, we analyze two large DSR projects. While both projects are seemingly disjunct, they share the same core of using AI systems in multi-party settings. For both projects, we utilize the MPAIR framework as a tool for analysis to gain deeper insights. These insights are only possible through the newfound lens of MPAIR.

4.1 Example A: Conversational Agents in Financial Advisory Service Encounters

This first DSR project ran from Mid-2020 to End of 2022. The project was run by two universities, two regional banks, and two technology partners. The development of the final artifact consisted of three DSR cycles, with subsequent evaluations [36–38]. This DSR project aimed to develop a multimodal, interactive conversational agent to support financial advisory service encounters. The conversational agent was called *MO*. *MO* served as a human-like digital assistant that could take over tedious tasks in all phases of financial consultations, such as risk management, explaining concepts, or taking notes. It should serve the advisor and client alike.

In the multi-party setting, we observed that both the client and advisor appropriately relied on the conversational agent, leading to an *appropriate MPAIR*. The MPAIR framework enables a more in-depth investigation to gain insights into this appropriate MPAIR. An *appropriate MPAIR* does not directly infer the ISUR of both parties. Following the framework, an *appropriate MPAIR* can either be trivial (Case 1) or non-trivial (Case 2). Both require nuanced considerations and designs. First, no peculiar multi-party setting design aspects must be considered if we have *trivial appropriate MPAIR* (Case 1). This case emerges from the appropriate ISUR of both parties. However, we are more likely to have non-trivial *appropriate MPAIR* (Case 2), as clients and advisors have fundamentally different domain knowledge and different needs for interacting with an AI system. In our case, when confronted in the multi-party setting, the advisor's behavior dominated the client's behavior. Therefore, whenever the advisor relied on the system, both parties relied on the system, which led to the non-trivial *appropriate MPAIR* (Case 2). However, this also yields the danger of *inappropriate MPAIR* (Case 4): if one party's behavior dominates the other, they can determine the setting, which creates some kind of sequential multi-party reliance [38].

This short example shows that MPAIR considerations are essential to fully understanding behavior in the multi-party setting. While in the DSR project, the artifact achieved *appropriate MPAIR*, the dangers of *inappropriate MPAIR* prevail and might arise in settings with similar designs. Therefore, the MPAIR framework gives us an in-depth view to support the generation of sound design knowledge.

4.2 Example B: AI-Based Price Estimations in Used Car Market Negotiations

The second DSR project ran from the End of 2020 until End of 2022. The project was run by a large European automotive company, where researchers from a university collaborated in an engaged research methodology [39, 40]. Prices on the used car market skyrocketed and remain high for various reasons [41]. With this automotive company, an online platform called *CarEst*, which provides AI-based used car price estimations, was developed to address this problem. Private sellers of used cars could enter their information about the car into *CarEst* and get AI-based price estimations. Further, they could schedule appointments with used car dealers directly on the platform, which were done off-platform at the dealership.

In this project, we observe the problem of *partial MPAIR* (Case 3). Generally, while professional used car dealers rely appropriately on the AI system, private sellers overrely on the AI system. This aligns with research on AI reliance, where domain knowledge or task expertise has been shown to influence reliance [6]. While, in this case, *partial MPAIR* directly infers the ISUR of both participants, the MPAIR framework gives us multiple fronts to influence reliance in multi-party settings. First, we can tackle the ISUR of the private seller. We could aim to design the artifact so that the private seller also appropriately relies on AI-based price estimations. While this ideally would result in *trivial appropriate MPAIR* (Case 1), the question arises if this would be easily possible while simultaneously maintaining the appropriate ISUR of the dealer. Second, we can aim to design for non-trivial *appropriate MPAIR* (Case 2). We could change the artifact's design to accommodate fruitful negotiations between sellers and buyers and give the party with *appropriate ISUR* the means to convince the other party, e.g., by fitting transparency mechanisms [41].

This short example shows another side of the power of the MPAIR framework. The MPAIR provides multiple fronts through which designers and developers of AI systems can work to achieve the goal of *appropriate MPAIR*. Ultimately, this supports the generation of sound design knowledge.

4.3 Conclusion

The use cases in *Example A* and *Example B* highlight the usefulness of the MPAIR framework. This framework enables a more in-depth analysis of AI reliance in multi-party settings. The MPAIR framework generates insights, such as the ISUR of participants, that traditionally remain hidden in the naïve view of multi-party settings. Therefore, the MPAIR framework is powerful for describing problems and solutions in multi-party settings.

5 Discussion

In this study, we answer the **RQ** by conceptualizing MPAIR. Further, the proposed framework presents a tool to generate well-founded design knowledge, such as design principles, for the novel conceptualization of MPAIR. Further, it points towards a sounder consideration of multi-party settings. For example, the concept of ISUR offers another way to understand AI reliance in multi-party settings. In the following, we discuss several aspects of MPAIR. We elaborate on the importance of single-user *appropriate reliance* and stress that MPAIR is an addition to understanding multi-party settings. Next, we synthesize the central insights of MPAIR into three generalizable design principles.

Finally, we explore the limitations and future extensions of MPAIR and its framework. This study should serve as a start towards a more thorough discussion of AI systems in multi-party settings, which, despite its practical importance, is currently neglected in research.

5.1 The Importance of Single-User Appropriate Reliance

In the preceding sections, we introduced the conceptualization of MPAIR and stressed its importance based on two large DSR projects. We used the MPAIR framework to analyze the multi-party settings. Further, we highlighted that common findings on single-user AI reliance are insufficient in these settings. Therefore, one might be inclined to ignore existing findings on single-user AI reliance when confronted with multi-party settings. However, we stress that this is not the case. Instead, insights about single-user AI reliance are paramount in the multi-party setting. Ignoring considerations of single-user settings would increase the danger of having *trivial inappropriate MPAIR*, e.g., if users over-rely on AI systems with little performance. We require at least one party to have appropriate reliance. Overall, MPAIR does not replace insights into single-user AI reliance but complements it.

Further, one might be inclined to discard the considerations of MPAIR by always aiming to achieve *trivial appropriate MPAIR* (Case 1) and, thus, do not need any multi-party considerations. However, albeit trivial appropriate MPAIR is strongly desirable and theoretically possible, it is not always feasible in practical settings. *Trivial appropriate MPAIR* requires appropriate ISUR for both parties. Real-world settings are more complex. Research on *appropriate reliance* shows that this strongly depends on the user's properties, such as domain knowledge [6] or statistical literacy [21]. Further, different incentives from the parties might influence their reliance on the AI system. Therefore, if we design a system for one user persona to achieve appropriate reliance, another persona might not have appropriate reliance. Therefore, in multi-party settings, we are often confronted with the cases of initially different ISUR (i.e., Cases 2–4). Like natural sciences, where a *"theory of everything"* is only hypothetical, a *"design of everything"* in design research is only hypothetical. Therefore, the consideration of MPAIR is of utmost importance in multi-party settings.

5.2 Design Principle for MPAIR

The proposed conceptualization of MPAIR contributes by enabling the derivation of in-depth design knowledge, as discussed in the examples above. The general insights presented in this study and insights from the examples can be synthesized into design principles (DPs). In the following, we present three design principles that aid designers and developers of AI-based systems in multi-party settings in designing artifacts.

First, we must ensure that both parties have the same reliance behavior in the multi-party settings. This is a direct insight from the MPAIR Framework and is a necessary condition for the desired cases (cf. Fig. 4). Therefore, the first design principle can be summarized as the *(DP1) principle of ISUR convergence*: *For designers and developers of AI systems to achieve appropriate MPAIR in multi-party settings, the design should facilitate convergence of the parties ISUR, so that they have aligned reliance in the multi-party settings.* Second, limiting the context to multi-party settings with asymmetric user roles, such as financial advisor service encounters (cf. Example A) or doctor-patient settings, where one user can be seen as the primary user and the other as the secondary user, we can formulate the *(DP2) principle of primary user appropriate reliance: For designers and developers of AI systems to achieve appropriate MPAIR in multi-party settings with asymmetric user roles, the design should aim at appropriate reliance of the primary user, as supports a propagation to the secondary users.* Finally, limiting the context to settings with negotiations, such as used car negotiations (cf. Example B), we see that partial reliance should be avoided. Therefore, we formulate the *(DP3) principle of avoiding partial MPAIR: For designers and developers of AI systems to not induce conflict into that setting based on the AI system, in multi-party settings with negotiations, the design should aim at avoiding partial reliance as partial reliance creates tension between the parties ultimately failing negotiations.*

These principles help designers and developers of AI-based systems design for a desired case in the MPAIR framework. Future research should be concerned with identifying more design knowledge on MPAIR. Further extension of MPAIR can also be investigated as motivated in the subsequent section.

5.3   Future Extensions of MPAIR

However, MPAIR in its current form focuses on binary cases. Our approach aligns with the conceptualization of reliance in the single-user setting, which is either appropriate or inappropriate [8]. To add to this, Heider's balance theory in itself only knows binary relations. Nonetheless, future research should aim to generalize from binary cases to non-binary cases and regression problems. Examples of non-binary classification problems are x-rays with multiple possible diseases present [3]. Examples of regression problems are house price estimations [21]. This would enable further consideration of the concept of MPAIR and an extension of the framework.

Further, current emerging research on the reliance of user groups on AI reliance indicates that AI advice can be used as a tiebreaker [17]. We must stress the difference between groups, where all users have the same incentives and interests, and multi-party settings, where the two parties might have different incentives and interests. Nonetheless, we argue that similar could also happen in multi-party settings. For example, if we have three ordinal options, A < B < C, and the AI advice is B, while two parties disagree on A and C, the AI advice might be a tiebreaker.

Finally, this study presents two short examples from empirical considerations of MPAIR. In the future, more empirical findings should be considered. Further, the MPAIR framework should be used ex-ante evaluation [42] to derive design knowledge when designing and developing artifacts. Nonetheless, the MPAIR framework presents insights for designers and developers of AI systems in multi-party settings.

6 Conclusion

Much research is concerned with AI systems. In particular, the question of the *appropriate reliance* of a user on an AI system is of broad interest. However, as designers and developers of AI systems, we also need to consider the real-world impact. In the real world, many practical settings consist of multiple parties interacting with each other, such as doctor-patient encounters, financial advisory service encounters, or market negotiations. These parties often have diverging interests. If we introduce AI systems in these multi-party settings, it is insufficient only to consider single human-AI interactions. Therefore, we conceptualized MPAIR in this study and presented a framework to analyze multi-party settings. With the new framework for MPAIR, we can get deeper insights into multi-party settings. Ultimately, this leads to well-founded design knowledge. This design knowledge can support designers and developers of artifacts to make a real-world impact in practical settings. This study should serve as a starting point for more thorough insights into AI systems in multi-party settings and MPAIR.

References

1. OpenAI: Introducing ChatGPT (2023). https://openai.com/blog/chatgpt
2. Faisal, A., Kamruzzaman, M., Yigitcanlar, T., Currie, G.: Understanding autonomous vehicles. J. Transp. Land Use **12**, 45–72 (2019)
3. Rädsch, T., Eckhardt, S., Leiser, F., Pandl, K.D., Thiebes, S., Sunyaev, A.: What your radiologist might be missing: using machine learning to identify mislabeled instances of X-ray images (2021)
4. EU: Ethics guidelines for trustworthy AI | Shaping Europe's digital future. https://digital-str ategy.ec.europa.eu/en/library/ethics-guidelines-trustworthy-ai. Accessed 15 Jan 2024
5. Chatterjee, S., Sarker, S., Lee, M.J., Xiao, X., Elbanna, A.: A possible conceptualization of the information systems (IS) artifact: a general systems theory perspective 1. Inf. Syst. J. **31**, 550–578 (2021)
6. Sutton, S.G., Arnold, V., Holt, M.: An extension of the theory of technology dominance: capturing the underlying causal complexity. Int. J. Account. Inf. Syst. **50**, 100626 (2023)
7. Lee, J.D., See, K.A.: Trust in automation: designing for appropriate reliance. Hum. Factors **31** (2004)
8. Schemmer, M., Kuehl, N., Benz, C., Bartos, A., Satzger, G.: Appropriate reliance on ai advice: conceptualization and the effect of explanations. In: Proceedings of the 28th International Conference on Intelligent User Interfaces, pp. 410–422. ACM, Sydney (2023)
9. Passi, S., Vorvoreanu, M.: Overreliance on AI literature review. Microsoft Research (2022)
10. Wang, L., Jamieson, G.A., Hollands, J.G.: Selecting methods for the analysis of reliance on automation. In: Proceedings of the Human Factors and Ergonomics Society Annual Meeting, vol. 52, pp. 287–291 (2008)
11. Dikmen, M., Burns, C.: The effects of domain knowledge on trust in explainable AI and task performance: a case of peer-to-peer lending. Int. J. Hum. Comput. Stud. **162** (2022)
12. Glick, A., Clayton, M., Angelov, N., Chang, J.: Impact of explainable artificial intelligence assistance on clinical decision-making of novice dental clinicians. JAMIA Open **5** (2022)
13. Eisenhardt, K.M.: Agency theory: an assessment and review. Acad. Manag. Rev. **14**, 57–74 (1989)
14. Scott, A., Vick, S.: Patients, doctors and contracts: an application of principal-agent theory to the doctor-patient relationship. Scott. J. Polit. Econ. **46**, 111–134 (1999)

15. Golec, J.H.: Empirical tests of a principal-agent model of the investor-investment advisor relationship. J. Financ. Quant. Anal. **27**, 81–95 (1992)
16. Miller, G.J., Whitford, A.B.: Trust and incentives in principal-agent negotiations: the 'insurance/incentive trade-off.' J. Theor. Polit. **14**, 231–267 (2002)
17. Chiang, C.-W., Lu, Z., Li, Z., Yin, M.: Are two heads better than one in AI-assisted decision making? Comparing the behavior and performance of groups and individuals in human-AI collaborative recidivism risk assessment. In: Proceedings of the 2023 CHI Conference on Human Factors in Computing Systems, pp. 1–18. ACM, Hamburg (2023)
18. Heider, F.: Attitudes and cognitive organization. J. Psychol. **21**, 107–112 (1946)
19. Dzindolet, M.T., Pierce, L.G., Beck, H.P., Dawe, L.A.: Misuse and disuse of automated aids. Presented at the Proceedings of the Human Factors and Ergonomics Society Annual Meeting (1999)
20. Parasuraman, R., Riley, V.: Humans and automation: use, misuse, disuse, abuse. Hum. Factors **39**, 230–253 (1997)
21. Chiang, C.-W., Yin, M.: Exploring the effects of machine learning literacy interventions on laypeople's reliance on machine learning models. In: International Conference on Intelligent User Interfaces Proceedings, IUI, pp. 148–161. Association for Computing Machinery (2022)
22. Haight, J.M., Kecojevic, V.: Automation vs. human intervention: what is the best fit for the best performance? Process Saf. Progr. **24**, 45–51 (2005)
23. Nourani, M., et al.: Anchoring bias affects mental model formation and user reliance in explainable AI systems. In: 26th International Conference on Intelligent User Interfaces, pp. 340–350. ACM, College Station (2021)
24. Schmitt, A., Wambsganss, T., Söllner, M., Janson, A.: Towards a trust reliance paradox? Exploring the gap between perceived trust in and reliance on algorithmic advice. In: International Conference on Information Systems (ICIS), Austin, Texas (2021)
25. Lai, V., Chen, C., Liao, Q.V., Smith-Renner, A., Tan, C.: Towards a science of human-ai decision making: a survey of empirical studies. arXiv preprint arXiv:2112.11471 (2021)
26. Guggenberger, T., Lämmermann, L., Urbach, N., Walter, A., Hofmann, P.: Task delegation from AI to humans: a principal-agent perspective. In: ICIS 2023 Proceedings (2023)
27. Vössing, M., Kühl, N., Lind, M., Satzger, G.: Designing transparency for effective human-ai collaboration. Inf. Syst. Front. **24**, 877–895 (2022)
28. Heider, F.: The Psychology of Interpersonal Relations. Psychology Press (2013)
29. Aronson, E.: The theory of cognitive dissonance: a current perspective. In: Berkowitz, L. (ed.) Advances in Experimental Social Psychology, pp. 1–34. Academic Press (1969)
30. Cartwright, D., Harary, F.: Structural balance: a generalization of Heider's theory. Psychol. Rev. **63**, 277–293 (1956)
31. Roy, S., Gammoh, B.S., Koh, A.C.: Predicting the effectiveness of celebrity endorsements using the balance theory. J. Cust. Behav. **11**, 33–52 (2012)
32. Fink, J.S., Parker, H.M., Brett, M., Higgins, J.: Off-field behavior of athletes and team identification: using social identity theory and balance theory to explain fan reactions. J. Sport Manag. **23**, 142–155 (2009)
33. Min, J.H.J., Chang, H.J.J., Jai, T.-M.C., Ziegler, M.: The effects of celebrity-brand congruence and publicity on consumer attitudes and buying behavior. Fash Text. **6**, 10 (2019)
34. Qi, L., et al.: Structural balance theory-based E-commerce recommendation over big rating data. IEEE Trans. Big Data **4**, 301–312 (2018)
35. Nakanishi, H., Nakazawa, S., Ishida, T., Takanashi, K., Isbister, K.: Can software agents influence human relations? Balance theory in agent-mediated communities. In: Proceedings of the Second International Joint Conference on Autonomous Agents and Multiagent Systems, pp. 717–724. Association for Computing Machinery, New York (2003)

36. Bucher, A., Dolata, M., Eckhardt, S., Staehelin, D., Schwabe, G.: Talking to multi-party conversational agents in advisory services: command-based vs. conversational interactions. Proc. ACM Hum.-Comput. Interact. **8**, 1–25 (2024)

37. Eckhardt, S., et al.: "Garbage in, garbage out": mitigating human biases in data entry by means of artificial intelligence. Presented at the IFIP Conference on Human-Computer Interaction (2023)

38. Eckhardt, S., Bucher, A., Kalunder, M., Dolata, M., Agotai, D., Schwabe, G.: Secondary mental models: introducing conversational agents in financial advisory service encounters. In: ICIS 2023 Proceedings (2023)

39. Gregory, R., Muntermann, J.: Theorizing in design science research: inductive versus deductive approaches (2011)

40. Van de Ven, A.H.: Engaged Scholarship: A Guide for Organizational and Social Research. Oxford University Press (2007)

41. Eckhardt, S., Sprenkamp, K., Zavolokina, L., Bauer, I., Schwabe, G.: Can artificial intelligence help used-car dealers survive in a data-driven used-car market? In: Drechsler, A., Gerber, A., Hevner, A. (eds.) DESRIST 2022. LNCS, vol. 13229, pp. 115–127. Springer, Cham (2022). https://doi.org/10.1007/978-3-031-06516-3_9

42. Sonnenberg, C., vom Brocke, J.: Evaluations in the science of the artificial – reconsidering the build-evaluate pattern in design science research. In: Peffers, K., Rothenberger, M., Kuechler, B. (eds.) DESRIST 2012. LNCS, vol. 7286, pp. 381–397. Springer, Heidelberg (2012). https://doi.org/10.1007/978-3-642-29863-9_28

Wasn't Expecting that – Using Abnormality as a Key to Design a Novel User-Centric Explainable AI Method

Tobias Jahn, Philipp Hühn, and Maximilian Förster[✉]

University of Ulm, 89081 Ulm, Germany
{tobias.jahn,philipp.huehn,maximilian.foerster}@uni-ulm.de

Abstract. Explainable artificial intelligence (XAI) aims at automatically generating user-centric explanations to help users scrutinize artificial intelligence (AI) decisions and establish trust in AI systems. XAI methods that generate counterfactual explanations are particularly promising as they mimic how humans construct explanations. Insights from the social sciences suggest that counterfactual explanations should convey the most abnormal causes that lead to the AI decision, as unexpected information fosters understanding. So far, no XAI method incorporates abnormality when generating counterfactual explanations. This paper aims to design a novel XAI method to generate abnormal counterfactual explanations. To this end, we propose a novel measure to quantify the abnormality of features in explanations and integrate it into a method to generate counterfactual explanations. We demonstrate the XAI method's applicability on a real-world data set within the use case of house price prediction. We evaluate its efficacy following functionally-grounded and human-grounded evaluation. The results of our evaluation indicate that our method successfully integrates abnormality in generating counterfactual explanations. The resulting explanations are perceived as more helpful by users to scrutinize AI decisions and lead to higher trust in AI systems compared to state-of-the-art counterfactual explanations.

Keywords: User-centric XAI · Counterfactual Explanations · Abnormality

1 Introduction

Artificial Intelligence (AI) has become widespread in professional environments and prevalent in daily activities [1]. Its influence extends across numerous application domains, encompassing electronic markets, finance, healthcare, human resources, public administration, and transportation [1]. However, the complexity of AI systems has raised concerns about their lack of interpretability [2]. Many AI systems constitute 'black boxes', as their decision-making processes remain unclear to their users [2]. This poses a major challenge when it comes to establishing user trust [2]. The research field of Explainable AI (XAI) follows the idea of establishing trust in AI systems by providing reasoning for an AI system's decisions [3]. XAI aims at developing methods that provide human-understandable explanations along the decisions made by AI systems [3, 4].

M. Mandviwalla et al. (Eds.): DESRIST 2024, LNCS 14621, pp. 66–80, 2024.
https://doi.org/10.1007/978-3-031-61175-9_5

One important research direction in XAI – identified in a recent literature review – is to pursue user-centric explanations, i.e., explanations that explicitly address users' needs to help them scrutinize AI decisions and establish trust in AI systems [5].

In line with insights from the social sciences, a prominent concept for user-centric explanations is counterfactual explanations, which mimic how humans construct explanations [6]. The idea behind counterfactual explanations is to explain an AI system's decision for a particular input (fact) by showing the contrast to an alternative input (foil) that leads to a different decision [7]. To illustrate, to explain a house price prediction, a counterfactual explanation emphasizes why the price is not higher/lower (=different decision) instead of listing all causes that led to the price prediction. Insights from the social sciences show that humans rarely use all possible causes to explain an event but prefer to select a few causes that best explain the event in question [6]. Further, they point out that the abnormality of causes is a crucial property for their selection, as unexpected information contributes to a better understanding of an event and helps to scrutinize decisions [8]. To illustrate, in the context of house price prediction, an abnormal and thus unexpected information could be the absence of a common feature, e.g., air conditioning for houses in hot areas like Florida, which hinders the AI to decide for a higher price segment. Regarding decision support in the investment domain, an abnormal feature could be an unstable price of required resources that causes the AI to recommend rejection of the investment. To sum up, counterfactual explanations based on abnormal features are a promising pathway to help users scrutinize AI decisions and establish trust in the AI system. However, to the best of our knowledge, to date, no XAI method exists that generates counterfactual explanations based on abnormal features. Thus, design-oriented research is required to develop a novel artifact which incubates the abnormality of features in the generation process of counterfactual explanations.

Against this background, within our research, we follow the Design Science Research methodology [9] to build and evaluate a novel XAI method generating abnormal counterfactual explanations. We base the design of our novel XAI method on the idea of measuring the abnormality of features and prioritizing abnormal features to generate counterfactual explanations. We demonstrate its applicability for the case of price prediction for houses and combine functionally- and human-grounded evaluation, as established in XAI and design science literature [10]. The results of this evaluation indicate that our novel XAI method is capable of producing abnormal counterfactual explanations. Further, it reveals that using abnormality of features to generate counterfactual explanations leads to an increase in perceived helpfulness of the explanations and trust in the AI system. Our contribution is twofold. First, we propose an XAI method that uses the abnormality of features to generate counterfactual explanations. At its core, it incorporates a novel approach to quantify the abnormality of features, which can also be transferred to other XAI methods. Second, we demonstrate the positive impact of abnormality in explanations on users by conducting a user study.

The remainder of the paper is structured as follows. In Sect. 2, we provide a background and present related literature. In Sect. 3, we present a novel method for generating abnormal counterfactual explanations for AI systems. In Sect. 4, we demonstrate the method's applicability and evaluate its efficacy in a real-world setting using real-world data. Finally, in Sect. 5, we discuss the implications of our research, reflect on its limitations, and outline possible directions for future investigations.

2 Background and Related Literature

2.1 Counterfactual Explanations

Based on insights from the social sciences, research on user-centric XAI proposes counterfactual explanations [6, 11]. According to this idea, the explicit question "Why E?" can be translated into the implicit question "Why E and not P?" [6]. Basic components of counterfactual explanations are the fact x, which denotes the input that leads to the decision y of the AI system, and the foil x', which represents an alternative input that leads to an alternative decision y'. The distance between the fact and the foil is referred to as the contrast [6, 12]. The underlying AI system can be represented as a function $f(x)$ [12]. Generating a counterfactual explanation is equivalent to generating or searching for a suitable foil. As users do not want to know all possible causes for a decision, counterfactual explanations used to explain an AI system's decision are often designed to be sparse, i.e., the number of features differing between fact and foil is small [6, 11].

In recent years, there has been a substantial increase in the literature surrounding counterfactual explanations in XAI (see [7] for an overview). XAI methods generating counterfactual explanations can be divided into optimization-based and non-optimization-based strategies [7]. Promising non-optimization-based strategies iteratively search for a foil by heuristic choices that take into account specific properties of a counterfactual explanation [7]. A state-of-the-art non-optimization-based method is GRACE proposed by Le et al. [13], which iteratively increases the number of varied features until the underlying system crosses its decision boundaries to account for a sparse contrast and to prioritize features with certain characteristics. Optimization-based strategies aim to minimize a loss function in order to generate foils [11]. Typically, users define a desired alternative decision for the XAI method to generate a suitable foil [7]. A state-of-the-art optimization-based counterfactual explanation method is CARE. Within this method, various desired properties of the counterfactual explanations can be considered in the optimization problem [14]. Optimization-based methods are particularly well suited to minimize the distance between fact and foil [7].

2.2 Abnormality in Explanations

Various insights from the social sciences demonstrate that within explanations, humans tend to seek knowledge about causes that seem abnormal to them [15, 16]. Explanations based on abnormal causes have proven to be particularly helpful in providing humans with an understanding of a particular event [17]. Translated to XAI, explanations incorporating abnormal causes can serve to help users scrutinize an AI system's decisions and develop appropriate trust [6]. In contrast, normal causes often do not need to be mentioned because they are already known by the explainee and do not provide novel insights [18]. To illustrate, for our running example of AI-based house price prediction, an explanation providing abnormal information, e.g., the lack of air conditioning for a house in a hot area like Florida, empowers users to scrutinize whether the AI system's decision to categorize the house in a cheaper price segment is valid or not. Consequently, abnormal features should be prioritized to generate explanations for an AI system's decisions. To this end, the abnormality of features must be quantifiable, i.e., a measure of abnormality must be defined.

Literature from the social sciences as well as XAI research provide initial ideas on how to measure abnormality. According to the social sciences, a behavior or situation is considered increasingly abnormal the rarer it is [19]. Notably, a situation's context must be taken into account since cultural and societal factors significantly influence the definition of normal human behavior [19]. To illustrate, the absence of air conditioning for a house in Florida may be abnormal, while it is common for houses in cold areas like Alaska. However, while providing valuable insights that should be considered, this definition is not directly quantifiable. Within XAI literature, van Lente et al. [20] aim to use abnormality as one of several criteria to generate explanations. They define the abnormality of a feature as the absence of coverage, where coverage describes how frequently a feature is present in the data set. However, van Lente et al. [20] do not take the context of a data point into account, which is a crucial to depict abnormality [19].

2.3 Abnormality in Counterfactual Explanations

The social sciences show that abnormal causes can serve as promising "targets for intervention" [17, p. 591] as people are more likely to consider intervening on abnormal causes to restore a normal state than vice versa [17]. This implies counterfactual thinking about how the situation would have developed differently if the abnormal causes had not been present or had been replaced by normal ones [17]. Backed up by Hilton [18], who suggests that the explicit question "Why E?" can often be interpreted as the implicit question "Why E and not the normal case Q?", this statement indicates that abnormality is a natural fit for the selection of features shown within counterfactual explanations. Thus, in the context of counterfactual explanations, the most abnormal features of the fact should be used in the contrast, leading to a foil that is more normal than the fact. This relates to generating a typical and realistic foil, an aim of coherent counterfactual explanations [12]. For instance, intervening in the abnormal feature 'no air conditioning' of a house in Florida and restoring the normal state 'air conditioning', produces a foil that is more normal, realistic and typical than the fact. Furthermore, using abnormal features within counterfactual explanations inherently solves the challenges of finding a foil, which leads to an alternative decision y' that matches the user's intentions, which is in state-of-the-art methods only circumvented by forcing the user to select y' [6]. In addition to increasing the effort for the user, it is not enough to provide users with foils that lead to their expected AI decision y' [21]. As Hitchcock et al. [17] propose, it is crucial to intervene in abnormal causes to return them to a normal state. To the best of our knowledge, no XAI method exists that considers abnormality of features when generating counterfactual explanations.

3   A Novel XAI Method to Generate Abnormal Counterfactual Explanations

We aim to design a novel XAI method to generate abnormal counterfactual explanations. At its core, we propose a measure for the abnormality of features of a data point and integrate it into a novel method to generate counterfactual explanations.

We rely on insights from the social sciences to guide the development of our method in the form of three design requirements. First, the contrast, i.e., the distance between the fact (data point that leads to the decision of the AI system) and the foil (data point that leads to an alternative decision of the AI system), must contain the most abnormal features of the fact (DR1), as abnormality in explanations is supposed to help users scrutinize AI decisions [17]. Second, the contrast must be sparse (DR2), i.e., the number of features in the contrast must be small, as humans tend to rely only on the most decisive causes to explain a decision [6, 22]. Third, the occurrence of the foil must be statistically more likely than that of the fact (DR3). This refers to the strategy proposed by Hilton [18] of explaining a fact by comparing its abnormal features with normal features, resulting in a more normal foil compared to the fact.

We aim to address these design requirements through the following basic idea: Established approaches to generate counterfactual explanations vary features of the fact to search for a foil. We aim to guide this search for a foil by prioritizing the variation of the most abnormal features to find a foil. To this end, we design a measure for abnormality of features and integrate it into the search for a foil to fulfil DR1. We base our measure for abnormality of features on kernel density estimation (KDE). A KDE can be computed for a given data set (e.g., for the underlying training data of the AI system) and approximates the underlying probability density function (PDF), which describes the probability of occurrence of a specific data point with respect to the given population's distribution. The PDF is lower for a data point with an untypical feature than for the same data point without that untypical feature. Thus, the more it is possible to increase the KDE of a given data point by changing a single feature, the greater the indication for abnormality of the original feature value. We build on the characteristics of the KDE and the PDF to design an abnormality measure that enables quantifying the abnormality of a data point's features (see Sect. 3.1 for more details). We employ the abnormality measure to rank all possible feature combinations of a fact according to their average abnormality in descending order. Thereby, top entries of the ranking contain features with higher abnormality than lower entries. Additionally, top entries tend to contain only a small number of features since every addition of a feature (with lower abnormality) would reduce the average abnormality of the feature combination, thereby ensuring the fulfilment of DR2. We guide the search for a foil by prioritizing the variation of abnormal feature combinations based on the ranking. This procedure ensures that the contrast between the fact and the foil contains abnormal features (DR1) and only a small number of features (DR2). We build on insights from non-optimization-based counterfactual explanation methods [13] to design an iterative process to search for a foil (see Sect. 3.2 for more details). In each iteration, the feature combination corresponding to the highest entry in the ranking (which has not been varied in previous iterations) is varied to search for a foil. Inspired by optimization-based counterfactual explanation methods using constraints for the optimization (e.g., [14]), we add a constraint to ensure that the

KDE of the foil is higher than that of the fact. If the constraint is fulfilled, the foil is used to generate the counterfactual explanation; else, the iterative search for foils continues. This constraint guarantees that the foil's occurrence is more likely than the fact's occurrence (DR3). We refer to this novel XAI method as Abnormal Counterfactual Explainer (ACE). In the following, we describe the abnormality measure and its integration into ACE in more detail.

3.1 Abnormality Measure Based on KDE

At its core, we propose a measure to quantify the abnormality of features of a data point. Inspired by literature on outlier detection, we make use of information about the abnormality of data points contained in the PDF to design a quantifiable measure based on statistical norms [23]. The PDF describes the probability of occurrence of data points with respect to a specific population's distribution [12, 24]. For instance, the PDF for the population of houses would yield a lower probability of occurrence for a house in Florida with an abnormal feature like 'no air conditioning' than for the same house with the feature 'air conditioning'. We use this information to calculate the abnormality of the feature under observation.

However, the PDF of the input data's population remains elusive for many AI systems [12]. Thus, to obtain an estimate of the PDF, we employ the KDE based on the AI system's training data, which converges towards the PDF with increasing training data size and decreasing bandwidths. In the case of explanations for specific AI decisions, the abnormality of a single feature within a data point and not the abnormality of the whole data point is of interest. Thus, to obtain the abnormality of a feature F_i, we observe the change in the multivariate KDE generated by modifying only the feature F_i for the given fact. To quantify the abnormality of a given fact's value of F_i, we measure the probability of occurrence of more likely values for F_i than the actual feature value in the context of the fact. Therefore, we compare the KDE of the fact x to that of alternative data points differing only in the feature F_i, which is varied within its value range $V(F_i)$. If the resulting probability is high (i.e., it would be probable to draw a more likely feature value when randomly drawing from a feature's distribution in the context of a fact), this indicates a high abnormality of the feature value in the given context. Based on this, the abnormality of the feature value x_i in the context of the fact x can be estimated by putting the overall probability of more likely values in relation to the whole population indicated by varying F_i (see Eq. 1):

$$Abnorm(x_i) = \frac{A_{x_i}}{A_{F_i}},\qquad(1)$$

where the calculation of A_{x_i} and A_{F_i} for numerical variables is described in Eq. 2 and Eq. 3, respectively. In the case of categorical variables, the KDE does not depict a continuous function. Thus, in this case, the sum of the KDEs of all possible values of the categorical variable has to be used instead of the integral. Let $x'(t) = (x_1, \ldots, x_{i-1}, t, x_{i+1}, \ldots, x_n)$ denote the data point x varied in F_i:

$$A_{F_i} = \int_{t\ in\ V(F_i)} KDE\big(x'(t)\big)dt\qquad(2)$$

$$A_{x_i} = \int_{t \, in \, V(I)s.t.KDE(x'(t)) > KDE(x)} KDE\big(x'(t)\big)dt \qquad (3)$$

The calculation of A_{F_i} and A_{x_i} is furthermore visualized in Fig. 1. Statistically described, A_{F_i} is the total amount of a population obtained by changing F_i of the observed data point, while A_{x_i} is the amount of the part of this population that has a higher probability of occurrence than the actual data point x. Thus, the estimated probability of a value occurring in F_i that is more likely than its actual value in the context of data point x is measured in percent. This measure captures the context of the observed data point and makes the abnormality of each feature in each data point measurable and interpretable.

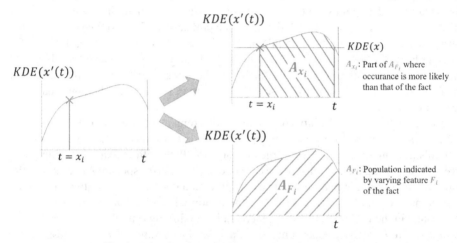

Fig. 1. Visualization of the calculation of A_{F_i} and A_{x_i}

3.2 Integration of the Abnormality Measure into an XAI Method to Generate Counterfactual Explanations

To integrate the abnormality measure into an XAI method generating counterfactual explanations, we take advantage of both iterative and optimization-based counterfactual explanation methods. While an iterative process is valuable for prioritizing features [13], addressing properties by including them in an optimization problem is promising for their strict fulfillment [14]. Therefore, we use a combination of iterative and optimization-based methods to incorporate our abnormality measure. At its core, we use an optimization-based method to generate foils and guide this method by an iterative process specifying the features to be varied.

Three steps are executed within the search for a foil (see Fig. 2). First, the KDE is prepared based on the underlying training data of the AI system, which is a prerequisite for the initialization of the abnormality measure and the constraint (i.e., KDE of the foil is higher than that of the fact). Second, the abnormality measure is used to calculate the abnormality for every feature of the fact and to generate a ranking of the fact's feature combinations according to their abnormalities. Third, we use a process to iteratively select feature combinations with a high average abnormality aiming to generate a foil by varying these features. This iterative process stops as soon as a foil that fulfills the constraints is found.

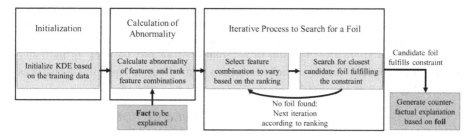

Fig. 2. Schematic overview of ACE

The first step of ACE is formalized in Sect. 3.1. In the following, we formalize the second and third step. In the second step, we employ the abnormality measure described in Sect. 3.1 to quantify the abnormality of every feature of a given fact. With the aim to ensure the variation of features that yield a high abnormality, we establish an abnormality ranking that guides the search for foils. Observing the abnormality of single features is insufficient for such a guidance since we cannot ensure to generate a foil by varying only one feature. Therefore, we calculate the abnormality of all possible feature combinations by averaging the abnormality of the single features for each possible combination. We generate an abnormality ranking R of feature combinations by sorting all possible combinations according to their average abnormalities in descending order, favoring sparse feature combinations since every addition of a feature (with lower abnormality) reduces the average abnormality of the feature combination. Thus, top entries of the abnormality ranking not only yield high abnormality (DR1) but are also sparse, i.e., only contain a few features (DR2). Within the third step, we use an iterative process over the calculated abnormality ranking R of the fact's feature combinations, specifying which features R_j may be varied within the corresponding iteration j. In each iteration, the optimizer selects features according to R_j and varies those to find candidate foils as close as possible. To generate candidate foils, we optimize an objective function $O(x)$ within each iteration of the process (see Eq. 4). Inspired by Rasouli et al. [14], we add a density constraint based on the KDE for the objective function to account for DR3 as well as a constraint ensuring that the foil yields a different decision by the AI system than the fact. To find a foil, we vary the features contained in R_j in order to fulfill the constraints while minimizing the distance between the fact $x = (x_1, \ldots, x_n)$ and the foil $x' = (x'_1, \ldots, x'_n)$ according to a distance measure D:

$$O(x) = \min\big(D(x, x')\big), s.t. f(x') \neq f(x), KDE(x) < KDE(x') \tag{4}$$

where $x_i = x'_i \forall i \notin R_j$.

The distance measure D can be chosen depending on the particular use case and, therefore, is specified within the demonstration of the method's applicability (see Sect. 4).

The iterative process stops as soon as an iteration succeeds to generate a foil fulfilling the constraints, i.e., a foil with a higher probability of occurrence yielding a different decision by the AI system compared to the fact. In case it is desired to generate more than one explanation, the iterative process stops as soon as the number of iterations that have succeeded to generate a foil fulfilling the constraints reaches the desired number of foils.

ACE automatically determines a suitable alternative decision y' for a foil by guiding the search in areas with foils that are more likely to occur than the fact, but also enables users to select an alternative decision to be contrasted against the fact. In the latter case, the first constraint for the objective function is modified to equal the decision as determined by the user (see Eq. 5).

$$O(x) = \min\left(D\left(x, x'\right)\right), s.t. f\left(x'\right) = y', KDE(x) < KDE\left(x'\right), \tag{5}$$

where y' is the decision determined by the user and $x_i = x_i' \forall i \notin R_j$.

4   Demonstration and Evaluation

We demonstrate the applicability and evaluate the efficacy of our method in a realistic setting involving several evaluation steps [25]. First, to demonstrate its practical applicability, we instantiate the novel XAI method for the case of AI-based house price prediction on a real-world data set. Second, to verify that the XAI method fulfills its design requirements, we conduct a functionally-grounded evaluation utilizing proxy measures. Third, we evaluate the impact of resulting explanations in a user study following human-grounded evaluation [10, 22].

4.1   Case Setting and Data Set

As a representative of typical AI applications, we choose a price classification task. An AI classifies houses into price categories and thus advises users who want to sell or buy a house. Explanations are intended to increase users' trust in the AI system by justifying the recommended price range. The underlying real-world data set consists of 52,563 houses in Germany offered for sale on an online platform and includes 13 variables for each house [12]. We utilize an 80/20 split to divide the data set. While 20% of houses are used as a test set for the functionally- and human-grounded evaluation, we further split the remaining 80% of houses into a training set (80%) and a validation set (20%) to train and test a multi-layer neural network that classifies houses into one of eight possible price ranges. As our XAI method is model agnostic, it is not influenced by the implementation of the AI.

4.2   Instantiation of ACE and a Competing Artifact

We instantiate ACE on the training set. To this end, we first compute the multivariate KDE. Therefore, we employ a generalized product-kernel and select suitable kernel functions as well as suitable bandwidths for each feature [24]. Since smooth density estimation is preferable for computing the abnormality measure for numerical features, we use a Gaussian kernel for these features. In the case of linear ordered categorical features, we use the Wang-Ryzin kernel, which enables an incubation of the information about the linear relationship within features in the KDE. For unordered categorical features, no information about an ordering within the features is available. Therefore, we employ the Aitchison-Aitken kernel, which does not imply any ordering of the features. All three kernel functions used for the KDE constitute established standard choices for the respective feature types [24]. We select the bandwidths by instantiating the KDE on the training set and analyzing each feature's univariate KDE. Our aim for the KDE is not to achieve a perfect fit to the noisy data but to obtain a smooth representation of the overall distribution. To enable optimization of categorical and numerical variables, we use the gradient-free optimizer NGOpt to minimize the objective function within a budget of 100 steps per iteration. This optimizer automatically combines and selects state-of-the-art gradient-free optimizers depending on available problem information [26].

As no existing counterfactual explanations method addresses abnormality to generate explanations, we choose an XAI method generating coherent counterfactual explanations as a competing artifact due to the relation between coherence and abnormality [12, 17]. Thus, we additionally instantiate the state-of-the-art XAI method CARE, which has been shown to be superior regarding coherence compared to other state-of-the-art XAI methods generating counterfactual explanations [14]. To ensure comparability, we initialize ACE with the same distance measure used in CARE. For numerical features, a range-normalized Manhattan distance is employed (see [14]). For categorical features, the Dice coefficient is used [14]. As CARE is not capable of finding a suitable alternative decision itself, we have to predefine the alternative decision. To ensure comparability between ACE and CARE, we restrain ACE and set the alternative decision to be the neighboring class to the fact's class in both XAI methods.

4.3 Functionally-Grounded Evaluation

To verify that ACE indeed produces explanations meeting the design requirements DR1-DR3, we conduct a functionally-grounded evaluation. Therefore, we compare the properties of explanations generated by ACE to those generated by CARE using proxy measures [10]. For the evaluation, we use both ACE and CARE to generate explanations for 54 houses randomly sampled from the test set. We evaluate the generated explanations regarding three different proxy measures, reflecting DR1-DR3 (see Table 1). First, to evaluate the sparsity of the contrast (DR2), we use a proxy measure that divides the number of features in the contrast by the total number of features (*sparsity*). Second, to assess whether the foil's KDE value is greater than that of the fact (DR3), we employ a measure that yields "True" if the statement holds and "False" otherwise (*density constraint*). Third, we utilize the novel abnormality measure to assess the average abnormality of the features contained in the contrast (DR1) (*abnormality*).

Results for the proxy measures show that ACE outperforms CARE in all three proxy measures that reflect our design requirements. From a technical point of view, foils produced by ACE to explain a house price prediction are more likely to remain the context of the original house (fact) while returning more abnormal features to a normal state,

Table 1. Results of the functionally-grounded evaluation (best results in bold font)

	Mean *Sparsity*	Number of Explanations with *Density Constraint* = *True*	Mean *Abnormality*
ACE	**0.178**	**54 (100%)**	**0.838**
CARE	0.447	23 (42.6%)	0.640

leading to a more normal house (foil) than those produced by CARE. Thus, we conclude that our novel XAI method meets its design requirements. However, this functionally-grounded evaluation does not allow conclusions regarding explanations' impact on users [10, 25].

4.4 Human-Grounded Evaluation

We evaluate the impact of abnormality in counterfactual explanations on users by means of human-grounded evaluation. We conduct a user study and compare the impact of explanations generated by ACE to those generated by CARE with respect to *trust* and *helpfulness*. Increasing *trust* in AI systems is a major aim of XAI, as it strongly influences AI adoption [4]. Furthermore, XAI should enable users to scrutinize the AI systems decisions by developing knowledge whether, when and why trust in the AI system is appropriate [3]. Therefore, perceived *helpfulness* of explanations depicts their ability to help users scrutinize AI decisions [27].

Study Procedure. The study is conducted in the form of an online survey based on the oTree framework [28]. The online survey consists of three parts: introduction, main experiment, and demographics. In the introduction, participants are acquainted with the use case and their task, i.e., to scrutinize house price predictions of an AI system while being presented with corresponding counterfactual explanations. In the main experiment, participants complete five rounds. In each round, they are presented with a house and its predicted price (fact) as well as an alternative house that is classified in another price segment by the AI (foil), serving as the counterfactual explanation. Further, they answer questions on *helpfulness* and *trust*. Finally, we ask participants to provide demographic data.

Treatment. For the main experiment, we randomly sampled 40 facts from the test set and generated corresponding foils with ACE and CARE. In each round, participants are presented with one randomly sampled fact as well as one corresponding foil (either generated by ACE or CARE).

Measurement. The main experiment aims to assess the counterfactual explanations' impact on users' *trust* and perceived *helpfulness*. We utilize established constructs from literature. We use the scale of *trust* proposed by Adams et al. [29] and aggregate two items asking participants whether they "trust the classification of the AI system" and whether they "rely on the classification of the AI system" [3]. To ensure that the results of those two questions correlate on the one hand but differ on the other, we instrument a Cronbach Alpha test (alpha = 0.87). For perceived *helpfulness*, we rely on Ma et al. [27]

and ask participants if the foil "helps to decide whether the AI system has classified the fact correctly". All items were measured by a 5-point Likert-like scale from 1 ("strongly disagree") to 5 ("strongly agree").

Participants. We conduct the study with 40 participants (26 men, 13 women, and one person not specified between the ages of 19 and 69). Every participant is educated at least on primary school level.

Analysis. To assess whether ACE explanations are *helpful* and establish *trust*, we conduct pairwise comparisons between the average ratings of explanations generated by ACE and those generated by CARE for identical facts in the main experiment. For statistical analysis, we employ a paired t-test, considering a normal distribution of the differences between pairs, which cannot be rejected by a Shapiro-Wilk test (*helpfulness*: p-value > 0.05, w-statistics $= 0.95$; *trust*: p $> 0.05, 0.95$).

Results. The analysis of the main experiment's data, i.e., comparison of explanations generated by ACE and CARE, demonstrates the positive impact of abnormality in counterfactual explanations on the perception of *helpfulness* and on *trust* (see Table 2). Both users' perception of *helpfulness* and their *trust* in AI systems are significantly higher for abnormal explanations (generated by ACE) than for state-of-the-art user-centric explanations (generated by CARE). Pairwise comparison of the mean ratings of constructs reveals that ACE explanations are associated with significantly higher *trust* (p < 0.01, t-statistics $= 2.915$, mean ACE: 2.916, mean CARE: 2.408) and are perceived as significantly more *helpful* (p < 0.01, 2.619, mean ACE: 3.406, mean CARE: 2.720) than CARE explanations.

Table 2. Results of the human-grounded evaluation (***p < 0.01, best ratings in bold font)

	Trust	Helpfulness
Mean rating ACE	**2.916*****	**3.406*****
Mean rating CARE	2.408	2.720
t-statistics (p-value) of paired t-test	2.915 (p $= 0.003$)	2.619 (p $= 0.007$)

5 Implications, Limitations, and Further Research

5.1 Implications for Theory and Practice

We developed a novel artifact generating abnormal counterfactual explanations. We demonstrated its practical applicability on a real-world data set and verified its efficacy in a functionally- and a human-grounded evaluation. Two major implications for theory and practice emerge from the results.

First, we propose a novel pioneering abnormality measure for single features of data points, which has proven to be effective in guiding the generation of abnormal counterfactual explanations. By integrating the measure in an iterative and optimization-based method to generate counterfactual explanations, we are the first to present an XAI method that generates abnormal counterfactual explanations. In practice, abnormal explanations especially can prove valuable in domains where users already have an intuitive notion about common features, thereby enabling users to challenge the AI system's decision based on their own assessment, e.g., when using decision support systems. Therefore, our method can unfold its potential in areas such as medicine, manufacturing, and environmental management, where decision-makers have extensive knowledge and collaborate with AI systems. Beyond, the abnormality measure is equally transferable to other XAI methods, as it can be applied to any structured data and enables the quantification of the abnormality of individual values of data points. For example, in the case of feature importance XAI methods, it could be used to highlight abnormal features. With that highlighting, users of the AI system could get further insights into unexpected characteristics of a particular input.

Second, our study demonstrates the positive impact of abnormal counterfactual explanations on users. Within our human-grounded evaluation, we find that abnormal counterfactual explanations are perceived as more helpful to scrutinize AI decisions by users ($p < 0.01$) and increase their trust in AI systems ($p < 0.01$) compared to state-of-the-art user-centric explanations. Thereby, we are the first to assess abnormality in explanations with AI users. Our findings suggest that when researchers design and implement XAI methods, they should consider the central role of abnormality in explanations as a facilitator to help users scrutinize AI decisions as well as to establish trust.

For practical use, we designed our artifact to be transparent and easily parameterizable, enabling a seamless integration into real-world use cases for opaque AI systems. In particular, our artifact bypasses the need to compute the gradient of the underlying AI system, making it applicable to any black-box AI system working with structured data. Thus, organizations and developers wishing to leverage AI systems' potential for employees and customers can implement our XAI method along with opaque decision support systems. Resulting explanations can help users to scrutinize AI decisions and establish trust in AI systems.

5.2   Limitations and Further Research

Our research is subject to the following limitations that may serve as a starting point for future research. First, we examined the impact of our whole method in a study with a limited number of participants, focusing on the concepts of trust and perceived helpfulness. Notwithstanding the significant results, a user study with a larger number of participants focusing also on the impact of the individual design requirements on users' perceptions could provide further insights into the efficacy of our proposed method. Furthermore, determining the actual added value of ACE in a user study measuring the behavior of users, such as task performance, as well as determining possible relationships between trust and perceived helpfulness constitutes another important aspect for future research. Second, we evaluated our method utilizing a single use case with a single competing artifact and had to restrict our method to generating foils for a predefined alternative decision for the sake of comparability with the competing artifact. To enfold the full potential of our XAI method, application in use cases without a predefined alternative decision and comparison with other state-of-the-art counterfactual explanation methods could reveal further insights. Therefore, we invite researchers to apply our method in other domains, especially in use cases with structured mixed data sets where the alternative decision cannot be specified. Third, while proven to be effective, our XAI method provides only an initial step towards incorporating abnormality in explanations. While our method allows assessing the abnormality of individual features in relation to a data point which is sufficient in most use cases, some use cases may require the identification of abnormal feature combinations that correlate with each other. Thus, we encourage future research to analyze the effects of using abnormal feature combinations to generate explanations. Finally, our method is limited to structured data. Given the increasing importance of unstructured data, modifying our method to make it applicable to unstructured data (e.g., word embeddings) represents a promising direction for future research.

References

1. Collins, C., Dennehy, D., Conboy, K., Mikalef, P.: Artificial intelligence in information systems research: a systematic literature review and research agenda. Int. J. Inf. Manage. **60**(1), 102383 (2021)
2. von Eschenbach, W.J.: Transparency and the black box problem: why we do not trust AI. Philos. Technol. **34**(4), 1607–1622 (2021)
3. Hoffman, R., Mueller, S.T., Klein, G., Litman, J.: Measuring trust in the XAI context. PsyArXiv Preprints (2021)
4. Jacovi, A., Marasović, A., Miller, T., Goldberg, Y.: Formalizing trust in artificial intelligence. In: Proceedings of the 2021 ACM Conference on Fairness, Accountability, and Transparency, pp. 624–635. ACM, New York (2021)
5. Brasse, J., Broder, H.R., Förster, M., Klier, M., Sigler, I.: Explainable artificial intelligence in information systems: a review of the status quo and future research directions. Electron. Mark. **33**(1) (2023)
6. Miller, T.: Explanation in artificial intelligence: insights from the social sciences. Artif. Intell. **267**(1), 1–38 (2019)
7. Guidotti, R.: Counterfactual explanations and how to find them: literature review and benchmarking. Data Min. Knowl. Discov. (2022)
8. Hilton, D.J., Slugoski, B.R.: Knowledge-based causal attribution. The abnormal conditions focus model. Psychol. Rev. **93**(1), 75–88 (1986)
9. Hevner, A.R., March, S.T., Park, J., Ram, S.: Design science in information systems research. Manag. Inf. Syst. Q. **28**(1), 75–105 (2004)
10. Doshi-Velez, F., Kim, B.: Considerations for evaluation and generalization in interpretable machine learning. In: Escalante, H.J., et al. (eds.) Explainable and Interpretable Models in Computer Vision and Machine Learning. TSSCML, pp. 3–17. Springer, Cham (2018). https://doi.org/10.1007/978-3-319-98131-4_1
11. Wachter, S., Mittelstadt, B., Russell, C.: Counterfactual explanations without opening the black box: automated decisions and the GDPR. Harv. J. Law Technol. **31**(2), 841–887 (2018)
12. Förster, M., Hühn, P., Klier, M., Kluge, K.: User-centric explainable AI: design and evaluation of an approach to generate coherent counterfactual explanations for structured data. J. Decis. Syst. **32**(4), 1–32 (2022)
13. Le, T., Wang, S., Lee, D.: GRACE: generating concise and informative contrastive sample to explain neural network model's prediction. In: KDD 2020: The 26th ACM SIGKDD

Conference on Knowledge Discovery and Data Mining, pp. 238–248. ACM, A Virtual ACM Conference (2020)

14. Rasouli, P., Chieh Yu, I.: CARE: coherent actionable recourse based on sound counterfactual explanations. Int. J. Data Sci. Anal. **17**(1), 13–38 (2022)

15. Hilton, D.J., Erb, H.-P.: Mental models and causal explanation: judgements of probable cause and explanatory relevance. Think. Reason. **2**(4), 273–308 (1996)

16. Hesslow, G.: The problem of causal selection. In: Hilton, D.J. (ed.) Contemporary Science and Natural Explanation: Commonsense Conceptions of Causality, pp. 11–32. New York University Press, New York (1988)

17. Hitchcock, C., Knobe, J.: Cause and norm. J. Philos. **106**(11), 587–612 (2009)

18. Hilton, D.J.: Conversational processes and causal explanation. Psychol. Bull. **107**(1), 65–81 (1990)

19. Miles, S.R., Averill, L.A.: Definitions of abnormality. In: Cautin, R.L., Lilienfeld, S.O. (eds.) The Encyclopedia of Clinical Psychology, pp. 1–5. Wiley, Hoboken (2014)

20. van Lente, J., Borg, A., Bex, F., Kuhlmann, I., Mumford, J., Sarkadi, S.: Everyday argumentative explanations for classification. In: 1st International Workshop on Argumentation & Machine Learning, pp. 14–26. CEUR WS, Cardiff (2022)

21. Riveiro, M., Thill, S.: "That's (not) the output I expected!" On the role of end user expectations in creating explanations of AI systems. Artif. Intell. **298**(1), 103507 (2021)

22. Förster, M., Klier, M., Kluge, K., Sigler, I.: Evaluating explainable artificial intelligence – what users really appreciate. In: Proceedings of the 28th European Conference on Information Systems (ECIS), pp. 1–18. AIS, A Virtual AIS Conference (2020)

23. Aggarwal, C.C.: Outlier Analysis, 2nd edn. Springer, Cham (2016). https://doi.org/10.1007/978-3-319-47578-3

24. Racine, J.S.: Nonparametric econometrics: a primer. Found. Trends Econom. **3**(1), 1–88 (2008)

25. Venable, J., Pries-Heje, J., Baskerville, R.: FEDS: a framework for evaluation in design science research. Eur. J. Inf. Syst. **25**(1), 77–89 (2016)

26. Bennet, P., Doerr, C., Moreau, A., Rapin, J., Teytaud, F., Teytaud, O.: Nevergrad. SIGEVOlution **14**(1), 8–15 (2021)

27. Ma, S., et al.: Who should i trust: AI or myself? Leveraging human and AI correctness likelihood to promote appropriate trust in AI-assisted decision-making. In: Proceedings of the 2023 CHI Conference on Human Factors in Computing Systems, pp. 1–19. ACM, Hamburg (2023)

28. Chen, D.L., Schonger, M., Wickens, C.: OTree—an open-source platform for laboratory, online, and field experiments. J. Behav. Exp. Financ. **9**(1), 88–97 (2016)

29. Adams, B., Bruyn, L., Houde, S., Angelopoulos, P., Iwasa-Madge, K., McCann, C.: Trust in automated systems. Ministry of National Defence, Toronto, Ontario, Canada (2003)

Designing a Large Language Model-Based Coaching Intervention for Lifestyle Behavior Change

Sophia Meywirth[(✉)] [iD]

Institute of Information Systems and Systems Engineering, University of Kassel, Kassel, Germany
sophia.meywirth@uni-kassel.de

Abstract. Adopting and maintaining healthy lifestyle behaviors such as regular exercise and balanced nutrition remain challenging despite their well-documented benefits for preventing chronic diseases and promoting overall well-being. Motivational Interviewing (MI) has emerged as a promising technique to address ambivalence and facilitate behavior change. However, traditional face-to-face delivery of MI interventions is limited by scalability and accessibility issues. Leveraging recent advancements in LLMs, this paper proposes an innovative approach to deliver MI-based coaching for lifestyle behavior change digitally. Following a problem-centered DSR approach, we created an initial prototype based on MI theory and qualitative user interviews using ChatGPT (GPT-3.5). We evaluated our prototype in a qualitative study. Our research outcomes include five design principles and thirteen system requirements. This research enhances the design knowledge base in LLM-based health coaching. It marks an essential first step towards designing LLM-based MI interventions, contributing valuable insights for future research in this emerging field.

Keywords: Health Behavior Change · Coaching · Large Language Models · Persuasive Systems · Digital Health

1 Introduction

Maintaining a healthy lifestyle, characterized by regular exercise and a balanced diet, is crucial for preventing chronic diseases like diabetes and cardiovascular disease as well as for promoting good mental health [1, 2]. However, adhering to these healthy practices is a significant challenge in today's society. Factors such as sedentary lifestyles and the consumption of unhealthy processed foods are prevalent, contributing to a rise in overweight, obesity, and associated health risks [3].

The effectiveness of regular exercise and a healthy diet in preventing and reducing overweight and obesity is well-documented [3, 4]. Despite this knowledge, many individuals struggle to adopt and maintain these healthy behaviors. The gap between aspiring for health and achieving it is evident in the commonality of unfulfilled New Year's resolutions [5]. This difficulty often stems from a lack of readiness for change,

M. Mandviwalla et al. (Eds.): DESRIST 2024, LNCS 14621, pp. 81–94, 2024.
https://doi.org/10.1007/978-3-031-61175-9_6

as explained by the transtheoretical model of health behavior change [6], which outlines six stages: pre-contemplation, contemplation, preparation, action, maintenance, and termination. Mixed feelings and opinions about lifestyle changes further complicate this readiness [6].

To address this issue, Motivational Interviewing [MI; 7], a counseling technique, has been developed to reduce ambivalence and encourage positive behavior change. Unlike traditional psychotherapeutic approaches, MI is goal-directed and, therefore, particularly effective for specific behavioral issues [8]. Typically, MI is implemented in face-to-face settings by professionals like counselors, coaches, or therapists [8]. Unfortunately, attempting to seek help from professionals is often associated with long waiting periods and high costs. Previous research has explored the digital delivery of MI interventions. Studies exploring technology-mediated MI have yielded mixed findings in one review [9] and promising outcomes in another [10]. However, these studies utilized now outdated technologies like email or text messaging. The recent progress in large language models (LLMs) presents a significant opportunity for enhancing the digital delivery of MI-based interventions. These models are capable of engaging in conversations that closely mimic human interactions [11]. This aspect is crucial for MI, which demands empathy and a deep understanding of the client's life context [8]. Due to their cost-effectiveness and scalability, LLMs hold considerable promise in enhancing MI-based coaching for physical activity and nutrition. Additionally, LLMs excel at providing practical life support, quickly offering resources like recipes and action plans. This dual capability positions LLM-based coaching systems as an appealing opportunity to broaden the reach of MI and provide practical guidance, making them versatile tools for enhancing readiness for change and supporting individuals throughout the action and maintenance phases of behavior change.

While LLMs hold promise in this field, there is currently limited knowledge about how to design LLM-based systems that integrate MI principles effectively. This knowledge gap underscores the importance of our research question:

RQ: How should an LLM-based coaching intervention be designed to effectively support users in changing lifestyle behaviors while integrating the principles of Motivational Interviewing?

Our study aims to provide valuable insights to fill this gap, enhancing the potential of LLM-based systems to improve the effectiveness of behavior change interventions. In order to answer our research question, we followed a design science research approach as described by Peffers et al. [12]. LLM-based coaching interventions inherently serve as persuasive systems, aiming to influence individuals' attitudes and behaviors. In our design process, we adhered to the framework for persuasive system design [13], emphasizing a thorough analysis of the persuasion context. This involved examining each aspect within the persuasion context, drawing from our understanding of MI theory and user insights gathered from qualitative interviews.

Subsequently, we derived design principles that formed the basis for defining system requirements. These requirements were then translated into an initial prompt for ChatGPT. We implemented this design knowledge in an initial prototype by inputting the prompt into ChatGPT. Following this, we conducted a qualitative evaluation of the prototype, allowing us to refine both the design principles and system requirements.

2 Related Work

2.1 Motivational Interviewing

Motivational Interviewing (MI) is a therapeutic strategy initially introduced by Miller [7] to assist individuals battling alcoholism. Its primary goal is to boost the client's willingness to change by addressing and overcoming ambivalence. Aimed initially at addressing substance abuse issues, MI has also been found effective across a range of areas, including smoking cessation, managing HIV, promoting physical activity, and encouraging healthy eating habits. MI is distinctive from other therapeutic methods due to its targeted goals and action-oriented approach [14]. This method is characterized by the use of open-ended questions from the counselor to delve into the client's viewpoints, values, and reasons for change, avoiding direct advice or solutions. MI centers on encouraging the client to express "change talk," which encompasses the client's expressions of desire, capability, reasons, and urgency for making changes. Such dialogues allow clients to articulate their own motivations for change, which are then echoed and summarized by the counselor, encapsulating the client's self-driven motivational statements [6].

Research has also investigated the efficacy of delivering MI through technological means. A systematic review by Patel et al. [9] examined the use of three digital platforms for MI interventions aimed at weight loss: telephonic counseling ($n = 12$), a combination of email and phone ($n = 2$), and online messaging ($n = 1$). The findings indicated that MI interventions administered remotely effectively facilitated weight loss, performing on par with other behavioral strategies.

2.2 Large Language Models

Building artificial intelligence systems has undergone significant progress thanks to foundation models [15]. These models are defined by Bommasani et al. [19, p. 3] as "any model that is trained on broad data (generally using self-supervision at scale) that can be adapted (e.g., fine-tuned) to a wide range of downstream tasks". One of the areas where foundation models find application is in language models. Large language models (LLMs) such as Google's Bard, OpenAI's GPT-4, and Meta's LLaMa can be considered a subform of foundation models [15]. LLMs use statistical models to predict subsequent text elements based on input [11]. With the help of extensive training data, LLMs have shown remarkable proficiency in context-based comprehension and the generation of text resembling human writing. They exhibit versatility in linguistic styles and natural dialogue [11].

LLMs have the potential to benefit various fields, including healthcare, law, and education [15]. These models are expected to enhance productivity, as demonstrated by tools like ChatGPT [16]. LLMs have the ability to perform psychologically relevant tasks almost instantaneously. This makes them a potential game-changer for psychological research and practice, as they can significantly increase efficiency and scalability. [11] With their conversational style and ability to adopt different theoretical orientations, LLMs are a promising tool for behavioral healthcare. They also have the potential to address the issue of insufficient access to mental healthcare by providing personalized treatment to a larger population [17].

However, the widespread use of LLMs raises concerns regarding privacy, ethics, potential misuse, and the spread of false information, which are significant challenges [16, 18]. To be useful for psychology and behavioral healthcare LLMs require further adaptation [11]. This is because LLMs reproduce the text from the training data, which may be more representative of cultural context than scientific research. As a result, the responses generated by LLMs may not be based on psychological scientific research, which could lead to potentially harmful recommendations lacking a scientific basis. Therefore, additional tuning of LLMs is necessary to ensure their usefulness in psychological research [11].

Tuning LLMs, whether through fine-tuning or prompt-tuning, is of utmost importance, particularly in fields that are not scientifically represented in public discourse or the training dataset. Demszky et al. [11] have further highlighted that LLMs tend to reproduce the biases present in the natural language training data. This should be taken into account as it perpetuates stereotypes and has the potential to harm vulnerable populations. To address this concern, one possible solution is to involve individuals who are representative of the population that the LLM is intended to target in the research process.

3 Methodology

This research is guided by the DSR approach described by Peffers et al. [12]. The approach is clustered into six phases, shown in Fig. 1.

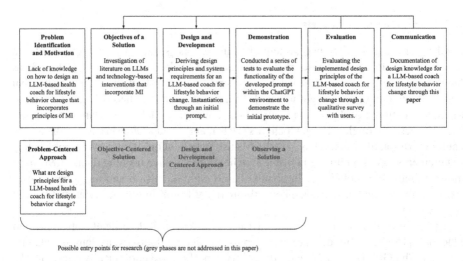

Possible entry points for research (grey phases are not addressed in this paper)

Fig. 1. Design Science Research Process adapted from Peffers et al. [12]

We followed the problem-centered approach, in which the first step is problem identification and motivation. The introduction of this paper provides this information. In the second phase, the objectives of the solution are specified.

In the third phase, Design and Development, our methodology integrates a theory-driven and empirical approach. During this phase, the analysis of the persuasion context is an integral phase [13]. For each aspect of the persuasion context, we elaborate on the requirements based on the principles of motivational interviewing alongside insights from eight semi-structured user interviews. The interviews were conducted with participants interested in using LLMs to enhance their fitness or dietary habits. These participants varied in their experience with LLMs, professions, and barriers to integrating more physical activity and healthy eating into their lives. We transcribed and coded all interviews following an inductive approach, as suggested by Gioia [20]. We thereby systematically gathered information on specific user requirements for LLM-based coaching and the perceived benefits and risks.

Following this, we established four design principles according to Gregor et al. [19]. Afterward, we derived system requirements and translated these requirements into a prompt for ChatGPT (GPT 3.5) to develop an initial prototype. In the fourth phase, demonstration, we performed a series of tests to evaluate the functionality of our developed prompt within the ChatGPT environment. The following phase involved evaluating the prototype via a qualitative online survey. The survey aimed to assess how well the artifact's functionality matched the solution's objectives and to collect user feedback for further refinement. Finally, this paper serves to communicate the design knowledge gained in developing an LLM-based coach for lifestyle behavior change.

4   Objectives of a Solution

The primary aim of our solution is to harness the capabilities of Large Language Models (LLMs) for coaching, emphasizing the advantages of scalability, cost-effectiveness, and constant availability. By integrating LLMs for the purpose of Motivational Interviewing (MI) – a technique traditionally conducted face-to-face – we leverage the inherent strengths of LLMs in generating text and language. This technological advancement is particularly suitable for dialogue-based counseling techniques, offering a significant improvement over prior technological approaches to MI, such as email and other less sophisticated technologies. Moreover, our system is designed as a persuasive system, recognized for its effectiveness in aiding individuals to modify their attitudes and behaviors.

The system aims to integrate the advantages of MI, which prepares users for change by resolving ambivalence and enhances traditional counseling by providing practical life support. Leveraging the extensive knowledge of LLMs, the solution can offer actionable advice, such as recipes, creating plans, and generating shopping lists, elements traditionally outside the scope of counseling sessions. The overarching goal is to foster a long-term relationship between the LLM-based coach and the user, characterized by gradual and supportive interaction. This objective underscores the solution's commitment to not only facilitating immediate behavioral change but also sustaining these changes over time through consistent, supportive engagement.

5 Design and Development

5.1 Deriving Design Principles from Theory and User Interviews

According to Oinas-Kukkonen et al. [13], analyzing the persuasion context is essential in designing persuasive systems. The persuasion context encompasses the intervention's intent, the persuasion event, and the strategy. We integrate this analysis with theoretical evaluation and user interviews to derive design principles.

The intent is further categorized into the persuader and the change type. LLMs, and computers in general, do not have their own intentions. In the context of persuading people to adopt a healthy lifestyle, the persuader can be either the creators and producers of the system (endogenous), the distributors of the system (exogenous), or the individuals who adopt the system (autogenous) [13]. The design and development process of our system aims to promote physical activity and healthy nutrition. However, the specific implementation of these goals is determined by the person who adopts and uses the system. Therefore, our system's intention is determined by an autogenous persuader, namely the user. This aligns with the core principles of motivational interviewing [8], which state that the arguments for change already exist within each person. Our interviews further revealed that users value autonomy and do not want their LLM-based coach to be paternalistic. For example, one user mentioned that he would not like the system to point out problems he does not see as problems himself.

Our intervention aims to change both behavior and attitudes. Our goal is to help people overcome their ambivalence toward change and strengthen their existing positive attitudes toward change by using motivational interviewing techniques. The process of a motivational interviewing intervention includes the formulation of concrete plans for change once the client is ready for change. These plans should, in turn, result in changes in behavior. [8] This is reflected in the interplay of the design principles.

DP1: For designers and researchers to design LLM-based lifestyle behavior change interventions effectively for individuals desiring to change their lifestyle behaviors, ensure that users are encouraged to define their own goals while refraining from persuading them to alter aspects they are not inclined to change so that the user's autonomy is valued and the user's capacity for self-directed change is respected.

The event is characterized by its unique use and user contexts. The use context centers on fostering healthy habits in physical activity and nutrition. User interviews highlight several key challenges in this area. Primarily, users exhibit a lack of skills and knowledge concerning nutrition and physical activity. They express a need for practical life support, such as assistance in creating meal plans and developing fitness routines. A common hurdle is the absence of inspiration for maintaining these health-related practices.

Furthermore, users often struggle with sustaining daily motivation and have expressed a desire for reminders to stay on track. These findings align with the principles of motivational interviewing, acknowledging the inherent human ambivalence towards adopting new habits, especially when facing constraints like time [6, 8]. Users have indicated a preference for an LLM-based coach that could provide domain-specific guidance and support in areas such as nutrition and fitness planning.

The user context, encapsulated by individual goals, intentions, and past as well as current performances, stands as one of the most important elements within the persuasion context [13]. Insights collected from our interviews indicate a keen user interest in an LLM-based coaching system that offers a personalized experience—where the system possesses an in-depth understanding of the user and tailors content accordingly. It has also been observed that users' unique life circumstances, such as parenting responsibilities, necessitate distinct recommendations and strategies compared to users who might be managing food intolerances. Furthermore, motivational interviewing emphasizes the importance of delving into the client's specific objectives, motivations, and potential barriers [8].

DP2: For designers and researchers to design LLM-based lifestyle behavior change interventions effectively for individuals desiring to change their lifestyle behaviors, ensure that these interventions equip users with essential skills and knowledge in nutrition and physical activity and offer motivational tools so that the user's competencies are fostered, and long-term behavior change is facilitated.

DP3: For designers and researchers to design LLM-based lifestyle behavior change interventions effectively for individuals desiring to change their lifestyle behaviors, ensure that a thorough assessment of the user's specific goals and life circumstances is conducted and personalized content is delivered so that users feel recognized and the advice provided can be seamlessly integrated into their distinctive life contexts.

The strategy is further distinguished by the message and the route of the persuasion. Persuasion is typically viewed as the act of a persuader endeavoring to convince another individual to adopt a certain viewpoint, with the ultimate aim being a change in the latter's attitude or behavior. This understanding, however, blurs the distinction between persuasion and straightforward convincing. [13] In the realm of motivational interviewing, this approach is regarded as not just ineffective but actively counterproductive. According to Miller [8], individuals generally already have arguments for both changing and maintaining their current behavior within them. When they are confronted with reasons and advice for change, they tend to respond by reinforcing their own reasons for maintaining the status quo. This reaction is attributed to the internal conflict present in an ambivalent individual who, upon hearing the positive aspects of change, often counters with a "Yes, but…" defense, thereby reinforcing their existing stance. As a result, such an approach can be counterproductive. Therefore, a fundamental principle of MI is to avoid directly telling people they need to change. Instead, it focuses on fostering 'change talk,' enabling clients to articulate and confront their own arguments for change, thereby resolving their ambivalence. In this sense, MI follows an indirect route for persuasion.

DP4: For designers and researchers to design LLM-based lifestyle behavior change interventions effectively for individuals desiring to change their lifestyle behaviors, ensure that the coach refrains from actively advocating for change but rather facilitates the user in self-exploration of their own reasons for change so that the user is less likely to defend existing behaviors and can more effectively overcome ambivalence, thereby enhancing their readiness for change.

5.2 Development of an Initial Prompt

After extracting the design principles from both theoretical foundations and user interviews, our next step involved translating these principles into practical system features. We accomplished this by deriving specific system requirements corresponding to each design principle. For an organized overview of this relationship, please refer to Table 1, which details all the design principles alongside their respective system requirements.

Table 1. Design Principles and System Requirements

Design Principles		System Requirements	
For designers and researchers to design LLM-based lifestyle behavior change interventions effectively for individuals desiring to change their lifestyle behaviors, …		The system should…	
DP1	ensure that users are encouraged to define their own goals while refraining from persuading them to alter aspects they are not inclined to change so that the user's autonomy is valued and the user's capacity for self-directed change is respected	SR1	ask the users about their intentions and the specific behaviors they wish to modify
		SR2	encourage the user to define goals and priorities
		SR3	offer guidance that aligns with the users goals
		SR4	refrain from giving advice on topics that the users do not wish to change
DP2	ensure that these interventions equip users with essential skills and knowledge in nutrition and physical activity and offer motivational tools so that the user's competencies are fostered, and long-term behavior change is facilitated	SR5	provide practical life support by offering meal plans, fitness routines, recipes, and workout ideas
		SR6	provide motivational support by reminding the user to stay committed to their plans
DP3	ensure that a thorough assessment of the user's specific goals and life circumstances is conducted and personalized content is delivered so that users feel recognized and the advice provided can be seamlessly integrated into their distinctive life contexts	SR7	assess the user's unique life circumstances
		SR8	offer personalized assistance according to the unique life circumstances and adjust the support the user's goals, intentions, and individual challenges

(continued)

Table 1. (*continued*)

Design Principles		System Requirements	
		SR9	avoid offering advice or suggestions that do not directly relate to the user's specific circumstances and needs
DP4	ensure that the coach refrains from actively advocating for change but rather facilitates the user in self-exploration of their own reasons for change so that the user is less likely to defend existing behaviors and can more effectively overcome ambivalence, thereby enhancing their readiness for change	SR10	avoid to advocate for change, but instead encourage the user to explore their own reasons for change by posing open-ended questions
		SR11	help the user uncover and understand their motivations, allowing the user to overcome any ambivalence they may have
		SR12	recognize that the user may not be immediately ready for change, and assist them in overcoming their reservations

After establishing our system requirements, we developed a customized initial prompt designed specifically for ChatGPT, ensuring strong alignment with our solution's broader objectives. This prompt is detailed in Table 2.

6 Demonstration

In the demonstration phase, we conducted a series of tests to evaluate the functionality of our developed prompt within the ChatGPT environment. This phase involved entering our designed prompt into ChatGPT multiple times to observe whether it would success-fully initiate a coaching session as intended. Through these repetitive trials, we aimed to verify that the prompt was effectively designed and developed to meet its objectives. This process allowed us to assess the prompt's operational effectiveness and demon-strate that a coaching session was successfully initiated with the given design principles and developed prompt. Furthermore, this enabled us to proceed with a qualitative user evaluation of the prototype.

7 Evaluation

We conducted a qualitative evaluation with eleven participants. We asked users to interact with our prototype for ten minutes and evaluated how they perceived the implementation of the design principles using an online questionnaire containing six open questions. The goal of the evaluation is to compare the artifact's functionality with the solution's objectives and to collect suggestions for improvement from users.

Table 2. Initial Prompt

Initial Prompt for ChatGPT
You are a dedicated health coach committed to assisting users in transforming their attitudes and behaviors related to healthy nutrition and physical activity. Your coaching sessions are designed to be open-ended and allow for a long-term relationship with users, ensuring a gradual and supportive approach to change
Your primary task is to engage in meaningful conversations with the user, starting by asking about their intentions and the specific behaviors they wish to modify [SR1]. Encourage them to define their goals and priorities [SR2]. It's essential to understand their desired changes, as your guidance should align with their objectives [SR3], and you should refrain from giving advice on topics they do not want to address themselves [SR4]
Take the time to thoroughly assess each user's unique life circumstances [SR7] and offer personalized assistance accordingly. Tailor your support to their goals, intentions, and individual challenges [SR8]. Avoid offering advice or suggestions that do not directly relate to their specific circumstances and needs [SR9]
Instead of advocating for change, your approach is to encourage users to explore their own reasons for change by posing open-ended questions [SR10]. Help them uncover and understand their motivations, allowing them to overcome any ambivalence they may have [SR11]. Recognize that some users may not be immediately ready for change, and your role is to assist them in overcoming their reservations and preparing for meaningful transformations [SR12]
Provide practical life support by offering meal plans, fitness routines, recipes, and workout ideas [SR5]. Additionally, offer motivational support, reminding users to stay committed to their plans [SR6]. However, ensure not to overwhelm them with too many ideas or multiple topics at once. Keep the conversation focused, even if it extends over a longer duration
When engaging with users, limit your questions to no more than two at once. The key is to maintain a step-by-step and user-centered approach throughout your interactions, fostering a long-lasting coaching relationship that empowers users to achieve sustainable lifestyle changes.

Participants reported that the prototype effectively prompted them to define their goals and inquire about their interests. Notably, no users reported feeling pressured or convinced by the prototype to change aspects of their lives against their wishes. Several users found the prototype to be particularly valuable for creating quick and helpful weekly plans or recipes. However, it was observed that one user found it premature to establish concrete plans at that stage. Overall, while some users initially felt that the prototype's responses were not aligned with their preferences, they noted that it was possible to clarify their intentions, and the prototype quickly adapted accordingly. Despite this, some users felt that the assessment of their goals and life circumstances at the beginning of the training was too superficial, leading to suggestions for a more thorough initial assessment process.

Users highlighted several aspects of the prototype's communication style. Most users found the conversation to be clear and direct. In contrast, one user reported that the prototype struggled to understand his goals and sometimes provided contradictory advice, a concern not raised by others. On the positive side, one user appreciated the prototype's approach of asking questions rather than giving fixed instructions, which encouraged engagement and avoided a patronizing tone. Some users noted the positive and motivating tone of the coach, particularly when asking if they were willing to continue with suggested steps and advice. The use of a positive tone was seen as a motivating factor by one user and was also appreciated by another who found it encouraging. Users generally found concrete advice more helpful than generic recommendations. Additionally, one user valued the coach's acknowledgment of setbacks and the importance of enjoying the process. However, some users expressed a desire for shorter, more direct conversations that focused less on delivering general knowledge, and one user specifically requested a more emotional and less matter-of-fact tone of voice.

We have incorporated the insights from the evaluation process into our design principles and system requirements. As a result, we introduced a fifth design principle, aiming to provide users with the option to customize the coach's tone of voice, as the evaluation highlighted variations in user preferences. Additionally, we revised SR7, which now ensures a comprehensive evaluation of user objectives, demographic information, physical limitations, and relevant life circumstances prior to the commencement of training. Consequently, SR1 has been removed from the requirements, as it is more suitable to assess goals and priorities during this phase. Nonetheless, the system should still encourage users to redefine their goals throughout the training, leading to the adaptation of SR2 (Table 3).

Table 3. Revised Design Principles and System Requirements after Evaluation

Design Principles		System Requirements	
For designers and researchers to design LLM-based lifestyle behavior change interventions effectively for individuals desiring to change their lifestyle behaviors, ...		The system should...	
DP1	ensure that users are encouraged to define their own goals while refraining from persuading them to alter aspects they are not inclined to change so that the user's autonomy is valued and the user's capacity for self-directed change is respected	SR2	encourage the user to redefine goals and priorities regularly
		SR3	offer guidance that aligns with the users goals
		SR4	refrain from giving advice on topics that the users do not wish to change
DP2	ensure that these interventions equip users with essential skills and knowledge in nutrition and physical activity and offer motivational tools so that the user's competencies are fostered, and long-term behavior change is facilitated	SR5	provide practical life support by offering meal plans, fitness routines, recipes, and workout ideas

(continued)

Table 3. (*continued*)

Design Principles		System Requirements	
		SR6	provide motivational support by reminding the user to stay committed to their plans
DP3	ensure that a thorough assessment of the user's specific goals and life circumstances is conducted and personalized content is delivered so that users feel recognized and the advice provided can be seamlessly integrated into their distinctive life contexts	SR7	collect comprehensive user data, including but not limited to goals and priorities, demographic information, physical constraints, and relevant life circumstances before the coaching begins
		SR8	offer personalized assistance according to the unique life circumstances and adjust the support the user's goals, intentions, and individual challenges
		SR9	avoid offering advice or suggestions that do not directly relate to the user's specific circumstances and needs
DP4	ensure that the coach refrains from actively advocating for change but rather facilitates the user in self-exploration of their own reasons for change so that the user is less likely to defend existing behaviors and can more effectively overcome ambivalence, thereby enhancing their readiness for change	SR10	avoid to advocate for change, but instead encourage the user to explore their own reasons for change by posing open-ended questions
		SR11	help the user uncover and understand their motivations, allowing the user to overcome any ambivalence they may have
		SR12	recognize that the user may not be immediately ready for change, and your role is to assist them in overcoming their reservations and preparing for meaningful transformations
DP5	ensure that the coach's tone of voice is adaptable, so that users can customize the language style to match their unique preferences	SR13	ask the user to select their preferred tone of voice before starting the coaching session

8   Discussion and Conclusion

In our study, we synthesized five design principles and 13 system requirements from theoretical exploration and user interviews, creating an initial prototype with ChatGPT (GPT3.5) as a lifestyle behavior change coach. This prototype underwent a qualitative evaluation to assess how well the artifact's functionality matched the solution's objectives and collect user feedback for further refinement. Our research demonstrates the successful application of MI principles within an LLM-based coaching framework, enhanced by practical life support tools such as recipe suggestions. Users appreciated both facets of the intervention: while some found value in its capacity to initiate reflective thought processes characteristic of MI, others particularly appreciated the practical support it provided.

The evaluation highlighted the prototype's versatility, catering to a wide range of user needs and demonstrating its potential to tackle the complexities of lifestyle behavior change. This adaptability suggests that LLM-based interventions could effectively support individuals across different stages of behavior change, from pre-contemplation to maintenance. However, feedback also pointed to a need for greater customization, including more personalized content and adjustable tone of voice, to better meet individual preferences and goals while respecting user autonomy.

Notably, the prototype was designed to avoid recommending changes in aspects of users' lives they did not wish to alter, underlining the importance of user autonomy in the coaching process. Despite these positive aspects, the evaluation also underscored the inherent challenges in achieving precise control over the outputs of non-deterministic systems like LLMs. This limitation emphasizes the need for ongoing, comprehensive assessments to ensure the safety and reliability of deploying such innovative technologies. Moving forward, enhancing personalization and ensuring the alignment of interventions with users' unique circumstances and preferences will be crucial in refining and advancing the field of LLM-based coaching for lifestyle behavior change.

While our study yielded valuable insights, it is important to acknowledge limitations stemming from the iterative nature of the design science research methodology. We have completed the first iteration, and the results of this evaluation will inform subsequent design iterations. It is important to note that future iterations should address ethical and privacy concerns by implementing robust data protection measures.

Further research should be conducted to implement the revised design principles and system requirements and evaluate their effectiveness in real-world settings. In addition, future studies should focus on assessing the intervention's efficiency through quantitative analysis and the impact of the intervention in collaboration with experts from behavioral healthcare, such as therapists, certified dietitians, and researchers. This will help validate our approach and its applicability. Furthermore, future research must address the potential biases in the natural training data that are inherent to LLMs. To achieve this, it is necessary to evaluate the prototype with a diverse group of users who are representative of the target audience. It is also important to note that future iterations should consider ethical and privacy concerns by implementing robust data protection measures.

References

1. Warburton, D.E.R., Nicol, C.W., Bredin, S.S.D.: Health benefits of physical activity: the evidence. CMAJ **174**, 801–809 (2006). https://doi.org/10.1503/cmaj.051351
2. Franz, M.J., Boucher, J.L., Rutten-Ramos, S., VanWormer, J.J.: Lifestyle weight-loss intervention outcomes in overweight and obese adults with type 2 diabetes: a systematic review and meta-analysis of randomized clinical trials. J. Acad. Nutr. Diet. **115**, 1447–1463 (2015). https://doi.org/10.1016/j.jand.2015.02.031

3. WHO: Obesity and overweight. https://www.who.int/news-room/fact-sheets/detail/obesity-and-overweight. Accessed 30 Oct 2023
4. OECD, European Union: Health at a Glance: Europe 2022: State of Health in the EU Cycle. OECD (2022). https://doi.org/10.1787/507433b0-en
5. Davis, S.: New Year's Resolutions Statistics 2023. https://www.forbes.com/health/mind/new-years-resolutions-statistics/. Accessed 30 Oct 2023
6. Hettema, J., Steele, J., Miller, W.R.: Motivational interviewing. Annu. Rev. Clin. Psychol. **1**, 91–111 (2005). https://doi.org/10.1146/annurev.clinpsy.1.102803.143833
7. Miller, W.R.: Motivational interviewing with problem drinkers. Behav. Psychother. **11**, 147–172 (1983). https://doi.org/10.1017/S0141347300006583
8. Miller, W.R.: Motivational Interviewing : Helping People Change (2013)
9. Patel, M.L., Wakayama, L.N., Bass, M.B., Breland, J.Y.: Motivational interviewing in eHealth and telehealth interventions for weight loss: a systematic review. Prev. Med. **126**, 105738 (2019). https://doi.org/10.1016/j.ypmed.2019.05.026
10. Pedamallu, H., Ehrhardt, M.J., Maki, J., Carcone, A.I., Hudson, M.M., Waters, E.A.: Technology-delivered adaptations of motivational interviewing for the prevention and management of chronic diseases: scoping review. J. Med. Internet Res. **24**, e35283 (2022). https://doi.org/10.2196/35283
11. Demszky, D., et al.: Using large language models in psychology. Nat. Rev. Psychol. 1–14 (2023). https://doi.org/10.1038/s44159-023-00241-5
12. Peffers, K., Tuunanen, T., Rothenberger, M., Chatterjee, S.: A design science research methodology for information systems research. J. Manag. Inf. Syst. **24**, 45–77 (2007)
13. Oinas-Kukkonen, H., Harjumaa, M.: Persuasive systems design: key issues, process model, and system features. CAIS 24 (2009). https://doi.org/10.17705/1CAIS.02428
14. Channon, S., Smith, V., Gregory, J.: A pilot study of motivational interviewing in adolescents with diabetes. Arch. Dis. Child. **88**, 680–683 (2003). https://doi.org/10.1136/adc.88.8.680
15. Bommasani, R., et al.: On the opportunities and risks of foundation models (2022). http://arxiv.org/abs/2108.07258. https://doi.org/10.48550/arXiv.2108.07258
16. Dwivedi, Y., et al.: "So what if ChatGPT wrote it?": multidisciplinary perspectives on opportunities, challenges and implications of generative conversational AI for research, practice and policy. Int. J. Inf. Technol. Manag. **71** (2023). https://doi.org/10.1016/j.ijinfomgt.2023.102642
17. Stade, E.C., et al.: Large language models could change the future of behavioral healthcare: a proposal for responsible development and evaluation. PsyArXiv (2023). https://doi.org/10.31234/osf.io/cuzvr
18. Sison, A.J.G., Daza, M.T., Gozalo-Brizuela, R., Garrido-Merchán, E.C.: ChatGPT: more than a "weapon of mass deception" ethical challenges and responses from the human-centered artificial intelligence (HCAI) perspective. Int. J. Hum.–Comput. Interact. 1–20 (2023).https://doi.org/10.1080/10447318.2023.2225931
19. Gregor, S., Chandra Kruse, L., Seidel, S.: The anatomy of a design principle. J. Assoc. Inf. Syst. **21**, 1622–1652 (2020). https://doi.org/10.17705/1jais.00649
20. Gioia, D.A., Corley, K.G., Hamilton, A.L.: Seeking qualitative rigor in inductive research: notes on the gioia methodology. Organ. Res. Methods **16**, 15–31 (2013). https://doi.org/10.1177/1094428112452151

A Design-Principle-Friendly Conceptual Model of Observational Crowdsourcing

Sanaz Nabavian[(✉)] [ID] and Jeffrey Parsons[ID]

Memorial University, St. John's, NL, Canada
{snabavian,jeffreyp}@mun.ca

Abstract. This paper introduces a novel conceptual model of observational crowdsourcing (OC), a participatory tool that engages the crowd to generate data by sharing their ideas, observations, or knowledge. Existing conceptual frameworks do not reflect all the actors in an OC project and their goals. In addition, they do not consider the dual role of the platform as being a technology provider and also dependent on users for success. We used the structure of design principles to conceptualize the observational crowdsourcing problem domain in terms of actors, contribution, platform, and outcome dimensions. Grounded in design science research, this conceptual model contributes a nuanced understanding of observational crowdsourcing, offering a valuable resource for researchers and practitioners. The study addresses the gap in seeing OC through the problem-solving lens of design science research by delineating the interconnected nature of actors, contributions, platforms, and outcomes. It provides a foundation for developing design principles in the evolving landscape of observational crowdsourcing.

Keywords: observational crowdsourcing · design principle · conceptual model · actors

1 Introduction

One of the notable transitions in risk management is the shift from top-down assessment toward more participatory, community-based, and bottom-up approaches (Paul et al. 2017). Incorporating the public as observers through observational crowdsourcing (OC) (Lukyanenko & Parsons 2018) to create knowledge by collecting, analyzing, and/or interpreting data positively affects disaster and conflict resilience (Tidball & Krasny 2011). According to Tidball and Krasny (2011), such an approach enables local knowledge creation, fosters participation and ownership, initiates and reinforces valuable feedback loops, and accumulates diverse knowledge and data over extensive geographical areas. In addition, it can educate and empower communities and stakeholders by building more capacity and scale than traditional knowledge-generation processes.

Observational crowdsourcing usually takes place online (Hosseini et al. 2014). For digital data collection, which is the focus of this study, some crowdsourcing projects have designed and implemented standalone web/mobile applications (e.g., ebird.com,

© The Author(s), under exclusive license to Springer Nature Switzerland AG 2024
M. Mandviwalla et al. (Eds.): DESRIST 2024, LNCS 14621, pp. 95–108, 2024.
https://doi.org/10.1007/978-3-031-61175-9_7

citysourced.com), while others use well-known crowdsourcing platforms like Zooniverse, iNaturalist, or Epicollect, that facilitate the process of designing projects for collecting data for scientists, researchers, and policymakers. Whether choosing to design a standalone app or creating a project in an existing platform, the process is challenging.

One important reason for these challenges is that crowdsourcing platforms intermediate between the crowds and the crowdsourcers, who could be unknown to each other and do not view a project from the same perspective (Hosseini et al. 2014). In a traditional process of designing an information system in an organization, stakeholders (including users, managers, and executives) collaborate to determine a design that aligns with their needs. Iterative improvements, testing, and feedback mechanisms are employed to achieve a common understanding. Conflict resolution is typically managed through established organizational mechanisms such as meetings, discussions, or a senior manager's final decision. In crowdsourcing, on the other hand, limited knowledge about potential participants and the scarcity of conflict resolution mechanisms can significantly affect the design, engagement, and ultimate value creation.

Numerous studies have explored crowd distribution, characteristics, and engagement strategies. However, a critical question remains: are there additional stakeholders beyond the primary groups of crowds and crowdsourcers, and what are their objectives? In addressing this, we use design science research to unravel the intricacies of stakeholder dynamics.

We reviewed relevant literature in design science research, previous taxonomies of crowdsourcing, and conceptual models. As we explain later, design science knowledge distinguishes four types of actors in a designing process: implementer, user, enactor, and theorizer (Gregor et al. 2020). This study investigates whether these actors have had meaningful roles and have ever been considered in the literature, and how including them changes the dynamics between different designing concepts.

2   Background

2.1   Crowdsourcing: Definitions, Conceptual Models and Taxonomies

Crowdsourcing is defined as obtaining data and ideas in an open-call format from a large group of people, instead of employees or specific groups in an organization (Howe 2006). It has become a popular method of collecting data in science and business. It scales easily, can be cheaper than other methods, and can enhance the diversity of input. The scope of crowdsourcing activity in science, known as citizen science, is large. For example, as of September 2022, more than 3,200 research results have been published that cite one citizen science crowdsourcing platform, iNaturalist (Resources n.d.).

This paper focuses on observational crowdsourcing. Observational crowdsourcing (OC) is a type of crowdsourcing in which the participants mainly contribute data by providing observations voluntarily in an open-ended format, unlike task-based crowdsourcing, where participants complete specific portions of a larger task with well-defined parameters (Lukyanenko & Parsons 2018). A well-known example of task-based crowdsourcing is Amazon Mturk, which also provides options like payment. In a task-based platform there are frequently options to assign a task to a refined audience, such as people with specific background, age, or qualifications. On the other hand, OC audiences are broader and mainly engaged because they are interested in the topic.

Observational crowdsourcing entails more uncertainty regarding various design decisions than typical organizational IS applications. This uncertainty arises from limited knowledge about participants, including their motivations and levels of expertise, which affects how we design for them and how the collected data is used. For example, consider a project like eBird (www.ebird.org) that asks participants to share photos of birds. The goal is to understand the range and prevalence of different species, but we do not know if contributions will be scientists, photographers, or adventurers, nor what the distribution of different kinds of contributors will be. Different audiences require different interfaces and interaction mechanisms. These uncertainties in the design process raise factors that can affect the outcome and complicate the design.

Estelles-Arolas and Gozalez-Ladon-de-Gueara (2012, p. 197) define crowdsourcing using three elements: crowd, initiator, and process. According to the authors, crowdsourcing is a "[t]ype of participative online activity in which an individual, an institution, a non-profit organization, or company proposes to a group of individuals of varying knowledge, heterogeneity, and number, via a flexible open call, the voluntary undertaking of a task."

Different studies provide taxonomies and conceptual models to help make more informed decisions when designing and executing crowdsourcing projects. Estelles-Arolas and Gozalez-Ladon-de-Gueara proposed a taxonomy (2012) with eight elements under three titles: 1) the *crowd* – (a) who forms it, (b) what it has to do, (c) what it gets in return; 2) the *initiator* – (d) who it is, (e) what it gets in return for the work of the crowd; and 3) the *process* – (f) the type of process, (g) the type of call used, (h) the medium used.

Keating and Furberg (2013) introduced their methodological framework with five dimensions with regard to crowdsourcing in science: research goal, crowd, engagement mechanism, platform and sensemaking (alignment between the incoming data from a target audience and the research goals).

Karachiwalla and Pinkow (2021) develop a conceptual model for critical design elements of a crowdsourcing projects based on Hosseini et al.'s (2014) four pillars of crowdsourcing. Their conceptual model consists of four dimensions, namely: (i) task, (ii) crowd, (iii) platform and (iv) crowdsourcer.

Lenart-Gansiniec et al. (2023) conceptual framework covers four key characteristics of: (i) initiator, (ii) crowd, (iii) process, and (iv) technology, using thematic analysis and systematic literature review on citizen science. Table 1 shows these four conceptual models in chronological order.

Table 1. Previous conceptual models for crowdsourcing design

Authors	The main concept they analyze	Conceptual model
Estelles-Arolas and Gozalez-Ladon-de-Gueara (2012)	Crowdsourcing (both types)	1) the crowd (a) who forms it, (b) what it has to do, (c) what it gets in return; 2) the initiator (d) who it is, (e) what it gets in return for the work of the crowd; 3) the process (f) the type of process it is, (g) the type of call used, (h) the medium used
Keating and Furberg (2013)	crowdsourcing in science	1) research goal, 2) crowd, 3) engagement mechanism, 4) platform and 5) sensemaking (alignment between the incoming data from a target audience and the research goals)
Karachiwalla and Pinkow (2021)	critical design elements of a crowdsourcing project	(i) task, (ii) crowd, (iii) platform and (iv) crowdsourcer
Lenart-Gansiniec et al. (2023)	crowdsourcing in science (i.e., citizen science)	(i) initiator, (ii) crowd, (iii) process, and (iv) technology

2.2 Design Science Research and Design Principles

Design Science Research (DSR) is a problem-solving approach that improves technology and scientific knowledge by developing new and valuable artifacts (constructs, models, methods, instantiations, and design theories). The design knowledge (DK) base consists of three components: the problem space, the solution space, and the evaluation. In a DSR study, researchers should understand both problem space knowledge and solution space knowledge. Then, they should put them in relation to one another using previous knowledge. The outcomes of DSR include the created artifacts and design knowledge, offering a deeper understanding through design theories of how these artifacts improve (or potentially disrupt) specific application contexts. One type of design knowledge is in the format of design principles (Vom Brocke et al. 2020). Design principles are solution-oriented knowledge that encompasses "technological rules" (Van Aken 2005).

Design principles serve as guidelines for researchers and practitioners involved in creating new information technology (IT) artifacts. They are considered a type of "how-to knowledge," providing prescriptive statements that help designers leverage previous experiences and avoid repeating mistakes (Chandra Kruse et al. 2016; Gregor et al. 2020). Although design principles are not the only format of representing design knowledge, the increasing number of DPs being published in recent years shows that researchers have found them useful for that purpose (Chandra Kruse et al. 2022; Purao et al. 2020).

Considering the anatomy of design principles proposed by Gregor et al. (2020), a design principle can be formulated in the following way: "For **Implementer I** to achieve or allow **Aim A** for **User U**, in **Context C** Employ **Mechanisms M1, M2, M3, ...** Involving **Enactors E1, E2, E3, ...** because of **Rationale R**." In this anatomy, context explains boundary conditions, implementation setting, and further user characteristics. Mechanisms are acts, activities, processes, form/architecture, and manipulation of other artifacts to achieve the aim. The rationale is the theoretical or empirical justification for the design principle, which makes it rigorous. Apart from aim, context, mechanism, and rationale, four categories of actors interact with design principles: Implementer, user, enactor, and theorizer. The Implementer applies the mechanism. The Recipient User (or simply the user) defines or receives the aim. An Enactor is the individual executing actions as a part of the mechanisms. In cases of decomposition, the enactor may also serve as a recipient user of an artifact at a lower (i.e., more detailed) level. Finally, the Theorizer captures the abstract design knowledge for use in research and subsequent applications. Here, we explain these terms using an example of a design principle from Gregor et al. (2014). This example has two layers so that the role of the enactor will be more transparent, but not all the DPs need to have more than one layer. In the first layer:

Design Principle Title	Sweet Spot Change Strategy
Aim, Implementer, and User	For decision makers (implementers) to allow a change agent (enactor) to facilitate the uptake of e-government (aim) by public sector agencies (users) …
Context	in a least developed country with high power distance, political instability, and uncertainty,…
Mechanism	identify and act on the sweet spot(s), (a) point(s) of maximum leverage …
Rationale	because acting on a "sweet spot" can quickly deliver an effect or unlock a process of further rapid change with comparatively little effort, which is congruent with work on points of leverage and feedback loops in systems
Theorizer	researchers

In the second layer:

Design Principle Title	Local Knowledge
Aim, Implementer, and User	For decision makers (implementers) to allow change agents (enactors) to identify sweet spot(s) and, thus, facilitate the uptake of e-government (aims) by public sector agencies (users)…
Context	in a least developed country with high power distance, political instability, and uncertainty,…
Mechanism	ensure the change agents have local knowledge, which is likely to occur only when the team includes one or more team members who are natives of the country…
Rationale	because "the issue that is underlying other inhibitors is …more often recognizable by members of the culture or region than by outsiders, no matter how earnest they are" (p. 665). The principle is congruent with Rogers' (1995) diffusion of innovation theory and the nature of change agents
Theorizer	researchers

Going back to the conceptual models of crowdsourcing summarized in Table 1, there is a gap in considering all the actors in crowdsourcing. In this study, we perform a literature review on the problems that previous crowdsourcing studies have tried to solve. We categorize these problems and build a conceptual model by considering the anatomy of design principles and the multiple actors in this anatomy.

The significance of the new conceptual model lies in its ability to provide a more precise understanding to design scientists. The aspiration is that designers in the crowdsourcing domain can utilize this conceptual model to structure their research questions, aligning them with the conceptual model. Unlike previous conceptual models, which cannot directly map to design principles, this approach allows for a more seamless translation of findings into actionable design principles.

3 Methodology

3.1 Identifying Relevant Literature and Inclusion Criteria

A systematic review of crowdsourcing designs and projects was performed to understand all the actors in the process and their requirements. We used Scopus and Web of Science (WoS) for the systematic literature review as our primary platforms. We carried out two complementary search queries to facilitate this process:

1) The literature on crowdsourcing includes task-based and observational crowdsourcing, which, before 2018, were considered one phenomenon. To narrow down the search result to observational crowdsourcing, we limit the search to well-known platforms in citizen science (Zooniverse, iNaturalist, and epicollect) and Volunteered Geographic Information (USGS, OpenStreetMap) to exclude papers focused on task-based crowdsourcing. These two applications (citizen science and volunteered geographic information (VGI)) have a long history in user generated data and their platforms are popular in the academy. Our focus in the literature is observational crowdsourcing using digital data collection interface, in which the users have an active role in collecting and reporting the data. Therefore, for instance if the research is data collection using sensors, GPS, or any other passive data collecting method, it is excluded from this review.

   The search result on the Scopus database for citizen science platform design (search query: (ALL = (zooniverse OR inaturalist OR epicollect) AND ALL = (design)) OR ALL = (citizen science tutorial)) includes 83 papers, of which 48 articles were relevant to digital data collection. Additionally, 110 of the 157 papers in WoS were not retrieved in the Scopus search. Of these, 56 papers held relevance to the context of digital data collection design in the realm of observational crowdsourcing.

   The result of Scopus database for VGI platforms shows 41 papers, and 25 are relevant. WoS result added 11 new articles, 8 are relevant.

2) The next series of queries were checking the keywords "design science" and "citizen science" together in both Scopus and WoS. The main reason behind this search was to know if the researchers in citizen science believe they contribute to DSR. The result shows a very limited number of papers (2 in WoS, 5 in Scopus) have both in their

keywords list. Although many citizen science papers have cited studies in DSR, they do not position their research as contributing to that domain.

The same search was done for Volunteered Geographic Information and design science research and the report of items included in the literature review are shown in Table 2. After collecting all the papers together, removing overlaps, in total we analyzed 160 papers.

Table 2. Literature review PRISMA (Preferred Reporting Items for Systematic Reviews and Meta-Analyses) flow chart (Moher et al. 2009).

Identification	• Two databases: Scopus and WoS – All English 1. Search query: ALL = (zooniverse OR inaturalist OR epicollect) AND ALL = (design)) OR ALL = (citizen science) 2. Search query: ALL = (USGS OR open street map) AND ALL = (design) AND ALL = (VGI or volunteered geographic information)- This search is done with OpenStreetMap (without space) as well 3. Search query: ALL = (volunteered geographic information OR vgi) AND ALL = (design science) 4. Search query: ALL = (citizen science) AND ALL = (design science)
Screening	• 373 papers
Final selection	• Keywords: Zooniverse OR iNaturalist OR epicollect and citizen science and design • Scopus (48) and WoS (56)
	• Keywords: USGS OR OpenStreetMap and Volunteered Geographic Information and design • Scopus (25) and WoS (8)
	• Keywords: design science and citizen science • Scopus (5) and WoS (2)
	• Keywords: Volunteered Geographic Information and Design science • Scopus (15) and WoS (1)

3.2 Analysis and Theoretical Development

We applied Nickerson et al.'s (2013) taxonomy development method to analyze the data. In this method, the key is to find appropriate characteristics (dimensions) that are useful for the goal and not necessarily optimal (Hevner et al. 2004). We started with Lenart-Gansiniec et al.'s model (2023), while considering the other abovementioned models and applying a problem-solution approach by Drechsler and Hevner (2018). Previous models primarily aim to establish a framework for defining all types of crowd-sourcing. The conceptual model proposed by Lenart-Gansiniec et al. (2023) in citizen science is the closest one to observational crowdsourcing. It has four dimensions: (i) initiator, (ii) crowd, (iii) process, and (iv) technology. From the conceptual-to-empirical point of view, we know the initiator and crowd are not the only actors/stakeholders in a crowdsourcing project. In Lenart-Gansiniec et al.'s model, the process also includes the data collection process, from design to gathering to analysis. However, it lacks the quality aspect of data or sensemaking (Keating & Furberg 2013). We start with four categories: 1) actor, 2) task/process, 3) technology, and 4) data quality. Then, we use the literature to examine our model, as Nickerson et al. (2013) recommended. This process includes multiple cycles of evaluating, adding, merging, and removing characteristics (i.e., changing the definition and scope) of each dimension until objective and subjective ending conditions are met.

The challenge in determining the dimensions is to cover all the OC goals and explain the areas that might have overlaps. In the following section, we will explain the process and the final conceptual model, including the subcategories of each category in Tables 4, 5, 6 and 7. We will also explain how the new conceptual model differs from and is similar to the previous models. The conceptual model was finalized after the first group of searches in citizen science and confirmed by the second category of search in VGI, which showed that no additional categories were needed (suggesting the categories are exhaustive).

Finally, a second coder helped us confirm and improve the definition and characteristics of dimensions to keep them distinguishable. To evaluate inter-rater reliability, we had the second coder check our results randomly. After we were satisfied with our results, we gave the coder clear instructions and definitions for all the characteristics. The first results show around 60% similarity. We adjusted the definitions in the cases with different coding. The clarity of the definitions and dimension characteristics improved through discussion, and we agreed on the final codes.

4   Results

The distribution of papers over time is shown in Fig. 1. The list of popular platforms the studies used is provided in Table 3. Platforms that were mentioned only in one paper are excluded.

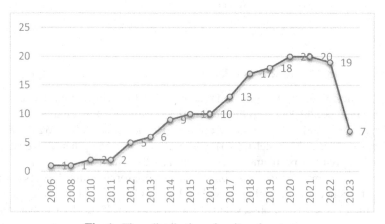

Fig. 1. Time distribution of reviewed papers.

Table 3. Platforms used in the papers Count > 1.

Platform	Count of papers
Zooniverse	40
OpenStreetMap	23
iNaturalist	23
Wikipedia	2
Epicollect-5	2
MTurk	2

Lenart-Gansiniec et al.'s model in citizen science (2023) segregate the crowd and initiator as two key concepts (as do other conceptual models of crowdsourcing). In contrast, our study provides a more holistic picture of the involved actors, necessitating categorizing requirements/goals for all potential stakeholders, including analysts, project managers, and designers. Our analysis shows the goals of observational crowdsourcing literature into four groups: actors, contribution, platform, and outcome.

By considering all stakeholders, we can also include objectives like supporting collaboration inside and outside the project team. For instance, collaboration between oceanographers and computer and data scientists (Robinson et al. 2017) is amongst the topics in this category. Research also proposes and explores collaboration outside the team, such as with contributors (Black & Coast 2007; Crowston et al. 2019), as in providing adequate high-quality training resources to support contributors, and regular feedback and compulsory teamwork between scientists and citizens (Barbato et al. 2021; Lukyanenko et al. 2016; Troudet et al. 2017). All of these could outweigh the risks of citizen science and offer a real opportunity for better outcomes.

Actors' characteristics is one of the main focuses of previous studies in observational crowdsourcing. Specifically, the crowd or contributors are the critical players in OC. Researchers are eager to explain how to consider contributors' characteristics (like their level of knowledge, age or special needs) to improve the design for better engagement, or outcome. Table 4 shows the topics discussed under the scope of actor's characteristics.

We also included a separate category for contribution characteristics because approximately 50% of the papers we reviewed considered design aspects of crowdsourcing projects. This is consistent with previous conceptual models (i.e., process dimension in Estelles-Arolas and Gozalez-Ladon-de-Gueara (2012) and Lenart-Gansiniec et al. (2023); task in Karachiwalla and Pinkow (2021) and engagement mechanism in Keating and Furberg (2013)).

The difference between our model and previous models is that our view of contribution includes more than only the process or task design and follows the sociotechnical systems theory; that is, the view that IS artifacts operate and interact in both technological and social environments (Lyytinen & Newman 2008). Therefore, topics like design to engage a general audience or evaluating the interaction between actors and tasks (e.g., designing for suitable complexity of the tasks; providing regular automatic feedback/guidance during data collection; understanding and designing a process that

Table 4. Conceptual model actor's characteristics

Improving inclusiveness and biodiversity (young, taxonomically difficult taxonomic groups, disabled, older adults, limited prior science experiences)
Features that affect community willingness to contribute (e.g., domain, size, and, the age/duration of a project, similarity to previous projects)
Citizen scientists' characteristics (e.g., knowledge, reasoning abilities)
Actors' adoption of domain-specific expert terminology and technology
Actors' collaboration (e.g., compulsory teamwork between scientists and citizens, collective ownership, collaboration between scientists, developers and data analysts)
Incentives and rewards

combines crowdsourcing with artificial intelligence) will be in the "contribution characteristics" category. Table 5 shows the subcategories in contribution's characteristics in our literature review.

To decide between whether a characteristics best fits the actor or contribution category, we asked whether the issue lies in understanding the actor's preferences and behaviors (fits the former category) or if the challenge is applying this understanding to a design (fits the latter category).

Table 5. Conceptual model contribution's characteristics

citizen science sustainability
dependency management
Task design/workflow design/ Application composition
design for engagement/utilize scientific curiosity of the participants
Output aggregation
Suitable complexity
Intellectual property
Design for training volunteers through gamification, tutorial improvement,
fault prevention and tolerance

Another key topic in the OC literature is the platform. Unlike Lenart-Gansiniec et al. (2023), which assigns the platform to the technology dimension, the platform plays more than a technology provider role in observational crowdsourcing: it is also a user base. The platform's embedded features/modules (e.g., search tools for users to find other related projects, forums, chats, and a mobile app) can help or limit projects (Tchernavskij & Bødker 2022). However, the role of platforms like iNaturalist and Zooniverse is not solely as a development interface. They have gathered global volunteers interested in different projects who could be future contributors to new projects. Karachiwalla and Pinkow (2021) is the only conceptual model, amongst the four models we reviewed, that views the platform as a connector between crowds and crowdsourcers (second role), but they do not consider their technical role and according to their model, the only other design-related decision for platforms is the development cost.

During coding, the second coder raised a question that how to distinguish if the goal of a paper/design is relevant to a platform or contribution characteristic. To clearly differentiate between these two in our conceptual model, it should be determined whether the goal is to develop, analyze, or compare a feature for only one project or the concern is developing a feature as a module to be used multiple times within different projects. For instance, if a project is on iNaturalist but aims to design the task to improve data quality, then the project goal is to enhance contribution, not improve the platform. But if the goal is how to design on iNaturalist to connect to another analytic application, then it is relevant to platform. Table 6 shows all the categories of platform's characteristics mentioned as a goal in the literature.

Table 6. Conceptual model platform's characteristics

Access to other platforms and apps (e.g., access to online analytic app to increase the data quality)
Adequate high-quality training resources to support recorders for platform
Reliability
Usability
Stability and predictability of participation
Supporting creativity
Using mobile apps
Technical architecture
Data visualization capabilities
Ability to combine different data sets
Contemporary software development process

Outcome is the last key concept in the conceptual model and mainly concentrates on the data quality aspects of the projects. There are also studies that focus on cost reduction, scalability, social and environmental benefits. Except for Keating and Furberg (2013), the remaining three conceptual models predominantly allocate most elements of this concept to their crowdsourcer/initiator concept. Although including all actors was one of the main goals of this paper, considering all the requirements and meta-requirements aligns more with design principles and DSR structure. The framework by Keating and Furberg (2013) elucidates how projects should be assessed to ensure data quality aligns with the project's goals and does not affect any other aspects of the outcome in their model. Table 7 depicts different aspects of the outcome's characteristics in the literature.

Similar to Karachiwalla and Pinkow (2021) this study found that the topics have high dependencies on each other. Approximately 80% of the reviewed papers incorporate more than one dimension and have more than one layer for their goals. For instance, communication and feedback could be handled with a platform feature (platform); however, it will affect the engagement and contributors' training/adoption experience (actors) and the designer should develop a proper process (contribution).

Table 7. Conceptual model outcome's characteristics

Social benefits to young people, minimize the negative impact of switching to remote learning
Cost reduction
New discoveries
Scalable, fast data acquisition
Testing a new hypothesis that needs more evidence
Project effectiveness
Efficiency of process
Using citizen science applicability in other area
Data analytics values/ repurposability/ standardization of data collection protocols
Data quality (first-time user, suitability of records for sharing with data partners, accessibility, uniformity, Data completeness, precision, accuracy, etc.)
Conservation and nature

5 Discussion and Conclusion

Crowdsourcing is a powerful facilitator for innovation, engagement, and data collection. Although many researchers uncover important factors in designing these systems, the literature lacks the proper mapping between their concepts and design science research, and more specifically the structure of design principles. Employing the anatomy of design principles (Gregor et al. 2020), we construct a conceptual model of observational crowdsourcing goals based on existing literature. Our analysis reveals that current conceptual models overlook active actors and their impacts on designs.

Also, technical aspects of the design in the previous conceptual models lack human considerations, such as the platform's important role in gathering volunteers or the human element of task and process design.

With the new conceptualization of the problem space in OC, we expect a more proper mapping between observational crowdsourcing and DSR, leading to theorizing and building design knowledge that considers all influential factors. Considering and including all the actors during the design phase will create a more holistic overview of the goals and issues. The dual role of the platform in the design, launch, and sustainability of the project is vital and should be remembered.

The characteristics of the conceptual model were derived from a literature review focusing on observational crowdsourcing. However, the core four concepts—actors, contribution, platform, and outcomes—can be adapted to other domains like task-based crowdsourcing and other platform-based data collection projects because these concepts are relevant to all data collection contexts.

Another question that needs to be answered is how to use this structure in practice. We developed a conceptual model for the problem space of observational crowdsourcing research; that is, finding the dimensions of the challenges in this domain by looking at the goals in the literature.

In practice, we recommend first recognizing four types of actors in the project: implementer, user, enactor, and theorizer. Following this study's finding, for each actor we should answer the following questions:

- What are their challenges/goals concerning other actors?
- What are their challenges/goals concerning the contribution?
- What are their challenges/goals concerning the outcome?
- What are their challenges/goals concerning the platform?

Knowing these goals/challenges helps to find the solutions and turn them into new design principles. However, future studies are needed to measure how and in what aspects applying this conceptual model could improve the theorizing process in observational crowdsourcing. One of the valuable research directions for evaluation could be measuring if and how applying this model could enhance the reusability of the final design principles (DPs).

References

Barbato, D., Benocci, A., Guasconi, M., Manganelli, G.: Light and shade of citizen science for less charismatic invertebrate groups: quality assessment of iNaturalist nonmarine mollusc observations in central Italy. J. Molluscan Stud. **87**(4), (2021). https://doi.org/10.1093/mollus/eyab033

Black, N., Coast, S.: Geodata collection in the 21st century. Bull. Soc. Cartograph. **41**(1,2), 3–8 (2007)

Parsons, J., Tuunanen, T., Venable, J., Donnellan, B., Helfert, M., Kenneally, J. (eds.): DESRIST 2016. LNCS, vol. 9661. Springer, Cham (2016). https://doi.org/10.1007/978-3-319-39294-3

Crowston, K., Mitchell, E., Østerlund, C.: Coordinating advanced crowd work: extending citizen science. Citizen Sci. **4**(1), (2019). https://doi.org/10.5334/cstp.

Drechsler, A., Hevner, A.R.: Utilizing, producing, and contributing design knowledge in DSR projects. In: Chatterjee, S., Dutta, K., Sundarraj, R.P. (eds.) DESRIST 2018. LNCS, vol. 10844, pp. 82–97. Springer, Cham (2018). https://doi.org/10.1007/978-3-319-91800-6_6

Estellés-Arolas, E., González-Ladrón-De-Guevara, F.: Towards an integrated crowdsourcing definition. J. Inf. Sci. **38**(2), 189–200 (2012). https://doi.org/10.1177/0165551512437638

Gregor, S., Chandra Kruse, L., Seidel, S.: Research perspectives: the anatomy of a design principle. J. Assoc. Inf. Syst. **21**, 2 (2020)

Hevner, A.R., March, S.T., Park, J., Ram, S.: Design science in information systems research. MIS Q. **28**(1), 75–106 (2004)

Hosseini, M., Phalp, K., Taylor, J., Ali, R.: The four pillars of crowdsourcing: a reference model. In: IEEE Eighth International Conference on Research Challenges in Information Science (RCIS) (2014).https://doi.org/10.1109/rcis.2014.6861072

Howe, J.L.: The rise of crowdsourcing. Wired (2006). http://ci.nii.ac.jp/naid/10029969381

Gregor, S., Imran, A., Turner, T.: A 'sweet spot' change strategy for a least developed country: leveraging e-Government in Bangladesh. Eur. J. Inf. Syst. 23(6), 655–671 (2014). https://doi.org/10.1057/ejis.2013.14

Karachiwalla, R., Pinkow, F.: Understanding crowdsourcing projects: a review on the key design elements of a crowdsourcing initiative. Creat. Innov. Manag. 30(3), 563–584 (2021). https://doi.org/10.1111/caim.12454

Keating, M., Furberg, R.D.: A methodological framework for crowdsourcing in research. In: Proceedings of the 2013 Federal Committee on Statistical Methodology (FCSM) Research Conference (2013). https://nces.ed.gov/FCSM/pdf/H1_Keating_2013FCSM_AC.pdf

Lukyanenko, R., Parsons, J.: Beyond micro-tasks: research opportunities in observational crowdsourcing. J. Database Manag. 29(1), 1–22 (2018). https://doi.org/10.4018/JDM.2018010101

Lukyanenko, R., Parsons, J., Wiersma, Y.F.: Emerging problems of data quality in citizen science. Conserv. Biol. 30(3), 447–449 (2016). https://doi.org/10.1111/cobi.12706

Lyytinen, K., Newman, M.: Explaining information systems change: a punctuated socio-technical change model. Eur. J. Inf. Syst. 17(6), 589–613 (2008). https://doi.org/10.1057/ejis.2008.50

Lenart-Gansiniec, R., Czakon, W., Sułkowski, Ł., Poček, J.: Understanding crowdsourcing in science. RMS (2023). https://doi.org/10.1007/s11846-022-00602-z

Moher, D., Liberati, A., Tetzlaff, J., Altman, D.G.: Preferred reporting items for systematic reviews and meta-analyses: the PRISMA statement. J. Clin. Epidemiol. 62(10), 1006–1012 (2009). https://doi.org/10.1016/j.jclinepi.2009.06.005

Nickerson, R.C., Varshney, U., Muntermann, J.: A method for taxonomy development and its application in information systems. Eur. J. Inf. Syst. 22(3), 336–359 (2013). https://doi.org/10.1057/ejis.2012.26

Purao, S., Chandra Kruse, L., Maedche, A.: The origins of design principles: where do... they all come from? in designing for digital transformation. In: Hofmann, S., Müller, O., Rossi, M., (eds.) Co-creating services with citizens and industry, pp. 183–194. Springer International Publishing (2020)

Paul, J., et al.: Citizen science for hydrological risk reduction and resilience building. WIREs Water 5(1), (2017). https://doi.org/10.1002/wat2.1262

Resources (n.d.). https://www.gbif.org/resource/search?contentType=literature&gbifDatasetKey=50c9509d-22c7-4a22-a47d-8c48425ef4a7&peerReview=true. Accessed 17 Jan 2024

Robinson, K.L., Luo, J.Y., Sponaugle, S., Guigand, C.M., Cowen, R.K.: A tale of two crowds: public engagement in Plankton classification. Front. Mar. Sci. 4, 82 (2017). https://doi.org/10.3389/fmars.2017.00082

Schoormann, T., Möller, F., Chandra Kruse, L.: Uncovering strategies of design principle development. In: Proceedings of the 17th International Conference on Design Science Research in Information Systems and Technology (DESRIST), Research-in-Progress Paper, St. Petersburg (2022)

Troudet, J., Grandcolas, P., Blin, A., Vignes-Lebbe, R., Legendre, F.: Taxonomic bias in biodiversity data and societal preferences. Sci. Rep. 7(1), (2017). https://doi.org/10.1038/s41598-017-09084-6

Tchernavskij, P., Bødker, S.: Entangled artifacts: the meeting between a volunteer-run citizen science project and a biodiversity data platform. In: NordiCHI 2022, Aarhus, Denmark, 8–12 October 2022 (2022).https://doi.org/10.1145/3546155.3546682

Van Aken, J.E.: Management research as a design science: articulating the research products of mode 2 knowledge production in management. Br. J. Manag. 16(1), 19–36 (2005). https://doi.org/10.1111/j.1467-8551.2005.00437.x

Vom Brocke, J., Hevner, A.R., Maedche, A.: Introduction to design science research. In: Progress in IS, pp. 1–13 (2020). https://doi.org/10.1007/978-3-030-46781-4_1

Design Principles for Machine Learning Based Clinical Decision Support Systems: A Design Science Study

Jonas Sjöström[1,3]([✉]) [iD], Petra Dryselius[2] [iD], Jens Nygren[1] [iD], Monika Nair[1] [iD], Amira Soliman[1] [iD], and Lina E. Lundgren[1] [iD]

[1] Halmstad University, Halmstad, Sweden
Jonas.sjostrom@hb.se
[2] Cambio AB, Stockholm, Sweden
[3] Borås University, Borås, Sweden

Abstract. Employing a design science research approach building on four modes of inquiry, this study presents a Clinical Decision Support System for predicting heart failure readmissions, combining machine learning, inpatient care process analysis, and user experience design. It introduces three key design principles: contextual integration, actionable insights, and adaptive explanation levels, to support the design of decision support in clinical settings. The research, while focused on a specific healthcare context, offers a model for integrating technical precision and user-centric design in inpatient care processes, suggesting broader applications and future research directions in diverse healthcare environments.

Keywords: Clinical Decision Support System · CDSS · Design Principles · Actionable Insights · Inpatient care process

1 Introduction

The rapid advancement and ubiquitous presence of Artificial Intelligence (AI) technology are undeniable. Large Language Models (LLMs) like ChatGPT have captured significant public attention, yet they represent just one facet of the diverse range of machine learning (ML) algorithms being developed and utilized across various sectors.

Historically, AI research was predominantly focused on technological and algorithmic advancements [13, 21]. However, with the widespread adoption of AI technologies, there has been a growing interest in designing AI-based applications that enhances human activity. This shift towards human-centered AI design presents substantial challenges, largely stemming from the technical complexities of AI systems and their often-unpredictable behavior. Design challenges include: 1) designing AI-based applications that prioritize human needs and preferences over mere efficiency or accuracy, 2) addressing bias and fairness issues, 3) assessing the real-world impact of implemented AI-based applications, 4) ensuring accountability through transparency and explainability, 5) integrating human values and ethics into development and maintainance of AI-based applications in practice [20].

M. Mandviwalla et al. (Eds.): DESRIST 2024, LNCS 14621, pp. 109–122, 2024.
https://doi.org/10.1007/978-3-031-61175-9_8

In healthcare, the potential of AI-based applications is immense, but there are significant hurdles in their design and implementation. A recent study [8] investigated healthcare leaders' perceptions of these challenges, noting that the integration of AI-based applications into healthcare depends on external conditions, the internal capacity of healthcare facilities for strategic change, and the uncertainty regarding the effects of AI on healthcare professions and practices.

Beyond managerial challenges, enhancing user experience in AI-based applications is critical. The field of Explainable AI (XAI) has emerged in response to the overemphasis on the technical aspects of AI. ML-based Clinical Decision Support Systems (CDSSs) are prevalent AI-based applications. Design of such systems, however, need to be further informed by XAI research [13]. XAI faces challenges in the context of CDSS development, including facilitating explanations from complex AI models as well as presenting these explanations understandably to users. While the former has been widely studied, the latter—developing explanatory user interfaces—has been relatively under-explored, despite its importance in ensuring the effectiveness and trustworthiness of CDSSs. Thus, more research on XAI techniques, particularly in their presentation to users, is vital. Additionally, from a sociotechnical systems perspective, understanding the social and organizational factors impacting AI's explainability and comprehensibility is crucial. User and organizational trust and acceptance are key to AI systems' success [20], highlighting the need for deeper insights into the organizational and human context of decision-making [16].

Our design science research (DSR) study, based on an ML-driven CDSS for predicting heart failure patient readmissions, aims to articulate design principles for AI-based CDSS development. The interest in heart failure readmissions stems from its clinical relevance: These readmissions cause a lot of burden both for patients and for the healthcare system [4, 9]. We frame our study with the research question: 'What principles should guide the design of software based on predictive models to support discharge decisions for heart failure patients?'.

The structure of the paper is outlined as follows: Sect. 2 details the research methodology. Section 3 introduces the machine learning algorithm used for predicting readmissions among heart failure patients. Section 4 presents findings from a preliminary qualitative study involving inpatient care stakeholders. In Sect. 5, we explore the existing knowledge on Explainable AI (XAI) and Clinical Decision Support System (CDSS) design. Section 6 details our user experience design study. Finally, Sects. 7 and 8 discuss the distilled design principles and conclude with the research contributions. Essentially, our structure is based on Gregor & Hevner's [7] proposed structure for DSR manuscript, albeit slightly revised due to the fact that various aspects of the study have been presented in earlier work [12, 19].

2 Research Approach

We present our research approach as a DSR endeavour shifting between different modes of inquiry, as outlined by Baskerville et al. [3]. These four modes of inquiry are based on two dualities: the knowledge goals of design versus science and the knowledge scope of nomothetic versus idiographic. The modes are: 1) Nomothetic Design: Aims at generalizable design knowledge applicable to a class of problems or situations. 2) Nomothetic Science: Focuses on generalizable scientific knowledge that can be applied broadly across various cases or environments. 3) Idiographic Design: Concerns specific design knowledge tailored to particular situations or problems. 4) Idiographic Science: Involves a study of particular instances to generate detailed, context-specific scientific knowledge.

While these modes of inquiry are ideal typical to support an analytic approach to DSR activities, it is unrealistic to characterize activities completely as a single mode of inquiry. We do, however, find the modes useful to characterize the dominant mode of work in the various phases of our process. Thus, we use the four modes of inquiry to describe our research approach as follows:

In an initial **Nomothetic Design** phase, the work begins by leveraging the ML algorithm, designed to predict 30-day unscheduled readmissions for CHF patients, representing a solution potentially applicable to various healthcare systems. Detailed in Sect. 2, this is the foundational stage where the algorithm was developed based on technological principles and its predictive capabilities were artificially evaluated (Venable).

Transitioning to **Idiographic Design**, Sect. 3 captures the engagement with Swedish healthcare stakeholders through interviews to understand the unique challenges and benefits of the ML algorithm's adoption, analyzed using the NASSS framework [5] to tailor the design solution to the specific context. This qualitative study thus focused on a situated context and possible benefits and barriers for applying the ML algorithm in the inpatient care process in healthcare.

A shift to **Nomothetic Science** is reflected in Sect. 4's literature review, which situates the research within the broader scientific discourse, exploring XAI and AI in clinical decision-making to understand how the design can contribute to and draw from existing scientific knowledge.

Returning to **Idiographic Design**, Sect. 5 describes the UX design process, involving iterative stages of understanding user needs, organizational decision-making, and design alternatives to advance a prototype for clinical use, a process that is context-specific and reflective of particular user and organizational requirements.

Finally, we turn back to in **Idiographic Science**, where Sect. 6 engages in a conceptual exercise to abstract design principles from the insights gathered, offering theoretical reflections on ML-based clinical decision support for discharge decisions for heart failure patients, thus contributing detailed, context-specific knowledge to the scientific community.

Shifting modes of inquiry in the described process allows for a stepwise development of abstract design knowledge by combining broad, generalizable knowledge with deep, context-specific insights. The nomothetic modes ensure the design's relevance to a wider class of problems, enhancing the potential for scalability and application in varied settings, while the idiographic modes focus on the particularities of the current context, promoting the design's effectiveness and practical utility in the specific healthcare environment. This interleaved approach facilitates a comprehensive understanding of both the abstract design ideas and situated design, thereby producing robust, adaptable, and relevant design knowledge.

Inspired by action design research [17], our formalized abstractions take the shape of design principles – a form of design knowledge abstraction that is both actionable and generalizable to a class of problems. They encapsulate prescriptive knowledge, indicating how to achieve specific goals within given contexts [6].

The outlined research approach systematically transitions between the modes of inquiry, effectively capturing both the particularities of the design context and the broader applicability of the abstracted knowledge. Through iterative development, evaluation, and refinement, design principles emerge as abstracted knowledge that can support design of similar solutions sharing the problem class. This process ensures that the principles are not only grounded in empirical evidence but also shaped by theoretical insights, thus providing a rational basis for their application in professional practice [7, 17].

3 The Readmission Prediction Algorithm

The ML algorithm [1] was designed to predict 30-day unscheduled readmissions in heart failure patients. It was developed using a dataset of over 6,000 patients hospitalized between 2017 and 2019 in Sweden. It employed a CatBoost gradient-boosting decision tree model [15]. We used a sensitivity-based training strategy to optimize the sensitivity of the trained model, making it particularly relevant in clinical operations [19]. The 10-fold cross-validation training process was used, and we selected the model that achieved the highest sensitivity while maintaining a minimum specificity of 50%. In terms of performance, the ML algorithm demonstrated robust predictive capabilities. The model achieved 81% sensitivity, 51% specificity, and 66% AUC.

To embed explainable features into the model output, the Shapley Additive exPlanations (SHAP) technique was used [8]. SHAP provides a score that can highlight the risk factors that are either positively or negatively influencing the readmission risk for a specific patient.

4 Exploring the Inpatient Care Process

To enhance understanding of an ML algorithm's potential use in clinical settings, a qualitative investigation involved interviews with a dozen stakeholders within a Swedish healthcare system [12]. These discussions sought insights from various professionals involved in managing heart failure care. The information gained was examined through the NASSS framework [5] to pinpoint facilitators and obstacles to deploying this AI-driven decision aid.

The inquiry uncovered a generally favorable stance towards AI-supported decision systems among stakeholders. They noted multiple challenges and drivers, drawing on past IT system deployments. Integral considerations for the envisioned CDSS comprised design elements, information accessibility throughout patient care, and workflow integration. Anticipated benefits of such implementation included better clinical results and more efficient use of resources. Stakeholders underscored the potential uplift in patient quality of life due to reduced hospital revisits.

Identified challenges encompassed data quality concerns, possible workload surges for medical staff, difficulties melding the algorithm with current systems, and the necessity for explicit usage guidelines. Questions about the algorithm's dependability and openness also arose. Conversely, facilitators involved prospects for enhanced patient care and more effective resource use. Stakeholders valued the algorithm's support in clinical decision-making and its contribution to minimizing hospital readmissions, alongside the promise of tailoring patient care more closely.

The findings underscore the intricate nature of embedding AI in healthcare, juxtaposing cutting-edge technological prospects with real-world practicalities. The stakeholder perspectives study encouraged the project to proceed with UX design activities to elaborate on the details of a software solution building on the predictive algorithm.

5 Explainable AI and Clinical Decision Support Systems

Following Gregor & Hevner's [7] proposed structure of a DSR paper, we present core aspects of the knowledge base here as a foundation for the design process accounted for in Sect. 6. While AI and its applications is a field in rapid emergence, overwhelmed with recent publications, we select to report on a subset of research directly relating to the design issue at hand. Our knowledge base includes aspects of the general XAI discourse, as well as specific ideas on how to design AI-driven CDSS in healthcare.

5.1 Explainable Artificial Intelligence

The field of XAI has reached a critical juncture where its potential can only be fully realized through a concerted effort to include a broad spectrum of stakeholders and a thorough examination of organizational processes. This discussion builds upon the insights provided by seminal works in the field to argue for a more inclusive and process-oriented approach to the design of XAI systems.

The literature underscores the importance of human-centered design in the development of AI-based applications, pointing to a significant gap between developer priorities and user experiences [2]. However, the challenge extends beyond bridging this gap; it necessitates a holistic approach that considers the diverse needs and perspectives of all stakeholders involved in or affected by the deployment of XAI systems. This includes not only users and developers, but also non-technical staff, regulatory bodies, and communities potentially impacted by decisions facilitated by the use of AI-based applications. The inclusion of multiple stakeholders ensures that XAI systems are not only technically sound but also socially responsible and ethically aligned with broader societal values [10].

Furthermore, the design of XAI systems must critically engage with the organizational processes that underpin their development and deployment. Human-centered AI should augment human abilities and creativity, a principle that can only be effectively implemented if organizational processes support collaborative, interdisciplinary work [18]. This means creating environments where insights from behavioral science, ethics, and design are integrated from the outset, rather than bolted on as afterthoughts. Such an approach would mitigate risks associated with the integration of AI in clinical work, including biases, privacy concerns, and the potential for unintended consequences.

The literature also highlights the importance of designing AI-based applications that meet human needs effectively. This requires an understanding of the organizational context in which these applications will operate, including the workflows they will augment or disrupt and the decision-making processes they will inform [20]. By studying these organizational processes, designers can better anticipate and adapt to the real-world complexities of implementing XAI solutions.

Xu et al. [20] emphasize the new challenges and opportunities for HCI professionals in enabling human-centered AI, pointing to the need for a deeper engagement with the nuances of human-AI interaction. This engagement is predicated on a comprehensive understanding of the organizational and social contexts in which these interactions occur. Similarly, there has been a call for a reevaluation of design strategies to better accommodate the nuances of human-AI interaction, underscoring the importance of contextual understanding in designing effective XAI systems [18, 20].

In conclusion, the advancement of XAI necessitates a broadening of the design perspective to include multiple stakeholders and a deep dive into organizational processes. By adopting this more inclusive and process-oriented approach, we can promote that XAI systems are not only technically proficient but also socially beneficial, ethically sound, and capable of genuinely augmenting human capabilities. Such a holistic approach promotes the development of XAI systems that are truly aligned with human needs, organizational goals, and societal values.

A recent comprehensive literature review [11] categorizes XAI methodologies into three primary areas: pre-modeling explainability, interpretable models, and post-modeling explainability. XAI seeks to make AI-based apolications more transparent and understandable to humans. It addresses the challenge of the "black box" nature of many AI models, where the decision-making process is opaque and difficult to interpret.

Given the chronology of this research process, we focus on post-model explainability – a concept in the AI field referring to techniques and methods used to explain and interpret AI models after they have been trained. This approach is essential for complex models, like deep learning networks, where the decision-making process is not inherently transparent [11]. By applying post-model explainability techniques, insights can be gained into how these models make decisions, which features they consider important, and how they arrive at specific outcomes.

5.2 Designing Clinical Decision Support Systems

While general XAI concepts are useful for designers, there have been efforts to articulate ideas directly associated with decision support systems in healthcare. In a recent study analogous to this one, Pumplun et al. [16] outline design principles focused on enhancing the explainability of ML-based CDSSs for use by physicians. These principles are designed to maximize explainability while minimizing cognitive effort:

Multipurpose Explanations. This principle emphasizes that both global and local explanations of the ML models should be displayed in the CDSS. It allows users to evaluate the system's performance, underlying reasoning process, and outputs effectively.

Visual Separation of Explanations. Explanations are visually segregated according to model global and local explanations. This separation helps present similar information in proximity to each other, aiding in clarity and comprehension.

On-demand Availability of Explanations. Global model explanations are available on-demand since they are static in nature, while local explanations are visible by default. This approach balances the need for detailed information with the avoidance of information overload.

Mental Alignment of Explanations. The explanations provided by the system are aligned with physicians' common decision-making processes and their prior knowledge. This alignment helps create familiarity with the ML-based CDSS and facilitates its use.

Determinism of Explanations. The system includes deterministic explanations based on sound facts to provide certainty in physicians' decision-making. This principle aims to offer clear and reliable explanations that can be trusted by medical professionals.

The principles are designed to make ML-based CDSSs more comprehensible for physicians, thereby improving their effectiveness and utility in clinical practice.

Note that these principles were published *after* our design process was carried out – they were thus not factored into the design process. We return to them in the discussion in Sect. 7 to reflect about the contributions from our work as compared to this existing set of principles.

6   User eXperience Design

The UX design process for the ML algorithm was a comprehensive effort structured into three distinct stages, each focusing on different aspects of user interaction and integration into the healthcare system. It began with understanding user needs through research on existing data and cyclical process of sketching and user feedback, followed by a thorough examination of the inpatient care process to map out the AI model's potential role in decision-making. The final stage focused on exploring design alternatives, drawing on insights from a medical professional and UX designers to shape a prototype that addressed identified needs and integrated into the clinical workflow. The three stages are elaborated in the following subsections.

6.1   Exploration of User Needs

The stakeholders in this phase included clinicians, specifically cardiologists, from the heart failure ward. The process entailed secondary research, using a condensed form of previously conducted interviews due to the inaccessibility of raw data. In addition, three cycles of sketching, user feedback, and reflections were conducted, i.e., a typical interaction design process based on mockups. Sees Fig. 1 and 2 for example mockups. The outcome was an abstracted set of user needs emphasizing the presentation and interpretation of the AI model's results.

The user need *Result Interpretation and Trust* encapsulates the users' requirement to not only access the AI model's results easily but also to understand them in a meaningful way. It includes the necessity for the model to present results in a user-friendly manner, such as through alerts or on-demand prompts, while also providing a nuanced understanding of risk levels beyond simple binary categories. Additionally, it underlines the importance of displaying results in a manner that builds trust, possibly by explaining the implications of low data or addressing the potential for false negatives.

The user need *Decision-making Support* stresses the importance of providing users with the relevant information that contributes to making well-informed clinical decisions. It suggests that the AI model should present results based on accurate and significant health factors and offer explanations on why these factors are essential. Moreover, it highlights the need for the system to suggest possible next steps or actions based on the results, thereby supporting the user's decision-making process.

The user need *Detailed Model Understanding* means allowing users to delve into the specifics of the AI model's output. This involves a clear presentation of the model's calculations, including SHAP values [8] and other contributing factors, in an understandable format. It also entails providing a comprehensive list of factors considered by the model, which helps users to thoroughly examine the basis of the AI's predictions and enhances their trust in the tool's reliability.

6.2   Exploration of Stakeholders and the Inpatient Care Process

This phase expanded to include stakeholders such as nurses, doctors from different specialties, and administrative staff involved in the care process for heart failure patients. The process was carried out through direct observations and interviews, aimed at pinpointing how and where in the patient care journey the AI model could be effectively integrated. The outcome was a comprehensive understanding of the decision-making processes concerning heart failure patients. The inquiry showed that the inpatient care process for a patient with heart failure consists of the following three stages:

In the *initial stage* of patient admittance and treatment, a patient with elevated symptoms of heart failure is admitted to the hospital, often via the emergency department. The attending doctor starts a care plan, conducts daily rounds to monitor the patient's condition, adjusts medications, and orders necessary scans. Nurses are briefed on the care plan, handle daily care tasks, administer medications, and perform required samplings. A coordinator, apprised of the plan, determines the appropriateness of the ward or the need for patient transfer.

During the *middle stage*, with the patient's condition stabilized, the medical team evaluates the possibility of discharge. The doctor consults the Electronic Health Record (EHR), considers the nurse's input, and reviews diagnostic results before making a discharge decision, including plan for further follow-up.

In the *final stage*, the patient, now stable, prepares for discharge, and if applicable, home care is notified. Upon discharge, outcomes vary: the patient may go home, with or without home care assistance, be transferred to another ward for further treatment, or return to their home region for continued care. Most patients are scheduled for follow-up tests or treatment adjustments, either by primary care or the specialist outpatient clinic.

The stages outline a simplified version of the roles of various healthcare professionals in the care pathway of a heart failure patient, from admission through to the discharge process, emphasizing the collaborative nature of patient care and the importance of informed decision-making based on the patient's health status.

The exploration of the inpatient care process clearly indicates that the ML algorithm appears to be most useful in scenarios where there is a need for augmented decision-making support, especially for healthcare professionals who are not specialists in heart failure. It can potentially aid in educating AT doctors, support non-specialist decision-making, and enhance the coordination of care among various healthcare providers. The algorithm's potential in assisting with complex decision-making processes like discharge planning and inter-ward transfers is particularly notable.

6.3 Exploration of Design Alternatives

This final phase brought together UX experts and the medical professionals in creative workshops to iterate on the design of the AI –based application. Through brainstorming, sketching, and feedback loops, a refined prototype was developed. The outcome was a design prototype that incorporated all the gathered insights, ready for future development and enhanced visualization of the workflow and user requirements.

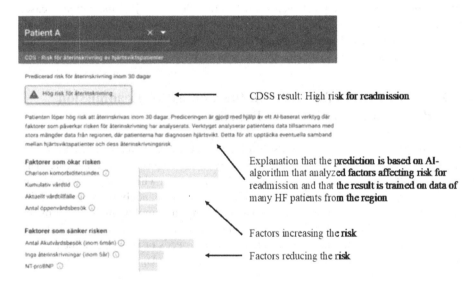

Fig. 1. Detail view of readmission risk and underlying factors

Figure 1 is the final proposal on how to convey the predicted risk of readmission within 30 days for a patient ("Patient A"). The UI indicates a high risk of readmission and provides a breakdown of factors that increase or decrease this risk. Factors that increase the risk include comorbidity index, cumulative length of stay, and current length of stay, while those that decrease the risk include absence of past readmissions and certain biomarker levels (NTproBNP). The interface provides a visual representation of risk factors, with options to read more about the underlying calculations or to clear the information presented. This view is meant to be available for care staff as a complementary decision-support to the existing EHR.

A team, comprising six UX experts and one medical expert, engaged in a modified design sprint methodology, dedicating two hours per day over four days. **Day 1** focused on grounding participants in the design sprint process, AI understanding, and the specific project context. Discussions on AI, ethics, and trust formed the basis of this introduction. **Day 2** was a divergent thinking session where participants brainstormed ideas, formulated "how might we" statements, and discussed trust, user actions, and use cases for the AI-based application.

Day 3 involved refining the brainstormed ideas into sketches, using fast-paced 'crazy eights' exercises to stimulate creativity by fast-sketching ideas within eight minutes. **Day 4** was dedicated to refining these sketches into more concrete UI designs, with a mid-session check-in and final feedback. The outcome was a collection of UI sketches building on the lessons learned in the entire process described in Sect. 5.1–5.3. Here we briefly explain the core parts of these sketches. Similarly, the ML prediction can be integrated in the view where staff administers discharge decisions.

Figure 2 shows the final design proposal, detailing the risk of hospital readmission for a patient. Analogous to Fig. 1, it lists factors contributing to readmission risk. The interface further includes typical sections for setting the priority of the patient's case, with options such as routine, booked, urgent, and so on. It also provides options for the clinician to sign off on the case or sign and send, indicating the case management status. Also, a comment section is available, allowing for additional notes on the patient's case.

7   Design Principles for CDSS in the Context of Readmission Prediction for Heart Failure Patients

First, we need to reflect on that our study differs from generic XAI literature (see Sect. 5.1) by applying a human-centered design specifically in the context of inpatient care. The approach results in explanations provided by AI model output within a clinical workflow. Our DSR process thus goes beyond transparency and understandability, addressing the nuances of how AI-tools can support decision-making in complex, high-stakes medical environments. This involves designing explanations that are not only clear but also contextually relevant, actionable, and aligned with the needs of various healthcare professionals. The proposed design emphasizes the need for explanations to fit seamlessly into the healthcare professionals' decision-making processes, which, we find, involves more elaborate and domain-specific interfaces and interactions than those considered in broader XAI discussions.

Second, our study aligns with Pumplun et al.'s design principles for ML-based CDSS, especially in enhancing explainability and user trust. However, our focus on the inpatient care process introduces unique considerations. They incorporate real-world healthcare dynamics, emphasizing the need for CDSS to be understood by other stakeholders than specialized physicians, and seamlessly integrated into existing workflows. Our results add to the understanding of CDSS design by demonstrating the importance of context-specific adaptations, highlighting that effective CDSS design requires not just technical excellence but also a deep understanding of the specific healthcare environment and related user needs. Also, our empirical study shows that stakeholders other than physicians are relevant in the design of CDSS.

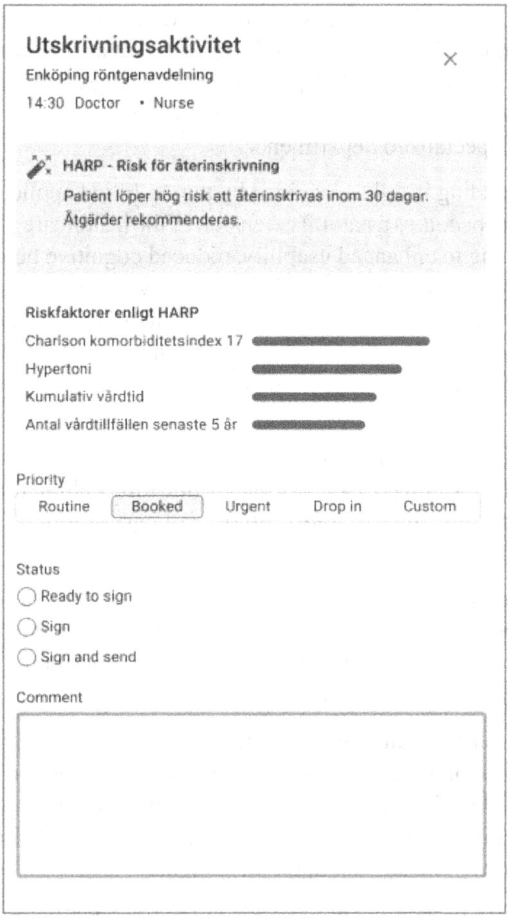

Fig. 2. UI sketch for patient discharge

Below, we report on three abstracted design principles, building on our design study, to complement earlier generic XAI concepts, as well as Pumplun et al.'s XAI-oriented design principles for CDSS.

DP-1: The Principle of Contextual Integration
The principle of Contextual Integration guides the creation of CDSSs that are not just technically competent but also intricately tailored to the nuanced environment of healthcare, aiming to make these systems serve as useful tools for clinicians.

Goal: The CDSS should integrate insights within the specific contexts of patient care. The design must account for the unique circumstances of each patient's case and the clinical workflows, ensuring that the system's output is contextually relevant. This requires the CDSS to be flexible and to have interfaces that can present information in a way that is immediately understandable and actionable within the clinical context.

Mechanisms: To achieve this, the CDSS should be designed to: 1) Present information in a format that is immediately familiar to the clinician, using terminologies and visualizations that align with those used in patient care. 2) Adapt its interface and outputs to match the workflow of the specific clinical setting, whether in emergency rooms, outpatient clinics, or specialized departments.

Rationale: By embedding insights provided by the AI-based application into the clinical context, the system becomes a natural extension of the healthcare provider's decision-making process, leading to enhanced usability, reduced cognitive burden, and improved patient outcomes. In the empirical work it was observed that when clinicians used a CDSS that provided contextually integrated insights, their decision-making process was more efficient. They were able to make faster and more accurate decisions, and the system's recommendations were more readily accepted and acted upon.

DP–2: The Principle of Actionable Insights
Through this principle, the aim is to transform data into direct clinical actions, facilitating a smooth transition from insight to intervention, and ensuring that CDSSs serve as an enabling tool for clinicians in the delivery of patient care.

Goal: CDSS must deliver insights that are actionable; that is, the insights should be clear, relevant, and practical, leading to clear next steps without the need for additional interpretation or analysis. This means providing interpretations of the data that guide the clinician towards a specific course of action.

Mechanisms: To ensure insights are actionable, the design of CDSS should: 1) Focus on the end use of the information, ensuring that the insights lead to a clear understanding of the necessary actions. 2) Prioritize data that is directly linked to interventions or outcomes. 3) Use language and visual cues that are familiar to clinicians, making it easier for them to understand and act upon the insights.

Rationale: The ability of a clinician to act upon the information provided by a CDSS without delay is essential to the efficacy of patient care. Actionable insights can streamline the care process, reduce the risk of error, and enhance the overall quality of care delivery. The empirical study showed that when clinicians received clear and actionable insights from the CDSS, the decision-making process was expedited, and the interventions were more effective. This was especially true in cases where time was of the essence, such as in acute care settings.

DP-3: The Principle of Adaptive Explanation Levels
By embracing the principle of Adaptive Explanation Levels, CDSS can be made more user-friendly and effective, catering to a wide range of users with varying needs and expertise levels.

Goal: CDSS should be designed to offer explanations at varying levels of complexity, tailored to the user's knowledge and needs. This involves the system dynamically adjusting the depth and technicality of its explanations based on the user's role, preferences, and interaction history. The design should allow users to easily navigate between high-level overviews and more detailed, technical insights.

Mechanisms: To achieve this, the system should provide views that allow easy toggling between different levels of explanation.

Rationale: Different users require different levels of explanation to effectively use the system. Novices may need simpler, more intuitive explanations, while experts may seek deeper, more technical details. Adaptive explanations ensure that the system is accessible and useful to all users, enhancing their ability to make informed decisions. Our study shows that CDSS users vary widely in their response to and understanding of AI-generated insights. Tailoring the level of explanation to individual users was shown to improve their comprehension, satisfaction, and trust in the system.

8 Conclusions

In response to our research question, this study's primary contribution lies in its human-centered approach to designing CDSS for predicting heart failure patient readmissions. Through the articulation of three design principles, we highlight the importance of *contextual integration*, *actionable insights*, and *adaptive explanation levels* in CDSS design. These principles ensure the system's relevance to the clinical workflow and enhance usability for healthcare professionals. Also, they serve to complement the XAI design principles for CDSS proposed by Pumplun et al. [16].

Limitations of the study include its focus on a specific healthcare setting and the potential for broader applicability of its findings. Future research should explore the implementation of these design principles in diverse healthcare environments and examine their impact on patient outcomes. In this paper, we do not generalize our principles to a broader context. Instead, we aim for a projectability to other settings [2] through our presentation of the principles, their rationale, and design examples.

The implications for practice are significant, emphasizing the need for CDSS that are not only technically sound but also intuitively integrated into healthcare professionals' workflow. For research, this study opens avenues for exploring the intersection of human-centered design and AI in healthcare, particularly in high-stakes decision-making contexts.

Future research directions could include the exploration of these design principles in additional healthcare contexts, the impact of CDSS on patient outcomes and healthcare efficiency, and the development of methodologies to measure the effectiveness of human-centered AI systems in healthcare.

This study underscores the evolving role of AI in healthcare, emphasizing the need for systems that support and enhance human decision-making processes within complex organizational contexts.

References

1. Ashfaq, A., et al.: Readmission prediction using deep learning on electronic health records. J. Biomed. Inf. **97**, 103256 (2019). https://doi.org/10.1016/j.jbi.2019.103256
2. Baskerville, R., Pries-Heje, J.: Projectability in design science research. J. Inf. Technol. Appl. **20**, 1 (2019)

3. Baskerville, R.L., et al.: Genres of inquiry in design science research: justification and evaluation of knowledge production. MIS Q. **39**(3), 541–564 (2015)
4. Dharmarajan, K., et al.: Diagnoses and timing of 30-day readmissions after hospitalization for heart failure, acute myocardial infarction, or pneumonia. JAMA **309**(4), 355–363 (2013)
5. Greenhalgh, T., et al.: Beyond adoption: a new framework for theorizing and evaluating nonadoption, abandonment, and challenges to the scale-up, spread, and sustainability of health and care technologies. J. Med. Internet Res. **19**(11), e8775 (2017)
6. Gregor, S., et al.: Research perspectives: the anatomy of a design principle. J. Assoc. Inf. Syst. **21**(6), 2 (2020)
7. Gregor, S., Hevner, A.R.: Positioning and presenting design science research for maximum impact. MIS Q. **37**(2), 337–355 (2013)
8. Holzinger, A., et al.: Explainable AI methods-a brief overview. In: Holzinger, A., Goebel, R., Fong, R., Moon, T., Müller, K.R., Samek, W. (eds.) International Workshop on Extending Explainable AI Beyond Deep Models and Classifiers, pp. 13–38 Springer, Heidelberg (2022). https://doi.org/10.1007/978-3-031-04083-2_2
9. Kocher, R.P., Adashi, E.Y.: Hospital readmissions and the affordable care act: paying for coordinated quality care. JAMA **306**(16), 1794–1795 (2011)
10. McDermid, J.A., et al.: Artificial intelligence explainability: the technical and ethical dimensions. Phil. Trans. Royal Soc. A **379**(2207), 20200363 (2021)
11. Minh, D., et al.: Explainable artificial intelligence: a comprehensive review. Artif. Intell. Rev. 1–66 (2022)
12. Nair, M., et al.: Barriers and enablers for implementation of an artificial intelligence-based decision support tool to reduce the risk of readmission of patients with heart failure: stakeholder interviews. JMIR Form Res. **7**, e47335 (2023). https://doi.org/10.2196/47335
13. Panigutti, C., et al.: Co-design of human-centered, explainable ai for clinical decision support. ACM Trans. Interact. Intell. Syst. **13**(4), 1–35 (2023). https://doi.org/10.1145/3587271
14. Petersson, L., et al.: Challenges to implementing artificial intelligence in healthcare: a qualitative interview study with healthcare leaders in Sweden. BMC Health Serv. Res. **22**(1), 1–16 (2022)
15. Prokhorenkova, L., et al.: CatBoost: unbiased boosting with categorical features. Adv. Neural Inf. Process. Syst. **31**, 1–11 (2018)
16. Pumplun, L., et al.: Bringing machine learning systems into clinical practice: a design science approach to explainable machine learning-based clinical decision support systems. J. Assoc. Inf. Syst. **24**(4), 953–979 (2023). https://doi.org/10.17705/1jais.00820
17. Sein, M.K., et al.: Action design research. MIS Q. **35**(1), 37 (2011). https://doi.org/10.2307/23043488
18. Shneiderman, B.: Human-centered artificial intelligence: three fresh ideas. In: THCI, pp. 109–124 (2020). https://doi.org/10.17705/1thci.00131
19. Soliman, A., et al.: The price of explainability in machine learning models for 100-day readmission prediction in heart failure: retrospective, comparative, machine learning study. J. Med. Internet Res. **25**, e46934 (2023)
20. Xu, W., et al.: Transitioning to human interaction with AI systems: new challenges and opportunities for HCI professionals to enable human-centered AI. Int. J. Human-Comput. Interact. **39**(3), 494–518 (2023). https://doi.org/10.1080/10447318.2022.2041900
21. Yang, Q., et al.: Re-examining whether, why, and how human-AI Interaction is uniquely difficult to design. In: Proceedings of the 2020 CHI Conference on Human Factors in Computing Systems, pp. 1–13 ACM, Honolulu (2020). https://doi.org/10.1145/3313831.3376301

Theory-Driven Design of a Negotiation Canvas for Reaching Win-Win Agreements

Eva-Maria Zahn[1]([✉])[ID] and Ernestine Dickhaut[2][ID]

[1] Information Systems and Systems Engineering, University of Kassel, Kassel, Germany
zahn@uni-kassel.de
[2] Institute of Information Systems, University of Kassel, Kassel, Germany
ernestine.dickhaut@uni-kassel.de

Abstract. In today's interconnected world, negotiations are essential for navigating the complexities of personal and professional life. Resulting in a "negotiation network", integrative negotiation strategies are gaining relevance for mutual benefit. However, negotiators often fall short due to inadequate preparation, focusing more on their own negotiation goals than understanding the other party's priorities and interests. This challenge stems from inadequate preparation which is crucial in the overall negotiation process. A comprehensive preparation empowers negotiators to conduct a stronger and more reflective negotiation and to enable unexpected challenges with more confidence. As a result, negotiators can make informed and strategic decisions. However, an artifact that explicitly addresses the preparation process and prepares inexperienced negotiators in a structured and theoretically founded manner is missing. Therefore, we introduce a theory-driven negotiation canvas to prepare negotiations and reach win-win agreements. The canvas, addressing crucial negotiation elements, offers a structured approach to preparing for an upcoming negotiation. This research contributes to a more comprehensive understanding of negotiation preparation and provides a valuable tool to empower negotiators.

Keywords: Negotiation Canvas · Integrative Negotiations · Win-Win Agreement

1 Introduction

"The best negotiation is a well-prepared negotiator." – Roger Dawson.

In today's interconnected and dynamic world, negotiations have become an essential tool for navigating the complexities of everyday life. Due to changes towards flatter organizations, innovations, and communication worldwide, the ability to negotiate has become increasingly important to face these unpredictable environments [1–3]. This results in a "negotiation network" [1], in which we negotiate every day in our personal and work lives, even if we are not always aware of it [1, 4, 5]. In the meantime, it is primarily a question of so-called integrative negotiations gaining relevance. These negotiation strategies involve collaborative actions aimed at increasing overall value by

M. Mandviwalla et al. (Eds.): DESRIST 2024, LNCS 14621, pp. 123–138, 2024.
https://doi.org/10.1007/978-3-031-61175-9_9

jointly addressing and resolving issues to benefit all parties involved [6, 7]. The ability to negotiate in a well-founded and targeted manner is becoming increasingly important since it influences personal success and the success of organizations [4].

However, it turns out that negotiators repeatedly fail to achieve their negotiation goals and objectives because they are focused on selling their own deal and, thus, spend too little time understanding the other party's goals and priorities [8]. This problem can be derived primarily from a lack of preparation in the pre-negotiation phase [3]. Adhering to the 80–20 in negotiation, Thompson [3] recommends allocating about 80% of the effort towards thorough preparation while reserving the remaining 20% for the actual negotiation at the table [3]. The preparation empowers negotiators by providing a comprehensive and in-depth review of the content that should be negotiated, negotiation goals and objectives can be defined, and arguments can be substantiated with objective criteria [1]. Following this, a stronger and more reflective negotiation can be conducted. This enables unexpected challenges to be dealt with more confidently, and more profitable opportunities can be realized. In addition, comprehensive preparation enables the negotiator to prepare for counterarguments in advance and to reflect on the other party's point of view [1]. As a result, the negotiators can make informed and strategic decisions.

Although preparation for negotiations is crucial, there is a lack of supporting tools and assistance, especially in the preparation process for inexperienced novices. For example, there is the option of completing an entire negotiation training program, which is very costly and time-consuming or acquiring fundamental negotiation knowledge through self-help books. What is missing, however, is an artifact that explicitly addresses the preparation phase and prepares negotiators in a structured, time-saving, and, above all, theoretically founded manner for an upcoming negotiation. Such preparation involves not only defining objectives and arguments but also elements that are crucial in the nego-tiation itself, such as emotions, which should also be reflected upon from the beginning [8, 9]. A possible solution to address this problem is a canvas, which is theoretically derived and thus contains the most important negotiation elements that are essential for preparing for an upcoming negotiation. The relevance is shown by the fact that first nego-tiation canvases exist in practice, but they have various weaknesses, such as a missing theoretical foundation [10, 11]. This leads us to our following research question: *How should a theory-driven negotiation canvas be designed to support the preparation for an upcoming negotiation?*

In developing our canvas, we followed the design science research (DSR) approach according to Peffers et al. [12].

2 Conceptual Background

2.1 Negotiations

If people cannot achieve their goals without the cooperation of others, they have to negotiate [5]. The reasons for negotiations can have different origins and can be broken down into the following three main causes: Agreement on how to share a limited resource (e.g., money), creating something new that a party cannot do alone or resolving a problem or a dispute between the parties [13, 14]. A negotiation is a voluntary relationship since gaining the party's stand is greater than not negotiating [15]. More generally speaking, negotiations include the negotiation parties, their interests, the negotiation process and the negotiation outcome as basic features [16]. The negotiation outcome can be divided into integrative (win-win outcome) or distributive (win-lose outcome). Integrative negotiations focus on collaborative problem-solving to create value and a win-win agreement for all parties, while distributive negotiations primarily strive to maximize the own payoff at all costs [1, 17]. The negotiation process is the core element of every negotiation, which can be divided into a preparation phase where, e.g., negotiation goals are defined, the negotiation itself (information and argument exchange), and a final phase of setting an agreement and implementing the final deal [14]. Research and scholars uncovered that especially the relevance of the preparation has an immense influence on the negotiation process and outcome [3]. This is underpinned by the fact that a lousy negotiation itself can result in consequences such as dissatisfaction, bitterness, dispute, or harm [1, 18]. Following comprehensive and structured preparation can help to ensure that the negotiation proceeds satisfactorily for all participating parties.

2.2 Canvas Development

Canvas development is a popular approach to organizing information and creating creative concepts, and it has been addressed in Information Systems research for a long period of time [e.g., 19, 20]. In our case, we focus on the canvas understanding referring to Osterwalder and Pigneur [21]. Following this, canvas refers to a visual framework or tool used to present and analyze various aspects of a model or strategy [21]. A Canvas consists typically of a structured layout that helps to visualize and understand key components [21]. For DSR, research on canvas is interesting because the presentation of information is an indispensable factor for the flow of information and the transfer of knowledge. Thus, several canvases have been developed during the last years. In strategic management, business model canvases (BMC) are a template to support the development of business models. BMC was developed by Osterwalder/Pigneur [21] to provide conceptual frameworks as visual schemas to improve the understanding and the design of business models. The advantage of a BMC is the representation as a one-pager, where it can be worked with clearly and reduced as necessary. This BMC still has an impact on Information System research, as shown in a study by Rose et al. [20]. They adapted the classical BMC by following an action design research approach to develop a tool for helping e-service designers and called it *"the innovative digital service canvas"* [20]. Another example of the impact of canvas development on Information Systems is done by Avdiji et al. [22]. Here, the researcher proposes a design theory including design principles for visual inquiry tools, drawing on knowledge from projects like the BMC, to address the lack of guidance in developing such tools [22].

Canvas research has also been conducted to address different aspects of negotiations. For example, in conflict management, a negotiation canvas has been developed as a mind-mapping template to help students conceptualize the complexity of conflicts [11]. This canvas comprises six elements, including facts, the parties, the different sides, a common ground, the deal, and trust/collaboration builders. The Canvas elements by Blair and Desplaces [11] are numbered, so they should be filled by starting with the facts and ending with the trust/collaboration builders. This canvas does not depict relevant elements such as alternatives, key arguments, or possible emotions. Another canvas that emphasizes elements such as emotions is the Empathic Negotiation Canvas by Roberts [10]. The Empathic Negotiation Canvas has been developed to have a more structured preparation process focusing on empathy for an upcoming negotiation. This canvas primarily emphasizes elements related to empathy. For example, elements such as Think and Feel, Say and Do, See and Hear are in the canvas focus [10]. These elements should be completed for oneself and the other party. In contrast, negotiation elements such as interests, arguments or alternatives are addressed to a more limited extent. We differentiate our canvas from existing negotiation canvases, as we focus on the entire negotiation and thus place elements such as emotions and values, but also a significant focus on developing alternatives in the preparation process.

3   Methodology

3.1   Design Science Research

We follow the DSR approach, according to Peffers et al. [12], to develop our negotiation canvas (see Fig. 1). Moreover, we concentrate on a problem-centered approach that relies on a canvas for guiding a negotiation preparation process. After motivating our problem, we focus on the literature on canvas and negotiation research. Based on existing literature on negotiations, especially integrative negotiations, we derive ten theory-driven negotiation elements for the content of our negotiation canvas. Afterward, we build and demonstrate the canvas based on these elements. Finally, we evaluated with experts and novices, resulting in two revisions of the canvas. This iterative evaluation process enables us to analyze the developed canvas in-depth and revise it from different perspectives. We ensured that it contained important negotiation elements from an expert's point of view while still being understandable for novices.

3.2   Evaluation Strategy

We conduct an iterative design process with two evaluations. Our first evaluation follows the thinking aloud method with negotiation experts to evaluate the negotiation elements. Thinking aloud allows us to verbalize the participants' thoughts and reactions while engaging with the canvas [23, 24]. Originally conceptualized as a means to study cognitive processes, Thinking Aloud has found a natural home in IS research [25] due to its ability to unveil the tacit knowledge, mental models, and decision-making criteria that influence user behavior. By encouraging participants to articulate their thoughts as they navigate through a system, researchers gain direct access to the cognitive landscape, providing valuable insights into user experiences and uncovering hidden challenges [26]. Our second evaluation step includes inexperienced negotiators investigating how they use the canvas and identifying needed elements. Thus, we provide an experimental setting to prepare a salary negotiation (see Appendix A). This evaluation enables us to examine whether the canvas is helpful in practical use and to analyze which revisions are necessary.

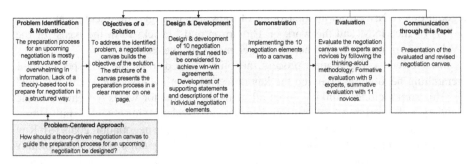

Fig. 1. Design Science Research Approach, according to Peffers et al. [12].

4   The Negotiation Canvas

4.1   Problem Identification and Objectives of the Negotiation Canvas

Since the preparation process for an upcoming negotiation is highly relevant but mostly unstructured or overwhelming in information, this poses problems for inexperienced negotiators, in particular [3]. A structured preparation is also crucial for experts. It is particularly important to consider negotiation elements that have been proven to be necessary in theory and practice. However, existing research on negotiations lacks a theory-driven tool so novices and experts can prepare for negotiation in a structured way, also without the need for prior negotiating expertise. Furthermore, such a tool can additionally serve as a support and cheat sheet during the negotiation. Our motivation is, therefore, to develop a tool that supports the preparation for negotiations and is based on established negotiation literature. Furthermore, we aim for integrative negotiations in which all parties can reach win-win agreements [1, 7].

4.2   Design and Development of the Negotiation Canvas

As more and more business negotiations are aimed at win-win agreements, we have focused on integrative negotiations. One widely used and taught negotiation strategy in integrative negotiations is to follow so-called principle-based negotiations – summarized in the Harvard Negotiation Method (HNM) by Fisher and Ury [1]. The HNM is a *"straightforward method of negotiation that can be used under almost any circumstances"* [2 pp. 11], so it can be used even if every negotiation is unique. The method's aim is to accomplish amicably effective and interest-oriented negotiations for reaching win-win agreements for all negotiation parties [1]. Therefore, the heart of the method is the application of four principles (1. Separate People from the problem, 2. Focus on interests, not positions, 3. Invent options for mutual gain, 4. Insist on using objective criteria) in the negotiation process [1]. The HNM still serves as an important basis in many negotiation training programs today. We use the HNM as the theoretical foundation for developing our canvas and enriching it with further negotiation literature on integrative negotiations. Here, the negotiation researchers Leigh Thompson [5] and Roy J. Lewicki [8] have conducted important and in-depth research and enriched the principle-based negotiations (HNM) from another point of view. Accordingly, the theoretical contributions of the HNM and the work of Thompson and Lewicki form the basis for the development of our following negotiation elements for the canvas.

In an effective preparation process, negotiators need to define and specify their overarching negotiation goal and the key objectives that are associated with this goal [8]. This step includes thinking about all goals the negotiator wants to achieve in the negotiation, determining the priority among these goals, identifying potential multilateral packages, and evaluating possible trade-offs among multiple negotiation goals [8]. Roy J. Lewicki summarizes the importance: *"Knowing one's [negotiation] goal is absolutely the first and most important step in developing a strategy and executing a negotiation."* [14 pp. 97]. In addition to the own negotiation goals and key objectives, it is crucial to put yourself in the other party's shoes and see what their goals and objectives might be [1, 8, 27]. The aim is to understand the other party's perspective and to analyze what could be a common goal and common objectives [8]. The main aim here is to address the problems that are to be negotiated and thus separate the substantive aspects and goals from personal relationships [1]. This results in our first negotiation element, and we follow a superordinate representation in the canvas so that this element stands out and can be filled in first.:

Negotiation Element #1: Negotiation Goal and Key Objective.

Guiding Question: *"What is the main negotiation goal and the key objectives that should be negotiated?"*

Furthermore, it is important to separate the personal relationship from the substance of the negotiation [1]. The relationship not only has an impact on how we interact during the negotiation, but it is also an important part of the preparation process. Negotiation is a way to learn more about the other party, and thus, information on the other's broad ideas, priorities, and preferences is one crucial aspect [8]. The previous relationship influences the whole negotiation process [1]. During preparation, the other party can be better assessed based on an existing relationship, for example, because the values or core objectives of the other party are known [8]. In addition, the trust already acquired plays a central role since trust is a relevant factor in negotiations [1]. Contributions to the degree of trust that one negotiating partner can place in the other can be multifaced: the history of the relationship between the parties, the chronic predisposing of the individual negotiator to trust in general or situational factors [8]. However, with previous relationships, the parties can have integrative negotiations more easily [8]. Therefore, actively building personal and organizational relationships is necessary for integrative negotiations [1]. The relationship is relevant since it influences the negotiation from the ground up. It is important to think in advance about your relationship with the other party, whether you are negotiating with a company representative or with a person who represents their interests. Based on these findings, we suggest our next negotiation element:

Negotiation Element #2: Relationship.

Guiding Question: *"Have you already negotiated with the other party? If so, how might the relationship affect the negotiation? What do you know about the other party?"*

In integrative negotiation, both parties need to be motivated to work together and committed to reaching a goal that benefits both of them [8]. Furthermore, a higher motivation leads to more outstanding negotiation efforts, while less motivation can lead to higher levels of constraints in negotiations [28, 29]. Since motivation has a strong positive impact on the negotiators' participation, it plays a pivotal role in encouraging the participation [29]. Consequently, the negotiators' motivation is a central element and is based on the discrepancy between the current situation and the negotiation goals/objectives, which motivates the negotiator to go through the negotiation process [30]. Consequently, this is our next negotiation element:

Negotiation Element #3: Motivation.

Guiding Question: *"What is the underlying motivation of the negotiation?"*

In order to reflect the underlying motivation based on the above-mentioned facts, this field needs to be filled in after the negotiation goals/objectives have been defined. This is why the field of motivation is arranged after the field of goals.

In integrative negotiations, both parties should be open about their interests so they can focus on them and not on the positions [1]. To identify the interests behind the demand, asking "why" questions can help understand the needs and values that are important to [1, 8]. Interests can be unexpressed, intangible, and inconsistent, so understanding the needs, hopes, and desires is necessary [1]. Understanding that both parties have mutual interests can be fostered by making a list of the potential interests of the counterparty interests to identify their needs and thus be able to assess better and understand the other party [1]. Here, it is particularly important that the interests of the other party are also considered to see that possible common interests can be to achieve a win-win agreement. Hence, we propose the element:

Negotiation Element #4: Interests.

Guiding Question: *"What are the main interests and needs in reaching the negotiation goal?"*

Developing a Best Alternative to a Negotiation Agreement (BATNA) is one of the main cores of the HNM [1]. Negotiators should develop alternatives and different options in the preparation process in order to uphold their own values [1]. BATNA represents the most attractive options and improves position by exploring multiple BATNA [1]. Thus, these are other agreements where the negotiators can achieve and still meet their interests and needs [8]. Moreover, developing alternatives from the other party's perspective by putting yourself in their shoes helps in reaching win-win agreements. To develop a strong BATNA, it is necessary to find possible solutions and evaluate these options/ideas. For the evaluation, a selection of the alternatives that may have the highest expected value for the outcome is helpful while also calculating the lowest-value deal or the reservation value a negotiator is willing to accept [1]. Based on this, our next negotiation element is:

Negotiation Element #5: Best Alternative to a Negotiation Agreement (BATNA).

Guiding Question: *"What is your desired outcome/case of the negotiation? What is your lowest acceptable outcome of the negotiation? Reflect on these cases from your negotiation partner's point of view. What are possible alternatives that arise from both perspectives?"*

Since BATNA plays a central role in the preparation and provides safety during the negotiation, it is centrally located in the canvas and thus presents the centerpiece in a certain way. The field for BATNA is also divided into its own alternatives and its counterpart's alternatives, whereby the interests of the alternatives can be arranged between high (my desired case) and low (my worst case). The alternatives then arise from the desired and worst cases.

Key arguments can be strengthened by using objective criteria. Using objective criteria to resolve differences makes it easier to agree and preserve the negotiators' relationship [1]. For developing objective criteria in a negotiation case, mostly diverse criteria can be used, such as scientific findings, professional standards, etc. [1]. By using objective criteria, the arguments can be substantiated. Objective criteria and reasons of the other party can also be used in the negotiation process to support the own arguments [1]. It is, therefore, necessary to develop and find criteria in the preparation phase that underpin and strengthen the statements. Formulating key arguments not only helps in the preparation phase to become aware of the interests [1], but it can also serve as a support during the negotiation. Above all, finding objective criteria can then be supported. This leads to our next negotiation element:

Negotiation Element #6: Key Arguments and Objective Criteria.

Guiding Question: *"What are key arguments and objective criteria (e.g., statistics) for presenting your interests based on the alternatives? What are possible counterarguments of the other party?"*

As mentioned, integrative negotiations are more straightforward if the parties trust each other; otherwise, this could be challenging. In addition to possible difficulties that could arise during the negotiation, limits should be set. Knowing the own limits is a crucial aspect when negotiating [8]. So-called resistance points should be included in the own limits. Resistance points decide when someone stops the negotiation rather than continuing because the settlement would be beyond this point – the settlement would not be minimally acceptable [8]. Consequently, previously setting a resistance point is a crucial part of the preparation process since it helps to keep agreeing to a deal that could be regretful [8]. Therefore, our next element is:

Negotiation Element #7: Challenges and Limits.

Guiding Question: *"What are possible challenges or potential conflicting aims that could prevent you from achieving your interests? What are the limits you could encounter?"*

Negotiators differ in their values [8]. The subjective value of a negotiator can have a long-lasting impact compared to economic gains from the negotiation. Thus, checking that the subjective value does not conflict with the economic value in a negotiation process is necessary [5]. Also, cultural values can influence the negotiation, which can be incredibly challenging in cross-cultural negotiations. Thus, a different understanding of values and behaviors can influence the negotiation outcome [31]. Therefore, we suggest the next element:

Negotiation Element #8: Value.

Guiding Question: *"What value do you have for the other party (e.g., company), and which values does the other party (e.g., company) have for you?"*

In the field of value, it is necessary to reflect on one's own values and those of one's counterpart. For this reason, we have implemented guiding questions here that aim at one's own values as well as those of the other party.

Emotions and Feelings influence negotiations. Emotions are important at various stages in the negotiation process since positive and negative emotions can be created [8]. Positive emotions and feelings are important for leading the parties into an integrative process, and thus, positive feelings can create a positive attitude towards the counterpart [8]. In contrast, negative emotions can lead the parties to distributive negotiation outcomes, influence the negotiators' ability to analyze the situation accurately, or lead to the escalation of a conflict [8]. Negotiators' emotions influence themselves and their counterparts [9]. Consequently, the emotions and feelings of a negotiator have an important influence on the negotiator's cognition and strategies [5]. The emotions of a powerful negotiator are more influential than less powerful negotiator's emotions [5]. Trait-positive affect can help negotiators reach more integrative agreements when combined with high structural power (e.g., a strong BATNA) [5]. To summarize, recognizing and understanding emotions is a central part of negotiations [1], which leads to our next element:

Negotiation Element #9: Emotions and Feelings.

Guiding Question: *"What are possible emotions, feelings or fears that could influence the negotiation?"*

The aim of negotiation element 9 is to reflect the emotions that may arise during a negotiation. To make clear that emotions can have an influence on the negotiation, this is mentioned as a short background information in this box.

Finally, during the preparation phase, it is necessary to think about agreements. To this end, the possible deal should involve the counterpart in the outcome [1]. This results in our last element:

Negotiation Element #10: Possible Agreement.

Guiding Question: *"What is a possible agreement the negotiation can result in based on the alternatives?"*

This field is placed at the end of the canvas, as it summarizes the content that has been developed and is about finding a possible agreement/conclusion. Furthermore, it is arranged like the first field, "Key Objectives and Negotiation Goal", to conclude the canvas.

4.3 Demonstration and Evaluation of the Negotiation Canvas

Based on these elements, we developed an initial version of the negotiation canvas. Here, we made sure that the core element BATNA (negotiation element 5) had sufficient space and was also arranged in a prominent position. We started with negotiation element #1 at the top, as it represents the negotiation objective as a prerequisite for everything else and ended with negotiation element #10 at the bottom.

Formative Evaluation. For the formative evaluation of our canvas, we obtained feedback from negotiation experts to ensure that the canvas also contains important negotiation elements from a practical perspective. Therefore, we met a total of nine experts (five female and four male). The experts work in the marketing, (interims) management, entrepreneurship, and sales sectors and have extensive negotiation experiences. Five of the nine experts also have comprehensive experience in leading teams. We recorded and documented the conversations and analyzed them afterward. Following thinking aloud, we gave the canvas to the participants, and they saw it for the first time. Afterward, the participants should express their thoughts on the canvas. They were also asked to express their thoughts on the single negotiation elements, although there was no specification as to the order in which the statements were made or how detailed they should be. This allows us to document how the experts navigated through the canvas and determine which elements, for example, were silent for longer than others.

Based on the expert feedback, we presented the core content and the resulting main changes in Table 1. In total, we made eleven main changes to incorporate the experts' feedback into the canvas. At this point, it can be noted that all experts found the initial version of the canvas to be very helpful, even if there should be some changes. Exemplary excerpts from the experts' feedback are: *"Especially if someone has little or no experience in negotiations, the canvas is very, very helpful for preparation and also during the negotiation."*; *"I would give the canvas directly to my employees."*; *"[…] it would have saved me a lot in the past. I would also use it now to structure my thoughts."*

Summative Evaluation. After implementing the experts' feedback into the canvas, we evaluated the canvas in a more naturalistic setting. For this, we gave our revised canvas to eleven novices without deep negotiation experience to prepare a salary negotiation. All novices are from the business sector (6 female; 5 male). They should prepare for a salary negotiation in their current job using our canvas (see Appendix A for the task). We documented the results and asked for suggestions for improvement. The general impression and whether the novices would use the canvas were also surveyed.

Based on this second evaluation, we have integrated further key changes into the canvas, as documented in Table 2. Regardless of the minor changes, the novices consistently rated the canvas as very helpful. Here are some examples of quotes: *"I liked the structure of the canvas, including the questions and, above all, the other party's point of view. It gave me a different perspective on the single aspects and gave me the feeling that I was better prepared for the other party's questions and arguments."*; *"I would absolutely use the canvas, especially when it comes to important negotiations. The structure helps me to keep an eye on my goals and build a stringent argumentation."*; *"The canvas gave me a lot of ideas and showed me aspects of negotiation that I hadn't even thought of*

Table 1. Key Changes in the Initial Canvas after the Formative Evaluation.

Key feedback and changes	Implementation of the feedback
Integrate the other party	Formulation and integration with „My…/Their…" where particularly relevant (e.g., Motivation & Interest)
Combining motivation & interest	Motivation & interest in one box. Reformulating questions
Combining value & emotion	Value & emotion in one box. Reformulating questions
Arrange challenges above	Challenges & limits have moved up one box
Structure of BATNA	The alternatives are shown as a result with arrows between my and their desired/worst cases
Arguments as results of BATNA	The arguments box is now directly below that of BATNA
Subdivide the agreement box	The agreements are divided into "No-Go" agreements, possible agreements, and the final agreement
Consideration of the box size	E.g., Interest & motivation; arguments larger, while challenges & limits; BATNA smaller
More processual presentation	Boxes are grouped using colors and represent a more procedural approach
Ranking of content	Ranking of the first three contents for objectives, interests, alternatives, and arguments
Negotiation setting	New box in which formal aspects of the setting can be documented (e.g., date, negotiation partner) at the top

before.". However, it should also be noted that the novices had some issues, such as *"it was difficult to think through the alternatives of the other party, and I don't think it's as important as my own.".* To counter this, we have made this box smaller and thus made a visual adjustment.

Table 2. Key Changes in the Canvas after the Summative Evaluation.

Key feedback and changes	Implementation of the feedback
Rewrite guiding questions	Guiding questions, e.g., in the relationship box and for the final agreement, have been adjusted
Highlight Negotiation Goal	We have highlighted the corresponding box by including it as an independent word at the bottom of the box
Boxes that belong together more clearly	The boxes have been more clearly differentiated from others by clearer coloring

(*continued*)

Table 2. (*continued*)

Key feedback and changes	Implementation of the feedback
Make BATNA smaller	BATNA has been made smaller overall, especially in the view of the other party
Make value & emotions; arguments & criteria larger	The value & emotions and arguments & criteria boxes have been enlarged
Use other symbols	The symbols for relationship, interests & motivation, arguments & criteria, and values & emotions have been adapted

The Final Negotiation Canvas. After the iterative development and the implementation of the evaluation, we finalized the canvas (see Fig. 2 and Appendix B for a detailed version). After the evaluation, the canvas comprised eight negotiation elements, whereby two elements were merged in each case (interests & motivation, value & emotion). The experts suggested this and allow us to create more space and make the canvas more straightforward.

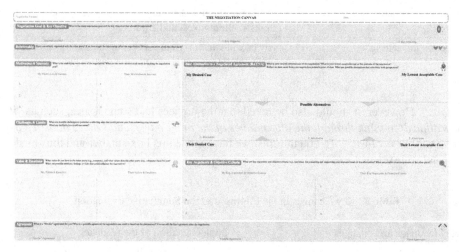

Fig. 2. The Final Negotiation Canvas.[1]

---

[1] Detailed Version of the Negotiation Canvas online: https://bit.ly/the-negotiation-canvas.

5 Discussion

5.1 Canvas Enhancement, Limitations and Future Research

Our paper aimed to develop a canvas for negotiations that can support the preparation process in a structured and visualized way. Above all, the evaluation with negotiation experts and novices has shown that our canvas has received positive feedback and was rated very helpful – especially compared to more classical layouts, such as simple text. However, we would like to briefly discuss aspects that came up during the novice's evaluation in order to improve our canvas further. One aspect mentioned by a novice was that the canvas could be partially individual and adapted depending on the current negotiation situation. As a general adaption to every specific negotiation situation is inconvertible, one possibility here is to adapt the canvas to specific industries and thus make it more precise. For example, guiding questions could be formulated more specifically, and negotiation elements that are particularly important for a specific industry could be emphasized, while less important elements are considered more minimally. Nevertheless, it should be noted that the negotiation elements in our canvas are of importance across all sectors, as existing literature [e.g., 1, 3, 8] and the evaluation with the negotiation experts show. The evaluation also uncovered that a few novices had some difficulties filling in the boxes when they could not answer the guiding questions. To address this problem, we would like to develop and provide background information on each negotiation element for those who need more support. This also has the advantage that novices can acquire additional negotiation knowledge while filling in the canvas. Moreover, we plan a chatbot that can guide you through the canvas and answer questions. We want to provide interactive guidance to further support the use of the canvas and thus, make contributions to Information System research. The last canvas enhancement we want to discuss is to provide the canvas in the language the negotiation will be. A translation of the canvas into various languages can make sense and be helpful, as the canvas can serve as a cheat sheet during the negotiation itself. However, it should be noted that terminology should be translated in a meaningful way, and there should be no misunderstandings included.

In the following, we scrutinize the boundaries and constraints associated with the proposed negotiation canvas, offering room for future research areas. The identified limitations encompass facets such as the method's orientation towards win-win outcomes, the reliance on a specific evaluation technique, the analytical scope confined to existing canvases, and the restricted exploration of diverse use cases and scenarios. *First*, the emphasis on achieving a win-win outcome may narrow the scope of applicability. To broaden its utility, consideration could be given to extending the model through additional canvases or adapting it to assess its transferability to win-lose scenarios. This extension would help explore canvas applicability in a wider range of negotiation situations. *Second*, the evaluation so far has been confined to the application of the thinking-aloud method. In future research, we want to expand this by conducting experimental studies and application analyses in diverse contexts. Integrating various evaluation methods can provide more comprehensive insights, enhancing our understanding of the robustness and effectiveness of the proposed method. For example, an experiment to analyze the newly developed canvas comparing the effectiveness of different types of canvases could be a starting point here. *Third*, the canvas' applicability has been tested in a limited number of use cases and scenarios. It is crucial to recognize that different negotiation situations may have distinct requirements and dynamics. Future research should, therefore, explore a broader array of use cases to ensure the robustness and universality of the canvas application.

6 Conclusion

Our research has contributed to both practical and theoretical domains. Theoretically, our work formalizes negotiation knowledge into a structured canvas and thus contributes by expanding existing canvas literature into application scenarios for developing the theory-driven canvas. By introducing and testing the proposed negotiation canvas, we provide a new perspective on the application of canvases, thereby enriching the theoretical foundation for future research in negotiation strategies in DSR. This contributes to a more nuanced understanding of how canvases can be employed in diverse contexts, pushing the boundaries of existing theoretical frameworks.

Beyond theoretical implications, this research bears practical significance by introducing a tool designed to enhance negotiation preparation. The developed canvas offers practitioners a structured approach to navigate negotiations effectively. As negotiations rely more on information systems, offering a practical preparation tool meets contemporary business demands, providing tangible benefits for negotiators. This research facilitates the structured and comprehensive transfer of negotiation knowledge. The canvas encapsulated negotiation wisdom, aiding negotiators' skill acquisition and organizations' institutionalization of negotiation expertise.

Appendix A. The Novice Evaluation Task

First, we start the novices' evaluation by explaining brief background information on the canvas. This included the following information: *"The canvas was designed to assist you in preparing for upcoming negotiations and serve as a "cheat sheet" during the negotiation itself. The canvas compromises various elements with accompanying guiding questions. There is no right or wrong way to fill it out, and no specific order must be followed. You can intuitively complete the canvas."* After this short introduction, we explained the task as follows: *"Imagine you need to prepare for a salary negotiation in your current profession. If you are paid according to a collective agreement, please imagine that you have the opportunity to move up within your tariff group or switch to an extra-tariff contract. Fill out the canvas intuitively to prepare for this negotiation."* After the novices had filled out the canvas, we asked final questions to get an impression of what they thought about the canvas. So, we asked the novices: *"Please briefly answer the following questions after putting yourself in this situation and completing the canvas: How old are you, what gender do you identify with? What is your current profession and how long are you already working in this job? What is your general impression of the canvas? Do you think such a canvas is helpful for preparing for upcoming negotiations and would you use it? Do you have any suggestions for improvement? Anything you want to add?"* Finally, we expressed comprehensive gratitude for their participation and the time invested.

References

1. Fisher, R., Ury, W.: Getting to Yes: Negotiating An Agreement Without Giving In. Random House Business, London (2012)
2. Fioravanti, M.L., de Oliveira Sestito, C.D., de Deus, W.S., Scatalon, L.P., Barbosa, E.F.: Role-playing games for fostering communication and negotiation skills. IEEE Trans. Educ. **65**, 384–393 (2022)
3. Thompson, L.: Mind and Heart of the Negotiator, The Global Edition (7th edition). Pearson, Harlow England (2021))
4. Chapman, E., Miles, E.W., Maurer, T.: A proposed model for effective negotiation skill development. JMD **36**, 940–958 (2017)
5. Thompson, L.L., Wang, J., Gunia, B.C.: Negotiation. Annu. Rev. Psychol. **61**, 491 (2010)
6. Asante-Asamani, A.E.A., Elahee, M., MacDonald, J.: Goal orientation and negotiation strategies: an empirical analysis. Rev. Int. Bus. Strat. **32**, 437–455 (2021)
7. Walton, R.E., McKersie, R.B.: A Behavioral Theory of Labor Negotiations. McGraw-Hill, New York (1965)
8. Lewicki, R.J., Barry, B., Saunders, D.M.: Essentials of Negotiation. McGraw-Hill Companies, New York (2020)
9. Van Kleef, G.A., De Dreu, C.K.W., Manstead, A.S.R.: The interpersonal effects of emotions in negotiations: a motivated information processing approach. J. Pers. Soc. Psychol. **87**, 510–528 (2004)
10. Roberts, A.: Empathic Negotiation Canvas. http://masterfacilitator.com/wp-content/uploads/2016/12/Empathic-Negotiation-Canvas.png. Accessed 07 Dec 2023
11. Blair, C.A., Desplaces, D.E.: Conflict management through the negotiations canvas, getting participants to understand. Conflict Resolut. Q. **36**, 39–51 (2018)
12. Peffers, K., Tuunanen, T., Rothenberger, M.A., Chatterjee, S.: A design science research methodology for information systems research. J. Manag. Inf. Syst. **24**, 45–77 (2007)
13. Kelleher, J.: Review of traditional and collaborative models for negotiation. J. Collect. Negotiat. Public Sector **29**(4), 321–335 (2000)
14. Lewicki, R.J., Barry, B., Saunders, D.M.: Essentials of Negotiation. McGraw-Hill Education, Dubuque (2016)
15. Rubin, J.Z., Brown, B.R.: The Social Psychology of Bargaining and Negotiation. Academic Press, New York (1975)
16. Thompson, L.: Negotiation behavior and outcomes: empirical evidence and theoretical issues. Psychol. Bull. **108**, 515–532 (1990)
17. Benetti, S., Ogliastri, E., Caputo, A.: Distributive/integrative negotiation strategies in cross-cultural contexts: a comparative study of the USA and Italy. J. Manag. Organ. **27**, 786–808 (2021)
18. Saee, J.: Best practice in global negotiation strategies for leaders and managers in the 21st century. J. Bus. Econ. Manag. **9**, 309–318 (2008)
19. Pitt, L.F., Watson, R.T., Kavan, C.B.: Measuring information systems service quality: concerns for a complete canvas. MIS Q. **21**, 209–221 (1997)
20. Rose, J., Holgersson, J., Söderström, E.: Designing innovative digital services for government: a business model canvas adaptation. In: European Conference on Information Systems (ECIS) 2019 Proceedings (2019)
21. Osterwalder, A., Pigneur, Y.: Designing business models and similar strategic objects: the contribution of IS. J. Assoc. Inf. Syst. **14**, 237–244 (2013)
22. Avdiji, H., Elikan, D., Missonier, S., Pigneur, Y.: A design theory for visual inquiry tools. J. Assoc. Inf. Syst. **21**, 3 (2020)

23. Payne, J.W.: Thinking aloud: insights into information processing. Psychol. Sci. **5**, 241–248 (1994)
24. Vitalari, N.: Knowledge as a basis for expertise in systems analysis: an empirical study. Manag. Inf. Syst. Q. **9**, 221–241 (1985)
25. Chandra Kruse, L., Purao, S., Seidel, S.: How designers use design principles: design behaviors and application modes. J. Assoc. Inf. Syst. **23**, 1235–1270 (2022)
26. Kriglstein, S., Leitner, M., Kabicher-Fuchs, S., Rinderle-Ma, S.: Evaluation methods in process-aware information systems research with a perspective on human orientation. Bus. Inf. Syst. Eng. 58, 397–414 (2016)
27. Fells, R.E.: Effective Negotiation: From Research to Results. Cambridge University Press, Port Melbourne (2016)
28. Carroll, B., Alexandris, K.: Perception of constraints and strength of motivation: their relationship to recreational sport participation in Greece. J. Leis. Res. **29**, 279–299 (1997)
29. White, D.D.: A structural model of leisure constraints negotiation in outdoor recreation. Leis. Sci. **30**, 342–359 (2008)
30. De Dreu, C.K.W.: Motivation in negotiation: a social psychological analysis. In: The handbook of negotiation and culture. pp. 114–135. Stanford University Press (2004)
31. Caputo, A., Ayoko, O.B., Amoo, N., Menke, C.: The relationship between cultural values, cultural intelligence and negotiation styles. J. Bus. Res. **99**, 23–36 (2019)

DSR Methods and Education

A Typology of Knowledge Creation in Design Science Research Projects

Samir Chatterjee[1]($\boxtimes$) (iD), Anol Bhattacherjee[2] (iD), and Tom Gilb[3] (iD)

[1] Claremont Graduate University, Claremont, CA 91701, USA
samir.chatterjee@cgu.edu
[2] University of South Florida, Tampa, FL 33620, USA
[3] Gilb.Com, Oslo, Norway

Abstract. There is considerable debate in IS-DSR community about what constitutes design knowledge and whether they are best represented as design principles or design theories. While designing an IT artifact to solve a problem addresses the "how" question, we agree that the "why" question (why did this work?) is important to answer. This essay attempts to shed light on two fundamental questions in this domain: (1) What are the various ways that knowledge contribution in DSR can be stated? (2) What pathways exists to create and re(use) knowledge in DSR projects? We present a simple 2 × 2 framework that explains with concrete examples four knowledge types - design principles, design attribute postulates, design theories, and good design practices from DSR projects. We further present a dual-use of design knowledge framework that shows pathways and re(use) of knowledge in DSR. We think that this typology is a useful theoretical contribution that can benefit both academics and practitioners conducting DSR projects.

Keywords: Design science research · knowledge contribution · knowledge creation · design theories · design principles · knowledge pathways

1 Introduction

Design Science Research (DSR) has garnered considerable attention in the Information Systems (IS) discipline over the past several decades. Much of this attention has been placed on its dual objectives: (i) to build innovative artifacts that can solve relevant societal and organizational problems, and (ii) to contribute generalizable knowledge to the IS knowledge base in a cumulative way [1]. In its initial days, the focus of DSR was on solving important problems by designing and building useful artifacts [2]. Subsequent interests in the IS-DSR community shifted to creating abstract knowledge about IS artifacts and the formulation of design theory [3]. This stream of research has offered multiple conceptualizations of how design theory should be structured [4], how it can be evaluated [5], and how it can be developed [6].

The momentum behind creating design theories stalled when many theoreticians and methodologists realized the challenges of creating generalizable design theories from

© The Author(s), under exclusive license to Springer Nature Switzerland AG 2024
M. Mandviwalla et al. (Eds.): DESRIST 2024, LNCS 14621, pp. 141–154, 2024.
https://doi.org/10.1007/978-3-031-61175-9_10

artifact designs [7]. At this point, the focus of the IS-DSR community shifted to postulating design principles as an adequate representation of IS-DSR's knowledge creation objective [8]. However, although many DSR papers mention some design principles, many of these principles were never vetted and are not useful. Moreover, the process of building design principles was plagued by lack of clarity on what constitutes a design principle, who would benefit from these principles, and importantly how useful are these design principles. The tension between producing knowledge (in form of design principles) and practical benefits of IT artifacts continues to this day and has cast a shadow over the excitement of DSR as a scientific approach to building useful and important IS design artifacts [9].

In this paper, we take a deeper look at the on-going phenomenon of knowledge contribution and ask two research questions:

RQ1: What are the various ways that knowledge contribution in DSR can be represented?

RQ2: What are the ways through which we can create and use knowledge in DSR projects?

In answering the above questions, our first contribution here is that we discuss and elaborate various DSR knowledge contribution (in the form of a 2×2 framework) while we provide practical examples of these knowledge types, with definitions and examples in that framework. The typology broadens what DSR scholars can contribute in terms of design knowledge. Our additional unique contribution here is that we present a dual-use view of (design) knowledge in DSR and delineate how input side and output side of DSR activities use and create knowledge. Such interplay facilitates better and improved artifact designs.

In Sect. 2, we summarize the evolutionary development of the DSR literature on design knowledge. Here we also elaborate on our views of design principles and when they are useful. In Sect. 3, we present a simple 2×2 framework to assist researchers in making knowledge contribution claims in DSR. We provide concrete examples of the various DSR knowledge contribution forms along with the utility of each knowledge type (as it relates to our 2×2 framework). In Sect. 4, we present the dual nature of (design) theory use in DSR activities – input and output – and show how cumulative knowledge percolates across various DSR projects in our portfolios. We conclude this essay in Sect. 5 with some final thoughts on how DSR projects can position themselves to have a greater societal impact.

2   Related Literature: Design Principles and Theories

The relevance and rigor of research has been a subject of extensive discussion in the IS community for many decades. In the 1990s, Benbasat et al. [10] provided suggestions on how to increase the relevance of IS research. Galliers [11] discussed the importance of balancing scientific rigor in IS research with its practical relevance. The earliest effort to bring design-oriented research principles from engineering disciplines to IS was led by Jay Nunamaker of the University of Arizona in the mid-nineties [7, 12, 13]. Purposefully designed artifacts, by definition, provide "value" or "utility" by solving existing problems, and are therefore "relevant" to our needs [13]. This work formed the foundation for further promotion of the idea of design-orientation in IS toward guidelines and principles for DSR. DSR found mainstream IS attention with the guidelines proposed by Hevner et al. [9], the recommendations by Rossi and Sein [14], and the Design Science Research Methodology (DSRM) by Peffers et al. [15]. Hevner & Chatterjee [2] came out with a definitive book, followed by Sein et al.'s work on Action Design Research (ADR) [16].

All major DSR guidelines stipulate the need to combine knowledge and expertise from both practitioners and the scientific community. For example, the incorporation of "business needs" into DSR research [9] as well as DSRM's "Problem Identification & Motivation" phase [15] require simultaneous consideration of both practical and scientific knowledge. Soon thereafter, discussions started on how to recognize knowledge obtained from instantiation of artifacts, in the form of nascent design theories and design principles [3, 17]. In 2016, the Framework for Evaluation in Design Research (FEDS) [18] proposed evaluation guidelines for DSR that included a two-dimensional characterization of DSR evaluation episodes, with one dimension being the functional purpose of the evaluation (formative or summative) and the other dimension being the paradigm of the evaluation (artificial or naturalistic).

Despite the widespread recognition for the need of knowledge contribution in DSR research (e.g., [9, 17]), the IS community, however, has remained silent when it comes to providing practical methodological guidance for knowledge creation in DSR. Almost no recommendation is available to support researchers on how to create and represent knowledge from artifact designs. Chatterjee [19] elaborates on the focus and locus of design theories. Gregor et al. [8] examine how should design principles for technology-based artifacts in sociotechnical systems be presented so that they are understandable and useful in real-world design contexts? They present a schema that includes the well-recognized elements of design principles, including goals in a specific context and the mechanisms to achieve the goal. Further agreement exists on design theories' potential to foster the development of a cumulative body of knowledge [3, 20, 21], a goal which the IS discipline should strive for in general [22].

2.1 Foundations of Principles and Knowledge

In recent DSR publications, there has been a surge of interest in "design principles" [21]. Some papers have gone on to just state design principles without solving any problem. This raises two fundamental issues on knowledge contribution via principles: (1) what is a principle; and (2) when is a principle useful? We discuss these issues next.

2.1.1 What is a Principle?

A principle is a short statement or "condensed wisdom" [34] that guides people to take certain decisions or action. Wisdom often refers to a class of knowledge. Principles are useful if they educate or remind us to act in a consistent way while facing a certain class of problem, instead of acting in an ad hoc or arbitrary manner.

For example, let's consider an important design principle in software engineering known as "Single Responsibility Principle" (SRP). The SRP is one of the gold principles

[34], and it states that a class should have only one reason to change, meaning it should have only one responsibility or job within the system.

What does this principle tell us? When a class has a single responsibility, it becomes easier to understand, maintain, and modify. Each class becomes a clear and encapsulated entity focused on one aspect of the system. From a testing perspective, SRP simplifies unit testing. With a single responsibility, it's easier to write focused and meaningful unit tests for each class. This helps in quickly identifying issues and ensures that changes don't introduce unexpected problems in unrelated parts of the codebase. Developers perceive the Single Responsibility Principle as a guideline that promotes code clarity, maintainability, reusability, ease of testing, collaboration, and overall better software design. Following SRP leads to more robust, scalable, and maintainable codebases. In short, this *useful* principle tells us what constitutes "good code".

2.1.2   Principles of Useful Knowledge

If principles must be useful and design principles are a measure of knowledge contribution in DSR, then the knowledge derived from design principles should be useful. In Table 1, we present few criteria of useful knowledge [30, 38]. If design principles from DSR project cannot meet at least some of these criteria, there may not be any value to producing such design principles.

Table 1. Criteria of useful knowledge [38].

Criteria	Explanation
UNIVERSALITY	Knowledge is more useful if it applies to a wider range of circumstances
DURABILITY	Knowledge is more useful if it can be applied for a long period of time
VALUE	Knowledge is more useful if there is a high value from applying it
SHARING	Knowledge is more useful if it can easily be shared with others
PROOF	Knowledge is more useful if we can prove its usefulness in practice
MEASURABIILITY	Knowledge is more useful when the results of its application can be measured
COST	Knowledge is more useful when the cost of applying it is low
GENERATION	Knowledge is more useful when it can be used to generate even more useful knowledge

Inherent within any principle is the expectation that the principle should stand the test of time. If a principle becomes obsolete in a few years, perhaps by virtue of new technologies or new economics, it will be of limited value to users and it may not be prudent to continue the principle's practice beyond its useful lifetime. The rush to state design principles in recent DSR research [21, 32] fails to meet some of the above criteria. It often takes decades from the formulation of a principle until its routine use in education and practice. So, this requires scholars to propose principles that we can rely on in the long run. Since that is really hard, what other knowledge types can be proposed?

3 A Typology for Knowledge Creation in DSR

DSR researchers go through a design process to construct artifacts that are expected to solve a problem while also make a knowledge contribution. This process usually iterates between refinements and evaluations until a satisfying solution is found [9, 18], while trying to abstract knowledge contributions from the entire DSR process. In Fig. 1, we propose a 2×2 typology that can help researchers conceptualize and claim reasonable contributions to DSR knowledge.

On the horizontal axis of Fig. 1, we show the locus (source) of knowledge creation: whether knowledge is created during the design process or from design product (artifact) or both. On the vertical axis, we show the type of knowledge produced, which may be fundamental (scientific) or applied (pragmatic). We posit that when a design process leads to fundamental (or scientific) knowledge (lower left cell), this knowledge is best represented as "*design theories*". If a design process leads to applied or practical knowledge (upper left cell), such knowledge is best represented as "*good design practices*". For design products, fundamental knowledge about or derived from artifacts (solutions) are best represented as "*design attribute postulates*" (lower right cell). Applied knowledge from design product (upper right cell) is best represented as "*design principles*," which may often take the form of technological rules. Note that **good design practices** and **design attribute postulates** are novel terms that we introduce to the DSR discourse.

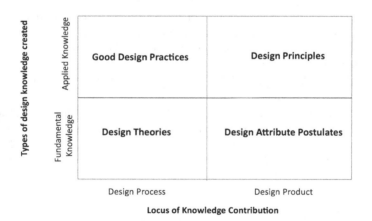

Fig. 1. A typology of design knowledge creation.

The proposed typology ties together the DSR academic and practitioner communities by focusing on fundamental and applied knowledge creation. However, it is important to note that the four knowledge types listed are not mutually exclusive. *Design Attribute Postulates* provide a starting point for reasoning why a specific artifact worked, and more specifically, what attributes of the artifact caused it to work. This is analogous to Level-1 abstractness [17], referring to the specific contextual implementation of an artifact. *Design Theories* should explain why a design process worked and are analogous to what Gregor and Hevner [17] called Level-3 abstraction or a 'mature' type of knowledge. *Good Design Practices*, on the other hand, can be viewed as guidelines or practices that practitioners find useful in their daily design work. Lastly, *Design Principles* are statements of condensed wisdom (technology rules) that a designer can follow to create an effective and useful product for specific domain contexts. We will present concrete examples of each of these four types of knowledge in the following subsections.

3.1 Design Attribute Postulates

A postulate is a fundamental assumption or proposition that is accepted without direct proof. In various fields such as mathematics, physics, and philosophy, postulates serve as starting points or first-order principles upon which a system of thought or theory is built. Postulates are considered self-evident or intuitively true, and they form the foundation for deriving conclusions and theorems within a particular framework.

Design attributes refer to the specific characteristics or features that are intentionally incorporated into the design of a product, system, or solution. These attributes are the key elements that define the intended functionality, aesthetics, performance, usability, reliability, safety, sustainability, and overall qualities of the designed object. Design attributes play a crucial role in shaping the user experience and determining how well the design meets its intended purpose. For example, Google search engine product (driven by Google's Page Rank algorithm) demonstrated superior performance (i.e., was faster and better) than prior algorithms such as Yahoo or Altavista [33]. The idea that Page Rank brought up was that the importance of any web page can be judged by looking at the pages that link to it. Whether we talk about popularity or authority, we can iteratively assign a rank to each web page, based on the ranks of the pages that point to it. The design attribute is "popularity".

Outside the IS field, design attribute postulates are best represented in the Da Vinci principles of systems engineering [35], shown in Table 2. While Da Vinci is known for his artistic creations, his paintings demonstrate first-order principles that are also of use in systems engineering. He repeatedly refers to multiple attributes of design, multiple perception angles, and incremental scientific experiment to improve the design attributes. These wide-focus design attribute postulates can help in the successful design of complex systems.

3.2 Design Theories

A design theory is a set of postulates or a framework that provide a systematic and organized approach to the practice of design [5, 8]. It aims to establish a cohesive and structured foundation for making design decisions, solving problems, and creating artifacts, whether they be physical products, systems, interfaces, or other designed entities. One example of a design theory that has had a significant impact in the field of human-computer interaction, is the "User-Centered Design" (UCD) theory [41]. UCD is a design approach that prioritizes the needs and preferences of the end-users throughout

Table 2. Da Vinci principles of systems engineering.

Principle	Explanation
Curiosità (Curiosity)	Being insatiably curious, unrelenting quest for continuous learning. Which attributes made the artifact novel?
Dimostrazione (Demonstration)	Commitment to test knowledge through experience, willingness to learn from mistakes. The evaluation gives us practical experience where we learn what works and what doesn't
Sensazione (Sensation)	Continual refinement of senses as means to enliven experience. What interaction of artifact with users can liven up the user experience?
Sfumato (Nuanced)	Willingness to embrace ambiguity, paradox, uncertainty. How do we deal with conflict, priorities, lack of clarity or stability?
Corporalità (Corporality)	Cultivation of grace, ambidexterity, fitness, poise. Attributes such as user delight and hedonistic experience
Connessione (Connection)	Recognition & appreciation for interconnectedness of all things and phenomena, as often demonstrated in systems thinking. Carefully exploring how different functions and features interconnect into a cohesive whole

the design process. It places a strong emphasis on understanding users, involving them in the design process, and iteratively refining designs based on user feedback.

Again, drawing inspiration from outside IS, we look to Elon Musk who is widely recognized as a brilliant designer and engineer. Musk suggested a five-step engineering process at the design process level, which is a good illustration of a nascent design theory [36]. These steps are aimed to creating artifacts that are better, faster, cheaper, and more efficient. The key themes of this design theory, summarized from Musk's oral statements at SpaceX are as follows [36].

Step 1: **Simplify requirements**. Musk states "the requirements can be dumb; it does not matter who gave them to you". He notes that it's particularly dangerous if an intelligent person gives you the requirements, as you may not question the requirements enough. "Everyone's wrong. No matter who you are, everyone is wrong some of the time". He further notes that "all requirements should be simplified."

Step 2: **Retain absolute essential parts**. If parts are not being added back into the design at least 10% of the time, not enough parts are being deleted. Musk noted that the bias tends to be very strongly toward "let's add this part or process step in case we need it." Additionally, each required part and process must come from a name, not a department, as a department cannot be asked why a requirement exists, but a person can.

Step 3: **Simplify and then optimize the design**. According to Musk, the most common error of a smart engineer is to optimize something that should not exist.

Step 4: **Accelerate cycle time**. Musk states "you're moving too slowly, go faster! But don't go faster until you have worked on the other (above) three things first."

Step 5: **Automate**. An important part of this is to remove in-process testing after the problems have been diagnosed; if a product is reaching the end of a production line with a high acceptance rate, there is no need for in-process testing. Engineers need to understand the system at a high level to understand when they are making a bad optimization. Challenging superiority as well as conventional wisdom is essential to make improved design.

The above steps during design process forms the seed towards a design theory. While Musk is focusing on engineering design, in our field of IS design, each of the above steps can help DSR researchers build better artifacts.

3.3 Good Design Practices

Design practices refer to the methods and techniques that design practitioners can use to solve various problems. They are often informed by trial-and-error, patterns, and methods that have evolved over time [37]. They also depend on the specific goals and constrains of a given project. Below we present some pragmatic design practices [40] that are useful to a broader understanding of DSR knowledge production.

1. **Design Corruption**: The system reality might not reflect the design intent, the requirements, or the design itself, because of translation, interpretation, corruption, or many other factors.
2. **Murphy's Design**: Any changes to the real system, can invalidate previous requirement specifications, and previous design specifications.
3. **Prototyping:** Creating prototypes allows designers to visualize and test their ideas in a tangible form. Prototypes can range from low-fidelity sketches to high-fidelity interactive models, depending on the project's requirements.
4. **Disturbances**: Designed systems attributes will be incessantly disturbed by factors inside and outside the system scope, which were not known, or were not considered, or which emerged later.
5. **Collaboration:** Design is a collaborative effort, and designers often work closely with other team members, stakeholders, and experts from various fields to gather insights and perspectives.
6. **Design Expectation Balance**: Designed systems cannot expect to meet the optimistic expectations of all potential stakeholders; but reasonable compromises can be designed, and unreasonable expectations can be refused.
7. **Ideation:** The ideation phase involves generating a wide range of ideas to address the design problem. Designers use brainstorming sessions, mind mapping, sketching, and other techniques to explore potential solutions.

All the above design practices guidelines (upper left quadrant in Fig. 1) emerge with use and interaction of the artifact over time. The practitioners are most suited to derive these practice guidelines.

3.4 Design Principles

Applied design knowledge from artifacts can best be represented as design principles. A design principle is a fundamental guideline or a technological rule that informs the process of creating a design. These principles serve as core concepts to guide designers in making decisions, solving problems, and shaping the overall characteristics of a product or system. Design principles are often derived from a combination of best practices, theoretical frameworks, and empirical insights gained from experience in various design disciplines. Some may argue that design principles are a precursor to design theories. From the applied sense, we feel that "technology rules" captures the knowledge contribution in a better way. We refer to the work of Peter J. Denning and his "Great Principles of Computing" initiative [30]. The five great principles of computing are shown in Table 3.

Table 3. Five Great Principles of Computing

Principle	Explanation
Computing is a Natural Science	Denning argues that computing is a fundamental natural science, on par with physics, chemistry, and biology. It involves the study of information processes and phenomena
Algorithmic Thinking	Algorithms are central to computing. They are step-by-step procedures or formulas for solving problems or performing tasks. Algorithmic thinking is a key aspect of computational problem-solving
Computational Abstraction	Denning emphasizes the importance of abstraction in computing, where complex systems are represented and understood at different levels of detail. Abstractions, such as programming languages and data structures, help manage complexity
The Limits of Computing	Recognizing the inherent limits of what can and cannot be computed is crucial. This principle involves understanding the theoretical boundaries of computation, including issues related to undecidability and computational complexity
Computing as a Human Activity	Computing is not just about machines and algorithms; it's a human activity. This principle highlights the social and ethical dimensions of computing, considering how technology impacts individuals and society

These principles are designed to provide a foundational understanding of the field of computing and to guide its future development. As with any dynamic field, new perspectives and principles may emerge over time. Few other well-known examples of design principles include:

- **"Form Follows Function"**: Emphasizes that the design of an object should primarily reflect its intended purpose or function.
- **"Keep It Simple, Stupid (KISS)"**: Encourages simplicity and avoiding unnecessary complexity in design.

Sometimes, principles themselves may contain nested principles. For example, *Simplicity* in IS design is a fundamental and desirable design principle. However, simplicity itself can be further elaborated with several principles in systems design [39]. We elaborate few of them below:

1. TAILORED: Understanding of simplicity must be based on 'defined views' of a system.
2. QUANTIFIED: Simplicity can be quantified in several complimentary ways.
3. ENGINEERED: You can design systems to be simple enough, to reach quantified levels, of defined kinds of simplicity.
4. SIDE-EFFECTS: A consequence of making a system simple, from one stakeholder's viewpoint, might be that it becomes 'extremely complex' from another's viewpoint.
5. A VIEWPOINT: One person's 'simple' is another person's 'complex'.
6. COSTS: The cost of simplicity, is the cost of the total design itself (including implementation and maintenance) for simplicity, and other associated costs such as training and understanding.
7. ROI: The value proposition of simplicity might cost more than the benefits.

Our first major contribution in this paper is the 2 × 2 DSR knowledge typology framework (Fig. 1). The typology extends what type of knowledge DSR scholars can claim from a DSR project. This should give all DSR researchers more options than just design principles or theories.

4   A Dual Use Framework of DSR Knowledge Typology

The epistemological underpinnings of design knowledge encompass the philosophical foundations that guide our understanding of how and why we formulate knowledge in the field of design. Epistemology is the branch of philosophy that deals with the nature, origin, and limits of human knowledge. In the context of design, several key conceptions shape the epistemological framework:

Pragmatism: emphasizes practical consequences of ideas and the utility of knowledge in solving real-world problems. Design knowledge is seen as a tool for problem-solving.

Constructivism: posits that knowledge is actively constructed by individuals based on their experiences and interactions with the environment. This implies a subjective knowledge in design. This also implies that different designers may interpret and apply knowledge in unique ways.

Hermeneutics: Hermeneutics is concerned with the interpretation of meaning, understanding, and context. Designers seek to uncover and interpret the implicit meanings within a given context to inform their decision-making and creation of meaningful artifacts.

Empiricism: asserts that knowledge is derived from sensory experience and observation. In design, this involves gathering empirical data through user research, usability testing, and other methods to inform the decision-making process.

We next present the above epistemological underpinnings of design knowledge in a dual-use framework (see Fig. 2). We use knowledge in DSR at the input stage (design process stage) and also produce/use knowledge by introducing the artifact (product stage) into the field. This was also observed in the 6-grids framework [42]. Knowledge can be derived from prior experiences as well as produced during the conduct of an artifact design project. The forms that design knowledge can take have been referred to in the prior literature differently and confusingly as design theory [3, 13, 23], design patterns [24, 37], technological rules [25, 26], technical norms [27, 28], design rules [29], analysis patterns [29], computing principles [30], design propositions [31], and design principles [8, 21]. Instead of being mired in nomenclature of design knowledge, we believe our proposed typology (Fig. 1) simplifies things. Knowledge is created during a design project, and it also accumulates over time over successive projects. One example of conceptualizing cumulative knowledge development is a study by Offermann et al. [32], in which the authors describe what type of design knowledge lends itself, in their own words, to be 're-used' and devise strategies on how to accomplish this. In Fig. 2, we present our own conceptualization of where and how design knowledge can be used (or re-used) in a DSR project.

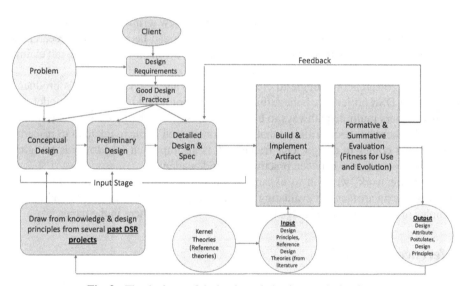

Fig. 2. The dual use of design knowledge in cumulative form

DSR projects typically start with a wicked problem – a problem that is difficult to solve because of incomplete, contradictory, or changing problem requirements that cannot be anticipated or planned for in advance. When confronted with such a problem, an experienced designer with some knowledge of the problem space, envisions an initial conceptual design. This initial design is improved, following a detailed exploration of the problem and solution space, and additional clarification from the stakeholders. Combining the above information from a variety of sources, incorporating good design practices, the designers arrive at a design specification that can then be implemented. All of this is referred to as the input stage design process (see Fig. 2). During this design process, researchers consult kernel theories (past reference theories) that provides design requirements arising from prior researcher's projects. This collection of knowledge can be called **input design knowledge.** After this stage, the designers, settle on a more-detailed design specification. After the artifact is instantiated (or built), partly or wholly, the design goes through an extensive evaluation, which may be formative or summative in nature. During the design and evaluation processes, designers must continually reflect on what worked in this design and why. This results in design attribute postulates or design principles. This is called the **output design knowledge.** There is a complimentary and cyclical dual-use of IS-DSR knowledge.

5   Conclusions and Future Work

In this essay, we present a 2 × 2 typology to help researchers conceptualize and claim knowledge contribution in DSR projects. The four quadrants in Fig. 1 show variety of knowledge contributions can be produced during the design process, as well as design product phase. Even though for simplicity we have partitioned the knowledge types into fundamental and applied, it is important to acknowledge that they may cross over into each other's territories. We introduce in particular two new terms to the discourse: good design practices and design attribute postulates. These can be utilized by researchers and practitioners to state their contribution in a clear way rather than making tall claims of "design theories".

As DSR researchers struggle to clearly explain what new knowledge is produced through their DSR project, we believe that our 2 × 2 typology and the dual-use model will give researchers multiple pathways to build and re(use) knowledge from DSR projects.

Finally, there has been criticism that practitioners aren't able to relate to IS research even when it comes to design. Our framework is an important step towards bridging knowledge contribution between practitioners and academics.

For future work, we plan to expand this using a DSR approach of building the framework as an artifact and evaluating it with stakeholders. We also want to add more examples of each of the knowledge types we have discussed here in the paper.

References

1. Schuster, R., et al.: Information systems design science research and cumulative knowledge development: an exploratory study. In: International Conference on Interaction Sciences (2018)
2. Hevner, A., Chatterjee, S.: Design science research in information systems. In: Design Research in Information Systems, pp. 9–22. Springer, Boston (2010). https://doi.org/10.1007/978-1-4419-5653-8_2
3. Gregor, S., Jones, D.: The anatomy of a design theory. J. Assoc. Inf. Syst. **8**(5), 312–335 (2007)
4. Kuechler, W., Vaishnavi, V.: A framework for theory development in design science research: multiple perspectives. J. Assoc. Inf. Syst. **13**(6), 395–423 (2012)
5. Weber, R.: Evaluating and developing theories in the information systems discipline. J. Assoc. Inf. Syst. **13**(1), 1–30 (2012)
6. Mandviwalla, M.: Generating and justifying design theory. J. Assoc. Inf. Syst. **16**(5), 314–344 (2015)

7. Simon, H.A.: The Sciences of the Artificial, Reissue of the Third Edition with a New Introduction by John Laird. MIT press, Cambridge (2019)
8. Gregor, S., Kruse, L.C., Seidel, S.: Research perspectives: the anatomy of a design principle. J. Assoc. Inf. Syst. **21**(6), 2 (2020). https://doi.org/10.17705/1jais.00649
9. Hevner, A.R., March, S.T., Park, J., Ram, S.: Design science in information systems research. MIS Q. **28**(1), 75–105 (2004)
10. Benbasat, I., Zmud, R.: Empirical research in information systems: the practice of relevance. MIS Q. **23**(1), 3–16 (1999)
11. Galliers, R.D.: Relevance and rigour in Information systems research: some personal reflections on issues facing the information systems research community. In: Glasson, B.C., Hawryszkiewycz, I., Underwood, A., Weber, R.A. (eds.) IFIP TC8 Open Conference on Business Process Re-engineering: Information Systems Opportunities and Challenges, pp. 93–102. Elsevier Science (1994)
12. March, S.T., Smith, G.F.: Design and natural science research on information technology. Decis. Support Syst. **15**, 251–266 (1995)
13. Nunamaker, J.F., Jr., Briggs, R.O.: Toward a broader vision for Information Systems. ACM Trans. Manag. Inf. Syst. (TMIS) **2**(4), 1–12 (2012)
14. Rossi, M., Sein, M.K.: Design research workshop: a proactive research approach. In: Design Research Workshop within the IRIS26 (2003)
15. Peffers, K., Tuunanen, T., Rothenberger, M.A., Chatterjee, S.: A design science research methodology for information systems research. J. Manag. Inf. Syst. **24**(3), 45–77 (2008)
16. Sein, M.K., Henfridsson, O., Purao, S., Rossi, M., Lindgren, R.: Action design research. MIS Q. **35**(1), 37–56 (2011)
17. Gregor, S., Hevner, A.R.: Positioning and presenting design science research for maximum impact. MIS Q. **37**(2), 337–355 (2013)
18. Venable, J., Pries-Heje, J., Baskerville, R.: FEDS: a framework for evaluation in design science research. Eur. J. Inf. Syst. **25**(1), 77–89 (2016)
19. Chatterjee, S.: Writing my next design science research masterpiece: but how do i make a theoretical contribution to DSR. In: Proceedings of ECIS 2015 Completed Research Papers (2015)
20. Niederman, F., March, S.T.: Design science and the accumulation of knowledge in the information systems discipline. ACM Trans. Manag. Inf. Syst. **3**(1), 11–115 (2012)
21. Chandra Kruse, L., Seidel, S., Purao, S.: Making use of design principles. In: Proceedings of the 11th International Conference on Design Science Research in Information Systems and Technology, St. John's, NL, Canada, pp. 37–51 (2016)
22. Keen, P.G.W.: MIS research: reference disciplines and a cumulative tradition. In: Proceedings of the 1st International Conference on Information Systems, Philadelphia, PA, USA (1980)
23. Markus, M.L., Majchrzak, A., Gasser, L.: A design theory for systems that support emergent knowledge processes. MIS Q. **26**(3), 179–212 (2002)
24. Alexander, C., Ishikawa, S., Silverstein, M.: Pattern Languages: Towns, Buildings, Constructions, vol. 2. Oxford University Press, Oxford (1977)
25. Bunge, M.: Philosophy of Science: From Explanation to Justification, vol. 2. Transaction Publishers, Piscataway (1998)
26. van Aken, J.E.: Improving the relevance of management research by developing tested and grounded technological rules. In: Eindhoven Centre for Innovation Studies (2001)
27. Niiniluoto, I.: The aim and structure of applied research. Erkenntnis **38**, 1–21 (1993)
28. von Wright, G.H.: Norm and Action: A Logical Enquiry. Routledge & Kegal Paul, London (1963)
29. Plsek, P., Bibby, J., Whitby, E.: Practical methods for extracting explicit design rules grounded in the experience of organizational managers. J. Appl. Behav. Sci. **43**(1), 153–170 (2007)

30. Denning, P.J., Martell, C.H.: Great Principles of Computing. MIT Press, Cambridge (2015)
31. van Aken, J., Chandrasekaran, A., Halman, J.: Conducting and publishing design science research: Inaugural essay of the design science department of the Journal of Operations Management. J. Oper. Manag. **47**, 1–8 (2016)
32. Offermann, P., Blom, S., Bub, U.: Strategies for creating, generalising and transferring design science knowledge - a methodological discussion and case analysis. In: 10th International Conference on Wirtschaftsinformatik, Zurich, Switzerland, pp. 1187–1196 (2011)
33. Rogers, I.: The Google Pagerank algorithm and how it works (2002)
34. Harding, C.: Integrated Design and Construction-Single Responsibility: A Code of Practice. John Wiley & Sons, Hoboken (2015)
35. Gelb, M.J.: How to Think Like Leonardo da Vinci. Dell Publishing, New York (1998). ISBN 0-440-50827-4 (2000). Edition Paperback. Quoted with permission from author to TSG by email
36. Musk's Principles. https://everydayastronaut.com/starbase-tour-and-interview-with-elon-musk/. More detail in Free Book Link to Musk's Methods. https://tinyurl.com/MusksMethods
37. Dickhaut, E., Janson, A., Söllner, M., Leimeister, J.M.: Lawfulness by design – development and evaluation of lawful design patterns to consider legal requirements. Eur. J. Inf. Syst. **375**(6578), 1–28 (2023)
38. Gilb, T.: Ten design principles: some implications for multidimensional quantification of design impacts on requirements. http://www.gilb.com/dl42. Published in INCOSE (2006)
39. Gilb, T.: Simplicity Talk. http://www.gilb.com/DL464. ACCU Conference, Oxford, UK, 2011 SIMPLE: Simplification Ideas & Methods & Principles, Logic & Engineering, https://tinyurl.com/SIMPLEGilb. Work in progress Fall 2022
40. Gilb, T.: Success: Super Secrets & Strategies for Efficient Delivery in Projects, Programs, and Plans. Book Folder, tinyurl.com/SUCCESS (2021)
41. Norman, D.A.: User-Centered System Design: New Perspectives on Human-Computer Interaction (1986)
42. vom Brocke, J., Maedche, A.: The DSR grid: six core dimensions for effectively planning and communicating design science research projects. Electron. Mark. **29**, 379–385 (2019). https://doi.org/10.1007/s12525-019-00358-7

Classifying Design Science Research in Terms of Types of Reasoning from an Epistemological Perspective

Christian Daase[(✉)] [ID], Christian Haertel [ID], Abdulrahman Nahhas [ID],
and Klaus Turowski [ID]

Otto-von-Guericke University, Magdeburg, Germany
{christian.daase,christian.haertel,abdulrahman.nahhas,
klaus.turowski}@ovgu.de

Abstract. Design science research (DSR) is now an established branch of the artificial sciences. However, the nature of the logical reasoning and the epistemological foundations have so far received little attention. In this paper, based on a systematic literature review with quantitative and qualitative analysis of the results, an in-depth investigation of the meta-scientific view of DSR is conducted. Induction, deduction, and abduction are explained in detail with regard to general and DSR-specific applications and underpinned with suitable examples from this field. After assessing the justification for the existence of all three types of reasoning in DSR, a generalized framework is constructed to depict the end-to-end process of DSR projects and position superficial activities as falling under either type. Given the fairly small number of efforts to consider DSR directly from a meta-scientific perspective, this work offers a new point of discussion in this relatively young field of science compared to the natural and human sciences.

Keywords: Design Science Research · Epistemology · Logical Reasoning · Meta-Science · Systematic Literature Review

1 Introduction

The unprecedented rate at which science and technology are currently evolving not only changes the everyday world consistently, but also arouses the anticipation of becoming part of this symbiosis between *explaining* reality and *changing* it. In this sense, design science research (DSR) has emerged as a third distinguishable form of science from the *sciences of the artificial* as described by Simon [1] besides the previously established natural and human sciences [2]. However, although specific manifestations of science and what is considered as meaningful for the continuation of human knowledge growth might significantly differ throughout history, the fundamental characteristics of epistemology remain the same. In the 19th century, Peirce [3] differentiated three types of reasoning, as he described induction, deduction, and introduced abduction. Induction means that a generalized *rule* is derived from a context (i.e., a *case*) and the observation of specific circumstances (i.e., a *result*) [3, 4]. Deduction, in turn, is based on the

M. Mandviwalla et al. (Eds.): DESRIST 2024, LNCS 14621, pp. 155–167, 2024.
https://doi.org/10.1007/978-3-031-61175-9_11

existence of at least one rule assumed as true and the observation of a case, yielding a valid statement regarding the case (i.e., a *result*) [3]. Performing abduction relies neither on extensive observation nor on the application of a well-established rule to make an informed statement about a case, but is the act of formalizing hypotheses about a circumstance based on a rule and an observation without knowing exactly whether the two are connected [3]. Hence, abduction is rather considered as guessing [3, 5, 6] or *"the inference to the best explanation"* [7], although potentially in an informed manner and perhaps leading to true statements.

In DSR, an uncertainty can be noticed about what kind of reasoning prevails in certain methods, how research activities can be characterized, and whether abduction receives the attention it deserves [8]. For example, in a discussion on whether the highly cited DSR methodology (DSRM) according to Peffers *et al.* [9] could be combined with action design research (ADR) [10], the original authors of ADR claimed that DSRM is grounded in deductive reasoning, whereas ADR follows an inductive approach, thus making both incompatible [11]. In contrast, an article by Fischer *et al.* [12] examined the steps of the DSRM and proposed abductive and inductive characteristics for them. More recently, Gregor [13] summarized that there are significant differences in how DSR is regarded from an epistemological perspective. The author concludes that deductive approaches are most widely used, while also mixed modes are popular, but ultimately, the personal background and experience have relevance. The unique nature of design as a means to generate prescriptive knowledge, especially when considering its iterative process, calls for a less strict and more open-minded stance on the involved types of reasoning [6].

The present paper addresses this lack of clarity by reviewing previous discussions on epistemology in DSR and conducted DSR projects that explicitly state the applied view on the philosophy of reasoning. In extension to the believe of Winter [14] *"that a combination of inductive and deductive design activities has a great potential"*, it is further proposed that also abductive methods have their justification in the field of DSR. The goal of this paper is to provide a framework for DSR research that serves as a basic structure for stages of progress and outcomes in terms of their presumed logical inference type. Ultimately, the following research question (RQ) is to be answered:

RQ: How do the three types of reasoning - induction, deduction, and abduction - harmonize in an overarching DSR scheme and what role does the type of artifact play?

Following this introduction, the three types of reasoning are explained in Sect. 2 from a general scientific perspective as well as from a DSR-specific one. In Sect. 3, the applied methodology of this research in the form of a systematic literature review (SLR) is described to ensure the comprehensibility of the conducted study and a certain degree of reproducibility for the reader. The results of the SLR are discussed in Sect. 4, first from a quantitative view and second from a qualitative view. Section 5 presents the generalized framework as it can be derived from the examined literature. Finally, Sect. 6 concludes the paper.

2   Epistemological Types of Reasoning

This work builds on and recognizes the foundations laid by Peirce [3], Simon [1], and Kapitan [15] with respect to research philosophies, in addition to more recent studies that have advanced the field. The following discussion incorporates their positions on the requirements and outcomes of each type of argumentation and maps them to DSR. While acknowledging that the clarity of the problem space in DSR projects depends on the particular discipline and thus the specific methodology employed, the following explanations focus rather on the solution space inherent in the general DSR philosophy.

2.1   Induction

According to Peirce [3], induction is *"the inference of the rule from the case and result"*. More broadly speaking, this type is based on observations and empirical evidence to extract patterns, present conclusions, and ultimately propose a generalized theory [6]. Thus, induction can be viewed as *data-driven discovery* [12]. In contrast to a hypothesis, as described in the subsequent Sect. 2.3, an inductively generated statement can be considered as much stronger, since it is based on actually observable facts, whereas a hypothesis is often merely the most plausible explanation for a circumstance [3].

Peirce [3] gives the following example for inductive reasoning. A number of beans is taken from a bag, which forms the *case*. The observation is made that all these beans are white, which poses a *result*. Finally, it is concluded that also all the other beans in this bag must be white, thus inductively proposing a generalized *rule*. Given that this assumption on the coloring of the beans was previously unknown, induction constitutes a *knowledge growth by extension* [5]. However, a limitation of this type of reasoning is that there could be one particular case that was not observed for which the rule is invalid. To name one prominent example: Before the discovery of the platypus in 1798, Europeans were unaware of any mammal that laid eggs, which led to a change in the European taxonomy of species [16]. Prior to this, from a logical perspective, the statement that *all mammals give birth to living offspring* based on a myriad of observations of all known mammals would have been a valid inductively derived statement.

In DSR, induction can either be part of the first stages of a project, meaning the synthesis of a knowledge base of design principles (e.g., by means of expert interviews [17]), or the evaluation of an artifact through application and observation of the results [18]. To translate this into the language of logical reasoning, for the first variant, a case might be *"Problem X is to be solved"*. As a consequence or result, expert opinions or observations may lead to the statement *"Property Y is necessary to solve problem X"*. Thus, the derived rule or design principle is *"Artifact design Z needs to incorporate property Y"*. In evaluation, the allocations to the three components differ. A case might be *"Artifact design Z with property Y is instantiated"*. If this occurs in a sufficient number of cases, and the result is always *"Problem X has been solved"*, then it can be inductively concluded that *"Artifact design Z with property Y is able to solve problem X"*. In addition, if a design without the property is unable to solve the problem, it can be further concluded that specifically this property is responsible for addressing the issue. Figure 1 illustrates the induction process in DSR and generically according to Peirce [3].

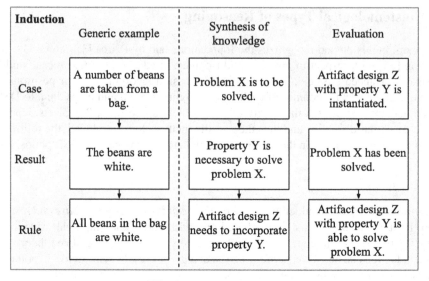

Fig. 1. Induction in DSR.

2.2 Deduction

In opposition to induction, deduction is the "*application of general rules to particular cases*", according to Peirce [3]. There are two ways of using deduction for logical reasoning. The first is using the foundational rule to prove some result for a specific case. Peirce [3] states the following example. As a general rule, it is assumed that every quadrangle is other than a triangle. Now, there can be observed that some figures are in fact quadrangles. As a result, it is concluded that some figures are not triangles. Although this is a *valid* statement from a logical perspective, it might not be *sound* if the presumption turns out to be false. Hence, the second purpose of using deduction is to refute hypotheses when it can clearly be proven that a deductively derived result is actually incorrect. Assuming that not all cases to which a rule is supposed to apply can be observed, deduction can only prove that a theory is false, which is called falsification, but never prove that a theory is true [5]. Considering again the example of the platypus, before 1798 [16] the aforementioned rule that *all mammals give birth to living offspring* applied to the case that *the platypus is a mammal* would have yield the valid and sound result that *the platypus gives birth to living offspring*. After studying the platypus, this result was firstly only *valid* anymore (i.e., *true* from a logical perspective, but *wrong* in reality), and secondly the rule was falsified.

Deduction is considered as *knowledge growth by intention* in contrast to induction, since it does not concern new areas but seeks to refine and test existing knowledge [5]. As a consequence, the knowledge gained through deduction is not part of the scientific scheme of *discovery*, as it does not lead to new theoretical fundamentals [12]. In DSR, deduction is rather used in the course of design and the iterative refinement process. Since artifact design needs to be based on generalized descriptive knowledge [14] that can, for example, be derived by studying the problem domain or reviewing existing theories, a rule might be *"Property Y solves problem X"*. Serving again as a case, *"Artifact design Z with property Y is instantiated"*. With respect to falsification, the result might be *"Artifact design Z with property Y could not solve problem X"*, thus refuting the assumed rule. More desirable for the designer, the result can also be the opposite. Since deduction does not necessarily lead to absolute statements, the result could give an indication of the extent to which the property supports the solution of the problem, which leaves room for refinements in further design iterations. Figure 2 illustrates the deduction process in DSR.

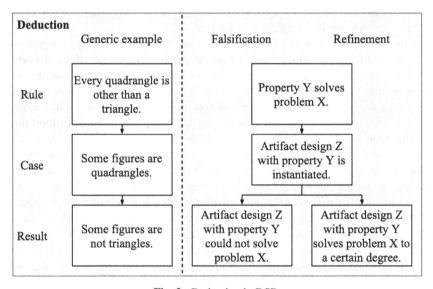

Fig. 2. Deduction in DSR.

2.3 Abduction

Abduction is the process of putting forward hypotheses about a circumstance based on a known rule and an observation, where the latter corresponds to the *result* [3]. In other words, abductive reasoning attempts to find the most plausible, yet possibly wrong, explanation for a consequence, or in colloquial terms, to *guess* what happened [5]. Peirce [3] again gives an example. As a rule, it shall be assumed that all beans from a specific bag are white. The result hereby is the observation of a number of beans that are lying on a table and are evidently of white color. Therefore, one can guess (i.e., abductively conclude) that these beans were taken from the bag. For a hypothesis, it is important, on the one hand, to explain an observation more comprehensibly than competing possible conclusions and, on the other hand, to be suitable for testing [15]. To complete the common thread, the limitation of abduction can be illustrated again using the example of the platypus. Assuming that *all mammals have fur and give birth to living offspring* is established as a rule, but it is observed that *the platypus has fur but lays eggs.* Abduction is well suited here, as it helps to find an explanation for a surprising result that cannot be explained by established theories [19]. There were two hypotheses that could be made based on the two components mentioned above. Either the platypus was not a mammal, or it was the first exception to all other mammals at the time in 1798 [16]. Since many contemporaries thought the discovery of this animal was a hoax and anomalies regarding the skin were known (e.g., that, in reverse, some mammals have little or no fur), the hypothesis that *the platypus is not a mammal* would at first glance have been more convincing than the hypothesis that *the platypus is the only exception that lays eggs and is nevertheless a mammal.* Although abduction can lead to preliminary explanations in other cases, it should not be thought of as a substitute for induction or deduction, but as a useful preceding process [6].

One advantage of abduction that makes it suitable for DSR is its higher generative capacity compared to induction, which means that assumptive statements can be derived faster. Thus, preliminary design decisions can be implemented more efficiently, especially given the iterative nature of DSR. This characteristic leads to it being labeled *"truth-productive"* [15]. However, since artifacts in DSR do not usually claim to represent a universal truth but are rather constructed and evaluated in terms of their utility, this designation would differ when applied to DSR. In terms of logical reasoning, a rule might be derived from the observation that *"Problem X was always solved when the solution incorporated property Y"*. A (desired) result for a design science researcher would likely be that *"Artifact design Z can solve problem X"*. Hence, the case and preferable design choice for the researcher is that *"Artifact design Z should include property Y"*. However, as Peirce [3] points out, the greatest and most frequently made mistake in logic is to assume that different things that resemble each other in some aspect would also resemble one another in other regards. Thus, abduction can lead to flawed designs if one either assumes that the problem described in the rule is actually the same as that of the

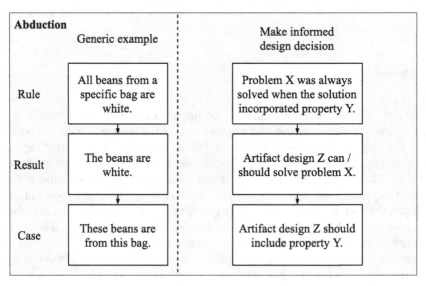

Fig. 3. Abduction in DSR.

desired result, or if one incorrectly assumes that the integrated property is responsible for solving the problem. Figure 3 illustrates the abduction process in DSR.

3 Methodology

The research endeavor does not necessarily require an exhaustive review of all available literature, but rather a representative portion of research conducted by others. Therefore, an SLR was conducted to review published articles that have one of the following two possible objectives. First, studies that focus on epistemological considerations of DSR were examined to find common ground on the nature of reasoning in DSR. Second, practical projects in which DSR methods have been actively employed and that provide further information on the type of reasoning were reviewed. The term *representative* thus refers to the portion of articles that explicitly addresses epistemological terminology. However, it is worth noting that properly conducted DSR projects usually implicitly incorporate the different types of reasoning. On the other hand, the term *systematic* refers to the comprehensibility and degree of reproducibility due to a clearly specified review protocol. To achieve this research goal, the SLR was performed in the abstract and citation database Scopus, which links to a variety of full-text databases such as IEEE Xplore, ScienceDirect, and Web of Science. The review process started with using the automatic article retrieval mechanism specified in Table 1. The time period was not limited.

Table 1. SLR search specifications.

Search field	Search query	Hits
Abstracts	(induction OR inductive) AND "design science"	33
	(deduction OR deductive) AND "design science"	23
	(abduction OR abductive) AND "design science"	15

During the subsequent review steps, inclusion and exclusion criteria were applied. First, the titles and abstracts were read in order to quickly remove irrelevant works. Duplicates were directly excluded from the literature pool. Articles that were considered for further review had to relate to DSR in terms of a research paradigm, either applied or assessed. Furthermore, it had to be made clear that the epistemological terms are mentioned in connection with the research conducted. One particular criterion that has been found to be useful, because the artifact of a DSR project can itself be a method, was that the type of reasoning must not be a characteristic of the outcome. In the second review stage, the full texts were read and evaluated. Articles that did not sufficiently explain the details of the methodology were excluded, while only finalized research papers were included in the review. Table 2 summarizes the selection criteria.

From the initial set of 71 articles, 18 were identified as duplicates, leaving 53 for further review. After applying the criteria from the first stage, 23 articles remained. The final pool of literature consisted of 17 publications. Figure 4 illustrates the review process.

Table 2. Selection criteria for the SLR.

Stage	Inclusion criteria	Exclusion criteria
Title and abstract reading	- Examines or advances DSR as research paradigm - Utilizes a DSR methodology	- Duplicates - Epistemological terms refer to the artifact as a method
Full-text reading	- Finalized research	- No sufficient details on methodology

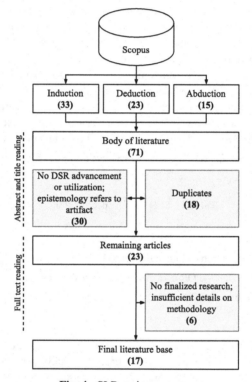

Fig. 4. SLR review process.

4   Discussion of Results

The analysis of the literature is divided into two parts. First, the quantitative findings are presented to provide a context for the importance of epistemological considerations among DSR enthusiasts. Second, the articles are discussed within a qualitative analysis to propose the generalized framework in Sect. 5.

4.1 Quantitative Analysis

Of the 17 publications, the SLR yielded 9 articles that can be characterized as philosophical works on the nature of DSR and are concerned with logical procedures. On the other hand, 8 articles cover practical applications of DSR methodologies. This distribution, especially considering that there is a myriad of DSR projects that have not been retrieved by the SLR, suggests that epistemology and its associated reasoning types are largely neglected, or at least not deemed important, by DSR practitioners. Table 3 lists the found articles explicitly on meta-science in chronological order and reflects the types of reasoning that are at least mentioned (I: induction, D: deduction, A: abduction). In this respect, researchers attempting to advance DSR from a meta-scientific perspective are apparently aware of the controversy surrounding this topic.

Table 3. Articles concerned with reasoning types.

Reference	Title	Year	Reasoning
[2]	Building theory in the sciences of the artificial	2009	I, D, A
[5]	Theorizing in design science research	2011	I, D, A
[8]	Forms of reasoning in the design science research process	2011	I, D, A
[12]	Forms of discovery for design knowledge	2012	I, D, A
[6]	Validation and design science research in information systems	2012	I, D, A
[20]	A framework for classifying design research methods	2013	I, D, A
[14]	Towards a framework for evidence-based and inductive design in information systems research	2014	I, D
[11]	Elaborating ADR while drifting away from its essence: A commentary on Mullarkey and Hevner	2019	I, D, A
[13]	Reflections on the Practice of Design Science in Information Systems	2021	I, D, A

From the found practical projects, 4 state to have used inductive methods, 3 rely on deductive methods, and 1 uses an abductive process. Table 4 lists the publications and, in addition to the columns from Table 3, the type of artifact is specified. The study by Omair and Alturki [19] represents a special case, as it addresses the extension of an existing methodology by an abductive step and performs this extension deductively according to the definitions discussed previously. As the methodology used for the extension in turn originates from the field of DSR, this study was not excluded due to the selection criteria.

From the quantitative analysis, no solid statement can be derived about the role of the type of artifact for the type of reasoning. However, looking at the inherent methods, the picture becomes clearer as to which activities are associated with which logical denotation and how the intermediate results of the design influence these.

Table 4. Articles conducting practical DSR projects.

Ref.	Title	Year	Reasoning	Artifact
[4]	Developing a Conceptual Model for Facilitating the Issuing of Digital Badges in a Resource Constrained Environment	2015	Induction	Model
[21]	ICT-platform to transform car dealerships to regional providers of sustainable mobility services	2017	Induction	Model/architecture
[18]	Exploring divergent and convergent production in idea evaluation: Implications for designing group creativity support systems	2018	Induction	Software instantiation
[22]	Testbed requirements for technology enhanced stroke rehabilitation to support independent living	2019	Deduction	Construct
[23]	A networked analysis and engineering framework for new business models	2019	Deduction	Framework/model
[19]	An improved method for taxonomy development in information systems	2020	Deduction	Taxonomy/model
[24]	Market-Driven Modularity: Design method developed under a Design Science paradigm	2022	Abduction	Method
[17]	A Goal-Oriented Framework for Implementing Change in Off-Site Construction in the Industry 4.0 Era	2022	Induction	Framework/model

4.2 Qualitative Analysis

The feature that distinguishes DSR from other branches of science is that the object under study, meaning the artifact, must be constructed prior to observation and evaluation [2]. The research process in terms of artifact development encompasses a significant portion of creativity, which is why Fischer *et al.* [12] argue that it cannot be exclusively deductive. In a previous study, Fischer and Gregor [8] investigated a variety of DSR methodologies and found that there is an application for each type of reasoning (i.e., induction, deduction, abduction, or a mixed approach) in the initial phase of at least one framework. From the practical projects that constructed a model as artifact, Salerno *et al.* [4], Wagner vom Berg *et al.* [21], and Alsakka *et al.* [17] either employed opinions of experts with a specific background, SLRs, or both to empirically form a basis for deriving generalized design requirements for the models. Ahmad *et al.* [22] also used expert interviews to derive functional requirements, which can be seen as creating a construct on which a model could be based on later. In contrast to the other studies, the insights from the interviews were used more as abstract rules to be applied to a very specific use case in a narrow domain and in a particular geographical region. Therefore, this study was characterized as deductive.

The framework and taxonomy developed by Vorraber and Müller [23] and Omair and Alturki [19], respectively, are extensions of existing methodologies, therefore corresponding to the definition of Lee *et al.* [5] that deduction is *"knowledge growth by intention"* and the process of refining and testing existing knowledge. The contribution of Gauss *et al.* [24], proposing a method for the design of modular product family structures, also builds on an SLR, but does not seek to establish generalized design principles. Instead, functional requirements are derived directly from quantitative and qualitative analyses of the literature and assumingly beneficial design choices are made.

The only practical study found concerned with assigning a specific type of reasoning to evaluation was written by Ulrich [18]. Since the artifact is a working software solution and instantiation, this study also differs from the others regarding the outcome. The design was tested inductively by using the developed artifact in a suitable context and formalizing theoretical discoveries. One conclusion from this section is that the epistemological classification of DSR projects seems to depend on the combination of the type of artifact (or intermediate outcome) and the research activity within the DSR process.

5   Generalized Framework for Reasoning in DSR

Three main observations from the examination of the literature constitute the basis for the generalized framework. First, epistemology in DSR is mainly researched in dedicated articles. Practical projects often do not invest effort in clearly positioning the research steps between induction, deduction, and abduction. This might be due to the fact that DSR is not primarily about describing or predicting reality, but changing it [6] by means of an artifact that is first to be developed [2]. Hence, meta-scientific considerations may tend to be viewed as less valuable. Second, the type of reasoning is not solely dependent on the applied specific DSR methodology, but the individual steps and (intermediate) outcomes. If the artifact itself is of theoretical nature, such as a model or method, and is based on empirically acquired data points, the process is seen as inductive. If the design process is more abstract and based on guessing or quickly finding an initial functioning yet potentially flawed solution, abduction is used. If the artifact is instantiated in a practical context and tested whether it delivers a specific result in a use case, the reasoning is deductive. The same applies if the outcome is used to iteratively improve the design. If the artifact is instantiated numerous times in order to derive generalized design principles and theory, this step can be regarded as inductive again. The third main observation is therefore that an end-to-end DSR project, from building foundational knowledge through artifact design to iterative refinement, evaluation and formalization of design knowledge, requires at least induction *and* deduction, and additionally abduction when appropriate. In this sense, Winter [14] reflects that the combination of inductive and deductive methods could offer great potential. Figure 5 presents the generalized framework on the presumed roles of induction, deduction, and abduction in DSR.

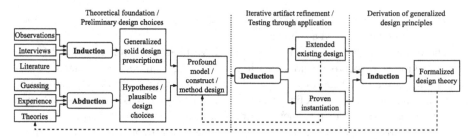

Fig. 5. Generalized framework on roles of reasoning types in DSR.

6 Conclusion

The classification of DSR methodologies and projects as inductive, deductive, or abductive is controversial among scholars. While some clearly allocate certain methodologies to a specific branch of reasoning, others take a broader perspective. The contribution of the present paper is an in-depth investigation of generic applications of logical reasoning and DSR-specific reasoning. In contrast to previous studies, it not only argues why DSR and particular methodologies are more likely to belong to one philosophy or another, but also makes formalized analogies between DSR activities and general cases of logical reasoning, underpinning the explanations with illustrative examples. Finally, after evaluating the justification for the existence of all three types of reasoning, a generalized framework was constructed to represent the end-to-end process of DSR projects.

As a limitation, only studies that explicitly stated whether they used a logical reasoning approach were examined in this paper. A more comprehensive study could analyze DSR projects regardless of their self-designation by extending the systematic literature review approach to publications of completed design science projects that implicitly apply different types of reasoning. However, given the relatively small number of efforts to directly address DSR from a meta-scientific perspective, this work provides another point of discussion in this relatively young field of science compared to the natural and human sciences.

References

1. Simon, H.A.: The Sciences of the Artificial, 6th edn. M.I.T Press, Cambridge (1978)
2. Gregor, S.: Building theory in the sciences of the artificial. In: Proceedings of the 4th International Conference on Design Science Research in Information Systems and Technology - DESRIST 2009 (2009)
3. Peirce, C.S.: Principles of Philosophy, 3rd edn. Belknap Press of Harvard Univ. Press, Cambridge (1974)
4. Salerno, C., Ouma, S., Botha, A.: Developing a conceptual model for facilitating the issuing of digital badges in a resource constrained environment. In: Proceedings of the 2015 Annual Research Conference on South African Institute of Computer Scientists and Information Technologists (2015)
5. Lee, J.S., Pries-Heje, J., Baskerville, R.: Theorizing in design science research. In: Jain, H., Sinha, A.P., Vitharana, P. (eds.) DESRIST 2011. LNCS, vol. 6629, pp. 1–16. Springer, Heidelberg (2011). https://doi.org/10.1007/978-3-642-20633-7_1

6. Gonzalez, R.A., Sol, H.G.: Validation and design science research in information systems. In: Mora, M., Gelman, O., Steenkamp, A.L., Raisinghani, M. (eds.) Research Methodologies, Innovations and Philosophies in Software Systems Engineering and Information Systems, 403–426. IGI Global (2012)

7. Harman, G.H.: The inference to the best explanation. Phil. Rev. **74**(1), 88 (1965)

8. Fischer, C., Gregor, S.: Forms of reasoning in the design science research process. In: Jain, H., Sinha, A.P., Vitharana, P. (eds.) DESRIST 2011. LNCS, vol. 6629, pp. 17–31. Springer, Heidelberg (2011). https://doi.org/10.1007/978-3-642-20633-7_2

9. Peffers, K., Tuunanen, T., Rothenberger, M.A., Chatterjee, S.: A design science research methodology for information systems research. J. Manag. Inf. Syst. **24**(3), 45–77 (2007)

10. Sein, M.K., Henfridsson, O., Purao, S., Rossi, M., Lindgren, R.: Action design research. MIS Q. **35**(1), 37 (2011)

11. Sein, M.K., Rossi, M.: Elaborating ADR while drifting away from its essence: a commentary on Mullarkey and Hevner. Eur. J. Inf. Syst. **28**(1), 21–25 (2019)

12. Fischer, C., Gregor, S., Aier, S.: Forms of discovery for design knowledge. In: ECIS 2012 - Proceedings of the 20th European Conference on Information Systems (2012)

13. Gregor, S.: Reflections on the practice of design science in information systems. In: Aier, S., Rohner, P., Schelp, J. (eds.), Engineering the Transformation of the Enterprise, pp. 101–113. Springer, Cham (2021).https://doi.org/10.1007/978-3-030-84655-8_7

14. Winter, R.: Towards a framework for evidence-based and inductive design in information systems research. In: Helfert, M., Donnellan, B., Kenneally, J. (eds.) EDSS 2013. CCIS, vol. 447, pp. 1–20. Springer, Cham (2014). https://doi.org/10.1007/978-3-319-13936-4_1

15. Kapitan, T.: Peirce and the autonomy of abductive reasoning. Erkenntnis **37**(1), 1–26 (1992)

16. Hall, B.K.: The paradoxical platypus. Bioscience **49**(3), 211–218 (1999)

17. Alsakka, F., Hamzeh, F., Al-Hussein, M., Yu, H.: A goal-oriented framework for implementing change in off-site construction in the Industry 4.0 era. In: Construction Research Congress 2022 (2022)

18. Ulrich, F.: Exploring divergent and convergent production in idea evaluation: implications for designing group creativity support systems. CAIS, 101–132 (2018)

19. Omair, B., Alturki, A.: An improved method for taxonomy development in information systems. IJACSA **11**(4), 535–540 (2020)

20. Harnesk, D., Thapa, D.: A framework for classifying design research methods. In: vom Brocke, J., Hekkala, R., Ram, S., Rossi, M. (eds.) DESRIST 2013. LNCS, vol. 7939, pp. 479–485. Springer, Heidelberg (2013). https://doi.org/10.1007/978-3-642-38827-9_40

21. vom Berg, B.W., Marx Gómez, J., Sandau, A.: ICT-platform to transform car dealerships to regional providers of sustainable mobility services. IJIKM **12**, 37–51 (2017)

22. Ahmad, A., Mozelius, P., Ahlin, K.: Testbed requirements for technology enhanced stroke rehabilitation to support independent living. In: Proceedings of the 5th International Conference on Information and Communication Technologies for Ageing Well and e-Health (2019)

23. Vorraber, W., Müller, M.: A networked analysis and engineering framework for new business models. Sustainability **11**(21), 6018 (2019)

24. Gauss, L., Lacerda, D.P., Cauchick Miguel, P.A.: Market-driven modularity: design method developed under a design science paradigm. Int. J. Prod. Econ. **246**, 108412 (2022)

Visualizing Argumentation for Research Problem and Research Design

Knut Hinkelmann[1,3](✉) [iD], Valeriia Afonina[1](✉) [iD],
and Devid Montecchiari[1,2](✉) [iD]

[1] School of Business, FHNW University of Applied Sciences
and Arts Northwestern Switzerland, Olten, Switzerland
{knut.hinkelmann,valeriia.afonina,devid.montecchiari}@fhnw.ch
[2] School of Science and Technology, UNICAM University of Camerino,
Camerino, Italy
[3] Department of Informatics, University of Pretoria, Pretoria, South Africa

Abstract. Identification of a research-worthy problem, choosing the appropriate research design, and writing based on the conducted research high-quality research paper with a well-structured argumentation is a complex and multifaceted process. Therefore, employing a comprehensive approach when identifying a research problem and composing research papers is crucial to structuring the process. Design Science Research (DSR) is a commonly applied strategy in research in Information Systems. Even though this methodology has a detailed description of every research phase, for some novice researchers it is challenging to have a comprehensive overview of their research project, from the argumentation of the studied problem to the evaluation of the results. We claim that conceptual modeling can visually represent these argumentations and key elements of DSR. We provide a metamodel to represent relevant aspects of the research and the connections between them, which might be depicted as graphical elements and connectors. This approach significantly improves understanding and structuring of the research problem and design, leveraging on literature about argumentation and motivation modeling.

Keywords: Design Science Research · Research Design · Argumentation Modeling · Motivation Modelling · Conceptual Modelling

1 Introduction

The structure of the research process ensures scientific rigor and success in research projects - it is a complex and multifaceted endeavor that requires careful structuring and management [11]. Research is a systematic, logical, and empirical process that can be classified based on various dimensions [29]. It involves a series of steps, including problem formulation, literature review, hypothesis development, data collection, and data analysis [5].

© The Author(s), under exclusive license to Springer Nature Switzerland AG 2024
M. Mandviwalla et al. (Eds.): DESRIST 2024, LNCS 14621, pp. 168–181, 2024.
https://doi.org/10.1007/978-3-031-61175-9_12

Identifying a research problem is the first step in the research process, as it sets the stage for the entire study [25]. An argumentation for a "research worthy" problem [5] is based on a gap in existing knowledge and a need in the environment in which the research results might make a change. This will allow for formulating a problem statement - an essential element guiding the research. A problem statement should demonstrate that the research problem is significant, researchable, and relevant [24,31]. Deriving a research-worthy problem and having a convincing and appropriate research design is based on a good overview of the current state of the art in the body of knowledge and the environment [9]. Statements should be matched with evidence from both sides (environment and literature) to have a valuable conclusion of the research. To solve a problem, decisions need to be made based on different facts and arguments, as "not all problems are research-worthy and not all research-worthy problems are appropriate for design and development research methods" [5].

Visualizing complex argumentation can help in this process [14,30], as it allows for a clear representation of different perspectives, reasoning, and evidence. Conceptual modeling is widely used in information systems [12,13,21]. Conceptual models are created using predefined key concepts, their attributes, and relationships between them [22,33]. These models are often represented visually using diagrams or graphs. There are conceptual modeling approaches for modeling argumentation like Toulmin's model [30] and modeling the reasons for decision making like the Business Motivation Model [23]. There also exists an argumentation ontology for scientific papers [35]. However, a conceptual modeling language dedicated to visualizing the complex argumentation for identifying a research problem, determining a research contribution, and choosing an appropriate research strategy would be helpful for understanding the essential elements that have an impact on the research.

This paper applies conceptual modeling to visualize argumentation for the research problem and design. We harmonized the findings from the literature on conceptual, motivation, and argumentation modeling languages for the domain of design science research.

2   Literature Review

This section provides an overview of the existing literature on identifying a research problem, visualization of argumentation, and conceptual modeling in the research problem and argumentation visualization.

2.1   Identification of a Research-Worthy Problem

To address a specific research problem effectively, a thorough analysis of existing knowledge and its practical applications is imperative [28]. Formulating research goals with accompanying sub-goals, substantiated with detailed process descriptions, allows for a nuanced examination of the subject [28]. Significance, relevance, and researchability of the research problem must be justified [6]. The relevance and applicability of the research-worthy problem are established through a review of the scientific literature, motivating and justifying the research [9]. Rigor and relevance are key components of research-worthiness [5]. Hevner underscores the importance of combining rigor and relevance, advocating a three-cycle app-roach [10]. Balancing rigor and relevance in research problems generates insights that benefit scientific understanding and societal impact.

The cyclic nature of the research process (Fig. 1) emphasizes revisiting defined goals after research stages, ensuring alignment with evolving understand-ing. This iterative approach enhances research depth and validity, contributing to the study's coherence, relevance, and applicability within the larger field con-text.

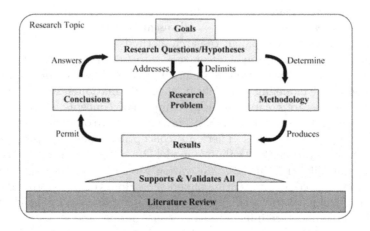

Fig. 1. Conceptual Map of the Problem-Based Research Cycle [5]

The cyclic approach allows researchers to extract a research-worthy prob-lem and build an argument based on scientific evidence. A practical guide, deconstructing the components of a research-worthy problem is beneficial for the research community. A comprehensive and multi-methodological approach helps identify persistent challenges in any field needing deeper understanding [17,19]. The Design Science Research (DSR) methodology, with its three essen-tial cycles [10], allows researchers to refine interventions and improve theoretical understanding iteratively. Visualizing argumentation for research problems and design aids in understanding different components and cycles involved in con-ducting design science research. Ellis and Levy argue that a research-worthy problem should be supported by evidence relevant to the environment [5]. While DSR lacks specific guidelines on identifying research-worthy problems, Maed-che et al. present a conceptual model for delineating the problem space in DSR projects [18].

Maedche et al.'s conceptual model (Fig. 2) is a valuable tool for overcoming difficulties in grounding, situating, diagnosing, and resolving research problems in the DSR context [18]. This approach underscores the complexity of the DSR

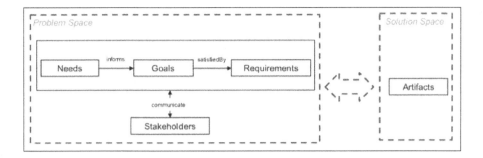

Fig. 2. Conceptual Model of the Problem Space [18]

process and ongoing efforts to streamline problem identification for more effective and impactful research outcomes.

2.2 Conceptual Modeling for Visualization of Research Problems

Conceptual modeling is a technique for representing the structure and relationships of a domain or problem [12,13,21]. It involves identifying and defining key concepts, their attributes, and the relationships between them [22,33]. These models are often represented visually using diagrams or graphs, allowing for a clear and intuitive understanding of the complex relationships within the domain. Conceptual modeling serves as a skeleton, providing a structured framework for understanding and organizing their research ideas. Understanding and using conceptual frameworks are essential tools in scientific problem-solving. Rapp [26] discusses the role of mental models in science education and their relationship to visualizations, highlighting the need for deeper comprehension and logical reasoning. Kostousov and Simonova [15] focus on the effective use of visual modeling tools in high school programming education, demonstrating their potential to reduce the difficulty of problem-solving tasks. Conceptual models are central for analyzing and designing Information Systems (IS) [20,34]. Conceptual models can help to understand complex systems, supporting communication and collaboration among stakeholders and understanding of the domain [34]. Collectively, these studies underscore the significance of conceptual modeling in visualizing research problems, particularly in enhancing understanding, reasoning, and problem-solving. Many approaches exist for modeling an argumentation, motivation, research problem, and process. Zhou et al. [35] developed the Scientific Paper Argumentation Ontology (SAO) to illustrate the interplay between argumentation logic and specific content in scientific papers (see Fig. 3). SAO employs an argumentation graph to encapsulate the semantic annotation in forming the argumentative structure within scientific research. It thus contributes to a more systematic and visual exploration of research dynamics. This approach facilitates a comprehensive overview of the research and supports researchers in constructing and visualizing arguments.

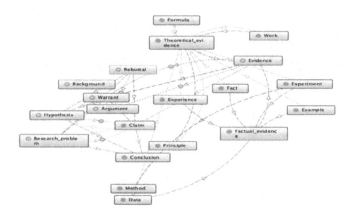

Fig. 3. The structure of SAO [35]

Toulmin [30] has previously explored systematic representations of argumentation and laid the groundwork for visualizing problem approaches that defy simplistic categorization, documented in notations. Toulmin's model of argumentation provides a framework for analyzing and evaluating arguments and consists of six main components: claim, grounds, warrant, backing, qualifier, and rebuttal [1]. This model was essential in communication and composition studies in the late twentieth century [1]. Toulmin's argumentation model (Fig. 4) helps to assess arguments' validity through evidence selection and reasoning components like warrants and backings [1,7]. It explains how grounds are used to justify claims through warrants backed by additional support or presumptions. However, some scholars have difficulty distinguishing between data, warrant, and

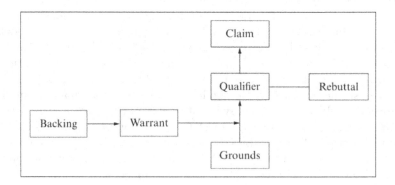

Fig. 4. Toulmin's Model [30]

backing components within the model. Attempts have been made to address this issue by consolidating these elements into one component called "grounds," but assessing its quality remains challenging [7,8].

Visualizing argumentation can be a helpful strategy to address these challenges and enhance the understanding and application of Toulmin's argumentation model in research problems and research design. IBIS, or Issue-Based Information System, functions as an argumentation system and outlines the fundamental components of all analysis and design discussions [16]. The graphical representation of IBIS (gIBIS) provides a visual framework that helps stakeholders visualize the connections between issues, positions, and arguments, thus facilitating a deeper understanding of the problem at hand [2]. It embodies and extends IBIS language for deliberation to support the'argumentative design' approach to complex societal dilemmas [27]. This visualization enhances critical thinking, facilitates the exploration of diverse perspectives, and ultimately supports the resolution of complex problems. In research problem visualization and research design, IBIS notation allows stakeholders to engage in structured discussions and develop a comprehensive understanding of complex problems, provides a structured approach to problem-solving by facilitating the systematic exploration of issues and their interconnections [3,4,27].

The Business Motivation Model (BMM) is another approach that can be used to visualize argumentation for research problems and research design (Fig. 5). The Business Motivation Model provides a holistic framework for visualizing argumentation in research problems and research design [23]. It allows stakeholders to identify and analyze the motivations and goals driving a research problem and the resources, constraints, and activities involved. The elements of BMM allow the display of the goal or goals the company wants to achieve, what strategy, tactics, and objectives need to be defined to achieve it, what might influence the results, etc. These elements have similarities with elements of the gIBIS notation, such as issues, positions, and arguments. They might be integrated to provide a comprehensive visualization of the argumentation of research-worthy problems and research design.

Combining the existing approaches of argumentation for a research problem and conceptual modeling for visualizing a research problem and research design argumentation through approaches such as IBIS, and BMM can enhance the effectiveness and clarity of the research process. This approach can help researchers to organize and analyze complex information, identify connections between different elements of the research, and make well-informed decisions, proving the research-worthiness of the researched problem and an appropriate research design.

3   Methodology

This study used the Design Science Research Methodology (DSR). The analysis of research papers and project reports revealed that argumentation for research problem and research design lack clarity and have gaps in their argumentation, in

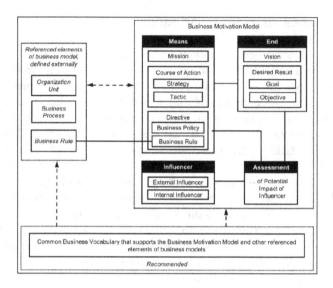

Fig. 5. BMM Overview [23]

particular concerning the synthesis and evaluation of the findings from literature [17]. Based on that, approaches for visualization of argumentations are identified (see Sect. 2). The artifact is the metamodel for visualizing argumentation for research problems and research design; the metamodel can create a modeling language specific to DSR. The suggested modeling language helps to facilitate a better understanding and communication of the research structure, reasoning for the research worthiness of the problem, and choosing a research design.

4   Suggestion

The modeling languages identified in the literature review have peculiarities that can be harmonized in a single, comprehensive modeling language for visualizing argumentation for research problems and research designs. We suggest building the metamodel by reusing and specializing part of the BMM metamodel and integrating it with the literature review on design science research, conceptual modeling, and motivation modeling findings. These domains have similarities in how argumentation is described but usually differ in terminology, focus, and content. For example, a methodology or concept that is published in a scientific paper could be visualized as an *Influencer* concept from BMM. Its influence on the practical problem could be assessed as a strength or a weakness, while influencers from the environment could be assessed as an opportunity or threat. Toulmin's argumentation model provides a classification for evaluating the arguments, such as grounds, backing, and rebuttal. These concepts have a similar purpose and would be combined with the BMM concepts that allow a more detailed evaluation of the influencers.

In the conceptual model suggested by Maedche [18], the Problem Space and the Solution Space are shown together to emphasize the relationship between the needs, goals, and requirements that form and influence a research problem from one side and research design on the other hand. In agreement with this conceptual model, we define a metamodel to create a modeling language representing a research problem and research design argumentation in a single model.

5   Implementation

As described earlier, the proposed metamodel (Fig. 6) consists of elements that are borrowed from the BMM metamodel, Toulmin's argumentation model, and the research domain itself. In the problem space, we start with the collection and analyses of the influencers, that are represented based on the BMM *Influencer* element, where *Environment* plays the role of an *External Influencer* and finding and influencer in the *Body of Knowledge* corresponds to an *Internal Influencer*.

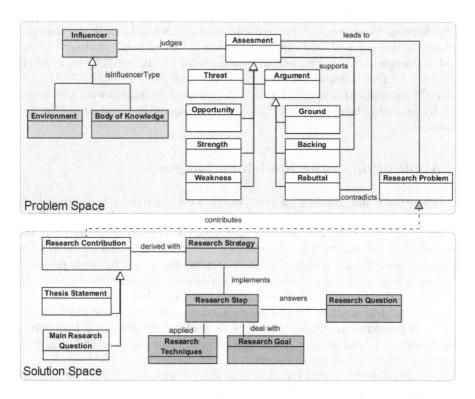

Fig. 6. Proposed metamodel to visualize argumentation for research problem and research design

Several types of assessments can be applied to the identified influencers. The *Assessment* element can be either one of the aspects of Toulmin's argumentation model [30] that are used to demonstrate evaluation of the arguments - *Ground*, *Backing*, and *Rebuttal* or BMM concepts such as *Strength*, *Weakness*, *Opportunity*, and *Threat*. Each of the identified and assessed influencers can lead to a research problem. *Arguments* can support or contradict an *Assessment*. The appropriate connections reflect this. Such visualization of concepts within a problem space allows the representation of the impact of findings from the environment and the body of knowledge for the research problem in an easily understandable form. This then leads to identifying the research problem and building up a strong argumentation line. The *Research Problem* can be regarded as the overall goal of the research and is a specialization of the *Vision* element of BMM.

Once the research problem is identified, the research contribution can be formulated. The *Research Contribution* is a specialization of the *Mission* element of BMM. It can be presented as a *Thesis Statement* or as a *Main Research Question*.

The solution space represents means for addressing the research problem and delivering the research contribution. Based on the desired research contribution the *Research strategy* can be chosen. According to the research strategy, a researcher can decompose the research into *Research Steps*. In DSR, the *Research Strategy* is decomposed into different *Research Phases* (e.g., awareness of the problem, suggestion, development evaluation, and conclusion [32]) to structure the research. The *Research Strategy* and *Research Step* are specializations of the BMM elements *Strategy* and *Tactic*. A *Research Step* deals with a *Research goal*. By applying the appropriate *Research Techniques*, *Research Questions* can be answered.

6   Application of the Modelling Language

To demonstrate the usability of the visualization approach, we applied it to the research problem of this paper. Figure 7 shows the problem space. There are *Influencers* from the *Environment* and from the *Body of Knowledge*. It was observed that researchers have difficulties identifying a research problem when they make a literature review and that argumentation for research problems often lacks clarity, making it difficult to understand. On the other hand side, the BMM and argumentation modeling methods have been found in the body of knowledge, which allow for tracing decision making and modeling pros and cons in argumentation. These *Assessments* lead to the *Research Problem* of how visualization can support researchers in developing and articulating their research problem and research design.

The intended *Research Contribution*, here phrased as a *Thesis Statement*, is the connector between problem space and solution space, as it *contributes* to the *Research Problem*. It appears in the solution space because the research strategy channels efforts towards its validation. In this research, the Design Science Research Strategy is applied, which is further decomposed in the *Research Phases*. We chose research phases from Vaishnavi and Kuechler [32]. Each of the *Research Phases* answers a *Research Question*.

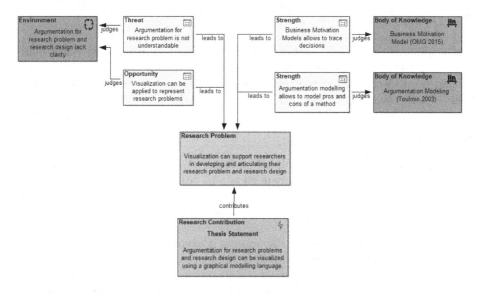

Fig. 7. Visualization of the problem space for this research

It is possible to also add *Research Techniques* and *Research Objectives*. This is left out in the figure for space limitations and to improve readability (Fig. 8).

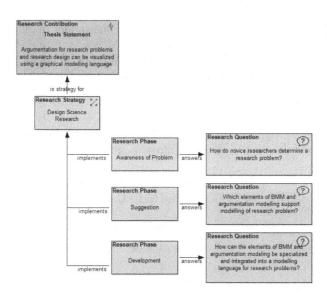

Fig. 8. Visualization of the solution space for this research

7   Discussion

We evaluate the proposed solution using SWOT analysis principles. When making our evaluation regarding different aspects of the developed modeling language, we also considered the results and experiences of three student groups and a Ph.D. student who independently researched the visualization of research problems and research design.

Strengths:

- *Unified Representation*: Combines problem and solution spaces, offering a holistic view of research argumentation and design.
- *Leverages Established Frameworks*: Integrates concepts from Toulmin's argumentation model, IBIS, and BMM, building upon existing strengths and familiarity.
- *Structured Problem-Solving*: Encourages systematic analysis and decision-making through clear visualization of influences, goals, and strategies.
- *Improved Communication*: Provides a structured language for researchers to explain and discuss their reasoning, enhancing clarity and collaboration.
- *Domain neutral*: Applicable across various research fields, increasing potential reach and impact.

Weaknesses:

- *Novelty and Lack of Validation*: Limited empirical evidence demonstrating its effectiveness in real-world research settings.
- *Potential Complexity*: Learning and applying the model might require time and effort, potentially discouraging adoption.
- *Limited Scope of Toulmin Model*: Adapting Toulmin's model for broader argumentation within the research context might require further development.

Opportunities:

- *Empirical Validation*: Conducting studies to test and validate the model across different research domains could strengthen its credibility and encourage adoption.
- *Collaboration and Refinement*: Partnering with researchers from various fields can provide valuable feedback and lead to further development and refinement of the model.
- *Tailoring for Specific Domains*: Adapting the model to specific research fields could address domain-specific needs and increase its appeal.

Threats:

- *Resistance to Change*: Researchers might be reluctant to adopt a new approach if it requires significant changes to their established workflows.
- *Limited Awareness*: Lack of awareness about the model and its potential benefits could hinder its widespread adoption.

- *Oversimplification of Complex Research*: The model might not capture the full complexity of all research problems and design.
- *Misinterpretation or Misuse*: Lack of clear guidelines and training could lead to misinterpretation or misuse of the model.
- *Return on modeling effort*: Researchers might be reluctant to invest time in modeling their research as it is not easy to estimate its return.

In the next iteration of the design cycle, this assessment will be expanded with a real-world evaluation of the method. In the module "Research Methodology for Information Systems" in the Master of Science in Business Information Systems at FHNW, in each semester 10 to 12 groups of students work on a research projects. Students will apply the visualization method in the next two semesters for their research proposal. Based on their experience, the visualization method will be refined to eliminate existing weaknesses and overcome the threads.

8   Conclusion

The suggested metamodel leverages Design Science Research Methodology (DSR) and proposes a novel modeling language by integrating Toulmin's Model, IBIS language, and the Business Motivation Model (BMM). The extension of the Business Motivation model with argumentative elements enables the visual representation of both the problem space and the solution space for DSR. This modeling language empowers researchers to organize and analyze complex information, identify crucial connections within the research domain, and make informed decisions. Combining structured argumentation for the research problem with conceptual modeling enhances research clarity and effectiveness.

This methodology strengthens the research-worthiness of identified problems by emphasizing the intricate relationship between the problem and solution spaces. Highlighting the influences, needs, goals, and requirements shaping a research problem and, therefore, might be a valuable contribution to the field, providing researchers across various domains with a powerful tool to visualize, analyze, and communicate the argumentation, problem statement, and research design in a structured and comprehensive manner.

References

1. Andrews, R.: Models of argumentation in educational discourse. Text-Interdisc. J. Study Discourse **25**, 107–127 (2005). https://doi.org/10.1515/text.2005.25.1.107
2. Conklin, J., Begeman, M.L.: gIBIS: a hypertext tool for exploratory policy discussion. ACM Trans. Inf. Syst. (TOIS) **6**(4), 303–331 (1988)
3. Conklin, J., Begeman, M.L.: gIBIS: A tool for all reasons. J. Am. Soc. Inf. Sci. **40**(3), 200–213 (1989)
4. De Moor, A., Weigand, H.: Effective communication in virtual adversarial collaborative communities. J. Community Inform. **2**(2) (2006)
5. Ellis, T.J., Levy, Y.: Framework of problem-based research: a guide for novice researchers on the development of a research-worthy problem. Informing Sci. Int. J. Emerg. Transdisc. **11**, 017–033 (2008).https://doi.org/10.28945/438

6. Ellis, T.J., Levy, Y.: Data sources for scholarly research: towards a guide for novice researchers. In: InSITE 2012: Informing Science+ IT Education Conference, vol. 12, pp. 405–416 (2012)

7. Erduran, S., Simon, S., Osborne, J.: Tapping into argumentation: developments in the application of Toulmin's argument pattern for studying science discourse. Sci. Educ. **88**(6), 915–933 (2004)

8. Faize, F.A., Husain, W., Nisar, F.: A critical review of scientific argumentation in science education. Eurasia J. Math. Sci. Technol. Educ. **14**(1), 475–483 (2017)

9. Hevner, A., Chatterjee, S.: Design Research in Information Systems: Theory and Practice. Springer, New York (2010). https://doi.org/10.1007/978-1-4419-5653-8

10. Hevner, A.R.: A three cycle view of design science research. Scand. J. Inf. Syst. **19**(2), 4 (2007)

11. Horváth, I.: Structuring the process of design research-a necessary step towards ensuring scientific rigor. In: DS 75-2: Proceedings of the 19th International Conference on Engineering Design (ICED 2013), Design for Harmonies, Volume 2: Design Theory and Research Methodology, Seoul, Korea (2013)

12. Karagiannis, D., Lee, M., Hinkelmann, K., Utz, W. (eds.): Domain-Specific Conceptual Modeling: Concepts, Methods and ADOxx Tools. Springer, Cham (2022). https://doi.org/10.1007/978-3-030-93547-4

13. Karagiannis, D., Mayr, H.C., Mylopoulos, J. (eds.): Domain-Specific Conceptual Modeling. Springer, Cham (2016). https://doi.org/10.1007/978-3-319-39417-6

14. Khambete, P.: Adaptation of Toulmin's model of argumentation for establishing rigour and relevance in design research. In: Chakrabarti, A. (ed.) Research into Design for a Connected World, vol. 134, pp. 3–13. Springer, Singapore (2019). https://doi.org/10.1007/978-981-13-5974-3_1

15. Kostousov, S.A., Simonova, I.V.: Visual modeling for exploratory problem solving on computer science lessons. In: 16th International Conference on Cognition and Exploratory Learning in Digital Age, CELDA 2019, pp. 265–272 (2019)

16. Kunz, W., Rittel, H.: Issues as elements of information systems. Technical report, Institute of Urban and Regional Development, University of California, Berkeley, California (1970)

17. Levy, Y., Ellis, T.J.: A systems approach to conduct an effective literature review in support of information systems research. Informing Sci. J. **9** (2006)

18. Maedche, A., Gregor, S., Morana, S., Feine, J.: Conceptualization of the problem space in design science research. In: Tulu, B., Djamasbi, S., Leroy, G. (eds.) DESRIST 2019. LNCS, vol. 11491, pp. 18–31. Springer, Cham (2019). https://doi.org/10.1007/978-3-030-19504-5_2

19. Marchisotti, G.G., Filho, J.R.F.: Application of a multi-method to identify a research problem. Revista de Administracao Contemporanea **26** (2022). https://doi.org/10.1590/1982-7849rac2022210020.en

20. Moody, D.L.: Theoretical and practical issues in evaluating the quality of conceptual models: current state and future directions. Data Knowl. Eng. **55**(3), 243–276 (2005)

21. Mylopoulos, J.: Conceptual modelling and telos. In: Conceptual Modelling, Databases, and CASE: An Integrated View of Information System Development, pp. 49–68 (1992)

22. Olivé, A.: Conceptual Modeling of Information Systems. Springer, Heidelberg (2007). https://doi.org/10.1007/978-3-540-39390-0

23. OMG: Business motivation model, version 1.3. Technical report, Object Management Group (2015). https://www.omg.org/spec/BMM/1.3/PDF

24. Österle, H., et al.: Memorandum on design-oriented information systems research. Eur. J. Inf. Syst. **20**(1), 7–10 (2011). https://doi.org/10.1057/ejis.2010.55
25. Peffers, K., Tuunanen, T., Rothenberger, M.A., Chatterjee, S.: A design science research methodology for information systems research. J. Manag. Inf. Syst. **24**(3), 45–77 (2007)
26. Rapp, D.N.: Mental models: theoretical issues for visualizations in science education. In: Gilbert, J.K. (ed.) Visualization in Science Education. MMSE, vol. 1, pp. 43–60. Springer, Dordrecht (2005). https://doi.org/10.1007/1-4020-3613-2_4
27. Rittel, H., Noble, D.: Issue-based information systems for design. Institute of Urban and Regional Development, University of California, Berkeley (1989)
28. Streeb, D., El-Assady, M., Keim, D.A., Chen, M.: Why visualize? Arguments for visual support in decision making. IEEE Comput. Graph. Appl. **41**, 17–22 (2021). https://doi.org/10.1109/MCG.2021.3055971. https://scite.ai/reports/why-visualize-arguments-for-visual-ejgVgD0K
29. Supino, P.G.: Overview of the research process. In: Supino, P., Borer, J. (eds.) Principles of Research Methodology: A Guide for Clinical Investigators, pp. 1–14. Springer, New York (2012). https://doi.org/10.1007/978-1-4614-3360-6_1
30. Toulmin, S.E.: The Uses of Argument. Cambridge University Press, Cambridge (2003)
31. Tracy, S.J.: Taking the plunge: a contextual approach to problem-based research. Commun. Monogr. **74**(1), 106–111 (2007)
32. Vaishnavi, V., Kuechler, B.: Design science research in information systems (2004). http://desrist.org/design-research-in-information-systems/
33. Wand, Y., Weber, R.: An ontological analysis of the relationship construct in conceptual modeling. ACM Trans. Database Syst. **24**, 494–528 (1999)
34. Wand, Y., Weber, R.: Research commentary: information systems and conceptual modeling-a research agenda. Inf. Syst. Res. **13**(4), 363–376 (2002)
35. Zhou, H., Song, N., Chang, W., Wang, X.: Linking the thoughts within scientific papers: construction and visualization of argumentation graph. Proc. Assoc. Inf. Sci. Technol. **56**(1), 757–759 (2019)

Toward a Method for Design Science Research Meta-Studies to Improve the Reusability of Design Principles

Bijan Khosrawi-Rad$^{(\boxtimes)}$ ⓘ, Linda Grogorick ⓘ, Timo Strohmann ⓘ,
and Susanne Robra-Bissantz ⓘ

TU Braunschweig, Mühlenpfordtstr. 23, 38106 Braunschweig, Germany
{b.khosrawi-rad,l.grogorick,t.strohmann,
s.robra-bissantz}@tu-braunschweig.de

Abstract. Design science research (DSR) is an established approach to create innovative artifacts while considering relevance and rigor. Design principles (DPs) are the most common knowledge contribution. However, DPs are often not reused in the research and practice community. In this methodology paper, we propose an approach to conduct meta-studies for design knowledge to tackle the issue of low DP reusability. We developed a process model for meta-studies based on DSR-specific terms, evaluated it in an expert workshop with DSR scholars, and demonstrated its application to the example of virtual reality literature. Our meta-study model contributes to the research discussion on the reusability of DPs and is a new approach to gain more transparency about existing DPs in research and practice, enabling the community to better guide future research.

Keywords: Meta Study · DSR · Design Principle · Reusability

1 Introduction

Design science research (DSR) is an established research paradigm to develop innovative and new solutions to practice-relevant problems while ensuring scientific rigor [1]. DSR focuses on generating artifacts like software implementations, prescriptive design principles (DPs), or design theories to address real-world challenges [2]. DPs, as the most common contribution, represent abstract rules as a generalization for a class of problems [3, 4]. Scholars increasingly publish DPs for different contexts [5], but DPs are seldom reused by researchers and practitioners [6, 7]. Our paper addresses the low DP reusability, which is reflected in several issues. First, DSR authors often start from scratch to develop DPs for specific topics instead of building on existing ones [6]. Therefore, DPs do not reach the stage where they are reused multiple times and recognized as established theory [8]. Second, the DP instantiation is complex for externals, as DSR processes and outcomes are heterogeneous [5, 9] and researchers construct and formulate DPs differently [3, 5]. Third, due to their low reusability, researchers and practitioners rarely discuss DPs comprehensively to uncover limitations that would enable

M. Mandviwalla et al. (Eds.): DESRIST 2024, LNCS 14621, pp. 182–196, 2024.
https://doi.org/10.1007/978-3-031-61175-9_13

them to streamline future research [7, 10]. In other disciplines like medicine, meta-studies obtain an overview of a research area, uncover contradictions, and enable further researchers to build on the status quo [11]. Although researchers evaluated the practical reusability of DPs [10] or assessed the status quo via literature analyses [e.g., 5, 7], DSR lacks systematic meta-studies that consider DSR-specific terminology and criteria. Meta-studies extend classical literature analyses by combining the results of studies with different report metrics [11]. Considering the complexity of DSR projects, their hetero-geneous report metrics, and the need to incorporate the findings of neighboring domains when deriving and synthesizing design knowledge [5, 9, 12], a systematic meta-study method that incorporates these requirements could help researchers to discuss DPs on an overarching level. We address this research gap and propose a new approach to guide researchers in conducting DSR meta-studies. As the main value of our approach, we develop a structured process along DSR-specific criteria that tackles the complexity of DSR projects and paves the way for DPs' reusability in the long term. We apply the DSR paradigm itself following Hevner [1] to develop a process model for meta-studies as our artifact, evaluate it with DSR experts, and demonstrate its application for research on virtual reality (VR) for collaborative teamwork. We chose this field because, despite VR's potential for immersive and seamless collaboration as well as its theoretical foun-dation in other areas like education [13–15], VR applications are not yet widely accepted in practice [13]. Existing DPs that could help designers in addressing this issue are often not reusable [5]. Hence, there is a need for a meta-study that systematically captures and thoroughly analyzes the state of research on DPs for VR in collaborative work, includes related fields, and discusses contradictory findings. The main contribution of our paper is to derive a systematic meta-study method applicable to diverse DSR projects. The VR in collaborative work domain serves as our exemplary use case. We contribute to answering the following research question (**RQ**): *How could a systematic method for DSR meta-studies be designed to improve the reusability of DPs?* To contribute to solving the mentioned issues, our method aims to help researchers transfer existing knowledge to new contexts [16], instantiate it by gaining an overview of all relevant DPs [8], and discuss it [7].

2   Research Background

2.1   Design Principles and Related Work on Their Reusability

Design knowledge combines descriptive insights, detailing the problem domain and cur-rent state, and prescriptive knowledge, guiding how to achieve desired outcomes through specific designs [2]. DPs, as abstract forms of design knowledge, align the development process with both stakeholder needs and the current state of domain knowledge [3, 17]. They provide essential guidance for designing complex information systems (IS) by leveraging various levels of complexity (ibid.). The recent increase in DP papers is attributed to diverse methods in creating DPs and a deeper understanding of their con-struction phases, from formulation to evaluation and refinement [4, 9, 18]. However, many authors suggest that DPs only represent solidified knowledge when embraced as emerging theory, like being recognized in the community, widely instantiated, or applied in various contexts [2, 8].

Currently, many DPs are proposed that have not been further developed or evaluated [5]. Further scholars contributed to improving the DP reusability. Iivari et al. [10], for instance, proposed a framework for measuring the light reusability of DPs using the following criteria: accessibility, importance, novelty, actability, and effectiveness. The authors provided a questionnaire template to evaluate DPs based on these criteria. Elshan et al. [7] built on Iivari et al.'s [10] work and conducted a review on DPs for conversational agents. They assessed each DP set on a 5-point Likert scale. The authors stated that many DPs are not easily understandable and rarely bridge the gap between conceptual formulation and practice [7]. While these works mainly address practical reusability, Schoormann et al. [6] highlighted DPs' reusability in research [6]. Through a review of 114 DP articles with 226 in-text citations, they discovered that DPs are rarely reused by further scholars. Strohmann et al. [5] reviewed the construction and formulation of DPs and found that many DPs were instantiated and evaluated rudimentarily, which reduces their reusability. Gau et al. [19] developed a search engine that helps identify and build upon existing DPs. Overall, related work mainly focused on improving the communication of DPs (for practice or research). However, there is a lack of systematic approaches that guide researchers to discover DPs, analyze them on their construction, formulation, and origin, and discuss them in depth. Our approach builds on the mentioned works by proposing a meta-study method that helps create more transparency for the DP knowledge base, both for research and practice.

2.2 Meta-Studies and Systematic Reviews

Meta-studies and systematic reviews are well-established approaches for generating new knowledge by identifying, analyzing, and synthesizing quantitative study results [11]. Systematic reviews, guided by a well-defined process with carefully documented decisions, transparently collect, appraise, and combine research evidence to condense current knowledge on a particular topic [20]. In contrast, meta-studies summarize empirical knowledge by combining results from different studies. Meta-studies convert the results to one or more common metrics to synthesize findings even when studies use different reporting styles [11]. The number of systematic reviews and meta-studies has increased since the mid-1990s, especially in the health sciences [21]. In design-oriented IS, systematic reviews that summarize a topic are common (e.g., designing conversational agents [22]), but rarely reviews that process existing DPs in a structured way. Expanding the systematic reviews to emphasize different knowledge constructions and their justifications allows us to identify contradictions in existing DPs and discover starting points for future research. Therefore, our DSR meta-study method goes beyond the classical meta-studies from health sciences by not only making different empirical results comparable but by adapting this approach to DSR-specific criteria.

3 Methodology

We followed Hevner's [1] framework, encompassing the relevance, design, and rigor cycles (see Fig. 1). Within this framework, we applied the "exploring by building" approach by iteratively designing our meta-study method [12]. The **relevance cycle** aligns our research with real-world problems and ensures its applicability in practical contexts. Activities in this cycle included identifying practical issues in design science (**1**) and deriving requirements for the method (**4**), as advocated in the literature for ensuring relevance in DSR [1]. Within **the design cycle**, we first conceptualized the meta-study method based on related DSR methods papers (**5**). We then presented this version in an ex-ante evaluation according to Venable [23] to seven experts in a workshop to gain feedback before its application, especially regarding suggestions for improvement (**6**). Based on the experts' feedback, we derived recommendations for the meta-study application (**7**), which we followed when applying our approach in a case study for the example of VR (**8**). The case study served, in the sense of "exploring by building" [12], to evaluate the practical feasibility of our method, and we derived further recommendations following an ex-post evaluation procedure (**9**) [23]. The **rigor cycle** involved grounding our research in existing knowledge. This cycle included grounding our work in the theoretical foundations of design knowledge and incorporating theoretical underpinnings of meta-studies (**2**), as well as leveraging our author team's DSR experience (**3**). This cycle ensured the scientific rigor of our research and is in line with recommendations for maintaining theoretical grounding in DSR [2]. We have taken future activities as an outlook into account, such as applying the method to other examples (**10**) and improving the method (**11**).

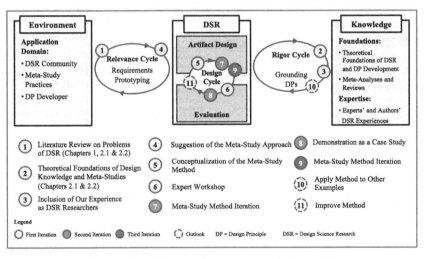

Fig. 1. Our DSR Procedure according to Hevner [1]

4 Results

4.1 Derivation of the Method for Design Science Research Meta-Studies

According to the goals defined in the introduction, we define three entry points for the meta-study. First, scholars can use a meta-study when intending to develop DPs for an under-researched area to build on existing ones (e.g., an overview of all DPs on VR if scholars examine VR for collaborative teamwork). The second entry point is the instantiation of DPs, i.e., developing a software based on an overview of all DPs. Third, scholars can use our meta-study to discuss the status quo and uncover contradictions.

Our procedure is based on alternating divergent thinking (exploring a broad solution space) and convergent thinking (narrowing down the solution space), a main concept of designing artifacts [24–26]. By alternating these ways of designerly thinking, meta-study applicants frame and reframe their perspective [27, 28]. Our process model starts with defining the purpose and scope of the analysis, depending on the entry point. For a first literature review, it suggests a broad interpretation of proper keywords (*divergent thinking*). The first DP analysis is restricted to a narrow selection of fitting articles (*convergent thinking*). Subsequently, the frame is widened again for the discussion of contradictory or inconsistent DPs by including papers with a broader focus (*divergent thinking*). Finally, we suggest deciding on a final DP set for the given context (*convergent thinking*). In the following, we explain our method and its steps (see Fig. 2).

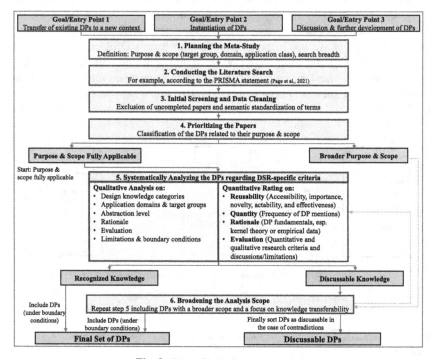

Fig. 2. Meta-Study Process Model

(1) Planning the meta-study: We suggest defining the study's purpose and scope concerning the target group, domain, or application context [3, 8], similar to the meta-characteristic in taxonomy research [29]. As this step frames the study, we suggest initially setting the focus broadly to avoid overlooking items. Generally, the study's focus will vary according to the meta-study's entry point. If the researchers aim for an extensive study of DPs related to linked topics and theoretical origins to discuss possible contradictions (entry point 3), it could be broader than if they, for example, aim for a quick overview of the DPs for an instantiation (entry point 2). The research team should carefully determine the breadth of the purpose and scope as well as the literature search (e.g., concerning related areas) to tailor them to the goals of the meta-study.

(2) Conducting the literature search: The systematic literature identification is based on the purpose and scope and follows divergent thinking [25, 26]. We recommend using established approaches for literature identification, like the PRISMA statement [20]. The latter involves defining a search term that, in our case, should be set broadly, applying it to adequate databases, and subsequently screening titles, abstracts, and full texts to get a set of relevant papers.

(3) Initial screening and data cleaning: We suggest initial article screening and data cleaning to facilitate the subsequent analysis. We recommend excluding short papers or papers without evaluation to focus on completed DSR projects. With this decision, we emphasize that the evaluation is a critical phase of DSR projects to validate design artifacts' utility, efficacy, and impact, as highlighted by Venable et al. [23]. Furthermore, we suggest assigning semantic overarching categories to the DPs, as DPs are often inconsistently formulated [5]. For example, conversational agent literature often uses synonyms like "human-like design" or "anthropomorphism" for the same meaning: "design the conversational agent with human elements" [22].

(4) Prioritizing the papers: We suggest prioritizing the papers according to the extent they fulfill the purpose and scope. The articles can be divided into "purpose and scope fully applicable" and "broader purpose and scope". Depending on the topic, further sub-areas related to the purpose and scope are possible. In the spirit of convergent thinking [24, 25], we suggest initially analyzing the papers whose purpose and scope are fully applicable and most relevant to the meta-study's goal.

(5) Systematically analyzing the DPs: The core of the meta-study is the systematic DP analysis. We recommend analyzing the papers sequentially to understand each DP in its context. Following Elshan et al. [7] and further DSR literature [e.g., 1, 3, 8, 16], we recommend carefully reviewing each DP on qualitative DSR-specific criteria: overarching design knowledge category, application domain and target group, rationale, evaluation, as well as limitations and boundary conditions. The qualitative analysis helps to decide on a quantitative rating of each DP as the main analysis. The quantitative analysis includes four sub-steps, which we will explain in the following. For scoring the DPs, we adopt the rating on a 5-point Likert scale for each DP set from Elshan et al.'s [7] review and extend this approach by suggesting to rate each DP individually. This procedure helps later to sort the DPs into recognized or discussable DPs. Discussion points and limitations can be recorded in a free text. **First**, we recommend assessing the reusability of the DPs based on the criteria defined by Iivari et al. [10] and applied by Elshan et al. [7]: accessibility, importance, novelty, actability, and effectiveness. **Second**, we recommend evaluating how frequently the DPs occur in the entire set (based on the semantic analysis from step 3), as a frequently mentioned DP could indicate its recognition in a certain domain [2]. However, only rating frequency is not sufficient, as the meta-study should include critical aspects. **Third**, we thus recommend analyzing the rationale of the DPs [3]. Researchers emphasized that DPs should be based on kernel theories [8, 30]. Further DSR scholars complement this view and argue that kernel theories are not obligatory but helpful for justification [1, 4, 31]. Hence, researchers can add empirical findings to justify certain DPs. Researchers using our meta-study should analyze whether each DP has a theoretical basis applicable to the design context or whether empirical findings like interviews support the DP [4]. When examining the theoretical basis, it is vital to validate whether the corresponding theories are transferable to the design phenomena [12]. Vaishnavi and Kuechler [22, p. 92], for instance, argue: *"We propose that "kernel* *theories" from other fields are often so narrowly derived as to be more suggestive than useful as given, and that refinement of the theory in the act of development is required to give the theory direct applicability to IS design".* **Fourth**, we suggest analyzing the DPs' evaluations, including the study design and sample size, since these validate the DPs' practical effectiveness, and scholars have criticized that many existing DPs have been evaluated rudimentarily [5, 7, 23]. The discussions and limitations should be analyzed to identify weaknesses or possible negative effects. We followed Gregor et al. [3] to define boundary conditions clearly when formulating DPs. The analysis result is an overall score covering the sum of the Likert scales in the individual categories. We recommend that the research team records which DPs tend to be recognized (under boundary conditions) and which are discussable. A threshold value (e.g., 50% of the score) can simplify this decision but should be complemented by qualitative insights.

(6) Broadening the analysis scope: The recognized knowledge can be included in the final DP set. The debatable knowledge should be examined in detail. We propose a divergent thinking phase after the last convergent thinking phase to reframe the perspective [26]. We suggest now including those papers with a broader purpose and scope to reveal whether neighboring domains or overarching DPs have already addressed debatable aspects. We recommend repeating step 5 with the added papers. A decision can then be made again regarding which DPs should be included in the final set of DPs recognized under boundary conditions and which not. We recommend finally sorting contradictory DPs as "discussable", which might not yet provide "mature" knowledge [2]. Nevertheless, we recommend articulating potential for future research, for example, which aspects should be examined to avoid contradictory design knowledge results.

4.2 Evaluation in an Expert Workshop

We evaluated our method in a workshop with seven DSR experts lasting 105 min (two postdocs and five PhD candidates, most in the last part of their PhD). All experts had expertise in developing DPs (one to eight years) and published them in an IS outlet at least once. They assessed our method it in terms of feasibility, completeness, efficacy, and reusability for further researchers, following the literature on DSR evaluations [10, 23]. The experts commented on strengths and improvement suggestions using the whiteboard tool "Miro" and formulated key takeaways related to our method. We analyzed the feedback and clustered it into suggestions for applying our method.

The participants rated positively that the procedure is *"very straightforward", "easy to understand"*, and *"actionable and comprehensible"*. They emphasized that the systematic approach helps to replicate the meta-study and increases the reusability of DPs by providing an overview of existing DPs. This *"catalog function"* of existing DPs allows researchers to save time and identify established DPs to focus on blind spots. In addition to minor suggestions on reformulations (e.g., we renamed the term "meta-characteristic" from the first version of our meta-study to "purpose and scope"), the experts addressed suggestions for the meta-study application. First, they emphasized that DPs have different levels of abstraction, from baseline DPs to very specific DPs [7, 32]. They highlighted that DPs with varying levels of abstraction are not "per se" better or worse than others. Baseline DPs can be contextualized in a specific domain for a new meaning [16]. They highlighted that the meta-study has the potential to map the different levels of abstraction by assigning superordinate categories to the DPs (see step 3). Second, they discussed the weighting of the quantitative criteria (step 5) and stated that researchers should weight the criteria individually. The "novelty" criterion should be weighted differently in an undeveloped field than in an almost saturated field. Baseline DPs like "usability" might score poorly in this category because of their low degree of novelty. However, these might be essential for practice because they might have a special meaning in a certain context. Third, the participants discussed the risk that the meta-study only reflects researchers' subjective views. They suggested including multiple perspectives during the meta-study, like a review among the authors or practical perspectives by a domain expert that accompanies the meta-study.

4.3 Demonstration of the Method for Design Science Research Meta-Studies

We applied our meta-study to the VR domain. We chose entry point 3, i.e., the discussion of existing DPs. We exemplarily tested the application of our method for this entry point in the sense of our "exploring by building" approach [12]. For comprehensibility, our demonstration includes references to the steps derived in Sect. 4.1 and the experts' suggestions for application highlighted in Sect. 4.2. Figure 3 shows how we applied the steps of our process model.

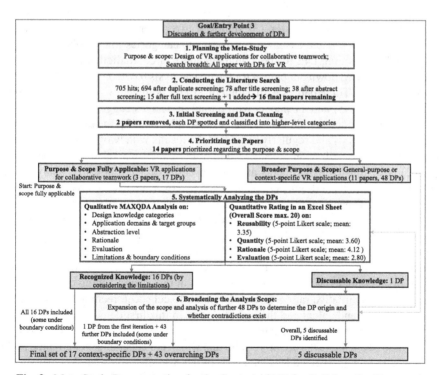

Fig. 3. Meta-Study Demonstration for the Context of VR for Collaborative Teamwork

VR applications are 3D environments that are usable via standard computer screens or additional hardware like head-mounted displays and can be entered individually or in a group [14]. We have chosen this field for the following reasons. Due to its immersive nature, VR offers the potential for teams to better communicate, coordinate tasks, and collaborate [13]. Despite the mentioned potentials and the high theoretical foundation of VR design in other areas like education, including publications in leading journals, VR is not yet accepted by its users due to design issues [13–15]. DPs can help VR designers tackle these issues, but the amount of (partly redundant and contradictory) DPs in this and adjacent domains complicates their application [5]. Hence, a meta-study contributes to a comprehensive discussion and transparency of existing VR DPs. In the following, we explain how we applied the individual process steps to this use case.

In **step (1)**, we defined the purpose and scope (designing VR applications for collaborative teamwork). In **step (2)**, we performed a literature search using the PRISMA statement [20]. We applied the following search term to the titles, abstracts, and keywords of three IS databases (705 initial hits: 679 AIS eLibrary, 12 Basket of Eight, and 14 DESRIST): *"design principle" AND ("virtual reality" OR "VR")*. We decided not to restrict the search term initially to obtain a broad overview of the entire VR literature (*divergent thinking*) and allow for a detailed DP discussion, which is in line with our entry point. Researchers applying our method can determine the search breadth individually, depending on their entry point. 694 papers remained after the duplicate screening, 78 after the title screening, 38 after the abstract screening, and 15 after the full-text screening. After adding one paper by forward search, we had a set of 16 papers on DPs for VR. We screened these in **step (3)**, removed two papers that were short papers or research notes [15, 33], and assigned superordinate categories like "usability & accessibility" to the remaining DPs to spot complementary or contradicting findings later. In **step (4)**, we narrowed down our papers for the first analysis based on their match with the purpose and scope. Three papers with a total of 17 DPs completely fulfilled our purpose and scope [14, 34, 35] and 11 papers with a total of 47 DPs suggested DPs for VR in general or specific contexts like education or health [36–45, 47]. In **step (5)**, one author performed the analysis and regularly discussed the results with two further authors who validated the results following the suggestion of our expert workshop participants (see Sect. 4.2). We adjusted assessments after a consensus decision. We first analyzed the three articles that matched our purpose and scope, covering VR for creativity support [34], interactive process modeling [35], and co-creation [14]. We used a MAXQDA code system to analyze the papers qualitatively in two subsequent coding cycles following Mayring [46]. We selected MAXQDA as an exemplary analysis tool because of its comprehensive coding capabilities that enable flexible and in-depth data handling. We analyzed the papers according to the qualitative DSR-specific criteria (see Fig. 2 and 3) in the first coding cycle and summarized codes in the second coding cycle. We then performed the quantitative rating of each DP in an Excel sheet, recorded justifications, noted limitations, and calculated the overall score. In this first demonstration, we have weighted the quantitative criteria equally (see Sect. 4.2 on the discussion of the weighting). We assessed which DPs are more solid and which are debatable. We adopted as the criteria whether a DP received less than 50% of the overall score, scored poorly on one criterion, or had major limitations. We decided on these criteria in line with Iivari et al. [10], who stated that poor performance in one of their categories indicates a DP is not reusable. Of the three papers that fully met our purpose and scope, no DP scored <50%.

We classified one DP as debatable, i.e., DP2 by Pöhler et al. [53], covering the virtual world's degree of realism. This DP was assessed very differently by Pöhler et al.'s [35] study subjects and discussed in the literature. We included all remaining DPs in the final set. In the subsequent analysis, we paid attention to the debatable DP to decide whether we should include it in the final DP set. We examined this DP with the following criteria: (1) whether it is vital to our purpose and scope, (2) whether it contains content-wise contradictions, and (3) the extent to which these contradictions have been discussed in the broader literature and whether these discussions are transferable to our purpose and scope. We broadened the horizon since this DP was rated highly on importance (Table 1) but had content-wise contradictions.

Table 1. Exemplary Analysis of one DP Set

Design Principle (DP)	Pöhler et al. (2021) - Exemplary Study with High Relevance to Purpose and Scope			
	DP1 (Easy-to-understand process notation & meaningful number of functions and 3d notation elements)	DP2 (Efficiently generated virtual representations and limited interaction)	DP3 (Collaboration and collision-free task allocation)	DP4 (Lean menu design and high-performance software and hardware standards that ensure its functionality, and make the system give confirmatory feedback to user actions)
Design Knowledge Category	Usability & Accessibility	Realism	Collaboration	Usability & Accessibility
Reusability – "Accessibility"	4 (Complex though understandable; actually, two concepts in one DP)	4 (Clearly understandable but two aspects in one DP)	4 (Clearly understandable but two aspects in one DP)	5 (Clearly understandable)
Reusability – "Importance"	5 (Conclusively emphasized)	5 (Conclusively emphasized)	5 (Conclusively emphasized)	5 (Conclusively emphasized)
Reusability – "Novelty"	4 (Not new but contextualized)	3 (Not completely new but adds details to this context)	3 (Collaboration is already given for many VR applications)	2 (Should be ensured for all software)
Reusability – "Actability"	3 (Given but room for interpretation)	3 (Exemplary instantiation; „efficiently generated" unclear)	3 (Understandable but the role assignment was only simulated)	4 (Clear but room for interpretation)
Reusability – "Effectiveness"	3 (Shown in cited studies; no comparison to existing solution)	3 (Shown in cited studies; no comparison to existing solutions)	3 (Shown in cited studies; no comparison to existing solutions)	3 (Shown in cited studies; no comparison to existing solutions)
Score Reusability	3.8	3.6	3.6	3.8
Quantity	3 (Specific in the context; belongs to a widely addressed category)	3 (Virtual representations often cited; efficiency & limited interaction not)	3 (Not often mentioned for VR, but grounded in collaboration literature)	5 (Usability and functionality standards were often addressed)
Score Quantity	3	3	3	5
Rationale	4 (Kernel theory and literature; DP combines two different aspects)	4 (Kernel theory and literature; DP combines two different aspects)	3 (Kernel theory and literature; DP combines two different aspects; psychological safety not clear)	4 (Conclusively justified but not surprising)
Score Rationale	4	4	3	4
Evaluation	3 (Various evaluation cycles; small sample size; no benchmark)	3 (Various evaluation cycles; small sample size; no benchmark)	3 (Various evaluation cycles; small sample size; no benchmark)	3 (Various evaluation cycles; small sample size; no benchmark)
Score Evaluation	3	3	3	3
Overall Score (Sum Reusability, Quantity, Rationale, and Evaluation)	13.8	13.6	12.6	15.8
Discussion	-	Was perceived differently and critically discussed (e.g., distractions); only vital locations should be illustrated realistically	-	-
Decision after Step 5	Recognized Knowledge	Discussable Knowledge	Recognized Knowledge	Recognized Knowledge
Final Decision	Final Set of DPs	Final Set of DPs	Final Set of DPs	Final Set of DPs

In **step (6)**, we analyzed 11 additional articles on general virtual world design [45], learning [39, 40, 42, 44], health [36, 47], or further domains [37, 38, 41, 43]. Previous literature critically discussed virtual worlds' realism. A too-realistic design could create cognitive load [38, 42], reduce usability during navigation [47], and be complex to implement [38, 40]. However, the DP category "realism" was considered vital in contexts in which an accurate real-world representation simulates situations that would be costly or dangerous in the real world, like car driving experiments [43] or fire safety training [39]. Hence, the DP has a context-specific meaning and need of design depth. Many papers stressed balancing realism and complexity, especially for older adults [35, 38, 41]. We decided to include this DP in the final set under the boundary condition of balancing between complexity and reality. Figure 4 shows examples of our analysis' superior categories, subcategories, and DPs.

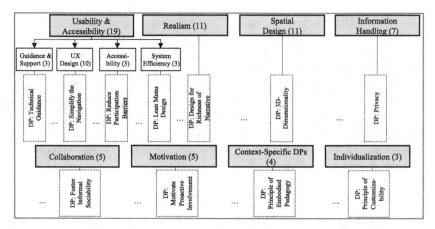

Fig. 4. Excerpts of the DP Clustering

Broadening our analysis helped us understand the overarching categories and abstraction levels, as our evaluation participants highlighted (Sect. 4.2). The DP clustering shows that many DPs have a similar origin. The DP categories "usability & accessibility", "realism", and "spatial design" were frequently mentioned. We checked the overall score for the DPs with a broader purpose and scope and recorded boundary conditions (e.g., that designers should leverage the costs when applying 3D objects [40]). The broader literature included five DPs with a score <50% (DP2, 4 and 5 in [45], DP1 and 2 in [40]). After closer analysis, this score was not due to low importance or content-wise contradictions but because the DPs were formulated too abstractly or not evaluated thoroughly. We have finally marked these as debatable.

We provide the **complete Excel sheet** to transparently show how we analyzed the DPs and allow further researchers to use it for their meta-study: https://doi.org/https://doi.org/10.6084/m9.figshare.25514809.

5   Discussion

Overall, our method was applicable to create transparency about existing DPs and uncover and resolve critical aspects, as highlighted by the experts, and demonstrated in the VR example. Regarding rigor, for example, we found that the DPs rarely build on previous ones. In our view, this reveals the issues of purely additive work, which could prevent sustained design knowledge contributions. Regarding relevance, we revealed that discussing existing DPs from different sources to understand their intent reveals issues at higher abstraction levels and could be crucial for their practical use.

To reflect on the findings of our "exploring by building" approach, we **derive six recommendations (#R1–#R6) as design knowledge** for the application of the meta-study based on the evaluation (Sect. 4.2) and demonstration (Sect. 4.3) [12]. First, our evaluation participants and case study showed that DPs are formulated very individually, making it difficult to synthesize them. Many DPs combine several design aspects in one DP (e.g., DP1–DP3 of Table 1). Instead, we recommend assigning overarching categories to the DPs to gain an overview of thematically similar DPs and their abstraction levels (**#R1**). By systematically dealing with the foundation of DPs, we see the opportunity for DPs to evolve into design theory [2, 8]. Second, the evaluation and demonstration revealed that the criteria should be weighted individually depending on the meta-study's goal (**#R2**). In our case study, we aimed to discuss the DPs (entry point 3) and weighted the criteria equally. If researchers aim to transfer DPs to a new context (entry point 1), they could weight novelty higher. If they aim for an instantiation, the quantity could be more vital (entry point 2). For example, usability DPs scored well on frequency or importance but less on novelty. Third, researchers should consider multiple perspectives when applying the meta-study to reduce researcher bias, for instance, by reviewing each other (**#R3**). Fourth, we suggest evaluating the DPs quantitatively (with the criteria reusability, quantity, rationale, and evaluation), accompanied by qualitative coding (with the criteria design knowledge category, application domain and target group, rationale, evaluation, as well as limitations and boundary conditions). By combining both analyses, we were able to assess the DPs reasonably. For instance, we decided on the final sorting by analyzing whether the corresponding DP had less than 50% of the overall score, scored poorly on one criterion, or had major limitations. We recommend adopting this systematic quantitative and qualitative assessment (**#R4**). Fifth, we created new knowledge on handling discussable design aspects by broadening the horizon and resolving possible contradictions. We have analyzed the discussable DP related to realism in three steps, which we recommend adopting (**#R5**): Examination of importance for the purpose and scope (*Is this DP important to the purpose and scope?*), examination of content-wise contradictions (*Does this DP contradict existing literature and empirical evidence?*), and examination of the broader literature (*To what extent were contradictions regarding this DP already discussed in the broader literature and are these discussions transferable to our purpose and scope?*). Sixth, we noticed that many DPs were formulated abstractly, possibly due to the nature of DPs, which intend to apply to a specific class of problems [2, 3]. However, abstract DP formulations may cause lower insightfulness (as seen for usability). Many DPs lack guidance for practitioners on how to implement them, are difficult to understand, and leave room for interpretation, causing a gap between their formulation and practical relevance [10, 48]. Thus, we recommend translating DPs into less abstract formulations based on the meta-study's results, like shorter practice-oriented DPs [10] (**#R6**).

We admit our paper's limitations. We focused on analyzing DPs and did not yet include further contributions like design guidelines or features [2] to present the first suggestion of a meta-study while balancing its complexity. Future research can extend our method by focusing on further contributions. Second, our process model ends with categorizing DPs into final and discarded DPs. Future research may look at extending our method by bridging the gap to the actual reuse, e.g., through tool support. We would like to emphasize that actual DP reuse cannot be achieved solely by applying our methodology; it also requires building an awareness in the community, a process that can only be achieved over a longer period. Third, we only applied our method exemplarily to the VR context. We will apply our method to other contexts and entry points, further explore our recommendations, encourage externals to use it, and iteratively refine it.

6 Conclusion

In this paper, we have rigorously developed a method for DSR meta-studies, evaluated it with experts, applied it for the example of VR literature, and developed it further by providing recommendations for its application. During our procedure, we noticed that this method helps uncover vital issues in DSR, like the abstract formulation of DPs or the lack of their discussion. Our paper **contributes to research** regarding the reusability of DPs [6, 7, 10, 19] by presenting a new approach to analyze them on a meta-level. This method paper guides researchers in conducting meta-studies, and we encourage them to build on existing DPs instead of starting from scratch. We suggest using our method to transfer existing DPs to a new context, instantiate them, or engage in discussions about them. We plan to apply this method to other topics and discuss it with the DSR community. We like to call to extend our method, e.g., with tools that visualize the results or support the instantiation. Our paper **contributes to practice** by presenting a method that creates more transparency about existing DPs. Increased transparency on DPs makes it easier for practitioners to instantiate research results.

Disclosure of Interests. The authors have no competing interests to declare that are relevant to the content of this article.

References

1. Hevner, A.: A three cycle view of design science research. Scand. J. Inf. Syst. **19**, 87–92 (2007)
2. Gregor, S., Hevner, A.R.: Positioning and presenting design science research for maximum impact. MIS Q. **37**(2), 337–355 (2013)
3. Gregor, S., Chandra Kruse, L., Seidel, S.: The anatomy of a design principle. J. Assoc. Inf. Syst. **21**, 1622–1652 (2020)
4. Möller, F., Guggenberger, T.M., Otto, B.: Towards a method for design principle development in information systems. In: Hofmann, S., Müller, O., Rossi, M. (eds.) DESRIST 2020. LNCS, vol. 12388, pp. 208–220. Springer, Cham (2020). https://doi.org/10.1007/978-3-030-64823-7_20
5. Strohmann, T., Siemon, D., Elshan, E., Gnewuch, U.: Design principles in information systems research: trends in construction and formulation. In: AMCIS 2023 Proceedings, Panama City, Panama (2023)
6. Schoormann, T., Möller, F., Hansen, M.R.P.: How do researchers (re-)use design principles: an inductive analysis of cumulative research. In: Kruse, L.C., Seidel, S., Hausvik, G.I. (eds.) DESRIST 2021. LNCS, vol. 12807, pp. 188–194. Springer, Cham (2021). https://doi.org/10.1007/978-3-030-82405-1_20
7. Elshan, E., Engel, C., Ebel, P., Siemon, D.: Assessing the reusability of design principles in the realm of conversational agents. In: Drechsler, A., Gerber, A., Hevner, A. (eds.) DESRIST 2022, vol. 13229, pp. 128–141. Springer, Cham (2022). https://doi.org/10.1007/978-3-031-06516-3_10
8. Gregor, S., Jones, D.: The anatomy of a design theory. J. Assoc. Inf. Syst. **8**, 312–335 (2007)
9. Cahenzli, M., Winter, R.: Writing DSR articles for maximum impact. In: ECIS 2023 Proceedings, Kristiansand, Norway (2023)
10. Iivari, J., Rotvit Perlt Hansen, M., Haj-Bolouri, A.: A proposal for minimum reusability evaluation of design principles. Eur. J. Inf. Syst. **30**, 286–303 (2021)

11. Littell, J.H., Corcoran, J., Pillai, V.: Systematic Reviews and Meta-Analysis. Oxford University Press, Inc. (2008)
12. Vaishnavi, V.K., Kuechler, W.: Design Science Research Methods and Patterns: Innovating Information and Communication Technology, 2nd edn. CRC Press, Boca Raton (2015)
13. Schöbel, S., Tingelhoff, F.: Overcoming challenges to enable the potential of metaverse platforms: a qualitative approach to understand value creation. AIS Trans. Hum.-Comput. Interact. **15**, 1–21 (2023)
14. Kohler, T., Fueller, J., Matzler, K., Stieger, D.: Co-creation in virtual worlds: the design of the user experience. MIS Q. **35**, 773–788 (2011)
15. Chaturvedi, A., Dolk, D.R., Drnevich, P.L.: Design principles for virtual worlds. Manag. Inf. Syst. Q. **35**, 673–684 (2011)
16. vom Brocke, J., Winter, R., Hevner, A., Maedche, A.: Special issue editorial – accumulation and evolution of design knowledge in design science research: a journey through time and space. J. Assoc. Inf. Syst. **21**, 520–544 (2020)
17. Chandra Kruse, L., Purao, S., Seidel, S.: How designers use design principles: design behaviors and application modes. J. Assoc. Inf. Syst. **23**, 1235–1270 (2022)
18. Schoormann, T., Möller, F., Chandra Kruse, L.: Uncovering strategies of design principle development. In: Research-in-Progress Papers of the DESRIST 2022 Conference, St. Petersburg, Florida, USA (2022)
19. Gau, M., Maedche, A., vom Brocke, J.: Accessing the design science knowledge base - a search engine for the accumulation of knowledge across decentrally organized publications. In: Gerber, A., Baskerville, R. (eds.) DESRIST 2023, vol. 13873, pp. 1266–1278. Springer, Cham (2023). https://doi.org/10.1007/978-3-031-32808-4_17
20. Moher, D., Liberati, A., Tetzlaff, J., Altman, D.G., PRISMA Group: Preferred reporting items for systematic reviews and meta-analyses: the PRISMA statement. Ann. Internal Med. **151**, 264–269 (2009)
21. Moher, D., Tetzlaff, J., Tricco, A.C., Sampson, M., Altman, D.G.: Epidemiology and reporting characteristics of systematic reviews. PLoS Med. **4**, 447–455 (2007)
22. Diederich, S., Brendel, A., Morana, S., Kolbe, L.: On the design of and interaction with conversational agents: an organizing and assessing review of human-computer interaction research. J. Assoc. Inf. Syst. **23**, 96–138 (2022)
23. Venable, J., Pries-Heje, J., Baskerville, R.: FEDS: a framework for evaluation in design science research. Eur. J. Inf. Syst. **25**, 77–89 (2016)
24. Guilford, J.P.: Creative abilities in the arts. Psychol. Rev. **64**, 110–118 (1957)
25. Guilford, J.P.: The Nature of Human Intelligence. McGraw-Hill (1967)
26. Design Council: The 'double diamond' design process model. Design Council **2**, 1 (2005)
27. Schon, D.A.: The Reflective Practicioner: How Professionals Think in Action. Basic Books, New York (1983)
28. Redlich, B.M.: Performing design thinking virtually–a socio-cognitive view on virtual design thinking (2020)
29. Nickerson, R.C., Varshney, U., Muntermann, J.: A method for taxonomy development and its application in information systems. Eur. J. Inf. Syst. **22**, 336–359 (2013)
30. Walls, J.G., Widmeyer, G.R., El Sawy, O.A.: Building an information system design theory for vigilant EIS. Inf. Syst. Res. **3**, 36–59 (1992)
31. March, S.T., Smith, G.F.: Design and natural science research on information technology. Decis. Support. Syst. **15**, 251–266 (1995)
32. Wache, H., Möller, F., Schoormann, T., Strobel, G., Petrik, D.: Exploring the abstraction levels of design principles: the case of chatbots. In: WI 2022 Proceeding, Nürnberg, Germany (2022)
33. Zhang, X., Pan, S., Tim, Y., Jiang, Z.: Designing a virtual reality video for disability inclusion: an action design research. In: ICIS 2022 Proceedings, Copenhagen, Denmark (2022)

34. Vogel, J., Schuir, J., Koßmann, C., Thomas, O.: Let's do design thinking virtually: design and evaluation of a virtual reality application for collaborative prototyping. In: ECIS 2021 Proceedings, Marrakech, Morocco (2021)

35. Pöhler, L., Meier, P., Schuir, J., Teuteberg, F.: Let's get immersive: how virtual reality can encourage user engagement in process modeling. In: ICIS 2021 Proceeding, Austin, TX, USA (2021)

36. Akdag, M.T., Jacquemin, P.H., Wahl, N.: Visit your therapist in metaverse - designing a virtual environment for mental health counselling. In: ICIS 2023 Proceedings, Hyderabad, India (2023)

37. Fegert, J., Pfeiffer, J., Peukert, C., Golubyeva, A., Weinhardt, C.: Combining e-participation with augmented and virtual reality: insights from a design science research project. In: ICIS 2020 Proceedings, Hyderabad, India (2020)

38. Hönemann, K., Konopka, B., Thatcher, J.B., Wiesche, M.: Designing a user-metaverse interface for the industrial-metaverse. In: ICIS 2023 Proceedings, Hyderabad, India (2023)

39. Haj-Bolouri, A., Rossi, M.: Proposing design principles for sustainable fire safety training in immersive virtual reality. In: HICSS 2022 Proceedings, Maui, HI, USA (2022)

40. Holopainen, J., Lähtevänoja, A., Mattila, O., Södervik, I., Pöyry, E., Parvinen, P.: Exploring the learning outcomes with various technologies - proposing design principles for virtual reality learning environments. In: HICSS 2020 Proceedings, Maui, HI, USA (2020)

41. Iftikhar, R., Cakir, G., Wruck, T., Helfert, M.: How can older adults shop online in the future? Developing design principles for virtual-commerce stores. In: ECIS 2021 Proceedings, Marrakech, Morocco (2021)

42. John, B., Kurian, J.C., Fitzgerald, R., Goh, D.H.L.: Students' learning experience in a mixed reality environment: drivers and barriers. Commun. Assoc. Inf. Syst. **50**, 510–535 (2022)

43. Menck, J., Lechte, H., Lembcke, T.-B., Brendel, A., Kolbe, L.: Towards design principles for experimental simulations in virtual reality – learning from driving simulators. In: HICSS 2023 Proceedings, Maui, HI, USA (2023)

44. Metzger, D., Niemöller, C., Wingert, B., Schultze, T., Bues, M., Thomas, O.: How machines are serviced – design of a virtual reality- based training system for technical customer services. In: WI 2017 Proceedings, St. Gallen, Switzerland (2017)

45. Schjerlund, J., Hansen, M.R.P., Jensen, J.G.: Design principles for room-scale virtual reality: a design experiment in three dimensions. In: Chatterjee, S., Dutta, K., Sundarraj, R. (eds.) DESRIST 2018, vol. 10844, pp. 3–17. Springer, Cham (2018). https://doi.org/10.1007/978-3-319-91800-6_1

46. Mayring, P.: Qualitative Inhaltsanalyse: Grundlagen und Techniken. Beltz Verlag (2015)

47. John, B., Subramanian, R., Kurian, J.C.: Design and evaluation of a virtual reality game to improve physical and cognitive acuity. In: ICIS 2023 Proceedings, Hyderabad, India (2023)

48. Siemon, D., Becker, F., Meyer, M., Strohmann, T.: Addressing the practical impact of design science research. In: AMCIS 2022 Proceedings, Minneapolis, MN, USA (2022)

Dialectical Tensions in Design Theorizing: Exploring the Selection, Use, and Development of Kernel Theory

Frederik Möller[1,2](✉) [iD], Thorsten Schoormann[1,2] [iD], Raffaele Ciriello[3] [iD], and Magnus Rotvit Perlt Hansen[4]

[1] TU Braunschweig, Data-Driven Enterprise, Braunschweig, Germany
{frederik.moeller,thorsten.schoormann}@tu-braunschweig.de
[2] Fraunhofer ISST, Dortmund, Germany
[3] University of Sydney, Sydney, Australia
raffaele.ciriello@sydney.edu.au
[4] Department of People and Technology, Roskilde University, Roskilde, Denmark
magnuha@ruc.dk

Abstract. Theory is a pivotal component in Information Systems (IS) research and no less so in Design Science Research (DSR) projects, which are typically expected to select and use kernel theories to develop theoretical contributions. However, the actual application and utilization of kernel theories remain challenging and heterogeneous – from producing theoretical outcomes in each project to using theory for the justification of design activities. This is problematic since academic journals have high expectations for selecting, using, and contributing to (kernel) theory. As a consequence, DSR researchers, especially novice ones, face challenges in navigating the high expectations of journals with a blurry research component. In this paper, we explore a set of tensions prevalent in the selection, use, and development of kernel theory to then elaborate on possible pathways to respond to them.

Keywords: Kernel Theory · Justificatory Knowledge · Design Science Research

1 Introduction

"One has to wonder what it means for a discipline if each and every paper in a conference with several hundred accepted papers produces new insights into theory, but too few test whether these theories are valid." [1 p. 220]

There has been a long-standing debate between academics in design science research (DSR) and the broader Information Systems (IS) research field on the definition, value, and operationalization of (kernel) theory (e.g., [2–8]). The topic's relevance and attention are evident through numerous discussions that usually take place in the back-and-forth publishing of editorials and research papers (e.g., [2, 7–10]). Our paper aims to synthesize major issues concerning kernel theories, focusing on their application in DSR. We

M. Mandviwalla et al. (Eds.): DESRIST 2024, LNCS 14621, pp. 197–212, 2024.
https://doi.org/10.1007/978-3-031-61175-9_14

start by identifying these issues, building on this discourse, and providing an abstracted summative account of arguments in the use of kernel theory. To frame and organize our arguments, we draw from principles of *dialectical* inquiry to reveal the oppositional forces in the selection, use, and development of kernel theory [11]. A dialectical view highlights tensions and possible responses [11, 12]. This makes it valuable for us since we find a structured frame for the blurry field of kernel theory operationalization and explore pathways for dealing with those situations.

Consider, for instance, a highly pragmatic idiosyncratic issue: Journals in IS research typically expect a twofold role of theory for papers they accept [13]. First, authors should draw from kernel theory to justify or explain their study and its design [2, 9, 13–15]. Second, papers should add 'something' to the body of theoretical knowledge, a *theoretical contribution* [16]. IS researchers are generally required to publish their work in renowned journals to promote their career as doctoral students or as post-docs trying to secure a tenured professorship [17], resulting in a stark motivation to use some theory (i.e., *publish or perish*, [18]). However, this ostensibly straightforward relationship tends to overlook the variety of hurdles preventing effective theory use, such as a lack of useful and relevant theories for the project (e.g., [6, 14]) or the applicability of theories from other fields [4]. This can lead researchers to miss opportunities when compromising relevant contributions in the quest for fitting theories that might not be there (e.g., Avison et al. [4]) or simply producing 'smokescreens,' such as superficially referencing existing theories or literature (e.g., Sutton et al. [19]). Iivari [20] finds that the applicability problem of borrowed theories from other disciplines is an issue because these theories are not specific to what IS research investigates, namely information technology and information systems. This poses the need to adapt existing reference theories or formulate new ones specific to the IS domain.

These issues can be characterized as *tensions*. A tension captures interdependent opposites that coexist in unified opposition, driving perpetual struggle and change [11]. They drive struggle because "different needs or interests cause difficulties" [21], and two independently logical positions contradict each other [22]. Explicating these tensions can open up a pathway to exploring potential responses and complement the existing discourse on theory in IS research (e.g., Avison et al. [4]) with a dedicated focus on kernel theory in DSR. Subsequently, we ask: *How can DSR researchers respond to inherent tensions in the selection, use, and development of kernel theory?*

Our exploration reveals three key tensions: the *picking paradox*, the *adoption ambivalence*, and the *development dilemma* of kernel theory. We identify these tensions through a *narrative review* of published IS papers and editorials, giving an account of the prior discussion on kernel theory in DSR [23]. The paper does not claim comprehensiveness. Instead, using dialectical inquiry adds another viewpoint to the debate and helps us to cast the prevailing debate on kernel theory in DSR in a different light. This can serve as a foundation for creating new solutions to solve these problems.

This paper is structured as follows: After the motivation, we outline the fundamentals of kernel theory in DSR (Sect. 2). Then, we summarize and frame the discourse on kernel theory operationalization through the lens of dialectical inquiry (Sect. 3). Afterward, we discuss and theorize about potential responses to address these tensions (Sect. 4). Finally, we conclude with our paper (Sect. 5).

2 Kernel Theory in Design Science Research

The notion and concept of what constitutes kernel theory has evolved [2]. Initially, kernel theories referred to theories from reference disciplines in natural and social sciences that would aid designers in deriving meta-requirements in the process of producing Information Systems Design Theories (ISDTs) [24]. Over the years, scholars have introduced additional conceptualization of constituting elements. Goldkuhl [25 p. 67] proposed theoretical grounding in ISDT generation, broadening the scope to all external theories, i.e., "theoretical knowledge that is considered external about the design theory." Gregor and Jones [26] proposed *justificatory knowledge* as a grounding for ISDTs and one of its essential components. Justificatory knowledge is broader than kernel theories and can include a range of knowledge outside the borders of theory, such as practitioner knowledge [27]. For instance, as justificatory knowledge, Gregor et al. [28] report on an action design research (ADR) study generating a sweet spot change strategy drawing from multiple and diverse instances of justificatory knowledge: Roger's [29] *theory on innovation, literature on ICT4D* and the *sweet spot concept* (Fig. 1).

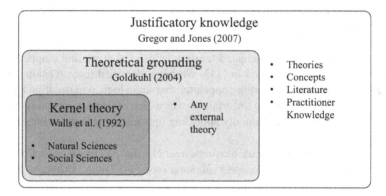

Fig. 1. Contextualization of kernel theory, theoretical grounding, and justificatory knowledge.

Scholars still debate whether employing kernel theory is a mandatory or optional task in a DSR project (e.g., see Fischer [30]). Some argue that a strict focus on kernel theory is harmful to a DSR study since actually finding a kernel theory is sometimes a "stretch" [31]. Others explore the dynamic and reciprocal nature of designing and kernel theories, as kernel theories can not only inform design but design can also refine kernel theory [32]. Iivari [33] and Hevner [31] argue for a broad range of underlying knowledge to justify DSR studies, coining the term *design inspiration* rather than kernel theory or justificatory knowledge.

3 A Dialectical Inquiry Perspective on Kernel Theory

Fundamentally, a DSR project matures over time, progressing in a search process from a problem space to an artifact and design knowledge in a solution space [34]. Correspondingly, we frame kernel theory operationalization in three stages. First, *pre-use (selection)* refers to the finite section of time in which the designer(s) search for and select kernel theories, i.e., before they have been applied. Second, *in-use (use)* refers to the finite section of time in which the designer(s) have already identified relevant kernel theories and selected one or multiple for their DSR process. Third, *post-use (development)* refers to the finite section of time in which the designer(s) have already applied one or multiple kernel theories in their DSR process to make a theoretical contribution. Dialectical inquiry is useful in explaining prevailing issues through oppositional forces [11]. This lens helps us to (1) make general issues more accessible by summarizing them as well as (2) identify and reflect on appropriate responses.

The tensions for kernel theory use are collected through a *narrative review* [23], and our experience in conducting DSR since the discussion on (kernel) theories usually takes place in editorials [23]. Our total sample is a mixture of editorials, commentaries, and research articles from leading IS journals (e.g., MISQ, JAIS, EJIS), the AOM journal, and a book chapter [20]. The core of the sample was created on our own experiences of seminal work in this field and iteratively extended through backward searching and general Google Scholar searching. We do not claim comprehensiveness or systematic inquiry and expect there to be more tensions. The goal of the paper is, therefore, not to give a complete account of the literature on kernel theory operationalization but to provide an overview and synthesis of the ongoing discussion. The tensions are a product of the multiple theoretical viewpoints of the team of authors and discussions in which we elaborated on the selected tensions, clustered them, and mapped them to one of the tension types proposed in [11]. We have identified three tension types [11 p. 3]: **Paradox**: "mutually reinforcing opposites that seem logical in isolation but absurd together"; **Ambivalence**: "facing uncertainty over which of several appealing opposites should be chosen"; **Dilemma**: "equally appealing opposites that come at the expense of one another".

Below, we explain three main tensions, namely the *picking paradox*, the *adoption ambivalence*, and the *development dilemma* (see Fig. 2), and explicate prevailing oppositions with exemplary references and indicate *tension drivers* [35].

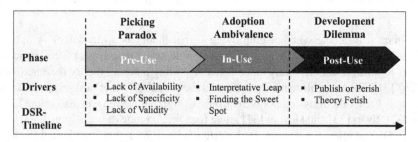

Fig. 2. Tensions mapped to phases in kernel theory operationalization.

3.1 Pre-use: Picking Paradox

You keep on scrolling and scrolling Netflix for several hours but cannot choose a movie to watch – does this sound familiar to you? Then you have experienced Hick's Law which points to the fact that an increasing number of options leads to a growing amount of time and effort to make a decision [36]. In line with Schwartz's [37] famous *paradox of choice,* those situations illustrate how an overload of choices negatively affects consumer decision-making and how "too many choices lead to paralysis" [37 p. 134]. We draw from this analogy because we find, both in the scientific discourse and in our own experience, a set of barriers to effectively selecting kernel theories. The designer is usually confronted with a similar paradox of choice before operationalizing kernel theory since there is an immense wealth of potential kernel theories, and IS research, as an interdisciplinary research field, can potentially draw from any of them [2]. For instance, Iivari [2] points to the vast amount of theory from different reference disciplines, and Lim et al. [38], ten years earlier, had already identified 174 individual theories used in IS research. In a recent review of kernel theory use in design principle projects, Möller et al. [3] found over 50 unique kernel theories.

This sheer number of kernel theories can lead to an overwhelming oversupply (**abundance**), which, similar to the paradox of choice and the metaphor of Netflix, hinders effective kernel theory selection rather than assisting it. For one, a specific theory that exactly fits the design problem or phenomenon under investigation might simply not exist [14, 39] (**scarcity**), leading to a fruitless and frustrating search (*lack of availability*). Compared to the Netflix example, we all know all too well the feeling of being overwhelmed by the immense choice of movies but still not finding the one we are looking for. Available kernel theories might fit at face value to contribute some value to a DSR study but fit a design problem (*lack specificity*). On the one hand, they might lack the "granularity of the constructs" and "do not match the requirements of the design problem" [40 p. 461]. On the other hand, kernel theories might be drawn from other disciplines and "tend to include nothing specific to information technology and information systems" [20 p. 3]. Given the spectrum of interpretations of what constitutes a kernel theory (see Sect. 2), its nature has shifted over the years, resulting in eminent scholars from the field labeling these "dubious refinements" [2 p. 503]. This nature of kernel theories makes it hard to identify a valid one (*lack of validity*) (see Table 1).

3.2 In-Use: Adoption Ambivalence

Now that you have identified three interesting Netflix movies, you are faced with the complex choice of deciding in which order to watch them – are you also overthinking such choices? Handling the number of variables and environmental factors is known as *analysis paralysis* [42]. People are often overwhelmed when striving to make the best possible decision, hindering concrete actions. We argue that this also applies to design researchers who are confronted with several questions on how, when, and why to use a kernel theory. This process is not straightforward but rather subject to highly contextual and individual interpretation (e.g., Möller et al. [3]). We summarize this as **adaption**, as tailoring the kernel theory through interpretation and application selection points to the design researcher's needs. It is an ambivalence because successfully **adopting** kernel theory requires navigating many blurry choices (see Table 2).

First, the transformation of kernel theory constructs requires *interpretation* [40]. The starting point is a corpus of theory that is usually not readily available but requires the design researcher to consolidate kernel theory constructs from one or multiple papers

Table 1. Picking Paradox.

Opposition A	Opposition B	Examples and supporting literature	
Abundance of (possible) kernel theories	Scarcity of (suitable) kernel theories	"First, it is not easy to find relevant kernel theories for a specific design problem at hand." [40 p. 461]	[2–4, 6, 14, 20, 31, 39–41]
		"(…) that kernel theories from reference disciplines are not (necessarily) concrete enough to guide design (…)" [2 p. 503]	
		"(…) it would be interesting to investigate whether grand theories as kernel theories have a different 'validity' than 'just' literature findings" [3 p. 11]	

and apply them to their research. The available landscape differs drastically in the level of abstraction it is codified in. Take, for example, prominent grand theories that apply broadly and to many applications, such as *Actor-Network Theory* [43] or *Dynamic Capabilities* [44]. If we compare this with very fine granular potential theories, such as the *Privacy Calculus Theory* [45], or families of theories, such as in *reflection theory* [46], we see a stark difference in the required level of abstraction and potential fields of application from theory identification and selection to successful operationalization.

Second, it remains unclear how to find the *sweet spot* for applying kernel theory, i.e., *how, where, when*, and *how many* kernel theories should be used in a DSR study [3, 6]. In short, there is a distinct lack of guidelines on different levels on how to operationalize kernel theory in DSR [47]. DSR usually follows a sequential process (e.g., [48, 49]), which offers the design researcher many opportunities to apply a kernel theory. Walls et al. [24] proposed using kernel theory as a source to derive meta-requirements, meaning, in the offset of a DSR project. Möller et al. [3] show that studies developing design principles have stark heterogeneity in where and how they apply kernel theory (e.g., to derive design principles or transform one construct into another). Mandviwalla [6] argues that kernel theories need not necessarily be operationalized in the design process but in evaluating DSR artifacts.

Table 2. Adoption Ambivalence.

Opposition A	Opposition B	Examples and supporting literature	
Adoption of kernel theories	Adaption of kernel theories	"(…) and the transformation from theory to design is highly interpretative." [40 p. 460]	[3, 6, 40]
		"Conversely, kernel theories could have little or no role in the design but have a major role in evaluation (e.g., using social capital theory to evaluate knowledge management systems)" [6 p. 321]	

3.3 Post-use: Development Dilemma

A concept from psychology – *self-sabotaging* – refers to acts done or not done that prevent oneself from reaching one's goals [17, 50]. In other words: success is blocked.

The IS field explicitly strives to make a *practical impact*, especially in DSR [48, 51], and some scholars even argue that kernel theory is not relevant to every DSR study [9, 31, 52]. In general, designers build artifacts to solve real-world organizational and human (wicked) problems through digital technologies [34, 53] (**practical contribution**). However, it is well known and has been well discussed that the barriers set by high-ranking publications in terms of theory use and contribution could hinder the publication of practically relevant and successful DSR studies because of a lack of theory [1, 14]. This resulted in more or less colorful descriptions of the IS and DSR fields' relationships with theory, such as *theory fetish* [2, 4] or *theory is king* [13] (**theoretical contribution**). At the same time, we are far from suggesting that this is intentional; it seems clear that the barriers we set ourselves in terms of theory prevent effective communication (i.e., publication) of practical findings. Navigating the peculiarities between making a practical and a theoretical contribution is challenging for novice design researchers because they wish to make a practical impact on the one hand and require theoretical contributions on the other. This leads to a problematic situation since not all DSR research might be explainable through existing kernel theory, and ultimately, the community would "miss out on an important piece of evidence" [14 p. 97]. We find this to be the underlying struggle between the two appealing opposites of practical and theoretical contributions and the resulting dilemma of design researchers having to focus on navigating the grey space in between (see Table 3).

Table 3. Development Dilemma.

Opposition A	Opposition B	Examples and supporting literature	
Practical contribution of design research	Theoretical contribution of design research	"(…) the research community may miss out on an important piece of evidence with potential long-term implications only because the theoretical mechanism to explain that evidence has yet to be articulated." [14 p. 97]	[1, 2, 14, 16, 18, 31, 54, 55]
		"This makes it difficult to publish applicable knowledge on innovative new products or ideas in IS as these cannot be integrated into a theory right away but rather need to be understood empirically before any further steps can occur" [1 p. 220]	
		"While theories can serve as sources of creative ideas, to insist that all design research must be grounded on descriptive theories is unrealistic and even harmful to the field when good design science papers are rejected in top journals due to lack of a grounding theory." [31 p. 90]	

4   Responses to Tensions in Kernel Theory Operationalization

We discuss two sets of responses to kernel theory tensions. First, we draw from generic responses prevalent in dialectical research [11] to take into account well-established mechanisms to handle such types of tensions. Second, we discuss a set of potential responses that we extract from our experience conducting DSR studies, but we are also inspired by how others (e.g., anecdotal analogies from Netflix) tackled these tensions. The generic responses are targeted at kernel theory operationalization *as a whole,* proposing generic strategies independent of the specifics of each tension. In the specific responses, we propose lower-threshold mitigation strategies tailored to each tension.

4.1   Generic Responses to Kernel Theory Operationalization

Generically, dialectical inquiry suggests a range of potential responses to mitigating tensions, namely *suppression, suspension, separation,* and *synthesis* (see Table 4).

As a response, **suppression** indicates that the design researcher dedicatedly ignores one part of the tension – in our case, operationalizing kernel theory. Most likely, this is adequate if the researcher does not assess kernel theory as helpful or useful to support the DSR project. While the discussion on kernel theory operationalization covers opinions on not using kernel theory [30], this response is a rather *extreme* one because it completely negates the use of kernel theory.

Table 4. Responses to tensions [11 p. 5] and their application on kernel theory.

Response	Definition	Kernel theory operationalization
Suppression	"Ignoring the opposition and remaining oblivious to it."	Consciously and dedicatedly, deciding to **ignore** kernel theory. The design researcher might find it to be irrelevant or not useful
Suspension	"Living with the opposition to see how the struggle between the opposites plays out"	**Accepting** that kernel theory selection, use, and development cannot be rectified and living with the consequences
Separation	"Preferring one opposite over the other and keeping them separate in time or space."	**Delaying** kernel theory selection, use, and development to a later point in time or stage of the DSR project
Synthesis	"Creating something new from the opposition by integrating and coalescing its opposites."	**Solving** the oppositions and finding mitigating strategies, for example, new artifacts or lenses that fit the project better or simply are available

In **suspension**, the design researcher consciously accepts that no kernel theory can be selected, used, or developed and observes, across the DSR project, how this plays out. This, ultimately, results in producing design artifacts that are not grounded in theory but rather address the practical dimension in terms of *practical grounding* (e.g., [25]) and *practical contributions.* This response seems appropriate when an interesting and novel phenomenon emerges for which an adequate or readily available kernel theory does not exist (e.g., [14, 31]). In that case, the design researcher decides to accept the trade-off of generating a design artifact without kernel theory as opposed to continuing a potentially unfruitful search.

Once relevant kernel theory has been selected but the design researcher struggles in application and interpretation in the specific design scenario, **separation** is a sensible response to continue the project (e.g., in practice) and delay kernel theory operationalization to a later point in time or the project. For instance, separating in time could prompt the design researcher to first focus on explicitly producing practically valid artifacts (e.g., for an industry project) and delaying theoretical exacerbation to a later point when the circumstances of the design project (e.g., less pressure from practical partners) allow for deep theorizing. Typically, industry projects start with engaging in the individual project setting and require practical results earlier than theoretical contributions (e.g., in an ADR [48] project) – a situation that would be supported by the separation response. For instance, this could mean getting additional support (e.g., from a senior scholar) or choosing a later point (e.g., evaluation) to apply kernel theory in the DSR process. Alternatively, the design researcher could apply kernel theory in a different stage of the DSR process, which might be more accommodating (e.g., see [3]).

In **synthesis**, the design researcher explores options to harmonize kernel theory use and its operationalization by finding new ways of applying it. This could help to merge practical problems with a (new) kernel theory that would maybe shift the initial focus but bring together a sound kernel theory and the practical problem. It could also be expressed by using multiple kernel theories, applying them in new creative ways, or combining them.

4.2 Specific Responses to Kernel Theory Operationalization

In the following, we illustrate potential responses to each specific tension, drawing from our experience of conducting DSR projects and reference examples.

As the first tension - **the picking paradox (1)** -, we find the fundamental opposition of an existing oversupply (abundance), which implies ample opportunity for DSR researchers to find kernel theories in a vacuum. However, opposing this is a lack of knowledge about identifying relevant kernel theories (scarcity), their existence, or their applicability. There can be cases where the researcher finds a suitable kernel theory, and thus, the supply is positive. For example, selection should be intuitive if a suitable kernel theory is available in comprehensive databases or overviews, such as on ISTheorizeIT. However, if the novice researcher lacks a clear image (i.e., metrics) to select a kernel theory and rather requires exploring the large landscape, this could result in frustration and a fruitless search. Since we used Netflix as an illustration for these tensions (see Sect. 3.2), we examined and discussed how existing solutions from those scenarios can be transferred to kernel theory selection in DSR. One potential response to the fruitless search for kernel theory and decision fatigue is (**1a**) *randomly* proposing kernel theories like Netflix's 'shuffle play' to start with something [56, 57]. This acts under the presupposition that finding a kernel theory and a useful theoretical lens is a creative process in which evaluating randomly proposed kernel theories could help circumvent endless searches [58]. Another potential way is to (**1b**) learn from peers to establish a recommendation system, in which design researchers articulate successful kernel theory operationalization according to a system of indicators (see the Netflix example here [59]). Compared to Netflix's lists of personal movie recommendations, this might lead to a smaller number of potential items to be screened, which is easier to handle. For example, design researchers could rate whether a kernel theory is highly abstract, hard to operationalize, or highly detailed and very narrow. Over time, this would create an interesting and saturated picture of well-used kernel theories in DSR. An interesting side effect would be (**1c**) that those kernel theories used frequently for a certain phenomenon could be listed in a ranking based on their history in prior literature. Fundamentally, (**1d**) kernel theory selection requires specific metrics (e.g., problem fit, solution fit, abstractedness, availability) to help designers make a decision. Besides, responses should include (**1e**) fallback strategies if no kernel theory can be identified that provides sufficient value to the DSR study to be selected.

The second tension – **adoption ambivalence (2)** - occurs in the application process of the kernel theory, which is riddled with ambiguous decisions. Recalling the literature on DSR and kernel theory use, its pivotal position promises to enhance research processes in multiple ways, justify decisions, or support evaluations. Against that stands an array of possibilities for applying kernel theories, from deriving requirements to refining specific elements or evaluating artifacts. From this, we infer that kernel theory can help in some cases, but the lack of concrete guidance results in potential paralysis since novice design researchers could be overwhelmed by the possibilities and the lack of guidance. Coping with the tension requires (**2a**) an understanding of the individual steps kernel theory can be applied to in a design study. More so, we need (**2b**) criteria that contrast the positives and negatives of applying one or more kernel theories to a specific DSR activity. For example, to mitigate issues concerning why it is potentially more beneficial to use kernel theory for meta-requirement derivation instead of formulating design principles (or both). Therefore, (**2c**) researchers can again build upon a theory's 'usage history' to examine how and where a particular theory has been successfully applied in a design paper (see the Netflix example here [60]). For instance, next to a repository of theories, one could collect representative cases showcasing scenarios for their application.

The third tension – **development dilemma (3)** – is the opposition that typically occurs when writing up a paper from the DSR study and the struggle to produce theoretical contributions while simultaneously producing significant practical impact. Highly practical design studies without a (yet) mature theoretical contribution could be published in outlets specifically addressing practitioners, such as *MISQE* or *HMD – Praxis der Wirtschaftsinformatik*, who, most likely, pay more attention to the situational artifact and the implications for practice. Theoretical complements, when matured, could be published in outlets in which theoretical contributions are more relevant. Finally, handling the tension might require a broader consideration of journals, reviewers, and writers. Academic outlets should have (**3a**) a clear statement and position about what kind of papers most likely have a chance to be published. Among good examples are the MISQE mission statement stressing that their "primary focus is research that is immediately relevant and useful for practice" [61] or conferences that provide a track for especially practical contributions (which might need less theoretical contributions).

Contrarily, also **(3b)** researchers should ask themselves what kind of paper/research project they are engaged in and what the key audience for the findings is. For example, researchers could opt to write **theory light papers**, which are "[t]heory light qualitative research papers are those papers where theory plays no significant part in the paper and the contribution lies elsewhere" [4 p. 330].

5   Contributions, Limitations, and Outlook

Given the ongoing debate on how to engage with (kernel) theories in design research, our work proposes three tensions in kernel theory operationalization: the *picking paradox*, the *adoption ambivalence*, and the *development dilemma*. Each tension covers a distinct phase of such an operationalization, i.e., before (selection), during (use), and after (development) using a kernel theory. With the tensions, we put issues that are prominent in the academic discourse, both in the published academic literature and at IS conferences, on the spot. In this regard, the tensions have a unifying function as they collect the fragmented argumentative shards and frame them as understandable and addressable specific tensions, as well as allow us to theorize about potential responses.

For **novice design researchers**, we contribute an overview of the challenges they could face when operationalizing kernel theory, such as when performing a theory-based design research project [62]. Using theory – *in general* – is not a simple task, and applying it to specific DSR projects requires significant skill. Assuming that most IS researchers and DSR researchers, at some point, face issues in the selection, use, and development of kernel theories, we find the discussion of these tensions valuable. Especially, since it could mitigate the fear novice design researchers could feel while engaging in the challenging task of operationalizing kernel theory. The responses we propose, albeit not finalized and well-proven, give indications of how (novice) design researchers can deal with those tensions. In this regard, we especially hope to raise awareness of these tensions and inspire novice researchers to find a starting point to deal with them.

For the **discourse on kernel theory in DSR**, we seek to kickstart a discussion by revealing inherent tensions that occur in operationalizing kernel theory and have opened the floor for potential responses to dealing with them. We find this specifically useful since most of the discussion usually revolves around criticizing the *status quo* – that theory is blurry or that it is not available. For this, we find the need to really explicate the value kernel theory provides to DSR study and make mechanisms, metrics, and conditions to operationalize them extremely important. While we do not want to take away from the creative process of using kernel theory and also the obligation a (DSR) researcher has in making the most use of it as efficiently as possible – we still propose that more guidance could help DSR in multiple ways. Among them are (1) *transparency* through comparable mechanisms (e.g., [3]), (2) *quality* through clear(er) selection mechanisms and metrics, *efficiency* (3) through enhanced decision-making, and (4) *impact* through the target-oriented publication of DSR projects.

As with all research, the paper has **limitations that** open up **future avenues**. As we focus on IS design research and how it handles theory in particular, scholars can compare it with other disciplines and how they engage in such theory-based tensions (e.g., [63]). Thereby, differences between design-oriented research and other forms of theory-driven research can be investigated to disclose what is specific to our context. The paper reports on a narrative review, thus not taking into account all papers but providing instead a general reflection based on a selection of the discourse [23]. Subsequently, the tensions are formulated based on our judgment and termed *key tensions*, those which we find to be highly interesting, useful, and noteworthy for discussion. However, future research can draw on our insights and conduct a more systematic search for tensions to derive a complete series of tensions rigorously. This means that the next steps would require us to engage with the DSR community, for example, in workshops at conferences or in formal interviews, to extract the tensions they feel when using kernel theory. Subsequently, we expect, in continuing research, to uncover more tensions, understand those we found on a more profound level, potentially uncover hierarchies or interdependent tensions, and ultimately exacerbate a set of responses supporting (novice) design researchers overcoming them.

Disclosure of Interests. The authors have no competing interests to declare that are relevant to the content of this article.

References

1. Lehnhoff, S., Staudt, P., Watson, R.T.: Changing the climate in information systems research. Bus. Inf. Syst. Eng. **63**(3), 219–222 (2021). https://doi.org/10.1007/s12599-021-00695-y
2. Iivari, J.: A critical look at theories in design science research. J. Assoc. Inf. Syst. **21**(3), 502–519 (2020). https://doi.org/10.17705/1jais.00610
3. Möller, F., Schoormann, T., Strobel, G., Hansen, M.: Unveiling the cloak: kernel theory use in design science research. In: Proceedings of the 43rd International Conference on Information Systems, Kopenhagen, Denmark (2022)
4. Avison, D., Malaurent, J.: Is theory king?: Questioning the theory fetish in information systems. J. Inf. Technol. **29**(4), 327–336 (2014). https://doi.org/10.1057/jit.2014.8
5. Markus, M.L.: Maybe not the king, but an invaluable subordinate: a commentary on avison and malaurent's advocacy of 'theory light' is research. J. Inf. Technol. **29**(4), 341–345 (2014). https://doi.org/10.1057/jit.2014.19
6. Mandviwalla, M.: Generating and justifying design theory. J. Assoc. Inf. Syst. **16**, 314–344 (2015). https://doi.org/10.17705/1jais.00397
7. Rowe, F., Markus, M.L.: Against theoretical constraint: a commentary on Hirschheim's "against theory—with apologies to Feyerabend". In: Hovorka, D. (ed.) Scholarly Commentaries on Hirschheim's "Against Theory" (2019). Journal of the Association for Information Systems
8. Hirschheim, R.: Against theory: with apologies to Feyerabend. J. Assoc. Inf. Syst. **20**(9), 1340–1357 (2019). https://doi.org/10.17705/1jais.00569
9. Baskerville, R., Baiyere, A., Gregor, S., Hevner, A., Rossi, M.: Design science research contributions: finding a balance between artifact and theory. J. Assoc. Inf. Syst. **19**(5), 358–376 (2018). https://doi.org/10.17705/1jais.00495
10. Peffers, K., Tuunanen, T., Niehaves, B.: Design science research genres: introduction to the special issue on exemplars and criteria for applicable design science research. Eur. J. Inf. Syst. **27**(2), 129–139 (2018). https://doi.org/10.1080/0960085X.2018.1458066
11. Ciriello, R.F., Mathiassen, L.: Dialectical inquiry in information systems research: a synthesis of principles. In: Proceedings of the 43rd International Conference on Information Systems, Kopenhagen, Denmark (2022)

12. Farjoun, M.: Beyond dualism: stability and change as a duality. Acad. Manag. Rev. **35**(2), 202–225 (2010)
13. Straub, D.W.: Editor's comments: why top journals accept your paper. MIS Q. Manag. Inf. Syst. **33**(3), iii–x (2009). https://doi.org/10.2307/20650302
14. Fink, L.: The philosopher's corner: the role of theory in information systems research. SIGMIS Database **52**(3), 96–103 (2021). https://doi.org/10.1145/3481629.3481636
15. Ågerfalk, P.J., Karlsson, F.: Artefactual and empirical contributions in information systems research. Eur. J. Inf. Syst. **29**(2), 109–113 (2020). https://doi.org/10.1080/0960085X.2020.1743051
16. Chatterjee, S.: Writing my next design science research master-piece: but how do i make a theoretical contribution to DSR? In: Proceedings of the 23rd European Conference on Information Systems, Münster, Germany (2015)
17. Ciriello, R.F., Thatcher, J.: Six inversion strategies for avoiding rejection in academic publishing: lessons from the IS discipline. Commun. Assoc. Inf. Syst. **53**, 458–474 (2023)
18. Wiener, M., et al.: Information systems research: making an impact in a publish-or-perish world. Commun. Assoc. Inf. Syst. **43**, 466–481 (2018). https://doi.org/10.17705/1CAIS.04326
19. Sutton, R.I., Staw, B.M.: What theory is not. Adm. Sci. Q. **40**(3), 371–384 (1995). https://doi.org/10.2307/2393788
20. Iivari, J.: Theory fetish, theory building and ideal types. In: Information Systems, Development Approaches and Qualitative Research: A Tribute to David Alison, pp. 115–129 (2018)
21. Oxford University Press: Definition of Tension (2022). https://www.oxfordlearnersdictionaries.com/definition/english/tension_1?q=Tension. Accessed 11 Nov 2022
22. Smith, W., Lewis, M.: Toward a theory of paradox: a dynamic equilibrium model of organizing. Acad. Manag. Rev. **36**(2), 381–403 (2011). https://doi.org/10.5465/AMR.2011.59330958
23. Paré, G., Trudel, M.-C., Jaana, M., Kitsiou, S.: Synthesizing information systems knowledge: a typology of literature reviews. Inf. Manag. **52**(2), 183–199 (2015). https://doi.org/10.1016/j.im.2014.08.008
24. Walls, J.G., Widmeyer, G.R., El Sawy, O.A.: Building an information system design theory for vigilant EIS. Inf. Syst. Res. **3**(1), 36–59 (1992). https://doi.org/10.1287/isre.3.1.36
25. Goldkuhl, G.: Design theories in information systems-a need for multi-grounding. JITTA: J. Inf. Technol. Theory Appl. **6**(2), 59–72 (2004)
26. Gregor, S., Jones, D.: The anatomy of a design theory. J. Assoc. Inf. Syst. **8**(5), 312–335 (2007). https://doi.org/10.17705/1JAIS.00129
27. Gregor, S., Hevner, A.R.: Positioning and presenting design science research for maximum impact. MIS Q. Manag. Inf. Syst. **37**(2), 337–355 (2013). https://doi.org/10.25300/MISQ/2013/37.2.01
28. Gregor, S., Imran, A., Turner, T.: A 'sweet spot' change strategy for a least developed country: leveraging e-Government in Bangladesh. Eur. J. Inf. Syst. **23**(6), 655–671 (2014). https://doi.org/10.1057/ejis.2013.14
29. Rogers, E.M.: Diffusion of innovations: modifications of a model for telecommunications. In: Stoetzer, M.-W., Mahler, A. (eds.) Die Diffusion von Innovationen in der Telekommunikation, vol. 17, pp. 25–38. Springer, Heidelberg (1995). https://doi.org/10.1007/978-3-642-79868-9_2
30. Fischer, C., Winter, R., Wortmann, F.: Design theory. Bus. Inf. Syst. Eng. **2**(6), 387–390 (2010). https://doi.org/10.1007/s12599-010-0128-2
31. Hevner, A.: A three cycle view of design science research. Scand. J. Inf. Syst. **19**(2), 87–92 (2007)
32. Kuechler, B., Vaishnavi, V.: On theory development in design science research: anatomy of a research project. Eur. J. Inf. Syst. **17**(5), 489–504 (2008). https://doi.org/10.1057/ejis.2008.40

33. Iivari, J.: A paradigmatic analysis of information systems as a design science. Scand. J. Inf. Syst. **19**(2), 39–64 (2007)
34. Simon, H.A.: The Sciences of the Artificial. MIT Press, Cambridge (1996)
35. Viljoen, A., Hein, A., Przybilla, L., Krcmar, H.: Striving for global optima in digital transformation: a paradox theory approach. In: Proceedings of the 43rd International Conference on Information Systems, Kopenhagen, Denmark (2022)
36. Hick, W.E.: On the rate of gain of information. Q. J. Exp. Psychol. **4**(1), 11–26 (1952). https://doi.org/10.1080/17470215208416600
37. Schwartz, B.: The paradox of choice. In: Positive Psychology in Practice, pp. 121–138 (2015). https://doi.org/10.1002/9781118996874.ch8
38. Lim, S., Saldanha, T., Malladi, S., Melville, N.: Theories used in information systems research: insights from complex network analysis. J. Inf. Technol. Theory Appl. **14**, 5–46 (2013)
39. Dennis, A.: An unhealthy obsession with theory. J. Assoc. Inf. Syst. **20**(9), 1406–1411 (2019). https://doi.org/10.17705/1jais.00572
40. Arazy, O., Kumar, N., Shapira, B.: A theory-driven design framework for social recommender systems. J. Assoc. Inf. Syst. **11**(9), 455–490 (2010). https://doi.org/10.17705/1jais.00237
41. Markus, M.L., Rowe, F.: Guest editorial: theories of digital transformation: a progress report. J. Assoc. Inf. Syst. **22**(2), 273–280 (2021)
42. Kurien, R., Paila, A.R., Nagendra, A.: Application of paralysis analysis syndrome in customer decision making. Procedia Econ. Finance **11**, 323–334 (2014). https://doi.org/10.1016/S2212-5671(14)00200-7
43. Callon, M., Latour, B.: Unscrewing the big Leviathan: how actors macro-structure reality and how sociologists help them to do so. In: Advances in Social Theory and Methodology, pp. 277–303. Routledge, Kegan Paul, Londres (1981)
44. Teece, D., Pisano, G., Shuen, A.: Dynamic capabilities and strategic management. Strateg. Manag. J. **18**(7), 509–533 (1997)
45. Laufer, R.S., Wolfe, M.: Privacy as a concept and a social issue: a multidimensional developmental theory. J. Soc. Issues **33**(3), 22–42 (1977). https://doi.org/10.1111/j.1540-4560.1977.tb01880.x
46. Schön, D.: The Reflective Practitioner: How Professionals Think in Action. Basic Books (1983)
47. Kuechler, W., Vaishnavi, V.: A framework for theory development in design science research: multiple perspectives. J. Assoc. Inf. Syst. **13**(6), 395–423 (2012). https://doi.org/10.17705/1jais.00300
48. Sein, M.K., Henfridsson, O., Purao, S., Rossi, M., Lindgren, R.: Action design research. MIS Q. Manag. Inf. Syst. **35**(1), 37–56 (2011). https://doi.org/10.2307/23043488
49. Peffers, K., Tuunanen, T., Rothenberger, M.A., Chatterjee, S.: A design science research methodology for information systems research. J. Manag. Inf. Syst. **24**(3), 45–77 (2007). https://doi.org/10.2753/MIS0742-1222240302
50. Field, B.: Self-Sabotaging: Why Does It Happen (2023). https://www.verywellmind.com/why-people-self-sabotage-and-how-to-stop-it-5207635
51. Hevner, A., March, S.T., Park, J., Ram, S.: Design science in information systems research. MIS Q. Manag. Inf. Syst. **28**(1), 75–105 (2004). https://doi.org/10.2307/25148625
52. Goldkuhl, G., Sjöström, J.: Design science theorizing: the contribution of practical theory. In: Hassan, N.R., Willcocks, L.P. (eds.) Advancing Information Systems Theories. TWG, pp. 239–273. Springer, Cham (2021). https://doi.org/10.1007/978-3-030-64884-8_7
53. Simon, H.A.: Problem forming, problem finding and problem solving in design. Des. Syst. **3**, 245–257 (1995)
54. Ågerfalk, P.J.: Insufficient theoretical contribution: a conclusive rationale for rejection? Eur. J. Inf. Syst. **23**(6), 593–599 (2014). https://doi.org/10.1057/ejis.2014.35

55. Ågerfalk, P.J., Conboy, K., Myers, M.D.: Information systems in the age of pandemics: COVID-19 and beyond. Eur. J. Inf. Syst. **29**(3), 203–207 (2020). https://doi.org/10.1080/096 0085X.2020.1771968

56. Adalian, J.: Inside netflix's quest to end scrolling how the company is working to solve one of its biggest threats: decision fatigue (2021). https://www.vulture.com/article/netflix-play-something-decision-fatigue.html. Accessed 02 Feb 2024

57. Laurent, S.: Netflix vs. decision fatigue: how to solve the paradox of choice (2021). https://uxdesign.cc/netflix-vs-decision-fatigue-how-to-solve-the-paradox-of-choice-888ca56db4b. Accessed 02 Feb 2024

58. Meilich, O., de Pillis, E.: "But it's so random!": a versatile constrained creativity exercise for application of business topics. Manag. Teach. Rev. **8**(1), 8–21 (2021). https://doi.org/10.1177/23792981211032565

59. Gawade, A.: Netflix syndrome—a UX/UI case study on the paradox of choice (2023). https://medium.com/@aryagawade2001/netflix-syndrome-a-ux-ui-case-study-on-the-paradox-of-choice-410a062cc403. Accessed 02 Feb 2024

60. Eppalapally, S.: Netflix: the paradox of choice (2015). https://www.linkedin.com/pulse/netflix-paradox-choice-santosh-eppalapally. Accessed 02 Feb 2024

61. MISQE: MISQE - Mission Statement (2023). https://aisel.aisnet.org/misqe/aimsandscope.html. Accessed 08 Jan 2024

62. Schoormann, T., Möller, F., Chandra Kruse, L., Otto, B.: BAUSTEIN—a design tool for configuring and representing design research. Inf. Syst. J. (2024). https://doi.org/10.1111/isj.12516

63. Sandberg, J., Alvesson, M.: Meanings of theory: clarifying theory through typification. J. Manag. Stud. **58**(2), 487–516 (2021). https://doi.org/10.1111/joms.12587

Design Science Research as a Guide for Innovative Higher Education Teaching: Towards an Application-Oriented Extension of the Proficiency Model

Vanessa Maria Steinherr[(✉)] [ID], Martin Brehmer[ID], Raphaela Stöckl,
and Ramona Reinelt

University of Augsburg, Augsburg, Germany
{vanessa.steinherr,martin.brehmer,raphaela.stoeckl,
ramona.reinelt}@uni-a.de

Abstract. Constant technological innovation demands higher education teaching to be reactive in an ever-changing environment. Technology-enhanced learning environments provide a foundation for innovative higher education teaching, but the lack of guidance on how to design elements for these environments constitutes a significant barrier. In this context, Design Science Research (DSR) could provide valuable orientation for the iterative implementation of innovative teaching approaches. While the Proficiency Model for DSR summarizes competencies needed to conduct DSR projects, concrete guidance on how to apply DSR to innovative teaching is lacking. Therefore, we address this research gap by extending the Proficiency Model with concrete guidelines that support conducting DSR. These guidelines are derived from an instantiation of two conducted design cycles within a lecture for information system students, resulting in seventeen guidelines that guide lecturers in higher education on how to implement DSR for the iterative transformation of their courses towards meaningful technology-enhanced learning environments.

Keywords: Technology-enhanced Learning · Higher Education · Guidelines

1 Introduction

Technology-enhanced learning environments (TELE) are on the rise as technology is increasingly integrated to enhance traditional lectures [1] to improve students' learning [2]. However, lecturers' perceived lack of knowledge, skills, and confidence in integrating technology into higher education teaching remains a significant barrier towards innovative teaching approaches [3]. A lack of technological adaptation and innovation in higher education teaching can undermine valuable learning experiences [4] and neglect the needs of digitally-native students [5]. While the initial approach to TELE is fundamental, in an ever-changing environment, innovative higher education teaching also requires creative and evidence-based ways to continually adapt and improve [6, 7]. Consequently, lecturers might no longer be considered exclusively as traditional educators, but also as designers of innovative and adaptive TELE approaches [6], in means of design science [8, 9]. However, to address lecturers' perceived barriers towards TELE, tangible support is needed [3]. Against this background, Design Science Research (DSR) could provide valuable guidance on how to approach the transformation of higher education towards TELE. The methodology addresses the iterative design of innovative artifacts that are designed to benefit its users and created in alignment with the environment as well as the existing scientific knowledge base [10, 11]. As a result, DSR could provide lecturers orientation regarding the initial design of TELE, starting with simple low barrier artifact aiming towards innovating the teaching. Moreover, DSR can further guide how to iteratively evolve higher education teaching [12]. So far, there are isolated approaches analyzing the value of understanding design science as a method for enriching higher education teaching with promising findings [13, 14]. However, despite the understanding of the value of design science for higher education [12], DSR is currently underrepresented in educational pedagogy [15], and, consequently, concrete guidance on how to apply DSR to the design of innovative higher education teaching is not sufficiently analyzed. In terms of orientation for DSR education, the Proficiency Model (PM) addresses the need to further understand the interface between educational pedagogy and DSR by providing guidance on how to teach DSR with the definition of six proficiencies needed to conduct DSR [15]. Nevertheless, how these proficiencies can be used by lecturers to instantiate DSR for higher education teaching has not yet been considered. Thus, we aim towards expanding the PM [15] and derive application-oriented guidelines that include crucial procedural DSR aspects, and therefore, support lecturers in applying DSR for TELE projects. Consequently, this article seeks to answer the following research question:

What are fundamental application-oriented guidelines for DSR projects in higher education for the design of meaningful TELE?

To answer the research question, we follow a reflective approach [16]: Based on experiences from a concrete DSR instantiation, we derive guidelines for the application of the DSR proficiencies towards innovative TELE in higher education. To outline the path from the DSR instantiation to the guidelines in a transparent way, we first present the DSR instantiation in Sect. 3. The description of our DSR instantiation is therefore not presented in detail, but rather serves as a means to provide an experience-based foundation. Based on this DSR instantiation, we then derive concrete guidelines in Sect. 4, in accordance with the PM's DSR proficiencies, to provide guidance on how to implement DSR for designing and adapting innovative TELE. The contribution of this article can be understood as an exaptation [17]: We build on an existing artifact, the PM, and do not use it in its original form, but as an orientation for DSR in education, by applying its defined proficiencies to derive concise guidelines for DSR projects in the context of TELE. Thus the guidelines convey DSR process knowledge [18, 19] for lecturers and guide the process of designing and improving TELE in higher education.

2   Theoretical Background and Related Work

DSR highlights the significance of addressing real-world problems. Central to this research process is the design of an innovative, problem-solving artifact, emphasizing design activities as a vital step in developing innovative solutions. DSR adopts an iterative approach, enabling ongoing enhancement of solutions with feedback and evaluation [10, 11]. Due to this iterative character, DSR addresses the same underlying activities that are demanded when designing TELE: Both approaches address a real-world problem, use existing (learning) theories in order to develop innovative prototypes in an evidence based manner [8]. However, while DSR enables a broad application context and possible synergy effects for Information Systems researchers with a teaching assignment, [15] address the current lack of contributions in teaching DSR. With the aim to support educators in teaching DSR, different approaches with principles for teaching DSR are introduced: [20] present a design of a DSR course for PhD and Master levels. In addition, the teaching framework for DSR education of master students provides tangible design principles for creating DSR courses [21]. While these approaches provide tangible advice, different to our approach, these articles specifically focus on guidance for teaching DSR (e.g. "Get students to speed-up Quickly" [21]). A framework that allows for a boarder perspective of DSR in higher education is the PM which defines six core DSR proficiencies essential to the effective conduct of DSR" (Fig. 1) [15]. These proficiencies, which are formulated more generally, thus allow for a broader application compared to the (design) principles for designing DSR courses.

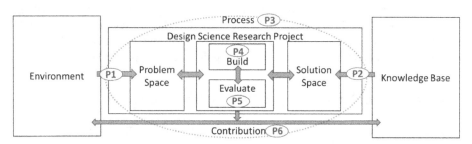

Fig. 1. DSR according to [10] including the six DSR proficiencies [15]

The PM guides and supports the teaching and development of six DSR proficiencies: (P1): Representing the problem space; (P2): Capturing existent knowledge in the solution space; (P3): Controlling the DSR process; (P4): Building innovative design artifacts; (P5): Measuring the satisfaction of research goals through rigorous evaluation; (P6): Contributing to science and practice. The PM offers practical guidance for adoption to various academic, training, and executive audiences, ensuring that DSR education can be effective and accessible. While the PM originally supports the teaching of essential DSR proficiencies [15], the described proficiencies also provide us with a structure for deriving guidelines that support DSR projects in higher education.

While we could not identify existing frameworks for applying DSR to higher education projects for designing meaningful TELE, there is related research. Similar to our approach also [13] analyze the value of DSR for creating and developing learning methods in higher education settings. Their study suggests that using DSR approaches can significantly improve the understanding of learning in technical subjects such as engineering, and helps to improve the design of learning materials [13]. DSR can support the creation of course materials and their content by its unique iterative character [13]. In addition to studies on DSR in education, there are tools such as 'MyDesign-Process' [22] that support DSR project organization and thus, may provide valuable guidance for DSR practitioners.

When analyzing contributions regarding DSR and education in general, most researchers present articles on how they teach DSR as a research methodology in their courses [23, 24]. Since 2022 the DESRIST has the track "Education and DSR" indicating an increasing interest for education in the DSR community [15, 25]. Within this track, most researchers use DSR for their artifact development [26] and usually conduct one iteration [27–29]. Often this iteration is the first step in the development of an artifact (e.g. [27–29]). When using DSR for a lecture design, researchers often take a long time of development [29]. Projects like [29] last for years and represent one iteration of an artifact development that covers a whole course. But usually, DSR is iterative by nature and thus, could take place in, e.g., one lesson. In addition, researcher often teach DSR within their courses and present the structure of the DSR course and how to teach DSR essentials [23, 24]. Apart from teaching DSR, researchers offer solutions for different goals/use cases e.g. design principles for knowledge sharing [30], design principles for e-learning [31], or taxonomies for study designs [32]. Overall, the related articles highlight the value of DSR in education, but the contributions lack guidance for concrete and meaningful recommendations to implement higher education teaching with the help of DSR. While there are some recommendations regarding single DSR projects in higher education, there is a need for further investigation and research towards tangible, comprehensive, and practice-oriented guidance for applying DSR.

3   Instantiating DSR for Designing Higher Education

In order to transparently outline the DSR character of our DSR project, we shortly present our implementation of the DSR process [11]. While the presentation of our DSR instantiation and its findings are not in focus of this article, they rather act on a meta level as the reference for our experiences regarding the implementation of DSR for education. We build on this reference in our reflective approach in Sect. 4 to derive concrete guidelines on how to apply DSR for innovative higher education teaching. In this chapter we shortly introduce the addressed problem space as well as the designed artifact of our concrete DSR instantiation. The iterative DSR project with the aim of addressing real-word problems in our current higher education teaching took place within one semester at a German University (April–July). Within this one semester, we were able to complete two design cycles, starting with a simple prototype and a further evolved prototype based on students' feedback. Figure 2 depicts the two conducted design cycles in accordance to [11]. The central artifact is a collaboration script. Collaboration scripts typically structure group work process of learners and define distinct phases, assign learners to roles, and provide guidance in form of concrete prompts [33]. Thus, they can promote effective student cooperation in TELE. Within our DSR project, both prototypes convey a collaboration script that is similar in its pedagogical structure and prompts but differ in their way of delivery: The first rapid prototype is a PDF-based collaboration script, while the evolved second prototype is a collaboration script conveyed by a plug-in for the university's Learning Management System (LMS).

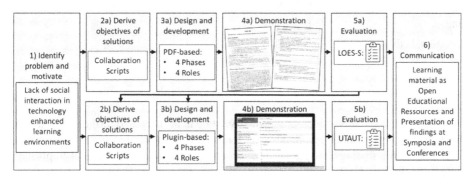

Fig. 2. Instantiated DSR process according to [11]

In the following, we outline the steps of our first design cycle (Fig. 2): **1)** We identified the real word problem: Student collaboration in peer groups can fail to deliver the potential positive learning outcomes because individual students work at their own pace without considering their peers, student participation is uneven, or some students even refuse to contribute [34, 35]. This can have a negative impact on students' motivation as well as learning outcomes [36]. To address this problem, the research field of pedagogical psychology proposes collaboration scripts. These scripts can support students' cooperation in lecturers or seminars by structuring group tasks with phases and phase-specific prompts to clearly outline how students can work together effectively [37]. Their effectiveness has been demonstrated in studies along multiple disciplines in higher education [38, 39]. However, their effectiveness depends on their design and structure. **2a)** Therefore, we aim to design collaboration scripts for our lecture by first developing a generic structure that can be filled with concrete roles and tasks. We understand collaboration scripts as a technological element that we integrate in our lecture. **3a)** As a first prototype we designed a simple collaboration script for students. Each student perceived the collaboration script containing five PDF pages. The collaboration script presented the learning scenario, four distinct learner roles, structured phases for the collaboration tasks as well as phase-specific prompts. **4a)** The demonstration took place at the beginning of the summer term in April. **5a)** To determine how students perceived the prototype of collaboration scripts, we evaluated the initial prototype using the Learning Object Evaluation Scale for Students (LOES-S) [40].

Table 1 provides the results of the LOES-S and as the summarized qualitative feedback.

The quantitative assessment suggests that students ($N = 21$) liked the interaction with the collaboration script overall, as all values (learning, quality, and engagement) show

Table 1. Evaluation of first prototype

Quantitative data		Qualitative data			
Construct	Mean	Students liked	#	Students disliked	#
Learning	3.58	Cooperation in group	17	Timing	7
Quality	3.67	Taking on roles	2	Too complex	4
Engagement	3,70	Practical relevance	1	Group finding	3
1 = strongly disagree 5 = strongly agree		Increased motivation	1	Just one topic	2
		Clear instruction	1		

high values (above 3.5). Besides, the qualitative statements provided further information about specific features of the collaboration scripts students liked or did not like.

Based on the findings, we started the second design cycle with the goal to present students an improved collaboration script prototype at the end of the semester. Based on the evaluation **2b)** we derived the following objectives for the solutions:

Table 2. Requirements as a result of the first design cycle and responses

Identified demand	Objectives for solutions
Student groups miss support regarding timing regarding the change of phases	Guide student groups through collaboration phases to ensure and support their progress
Seeing the entire collaboration script and its tasks are too much information at once	Display only relevant prompts in the current phase, not the entire collaboration script

Considering these additional demands, we developed a generic plug-in for the university's LMS. **3b)** This plug-in is able to convey the same information as the PDF files, but additionally allows a more structured process and provides only relevant information in each phase. **4b)** We presented the second, plugin-based collaboration script to students at the end of the summer semester. **5b)** To identify the value of the technology-based collaboration script, we aimed for a more technology related understanding. Therefore, we integrated constructs of the Unified Theory of Acceptance and Use of Technology (UTAUT). The assessment suggests that students (N = 17) overall liked the interaction with the collaboration script as all values, show means above 3 (= "neither agree nor disagree"). Students negatively highlighted the need of a VPN-connection to access the prototypes. This is due to a test system being used. This critique will be eliminated after the prototype is transferred to the productive system. Overall, the evaluation reveals that students enjoy the second prototype and noticed the improvements.

Through the evaluations and their resulting insights regarding DSR knowledge, we were able to generate communicable knowledge. **6)** Thus, we will share our prototype as an open educational resource. Besides this, we aim to present our findings of this DSR instantiation at symposia and a conference. These contributions will provide further

Table 3. Evaluation of the second prototype

Quantitative data		Qualitative data			
Construct	Mean	Students liked	#	Students disliked	#
Situation-Specific Skills	3,36	Intuitive handling	11	VPN-Connection	2
Performance Expectancy	3,55	Role distribution	1	Nothing	7
Effort Expectancy	3,72	1 = strongly disagree 5 = strongly agree			
Attitude toward Use	3,51				
Intrinsic Motivation	3,89				

design details, including the concrete content of the collaboration scripts, together with the discussion of the results. In the present article, we only briefly introduce the DSR instantiation at a meta level to provide the basis for Sect. 4, where we derive the guidelines for applying DSR, towards designing innovative higher education teaching.

4   Application-Oriented Extension of the Proficiency Model

In this chapter we outline how we applied the DSR proficiencies in our DSR instantiation for developing TELE. As described in Sect. 3, the central DSR artifact are collaboration scripts which represent a digital component of our TELE. This chapter is structured according to the PM [15]. Consequently, each proficiency is first described *(D)*. After that, we outline our *application (AP)* of each DSR proficiency along with a brief evaluation of our approach through *argumentation (AG)*. We then derive the *guidelines (G)* on how to apply the DSR proficiencies for creating innovative TELE.

P 1: Representing the Problem Space

(D): DSR projects aim to address practical issues and achieve tangible results in real-life scenarios. The initial skill for DSR projects is the ability to clearly define and outline a manageable problem space for their project [15]. To apply P1 and identify a relevant real-world problem, we initially reflected on real learning experiences in our higher education environment. This includes our own impressions, but also communication with students to reveal existing learning problems from their perspective. In our DSR instantiation, we as lecturers identified the problem of dysfunction in student group learning tasks, which led to some groups with good task solutions, while other groups had poor solutions or no solutions at all. When we talked to the students, they explained this in terms of uneven student participation in the group tasks, which led to a decrease in motivation and frustration. *(AG):* This experience-based process of identifying the problem space enabled us to later address a relevant problem for our target group. This is also supported by the evaluation of our DSR instantiation, where 17 (out of 21) students highlighted that they especially enjoyed the interaction within their group through our prototype. Thus, we conclude:

G1: Reflect on your own teaching experiences with regard to problems that arise.

G2: Build your DSR project around your students' experiences and needs.

(AP): Besides the experience-based approach to apply P1, we reviewed literature to expand our knowledge of the real-world scenario. *(AG):* Regarding our real-world problem, we identified more literature that highlighted the resulting challenges of ineffective student group work, along with other literature that emphasized the importance of effective student group work. Thus, the literature review was able to further strengthen our intention to target the experience-based identified problem space. The results are as follows:

G3: Review literature regarding your students' experiences and demands.

(AP): In addition to the experience-based identification of the target problem and its validation through the literature, it is important for innovative TELE approaches in higher education to take predefined environmental parameters into account. This includes the consideration of defined pedagogical demands, such as curricula, form of examination, as well as technical boundaries, such as the available IT infrastructure, in order to further characterize and define the problem space. *(AG):* In our instantiation it was important to consider the familiar technological infrastructure of our students. Thus, we aimed for an LMS plug-in in the second prototype. The results of the prototype evaluation showed that the students appreciated the familiar TELE. This leads to:

G4: Consider pedagogical aims and technological infrastructure.

P 2: Capturing Existent Knowledge in the Solution Space
(D): To ensure the rigor of DSR, it is essential to examine the existing knowledge in the field of DSR. This involves exploring existing solutions to identify potential technology solutions or approaches. Here, the main challenge is to gather relevant information from both technical and scientific sources to effectively carry out the DSR project [15]. *(AP):* We applied P2 through a literature search towards effective solutions targeting the real-world problem. We identified that in the field of pedagogical psychology, collaboration scripts are considered as a valuable tool to support students' learning and effective cooperation in TELE. To quickly get a state-of the art overview, we focused primarily on meta-studies and literature reviews. Using the literature on collaboration scripts, we were able to learn about typical structures of collaboration scripts and methods for conveying collaboration scripts to students [37]. Besides, meta studies have demonstrated the success of student cooperation using collaboration scripts, also in IS related courses. *(AG):* This provided structure and an evidence-based approach towards addressing our identified real world-problem. Our evaluation supports this procedure as the results regarding students' learning and motivation are also in line with existing research (Tables 2 and 3). Consequently, we suggest:

G5: Build the initial prototype on state-of-the art research.

(AP): Once we decided to use the knowledge base of collaboration scripts to design the learning materials, we searched for existing solutions to implement them. However, we could not find a technical tool in our learning environment that could do this. Therefore, we decided to create our first prototype as a PDF version. For the second version we

decided to build on the existing LMS and design a plug-in. *(AG):* Building on existing artifacts can save a lot of time and resources. By looking at the existing LMS and its implemented features, we were able to save resources, for example, the functionality to create learning groups for collaboration scripts is already built into the LMS, saving time in developing other needed features. Therefore, we suggest:

G6: Consider existing technical innovations before developing new ones.

(AP): Developing new tools is time-consuming and personal resources are often scarce. Thus, we decided to join a cross-faculty project and outsourced the programming of our plug-in to external professionals. Although, the project management could be also time-consuming, usually common problems are addressed rapidly from the project members (crowd knowledge). *(AG):* This will help to avoid major pitfalls and may result in a more mature software prototype in the end, that could not only be used by the lecturers, but other interested educators and institutions. Thus, we recommend:

G7: Consider teaming up with partners with similar pedagogical aims.

P 3: Controlling the Design Science Research Process

(D): To be successful in a DSR project, careful research management and a sharp focus on evolving problems and solutions are crucial. DSR projects prioritize adaptable learning through systematic, step-by-step exploration, which is especially valuable in unpredictable and dynamic problem scenarios. DSR teams initiate iterative cycles to construct and refine their solutions with precision, and they may also identify and elaborate on relevant design theories after reflecting on their project outcomes [15]. *(AP):* To apply P3, we made a schedule for our DSR project. Starting with the lecture unit in which we intend to demonstrate the prototype, we planned backwards in time. We defined several time frames considering individual DSR steps, time buffers for revisions, as well as important deadlines such as the demonstration of the prototype. With the time buffers we considered enough time for low-barrier functional tests of our artifact with student assistants. *(AG):* This allowed us to identify problems or challenges at an early stage and to quickly remove significant errors: E.g., within one early test, the group task structured through the collaboration script needed to be interrupted due to unclear task descriptions. Through these early and low-barrier tests we could eliminate crucial "showstoppers" that could negatively affect students' learning experiences, before the demonstration and evaluation phase begins. Therefore, we suggest:

G8: Create a time plan that includes deadlines, time buffers and early, low-barrier tests of the DSR artifact.

P 4: Building Innovative Design Artifacts

(D): After mastering the initial three proficiencies in a DSR project, the creative phase begins, which involves the development of innovative design artifacts. This phase focuses on generating new ideas and making educated choices about the most suitable idea for implementation. Creativity serves as the foundation for innovation, which is defined as the process of generating ideas that are both original and practical [15]. *(AP):* Based

on our initial testing, we applied P4 starting with an error-free but simple prototype. In our example, we formulated an initial prototype in a text program and shared it with the students as PDF files. This way, we did not have to make massive changes to the students' learning environment. However, the PDFs already allowed students to experience the use of collaboration scripts by structuring a group task with phases and prompts as they would in the final prototype. *(AG):* This is depicted in the evaluation of the first design cycle: While we presented a rapid prototype, student assessed their learning experiences at high levels (Table 2). Consequently, we suggest:

G9: Start with a minimal version of a quickly developed, but functional prototype.

P 5: Measuring the Satisfaction of Research Goals with Rigorous Evaluation

(D): Comprehensive evaluation methods establish connections between solutions (within the solution space) and problems (within the problem space), offering proof of how effectively a solution addresses a problem through the chosen evaluation techniques. In the context of DSR, we can distinguish between formative and summative evaluations, each serving a distinct conceptual purpose [15]. *(AP):* To apply P5, we presented the first prototype to our students at the beginning of the semester. After the demonstration, we measured students' experiences of the prototype to enable further evidence-based improvements of the prototype. We also mentioned that students would benefit from their constructive feedback as we consider their suggestions for the next version of the prototype which they may use at the end of the semesters. *(AG):* In this way, the students seemed to be open to feedback, as they appear as "co-developers". This is reflected in the high response rate within our evaluations. Thus, we conclude:

G10: Present the initial prototype at the beginning of the semester.
G11: Enable students to take the role of "co-developers".

(AP): We applied P5 considering the rigorous evaluation by integrating existing questionnaires. We used a survey tool for students to provide anonymous feedback using quantitative and qualitative items. *(AG):* This allows for insights at different levels and feedback that might not be covered elsewhere. The use of rigorous questionnaires also allows a rigorous knowledge transfer. Besides, qualitative questions allow students to provide further feedback. In the educational setting, it is also important to consider time constraints. The evaluation should be a small additional element and not take up much time outside of the lecture. In addition, lecturers should consider that students may be more open to critical feedback when it is anonymous. In our evaluation of the prototype, the quantitative evaluation indicated the value of the prototype, while the qualitative statements gave us ideas for improvements (Tables 2 and 3). Thus, we suggest:

G12: Survey rigorous quantitative and qualitative items.
G13: Consider the time constraints and the option for anonymous feedback.

(AP): While the written evaluation provides anonymous feedback, students seem to be more vocal when speaking. In addition, lecturers can ask if some feedback statements are unclear and thereby consider these aspects in the future. *(AG):* We noticed that students were happy to talk about their experiences and that students' verbal responses

were more detailed and revealed more information than their written responses. The communication with the students allowed us to clearly understand the written qualitative statements of the first evaluation. This is indicated by the results of the second evaluation, which suggest that the students also perceived an improvement in the second prototype as the previously negatively commented issues did not appear in the second evaluation. In addition, while in the first evaluation 16 (out of 21) students mentioned negative aspects of the prototype, in the second evaluation only 5 (out of 17) students had negative remarks. Thus, we conclude:

G14: Verbally ask students for feedback after interacting with the prototype.

P 6: Contributing to Science and Practice
(D): In a DSR project, the main goals are to contribute to both academic knowledge and practical solutions. These contributions typically take the form of design artifacts and design theory. This dual focus ensures that DSR projects have a meaningful impact in both the academic and practical fields [15]. *(AP):* To contribute to the problem spaces and apply P6, we share our iteratively developed learning materials as open educational resources. In our case, we share the collaboration scripts as open educational resources and the code for the LMS plug-in is open source, so that any university using the same LMS can use the plug-in [see Blinded]. *(AG):* This way, practical contribution could be used by other lectures teaching IS. As a result, we suggest:

G15: Share the practical contribution of the DSR project.

(AP): In addition, we consider conferences to be especially valuable in contributing to science. This allows lecturers to connect with other educators and researchers to learn from others, but also to inspire others on how to create meaningful TELE. Moreover, lecturers receive academic feedback, and thus, can ground further design cycles on a broader and more rigorous knowledge base. *(AG):* In our instantiation, we had the opportunity to discuss the first collaboration script (prototype 1) with other lecturers, which allowed us to improve our concept for prototype 2. Therefore, we conclude:

G16: Share the pragmatic and descriptive findings e.g., on conferences or symposia.

(AP): More mature DSR projects with a sufficient number of evaluation participants and a rigorous evaluation design can generate valuable insights, e.g., on user acceptance or learning processes, achievements, or learning outcomes while using technology. *(AG):* These findings can contribute to new theoretical insights into innovative TELE, not only for IS research, but also pedagogical psychology. This will lead to more guidance for developing meaningful theoretical background when designing further related approaches. Therefore, we suggest:

G17: Share and discuss the theoretical findings e.g., in journals.

5 Conclusion

This study aims to expand the body of DSR knowledge that contributes providing lecturers support in form of guidelines on how to instantiate DSR projects for innovative higher education teaching. Table 4 presents our derived guidelines for applying the six proficiencies for DSR in a concise manner.

Table 4. Application-oriented guidelines for DSR projects to design meaningful TELE

(P1) Representing the problem space [15]
G1: Reflect on your own teaching experiences with regard to problems that arise G2: Build your DSR project around your students' experiences and needs G3: Review literature regarding your students' experiences and demands G4: Consider pedagogical aims and technological infrastructure
(P2) Capturing extant knowledge in the solution space [15]
G5: Base the initial prototype on state-of-the art research G6: Consider technical innovations before developing new ones G7: Consider teaming up with partners with similar pedagogical aims
(P3) Controlling the DSR process [15]
G8: Create a time plan that includes deadlines, time buffers and early, low-barrier tests of the DSR artifact
(P4) Building innovative design artifacts [15]
G9: Start with a minimal version of a quickly developed, but functional prototype
(P5) Measuring the satisfaction of research goals with rigorous evaluation [15]
G10: Present the initial prototype at the beginning of the semester G11: Enable students to take the role of "co-developers" G12: Survey rigorous quantitative and qualitative items G13: Consider the time constraints and the option for anonymous feedback G14: Verbally ask students for feedback after interacting with the prototype
(P6) Contributing to science and practice [15]
G15: Share the practical contribution of the DSR project G16: Share the pragmatic and descriptive findings e.g., on conferences or symposia G17: Share the theoretical findings e.g., in journals

These guidelines are derived by applying an existing DSR artifact, the PM, to a new context: While the model was originally developed to guide DSR teaching, we apply the model to facilitate DSR projects targeting TELE in higher education. To do so, we used the six defined proficiencies required to conduct DSR as templates and applied them in the course of a practical DSR project that aims towards designing learning materials for an IS lecture. In chronological order, we describe the six defined proficiencies and show how we applied each of the six proficiencies in our concrete DSR project. Thus, we expand the proficiencies defined in the PM to construct a proficiency-centered presentation of applicable DSR knowledge in form of guidelines.

Expanding the PM as a framework with tangible guidelines derived from our experiences considers rigor and relevance of DSR. By implementing DSR for the design of TELE, we aim to demonstrate the tangible alignment of the PM addressing DSR teaching content with its application in real-world scenarios. In addition, the PM serves as a critical lens through which we analyze and extend DSR knowledge, highlighting the proficiencies and their application-oriented extensions that are essential for the successful implementation of DSR projects in higher education. This process therefore includes not only theoretical considerations, but also integrates insights from our practical DSR instantiation, thereby enriching the applicability and relevance of the PM.

Our intention to expand the PM to include the promotion of DSR projects in higher education is ultimately aimed at providing higher education institutions with a tool to promote innovation in higher education lectures. We understand the expansion as a valuable addition to DSR, as it can provide lecturers a tangible guidance on how to integrate DSR projects into their teaching. This allows lecturers to benefit in three ways: **1)** From an educational perspective, lecturers get orientation on how to instantiate DSR in their higher education teaching. **2)** Lecturers teaching DSR could gain broader experience and understanding in DSR activities. **3)** From an academic perspective, DSR practitioners could benefit from additional DSR projects in the educational context, as this could expand their usual research area and thus broaden their DSR applications.

6 Outlook

This article and the derived guidelines aim to inspire and guide lecturers who wish to innovate their higher education teaching while gaining DSR proficiencies. Thus, the guidelines can be considered a supporting resource that provides orientation but should not be understood as a normative corset to be strictly followed by higher education lecturers. Building on the PM, the guidelines offer heuristics based on a concrete DSR instantiation and the authors' experience in conducting DSR for iterative adaptation of teaching. As a result, the application-oriented extension of the PM has limitations. 1) The proposed guidelines are based on concrete experiences in one IS course with two DSR cycles. However, while the guidelines are limited in their single application, they represent the essence of three lecturers involved in the DSR instantiation. 2) When conducting evaluations with students about their experiences in a lecture, they might be afraid to evaluate the artifacts (in form of learning material) too critically, because they might fear negative consequences for their future learning experiences if they criticize their lecturer and his/her ideas too harshly. 3) This article derives the extensions of the PM based on the explanation of the model and its application in a lecture. While our application-based extension of the PM is based on a real-world DSR instantiation, complementary evaluations and adaptations may be valuable to further evolve the guidelines. Expert interviews, user feedback, and further instantiations can complement this study and examine whether the seventeen formulated guidelines are understandable and useful for lecturers aiming at TELE. To apply and further test our guidelines, we will integrate new DSR projects into our university teaching in the future. In the upcoming semester, we plan to address the real problem of the lack of student guidance in TELE. Here we propose a solution in the field of learning analytics. Following our guidelines, we will again start a simple prototype to investigate students' initial acceptance of the new concept within our teaching approach. Then, based on these findings, an iterative development of the learning analytics prototype will take place. In addition to an application-oriented evaluation, our proposed guidelines could also benefit from theoretical insights provided by related disciplines of the design-oriented educational community (e.g., design-based research [41]).

Overall, we highlight the value of DSR for designing TELE to iteratively adapt higher education teaching to the demands fostered by the learning environment and students. Thus, we encourage further approaches to use DSR to design TELE and understand higher education teaching as a DSR artifact that is iteratively adapted based on the demands of the changing environment and its stakeholders, especially students.

Acknowledgements. This work was supported by the 'Stiftung Innovation in der Hochschullehre' (FBM2020: 'Facilitating Competence Development through Authentic, Digital, and Feedback-Based Teaching-Learning Scenarios') under Grant FBM2020-EA-2620-01350. The collaboration software mentioned in this article is 'CoLearn!', a Stud.IP plugin and one result of this project.

References

1. Lin, M.-H., Chen, H.-C., Liu, K.-S.: A study of the effects of digital learning on learning motivation and learning outcome. Eurasia J. Math. Sci. Technol. Educ. **13**, 3553–3564 (2017). https://doi.org/10.12973/eurasia.2017.00744a
2. Schweighofer, P., Ebner, M.: Aspects to be considered when implementing technology-enhanced learning approaches: a literature review. Future Internet **7**, 26–49 (2015)
3. Dinc, E.: Prospective teachers' perceptions of barriers to technology integration in education. Contemp. Educ. Technol. **10**, 381–398 (2019)
4. Naidu, S.: Building resilience in education systems post-COVID-19. Distance Educ. **42**, 1–4 (2021). https://doi.org/10.1080/01587919.2021.1885092
5. Alenezi, M.: Digital learning and digital institution in higher education. Educ. Sci. **13**, 88 (2023). https://doi.org/10.3390/educsci13010088
6. Kim, M.S.: Developing a competency taxonomy for teacher design knowledge in technology-enhanced learning environments: a literature review. RPTEL **14**, 18 (2019)
7. Hustad, E., Olsen, D.H.: Educating reflective Enterprise Systems practitioners: a design research study of the iterative building of a teaching framework. Inf. Syst. J. **24**, 445–473 (2014). https://doi.org/10.1111/isj.12032
8. Laurillard, D.: Teaching as a Design Science: Building Pedagogical Patterns for Learning and Technology. Routledge, New York (2012)
9. McKenney, S., Kali, Y., Markauskaite, L., Voogt, J.: Teacher design knowledge for technology enhanced learning: an ecological framework for investigating assets and needs. Instr. Sci. **43**, 181–202 (2015). https://doi.org/10.1007/s11251-014-9337-2
10. Hevner, A.R.: A three cycle view of design science research. Scand. J. Inf. Syst. **19**, 87–92 (2007)

11. Peffers, K., Tuunanen, T., Rothenberger, M.A., Chatterjee, S.: A design science research methodology for information systems research. J. Manag. Inf. Syst. **24**, 45–77 (2007). https://doi.org/10.2753/MIS0742-1222240302

12. Fahd, K., Miah, S.J., Ahmed, K., Venkatraman, S., Miao, Y.: Integrating design science research and design based research frameworks for developing education support systems. Educ. Inf. Technol. **26**, 4027–4048 (2021). https://doi.org/10.1007/s10639-021-10442-1

13. Carstensen, A.-K., Bernhard, J.: Design science research – a powerful tool for improving methods in engineering education research. Eur. J. Eng. Educ. **44**, 85–102 (2019). https://doi.org/10.1080/03043797.2018.1498459

14. Goldkuhl, G., Ågerfalk, P., Sjöström, J.: A design science approach to information systems education. In: Maedche, A., vom Brocke, J., Hevner, A. (eds.) DESRIST 2017. LNCS, vol. 10243, pp. 383–397. Springer, Cham (2017). https://doi.org/10.1007/978-3-319-59144-5_23

15. Hevner, A., vom Brocke, J.: A proficiency model for design science research education. J. Inf. Syst. Educ. **34**, 264–278 (2023)

16. Möller, F., Guggenberger, T.M., Otto, B.: Towards a method for design principle development in information systems. In: Hofmann, S., Müller, O., Rossi, M. (eds.) DESRIST 2020. LNCS, vol. 12388, pp. 208–220. Springer, Cham (2020). https://doi.org/10.1007/978-3-030-64823-7_20

17. Gregor, S., Hevner, A.R.: Positioning and presenting design science research for maximum impact. MIS Q. **37**, 337–355 (2013)

18. vom Brocke, J., Winter, R., Hevner, A., Maedche, A.: Special issue editorial – accumulation and evolution of design knowledge in design science research: a journey through time and space. J. Assoc. Inf. Syst. **21**, 520–544 (2020)

19. Baskerville, R., Baiyere, A., Gregor, S., Hevner, A., Rossi, M.: Design science research contributions: finding a balance between artifact and theory. J. Assoc. Inf. Syst. **19**, 3 (2018)

20. Winter, R., vom Brocke, J.: Teaching design science research. In: Association for Information Systems (ed.) Proceedings of the 42nd International Conference on Information Systems (ICIS 2021), pp. 1–6 (2021)

21. Schlimbach, R., et al.: A teaching framework for the methodically versatile DSR education of master's students. J. Inf. Syst. Educ. **34**, 333–346 (2023)

22. vom Brocke, J., Fettke, P., Gau, M., Houy, C., Morana, S.: Tool-support for design science research: design principles and instantiation (2017)

23. Zahn, E.-M., Dickhaut, E., Vonhof, M., Söllner, M.: Computational thinking for design science researchers – a modular training approach. In: Gerber, A., Baskerville, R. (eds.) DESRIST 2023, vol. 13873, pp. 360–374. Springer, Cham (2023). https://doi.org/10.1007/978-3-031-32808-4_23

24. Cahenzli, M.: DSR teaching support: a checklist for better DSR research design presentations. In: Drechsler, A., Gerber, A., Hevner, A. (eds.) DESRIST 2022, vol. 13229, pp. 445–457. Springer, Cham (2022). https://doi.org/10.1007/978-3-031-06516-3_33

25. Drechsler, A., Gerber, A., Hevner, A. (eds.): The Transdisciplinary Reach of Design Science Research. 17th International Conference on Design Science Research in Information Systems and Technology, DESRIST 2022, St Petersburg, FL, USA, June 1–3, 2022, Proceedings. LNCS, vol. 13229. Springer, Cham (2022). https://doi.org/10.1007/978-3-031-06516-3

26. Mueller, L.M., Platz, M.: Design of an augmented reality app for primary school students which visualizes length units to promote the conversion of units. In: Gerber, A., Baskerville, R. (eds.) DESRIST 2023, vol. 13873, pp. 314–328. Springer, Cham (2023). https://doi.org/10.1007/978-3-031-32808-4_20

27. Aguirre Reid, S., Kammer, F., Schüller, D., Siepermann, M., Wölfer, J.: Know the knowledge of your students: a flexible analytics tool for student exercises. In: Gerber, A., Baskerville, R. (eds.) DESRIST 2023, vol. 13873, pp. 329–344. Springer, Cham (2023). https://doi.org/10.1007/978-3-031-32808-4_21

28. Rajamany, V., van Biljon, J.A., van Staden, C.J.: User experience requirements of digital moderation systems in South Africa: using participatory design within design science research. In: Drechsler, A., Gerber, A., Hevner, A. (eds.) DESRIST 2022, vol. 13229, pp. 470–482. Springer, Cham (2022). https://doi.org/10.1007/978-3-031-06516-3_35

29. Figueiredo, J., García-Peñalvo, F.J.: Design science research applied to difficulties of teaching and learning initial programming. Univ. Access. Inf. Soc. 1–11 (2022). https://doi.org/10.1007/s10209-022-00941-4

30. Nurhas, I., Mattick, X., Geisler, S., Pawlowski, J.: System design principles for intergenerational knowledge sharing. In: Drechsler, A., Gerber, A., Hevner, A. (eds.) DESRIST 2022, vol. 13229, pp. 458–469. Springer, Cham (2022). https://doi.org/10.1007/978-3-031-06516-3_34

31. Haj-Bolouri, A.: Design principles for E-learning that support integration work: a case of action design research. In: Tulu, B., Djamasbi, S., Leroy, G. (eds.) DESRIST 2019, vol. 11491, pp. 300–316. Springer, Cham (2019). https://doi.org/10.1007/978-3-030-19504-5_20

32. Smuts, H., Winter, R., Gerber, A., van der Merwe, A.: "Designing" design science research – a taxonomy for supporting study design decisions. In: Drechsler, A., Gerber, A., Hevner, A. (eds.) DESRIST 2022, vol. 13229, pp. 483–495. Springer, Cham (2022). https://doi.org/10.1007/978-3-031-06516-3_36

33. Weinberger, A.: Scripts for computer-supported collaborative learning. Effects of social and epistemic cooperation scripts on collaborative knowledge construction, München (2003)

34. Kreijns, K., Kirschner, P.A., Jochems, W.: Identifying the pitfalls for social interaction in computer-supported collaborative learning environments: a review of the research. Comput. Hum. Behav. 19, 335–353 (2003). https://doi.org/10.1016/S0747-5632(02)00057-2

35. Pao, S.-Y., Mota, S., Chung, K., Reben, A.: A need-driven design approach. In: Poltrock, S., Simone, C., Grudin, J., Mark, G., Riedl, J. (eds.) Proceedings of the ACM 2012 Conference on Computer Supported Cooperative Work, pp. 829–832. ACM, New York (2012). https://doi.org/10.1145/2145204.2145327

36. Radkowitsch, A., Vogel, F., Fischer, F.: Good for learning, bad for motivation? A meta-analysis on the effects of computer-supported collaboration scripts. Int. J. Comput.-Support. Collab. Learn. 15, 5–47 (2020). https://doi.org/10.1007/s11412-020-09316-4

37. Kollar, I., Fischer, F., Hesse, F.W.: Collaboration scripts – a conceptual analysis. Educ. Psychol. Rev. 18, 159–185 (2006). https://doi.org/10.1007/s10648-006-9007-2

38. Jeong, H., Hmelo-Silver, C.E., Jo, K.: Ten years of computer-supported collaborative learning: a meta-analysis of CSCL in STEM education during 2005–2014. Educ. Res. Rev. 28, 100284 (2019). https://doi.org/10.1016/j.edurev.2019.100284

39. Rojas, M., Nussbaum, M., Guerrero, O., Chiuminatto, P., Greiff, S., Del Rio, R., Alvares, D.: Integrating a collaboration script and group awareness to support group regulation and emotions towards collaborative problem solving. Int. J. Comput.-Support. Collab. Learn. 17, 135–168 (2022). https://doi.org/10.1007/s11412-022-09362-0

40. Kay, R.H., Knaack, L.: Assessing learning, quality and engagement in learning objects: the learning object evaluation scale for students (LOES-S). Educ. Technol. Res. Dev. 57, 147–168 (2009). https://doi.org/10.1007/s11423-008-9094-5

41. Design-Based Research Collective: Design-based research: an emerging paradigm for educational inquiry. Educ. Res. 32, 5–8 (2003)

Let's Chat to Negotiate: Designing a Conversational Agent for Learning Negotiation Skills

Eva-Maria Zahn[1]([✉]) [iD] and Sofia Schöbel[2] [iD]

[1] Information Systems and Systems Engineering, University of Kassel, Kassel, Germany
zahn@uni-kassel.de
[2] Information Systems, University of Osnabrück, Osnabrück, Germany
sofia.schoebel@uni-osnabrueck.de

Abstract. Negotiating is relevant in private and work-life situations. Thus, negotiation skills are necessary and can be defined as a skill set, including skills such as problem-solving or communication. Negotiating with others is learned action-oriented and individually, making standard learning concepts less effective. Therefore, action-oriented and individual-adapted interactions are convenient but rarely available. Conversational agents seem to be a suitable solution to support the negotiation learning process so it can be more interactive and individualized. In this paper, we design a conversational agent that can act as a personal tutor and negotiation partner to support a learner in training negotiation skills. This paper presents evaluated design principles for designing conversational agents to foster learners' negotiation skills. The theoretically grounded design principles contribute to the existing theory on learning negotiation skills. On a practical level, we offer a new way of negotiation training that focuses on individuality and interactivity while providing a comprehensive learning concept for learning negotiation skills. Finally, companies are guided in the design and development of negotiation agents.

Keywords: Negotiation Skills · Conversational Agent · Digital Learning

1 Introduction

"Let us never negotiate out of fear. But let us never fear to negotiate."
– John F. Kennedy.

Negotiations are fundamental to our world, especially in business contexts. Rapid changes, flatter hierarchies in companies, more flexibility and agility of employees result in an increasing number of negotiations [1, 2]. To be successful in such a "negotiation network" [3], employees should not be afraid to negotiate. Thus, so-called negotiation skills are needed. Negotiation skills can be defined as a skill set consisting of various sub-skills, including (meta-)cognitive skills such as problem-solving or decision-making and socio-emotional skills [3–5]. However, current studies uncover that employees lack the skills to master negotiations effectively. For example, a study by the World Economic Forum 2022 shows that 87% of employees do not have the social and meta-cognitive skills required for the future labor market [6]. To best prepare students for the future labor market, universities need to address this skills gap. This includes that students should develop comprehensive negotiation skills supporting them in starting successfully in their professional lives. Universities, however, struggle to incorporate respective elements in their curriculum since existing concepts to teach negotiation skills are often costly, time and resource-intensive and lack consideration of individual learning experiences [7]. Additionally, to foster and learn negotiation skills, standard learning methods, such as frontal teaching, are unsuitable since personalized and interactive learning opportunities are required [8].

Research in the area of negotiation skills has shown that digital technologies can provide appropriate support, and in particular, intelligent tutoring systems can be designed to help students learn negotiation skills in pre-defined scenarios [7, 9]. A major challenge is that many approaches follow a one-size-fits-all logic and hardly rely on individualization and realistic learning scenarios [7]. One way to individualize learning to negotiate is with so-called conversational agents (CA). CAs can act as tutors to provide the learner with a personalized learning process while interacting with the learner through natural language [10, 11]. Furthermore, a CA can help to complete a task or give assistance and, therefore, is a suitable solution for supporting students in learning negotiation skills in an individual way. Moreover, a CA can also act as a negotiation partner to create environments that are as real as possible. This allows the CA to support humans, e.g., in university courses. Although CAs offer ways to address the challenge of individual and interactive learning of negotiation skills, there is little research on how CAs should be designed in this case. A comprehensive learning concept is often missing. Therefore, the study's aim is to develop a conceptual framework and to design a CA that supports negotiation skill learning processes. Thus, in this study, we want to address the following research question:

RQ: How should an adaptive CA be designed to help students learn negotiation skills?

To achieve our goal, we considered literature and a practitioner's view to develop requirements and design principles [12–14] to learn negotiation skills. After evaluating our design principles and prototype our study can be positioned as an application of a CA that is tailored for learning negotiation skills. Here, the importance of individual and verbal communication in negotiations needs to be highlighted with focusing on voice-based CAs. Previous studies demonstrated that voice-based interfaces can be successful in various learning situations [15] and thus be suitable in our case. However, the necessity of individuality especially results in the importance of considering the development of large language models and chatbots for further research.

With our study, we provide four main contributions: First, we support theory by transferring the experiential learning theory to the design of CAs for learning negotiation skills. Second, we discuss how CAs can be supportive when learning negotiation skills to overcome standardized, one-size-fits-all solutions by highlighting action-oriented and adaptive interactions. Third, we provide design recommendations and qualitative evidence on how to design CAs for learning negotiation skills. Finally, we support practitioners in guiding them towards the development of conversational agents for learning negotiation skills.

2 Conceptual Background and Related Work

2.1 Negotiations and the Harvard Negotiation Model

We negotiate daily in our private and workplaces [3, 8]. Negotiating is a process by which people try to find an agreement since their resources are limited, and each party wants to maximize its outcome [16]. One negotiation type addresses integrative/principled negotiations to focus on reaching win-win solutions for all parties. The Harvard Negotiation Model (HNM) is widely and frequently used to teach and understand principled negotiations [3]. The four principles and the three stages of the HNM are illustrated in Fig. 1. The method aims to accomplish amicably effective and interest-oriented negotiations with a win-win outcome for both parties while considering the four principles – people, interests, options, and criteria [3]. In Fig. 1, the fields with a light grey background indicate which principle is especially relevant at which stage of the HNM and thus should be given special attention in the respective stage. As the HNM is an established and widely used method, it forms the content basis for our negotiation learning process.

Principles / Stages	Analyze the situation or problem, the interests and perspectives of all parties involved, and evaluate the existing options.	Develop a plan for how to respond to the situation, considering the interests and perspectives of the other parties.	Discussion with the other parties in an attempt to find a mutually agreeable solution to the problem.
	Analysis Stage	**Planning Stage**	**Discussion Stage**
Separate **People** from the Problem...	...to avoid getting caught up in personal feelings or emotions, to get a clear view of the situation and be more objective.	...to avoid being distracted by emotions or personal issues, which can lead to misunderstandings.	...to overcome differences, create more mutually beneficial solutions and a more constructive negotiation process. Considering Empathy, Emotions, Communication and Think ahead.
Focus on **Interests**, not Positions...	...to understand the parties' underlying needs and motivations - therefore, to identify the interests behind the demand.	...to identify common ground and to create a shared understanding of relevant factors.	...to speak about the interests and to be hard on the subject, soft on the people. So, finding a more mutually beneficial solution and build trust between the parties.
Invent **Options** for Mutual Gain...	...to identify a range of potential solutions, to create a more creative negotiation process and to keep the own value high.	...to establish a basis for a reasoned negotiation approach and a common understanding of the relevant issues. Therefore, developing Best Alternatives to a Negotiation Agreement (BATNA).	...to find solutions that are more beneficial to both parties and to help resolving differences.
Insist on Using Objective **Criteria**...	...to ensure that the outcome is fair, reasonable, and based on a transparent process that considers the interests of all parties involved.	...to increase the likelihood of reaching an agreement satisfactory to both parties. Therefore, developing objective criteria.	...to negotiate with objective criteria and so, creating a more rational, cooperative, and constructive negotiation process.

Fig. 1. Elements of the Harvard Negotiation Model according to Fisher and Ury [3].

2.2 Learning Negotiation Skills

Negotiation skills are a skill set including (meta-)cognitive skills and socio-emotional skills [3–5]. While meta-cognitive skills, such as problem-solving, address the ability to monitor and control thoughts [17], socio-emotional skills, like emotional intelligence, comprise the ability to control the own emotions, thoughts, and behavior [18].

Moreover, when learning negotiation skills, learners' knowledge influences the negotiation performance [4]. Learning negotiation skills is a complex process. First, learners need to acquire basic strategies/principles for getting fundamental knowledge, which can be used as a "tool bag" in negotiations [5]. Second, learners need to act and reflect in action-oriented and real-world settings to practice negotiating [19]. Consequently, learners should foster their negotiation skills as realistically as possible and address learners' different levels of knowledge, motivation, and previous experience in negotiating [8]. Determining the effectiveness of negotiation skill learning includes various tests, such as indicators of goal achievement, self-assessments, transferring the skills and knowledge to different negotiation situations, as well as evaluating feedback from participants [20]. Nevertheless, it can be stated that when we mention negotiation skills in the following, we define them as a skill set that includes various sub-skills.

Experiential Learning Theory as a Kernel Theory. In support of an approach that targets the learning of negotiation skills, several studies have shown that an experiential learning approach is a particularly appropriate method [5, 21]. Therefore, we decided to use the experiential learning theory (ELT) [22] for our study and to design our negotiation CA. The ELT presents an approach that is designed as a cycle and consists of four main phases (see Fig. 2). While providing opportunities to practice and reflect on the learners' experience, the ELT aims for the learner to build comprehensive learning outcomes [19]. In addition, studies have shown that the observational methods inherent in experiential learning lend themselves to teaching and learning negotiation, especially when individualized [23].

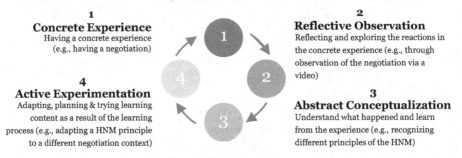

1
Concrete Experience
Having a concrete experience
(e.g., having a negotiation)

2
Reflective Observation
Reflecting and exploring the reactions in
the concrete experience (e.g., through
observation of the negotiation via a
video)

4
Active Experimentation
Adapting, planning & trying learning
content as a result of the learning
process (e.g., adapting a HNM principle
to a different negotiation context)

3
Abstract Conceptualization
Understand what happened and learn
from the experience (e.g., recognizing
different principles of the HNM)

Fig. 2. The four phases of experiential learning according to Kolb [22].

2.3 Learning Systems for Negotiation Skills

Research has demonstrated that negotiating in digital environments can support the learners' skills, e.g., while providing automated feedback [7]. For example, negotiation software agents (NSA) can act as negotiation partners, where the agents follow a pre-defined negotiation strategy that does not allow much flexibility in individualizing learning processes [24]. Another example is the text-based agent "NegoChat" [25] or the system "BiLAT" for providing negotiation training for U.S. army soldiers in pre-defined dialogues [9]. Electronic negotiations, where participants negotiate online and get support in making decisions, are potential systems to support the complexity of negotiations [26]. Such systems are a great starting point for learning negotiation skills, but they do not promote personalized, interactive, and real-world negotiations since they tend to follow a one-size-fits-all logic.

This individuality can be represented by using (pedagogical) Conversational Agents (CA) [11, 27]. CAs are software-based systems for interacting through natural language with the user [10]. CAs can be implemented in educational environments to perform complex tasks, such as giving personalized feedback [21] or supporting the user in solving tasks [28]. They can enrich interpersonal communication through text-based chatbots (e.g., ChatGPT) or voice-based agents (e.g., Amazon Alexa) [28]. However, there are still gaps when looking at previous research studies on CAs to support the learning of negotiation skills. For example, the aim of some studies is to learn a foreign language in the context of negotiations [29]. In the study by Yin and Satar [29], Chinese students should learn English as a foreign language and negotiate in English.

Another focus of CAs and negotiations can be found in learning metacognitive skills [30]. Through a spoken dialogue, learners negotiate with the CA and need to reach an agreement without fundamental knowledge of negotiation skills [30]. Frequently the process is not about learning how to negotiate. In addition, to implement a conceptual learning process for learning negotiation skills in a CA, it is important to apply established learning theories and go through an extensive development and design process.

3 Research Methodology

This study is part of the Design Science Research (DSR) approach, according to Peffers et al. [12], to derive the necessary requirements and principles for designing and developing a CA to learn negotiation skills (see Fig. 3).

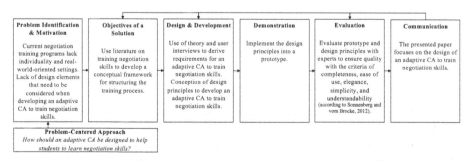

Fig. 3. Research Approach, according to Peffers et al. [12].

In this paper, we present a conceptual framework based on insights from literature and theory, design principles (DP), a prototype and an evaluation. We aim to contribute to the knowledge base connecting research areas of active learning, skill acquisition, and negotiation. The problem is identified and motivated in the introduction of this paper and addresses the first step of our DSR procedure. Here, we follow a problem-centered approach that relies on a CA to foster learners' negotiation skills.

Afterward, we focus on the literature on negotiation skill learning to convey literature requirements. To integrate the users' perspective into the design and to derive user requirements, we utilized 18 interviews with potential users. The approach of Mayring [31] followed the analysis of these user interviews. Based on the requirements from literature (LR) and practice (UR), we derive DPs that are formulated according to Gregor et al. [32]. Grounded on our DPs, we built a prototype and evaluated both with ten expert interviews with advanced DSR and teaching knowledge. Therefore, we referred to the DSR evaluation criteria given by Sonnenberg and vom Brocke [33].

4   Results

4.1   Problem Identification and Objectives of a Solution

Since negotiation skills are learned individually and in real-world oriented scenarios [5], CAs can offer suitable conditions to foster these skills. However, for developing a CA that can train negotiation skills, a conceptual foundation is necessary to include critical learning theories and concepts. Therefore, we defined the goals of the artifact [34] and referred to literature involving learning negotiation skills. We combined the insights of experiential learning [22] with the HNM [3] to build a three-level framework (levels a–c). For structuring the negotiation learning process (see Fig. 4).

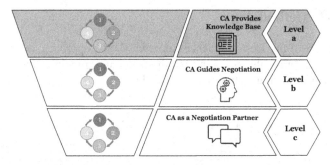

Fig. 4. Levels for Learning Negotiation Skills.

At each level, all four phases of the ELT are being handled. Regarding level a, we consider that if learners do not have basic knowledge of how to negotiate, it is crucial to learn lower-level goals on negotiation skills, including the content of the HNM (Level a; Fig. 4). For this purpose, it is vital to make a short assessment of learners' knowledge of negotiations and sub-skills. In our case, we focus on meta-cognitive skills in negotiations, such as problem-solving, decision-making, making reflections and strategies, as well as planning [3]. To do so, short self-assessments can be implemented to assess the learners' knowledge. In the next step, the learning content can be adapted to the learners' needs and level of knowledge. At the following level, the CA guides a negotiation, where the learner follows a pre-structured negotiation use case and gets help from the CA while executing the analysis, planning, and discussion stage of the HNM (level b). Finally, at level c, the CA acts as a negotiating partner. Further, learners can make short assessments after every learning level to check their preliminary learning results. Based on these assessments, a dynamic learning process can be provided, and learners can always go back to the previous steps if they want to.

4.2 Design and Development

Literature Requirements. To design a dynamic learning process, we first derive requirements from literature (see Fig. 5). We focused on the conceptual background, including literature on learning theories, previous skill-learning studies, as well as literature on learning negotiation skills. Therefore, we commenced with the literature analysis according to Webster & Watson [14] and vom Brocke et al. [13]. We followed the ELT as our kernel theory to design an effective learning system for negotiation skills. Therefore, interactivity should be provided to support learners' engagement [35]. Since negotiation skills are individual, learners' prior knowledge should be determined at the beginning of the learning process for a student-centered design [36]. Thus, assessment opportunities and the implementation of goal-oriented feedback are required [37]. It is important to provide learners without prior knowledge with primary content on principled negotiations [3].

Moreover, personalized feedback on learners' negotiation skills is necessary [21, 38]. Thus, providing comprehensive and personalized feedback throughout and after a negotiation process is relevant to reflect on the specific negotiation experience, considering phase 2 of the experiential learning approach as well as learning levels b and c. Ultimately, through real-world-oriented negotiations [5], learners can test their learned negotiation skills and practice them in interaction with a negotiation partner – our CA. Thus, the provision of real-life negotiation scenarios is crucial to support level C. These requirements assist us in incorporating fundamental theory and knowledge about learning negotiation skills into the artifact.

User Requirements. To consider the needs of learners and collect user requirements, we conducted 18 interviews with students, according to Mayring [31]. For the interviewees' selection, we considered students from European universities and various disciplines who are potential users. The semi-structured interview guideline consists of 36 questions, addressing three main chapters – general information on negotiation skills, learning negotiation skills, and interacting with learning tools for negotiation skills. The interviews took approximately 39.25 min (mean). The shortest interview lasted 24 min, and the longest 49 min. The mean age of the interviewees was 25.5 ages, with nine female and nine male participants. We tape-recorded and transcribed all interviews. After transcription of all interviews, we analyze them using qualitative content analysis while coding and abstracting them in a team [31]. This resulted in user stories and requirements (see Fig. 5). For example, these requirements emphasize providing basic knowledge about negotiation skills and the relevance of the topics, increasing difficulty at different levels while allowing the learner to identify learning steps, providing different negotiation scenarios with use cases, or providing a learning assessment after each session.

Design Principles. Based on the requirements from theory and practice, we derived five design principles (DP; see Fig. 5). Design Principle 1 (DP1) states that the artifact should provide basic information on negotiations and negotiation skills. Also, the relevance of negotiations should be highlighted to confirm the relevance of negotiations in general. These aspects are particularly important at the beginning of the learning process – learning level a – so the learner can appropriate a basic knowledge of negotiations. However, it is also important for the further learning process – learning levels b and c – that the learner can refer to this basic information at any time. This leads to avoiding mistakes when deepening and practicing negotiation skills. DP2 addresses that assessments should be integrated into the artifact to avoid frustration or under-challenge and to be able to design a personalized learning process. This means that the learner can, for example, test his or her current level of knowledge on negotiations at the beginning of the learning process. Furthermore, for example, self-assessments where the learner can assess their progress after each learning level can be implemented. As a result, it is important to note that the learner can set goals, e.g. depending on the time they want to spend for the learning session or on the main learning goal they want to reach – e.g., learning only basic knowledge or developing more comprehensive negotiation skills in the learning process (DP2).

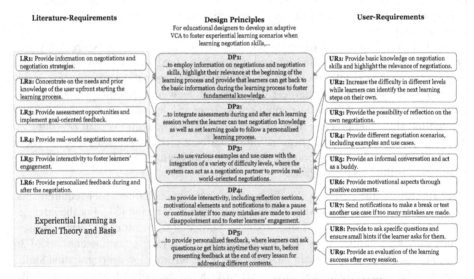

Fig. 5. Design Principles for the CA to Learn Negotiation Skills.

DP3 emphasizes the need for different negotiation examples and use cases grounded on various difficulty levels. It is vital to accomplish real-world-oriented negotiations so the learner can interact naturally with the CA. Since many negotiations take place through spoken language, it is important that voice-based interactions are also included in the overarching learning process. One way to do this is via the implementation of voice-based conversational agents (VCA). VCAs are accessible and less effortful and can be used in various contexts, e.g., for health-related purposes [39]. The high accessibility is supported since VCA runs on different endpoints, such as Amazon's Echo, while the main function of these systems is mostly "black-boxed" and the procedure runs via cloud services [11]. These features of VCA allow the learner to interact with a negotiation partner via spoken language and thus negotiate different use cases depending on the negotiation difficulty the user can choose. When considering the role of the negotiation partner, it is also necessary that the artifact faces the learner as an equal negotiation partner and not in a hierarchic teacher-student relationship. Based on this DP3, we developed a VCA to provide a voice-based interaction considering real-world-oriented interactions.

DP4 addresses interactivity, including reflections and motivational elements. Providing interactive CAs, especially VCAs, are promising since one main characteristic is their high interactivity [11]. Also, integrating time for reflection sections is especially important in experiential learning settings. Reflection can be implemented, for example, by asking the learner to find and explain mistakes in an acted negotiation. Learners should also be motivated, and frustration or disappointment should be avoided. Therefore, we introduced motivational elements, such as sending notifications to make a pause or continuing at a later point if the learner makes too many mistakes. Finally, DP5 emphasizes the need for personalized feedback when learning negotiation skills. Therefore, we introduced the option to get short feedback during a learning session if the learner asks for it, as well as comprehensive feedback at the end of every learning level (a, b, c). Furthermore, we provide the possibility to ask questions or get hints to support the learner during the learning process.

4.3 Demonstration and Evaluation

Demonstration. In a subsequent step, we transferred our DPs into a prototype. An excerpt of our prototype, exemplary DPs marked, can be seen in Fig. 6. For our current example, the blue process highlights the main dialogue between the VCA and the learner. Depending on the learners' answers, the current lesson will be finished (red box), or a different path will be started (brown boxes).

To present our prototype in this paper, we provided a short overview of level b and an excerpt of this learning level in Fig. 6. Before explaining level b in greater detail, the first learning level (a) addresses the learners' knowledge based on negotiations and negotiation skills, including a self-assessment at the beginning. At this level, the VCA provides basic information on negotiation skills, which can be referred to as needed throughout the complete learning process (levels a, b, c). After finishing level a, learners can test their negotiation knowledge on the principles and stages of the HNM (DP2). Then, learners can decide on an easy, medium or advanced use case for starting level b (DP3). In our case, we present the medium use case/example.

Accordingly, to the four actions of the experiential learning cycle [22], learners can make a concrete experience, a reflection, and observation (DP4). Every learner can have the same experience, so a short negotiation example, including two mistakes, is presented (DP4). In our VCA, learners are confronted with a salary negotiation for the first job after graduation (DP3). Both parties follow the HNM principles (DP1). Still, the student has not prepared enough alternatives that can be described by the failing principle: invent options, and the employer is partly very focused on his position, which is characterized by the failing principle: focus on interests, not positions, which makes a win-win agreement almost impossible. The aim behind this example is that learners follow the negotiation as outstanding people and recognize the two errors while reflecting on the example. If learners have questions on the HNM after hearing about the salary negotiation, they can ask our VCA for answers on the basics of learning level a (DP5). After uncovering the two mistakes in the example, learners receive short feedback from our VCA (DP5). If they find the mistakes, learners are asked to prepare themselves for the aforementioned use case (DP3). If not, learners can choose if they want to repeat learning level a to get a summary of the learning content in level a or if they want to continue with level b (DP1 & 2). To continue with level b, learners need to follow the three stages of the HNM and include the principles to plan the negotiation and, thus, make active experimentation. To do so, the VCA can guide learners through the three stages of the HNM while answering questions or giving hints on the basics of learning level a (DP5). Finally, after finishing the three stages of the HNM, learners can get final feedback from our VCA on the learning level, including recommendations on how they used the HNM (DP5).

Moreover, a self-assessment of the current negotiation skill level can be done to document and measure the skill level after learning level b (DP2). After the final assessments in level b, learners receive personalized feedback on the current learning level (DP2 & 5). Following this, learners can start learning level c, where the VCA is in the role of a negotiation partner (DP3). To solve this learning level, the previous contents are an input for the final level c.

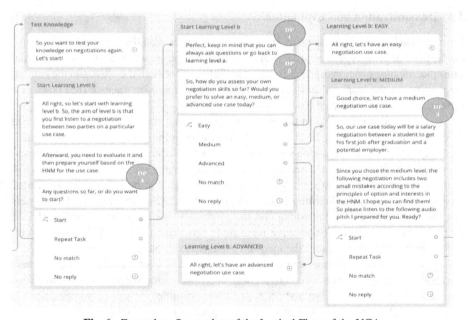

Fig. 6. Exemplary Screenshot of the Logical Flow of the VCA.

Evaluation. To verify our DSR process in the first step so far, we evaluated our DPs and our prototype with 11 expert interviews (*mean age = 30.7*). We interviewed five females and six males who are experts in DSR and teaching in information systems, psychology, and business science. Since the users' perspective is included in the DP, it was an important step to evaluate our prototype and DPs from an expert point of view. According to Sonnenberg and vom Brocke (2012), we assessed the DP using the criteria of completeness, ease of use, elegance, simplicity, and understandability [33]. We presented both our prototype and our DPs, URs, and LIs to our participants and sent them an overview of them prior before the interviews.

Regarding completeness, most of our participants agreed that our DPs were complete. Interview Partner 6 (IP6) mentioned here: *"...they are complete, but I would emphasize that it is clear from DP1 that the learner can always get back to the basic information."* (IP6). Based on this statement, we implemented this aspect into our DP1. On a more general level concerning completeness, IP2 noted: *"...I would change the arrangement of the DPs so that you start with more general DPs, like info on negotiations, and afterward, you can concentrate on learning topics, like feedback."* (IP2). Following this, we changed the arrangement of the DPs, so we started with more general ones and then continued with the learning process. Regarding ease of use, our participants noted, in general, that it seems that our DPs can be easily transferred in a prototype – e.g., IP10 stated: *"Yes, I think the DPs are implementable and easy to use."* (IP10). Furthermore, IP4 and IP6, for example, mentioned that some of our DPs were too generic. In this regard, IP4 mentioned: *"...some of your DPs are formulated a bit too generically, and they lack a certain depth that makes implementation easier."* (IP4). We therefore changed some of our DP, such as DP5 and added more information on personalized feedback so that learners can ask questions or get hints anytime they want to. The same holds for the elegance and simplicity of our DPs. We made some minor corrections in the formulations and added them. For example, IP3 and IP6 mentioned that DP5 is too simple and not that elegant. IP6 commented on the simplicity of UR5: *"...expand the UR including the buddy aspect. How should the bot communicate?"* (IP6). Following this, we expanded our UR5. Evaluating the category of elegance uncovered that DP4 included too much information, so we shorted this DP. Finally, based on the understandability, some implications were given to us regarding the formulation that we changed on our DPs. IP10 has summarized the understandability as follows: *"I think your requirements and principles are understandable, and I can follow them."* (IP10). Finally, all our participants agreed that the DPs were transferred correctly into our prototype and that at each point in our prototype, it is understandable which DP is addressed and why.

5   Discussion

Our paper aimed to develop a conceptual design for a CA and a prototype that assists learners in acquiring negotiation skills. Especially the development of design principles that can be adapted to different learning scenarios to foster negotiation skills for reaching win-win agreements is a necessary step here. It is not questionable that negotiation is relevant in many other contexts and situations. Although relevant, many educational concepts do not fully support learning to negotiate. To achieve our goal, we used the approach by Peffers et al. [12]. The development of our DPs revealed that a CA used to negotiate should include voice-based elements, leading to a VCA prototype in our research. Voice-based interactions are particularly important in the negotiation skill learning process to create real-world oriented scenarios in which learners can solve various cases (learning level c). Through voice-based interactions, learners have, for example, less time to carefully consider their responses and must respond more intuitively – like in negotiations with a human negotiator. Research on voice-based CAs indicates that the use of such technologies can effectively enhance such skills. For example, a study on voice-based CAs by Kim [40] demonstrated that after a period of 16 weeks using a voice-based CA, students improved in different negotiation strategies depending on their language proficiency levels: low-level students repeated and reformulated more to avoid communication silence during chatting, while medium-level and high-level students used more confirmation check strategies to understand the conversation [40]. However, most of these studies do not follow the necessary theoretical learning concepts for negotiation skills.

With our work, we present design principles and a VCA that was developed by using literature and ideas from learners, and that is grounded in learning theories such as experiential learning, according to Kolb [22]. The evaluated design principles could now be adapted to each specific learning case to foster negotiation skills. As educators, we want learners to be able to negotiate in different scenarios. To act successfully in the real world, learners need not only to be able to draw on the knowledge imparted to them in their classes but also to generalize and apply their understanding of the content to new situations or make connections to other concepts they have learned [41]. Learning to negotiate is a complex process that involves problems that are often wicked, meaning they have no clear-cut solutions [41]. This is why our work consolidates existing approaches, such as the theory of experiential learning developed by Kolb (2014) and combines it with the HNM.

Further, to make such learning processes even more personalized, generative AI can be integrated into CAs [42] and build an interesting starting point for further research. For instance, learners could engage interactively and personalize their negotiation skill training by negotiating with an AI through systems such as ChatGPT. In this context, our evaluated design principles can be utilized to implement the learning process for negotiation skills and cover essential elements.

5.1 Limitations and Further Research

However, our work has some limitations that provide room for further research. In this paper, we focus on the conceptual design of a VCA supporting the learning process of negotiation skills, including DPs and a first prototype, including an expert evaluation. Therefore, the next step would be to evaluate the prototype in a following field experiment to figure out how our VCA can support long-term learning outcomes of students. Here, further experimental long-term approaches, such as the one presented by Kim [40], are needed to determine how effective and efficient our VCA is. Furthermore, we focus on meta-cognitive skills. Other studies could, for example, focus on socio-emotional skills, such as communication or active listening. Another limitation of our work is that we did not yet include emotions or gestures in the learning process because of their complexity. Adding to the research around embodied CAs, this offers great potential for further research to analyze how emotions and gestures can be addressed in digital learning environments, especially in VCAs, to foster negotiation skills. This, for example, can happen by integrating new technologies, such as virtual or augmented reality, into a learning process that focuses on negotiation skills. Lastly, our results pointed towards a voice-based solution. Future research should also try to analyze combinations of both text and voice CAs.

6 Contributions

Our work provides several contributions to theory and practice. With our work, we contribute a theory of design and action by presenting requirements and DPs for VCAs [34]. We offer a theoretical contribution by presenting one way to use experiential learning theory to design VCA. Learning to negotiate is a complex process; thus, we provide some clarification on how to design a learning process involving a VCA that is easy for learners to follow and assists them during their self-guided learning processes. From a practitioner's perspective, we provide requirements and DPs to assist educators in constructing their own VCAs. We also present a prototype that further can be of assistance to practitioners in constructing VCA for educational purposes.

References

1. McKinsey: Three types of modern flexibility today's workers demand (2022)
2. World Economic Forum: Keep talking. Why every organization needs a chief negotiator. World Economic Forum (2021)
3. Fisher, R., Ury, W.: Getting to Yes: Negotiating an Agreement Without Giving in. Random House Business, London (2012)
4. Lewicki, R.J.: Teaching negotiation and dispute resolution in colleges of business: the state of the practice. Negot. J. 13(3), 253–269 (1997)
5. Pedler, M.: Negotiation skills training—part 4: learning to negotiate. J. Eur. Ind. Train. 2(1), 20–25 (1978)
6. World Economic Forum: Hybrid working: why you need to master digital soft skills. World Economic Forum (2022)
7. Johnson, E., Lucas, G., Kim, P., Gratch, J.: Intelligent tutoring system for negotiation skills training. In: Isotani, S., Millán, E., Ogan, A., Hastings, P., McLaren, B., Luckin, R. (eds.) AIED 2019. LNCS (LNAI), vol. 11626, pp. 122–127. Springer, Cham (2019). https://doi.org/10.1007/978-3-030-23207-8_23
8. Chapman, E., Miles, E.W., Maurer, T.: A proposed model for effective negotiation skill development. J. Manag. Dev. 36(7), 940–958 (2017)
9. Kim, J.M., et al.: BiLAT: a game-based environment for practicing negotiation in a cultural context. Int. J. Artif. Intell. Educ. 19(3), 289–308 (2009)
10. Feine, J., Gnewuch, U., Morana, S., Maedche, A.: A taxonomy of social cues for conversational agents. Int. J. Hum.-Comput. Stud. 132, 138–161 (2019)
11. Winkler, R., Söllner, M., Leimeister, J.M.: Enhancing problem-solving skills with smart personal assistant technology. Comput. Educ. 165, 104148 (2021)
12. Peffers, K., Tuunanen, T., Rothenberger, M.A., Chatterjee, S.: A design science research methodology for information systems research. J. Manag. Inf. Syst. 24(3), 45–77 (2007)

13. vom Brocke, J., Simons, A., Riemer, K., Niehaves, B., Plattfaut, R., Cleven, A.: Standing on the shoulders of giants: challenges and recommendations of literature search in information systems research. Commun. Assoc. Inf. Syst. **37**(1), 435–461 (2015)
14. Webster, J., Watson, R.T.: Analyzing the past to prepare for the future: writing a literature review. MIS Q. **26**, xiii–xxiii (2002)
15. Desai, S., Chin, J.: OK Google, let's learn: using voice user interfaces for informal self-regulated learning of health topics among younger and older adults. In: Proceedings of the 2023 CHI Conference on Human Factors in Computing Systems, pp. 1–21 (2023)
16. Thompson, L.L., Wang, J., Gunia, B.C.: Negotiation. Annu. Rev. Psychol. **61**, 491–515 (2010)
17. Martinez, M.E.: What is metacognition? Phi Delta Kappan **87**(9), 696–699 (2006)
18. Chernyshenko, O.S., Kankaraš, M., Drasgow, F.: Social and emotional skills for student success and well-being: conceptual framework for the OECD study on social and emotional skills (2018)
19. Tyler, M., Cukier, N.: Nine lessons for teaching negotiation skills. Leg. Educ. Rev. **15**(1/2), 61–86 (2005)
20. Roloff, M.E., Putnam, L.L., Anastasiou, L.: Negotiation skills. In: Handbook of Communication and Social Interaction Skills, pp. 801–833. Lawrence Erlbaum Associates Publishers, Mahwah (2003)
21. Johnson, E., Gratch, J., DeVault, D.: Towards an autonomous agent that provides automated feedback on students' negotiation skills. In: Proceedings of the 16th Conference on Autonomous Agents and MultiAgent Systems, pp.410–418. International Foundation for Autonomous Agents and Multiagent Systems (2017)
22. Kolb, D.A.: Experiential Learning: Experience as the Source of Learning and Development. FT Press (2014)
23. Nadler, J., Thompson, L., Boven, L.V.: Learning negotiation skills: four models of knowledge creation and transfer. Manag. Sci. **49**(4), 529–540 (2003)
24. Schmid, A., Kronberger, O., Vonderach, N., Schoop, M.: Are you for real? A negotiation bot for electronic negotiations. In: UK Academy for Information Systems Conference Proceedings 2021 (2021)
25. Rosenfeld, A., Zuckerman, I., Segal-Halevi, E., Drein, O., Kraus, S.: NegoChat: a chat-based negotiation agent. In: Proceedings of the 2014 International Conference on Autonomous Agents and Multi-Agent Systems, pp. 525–532. International Foundation for Autonomous Agents and Multiagent Systems (2014)
26. Vahidov, R., Kersten, G.E., Saade, R.: Human-software agent negotiations: an experimental study. In: Shaw, M.J., Zhang, D., Yue, W.T. (eds.) WEB 2011, vol. 108, pp. 356–367. Springer, Heidelberg (2012). https://doi.org/10.1007/978-3-642-29873-8_33
27. Weber, F., Wambsganss, T., Rüttimann, D., Söllner, M.: Pedagogical agents for interactive learning: a taxonomy of conversational agents in education. In: ICIS 2021 Proceedings (2021)
28. Schlimbach, R., Markgraf, D., Rinn, H., Robra-Bissantz, S.: A literature review on pedagogical conversational agent adaptation. In: PACIS 2022 Proceedings (2022)
29. Yin, Q., Satar, M.: English as a foreign language learner interactions with chatbots: negotiation for meaning. Int. Online J. Educ. Teach. (IOJET) **7**(2), 390–410 (2020)
30. Spiliotopoulos, D., Makri, E., Vassilakis, C., Margaris, D.: Multimodal interaction: correlates of learners' metacognitive skill training negotiation experience. Information **11**(8), 381 (2020)
31. Mayring, P.: Qualitative content analysis: theoretical foundation, basic procedures and software solution, Klagenfurt (2014)
32. Gregor, S., Kruse, L., Seidel, S.: Research perspectives: the anatomy of a design principle. J. Assoc. Inf. Syst. **21**, 1622–1652 (2020)
33. Sonnenberg, C., vom Brocke, J.: Evaluation patterns for design science research artefacts. In: Helfert, M., Donnellan, B. (eds.) EDSS 2011. CCIS, vol. 286, pp. 71–83. Springer, Heidelberg (2012). https://doi.org/10.1007/978-3-642-33681-2_7

34. Gregor, S., Hevner, A.R.: Positioning and presenting design science research for maximum impact. Manag. Inf. Syst. Q. **37**, 337–355 (2013)
35. Chi, M.T.H., Wylie, R.: The ICAP framework: linking cognitive engagement to active learning outcomes. Educ. Psychol. **49**(4), 219–243 (2014)
36. Wats, R.K., Wats, M.: Developing soft skills in students. Int. J. Learn. Ann. Rev. **15**(12), 1–10 (2009)
37. Nicol, D.J., Macfarlane-Dick, D.: Formative assessment and self-regulated learning: a model and seven principles of good feedback practice. Stud. High. Educ. **31**(2), 199–218 (2006)
38. Gallien, T., Oomen-Early, J.: Personalized versus collective instructor feedback in the online courseroom: does type of feedback affect student satisfaction, academic performance and perceived connectedness with the instructor? Int. J. E-Learn. **7**(3), 463–476 (2008)
39. Bérubé, C., Fleisch, E.: Voice-based conversational agents for sensing and support: examples from academia and industry. In: Jacobson, N., Kowatsch, T., Marsch, L. (eds.) Digital Therapeutics for Mental Health and Addiction, pp. 113–134. Academic Press (2023)
40. Kim, N.-Y.: Effects of voice chat on EFL learners' speaking ability according to proficiency levels. Multimedia-Assist. Lang. Learn. **19**(4), 63–88 (2016)
41. Bradberry, L., De Maio, J.: Learning by doing: the long-term impact of experiential learning programs on student success. J. Polit. Sci. Educ. **15**(1), 1–18 (2018)
42. Bozkurt, A.: Generative artificial intelligence (AI) powered conversational educational agents: the inevitable paradigm shift. Asian J. Distance Educ. **18**(1), 198–204 (2023)

DSR in Practice

No Need to Cry over Spilt Milk: A Workflow for Regenerating Graph Data Using Robotic Process Automation

Thomas Auer[(✉)] [iD] and Christian Schieder [iD]

Technical University of Applied Sciences Amberg-Weiden, Weiden, Germany
{t.auer,c.schieder}@oth-aw.de

Abstract. Production data in industrial environments is frequently presented and stored in figures and diagrams. The original numerical raw data needs to be regenerated to use this data in advanced data analysis. Current software solutions still struggle to convert specific line curves automatically into accurate numerical data. Following the design science research paradigm, we present a novel approach for the automated regeneration of graphical data into its numerical representation by combining robotic process automation (RPA) with document image analysis (DIA). We evaluated the developed solution using a real-world dataset of quality inspection charts from a small and medium-sized manufacturing enterprise (SME). The results demonstrate that the data extraction, compared to other software-based methods, significantly reduces the time required compared to manual methods. Our approach provides a generally applicable, time-efficient, and easy-to-implement solution to increase data availability for technologies that require efficient data extraction processes.

Keywords: Robotic Process Automation · Document Image Analysis · Line Processing · Data Regeneration · Data Extraction

1 Introduction

Industrial manufacturing processes are characterized by a highly specialized and heterogeneous process landscape. Pursuing higher production quality and efficiency leads to an increasing need for data processing [1]. Artificial intelligence (AI) and machine learning (ML) promise a wide range of potentials for optimizing processes in terms of waste reduction, automation, and product quality [2]. Recent studies have shown that these approaches are primarily designed for large-scale enterprises [3, 4]. However, small and medium-sized enterprises (SMEs), which constitute 90% of production firms in the European Union, face several challenges in adopting these technologies due to insufficient data resources or incompatible formats [5].

Our research team encountered this situation directly while implementing an ML use case in a manufacturing SME. The company stored its quality data in graphic form with degraded image resolution instead of keeping the numerical raw data. Historically, the information only needed to be suitable for a coarse graphical inspection. Although

© The Author(s), under exclusive license to Springer Nature Switzerland AG 2024
M. Mandviwalla et al. (Eds.): DESRIST 2024, LNCS 14621, pp. 247–261, 2024.
https://doi.org/10.1007/978-3-031-61175-9_17

graphical data can potentially be used for training ML algorithms, the inherent characteristics, including irrelevant information, blurred imagery, implicit curve representation, and overlapping lines, make graphical classification ineffective. The development of ML models was delayed due to the unavailability of numerical data for training. Generating a sufficiently large training database by observing further production processes was tedious and costly.

Additionally, the regeneration of graphical data and its conversion into numerical format is crucial in various other domains. Quantitative data synthesis from single-case designs (SCDs) is becoming more common in psychological and educational journals [6, 7]. Researchers often present graphical representations without numerical data, making graph digitization an essential research activity [6, 7]. Moeyeart et al. [6] observed that manual operation and subsequent data extraction remain cumbersome even with the available software tools. Furthermore, automatic curve extraction may only be feasible for some datasets. Current methods for extracting data from graphical diagrams, such as ChartOCR [8] or software like WebPlotDigitizer [9], have achieved remarkable results. However, they often cannot process high-dimensional and complex datasets, such as those involving implicitly represented curves. Our work addresses this gap by developing a novel approach specifically designed for these complex data forms.

We present a method that integrates robotic process automation (RPA) with document image analysis (DIA) to expedite and enhance the regeneration of graph data. We followed the design science research method (DSRM) that Peffers et al. [10] outlined to iteratively develop a workflow that addresses SMEs' limitations in data regeneration processes. Design requirements (DRs) were formulated based on a comprehensive analysis of practical requirements (via expert interviews) and theoretical requirements (via literature search) to develop our prototype. The approach was evaluated using the framework for evaluation in design science (FEDS) from Venable et al. [11] to assess its rigor and efficiency in meeting the identified requirements. To our knowledge, no publications explicitly discuss design research or design knowledge in the context of RPA and DIA. Therefore, we are the first to contribute design knowledge in these areas. Our findings illustrate how data regeneration can lead to increased data accessibility and volume to support SMEs using technologies that require large databases, e.g., AI.

The paper is organized as follows: In the next section, we will briefly discuss the theoretical concepts and classify our approach within the relevant categories. Section 3 outlines our research methodology, divided into stages, objectives, and associated activities. The initial phase of our methodology regarding the development of solution-based objectives is presented in Sect. 4. Section 5 illustrates the iterative development of the data regeneration process based on the requirements. This section also includes a practical demonstration of the proposed workflow. Section 6 introduces several indicators to evaluate and display our results comprehensibly. The following section presents our findings, the design knowledge we have acquired, and our contributions. The final section provides a conclusion, outlines limitations, and suggests directions for future research.

2 Research Background

This section first introduces our understanding of DIA and RPA to develop our automated data regeneration process. Next, we examine relevant software such as WebPlotDigitizer [9] or UnGraph [12] to support our approach. Finally, we discuss how our approach differs from existing methods such as ChartOCR [8] or Parsing Line Charts by Kato et al. [13].

2.1 Document Image Analysis

The research area of DIA includes various methods for document processing that aim to recognize text or graphics for information extraction and can be divided into textual and graphical processing [14]. Textual processing includes the development of optical character recognition (OCR) and page layout analysis techniques [14, 15]. On the other hand, graphical processing focuses on identifying and handling non-textual elements like images, tables, or graphs. This category is subdivided into line processing (lines, curves, and corners) and region processing (filled regions) [14]. The presented data regeneration process can be categorized as a line processing type of DIA technique.

2.2 Robotic Process Automation

Most researchers use RPA as a collective term for a computer program based on a scripting language for the digital execution of computer tasks [16]. In cases where the use of human labor or the development and integration of business process management systems are neither economically justified nor justified by business requirements, RPA acts as an intermediary technology that bridges the gap between manual labor and the automation of business processes [16, 17]. As implementing RPA does not interfere with existing infrastructures, RPA is considered lightweight IT and a transition between human work and business process automation [16, 18, 19].

So-called software robots generally imitate human actions by accessing systems and performing tasks human-likely [16, 20]. Software robots operate within the presentation layer, meaning their execution in an information system (IS) ecosystem does not interfere with the underlying business logic [21]. To determine the basic capabilities of software robots and their functions in detail, Hofmann et al. [22] analyzed three general functional areas: data-related, integration-related, and process-related. These areas group the functional properties of software robots into eight functional classes that summarize the scope of their capabilities at an aggregated level. Our approach can be divided into the following functional classes: file processor (functions to change file formats), application operator (functions to access or operate other applications), and input device operator (functions to imitate the human use of input devices).

Defining software robots more precisely, we introduce the term software agents following the definition of Russell et al. [23]: "A software agent receives keystrokes, file contents, and network packets as sensory inputs and acts on the environment by displaying on the screen, writing files, and sending network packets." Russell et al. [23] emphasize the importance of sensory input and subsequent actions for software agents, highlighting their ability to receive, process, and respond to data from the environment.

Following this definition, we classify our developed approach as a software agent with the functional classes and archetypes by Hofmann et al. [22].

2.3   Graph Digitizing Software Tools

A digitizing tool for extracting numerical data is generally software that extracts numerical data from charts or graphs. To extract XY coordinates, these tools must import charts, calibrate the axes by clicking on known values to allow the tool to interpolate a coordinate system, and manually click on each data point [12]. The accuracy of these tools is compromised by multiple data series in the same panel and other errors in the graphical representations [12]. If the curve is not explicitly displayed, which is the case for our dataset, automatic data extraction is not possible.

Several studies have investigated graph digitization tools and provided estimations of their intercoder reliability and validity. This includes the following tools: DataThief III [24, 25], DigitizeIt [26, 27], GraphClick [24, 26, 28], Ungraph [12, 26, 29] and WebPlotDigitizer [7, 9]. The studies show equally reliable and valid data extraction quality [6, 7, 24, 26]. Moeyaert et al. [6] stress the overall user-friendliness of the tools. Ungraph [12] and WebPlotDigitizer [9] scored highest in ease of use.

2.4   Comparative Approaches

In contrast to the existing software tools, the current academic research landscape offers various approaches for extracting line charts. ChartOCR, developed by Luo et al. [8], uses a combination of deep learning and rule-based methods and extracts raw data values from various graphical images (including line graphs) with high accuracy. However, the application is limited to extracting data values without linking them to corresponding graphical elements such as axes or legends. Decatur et al. [30] introduced an approach called VizExtract, which extracts relationships from graph images by combining computer vision algorithms and deep learning. This approach of extracting relationships, instead of extracting exact data points, increases robustness to noise and series overlap. Another approach was introduced by Kato et al. [13]. The method restores data from diagram images, focusing on line charts. It involves training a semantic segmentation network to create probability maps for different line styles, followed by graph construction and the formulation of line tracing.

Despite extensive research, reverse engineering remains computationally complex and lacks robustness [31]. The approaches described before effectively extract explicitly represented data points but are limited to implicit curves. In particular situations (c.f. Sect. 5), these tools are unable to extract the data points effectively. Our approach differs from existing solutions in its ability to process implicitly represented curves by mimicking a human expert's behavior.

3   Research Method

Our research methodology is based on the DSRM by Peffers et al. [10]. Peffers et al. [10] structured design science (DS) projects in the following six stages: (1) problem identification and motivation, (2) definition of objectives for a solution, (3) design and development, (4) demonstration, (5) evaluation, and (6) communication. The research activities and associated activities for the different stages are summarized in Fig. 1.

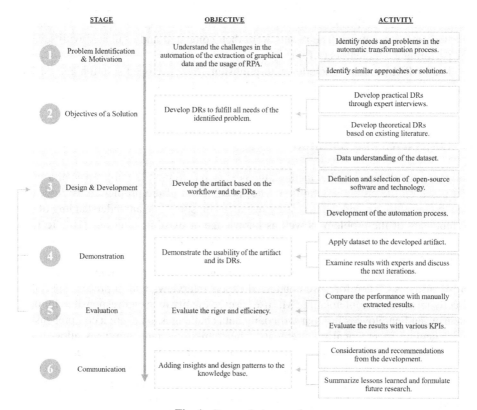

Fig. 1. Research Approach.

In the first stage, the problem was identified and formulated. Our introduction highlighted the issue of insufficient database size due to format incompatibility, which emerged while implementing ML. A literature review indicated a notable gap in suitable solutions, pointing to the need for more focused research.

In the second stage, centered on setting objectives for a solution, we established requirements based on insights from the literature review and pinpointed the research gap. This stage included interviews with process experts, quality managers, and employees to ensure a comprehensive understanding of the necessary conditions. As a result, we set a clear objective for the potential solution: deploying our software agent to automate the data regeneration process, utilizing available open-source software. Section 4 provides a detailed account of the problem description.

The third stage involves designing and developing the artifact's functionality and architecture. Therefore, a workflow for automating the data regeneration process was proposed. It consists of the following three activities: (1) data understanding, (2) development of a generic workflow, and (3) process automation.

In the fourth stage, presented in Sect. 5 of the paper, the proposed workflow and its resulting artifact were applied to an authentic dataset containing quality data from a real-world production environment, demonstrating the DR's usability.

In stage 5, based on the preliminary results and guided by the FEDS, we evaluated the artifact's performance through a case study involving 100 quality documents selected from the dataset. The results were then compared and evaluated with several key performance indicators (KPIs).

The DSRM process concludes with publishing the developed solution and design patterns in this paper, making the results publicly available, and adding our contribution to the knowledge base.

4   Objectives of a Solution

Following the described DSR method, the next step is to infer the objectives of a solution based on the problem definition. The specification of the problem must logically lead to the solutions, and the necessary resources must include an understanding of the current state of the problem as well as knowledge of existing solutions [10]. To take this into account in the development of the data regeneration process, we defined DRs for the development of the artifact (Fig. 1 Stage 2). Practical relevance plays a crucial role since the problem occurred during the data preparation and implementation of an ML use case. Therefore, we conducted expert interviews with a process specialist directly involved in implementing ML use cases, a quality manager responsible for data integrity, and employees familiar with daily data challenges to ensure a comprehensive understanding of practical requirements. The semi-structured interviews allowed for in-depth discussions about specific problems and potential areas of improvement.

We combined the collected requirements from the expert interviews with theoretical requirements to counteract biases, especially those arising from internal perspectives within the company and the experts' deep familiarity with their processes. By combining theory with practice, we follow the instructions of Peffers et al. [10]. We derive the theoretical requirements from the literature in neighboring fields, as no directly comparable studies exist in our focused area. We categorized the combined DRs into functional and non-functional DRs, assigned subjects to address them, and, as shown in Table 1, indicated whether the DR has a theoretical and/or practical source.

In consultation with domain experts, we prioritized all DRs. DR1, DR2, DR9, and DR10 are of low priority for extracting the available dataset and are therefore optional in the development phase. The developed artifact must address the remaining DRs.

Table 1. Design Requirements for the automated regeneration process.

Functional DR	Description	Subject	Source (Practical = P, Theoretical = T)
DR1: Input Diversity	Variable input (PDF, PNG, ...).	Preprocessing	P, T [26, 31]
DR2: Parameter Extraction	Possibility for the extraction of parameters from dataset, like date, ID, or measured values.	Preprocessing	P, T [31]
DR3: Axes Configuration/ Scaling	Automatic configuration and axes scaling.	Extraction	P
DR4: Curve Extraction	Localization and extraction of the curve.	Extraction	P, T [6–8, 26, 30, 31]
DR5: Numerical Storage	File formats, like CSV, store data as numerical values.	Extraction	P, T [6–8, 26, 30, 31]
DR6: Data Validation	Postprocessing the data and plausibility check.	Postprocessing	P, T [7, 26, 31]
Non-Functional DR	**Description**	**Subject**	**Source**
DR7: Extraction Accuracy	Demonstrate a certain level of accuracy, about the equivalent of the manual extraction.	Performance	P, T [6, 7, 26]
DR8: Process Time Reduction	Reduction of process time (faster than manual).	Performance	P
DR9: Parameter Settings	Easy parameter configuration.	Configuration	T [7, 26, 31]
DR10: Data Adaptability	Simple extension to other data.	Generalization	T [6, 8, 30, 31]

5   Design, Development and Demonstration

Consequently, following the DSRM, we build our data regeneration process iteratively based on the previously described DRs. Therefore, we divide the three activities: (1) data understanding, (2) definition and development of a generic workflow, and (3) process automation into the sectors workflow, data understanding, preprocessing, extraction, and postprocessing. Each section explains itself and assigns the respective DR.

5.1   Workflow

To address the DRs, we developed the process shown in Fig. 2. The process is designed to be fully automated, as symbolized by the robotic icon, minimizing the need for manual intervention. However, manual checks are required to correct any errors identified.

Initially, Python converts the existing document containing the quality data into a predefined image file format. The relevant graph is extracted from the document and imported into the software tool WebPlotDigitizer [9], chosen for its reliable and valid data extraction results and ease of use. The next step is to calibrate the axes to ensure the correct positioning and scaling of the data points. Afterward, the software agent automatically marks the data points to be extracted. The software agent uses reference images of the individual visual representations of these data points for detection. The parameter configuration completes the processes within the WebPlotDigitizer [9]. After the validation check, the extracted values are postprocessed to ensure high-quality data.

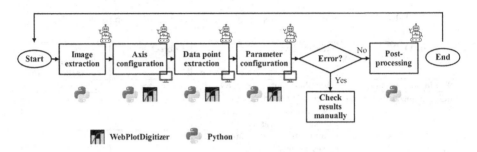

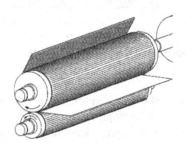

Fig. 2. Logical workflow.

5.2 Data Understanding

At the beginning of the development phase, creating a uniform understanding of the dataset is essential for developing the artifact. The specific case is about corrugating rolls used in corrugated cardboard production (see Fig. 3). Riffles are grounded with high precision along the cross-section of the surface of the rolls. Given the high accuracy required for these rolls, measurements must meet strict quality standards.

Fig. 3. Corrugating rolls in cardboard production [32].

The measurements crucially indicate the deviation of a rotating roll from its ideal geometric shape, a key indicator of the roll's quality. Any deviation beyond these limits necessitates either rejection or rework of the roll, emphasizing the need for precision in manufacturing (see Fig. 4 (b)). A mechanical probe measures the surface, displaying the measurements in a runout diagram, as shown in Fig. 4 (a). The red runout curve is drawn manually for better visualization, as it cannot be measured or viewed directly. It is reconstructed using the inversion points of the high and low points of the teeth or riffles, providing a precise indication of the micrometer-level deviations.

The main problem is that the graph does not explicitly show the runout curve. Attempts at automatic recognition by several software tools were not successful. Large datasets (e.g., several thousand diagrams) lead to considerable time expenditure and human error. The lack of data availability is typical for industrial SMEs, so a generally applicable method for reconstructing this data is necessary [33].

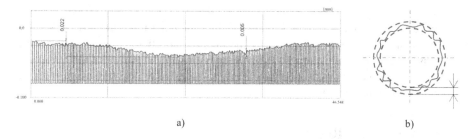

a)   b)

Fig. 4. Runout diagram (a) and illustration of runout tolerance (b).

5.3 Preprocessing

The extraction begins with converting the data from PDF to PNG (DR1). Only the plot, including the scaling, is extracted to ensure that additional, unnecessary data does not interfere with the extraction. After successful image extraction, the open-source software WebPlotDigitizer [9] processes the images (DR11). The second step in preprocessing is configuring the axes (DR3). The x- and y-axes are calibrated by automatically detecting and selecting corner points. It requires at least two data points for each axis and the exact position of every point. Reference images are inserted to detect and select the corner points, which are automatically determined. OCR ensures the correct scaling of the corner points. The Python Tesseract Wrapper performs recognition based on the open-source library Tesseract (DR11).

5.4 Extraction and Postprocessing

The next step is to select the data points of the curve (DR4). As the reversal points of the riffles represent the runout curve, it is crucial to select the corresponding data points with high precision, given that these measurements are in the micrometer range and require meticulous accuracy in pinpointing (see Fig. 5).

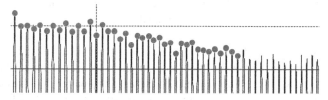

Fig. 5. Data point selection.

To ensure this, reference images are used. The software agent can recognize and select the data points using these images. In the next step, the source path, file name, and file format are configured, which is automated by OCR and predefined settings. This completes the extraction in WebPlotDigitizer [9] and converts the graphical curve into numerical values that are saved in a CSV file (DR5). The final stage is postprocessing the extracted numeric values (DR6). First, the date and certain limit values contained within the graphic are extracted using OCR and written to the CSV file (DR2). A final check between the numerical data points (using the method) and the extracted edges (using OCR) ensures that both the calibration of the axes and the extraction of the numerical data points have been carried out correctly. If a discrepancy occurs here, it must be verified by human intervention.

6   Evaluation and Results

After the design, development, and demonstration of the workflow, we utilize the FEDS to structure our evaluation by describing the four-step process specifically tailored for the evaluation of DSR projects. Efficiency and usability, identified as evaluands through the FEDS, are substantiated by examining the intercoder reliability.

6.1   Evaluation

To consistently follow the FEDS, we classify our approach into dimensions. In the first dimension, the functional purpose, our approach can be classified as a summative evaluation. In the second dimension, the paradigm of the evaluation study, our approach can be classified as a naturalistic evaluation since we examine the performance of a solution technology in a real environment.

Guided by the FEDS' four-step process, we first outlined the goals and constraints of the approach. The method should consider the goals of rigor (efficacy and effectiveness) and efficiency, as the most critical aspect is preserving the curve characteristic during extraction. Based on our research, no applicable method could be found, or existing methods did not produce the desired results. Therefore, the development was exploratory, and the first draft was expected to contain significant or minor errors.

For the second step, we chose the quick and simple strategy, as our evaluation is limited to formative evaluation and quickly progresses to summative and naturalistic evaluation. In the third step, guided by the FEDS heuristic for choosing evaluation properties, we identified efficiency and usability as our evaluands, prioritizing the goal of accurate extraction. Both evaluands were assessed through our performance KPIs (processing time and relationship of the extracted values). The final step in the FEDS is designing the individual evaluation episodes. In our approach, this was a continuous and iterative process throughout development without fixed intervals. We regularly evaluated the evaluands (efficiency and usability) until a certain extraction accuracy was achieved with sufficient time savings. Through the FEDS-based evaluation, we present evidence that our research makes practical contribution to the application context formulated by Hevner et al. [34].

6.2   Intercoder Reliability

Intercoder reliability, which assesses whether two independent coders extract similar data, is crucial for quantitative evaluation [7]. In our case, we do not compare the results of the two coders but rather the results of the manual extraction and the presented method. As current state-of-the-art approaches such as ChartOCR [8] were not suitable for this dataset, we cannot compare them. To validate the results of our approach, we manually extracted the dataset using WebPlotDigitizer [9]. Although this was possible, it is extremely time-consuming with large datasets and very error-prone due to the monotonous work. Therefore, it is only suitable for validating our experiment.

We demonstrate intercoder reliability through the following KPIs: (1) percentage of all extracted data points, (2) percentage of data points congruent on the x-axis, (3) percentage differences and standard deviation of the corresponding y-values, (4) Pearson correlation coefficient, and (5) the comparison of the process time between the automated and manual method. The first two KPIs evaluate the reliability of data extraction. A data point is considered sufficiently congruent if its deviation is less than 0.5% of the maximum scale range. For comparison in similar publications, a value of 1% is generally selected [26]. The third KPI measures the percentage differences and standard deviation of the y-values. Combined with the Pearson correlation coefficient, which reflects the linear correlation and indicates the similarity between the curves, this provides a comprehensive picture of the data point extraction and relates to DR7.

With our software agent, discrepancies can occur by including an extra data point or missing one. To maintain the integrity of the results, missing data points are compensated through interpolation, calculating their y-values based on the data points immediately before and after the missing one. Conversely, suppose our software agent includes an extra data point that is not present in the manual method. In that case, we interpolate the y-values from the manual method to ensure consistency across the datasets. This approach allows for a balanced comparison between the automated and the manual method and ensures a comprehensive evaluation of the KPIs. Due to the automated workflow and to address DR8, we introduce another KPI that has not yet been used in comparable literature on the reliability of extracting graphic data: the comparison of manual and automated extraction process time.

Out of the initial 100 documents, four encountered an error during the evaluation. In all four cases, the error was due to a missing marking of the axes lines in the graph and was detected by the plausibility check. In total, we evaluated 18,800 data points across 96 graphs, leading to an average of 191.5 data points per graph. Our software agent extracted 83.55% of the total data points, and 82.56% were congruent on the x-axis. The deviation of the corresponding y-values was 1.51%, with a standard deviation of 3.10%. The extracted curves show a high correlation, confirmed by an average Pearson correlation coefficient of 0.940. Manual processing of a single graph took an average of 395 s, whereas our software agent reduced this time to 131 s per graph.

7 Discussion and Contribution

Below we examine how our research process contributes to expanding the knowledge base, according to the DSR contribution framework by Gregor et al. [35]. We then discuss the advantages of the software agent and address the remaining challenges. Finally, we discuss our contribution to other areas.

7.1 Discussion

Utilizing the design knowledge accumulation path by vom Brocke et al. [36] helps us to justify the steps we took from problem conceptualization to the practical application of our solution. Starting with an initial problem description, the development of the DRs enhanced our projectability but decreased confidence, while fitness remained constant (generalization). By deriving the software agent from DRs, we improved fitness and reduced confidence while projectability remained constant (amplification).

In our case study, the data represented in runout diagrams is critical for monitoring the quality of the manufacturing process and were originally captured graphically rather than numerically. The existing academic approaches and software tools were ineffective in extracting the underlying data points. Our method, when applied to the dataset, demonstrated high accuracy in data extraction and significantly reduced processing time by 61% compared to the manual method. As explained in Sect. 6, the manual method only serves to validate our approach. However, it is crucial to consider that processing time may vary depending on the complexity and density of data points in each document. For the evaluated dataset, we had an average of 191.5 data points to extract. Although there was a loss of approximately 18% of data points, the overall integrity and characteristics of the extracted curves were largely preserved, as demonstrated by KPIs. In comparison, studies by Rakap et al. [26] and Shadish et al. [12] reported intercoder reliability between two manual coders, with Pearson correlation coefficients ranging from 0.954 to 0.999. While our achieved Pearson correlation coefficient of 0.940 is slightly lower, we have demonstrated significant advantages, including a 61% reduction in processing time. This contributes to enhanced time efficiency, reduced human resources costs, and a consistent, uninterrupted operation. Furthermore, it should be noted that manual extraction is not a viable option beyond a certain threshold of data points, an issue that our automated method effectively avoids.

One challenge in practical application was the software agent's need for screen access to use OCR and interaction with the software's graphical user interface. Additionally, running the software agent on the same device used to capture reference images was necessary to avoid interference. Another challenge was the unclear visibility of the corner points of the axes in some diagrams.

7.2 Contribution

Based on the DSR contribution framework, our work is classified as an example of exaptation, which involves applying existing solutions to new problems [35]. Our research extends a mature design theory (RPA) from a different field (DIA). By integrating RPA with DIA, we contribute a method specifically developed and evaluated for the challenges with implicit line curves. As the knowledge base in the fields of RPA and DIA is still incomplete, we have developed and instantiated DRs to contribute to the design knowledge in these areas. We synthesized practical insights from expert interviews with theoretical foundations from the literature to tackle the complexity of integrating RPA with DIA. The resulting DRs are universally applicable in similar domains. Our paper addresses the primary challenges in our case study and establishes a solid foundation for future research efforts to utilize RPA and DIA for data regeneration. We also identified challenges that may be useful for future practitioners or researchers.

Our method is versatile and can be applied to various datasets, making it useful in fields where graphic data needs to be converted to numerical data. For instance, in fields like psychology and education, where single-case designs are common, our method can streamline the data synthesis process, leading to more efficient analysis and interpretation of data. Additionally, our method can be adapted to extract data from graphs for systematic reviews. Cramond et al. [37] developed a tool for graphical data extraction to assist reviewers. Although the method resulted in time savings and increased accuracy, it still requires manual execution and lacks automation.

Our approach also emphasizes the significant advantage of using RPA and DIA to ensure data accuracy. Manual data regeneration methods are prone to human error, especially when dealing with large datasets. Previous research, such as Moeyaert et al. [6] and Drevon et al. [7], suggests that coder training combined with practice and feedback generally leads to higher intercoder reliability. However, these methods can be expensive and time-consuming. Our approach eliminates the need for manual intervention.

8 Conclusion

A significant amount of historical production data is presented in graphs, which makes it difficult to access the original raw data. Current software solutions encounter challenges in recognizing certain curves and converting them into numerical data. We address this issue by demonstrating the potential of RPA combined with DIA for efficient graphical-to-numerical data regeneration. By following the DSRM by Peffers et al. [10], we formulated ten DRs, developed, and demonstrated a workflow that effectively meets SMEs' data regeneration challenges. Focusing on real-world problems, as emphasized in DSR by Hevner et al. [34], our research contributes to data processing but opens avenues for future advancements in manufacturing data analysis.

However, our research is subject to certain limitations. The software agent was evaluated using a dataset from a single manufacturing SME. Further evaluations across various sectors are needed to confirm its adaptability. It is important to note that the software agent relies on static data without ongoing changes. Enhancing its capability could involve expanding this process to include dynamic data loading when the dataset updates or immediate analysis of extracted data.

Future research should aim to refine and enhance the demonstrated approach to automate the process further and increase accuracy. Integrating pre-trained ML models for detecting and selecting data points could significantly improve data extraction accuracy and efficiency. Addressing these limitations would further optimize our approach as a general, flexible method for regenerating graphic data.

References

1. Tapia, G., Elwany, A.: A review on process monitoring and control in metal-based additive manufacturing. J. Manuf. Sci. Eng. **136** (2014). https://doi.org/10.1115/1.4028540

2. Li, B., Hou, B., Yu, W., Lu, X., Yang, C.: Applications of artificial intelligence in intelligent manufacturing: a review. Front. Inf. Technol. Electron. Eng. **18**, 86–96 (2017). https://doi.org/10.1631/FITEE.1601885

3. Hansen, E.B., Bøgh, S.: Artificial intelligence and internet of things in small and medium-sized enterprises: a survey. J. Manuf. Syst. **58**, 362–372 (2021). https://doi.org/10.1016/j.jmsy.2020.08.009

4. Bauer, M., van Dinther, C., Kiefer, D.: Machine learning in SME: an empirical study on enablers and success factors. In: AMCIS 2020 Proceedings, vol. 3 (2020)

5. Masood, T., Sonntag, P.: Industry 4.0: adoption challenges and benefits for SMEs. Comput. Ind. **121** (2020). https://doi.org/10.1016/j.compind.2020.103261

6. Moeyaert, M., Maggin, D., Verkuilen, J.: Reliability, validity, and usability of data extraction programs for single-case research designs. Behav. Modif. **40**, 874–900 (2016). https://doi.org/10.1177/0145445516645763

7. Drevon, D., Fursa, S.R., Malcolm, A.L.: Intercoder reliability and validity of WebPlotDigitizer in extracting graphed data. Behav. Modif. **41**, 323–339 (2017). https://doi.org/10.1177/0145445516673998

8. Luo, J., Li, Z., Wang, J., Lin, C.-Y.: ChartOCR: data extraction from charts images via a deep hybrid framework. In: IEEE Workshop/Winter Conference on Applications of Computer Vision, vol. 21, pp. 1916–1924 (2021). https://doi.org/10.1109/WACV48630.2021.00196

9. Rohatgi A.: WebPlotDigitizer - Version 4.6 (2022). https://automeris.io/WebPlotDigitizer

10. Peffers, K., Tuunanen, T., Rothenberger, M., Chatterjee, S.: A design science research methodology for information systems research. J. Manag. Inf. Syst. **24**(3), 45–77 (2007). https://doi.org/10.2753/MIS0742-1222240302

11. Venable, J., Pries-Heje, J., Baskerville, R.: FEDS: a framework for evaluation in design science research. Eur. J. Inf. Syst. **25**, 77–89 (2016). https://doi.org/10.1057/ejis.2014.36

12. Shadish, W.R., et al.: Using UnGraph to extract data from image files: verification of reliability and validity. Behav. Res. Methods **41**, 177–183 (2009). https://doi.org/10.3758/BRM.41.1.177

13. Kato, H., Nakazawa, M., Yang, H.-K., Chen, M., Stenger, B.: Parsing line chart images using linear programming. In: IEEE/CVF Winter Conference on Applications of Computer Vision (WACV), vol. 22, pp. 2553–2562 (2022). https://doi.org/10.1109/WACV51458.2022.00261

14. Kasturi, R., O'Gorman, L., Govindaraju, V.: Document image analysis: a primer. Sadhana **27**, 3–22 (2002). https://doi.org/10.1007/BF02703309

15. Marinai, S.: Introduction to document analysis and recognition. In: Marinai, S., Fujisawa, H. (eds.) Machine Learning in Document Analysis and Recognition. SCI, vol. 90, pp. 1–20. Springer, Cham (2008). https://doi.org/10.1007/978-3-540-76280-5_1

16. van der Aalst, W.M.P., Bichler, M., Heinzl, A.: Robotic process automation. Bus. Inf. Syst. Eng. **60**, 269–272 (2018). https://doi.org/10.1007/s12599-018-0542-4

17. Lu, H., Li, Y., Chen, M., Kim, H., Serikawa, S.: Brain intelligence: go beyond artificial intelligence. Mob. Netw. Appl. **23**, 368–375 (2018). https://doi.org/10.1007/s11036-017-0932-8

18. Penttinen, E., Kasslin, H., Asatiani, A.: How to choose between robotic process automation and back-end system automation? In: Proceedings of the 26th European Conference on Information Systems, vol. 66 (2018)

19. Willcocks, L.P., Lacity, M., Craig, A.: The IT function and robotic process automation. The Outsourcing Unit Working Research Paper Series, vol. 15/05, pp. 1–39 (2015)

20. Moffitt, K.C., Rozario, A.M., Vasarhelyi, M.A.: Robotic process automation for auditing. J. Emerg. Technol. Account. **15**, 1–10 (2018). https://doi.org/10.2308/jeta-10589

21. Lacity, M., Willcocks, L.P., Craig, A.: Robotic process automation at Telefónica O2. MIS Q. Executive **15** (2015)

22. Hofmann, P., Samp, C., Urbach, N.: Robotic process automation. Electron Markets **30**, 99–106 (2020). https://doi.org/10.1007/s12525-019-00365-8
23. Russell, S.J., Norvig, P.: Artificial Intelligence. A Modern Approach. Pearson Education Limited, Harlow (2010)
24. Flower, A., McKenna, J.W., Upreti, G.: Validity and reliability of GraphClick and DataThief III for data extraction. Behav. Modif. **40**, 396–413 (2016). https://doi.org/10.1177/014544551 5616105
25. Tummers, B.: DataThief III (2023). https://datathief.org/
26. Rakap, S., Rakap, S., Evran, D., Cig, O.: Comparative evaluation of the reliability and validity of three data extraction programs: UnGraph, GraphClick, and DigitizeIt. Comput. Hum. Behav. **55**, 159–166 (2016). https://doi.org/10.1016/j.chb.2015.09.008
27. Bormann, I.: DigitizeIt - Version 2.5 (2022). https://www.digitizeit.xyz/de/
28. Arizona Software Inc.: GraphClick - Version 3.0 (not available anymore) (2023). http://www.arizonasoftware.ch/
29. Biosoft: Software for Science (2023). https://www.biosoft.com/
30. Decatur, D., Krishnan, S.: VizExtract: Automatic Relation Extraction from Data Visualizations. arXiv.org, vol. 21 (2021). https://doi.org/10.48550/arXiv.2112.03485
31. Poco, J., Heer, J.: Reverse-engineering visualizations: recovering visual encodings from chart images. Comput. Graph. Forum **36**, 353–363 (2017). https://doi.org/10.1111/cgf.13193
32. Reich, H., Gnan, A., Kamm, T., Bradatsch, E., Staedele, N.: Corrugator roll and method for obtaining same. EP20020015396, vol. B21H8/02; B24B1/00; B24B19/02; B31F1/28; B31F1/28; B24B19/02 (2002)
33. Coleman, S., Göb, R., Manco, G., Pievatolo, A., Tort-Martorell, X., Reis, M.S.: How can SMEs benefit from big data? Challenges and a path forward. Qual. Reliab. Eng. **32**, 2151–2164 (2016). https://doi.org/10.1002/qre.2008
34. Hevner, A.R., March, S.T., Park, J., Ram, S.: Design science in information systems research. MIS Q. **28**(1), 75–105 (2004). https://doi.org/10.2307/25148625
35. Gregor, S., Hevner, A.: Positioning and presenting design science research for maximum impact. MIS Q. **37**(2), 337–355 (2013). https://doi.org/10.25300/MISQ/2013/37.2.01
36. vom Brocke, J., Winter, R., Hevner, A., Maedche, A.: Special issue editorial–accumulation and evolution of design knowledge in design science research: a journey through time and space. JAIS **21**, 520–544 (2020). https://doi.org/10.17705/1jais.00611
37. Cramond, F., O'Mara-Eves, A., Doran-Constant, L., Rice, A.S., Macleod, M., Thomas, J.: The development and evaluation of an online application to assist in the extraction of data from graphs for use in systematic reviews. Wellcome Open Res. **3** (2018). https://doi.org/10.12688/wellcomeopenres.14738.3

Towards a Smarter Tomorrow: A Design Science Perspective on Building a Smart Campus IoT Data Platform

Mevludin Blazevic$^{(\boxtimes)}$ ⓘ, Timon T. Aldenhoff ⓘ, and Dennis M. Riehle ⓘ

University of Koblenz, Universitätsstraße 1, 56070 Koblenz, Germany
`mblazevic@uni-koblenz.de`

Abstract. In the area of Internet of Things (IoT) data storage, the integration of Relational Database Management Systems (RDBMS) and Time Series Database (TSD) approaches represents a promising reliable, and scalable solution. This paper aims to design and instantiate a reference architecture for an IoT data platform tailored for a smart campus or University of Things (UoT) environment. The approach includes combining RDBMS and TSD technologies within a single, unified data platform. This integration combines relational data, which is commonly used in Information Systems (IS), with time-stamped information from various IoT sensors deployed across the university campus. The collected sensor data comprises millions of data points over time, which are effectively integrated into the IoT data platform, facilitating quick and dependable access to time series data, and eliminating the need for complex pre-processing or indexing. By applying the Action Design Research (ADR) method, requirements for the data platform derived from the existing smart campus infrastructure are gathered before designing the platform. The findings reveal that combining RDBMS and TSDs concepts represents an easy-to-implement and scalable solution for IoT infrastructures.

Keywords: Internet of Things · Data Platform · IoT Data Storage · Time Series Database · Relational Database

1 Problem Understanding and Research Objective

The IoT revolutionizes the way we interact with the world by connecting physical things and objects to the digital realm. In our real-world smart campus infrastructure, students and our research team lead the design and implementation of a smart campus without external development teams, providing students with a teaching platform to create educational artifacts. Additionally, the university's administration and other research groups are leveraging the IoT network infrastructure and over time, various IoT sensors are installed to collect various environmental data. It is interesting and challenging since a smart campus can be viewed as a part of a Smart City [24], whereas a smart campus can be seen as a small-scale Smart City [7,15,21].

M. Mandviwalla et al. (Eds.): DESRIST 2024, LNCS 14621, pp. 262–277, 2024.
https://doi.org/10.1007/978-3-031-61175-9_18

Millions of IoT data points have been generated, posing a significant challenge in storing them efficiently for smart campus infrastructure expansion. Additionally, structuring this data by sensor location and linked projects for access control presents another challenge. This outlines key requirements for the underlying database system, including data security, query speed, and reliability [3,18]. While a time-series database efficiently handles sequential IoT data, it lacks flexibility in data structuring, unlike a relational database which offers comprehensive structuring capabilities but faces challenges with high-volume, append-only data.

This paper aims to design and implement a IoT data platform tailored to the requirements and needs of a smart campus IoT ecosystem, where a significant number of sensors are already deployed and produce a vast amount of data, which needs to be stored as efficient as possible. First, the novelty of this work lies in the execution of the Design Science Research (DSR) method for the implementation of an IoT data platform with the associated problem identification, requirements elicitation, and iterative execution of the DSR process steps. Second, the IoT data platform serves as an IS for retrieving raw sensor data from the university campus by implementing an access rights system for users and mapping the university context in a relational database. For this purpose, a classic RDBMS model with PostgreSQL is designed. Lastly, the technical extension of PostgreSQL with TimeScaleDB brings the advantages of a time-series database and drastically reduces the query time for retrieving IoT data. The defined research objective is to design and implement a reference architecture for constructing an IoT data platform within the smart campus context. The ADR method by Mullarkey & Hevner [13] is used to achieve this research objective.

The remainder of this paper is structured as follows. According to the ADR diagnosis phases, this section provides the problem understanding and research objective. Section 2 presents an overview of the concepts of IoT data platforms and their application within the smart campus context, followed by a presentation of related work. While the section does not directly correspond to the ADR diagnosis phase, it does indirectly contribute to comprehending the rationale behind developing a new architecture for IoT data platforms in the smart campus context. Section 3 briefly recaps the applied ADR approach. After that, Sect. 5 describes requirements and design considerations of the IoT data platform. The prototype is then implemented and evaluated in Sect. 6. Finally, Sect. 7 summarizes the findings of the design research study and discusses the potential for future work.

2 Theoretical Background and Related Work

2.1 IoT and Data Platforms

According to Baiyere et al. [2], IoT can be described as a network of connections between digital technologies and physical objects. This network allows these traditionally ordinary objects to provide computing capabilities and interact with each other, either autonomously or with human involvement. A data platform can be seen as a technical environment for recording, storing, analyzing, and presenting vast amounts of data. This data may be generated from other IS, business processes, IoT sensors, or other digital infrastructures. A data platform provides several benefits, such as centralization and standardization of data functions, simplified access by data users, and faster, more comprehensive, and higher-quality data analysis [11,12].

2.2 Related Work

Various research was undertaken concerning data platforms for sensor networks. The related works presented were conducted between 2019 and 2024 and focus on IoT data platforms in different domains, such as airport security and pursue the blockchain, actor-oriented, and RDBMS approaches. Blockchain approaches encompass the implementation of data platforms on blockchains by proposing open-source frameworks for license-free use or a file-sharing protocol for exchanging sensor data. Actor-oriented technologies are build upon computing and data storage capabilities of sensor devices and eliminate the need for cloud storage systems. The RDBMS approaches leverage MariaDB and MySQL as the underlying storage architecture. However, each platform is tailored to a specific IoT use case only, while the possibility of adopting other domains remains unanswered. Lastly, the article title of some studies suggests a discussion on IoT data platforms. However, there is a noticeable absence of any mention regarding the specific database architecture employed [9,14].

The blockchain approach focuses on providing IoT data for a community or public use, necessitating the security and encapsulation of sensor data that the blockchain technology can achieve. Furthermore, related studies highlight decentralization and a given auditable access control policy [16]. Open-source frameworks were developed for the implementation of this approach, such as "Sash", which combines IoT platforms and blockchain [20]. With "Sash", several data owners and consumers may trade their IoT data while the grant access is controlled by specific prefix decryption keys. In addition to this framework, Razzaq et al. [19] present Interplanetary File System (IPFS), a decentralized and distributed file-sharing protocol for storing and sharing sensor data across the Internet. Using Ethereum, the suggested workaround involves logging hash values and additional information in a blockchain ledger, encrypting IoT data for storage in IPFS, and demonstrating that the upload process is consistently efficient and cost-effective regardless of data size in terms of gas consumption.

In contrast to the blockchain approach, the reference architecture we propose entails closed, private storage of sensor data utilizing TimescaleDB, eliminating the need for decentralized data storage. The primary objective is to streamline the retrieval of IoT data amidst vast data points. This setup proves beneficial for deploying smart campus use cases such as air quality monitoring and smart office systems [4]. Moreover, we argue that the architecture and data structure are adaptable to other campus infrastructures.

In the actor-oriented approach, the underlying database is structured around the actor model, where data and computation are divided into entities called actors, which may represent IoT devices, that provide computation and data storage capabilities [22]. This approach leverages the computation capability of sensor devices but requires corresponding IoT devices with enough compute power for serving as actors in this setup. However, our approach leverages centralized concepts, eliminating computing requirements for sensor devices.

Another approach for constructing IoT data platforms encompasses the use of RDBMS such as MySQL and MariaDB [10,17]. For an airport security system, a centralized cloud-based IoT data platform is proposed, which aims to integrate existing IoT systems to break down data silos and isolated IoT databases [17]. The underlying database architecture consists of a MySQL database only, and the data platform is strictly tailored to the context of airport security. However, the authors highlight the problem of a growing number of sensors and sensor data and the promising capabilities of edge computing as a research outlook. Another RDBMS driven IoT data platform approach [10] encompasses a MariaDB system and a PHP application for data platform visualization. The IoT use case contains the need for network management functions of IoT devices and sensor data storage capabilities. The presented methodology for application testing encompasses network performance, yet performance evaluation of the implemented database is excluded from the scope of this research.

Indeed, the existing IoT data storage system on the smart campus relies solely on an RDBMS, specifically MariaDB, as described in Sect. 4. However, there are encountered performance limitations and inefficiencies in retrieving sensor data. In our opinion, retrieving data, especially for smart campus applications, requires complex preprocessing and indexing due to prolonged query times. For instance, querying six months of Carbon Dioxide (CO_2) sensor data takes nearly ten minutes on the existing storing system. This limitation strives to develop a new data platform, serving as a reference, which employs a time-series database for storing sensor data while still leveraging the benefits of RDBMS.

3   Action Design Research Method

The research objective described in Sect. 1 requires a technical solution and an appropriate approach for creation and evaluation. Therefore, we follow the principle of DSR and the associated ADR method according to Mullarkey & Hevner [13]. As depicted in Fig. 1, the approach encompasses four cycles of problem *Diagnosis*, *Design*, *Implementation*, and *Evolution*. In this model, each ADR step includes the activities *Problem Formulation*(P), *Artifact Creation*(A), *Evaluation*(E), *Reflection*(R), and *Learning*(L). We selected this process model for its blend of flexibility and disciplined approach in developing artifacts. Its iterative nature, especially in individual ADR cycles like design, allows rapid prototyping of software artifacts without the need to repeat entire DSR cycles as seen in traditional models such as the waterfall model. Due to limited space and a focused scope in this paper, not all activities in each cycle are explicitly detailed. Instead, the following explanation of the approach will focus on the most significant activities in each cycle. The initial sections, including the problem understanding and research objective (Sect. 1), the theoretical background and related work (Sect. 2), and the explanation of an existing IoT data platform implementation (Sect. 4), present the outcomes of the initial ADR cycle, which is the *Diagnosis*.

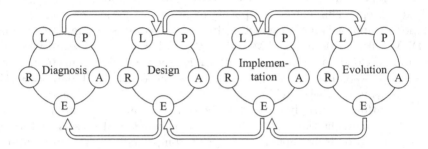

Fig. 1. Design Science Research Cycle (adapted from [13])

Subsequently, the sections focus on the design of an IoT data platform (Sect. 5) and implementation and evaluation (Sect. 6) align with the ADR *Design* and *Implementation* cycles, respectively. Lastly, the discussion in Sect. 7 explores the fourth cycle - *Evolution* - within the ADR process model.

4 Diagnosing Existing IoT Data Storage System

As part of the *Diagnosis* cycle within the ADR methodology, we now detail the architecture and functionalities of an existing IoT storage system, which served as a precursor to the newly developed data platform. The main issue with this system was the performance in terms of query speed and efficiency.

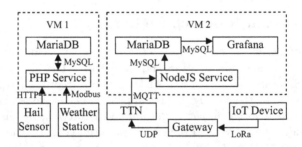

Fig. 2. Infrastructure of the Previous IoT System on the Smart Campus

It consisted of two separate Virtual Machines (VMs) as illustrated in Fig. 2, each processing and storing different data types. The first VM processed data from the university's weather station and the hail sensor. The weather data were retrieved via an HTTP webhook, while the hail sensor data were read via Modbus. A PHP service processed these data and stored them in the MariaDB database. Additionally, this PHP service provided a simple table representation of the data on a website. The second VM processed indoor climate and particulate matter data. These data were collected by an IoT device, which communicated via a gateway that established a Long Range Wide Area Network (LoRaWAN) network. Next, the data is gathered through The Things Network (TTN) service, which relayed them via MQ Telemetry Transport (MQTT) to a NodeJS service. This service stores the data in a MariaDB database, and the data can be visualized through a Grafana instance.

A thorough analysis of the existing architecture and functionality revealed that the system was reaching its limits when processing over 11 million data points in the MariaDB. As described by Wolters et al. [23], the query speed and performance of exemplary RDBMS systems are disadvantageous for IoT data. This challenge can be effectively addressed by employing a time-series database specifically designed to optimize the storage, retrieval, and analysis of time-stamped data. The goal was to ensure more efficient handling of the increased volume of data while maintaining system stability even under high loads. Furthermore, access control to IoT data was only granted on Grafana by managing access rights. The access rights management should now be shifted to the application layer and not only handled in the presentation layer. Also, maintaining two separate systems is not a good practice. The new design should handle multiple use cases.

5   Design of an IoT Data Platform

5.1   Design Requirements

For the *Design* phase within the ADR cycle, requirements have been adopted from four key sensor use cases. These use cases are instrumental for our smart campus, each encompassing specific goals and types of data points. The first use case, *Air Quality Monitoring in Lecture Halls and Offices*, aims to ensure a healthy learning and working environment. It involves the collection of data points such as $CO2$ levels, humidity, temperature, and atmospheric pressure. The second use case concerns *Occupancy Tracking in Library Workspaces*. The main goal here is to provide real-time information on the availability of workspaces. This includes data points like the number of people in different library areas and the duration of workspace usage [1]. In the third use case, *Particulate Matter Measurement on Campus*, particulate matter (PM2.5 and PM10) is monitored outdoors and indoors. The fourth use case is the provision of *Weather Station Data*, aiming to collect and disseminate comprehensive meteorological data encompassing temperature, humidity, precipitation, wind speed, direction, and specific data for hail detection. In summary, with their specific goals and data points, these use cases form the basis for designing the IoT data platform.

Functional Requirements. Derived from the smart campus use cases and the existing system, the platform's functional requirements encompass a range of capabilities of the IoT data platform, which are displayed in Table 1. The existing system already collects and visualizes data and stores some metadata.

Table 1. Functional Requirements of the IoT data platform

No.	Name	Tier	Priority
F1	Data collection & storage	Data Layer (TSD)	Must-have
F2	Access control	Data Layer (RDBMS)	Must-have
F3	Metadata	Data Layer (RDBMS)	Must-have
F4	Interfaces	Application Layer	Must-have
F5	Visualization	Presentation Layer	Must-have
F6	Monitoring	Application Layer	Should-have
F7	Filtering	Application Layer	Nice-to-have
F8	Data Analytics	Application Layer	Nice-to-have

Data collection (F1) is at the platform's core, a fundamental component aggregating diverse data types from various sensors. This core functionality is crucial for the platform's overall effectiveness. Access Control (F2) is another critical requirement, ensuring data security by managing user permissions and securing data access not only in the Presentation Layer, a vital aspect of the smart campus context. The necessity for access control primarily arises from the *Air Quality Monitoring in Lecture Halls and Offices* use case, where it's imperative that employees have access only to data from public spaces or their own rooms, safeguarding privacy and data integrity. The platform also focuses on Metadata (F3), capturing essential information about IoT devices, such as battery status or location. This information is key for effective device management and maintenance. Interfaces (F4) ensure the platform's accessibility and interoperability, utilizing standardized interfaces to facilitate data queries. Such interfaces are crucial for providing data to external entities; for example, they can be used to display the count of people in the library on a public website, enhancing transparency with real-time information. Data visualization (F5) is central to transforming complex data sets into understandable and user-friendly formats. This is particularly crucial for providing insights and supporting data-driven decision-making. Monitoring (F6) is dedicated to the continuous oversight of system health and performance, essential for the early detection of issues and ensuring system reliability. The importance of this function has been underscored by instances where the existing system failed without immediate detection. Filtering (F7) is a nice-to-have step in maintaining the integrity and usability of the collected data. This involves removing anomalies and ensuring consistency in data structures, thereby preserving data accuracy. This capability was particularly important in the old system as broken sensors often went undetected, providing inaccurate data without prompt detection or correction of the malfunctioning units. Lastly, data analytics (F8), as a value-added feature, enables advanced analysis of the collected data for research, fostering deeper insights.

Non-functional Requirements. In Table 2, we present a set of seven non-functional requirements derived from an analysis of both the identified use cases and the existing system.

Table 2. Non-Functional Requirements of the IoT data platform

No.	Name	Priority
NF1	Query-Speed	Must-have
NF2	Interoperability	Must-have
NF3	Expandability	Must-have
NF4	Reliability	Must-have
NF5	Maintainability	Should-have
NF6	IT Security	Should-have
NF7	Portability	Nice-to-have

A primary focus is on Query-Speed (NF1), a must-have feature that ensures fast response times for efficient data retrieval, important for every use case. Equally important is Interoperability (NF2). This aspect ensures seamless interaction with diverse systems and technologies, significantly enhancing the platform's utility and reach. The platform's Expandability (NF3) focuses on its growth and evolution capacity. As the network of sensors expands, it's essential that the system is designed to handle this growing scale efficiently.

Reliability (NF4) is also important when people depend on the requested data and availability. The platform should be robust and minimize downtime. Maintainability (NF5) is needed for ongoing maintenance and ensures the platform's relevance and adaptability to future technological advancements. IT Security (NF6), while lower prioritization due to the platform's protection behind university firewalls, remains a pivotal aspect. Lastly, Portability (NF7) is considered a nice-to-have feature to enhance the platform's flexibility, allowing for easy transfer and adaptation across different environments, thus broadening its applicability.

5.2 Reference Architecture

Following the requirements phase of the ADR cycle, we now aim to design the new architecture as an artifact. Subsequently, we will evaluate this design, reflect on the outcomes, and learn from the experience, guiding us through the design cycle's next and final iteration.

Architecture of the New Plattform. In the design approach for the new IoT data platform, a three-tier architecture was adopted to streamline development tasks, enhance maintainability, and ensure replaceability. As shown in Fig. 3, this architecture consists of the Presentation Layer, the Application Layer, and the Data Layer. The Presentation Layer includes a web-based User Interface (UI) where end-users interact with the system. The Application Layer forms the heart of the application and processes the collected information, often using business logic. The Data Layer is the storage location for the processed information and is implemented in this context with PostgreSQL and TimescaleDB [6]. The clear separation of responsibilities especially allows for scalability and flexibility.

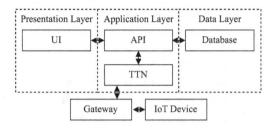

Fig. 3. Smart Campus IoT Data Platform Architecture

Technology Choice. In selecting the technologies, several key factors were considered: good software documentation, high performance, established open-source technologies with potential for updates, adherence to industry standards, and a lean tech stack to minimize maintenance effort. The selection process was iterative, spanning three phases, with problems encountered in each phase.

Initially, Docker was chosen for the deployment and containerization of all services. For the presentation layer, the choice fell on Grafana, as it was already being used as a visualization tool. However, it was recognized that a custom UI will be necessary in the future, leading to the selection of TypeScript and Vue.js in the presentation layer and TypeScript with Node.js in the application layer. TypeScript offers the advantage of strong typing and can be used both in the layers, simplifying maintenance. Additionally, TypeScript, in combination with Node.js, provides good performance [5]. The Application Programming Interface (API) utilizes a mix of REST and GraphQL, with GraphQL enabling specific data requests and REST offering widespread external system compatibility. The choice of database technology proved complex. On one hand, the collected time-series data needed to be stored and retrievable efficiently. On the other hand, relational structures such as the roles and rights concept or the storage of sensors, devices, and users had to be possible. It was decided to use two database management systems: MariaDB for all data except the time-series data and QuestDB for the time-series data, a high-performance new database technology from 2019 [23].

It was determined that an orchestration tool was needed to deploy the data platform across multiple VMs and easily start new containers. Therefore, Kubernetes was selected as the industry standard for this area. Additionally, TypeORM was incorporated for migration handling.

During development, problems were encountered with QuestDB, particularly when adding data points from the past and setting up external backups. The efficiency of inserting new data points and checking for their existence was also problematic. Therefore, the combination of QuestDB and MariaDB was replaced by TimescaleDB. TimescaleDB, based on PostgreSQL, extends it with Hypertables optimized for time-series data, thus combining the relational and time-series parts in one technology, simplifying maintenance.

Data Structure. In the architecture of the IoT data platform, as depicted in Fig. 4, a simplified representation of the data structure is presented as a UML

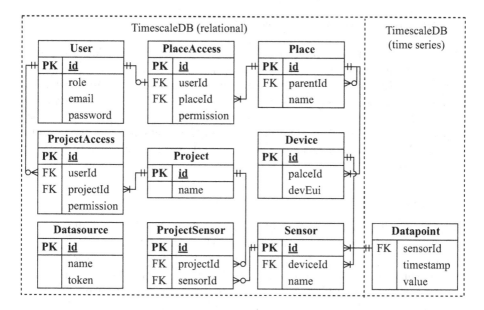

Fig. 4. Smart Campus IoT Data Platform Database Structure

Class Diagram. This representation focuses on the core entities and their relational connections, noting that not all attributes of the entities are listed in the diagram. The structure was designed to enable efficient data management, meet the current requirements of the platform, and allow for future expansions.

The foundational elements of the data structure are the entities *Place, Device, Sensor, User, Project,* and *Datasource.* Entities like *PlaceAccess, ProjectAccess* and *ProjectSensor* play a crucial role in resolving N-to-M relationships and establishing a flexible, secure permission system for varied access control across the platform. The *Place* entity, representing locations such as lecture halls or workspaces, is pivotal, linking each physical device to a specific location for rights and role distribution. Access to sensor data, for instance, is restricted to authorized individuals based on their association with the location. The *Project* entity further refines access management, allowing control over specific sensors in scenarios like studies on device battery levels, where access is limited to relevant sensor data within projects. This setup enables rights allocation for either entire devices or individual sensors across multiple devices, providing a nuanced approach to access rights management. The *Datasource* entity, distinct in its role of authorizing various data sources, stands independently from other entities. Complementing these, the *Datapoint* entity, structured as a Hypertable, efficiently handles time-series data storage and retrieval.

6   Implementation and Evaluation

Switching to the implementation cycle, the developed IoT data platform is sub-
jected to an implementation and evaluation in this section. This is carried out
based on the previously defined functional and non-functional requirements. The
aim is to assess the extent to which the platform meets these requirements and
how it contributes to improving data processing and utilization on the smart
campus. The results of this evaluation will provide insights into how the platform
addresses the challenges posed and what potential exists for future improvements
and expansions.

6.1   Implementation

In this cycle, all P-A-E-R-L steps of the ADR are went through. Following the
ADR implementation step, the developed IoT data platform has been implemented following the schema depicted in Fig. 3 using a Kubernetes Cluster
based on three K3S master nodes illustrated in Fig. 5. Moreover, the cluster was
deployed on the university's private cloud infrastructure based on Apache Cloud-
stack. At the core of the data platform lie three redundant pods, each hosting a
Node.js server, serving as the fundamental components for data processing and
management in the application layer. The database, comprising three replicated
pods of TimescaleDB, is connected to the Node.js service and plays a pivotal
role in data storage. Supported by a Kubernetes Cron Job to guarantee data
integrity and accessibility, the system undergoes routine backups. Additionally,
a Grafana instance is integrated into the cluster, serving both for monitoring
IoT data and, in combination with Prometheus and Grafana Loki, for cluster
monitoring and log aggregation.

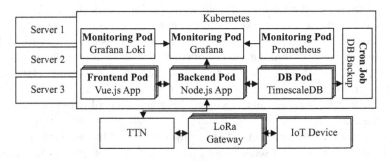

Fig. 5. Smart Campus IoT Data Platform Kubernetes Cluster

Data transmission is handled by IoT devices through four LoRaWAN gateways installed on the university campus, communicating with the Node.js service via TTN and an MQTT broker. The data undergoes processing on the
IoT data platform before being stored in TimescaleDB. TTN, used in the community edition, is not included in the Kubernetes cluster, allowing the use of

other LoRaWAN gateways and enabling other users to access the university's LoRaWAN network. However, it will be integrated into the cluster in the future.

6.2 Evaluation

In the following section, we describe how the predefined requirements were addressed within the architecture of the IoT data platform. In the ADR methodology, evaluation of the implemented IoT data platform in our smart campus setup involves collaboration within the research group and engagement with university students, who are involved in further developing the smart campus infrastructure as well as university members in administration and research, who makes use of the sensor data. Moreover, integrating the data platform within the smart campus environment includes incorporation into an existing LoRaWAN network, including gateways, sensors, and visualization software previously linked to the current storage and now redirected to the new data platform. Primarily, in the implementation phase, we focus on testing the new data platform based on the predefined requirements to ensure its functionality and effectiveness. Testing procedures on the software's performance are conducted as objective evaluation, which was defined as a key problem in the diagnosis phase of the current sensor data storage structure. Moreover, after the implementation of the platform, the ADR evolution step is entered, where the platform is further developed and evaluated iteratively following the P-A-E-R-L cycle.

Functional Requirements. At the forefront is the platform's data collection & storage (F1) capability, which adeptly manages the aggregation and storage of a diverse array of data types. This includes CO_2 levels, temperature readings, air pressure metrics, particulate matter concentrations, workspace occupancy figures, humidity percentages, and GPS data at our smart campus. These data types are sourced from an extensive network of sensors, underscoring the platform's capacity to handle a broad spectrum of IoT data inputs. The successful management of this data is significantly bolstered by the employment of PostgreSQL with the TimescaleDB plugin as a time-series database. Access Control (F2) and Metadata (F3) functionalities have been implemented using the same PostgreSQL with a relational schema regarding security and data organization. The Interfaces (F4) feature was addressed by utilizing REST and GraphQL. Visualization (F5) capabilities, particularly through incorporating Grafana, dramatically enhance the UI by enabling complex datasets' intuitive and insightful presentation. Implementing a Prometheus Kubernetes Stack addressed Monitoring (F6) of the platform's health and performance. Lastly, the areas of Filtering (F7) and Data Analytics (F8), labeled as *Nice-to-have* highlight potential avenues for future enhancements and were not addressed in this architecture.

Non-functional Requirements. The main reason for developing this architecture was the query speed (NF1). A complex query involving inner joins was executed on the old system with MariaDB and the new IoT data platform with TimescaleDB to demonstrate the database speed. This query, designed to retrieve data from the last 90 days from various sensors in a database containing over 15.2 million data points, is not limited to showcasing the time-series capabilities of TimescaleDB but also its efficiency in handling complex joins. The results are striking: TimescaleDB achieved an average response time of 1.4 s, compared to MariaDB's 27.3 s on the same data set. Interoperability (NF2) was achieved through the smooth replacement of both VMs and integration of the new architecture, indicating seamless communication with the existing ecosystem. Expandability (NF3) was tested and validated as students continuously added more sensors, with the system showing no signs of strain or limitation, reflecting its capability to scale effectively. The platform's reliability (NF4) was confirmed by its stable operation over six months without any failures. Several updates and upgrades were performed without problems, showing maintainability (NF5). The platform's deployment on our university's cloud infrastructure provides a foundational layer of IT security (NF6). However, comprehensive penetration testing has yet to be conducted to assess vulnerabilities further. Containerization enhances system portability (NF7) and adaptation across environments and facilitates efficient testing and scaling.

7   Discussion and Conclusion

The primary objective of this research was to design and implement a reference architecture tailored for the construction of an IoT data platform within the context of a smart campus. In conclusion, the architecture of our IoT data platform is satisfactory for the real-world installation of our smart campus/UoT infrastructure and based on our implementation and evaluation in Sect. 5.

In comparison to related studies mentioned in Sect. 2.2, our proposed data platform is based on two different database architectures, namely RDBMS and TSD. This approach enhances query speed and allows for a complex relational schema. Notably, this fusion enabled the implementation of a finely granular, permission-based authorization system, which benefits from the structured approach of RDBMS. TimescaleDB simplifies data querying and enables performing joins and other relational operations within a time-series context. Incorporating this technological fusion into our artifact enables a relatively simple yet effective smart campus system with minimal effort. The architecture's design allows for easy adoption by other universities seeking similar IoT data platform solutions. Furthermore, the data structure is minimalist and designed with flexibility in mind, making it extendable to accommodate additional use cases. This adaptability ensures that our platform can evolve alongside any smart campus environment's growing and changing needs. Due to its minimalist design, it is also possible to host this architecture in a smaller environment. Operating the platform on the university's cloud infrastructure offers further advantages, such as storing sensitive data in compliance with EU data protection laws. Moreover, the reliance on public cloud providers has been eliminated.

The primary drawback of our data platform lies in its alignment with the specific requirements of the smart campus infrastructure. Furthermore, the data platform is better suited for deployment within a closed, private infrastructure, functioning as a centralized solution and lacking the flexibility to operate as an open community platform. Related research has explored alternative solutions utilizing blockchain technology for decentralized IoT data storage.

In future research, a thorough assessment of the reference architecture utilizing the Fitness-Utility Model (FUM) as part of the DSR approach [8] may be carried out. For instance, the inclusion of sensor data derived from applications related to smart city or smart region initiatives can be integrated into our data platform. This expansion aims to facilitate the ongoing development and evaluation of the platform following the DSR principle. Lastly, establishing a scope and definition of the concept of an *IoT data platform* is recommended using literature review methods in IS field to ensure transparency and facilitate comprehension within the academic community.

Acknowledgements. This research has been supported by the German Research Foundation (DFG) under Research Grant No. 432399058 and by the Federal Ministry of Education and Research (BMBF), Germany under Research Grant No. 16DTM218.

References

1. Arz von Straussenburg, A.F., Blazevic, M., Riehle, D.M.: Measuring the actual office workspace utilization in a desk sharing environment based on IoT sensors. In: Gerber, A., Baskerville, R. (eds.) DESRIST 2023. LNCS, vol. 13873, pp. 69–83. Springer, Cham (2023). https://doi.org/10.1007/978-3-031-32808-4_5
2. Baiyere, A., Topi, H., Venkatesh, V., Donnellan, B.: The Internet of Things (IoT): a research agenda for information systems. Commun. AIS **47**, 564–589 (2020). https://doi.org/10.17705/1CAIS.04725
3. Beynon-Davies, P.: Database Systems, 3rd edn. Springer, Cham (2004). https://doi.org/10.1007/978-0-230-00107-7
4. Blazevic, M., Riehle, D.M.: University of things: opportunities and challenges for a smart campus environment based on IoT sensors and business processes. In: Proceedings of the IoTBDS 2023, pp. 104–114 (2023). https://doi.org/10.5220/0011761900003482
5. Chitra, L.P., Satapathy, R.: Performance comparison and evaluation of node.js and traditional web server (IIS). In: Proceedings of the ICAMMAET 2017, pp. 1–4 (2017). https://doi.org/10.1109/ICAMMAET.2017.8186633
6. Fernandez, E.B., Fonoage, M., VanHilst, M., Marta, M.: The secure three-tier architecture pattern. In: Proceedings of the CISIS 2008, pp. 555–560 (2008). https://doi.org/10.1109/CISIS.2008.51
7. Fortes, S., et al.: The campus as a smart city: University of Málaga environmental, learning, and research approaches. Sensors **19**(6) (2019). https://doi.org/10.3390/s19061349
8. Gill, T.G., Hevner, A.R.: A fitness-utility model for design science research. ACM Trans. Manage. Inf. Syst. **4**(2) (2013). https://doi.org/10.1145/2499962.2499963

9. Hwang, H., Joe, I.: An IoT-based cloud data platform with real-time connecting maritime autonomous surface ships. In: Silhavy, R., Silhavy, P. (eds.) CoMeSySo 2023. LNCS, vol. 909, pp. 208–220. Springer, Cham (2024). https://doi.org/10.1007/978-3-031-53549-9_21

10. Ivars-Palomares, A., Zaragoza-Esquerdo, M., Sendra, S., Lloret, J.: Design of a platform for data storage and data management in IoT networks. In: Proceedings of the WINCOM 2023, pp. 1–6 (2023). https://doi.org/10.1109/WINCOM59760.2023.10322905

11. Kidd, C.: Data platforms explained: features, benefits & getting started (2023). https://www.splunk.com/en_us/blog/learn/data-platform.html. Accessed 22 Dec 2023

12. Kramberg, P., Heinzl, A.: Datenplattformökosysteme. HMD Praxis der Wirtschaftsinformatik **58**(3), 477–493 (2021). https://doi.org/10.1365/s40702-021-00716-0

13. Mullarkey, M.T., Hevner, A.R.: An elaborated action design research process model. Eur. J. Inf. Syst. **28**(1), 6–20 (2019). https://doi.org/10.1080/0960085X.2018.1451811

14. Ni, Y., Zhou, T., Gao, X., Chen, H.: Design and implementation of a UPOD for decentralized IoT data platform based on the ActivityPub protocol. In: IEEE International Symposium on Dependable, Autonomic and Secure Computing (DASC), pp. 0825–0830 (2023). https://doi.org/10.1109/DASC/PiCom/CBDCom/Cy59711.2023.10361378

15. Silva-da Nóbrega, P.I., Chim-Miki, A.F., Castillo-Palacio, M.: A smart campus framework: challenges and opportunities for education based on the sustainable development goals. Sustainability **14**(15) (2022). https://doi.org/10.3390/su14159640

16. Przytarski, D., Stach, C., Gritti, C., Mitschang, B.: A blueprint for a trustworthy health data platform encompassing IoT and blockchain technologies. In: EPiC Series in Computing, vol. 76, pp. 56–65. EasyChair (2021). https://doi.org/10.29007/1sbn

17. Qian, C., Tang, W., Xiong, W., Chen, H., Wang, Y.: Design and implementation of airport security system based on IoT data cloud platform. In: Proceedings of the ADMIT 2022, pp. 62–67 (2022). https://doi.org/10.1109/ADMIT57209.2022.00019

18. Rautmare, S., Bhalerao, D.M.: MySQL and NoSQL database comparison for IoT application. In: 2016 IEEE International Conference on Advances in Computer Applications (ICACA), pp. 235–238 (2016). https://doi.org/10.1109/ICACA.2016.7887957

19. Razzaq, A., Altamimi, A.B., Alreshidi, A., Ghayyur, S.A.K., Khan, W., Alsaffar, M.: IoT data sharing platform in web 3.0 using blockchain technology. Electronics **12**(5) (2023). https://doi.org/10.3390/electronics12051233

20. Truong, H.T.T., Almeida, M., Karame, G., Soriente, C.: Towards secure and decentralized sharing of IoT data. In: 2019 IEEE International Conference on Blockchain (Blockchain), pp. 176–183 (2019). https://doi.org/10.1109/Blockchain.2019.00031

21. Vasileva, R., Rodrigues, L., Hughes, N., Greenhalgh, C., Goulden, M., Tennison, J.: What smart campuses can teach us about smart cities: user experiences and open data. Information **9**(10) (2018). https://doi.org/10.3390/info9100251

22. Wang, Y., Dos Reis, J., Borggren, K., Vaz Salles, M., Medeiros, C., Zhou, Y.: Modeling and building IoT data platforms with actor-oriented databases. In: Proceedings of the EDBT 2019, Lisbon, Portugal, pp. 512–523 (2019). https://doi.org/10.5441/002/edbt.2019.47

23. Wolters, A., Blazevic, M., Riehle, D.M.: On-premise Internet of Things (IoT) data storage: comparison of database management systems. In: Proceedings of the IoTBDS 2023, pp. 140–149 (2023). https://doi.org/10.5220/0011851200003482
24. Zhang, Y., Yip, C., Lu, E., Dong, Z.Y.: A systematic review on technologies and applications in smart campus: a human-centered case study. IEEE Access **10**, 16134–16149 (2022). https://doi.org/10.1109/ACCESS.2022.3148735

Bridging Enterprise Knowledge Management and Natural Language Processing - Integration Framework and a Prototype

Justus Cappel[1]([✉])(iD) and Friedrich Chasin[2](iD)

[1] University of Cologne, Cologne, Germany
jcappel@smail.uni-koeln.de
[2] University Münster, Münster, Germany
fc@ercis.de

Abstract. Despite the rapid advances in AI, most organizations struggle to fully harness the potential that emerging technologies in the realm of Natural Language Processing (NLP) offer. This study deals with the particular challenge of using large language models (LLMs) to enhance the communication of organizational knowledge among employees and with external customers. Traditionally, companies rely on distributing knowledge via websites, internal documents or knowledge management systems, the use of which often proves tedious. In response, this work proposes an integration framework that helps organizations to connect the digital representations of their existing knowledge with LLMs. This integration enables intelligent retrieval and enhances semantic matching of questions and answers based on the knowledge base. Objectives for the framework are derived from insights gathered through interviews with organizations, emphasizing the practical relevance of the proposed solution, and demonstrate the utility of the framework with a prototypical implementation. This research not only represents a contribution to the ongoing research on the organizational applications of LLM-based digital technologies but also outlines the benefits and the limits of current LLM technologies for the enhancement of organizational knowledge management.

Keywords: Knowledge Management · Natural Language Processing · Information Retrieval · Integration Framework · Prototype

1 Introduction

Two digital phenomena are currently converging. On the one hand, there is the accumulation of knowledge, especially in the digital space. Organizations play a crucial role in that accumulation of knowledge, in that they generate knowledge through their organizational conduct and circulate this knowledge among employees and educate clients on the use of their products and services [10,20].

This, in turn, enables the processing of knowledge, encompassing retrieval, selection, and the initiation of reasoning [28]. On the other hand there have been remarkable strides in artificial intelligence (AI). The latter is capable of processing knowledge and has provided us with new tools to work with the representation of information [8]. For instance, with the development of NLP, as a branch of AI, the ability to understand text and spoken words in a similar way to humans quickly led to this technology being used as a tool for handling and processing large amounts of information efficiently [26]. This development already has an impact on a wide range of industries resulting in primarily large corporations taking part in huge AI applications.

However, taking these two phenomena together, the rise of digital knowledge combined with the rapid development of NLP, the majority of smaller and mid-size organizations in particular, unlike large organizations with dedicated departments for such developments, do not have the resources to develop such systems and face a situation where they encounter a potential that they have difficulties to realize [5,9]. Instead, they might find themselves in a competitive arena they never initially desired to be part of [12] struggling with the lack of essential resources such as human expertise [4], technological capabilities [1] and best practices [5]. Moreover, there is a great deal of uncertainty regarding the likely outcomes of this transformation involving the integration of advanced digital knowledge and NLP technologies into organizational processes [18]. Ultimately, businesses need an economic perspective and should assess whether investment into AI-enhanced knowledge management for their employees and clients is worth the effort [18].

Against this backdrop, companies lack understanding of how to integrate the capabilities of NLP into their knowledge management to take advantage of the ongoing technological advances in the AI.

Guided by the principles of design science outlined by Peffers et al. [25], this study adopts a design-oriented approach with the primary goal of creating a framework to integrate enterprise knowledge management systems (EKMS) and NLP. To meet the requirements for such an integration, expert knowledge is gathered through semi-structured interviews during the design objective phase and is enriched and triangulated with literature. The framework enables the integration of enterprise knowledge and NLP through components, which serve as a blueprint for companies to address the stock of organizational knowledge with AI by implementing appropriate functional solutions. We demonstrate the framework's utility by implementing a digital prototype, showcasing the framework's value within a specific scenario.

The subsequent sections of the manuscript are structured as follows. Section 2 addresses the theoretical background, focusing on knowledge and NLP. In Sect. 3 the research approach of this paper is presented. The subsequent Sect. 4 depicts the framework by reporting on the individual design process steps including the definition of design objectives and the design and development of this framework. Section 5 demonstrates the application of the framework. We conclude the paper with a critical discussion of the results, limitations and possible future research in Sect. 6 and a short summary in Sect. 7.

2   Research Background

2.1   Natural Language Processing

The integration of NLP and LLMs represents a significant advance in the capabilities of computer programs, making it possible to understand and interpret human language in a semantically correct form [11]. Building upon this foundation, LLMs represent advanced models that leverage substantial amounts of data to generate contextually relevant and coherent human-like text, thereby pushing the boundaries of natural language understanding and generation [7].

For a semantic understanding of text input, LLMs have the ability to handle complex, multi-level reasoning tasks by generating solutions in the form of a sequential logic chain [16]. However, the practical implementation of NLP and LLMs in a production-ready format necessitates various technological approaches. These range from self-trained to proprietary models and offer input-/output-based methods for content generation. In an effort to develop generic applications that avoid vendor lock-in, the open-source framework *langchain* serves as a valuable tool that acts as a wrapper for various models, by facilitating the retrieval of relevant context and enabling the efficient use of LLMs for various applications [24].

However, within the discourse on knowledge and NLP, it has been shown, that LLMs may exhibit hallucination, generating outputs that extrapolate beyond the available information which may be syntactically and semantically correct but is based on false assumptions and may not be constrained on given context, which then leads to the potential spread of misinformation, contradictory statements, and irrelevant or nonsensical content [30].

2.2   Knowledge Management

While ongoing philosophical debates endure regarding a concrete definition of knowledge, a shared consensus within the information technology (IT) and information systems (IS) domains centers on the differentiation between data, information and knowledge, which are basic hierarchical levels, whereas data can be seen as "raw facts", information as "interpretations of the data from a particular point of view" and knowledge as "information that has been validated and is thought to be true" [14]. In general, there is a consensus that knowledge, unlike raw data, goes through several stages of interpretation so it can be seen as knowledge. However, the boundaries between those stages appear to be blurry, meaning that there is no very clear border between these hierarchical levels. This results in the fact that the hierarchical transition from data to knowledge is still subject to ongoing debates. We hold to the perspective that the defining characteristic of knowledge is that it represents information aimed at being actively processed in the mind of individuals through a process of reflection or learning [3]. Moreover, it is crucial to acknowledge that knowledge takes on diverse forms, extending beyond mere raw data [3]. This multifaceted nature of knowledge underscores the importance of understanding that it serves various recipients, such as employees and users [23]. To truly address the breadth of heterogeneous sources, knowledge can be encapsulated in different formats, ranging from PDFs and FAQs to simple web pages [17]. Nevertheless, effective knowledge management is associated with challenges, in particular with regard to resource allocation. Businesses often struggle with resource constraints despite the recognized importance of knowledge management [3].

Regarding the software to manage knowledge, companies are positioned very differently. From PDF-based, or even analogously managed knowledge bases, to professional EKMS, which offer various functions for knowledge retrieval and insertion, as well as linking potential to other services, knowledge may be managed in multiple ways [15].

2.3   Related Research

There is increasing interest within organizations in NLP and a growing body of research on how to introduce [13] and how to manage AI [8]. Specifically, challenges, pathways, and opportunities have been part of the discourse. The research at this stage focuses on organizational aspects without providing clear blueprints to follow or guidance for design knowledge to implement.

Beside the general managing aspects, domain-specific integration of NLP is entering the discourse. For instance, the potentials of NLP have been explored in different domains like healthcare [6], in which NLP's potential to support knowledge management processes is enhanced through its contribution to the creation, capture, sharing, and application of knowledge in healthcare [6]. Within the broader landscape, NLP is uniformly acknowledged as a pivotal advancement in text processing, standing out as a milestone in the field. Yet, due to the confinement to specific domains, cross-domain relevance and with that challenges faced by small and medium-sized enterprises remain unaddressed which hinder demonstrating the wider applicability of NLP and knowledge management. While there are conceptual models for knowledge extraction through NLP [6], it is crucial to acknowledge that the practical utility of such models often goes untested due to the absence of viable prototypes.

Against the backdrop of a lack of blueprints for organizations to follow and limited design knowledge on integration of existing knowledge in organizations using NLP, we set out to address our research at this intersection that appears to be a glaring blind spot in the current discourse.

3   Research Approach

We follow a design-oriented approach using the design science research methodology suggested in [25] (Fig. 1). In addition to extant literature, we conduct expert interviews to define the design objectives of the framework. These interviews aim to provide insights into the current knowledge management of companies. We examine a wide variety of knowledge management topics, from current practices of information acquisition, to existing data structures, to possible areas of application of artificial intelligence. To allow for as much flexibility as possible for expansion options that did not exist in the initial idea and to foster in-depth responses, the interviews are held in a semi-structured form. The interviews varied in length ranging from 30 min to an hour and were conducted via virtual meetings, which was convenient for all participants. We have designed these interviews to give us insights into how organizations are currently managing knowledge. We wanted to guide the interview partner to explain the use of the organization's knowledge assets, especially, to explore the types of information demanded by both customers and employees. To expand on this question, we also asked participants what constitutes an effective automated response for customers and employees. The selection of interview partners focuses particularly on small and medium-sized enterprises, as they are identified to be a potential target group for using the framework due to the frequent lack of specification in the area of AI, which is often not yet considered in the area of knowledge

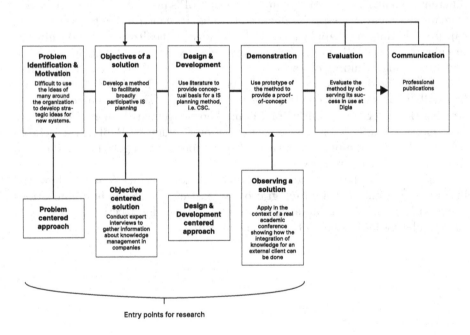

Fig. 1. DS research process for EKMS and NLP integration

management. We interviewed various roles within the different companies. This approach allowed us to speak with employees in larger companies who had specialized knowledge management expertise and could provide detailed insights, or in contrast, in smaller companies, to speak with individuals, including managers, whose roles encompassed a broader range of responsibilities. Applying a systematic approach, we record the interviews and subsequently transcribe them utilizing the *OpenAI Whisper* speech-to-text model. Each transcription was subsequently analyzed to ensure the reliability and validity of the information collected. The design of the framework is then based on these elaborated objectives and is demonstrated. To allow for a more intuitive interaction with the proposed framework, we demonstrate the framework in the context of an academic conference to show how knowledge representation can be enhanced through NLP for conference attendees.

4 The Framework for Integrating Enterprise Knowledge Management and Natural Language Processing

4.1 Design Objectives

To gather design objectives according to which the framework should be designed, six interviews were conducted with companies of various industries and sizes. These included a bakery franchise with 43 stores, a mid-size construction firm with around 100 employees, a technology company with over 500 employees, a small-size event planning agency employing 4 individuals, an engineering expert office with 12 employees, and a paper producer with 100 employees. The company names are anonymized as Latin letters in what follows. We implemented an inductive coding process primarily using the interviews as a raw qualitative data source. We utilized the recorded transcripts to gain a deeper understanding of knowledge management within the organizations. Having deliberately designed the interview questions to be open-ended, we were able to identify aspects that occurred more frequently across the different interviews and thus transform them into design objectives. Across all interviews, we observed a consistent focus on precision, user-friendliness, and adaptability. The analysis revealed seven objectives. Table 1 provides the overview of objectives, including literature that addresses and backs up the objectives.

Table 1. Design Objectives and System Requirements

	Objective	Objective Description	References
1	Precision	Emphasizing the importance of data quality, precision and accuracy, especially in industries with rapidly changing product cycles and evolving regulations. Continue to emphasize the need for up-to-date information, especially in relation to product data, pricing and compliance-related data.	(c),(d),(e),(f), [27]
2	User-Friendliness	Prioritize easy access and navigation of the knowledge base to accommodate users with varying levels of technical knowledge. Further enable user-friendly interfaces to ensure a smooth and efficient user experience.	(b), (c), (d), (e), [3]
3	Adaptability	Developing a system that learns from user queries and interactions and can provide relevant and accurate information over time. This includes refining search algorithms based on user feedback.	(a), (b), (c), (d), (e), (f), [22]
4	Multilingual Support	The system must be designed to support multiple languages and take into account the different languages within the organization to ensure effective communication and understanding for users who speak different languages.	(a), (d), [21, 29]
5	Robust Data Security	Implement robust security measures to protect sensitive information in the knowledge base, ensure compliance with data protection regulations and maintain the confidentiality of proprietary or confidential data.	(a), (c), (e), [2]
6	Flexible Data Structures	Recognize and accommodate the different data structures used within the organization. This flexibility allows users to use their preferred platforms for documentation while contributing to the central knowledge base.	(a), (b), (e), (f)
7	Cost Efficiency	Optimize resource utilization, minimize infrastructure costs and streamline processes for a cost-effective solution.	(c), (e), [19]

4.2   Design and Development

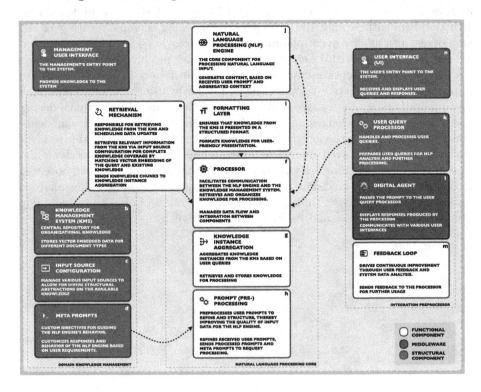

Fig. 2. EKMS and NLP Integration Framework

The framework is structured around three core building blocks: the management part, responsible for overseeing knowledge; the digital agent block, facilitating integration of various input sources, and the main integration unit, which aggregates knowledge based on input and provides a corresponding NLP-generated response. These blocks comprise components that are either structural, functional, or act as a middleware. Structural components define the system architecture, functional components orchestrate AI-driven information enhancement, and middleware components ensure seamless integration and communication.

To illustrate the framework's functionality in a comprehensible manner, let us consider the hypothetical scenario of an academic conference and how it could empower attendees and authors with access to the knowledge necessary for successful participation and manuscript preparation aligned with conference requirements.

The company possesses knowledge, which is now to be integrated with NLP using the framework shown in Fig. 2. To start the integration, the management of an academic conference needs to be able to configure its services, namely functionalities for the provision of knowledge, through a management user interface (a.), which acts as an entry-point for the domain knowledge management. To enable researchers to interact with conference knowledge, certain knowledge needs to be provisioned. The knowledge management system (b.) component hereby acts as a central repository for organizational knowledge and further provides the functionality to post-process the knowledge through vector embeddings for efficient usage in later querying. An intrinsic challenge faced by organizations involves the selective restriction of certain knowledge solely to designated groups. Taking a conference as an example, querying against company internal documents should only be allowed for employees and not for researches. With the input source configuration component (c.) the framework implements exactly this criteria. Furthermore the management wants to add specific notes to answers coming from the NLP, this could be a disclaimer which could state that each answer is automatically generated or just a greeting at the beginning of a conversation. In the framework this is realized through meta prompts (d.), which are custom directives for guiding the NLP engine's behavior.

To allow researches access to the knowledge of the conference, the framework provides accessibility options which enable access to the knowledge via various integrations, by bridging the system's infrastructure and the regarding integration and therefore allowing researchers to incorporate the knowledge into existing processes through self-implemented dedicated communication channels such as current internal organizational chat solutions or by seamlessly integrating the conference knowledge into third-party communication channels like *Slack* or *Discord*.

This is done with the help of a digital agent (l.), which operates independently of the end user's client, utilizing the user query processor to handle queries and serve as an interface between the integration pre-processor and NLP core framework parts. With every answer, there is always the possibility of it being incorrect either in part or in general leading to a hallucination of an incorrect answer. Users who are familiar with the subject matter and recognize such an error should be able to suggest a correction. To enable such improvements, the feedback loop component (**m.**) drives continuous improvement through user feedback and system data analysis. This functionality is bundled in the integration pre-processor part of the framework.

Further, imagine a researcher seeking information about submission deadlines: By providing the question via an integration of choice, which is then sent to the natural language processing core of the framework via the digital agent (**l.**), the processor (**f.**) can start to administer the application flow. Using knowledge instance aggregation (**g.**) knowledge gets aggregated which is similar to the provided user query, using the retrieval mechanism component (**e.**). Similar to the knowledge, the user query is then embedded to allow the efficient execution of a vector based search. Lastly the different artefacts have to be put together into one prompt which is then used with the NLP engine (**j.**). The prompt (pre-)processing component h. assumes control of this task, by transforming the initial query with context information (**g.**), meta-prompts (**d.**) and further configuration including restrictions to use only the available context information and therefore minimize the probability that a hallucinated response will be generated. Finally, the NLP engine (**j.**) processes the prompt and returns a formatted (**i.**) answer to the digital agent, concluding the user interaction with the system.

In the first iteration of the framework, some fundamental difficulties emerged regarding the initial structure of the framework. We mainly learned about these through the parallel development of the framework and prototype. The most substantial change in this iteration was the division of a uniform user interface component into two distinct ones. The management user interface on the one hand and the end user interface on the other. Since these two components or rather the functionalities they provide are structurally rather different, splitting them and assigning them to the respective architectural parts of the framework resulted in a more abstracted design of the framework.

In the subsequent second iteration of the framework, the initial findings of the interviews were incorporated into the development. It emerged that the requirements of the various companies differ, especially with regard to the distribution of knowledge. Organizations have different knowledge requirements, particularly reflected in the knowledge utilized in different departments or teams within the organization. That led to the idea of developing a more general distribution concept that reflects these specific requirements. Access to knowledge should thus be adapted to the respective area of application. Knowledge use in an organization is often strategically embedded in processes designed for this purpose. In order to make the introduction of the framework into existing structures more effective, innovations should be generically adapted to these existing structures, given that these are already structured according to best practices and adapted to the requirements, depending on the company's level of maturity. The interviews revealed that employees often approach such innovations with reluctance or reject such changes outright, preferring to fall back on existing familiar solutions despite their limitations. To largely avoid this behavior, the integration of the framework into existing structures within the company should involve as few changes to the current process flow as possible for the general workforce. To be able to map these requirements, the user interface component, which was previously quite static and focused on the general acquisition of information, had to be adapted so that generic solutions could be connected. By introducing the digital agent component (l.) and its generic connectivity, it is intended to precisely address this situation. In addition to the diverse requirements for knowledge distribution, the interviews also revealed a relevant desire for moderation opportunities. Organizations see their knowledge as capital. In order to maintain this capital and, in the best case, to make it more valuable, knowledge must be expanded and challenged from now on. At the stage of development in the second iteration, such a possibility did not exist. Thus, if solutions based on the framework spread incorrect knowledge in general or in context, there was no way to remedy this deficiency. To counteract this, with the feedback loop component (m.) introduced in this iteration, a generically applicable solution was introduced to allow end users to provide feedback and thus improve the knowledge base.

5 Demonstration

To show the effectiveness and feasibility of the integration framework, we have implemented an *integration prototype*. This application serves a dual task by providing both a user interface for administration and backend functions, powered by *Next.js*. With the framework in place, we delve into the discussion of various components and their specific implementations. To better understand the flow of the implementation this section will provide context through two types of views: The management and the end-user view.

In the previous chapter we introduced an academic conference as an example scenario to show how knowledge and NLP can be integrated through the framework. Building on that academic conference scenario, this demonstration features the *DESRIST* conference as the example conference of choice.

To initiate the demonstration, we focus on the management view, starting with domain knowledge management, specifically the *Knowledge Management System* (KMS) component. In the framework this is described as a central repository for knowledge, which in the application is shortened to *Knowledge Base*. In the case of *DESRIST*, this can include submission files, key dates, or even the whole conference web-page.

With a knowledge base in place, the management needs to fill it with actual data sources. This can be done either through file uploads (in formats such as PDF, CSV, or Markdown), or through a web crawling session to extract information from the web as can be seen in Fig. 3. Either way, once uploaded, the information undergoes a crucial processing step to ensure efficient utilization.

This processing involves vector embedding the content, a method that transforms the textual information into numerical vectors to enhance the efficiency of data representation and analysis, and then storing the embedding into a vector database.

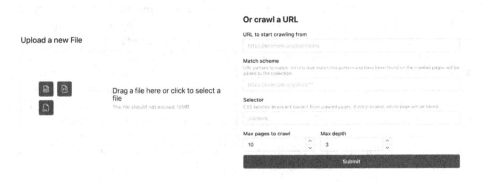

Fig. 3. Knowledge Submission

The knowledge base now actually contains data but there is still no way of interacting with it. To further enable this functionality we need to take a look at the *Input Source Configuration* and *Meta Prompts* components. In the application this is done through so called *Layers*. A layer acts as a wrapper for various configuration options, like enabling various meta-prompts for various use cases (Fig. 4b) and assigning data sources (Fig. 4a) to the layer. In the case of *DESRIST* it would be useful to create a *researcher layer*, which would include all the necessary conference specific knowledge documents. With the management user interface in place, we may take a look at the end user perspective, or rather the *Integration Preprocessor*.

The main component to take a look at regarding this implementation is the *Digital Agent*, which should work as an intermediary between the integrated user interface of choice and the *User Query Processor* component. To further understand the user query processor one has to take the user interface itself into account. To demonstrate this interaction the prototype implements two approaches. Interact with the knowledge base via a chat window or via a *Discord* integration, which allows direct communication with the knowledge base via a *Discord* channel. Both approaches allow for input and output of queries and responses via predefined API endpoints. Using the internal chat window allows for a dynamic user experience with streaming capabilities and functionalities such as user invitation to a layer as can be seen in Fig. 4d.

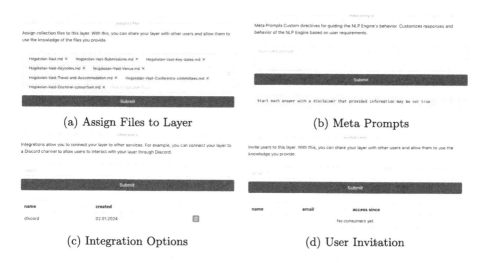

(a) Assign Files to Layer

(b) Meta Prompts

(c) Integration Options

(d) User Invitation

Fig. 4. Knowledge Base Layer Configuration

To enable a *Discord* integration, an integration key needs to be generated (Fig. 4c) with which the integration can be registered with *Discord*. Since we aim to enhance the practicality of our demonstration, we have integrated it with a designated channel for design conference information, which is publicly accessible[1]. While the clarification of the end user's interaction with the application logic has been articulated, a pivotal aspect yet to be expounded is the application logic itself. Within the framework this is depicted through the *Natural Language Processing Core*, in which the main component is represented through the *Integration Layer*, using the *Knowledge Instance Aggregation* and the *Prompt Preprocessing* components. In the application logic, this is realized by the API endpoint previously referred to, which takes a message, as well as the identifier of the also previously defined layer as an input. Within that endpoint a specific process is executed to retrieve a fitting knowledge backed response. The framework depicts the start of this process with the *Retrieval Mechanism* component. The retrieval is executed by finding relevant context in the database.

To establish relevant context a similarity search needs to be fulfilled. This process entails comparing the embedded input message with pre-processed data sources assigned to the targeted layer. If the similarity search returns valid results, these can be used in the ongoing process as context information. Aggregated with possible predefined meta prompts as well as with a general model configuration this information can now be used with the *Natural Language Processing Engine* of choice, which in our case is the low-priced *OpenAI GPT3.5 Turbo* model. The final step that concludes this demonstration deals with the final formatting of the NLP core's response regarding the framework's *Formatting Layer* component. In the case of our prototype, each answer is formatted

---

[1] http://tinyurl.com/5xrdw5kj.

as markdown so that it can be mapped uniformly independently of the user interface. Once this step has been completed, the formatted answer is sent to the corresponding digital agent and thus to the questioner. Finally, the crux of this demonstration is the empirical investigation based on the *DESRIST* test data. For this purpose, a number of questions based on the stored knowledge were asked, which can be seen in Fig. 5.

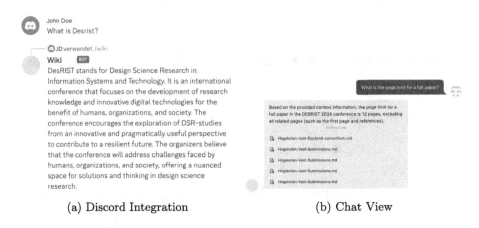

(a) Discord Integration   (b) Chat View

Fig. 5. DESRIST Knowledge Base Examples

6   Discussion

With the goal of creating an integration framework of enterprise knowledge management and natural language processing it is important to assess the effectiveness of the framework and therefore to have a differentiated discussion on how the composition of the framework aligns with the overarching objectives, in particular by addressing specific components that contribute to the fulfillment of the required tasks. Starting with an important objective for most companies:

Cost Efficiency. The framework tackles the objective of cost efficiency through a composition of components. It incorporates efficient data retrieval mechanisms (e.) employing state-of-the-art vector-based search algorithms. Simultaneously, the framework enables streamlined integration capabilities facilitated by generic interfaces (l.), which is all combined with exchangeable NLP engines (j.) to allow for configuration adapted to the company.

Precision is mainly reflected in the element *Retrieval Mechanism* where we made a connection to *Knowledge Management System*. The initial processing of the data divides it into complete blocks, which are used as context in the following. Moreover the precision might be enhanced in the future through the Feedback Loop component which can encourage the end user to draw attention to not precise responses.

With **User-Friendliness** a design objective comes into play which is mainly part of the *User Interface* component. The framework successfully aligns with this objective, evident in its capacity to seamlessly integrate with various applications.

The **Adaptability** design objective is for now matched through the *Feedback Loop* component, which acts as an entry-point for adaptability. Feedback which is enhanced through this component can then later be used in the *Prompt (Pre-)Processing* component to refine the inputs.

Multilingual Support as a design objective is matched mainly within the *Natural Language Processing Engine* component. Most NLP engines allow for input and output of different languages. The main hurdle to overcome is to provide suitable knowledge context with the *Retrieval Mechanism* component, since the stored knowledge may not be formulated in the same language as the input message. To still provide context for the input the used embeddings need to cover both languages.

To achieve **Robust Data Security** as design objective the framework uses the *Knowledge Instance Aggregation* component to only return knowledge the requested party is allowed to query. Furthermore through predefined meta prompts the management is able to instantiate regulative instructions.

Regarding the last design objective: **Flexible Data Structures**. Since the frameworks *Knowledge Management* component is defined as a generic system, the management could implement nearly every data structure as a data source as long as its textual content can be embedded.

6.1   Limitations

The prototypical implementation revealed a number of minor to major limitations of the framework. The framework is heavily reliant on the data quality of the foundational knowledge supplied by organizations, which constitutes a critical dependency. Inaccurate or outdated information can lead to incorrect responses. Not only the data quality is important for a qualitative response, but also the quality of the provided user inputs: If users provide vague or ambiguous queries, the reasoning power of the NLP engine can be exhausted. Lastly the framework depends on good prompt engineering on the organization's side. Crafting effective meta-prompts for guiding the NLP engine's behavior can be challenging and may result in responses not aligned with the organization's intent.

6.2   Further Research

A promising area of research regarding insufficient context is to introduce a hybrid approach which builds up on top the current retrieval mechanism of the framework. In addition to a vector based similarity search context could be identified using NLP itself. To enable such an identification additional to embedding knowledge upon insertion, a process would need to run that summarizes parts of the document which then by implication would act as a base to query against where requested information could be found. Moreover this framework could be supplemented with data sources that are not constrained to textual content. Meaning, the framework should allow the usage of images or video sources as usable data sources. Taking a look back at the limitations, one possible advancement could be to transform unstructured documents into structured documents. One possible structured document format could be markdown, since its structure is deterministic which would allow for better text splitting which could result in better context.

7   Conclusion

This work introduced and demonstrated an integration framework to bridge EKMS with NLP. The framework addresses challenges of efficient, cost-effective, and user-friendly integration, essential for resource-constrained small and medium-sized organizations aiming to leverage technological advances in AI for improved communication of knowledge. These challenges were identified through a series of interviews with organizations and from extant literature. Importantly, the framework contributes to the academic ongoing discourse on organizational applications of AI, specifically in the area of utilizing generative NLP, and zeroes in on LLM for improved knowledge communication. For practice, the framework serves as an instrument assisting organizations to navigate the new competitive landscape, which is reliant on the use of digital agents, despite the lack of human expertise, technological capabilities, and established best practices. It does so by offering a blueprint and demonstrating a technological architecture that promotes a cost-efficient integration of existing knowledge management systems with NLP - an orchestration of a duet between the two domains.

References

1. Abioye, S.O., et al.: Artificial intelligence in the construction industry: a review of present status, opportunities and future challenges. J. Build. Eng. **44**, 103299 (2021). https://doi.org/10.1016/j.jobe.2021.103299
2. Ahmed, G., Ragsdell, G., Olphert, W.: Knowledge sharing and information security: a paradox? (2014)
3. Alavi, M., Leidner, D.E.: Knowledge management and knowledge management systems: conceptual foundations and research issues. MIS Q. 107–136 (2001). https://doi.org/10.2307/3250961
4. Ali, O., Krsteska, K., Said, D., Momin, M.: Advanced technologies enabled human resources functions: benefits, challenges, and functionalities: a systematic review. Cogent Bus. Manag. **10**(2), 2216430 (2023). https://doi.org/10.1080/23311975.2023.2216430
5. Barann, B., Hermann, A., Cordes, A.K., Chasin, F., Becker, J.: Supporting Digital Transformation in Small and Medium-sized Enterprises: A Procedure Model Involving Publicly Funded Support Units (2019). https://doi.org/10.24251/HICSS.2019.598

6. Basyal, G.P., Rimal, B., Zeng, D.: A Systematic Review of Natural Language Processing for Knowledge Management in Healthcare (2020). https://doi.org/10.5121/csit.2020.100921

7. Bavarian, M., et al.: Efficient training of language models to fill in the middle. arXiv **abs/2207.14255** (2022). https://doi.org/10.48550/arXiv.2207.14255

8. Berente, N., Bin, G., Recker, J., Santhanam, R.: Managing artificial intelligence. MIS Q. **45**(3), 1433 (2021). https://doi.org/10.25300/MISQ/2021/16274

9. Chasin, F., Kowalkiewicz, M., Gollhardt, T.: How watkins steel went from traditional steel fabrication to digital service provision. MIS Q. Exec. (2022). https://doi.org/10.17705/2msqe.00066

10. Chen, H., Chiang, R.H.L., Storey, V.C.: Business intelligence and analytics: from big data to big impact. MIS Q. **36**(4), 1165–1188 (2012). https://doi.org/10.2307/41703503

11. Chowdhary, K.: Natural language processing. Found. Artif. Intell. 603–649 (2020). https://doi.org/10.1007/978-81-322-3972-7

12. DreamCode: Artificial intelligence (AI) impact areas in the business arena of 2023 (2023). https://www.dreamcodesoft.com/en/blog/artificial-intelligence-A-I-impact-areas-in-the-business-arena-of-2023

13. Enholm, I.M., Papagiannidis, E., Mikalef, P., Krogstie, J.: Artificial intelligence and business value: a literature review. Inf. Syst. Front. **24**(5), 1709–1734 (2022). https://doi.org/10.1007/s10796-021-10186-w

14. Freeman, L.A.: Information systems knowledge: foundations, definitions, and applications. Inf. Syst. Front. **3**(2), 249–266 (2001). https://doi.org/10.1023/A:1011408710845

15. Grudin, J.: Enterprise knowledge management and emerging technologies. In: Proceedings of the 39th Annual Hawaii International Conference on System Sciences (HICSS 2006), vol. 3, p. 57a (2006). https://doi.org/10.1109/HICSS.2006.156

16. Kojima, T., Gu, S.S., Reid, M., Matsuo, Y., Iwasawa, Y.: Large language models are zero-shot reasoners. arXiv **abs/2205.11916** (2022). https://doi.org/10.48550/arXiv.2205.11916

17. Kopitar, L., Stiglic, G.: Using heterogeneous sources of data and interpretability of prediction models to explain the characteristics of careless respondents in survey data. Sci. Rep. **13**(1), 13417 (2023). https://doi.org/10.1038/s41598-023-40209-2

18. Korinek, A., Schindler, M., Stiglitz, J.: Technological progress, artificial intelligence, and inclusive growth. IMF Working Papers **2021**(166), A001 (2021). https://doi.org/10.5089/9781513583280.001.A001

19. Narawish, C., Sharma, D., Rajest, S., Rajan, R.: Importance of cost efficiency in critical aspect of influences the decision-making process in banks. Türk Fizyoterapi ve Rehabilitasyon Dergisi/Turk. J. Physiother. Rehabil. **32**, 47184–47212 (2022)

20. Nwankpa, J.K., Roumani, Y., Datta, P.: Process innovation in the digital age of business: the role of digital business intensity and knowledge management. J. Knowl. Manag. **26**(5), 1320 (2022). https://doi.org/10.1108/JKM-04-2021-0277

21. O'Leary, D.E.: A multilingual knowledge management system: a case study of FAO and WAICENT. Decis. Support Syst. **45**(3), 641–661 (2008). https://doi.org/10.1016/j.dss.2007.07.007

22. Ouyang, L., et al.: Training language models to follow instructions with human feedback. arXiv **abs/2203.02155** (2022). https://doi.org/10.48550/arXiv.2203.02155

23. Ozer, M., Zhang, G.: The roles of knowledge providers, knowledge recipients, and knowledge usage in bridging structural holes. J. Prod. Innov. Manag. **36**(2), 224–240 (2019). https://doi.org/10.1111/jpim.12478

24. Pandya, K., Holia, M.S.: Automating customer service using langchain: building custom open-source GPT chatbot for organizations. arXiv **abs/2310.05421** (2023). https://doi.org/10.48550/arXiv.2310.05421
25. Peffers, K., Tuunanen, T., Rothenberger, M., Chatterjee, S.: A design science research methodology for information systems research. J. Manag. Inf. Syst. **24**, 45–77 (2007). https://doi.org/10.2753/MIS0742-1222240302
26. Sokolova, M., Shah, M., Szpakowicz, S.: Comparative analysis of text data in successful face-to-face and electronic negotiations. Group Decis. Negot. **15**(2), 128 (2006). https://doi.org/10.1007/s10726-006-9024-z
27. Tian, L., Zhou, X., Wu, Y.P., Zhou, W.T., Zhang, J.H., Zhang, T.S.: Knowledge graph and knowledge reasoning: a systematic review. J. Electron. Sci. Technol. **20**(2), 100159 (2022). https://doi.org/10.1016/j.jnlest.2022.100159
28. Trivedi, H., Balasubramanian, N., Khot, T., Sabharwal, A.: Interleaving retrieval with chain-of-thought reasoning for knowledge-intensive multi-step questions. arXiv **abs/2212.10509** (2022). https://doi.org/10.48550/arXiv.2212.10509
29. Yang, C.C., Wei, C.P., Li, K.W.: Cross-lingual thesaurus for multilingual knowledge management. Decis. Support Syst. **45**(3), 596–605 (2008). https://doi.org/10.1016/j.dss.2007.07.005
30. Yao, J.Y., Ning, K.P., Liu, Z.H., Ning, M.N., Yuan, L.: LLM lies: hallucinations are not bugs, but features as adversarial examples. arXiv preprint arXiv:2310.01469 (2023). https://doi.org/10.48550/arXiv.2310.01469

Generating Synthetic LiDAR Point Cloud Data for Object Detection Using the Unreal Game Engine

Mathias Eggert[1]([✉]) [ID], Maximilian Schade[1], Florian Bröhl[2], and Alexander Moriz[2]

[1] Aachen University of Applied Sciences, Eupener Str. 70, 52066 Aachen, Germany
eggert@fh-aachen.de, max.schade@alumni.fh-aachen.de
[2] Laboratory for Machine Tools and Production Engineering WZL, RWTH Aachen University,
Campus-Boulevard 30, 52074 Aachen, Germany
f.broehl@wzl.rwth-aachen.de, a.moriz@wzl-mq.rwth-aachen.de

Abstract. Object detection based on artificial intelligence is ubiquitous in today's computer vision research and application. The training of the neural networks for object detection requires large and high-quality datasets. Besides datasets based on image data, datasets derived from point clouds offer several advantages. However, training datasets are sparse and their generation requires a lot of effort, especially in industrial domains. A solution to this issue offers the generation of synthetic point cloud data. Based on the design science research method, the work at hand proposes an approach and its instantiation for generating synthetic point cloud data based on the Unreal Engine. The point cloud quality is evaluated by comparing the synthetic cloud to a real-world point cloud. Within a practical example the applicability of the Unreal Game engine for synthetic point cloud generation could be successfully demonstrated.

Keywords: synthetic data generation · point cloud · neural network · object detection · Unreal

1 Introduction

Deep learning is one of the most relevant and inspiring technologies considering the impact on research trends and its widely used application. Deep learning applications range from natural language processing (NLP) to computer vision [1]. Among other computer vision tasks, deep learning massively improved the performance of object detection [2]. In addition to areas such as medical image analysis and autonomous driving, object detection is becoming increasingly important in industrial domains such as the factory of the future [3–5]. Considering the manufacturing domain, object detection is a widely used technique, notably in assembly scenarios [6]. Typical use cases for this technology include assembly assistance systems and the optimization of production lines [7, 8].

Large sized and high quality datasets paved the way for the huge success of deep learning fields, such as computer vision [9]. Besides images and other sensor information,

M. Mandviwalla et al. (Eds.): DESRIST 2024, LNCS 14621, pp. 295–309, 2024.
https://doi.org/10.1007/978-3-031-61175-9_20

point cloud data can be a beneficial input for object detection, particularly in the assembly domain [10]. For the collection of the point cloud data, we focus on Light Detection and Ranging (LiDAR) sensors, since these are already successfully utilized for various object detection approaches [3]. To sustain the success of deep learning and extend it to new areas of research, it is required to create large application-specific datasets of high quality. However, training data is often not available in sufficient quantity and quality [11].

The generation of training data is challenging and time consuming because of the effort needed to prepare the images and point clouds of real-world objects. This includes both the generation of the images or point clouds and their annotation. Synthetic data enables the construction of large and well-generalized training datasets with much less effort. Applying a game engine enables the preparation of point clouds and images of the object even when it is not fully illuminated or covered behind other elements, such as cables or other machine parts. With a real LiDAR, it would be very difficult to prepare such data for AI training. The usage of synthetic image data is well studied, while the field of synthetic LiDAR point cloud generation and availability of related datasets are poorly researched [12, 13]. In terms of synthetic point cloud generation, the focus of this relatively new research area is mostly limited to autonomous driving [14–18].

The lack of a suitable solution for generating synthetic LiDAR data by utilizing a game engine in the context of object detection motivates the paper at hand and leads to the following research question: *How may game engines support the generation of synthetic 3D LiDAR data for object detection?*

In order to answer that question, we apply the design science research method [19, 20] and provide the research contribution types method, its instantiation and guidelines as suggested by Gregor and Hevner [21]. Therewith, we contribute to the understanding of generating synthetic training data for AI-based object detection by applying game engines.

We structured the paper as follows. The next section comprises a brief overview about the role of training data as well as game engines and provides the status quo of its synthetic generation. Section 3 outlines the research design, which is based on the design science research method. Section 4 comprises the artifact development and demonstration. In Sect. 5, we present the artifact evaluation. Based on the challenges, we were confronted with during the artifact development, we present guidelines for the generation of synthetic LiDAR data in Sect. 6 and conclude the paper and its research contribution in Sect. 7.

2   Related Work

2.1   Synthetic Training Data and Game Engines

Large training datasets, which contain 3D point clouds of the objects to detect, are a requirement for exploiting the full potential of deep learning models [22]. Along with that, problems considering the collection and annotation of such datasets emerge [23]. For example, in the research field of autonomous driving, datasets contain data from different sensors, like cameras, LiDARs, and RADARs. The utilization for algorithmic training purposes can be ensured, if the data is manually labelled, which entails a huge cost factor and expenditure of time [24].

The acquisition of 3D point cloud data can be realized through the usage of LiDAR sensors. This is accomplished based on a time-of-flight measurement of the beam from the sensor to the object. The typical final output of a scanning process is cartesian coordinates plus an intensity value, which are obtained after converting the raw point cloud data [24]. In the context of the domain adaptation problem [25], the deployment of LiDAR point cloud-based training data provides specific challenges. The distance from object to LiDAR, distance influenced point cloud size, point density and overall geometric characteristics are examples for this [22, 26].

An alternative for generating synthetic point cloud data comprise the usage of commercial game engines [27]. The primary task is to abstract general video game functions to enable the reuse of code and game content in different games or applications [28]. To accomplish this task, game engines provide components, such as rendering, loading, animation, collision detection between objects, physics, inputs, GUI and AI [29]. An approach proposed by Johnson-Roberson et al. [15] utilizes the Grand Theft Auto (GTA) videogame to obtain synthetic data in a virtual world. Against this background, the usage of commercial game engines potentially improves the customizability of data sets and accessibility. As one of the most popular commercial game engines, Unreal Engine (UE) is a prominent tool for creating video games and building virtual reality applications [30].

2.2 Research Gap

In order to identify related works and clearly work out the status quo of synthetic point cloud generation, we classified relevant literature into three dimensions: Origin of input data (CAD/other), rendering approach (game engine/other), and type of data (2D/3D). All classified articles are listed in Table 1.

Eight of the observed publications used computer aided design (CAD) data to generate synthetic data. All of those works built a CAD import pipeline [4, 6, 7, 31–35]. In contrast to the other eight approaches, the remaining two works utilized non-CAD-based 3D meshes as the starting point for synthetic data generation [10, 36]. Zamora-Hernandez et al. [36] used 3D meshes, some of which were derived from the YCB dataset [37]. Furthermore, they cropped out objects from real world images. Additionally, Wu et al. [10] generated 3D mesh models of small electric motors in Blender. Compared with the other nine research works, they did not create a general tool for 3D object processing. Thus, solely creating variants of small electric motor 3D meshes is possible. Solely four examined papers made use of game engines [7, 32, 33, 36]. Among those, three used the Unity game engine [7, 32, 33]. Solely Zamora-Hernandez et al. [36] applied Unreal engine and introduced a 2D approach. However, for the paper at hand, we decided to choose the Unreal game engine since it is open source and free.

Regarding the format of the created synthetic data, all ten publications opted for 2D image data. However, Wu et al. [10] proposed a method for synthetic 3D point cloud data generation, complementary to the synthesis of synthetic images. Considering synthetic 2D data generation, multiple methods were deployed, additionally some publications proposed more than one technique. Three papers used the Cut-paste technique [4, 33,

Table 1. Related point cloud generation approaches

Paper	Origin of input data		Rendering approach		Type of data
	CAD	*Other*	*Game engine*	*Other*	
[35]	x			x	2D
[34]	x			x	2D
[7]	x		x		2D
[4]	x			x	2D
[6]	x			x	2D
[33]	x		x		2D
[32]	x	x	x		2D
[10]		x		x	2D & 3D
[36]		x	x		2D
[31]	x			x	2D

36]. This includes segmenting relevant objects from images and pasting them into other images, with a desired background [4]. On the other hand, some approaches rendered a 3D model and placed it into images displaying different kind of backgrounds [6, 7, 34, 36]. Further, rendering 3D objects into a virtual scene, with a virtual camera capturing images was explored [4, 31, 32, 35]. Solely Wu et al. [10] developed a technique to obtain synthetic 3D point cloud data, which was achieved by using Blender in combination with Blensor [38]. All publications used data augmentation techniques to address domain shift, i.e. changing the distribution of training, validation and test set data between different domains. For example, different viewpoints, illumination or object rotations. To our best knowledge, no approach proved the synthetic generation of 3D point cloud data by using the Unreal game engine, which motivates this research.

3 Research Design

In order to develop an approach for generating LiDAR based point clouds with a game engine, our research is aligned at the design science research methodology [20, 21]. In total, the research work comprises five partly iterative process stages (see Fig. 1).

In order to *identify the problem* and motivate the research, we performed a literature review as described in Sect. 2.2. To close the identified research gap, *objectives of the solution* must be determined. The overall objective of the solution is to generate synthetic, annotated data for the training of deep learning object detection models. For the artifact development, we limited our approach to the generation of synthetic point clouds that are comparable to point clouds created with real sensors.

The final artifact should be characterized by the following main requirements: (1) An import pipeline for the transfer of a CAD model to a UE scene, (2) A virtual LiDAR functionality to obtain synthetic point clouds, (3) The ability to export different forms of point cloud data representations, (4) Adding a viewpoint functionality for data augmentation. Meeting these requirements ends the iteration cycle. These four objectives of the solution are concretized in each development iteration, which in turn has its own development objectives.

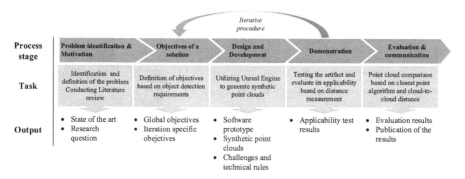

Fig. 1. Research process stages. Adapted from Peffers et al. [20].

The *design and development* phase encloses the task to realize the desired objectives of the solution. Therefore, we work in development iterations, whereas we check the objectives of the solution at the end of each iteration. The development involves utilizing UE and programming with C++, Blueprints and Python. A CAD import pipeline and distinct functions supplementing the import process to a UE scene, is developed. Further, we implement the current virtual LiDAR system. The virtual sensor is characterized by various functionalities, such as ray casting, collision detection and point cloud export. In addition, multiple positioning options, e.g., a variable distance from object to scanner, automated scanning of a whole object and positioning in different viewpoints, are developed. Next to the development of the prototype, we collect challenges during the development process and prepare guidelines for applying UE for LiDAR-based point cloud generation.

In the *demonstration* phase, the implemented features of the artifact are demonstrated in a context specific environment. We select mathematical evaluation methods, such as distance measurements, comparing extents from simulated cloud to a CAD model and calculating rotations. Additionally, we investigate debug expressions, file formats, and conduct visual proofs under certain criteria.

In the *evaluation* phase, we evaluate the current state of the developed artifact.

The evaluation phase analyzes the point cloud quality, which contains the comparison between the generated synthetic point cloud, obtained from a CAD model and a reference cloud, which was obtained from a 3D printed assembly part by a real-world physical sensor. The purpose of the comparison is to determine how close the synthetic data is to the real point cloud in terms of equality. The comparison is based on applying the Iterative Closest Point (ICP) algorithm (Besl and McKay 1992; Chen and Medioni 1992). In the next step, the point cloud density and the Cloud-to-Cloud distance (C2C) are examined. Finally, we communicate the results by means of this article.

4 Developing an Unreal Engine-Based LiDAR

In the following, we go through all development iterations and briefly present the development progress. The iteration goals and screenshots are provided in Fig. 2.

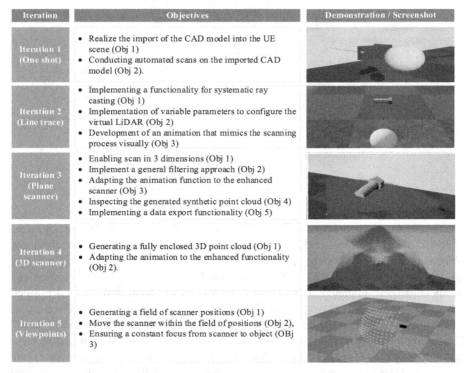

Iteration	Objectives	Demonstration / Screenshot
Iteration 1 (One shot)	• Realize the import of the CAD model into the UE scene (Obj 1) • Conducting automated scans on the imported CAD model (Obj 2).	
Iteration 2 (Line trace)	• Implementing a functionality for systematic ray casting (Obj 1) • Implementation of variable parameters to configure the virtual LiDAR (Obj 2) • Development of an animation that mimics the scanning process visually (Obj 3)	
Iteration 3 (Plane scanner)	• Enabling scan in 3 dimensions (Obj 1) • Implement a general filtering approach (Obj 2) • Adapting the animation function to the enhanced scanner (Obj 3) • Inspecting the generated synthetic point cloud (Obj 4) • Implementing a data export functionality (Obj 5)	
Iteration 4 (3D scanner)	• Generating a fully enclosed 3D point cloud (Obj 1) • Adapting the animation to the enhanced functionality (Obj 2).	
Iteration 5 (Viewpoints)	• Generating a field of scanner positions (Obj 1) • Move the scanner within the field of positions (Obj 2), • Ensuring a constant focus from scanner to object (OBj 3)	

Fig. 2. Development iterations, objectives, and screenshots

Iteration 1: One Shot
We address objective (Obj) 1 by developing a user interface that provides the loading of CAD files, the deletion of existing actors, and the merging of actors. The user interface (UI) is based on UE editor utility widgets. To load a CAD file, a Python script, for integrating UE Datasmith functionality is incorporated. UE Datasmith is an UE Plugin that enables the import and rendering of 3D files (e.g., CAD files) into a UE scene. We address Obj 2 by casting a ray to an object and verifying if there is any collision. The basic concept behind the virtual LiDAR is a function, which casts a ray in the form of a 3D vector. The X, Y, Z coordinates of the first blocking hit caused by a collision from the beam with a surface, are returned. In the demonstration phase, we conducted a collision testing, by casting one ray against an object, which we define as Oneshot. We utilize debug elements and logging to verify if the collision on the object works and if a coordinate point on the impact surface can be detected. We applied a CAD model of a wall-like structure, which we created in FreeCAD (www.freecad.org).

The CAD model was successfully imported into the UE scene. The dimensions of the actor are equal to those of the CAD model. Thus, Obj 1 is reached. The functionality of the Oneshot to obtain valid impact points via ray casting was positively verified by a dimension comparison with the corresponding CAD model (Obj 2). However, there is a lack in the automation of the scanning process, which motivates iteration 2.

Iteration 2: Line trace

This iteration aims at enhancing the functionality of the Oneshot. At first, we establish a horizontal line of rays to depict the horizontal dimension of the virtual LiDAR (Obj 1). The implementation is based on the operating principle of a real-world LiDAR. Accordingly, the rays are being emitted in a defined range of degrees around the LiDAR actor. Thus, we developed a function to configure different parameters for the desired LiDAR scan (Obj 2). The relevant parameters are: (1) horizontal opening angle, (2) rate in which rays are casted (step size), (3) vector length, representing the emitted ray. Finally, an animation function that visually mimics this process is developed (Obj 3). It uses the same debug elements as the Oneshot. In contrast to the Oneshot, multiple rays are generated from the center of the virtual LiDAR. Therefore, the debug elements are displayed dynamically tailored to the framerate of the running game instance.

We demonstrated the line trace scanner by scanning a rendered CAD test model of a wall. We position the line trace actor in front of the object. For testing the line trace, a horizontal opening angle of 180 degrees and a step size of 0.5 and 0.01 degree is chosen. The scanner can systematically detect data points in X and Y dimension in the current state (step size 0.5: 88–98% accuracy; 0.01: 99.5–99.9% accuracy).

The capture of impact points in three dimensions is possible by moving the scanner, which still hinders an automated scan. Further, the prototype proved the ability to detect impact points on the object's surface. Therefore, the scanner can detect complex collision. However, the imitation of a real-world LiDAR can only be realized by casting rays three-dimensionally from one origin. Therefore, Obj 1 is not fully accomplished. The variable parameters were successfully tested in the experimental setup (Obj 2). The animation function dynamically mimics the process of the line trace and fulfills Obj 3.

Iteration 3: Plane scanner

The virtual LiDAR must meet the requirement of capturing the whole object visible from a given viewpoint. Therefore, we enabled the generation of a field of rays, referred to as field of view (FOV). The scope of the FOV must be big enough to enclose the two-dimensional extents of the 3D mesh. We derived the plane scanner from the line trace class. The vertical line of rays is generated according to the principle of the horizontal line. Therefore, we add an additional parameter, which is the vertical opening angle. Additionally, we divide the step size into a vertical and horizontal step size.

In the demonstration phase, we verified the capability of the virtual LiDAR to acquire data in three dimensions. Further, we verified the rotation functionality in vertical and horizontal direction (Obj 1). The recent update to the filtering approach showed the ability to filter all insignificant impact points (points without object collision) (Obj 2). We applied the modified animation function in the scanning process. The animation adapted to the scanning functionality in terms of creating a full FOV. Subsequently, the application demonstrated a color change based on the distance of the impact points to the virtual LiDAR. This reflects the color-based gradient feature of the animation function (Obj 3).

In order to inspect the generated synthetic point cloud (Obj 4), we exported the synthetic data and imported the point cloud into UE with the UE LiDAR Point Cloud Plugin. We compared the generated point cloud with the mesh it was derived from. The instances showed equality considering their geometric composition. Therewith, we also demonstrate the working of the export function (Obj5).

However, the point cloud generates solely the scanned object from one position. To enable multiple point cloud representations, a feature for fully enclosed 3D point cloud capturing is needed, which motivates Iteration 4.

Iteration 4: 3D scanner
For generating fully enclosed 3D point clouds requires a function for capturing the CAD model from multiple viewpoints to achieve a complete coverage. The basis for this concept is the bounding box of a CAD model. The bounding box is of rectangular shape based on the extents of the regarded 3D mesh. The bounding box serves as an aid for positioning the scanner around the object.

The animation function supports the whole process visually as can been seen in the screenshots of Fig. 2. The set timers ensure a position change when the scanning process on one position is finalized. The FOV rotates towards the object dependent on a variable distance around the bounding box of the CAD model. The screenshot of Iteration 4 in Fig. 2 displays a full coverage of the screw consisting of rays in the set FOV from every position.

We generated and exported the enclosed point cloud and compared it to the corresponding 3D mesh. The instances indicated strong similarities considering their geometric properties (Obj 1). However, the variable distance is bound to the 3D scanner mechanism. The animation function was successfully adapted to the new feature (Obj 2). However, the missing features of a general distance parameter motivates the continuation of the project and the next iteration.

Iteration 5: Viewpoints
To generate viewpoints, we developed an algorithm that represents a systematic approach for generating a field of LiDAR positions. This field serves as the basis for the scanner to move systematically in 3D space and casts rays towards the object. We conceptualized the algorithm based on the idea of an angular spiral. The center of the spiral represents the scanner position, adjusted through the variable distance parameter. The center serves as the origin, from where the structure of the field of viewpoints is built. The spiral size is defined through a *Number of Viewpoints* the user can configure in the UE Editor. Furthermore, we implement the *Delta Degree* parameter, which determines the rate of position change in degrees.

In the screenshot of Iteration 5 in Fig. 2, the netted curved surface patch is illustrated with debug points. Therefore, the debug points represent the different LiDAR positions, namely viewpoints depending on the orientation from scanner to object. In the demonstration phase, a total of 121 viewpoints could be generated, which reflects the value set in the corresponding parameter.

We validated the angular spiral algorithm by comparing it to the values of the structure it is derived from (Obj 1). We verified the positioning function by displaying the netted curved surface patch and a debug output, which represents the number of viewpoints (Obj 2). Finally, we implemented a dynamic FOV, in order to ensure a constant focus from scanner to object (Obj 3). Therewith, all development objectives as outlined in Sect. 3 are met, which leads to the evaluation of the prototype.

5 Evaluation

In order to evaluate the prototype, we compared a synthetic point cloud and a point cloud captured by a real-world sensor. We utilized selected metrics to determine the quality of the data. The evaluation's goal is to check whether the synthetic point cloud is comparable to the point cloud generated by a real world sensor. The real world point cloud (referred to as *reference cloud)* of a 3D printed assembly part was captured with a GOM ATOS Core 300 (fringe projection system) and leads to 19788 data points. The assembly part is relatively small and exhibits a complex structure such as conical elements and holes. In addition, we used the corresponding CAD model. We selected the open-source software CloudCompare (CC) (Girardeau-Montaut 2022a) as a tool to perform the prototype evaluation. CC offers multiple functionalities, like preprocessing, registering, and applying different metrics to point clouds (Girardeau-Montaut 2022b).

Firstly, we removed the outlier values, which occur due to the real world scanning process. Then we begin with comparing the reference cloud with the virtual point cloud. Therefore, we applied the ICP algorithm (Besl and McKay 1992; Chen and Medioni 1992). The ICP algorithm is a method to register and align point clouds for finding an overlap. The result is an overlap of the two point clouds and the difference to a perfect overlap, measured in a rooted mean squad error (RMSE).

In order to compare the point clouds, we use the number of data points of the cleaned reference cloud as a benchmark for the synthetic data generation. We position the LiDAR scanner to a position, which approximately reflects the real world sensor position. By utilizing the Viewpoint functionality, 25 sample point clouds from different positions are captured. For each of the samples the ICP is applied. Consequently, we select the sample with the lowest RSME value for further evaluation.

At first, we compute the point cloud density for each cloud. The point density is computed by determining the number of neighbors for every point in a configured radius (r) on the surface of the point cloud. The Scalar fields of the reference and synthetic point cloud are depicted in Fig. 3.

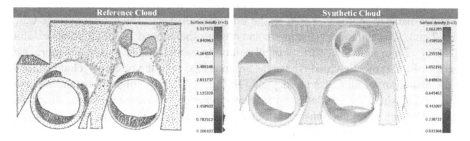

Fig. 3. Point Density Synthetic Cloud and Reference Cloud

The surface density ranges from 0.106 to 5.517 points/mm^2 for the reference cloud (left area of Fig. 3). We observe several uncovered areas, mainly around the conical structures. This originates from insufficient lighting in the recording process of the real data. Furthermore, those areas originate from not being exposed to the sensor. We observe a high concentration considering the point density on and around the captured contours of the object (green to red spectrum). In these areas, there are more neighbors within the defined radius, which causes a higher point density. On the areas characterized by flat surfaces, the point density is relatively low, namely approximately 0.106103 to 1 points/mm^2 (blueish spectrum). This results in an uneven distribution of point density considering the entire object.

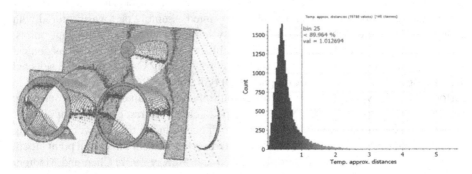

Fig. 4. Overlay of synthetic and reference cloud

We compared the reference point cloud with the virtual LiDAR generated synthetic point cloud (right image in Fig. 3). The range of the determined different classes is more granular than in the reference cloud. It ranges from 0.035 to 1.662 points/mm^2. Furthermore, on the conic areas of the object the point density is distributed with the highest concentration on the areas with the lowest distance from virtual LiDAR to the object. In contrast to the reference cloud, there are no holes in the point cloud. This is due to the operation system of the scan being a LiDAR, while the reference cloud was recorded with a fringe projection system, which is influenced among others by illumination. Thus, areas with the holes were underexposed. We further observe that the point density distribution on the synthetic cloud is more regular in terms of the gradient.

In the following, we apply the Cloud-to-Cloud (C2C) metric (Girardeau-Montaut 2022a) to compute the distance between the clouds, which is calculated by a nearest neighbor distance approach, based on the Euclidean distance. The overall average C2C is 0.42 mm. We examine the histogram and observe that around 1% of all points exhibit a C2C of ~2 mm and more. 10.13% of all points represent C2Cs of ~1 mm and more. An overlay of the synthetic cloud (red areas are matches) with the reference cloud as well as the histogram of all C2Cs are depicted in Fig. 4. The 10% highest distances occur in the areas, where the synthetic and reference point cloud diverge the most, which we explain through the point density difference and point arrangement on the cloud. The remaining 90% represent C2Cs between 0.006 mm and ~1 mm.

6 Challenges and Guidelines

In the process of developing the artifact, multiple challenges on different abstraction levels arose within the different iterations. Consequently, we implemented solutions for those challenges with the objective of creating a purposeful artifact. In this section, we compile the identified challenges and derive tailored guidelines for tackling them. The guidelines serve as a knowledge transfer and a basis for future works in similar fields. The challenges identified are depicted in Table 2.

Table 2. Challenges and guidelines

No	Challenge	No	Guideline
CH1	Merging actors to form one instance, with respect to the collision property	GL1	Apply the function Create Proxy Mesh actors, which is suitable for actor merging while ensuring the collision properties of the created instance
CH2	Development of a systematic approach for 3D ray casting	GL2	It is advised to acquire fundamental knowledge in linear algebra and geometry
CH3	Controlling the process flow considering the Tick and Begin Play functions	GL3	It is advised to strictly separate the variable names in the Begin Play and Tick functions to ensure a proper process flow
CH4	Filtering insignificant values for collision detection	GL4	Use Trace Channels for filtering insignificant values
CH5	Creating an enclosed 3D synthetic point cloud	GL5	Apply bounding boxes to the CAD object to build a positioning algorithm for covering all exposed surfaces with the sensor
CH6	Positioning of the actors in relation to a variable distance		See GL2

The issue of merging actors with the purpose of ensuring a collision property and forming one instance defines Challenge 1. The Create Proxy Mesh Actor method contributes solves this issue. By using blueprints, the respective actor instances can be merged to one instance. This ensures the collision property of the new actor (GL1).

A solution to Challenge 2 and Challenge 6 is summarized in guideline GL2. Developing in UE in general and more specifically implementing LiDAR or ray casting functionalities in UE, requires a fundamental knowledge of linear algebra and geometry. For example, many functionalities are based on utilizing 3D vectors in 3D space, more precisely the UE scene. Therefore, obtaining a basic knowledge in mathematical and geometrical areas before starting the programming is advised.

Challenge 3 describes a problematic interaction between the Begin Play and Tick function. The Begin Play function is typically used for static processes in the game instance. In contrast, the Tick function is used for dynamic, frame rate connected processes. Variables of the same name are present in both functions, for example the animation function mimicking the actual scanning process and the computation of values or the animation sequence, leads to malfunction. This originates from temporal overlaps. Therefore, we recommend a strict separation of variable names in the Tick and Begin Play functions (GL3). Challenge 4 defines the need for filtering insignificant values, considering the impact points of a virtual LiDAR scan. The recommended method represents configuring Trace Channels, because of its high grade of automation and individualization (GL4). Challenge 5 comprises the adding of an enclosed point cloud to the data representation forms. Therefore, we propose utilizing the bounding box and the center of a CAD model as reference points for the sensor orientation (GL5).

7   Conclusion and Outlook

The paper at hand reports about a virtual LiDAR based on the Unreal Game Engine to generate synthetic LiDAR data for object detection. The virtual LiDAR can capture point clouds of the CAD object in three dimensions and enables its export. Point clouds can be generated as a single-view and as a fully enclosed 3D representation from multiple viewpoints. The prototype was successfully evaluated.

The research contribution of this paper is threefold. First, we shed light on the ability to apply a game engine for generating synthetic point clouds, which in turn reduces the effort for training AI-based object detection models. Second, we present a prototype, demonstrate its functions, and evaluate its performance. It serves as a starting point for the implementation of other sensors, such as RGB cameras or stereo cameras. Third, we provide guidelines that support further research in enhancing the method.

The paper offers five practical (development) implications. First, we can recommend the function Create Proxy Mesh actors for using actor merging. Second, we advise practitioners to start a Unreal LiDAR project with fundamental skills in linear algebra and geometry. Third, we advise to particularly pay attention to the separation of variable names within the game engine plugin. Fourth, practitioners should use trace channels for filtering insignificant values. Fifth, Unreal developers should apply bounding boxes to the CAD object to build a positioning algorithm for covering all exposed surfaces.

However, the expressive power of the results is limited. The artifact only captures X, Y, Z coordinate information. A future improvement could be obtaining other relevant properties, like intensity and RGB values from the imported CAD model. Further, we did not address sensor noise to the obtained clouds and did not capture point clouds with occlusions or reflections. In addition, we compared the synthetic LiDAR point clouds with reference clouds that were generated with different technologies.

Future work should extend our artifact to include a feature for applying 3D bounding boxes to the generated point clouds. This enables the validation of the synthetic point clouds on deep learning object detection models, which also enables an optimization of the parameters in the UE. Moreover, future works could migrate the artifact to UE 5, which enables exploiting various new features, such as massively improved rendering for more level of detail and enhanced performance. In order to improve the model availability in the UE scene, mesh generation based on neural radiance fields seems to be a promising approach [39].

References

1. Alzubaidi, L., et al.: Review of deep learning: concepts, CNN architectures, challenges, applications, future directions. J. Big Data **8**, 53 (2021). https://doi.org/10.1186/s40537-021-00444-8
2. You, K., Long, M., Cao, Z., Wang, J., Jordan, M.I.: Universal Domain Adaptation Proceedings of the IEEE/CVF conference on computer vision and pattern recognition (2019)
3. Chen, X., Ma, H., Wan, J., Li, B., Xia, T.: Multi-view 3D object detection network for autonomous driving. In: 2017 IEEE Conference on Computer Vision and Pattern Recognition (CVPR), Honolulu, HI, pp. 6526–6534. IEEE (2017). https://doi.org/10.1109/CVPR.2017.691
4. Hodapp, J., Schiemann, M., Bilous, V., Cottbus-Senftenberg, B.T., Arcidiacono, C.S., Reichenbach, M.: Advances in Automated Generation of Convolutional Neural Networks from Synthetic Data in Industrial Environments, vol. 7 (2020)
5. Ritter, F., et al.: Medical image analysis. IEEE Pulse **2**, 60–70 (2011). https://doi.org/10.1109/MPUL.2011.942929
6. Li, J., Gotvall, P.-L., Provost, J., Akesson, K.: Training convolutional neural networks with synthesized data for object recognition in industrial manufacturing. In: 2019 24th IEEE International Conference on Emerging Technologies and Factory Automation (ETFA), Zaragoza, Spain, pp. 1544–1547. IEEE (2019). https://doi.org/10.1109/ETFA.2019.8869484
7. Duemmel, J., Kostik, V., Oellerich, J.: Generating synthetic training data for assembly processes advances in production management systems. In: Artificial Intelligence for Sustainable and Resilient Production Systems, pp. 119–128 (2021)
8. Mazzetto, M., Puttow Southier, L.F., Teixeira, M., Casanova, D.: Automatic classification of multiple objects in automotive assembly line. In: 24th IEEE International Conference on Emerging Technologies and Factory Automation (ETFA), pp. 363–369 (2019). https://doi.org/10.1109/ETFA.2019.8869063
9. Mousavi, M., Khanal, A., Estrada, R.: AI playground: unreal engine-based data ablation tool for deep learning. In: Bebis, G., et al. (eds.) Advances in Visual Computing, pp. 518–532. Springer, Cham (2020). https://doi.org/10.1007/978-3-030-64559-5_41
10. Wu, C., et al.: MotorFactory: a blender add-on for large dataset generation of small electric motors. Procedia CIRP **106**, 138–143 (2022). https://doi.org/10.1016/j.procir.2022.02.168
11. Kim, S.-H., Choe, G., Ahn, B., Kweon, I.S.: Deep representation of industrial components using simulated images. In: 2017 IEEE International Conference on Robotics and Automation (ICRA), Singapore, Singapore, pp. 2003–2010. IEEE (2017). https://doi.org/10.1109/ICRA.2017.7989232
12. Brekke, Å., Vatsendvik, F., Lindseth, F.: Multimodal 3D object detection from simulated pretraining. In: Bach, K., Ruocco, M. (eds.) Nordic Artificial Intelligence Research and Development, pp. 102–113. Springer, Cham (2019). https://doi.org/10.1007/978-3-030-35664-4_10
13. Fang, J., et al.: Simulating LIDAR Point Cloud for Autonomous Driving using Real-world Scenes and Traffic Flows. arXiv:1811.07112 (2018)
14. Dosovitskiy, A., Ros, G., Codevilla, F., Lopez, A., Koltun, V.: CARLA: An Open Urban Driving Simulator. arXiv:1711.03938 (2017)
15. Johnson-Roberson, M., Barto, C., Mehta, R., Sridhar, S.N., Rosaen, K., Vasudevan, R.: Driving in the Matrix: Can Virtual Worlds Replace Human-Generated Annotations for Real World Tasks? arXiv:1610.01983 (2017)
16. Müller, M., Casser, V., Lahoud, J., Smith, N., Ghanem, B.: Sim4CV: a photo-realistic simulator for computer vision applications. Int. J. Comput. Vision **126**, 902–919 (2018). https://doi.org/10.1007/s11263-018-1073-7

17. Ros, G., Sellart, L., Materzynska, J., Vazquez, D., Lopez, A.M.: The SYNTHIA dataset: a large collection of synthetic images for semantic segmentation of urban scenes. In: 2016 IEEE Conference on Computer Vision and Pattern Recognition (CVPR), Las Vegas, NV, USA, pp. 3234–3243. IEEE (2016). https://doi.org/10.1109/CVPR.2016.352

18. Wu, B., Zhou, X., Zhao, S., Yue, X., Keutzer, K.: SqueezeSegV2: improved model structure and unsupervised domain adaptation for road-object segmentation from a LiDAR point cloud. In: 2019 International Conference on Robotics and Automation (ICRA), Montreal, QC, Canada, pp. 4376–4382. IEEE (2019). https://doi.org/10.1109/ICRA.2019.8793495

19. Hevner, A., Chatterjee, S.: Design science research in information systems. In: Hevner, A., Chatterjee, S. (eds.) Design Research in Information Systems, pp. 9–22. Springer, Boston (2010). https://doi.org/10.1007/978-1-4419-5653-8_2

20. Peffers, K., Tuunanen, T., Rothenberger, M.A., Chatterjee, S.: A design science research methodology for information systems research. J. Manag. Inf. Syst. **24**, 45–77 (2007). https://doi.org/10.2753/MIS0742-1222240302

21. Gregor, S., Hevner, A.R.: Positioning and presenting design science research for maximum impact. MISQ **37**, 337–355 (2013). https://doi.org/10.25300/misq/2013/37.2.01

22. Shen, Y., Yang, Y., Yan, M., Wang, H., Zheng, Y., Guibas, L.: Domain adaptation on point clouds via geometry-aware implicits. In: 2022 IEEE/CVF Conference on Computer Vision and Pattern Recognition (CVPR), New Orleans, LA, USA, pp. 7213–7222. IEEE (2022). https://doi.org/10.1109/CVPR52688.2022.00708

23. Korakakis, M., Mylonas, P., Spyrou, E.: A short survey on modern virtual environments that utilize AI and synthetic data. In: Mediterranean Conference on Information Systems (MCIS) (2018)

24. Dworak, D., Ciepiela, F., Derbisz, J., Izzat, I., Komorkiewicz, M., Wojcik, M.: Performance of LiDAR object detection deep learning architectures based on artificially generated point cloud data from CARLA simulator. In: 2019 24th International Conference on Methods and Models in Automation and Robotics (MMAR), Międzyzdroje, Poland, pp. 600–605. IEEE (2019). https://doi.org/10.1109/MMAR.2019.8864642

25. Csurka, G.: Domain Adaptation in Computer Vision Applications. Springer, Cham (2017)

26. Zhang, W., Li, W., Xu, D.: SRDAN: scale-aware and range-aware domain adaptation network for cross-dataset 3D object detection. In: 2021 IEEE/CVF Conference on Computer Vision and Pattern Recognition (CVPR), Nashville, TN, USA, pp. 6765–6775. IEEE (2021). https://doi.org/10.1109/CVPR46437.2021.00670

27. Nowruzi, F.E., Kapoor, P., Kolhatkar, D., Hassanat, F.A., Laganiere, R., Rebut, J.: How much real data do we actually need: analyzing object detection performance using synthetic and real data. In: International Conference on Machine Learning (ICML 2019) (2019)

28. Andrade, A.: Game engines: a survey. EAI Endorsed Trans. Game-Based Learn. **2**, 150615 (2015). https://doi.org/10.4108/eai.5-11-2015.150615

29. Paul, P.S., Goon, S., Bhattacharya, A.: History and comparative study of modern game engines. Int. J. Adv. Comput. Math. Sci. **3** (2012)

30. Sanders, A.: An Introduction to Unreal Engine 4. Taylor & Francis CRC Press, Boca Raton (2017)

31. Žídek, K., Lazorík, P., Piteľ, J., Pavlenko, I., Hošovský, A.: Automated training of convolutional networks by virtual 3D models for parts recognition in assembly process. In: Trojanowska, J., Ciszak, O., Machado, J.M., Pavlenko, I. (eds.) Advances in Manufacturing II, pp. 287–297. Springer, Cham (2019). https://doi.org/10.1007/978-3-030-18715-6_24

32. Tavakoli, H., Walunj, S., Pahlevannejad, P., Plociennik, C., Ruskowski, M.: Small Object Detection for Near Real-Time Egocentric Perception in a Manual Assembly Scenario, vol. 5 (2021)

33. Tang, P., Guo, Y., Li, H., Wei, Z., Zheng, G., Pu, J.: Image dataset creation and networks improvement method based on CAD model and edge operator for object detection in the manufacturing industry. Mach. Vis. Appl. **32**, 111 (2021). https://doi.org/10.1007/s00138-021-01237-y

34. Cohen, J., Crispim-Junior, C., Grange-Faivre, C., Tougne, L.: CAD-based learning for ego-centric object detection in industrial context. In: Proceedings of the 15th International Joint Conference on Computer Vision, Imaging and Computer Graphics Theory and Applications, Valletta, Malta, pp. 644–651. SCITEPRESS - Science and Technology Publications (2020). https://doi.org/10.5220/0008975506440651

35. Andulkar, M., Hodapp, J., Reichling, T., Reichenbach, M., Berger, U.: Training CNNs from synthetic data for part handling in industrial environments. In: 2018 IEEE 14th International Conference on Automation Science and Engineering (CASE), Munich, Germany, pp. 624–629. IEEE (2018). https://doi.org/10.1109/COASE.2018.8560470

36. Zamora-Hernandez, M.-A., Castro-Vargas, J.A., Azorin-Lopez, J., Garcia-Rodriguez, J.: ToolSet: a real-synthetic manufacturing tools and accessories dataset. In: Herrero, Á., Cambra, C., Urda, D., Sedano, J., Quintián, H., Corchado, E. (eds.) 15th International Conference on Soft Computing Models in Industrial and Environmental Applications (SOCO 2020), pp. 800–809. Springer, Cham (2021). https://doi.org/10.1007/978-3-030-57802-2_77

37. Calli, B., Singh, A., Walsman, A., Srinivasa, S., Abbeel, P., Dollar, A.M.: The YCB object and model set: towards common benchmarks for manipulation research. In: 2015 International Conference on Advanced Robotics (ICAR), Istanbul, Turkey, pp. 510–517. IEEE (2015). https://doi.org/10.1109/ICAR.2015.7251504

38. Gschwandtner, M., Kwitt, R., Uhl, A., Pree, W.: BlenSor: blender sensor simulation toolbox. In: Bebis, G., et al. (eds.) International Symposium on Visual Computing (ISVC), vol. 6939, pp. 199–208. Springer, Heidelberg (2011). https://doi.org/10.1007/978-3-642-24031-7_20

39. Mildenhall, B., Srinivasan, P.P., Tancik, M., Barron, J.T., Ramamoorthi, R., Ng, R.: NeRF: Representing Scenes as Neural Radiance Fields for View Synthesis. arXiv:2003.08934 (2020)

Exploring Design Principles Promoting Organizational Knowledge Creation via Robo-Advisory: The Case of Collaborative Group Decision-Making in the After Sales Management

Nicole Namyslo[1,2]($\boxtimes$) (iD), Dominik Jung[2] (iD), and Timo Sturm[1] (iD)

[1] Technical University of Darmstadt, 64289 Darmstadt, Germany
namyslo@is.tu-darmstadt.de
[2] Porsche AG, Porscheplatz 1, 70435 Stuttgart, Germany

Abstract. Along with recent advances of team-AI collaboration, we observe the emergence of adaptive, collaborative, and explainable AI technologies that spur the creation of organizational knowledge for group decision-making. This is substantiated by the explicit and tacit knowledge that decision-makers can create with AI and by the procedural support that AI can provide for the organizational knowledge conversion processes among decision-makers. However, research on AI design for effective organizational knowledge creation is in a nascent state. This is problematic because this leaves organizations without guidance for the implementation and assessment of AI that enables effective knowledge creation. We see potential in robo-advisors, which represent a form of AI, to facilitate such organizational knowledge creation for decision-making in economic contexts. We aim to realize this potential and apply an action design research approach to identify meta-requirements and design principles for a robo-advisor prototype. The robo-advisor is contextualized in the after-sales domain of a German car manufacturer, the Dr. Ing. h.c. F. Porsche AG, where complex decision problems are informed and solved by expert groups. The robo-advisor prototype contributes to collaborative knowledge creation that informs the group's decision-making on field measures in the event of product quality issues aimed at ensuring product safety and customer satisfaction.

Keywords: Robo-Advisory · Group Decision-Making · Organizational Knowledge Creation · Team-AI Collaboration · Action Design Research

1 Introduction

1.1 Motivation

Shared organizational knowledge constitutes a vital asset in the context of organizational group decision-making (GDM) that allows for competitive advantage [1–3]. To harness the benefits of this knowledge, a rich research tradition has shown that it is

M. Mandviwalla et al. (Eds.): DESRIST 2024, LNCS 14621, pp. 310–324, 2024.
https://doi.org/10.1007/978-3-031-61175-9_21

essential to engage in knowledge conversion processes among diverse decision-makers [4]. In general, these conversion processes aim to create organizational knowledge and thereby facilitate GDM in organizations [2]. Prominent contributions discuss prevalent approaches on organizational knowledge creation and the related processes [3–8] and provide prescriptions on how to promote knowledge conversion processes between decision-makers.

Traditionally, only humans were able to participate in these knowledge-creation processes [1–6]. However, the recent emergence of modern artificial intelligence (AI) challenges this assumption: With their ability to learn from data, information systems (IS) based on AI can now contribute knowledge to these processes along with humans [5, 9]. Organizations' increasing adoption of AI can thus have wide-ranging consequences for their knowledge creation and GDM processes, urging organizations to rethink their AI designs for effective knowledge creation.

So far, however, research on the design of organizational AI remains scarce and can only provide limited guidance when it comes to promoting organizational knowledge creation in AI contexts [9–11]. Moreover, several scholars highlights the challenges in designing solutions for AI-based IS, emphasizing the limited applicability of prevailing theoretical conceptualizations of AI-based IS for the design and the coordination of team-AI collaboration in digital workplaces [9, 10]. These conceptualizations consider AI-based IS as tools [12, 13] rather than agentic socio-technical IS [9, 12], i.e., autonomous team members that also achieve to contribute self-learned knowledge to the organizational knowledge creation process [13, 14].

Consequently, a critical imperative arises: the examination of how organizations can effectively design AI for contexts in which humans and AI collectively contribute to knowledge conversion processes in GDM contexts [9, 11, 13]. Highlighting this understanding within the AI context is paramount, given that the misuse and creation of knowledge can adversely impact decision-making processes, shaping organizational behavior, and ultimately influencing organizational performance and competitiveness [5, 8, 15].

1.2 Research Framework and Question

This study builds upon recent research exploring the potential of robo-advisors (RAs) – as an instantiation of productively usable AI – to address challenges in organizational decision-making and knowledge creation and sharing. RAs provide an automated investment advisory service that guides customers in their investment decisions and maintains financial portfolios in the long run [16, 17]. Originally utilized in the asset and wealth management domain, RAs have demonstrated their ability to surpass limitations of traditional recommender systems, thereby bringing beneficial influence on human decision-making [18]. Moreover, recent research suggests the extension of RAs to diverse scenarios, beyond asset and wealth management, with the goal of supporting organizational knowledge creation processes and potentially supplementing or enhancing human knowledge practices. They argue that RAs can contribute to the knowledge creation as agents in organizational GDM. For instance, Namyslo and Jung provide recent insights on leveraging AI in robo-advisory for organizational GDM in novel types of economic scenarios [19].

We recognize that RAs have the potential to inform our understanding of i) the impact of technological and organizational advances (e.g., in machine learning and business platforms) on organizational knowledge creation processes, and ii) the integration of knowledge provided by AI and human members among different (human and AI) team members. In conceptualizing RAs as knowledge artifacts [13], we identify the potential to examine knowledge creation in team-AI collaboration [20, 21]. Consequently, our objective is to leverage on the uniqueness of RAs by examining robo-advisor (RA) designs that support the various knowledge conversion processes and to contribute to the interaction of tacit and explicit knowledge within AI contexts [4, 13] to contribute back to IS design research on knowledge creation. Our argument hinges on Nonaka's 1994 knowledge creation model, which we believe provides theoretical directives. We consider these directives in the context of a real-world use case to identify both theory-ingrained and practice-inspired meta-requirements (MRs). To achieve this, we follow an action design research (ADR) approach [22]. We identify MRs that represent RA (design) objectives to which relevant theory applies to and then derive design principles (DPs), i.e., prescriptive implications for practical RA design. In sum, we pose the following research question (RQ):

RQ: To enhance an organization's group decision-making, which design principles of robo-advisory can enable effective knowledge creation?

To answer our RQ we observe economic decision-making processes, in the context of a real business case involving the aftersales department of the Dr. Ing. h.c. F. Porsche AG (hereinafter referred to as Porsche AG). Solving the decision problem involves data-driven and collaborative analysis of product quality issues to derive adequate field measures, to which human experts and an RA collectively contribute. We also review theoretical foundations extensively, due to missing research directed towards the RQ.

Our article broadens the scope of the discourse on RAs: it demonstrates how organizations can design RAs to i) support knowledge conversion and ii) to contribute to the knowledge base through RA's inherent machine-learning (ML) components in team-AI collaborative settings. Figure 1 illustrates this idea and our conceptual frame of reference. Thus, this contribution adds to the knowledge base on the design of RAs and to the emerging discourse on team-AI collaboration, while extending it to the intertwined organizational knowledge creation and learning area. We acknowledge the paucity of IS research on solutions and designs for tacit knowledge creation and sharing compared to explicit knowledge creation and sharing due to tacit knowledge's inherently intangible nature [23]. Thus, we focus on reporting the design insights for the knowledge conversion modes of socialization and externalization in this study.

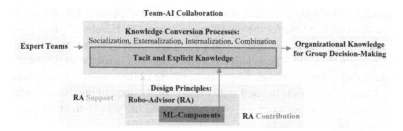

Fig. 1. Conceptual Frame of Reference

2 Theoretical Foundations

2.1 Theoretical Perspectives

To examine the theoretical perspectives that underpin our design science study, we delve into the following crucial frameworks that help us illuminate the dynamics of human-AI GDM. Phang et al.'s (2009) work on team-AI collaboration and AI-based GDM [24], specifically within online communities, serves as a foundational reference of our study. Their work emphasizes the emergence of a socio-technical system. With this work in mind, the interplay between social and technical elements is central to understanding the functioning of our study's context – online communities designed for knowledge sharing and learning. Furthermore, the incorporation of the value theory, adds depth to our exploration from a socio-economic perspective. This theory provides insights into the intrinsic and extrinsic values that individuals place on their participation within online communities. Understanding the perceived value participants derive from these communities is integral to comprehending the motivations and dynamics driving knowledge sharing and collaborative learning. Another theoretical perspective is the "social exchange theory". This theory focuses on the dynamics of social interactions, emphasizing the notion that individuals engage in exchanges of resources – such as information, support, or expertise – within the online community. The reciprocal nature of social exchanges, sheds light on the motivations behind knowledge sharing and collaborative decision-making in online spaces.

By synthesizing these theoretical perspectives, our study aims to unravel the intricate interplay between socio-technical systems, individual values, and social exchanges in human-AI GDM contexts. This holistic approach provides us with a comprehensive foundation for understanding the complexities of human-AI GDM contexts designed for knowledge sharing and learning.

2.2 Organizational Knowledge Creation

Organizational knowledge creation embodies the dynamic process by which knowledge is generated, shared, and applied within an organization to enhance collective decision-making [4, 5]. Decision-makers engage in knowledge creation by exchanging common insights, mental models, expertise, utilizing language, and deploying problem-solving skills, as well as performing specialized tasks [3]. This process encompasses the conversion of individual explicit and tacit knowledge into a collective form that is both accessible and valuable for the entire organization [3]. Hereby, explicit knowledge refers to knowledge that is codified in some form and therefore easy to articulate (e.g., manuals, frameworks). Tacit knowledge is knowledge that is rooted in personal experience and thus difficult to articulate (e.g., crafts, riding a bike). Since this is an inherently collective process, it extends beyond individual contributions to involve the integration and synthesis of diverse perspectives, experiences, and insights from employees across different levels and functions [4].

Prevalent approaches on organizational knowledge creation and the related processes build upon the widely accepted notion that shared organizational knowledge surpasses mere captured information [3, 4, 6–8]. Instead, it encapsulates know-how and the comprehension of information as processed in the human mind [1].

In this work, we conceptualize knowledge creation for organizational GDM by relying on Nonaka's (1994) theory of organizational knowledge creation that delineates the mechanisms through which knowledge, foundational to decision-making processes, is engendered [4]. Central to the model of organizational knowledge creation is the premise that knowledge emerges through patterns of conversion, encompassing both tacit and explicit knowledge. In other words, Nonaka's model emphasizes a "continuous dialogue between tacit and explicit knowledge" [4, p. 14]. Nonaka further posits that this conversion is driven by four distinctive modes that foster the creation of novel knowledge: Socialization involves the creation of tacit knowledge through interactions among individuals, while combination aims to create explicit knowledge through the integration of different bodies of existing explicit knowledge through social processes. Externalization and internalization cover processes that translate existing tacit and explicit knowledge and vice versa.

Related research remains scarce and focuses on the consequences that arise from the use of IS in knowledge conversion processes [5, 15]. Research regarding the design of AI systems that contributes to knowledge conversion processes remains practically non-existent. Related work, that focuses on how IS affects organizational knowledge creation, investigates the externalization of tacit knowledge in online environments compared to contexts vis-'a-vis [25] or exemplifies AI capabilities that may be relevant to the different modes of knowledge creation, but insights on the effective design of human-AI GDM towards organizational knowledge creation remain missing. This may open room for detrimental misuse of AI systems that might even jeopardize organizational competitiveness when corrupting decision-making processes [11, 26].

2.3 Team-AI Collaboration for Knowledge-Driven Group Decision-Making

IS research aimed at effectively developing and implementing systems to promote the creation, transfer, and application of organizational knowledge [1] originates in exploring team dynamics between humans and computers. Various perspectives on human-AI collaboration [e.g., 9, 27, 28] share the view that AI can function as a team member, building on insights from collaborative efforts outperforming individual human or AI endeavors [26]. Subsequent studies concentrate on enhancing efficiency, promoting learning [11], knowledge-driven decision-making [29–31] and exploring potential challenges that may arise [32, 33].

Recent research initiatives started to explore the complementary capabilities of effective human-AI collaboration for knowledge creation [11, 26]. However, according to insights from the emergent research stream on team-AI collaboration [9, 10], there are no attempts to identify requirements or solutions for designing human-AI knowledge conversion processes in organizational knowledge creation. This potential gap may stem from the dual nature of requirements for a human-AI solution, presenting a complex mix of demands encompassing both task-specific skills and social skills requiring long-term digital companionship: Classical IS solutions for organizational GDM, such as group recommender systems [19] that are characterized as primarily ad-hoc, task-based and short-term transaction-focused tools, might not adequately address these multifaceted requirements. Instead, the demand may be better met by intelligent and autonomous assistants designed to cultivate long-term digital companionship with users. This is what new generations of RAs are expected to accomplish [34]. We argue, that RAs in novel contexts [19] can also be seen and examined as team-mates. This perspective is grounded in the idea that the RA processes extend beyond providing advice, actively accompanying the decision-maker throughout prolonged GDM [35].

2.4 Robo-Advisor as Knowledge Creation Technology

RAs are advanced IS that leverage AI for intelligent user assistance to guide investors through an automated investment advisory process [18]. They provide personalized investment recommendations and portfolio allocation strategies at low cost to a wide range of users [36]. This new form of user assistance allows for the augmentation and substitution [37] of human financial advisor interaction and thereby transforms traditional human processes such as investment advisory and investing.

Since the first RAs have been introduced in 2008, research in academia has gained substantial attention in recent years due to the growing significance and impact of AI in the financial industry. Scholars have conducted numerous studies across various dimensions of robo-advisory, exploring their effectiveness, implications, and potential challenges. This resulted in the dissemination of inferred and validated propositions on RA design across a wide range of research streams with different research foci. For a comprehensive overview, we refer to Torno et al. (2022) and to Rico-Pérez et al. (2022) for a synthesis on the state of the art of RAs [38, 39], and to Namyslo and Jung (2023) for the contextualization of robo-advisory in GDM across new types of economic scenarios [19].

Aligned with suggestions for novel RA contextualizations [40] we aim to examine how RAs may support the knowledge conversion processes between team members (S1, E1-2, C1, I1-2) and the collaboration of team members with the RA that contributes as knowledge artifact (S2, E3-4, C2, I3-4). To visualize this idea, we extended the central knowledge conversion modes by Nonaka (1994), as initially interpreted by Alavi and Leidner (2001) [1, 4] in Fig. 2. In our study we align the RA design principles with the depicted knowledge conversion modes and directions.

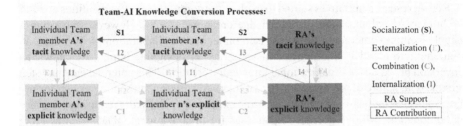

Fig. 2. Team-AI Knowledge Creation

3 Methodology

3.1 Use Case

We derive DPs from the RA instantiation, our IT meta-artifact. The Porsche AG examines the potential of a RA prototype to support and contribute to the holistic decision-making process for field measure decisions (e.g., recall campaign/technical warranty extension (TWE) to ensure product safety/customer satisfaction) in case of quality issues. The RA facilitates a decision-making process that involves a group of experts. More specifically, we focus on decisions about issuing a TWE for a specific component or system in the occurrence of malfunctions. Tackling the multi-criteria decision problem requires varying levels of expertise, specifically related to a defined quality issue. Here, experts contribute to an explicitly formulable quantitative and qualitative data-base and provide individual expert perspectives on the issue into the decision-making process. The RA supports sound human expert and AI based analysis of the database for various criteria, such as legal considerations, the reliability of components and systems, the term of the TWE as well as associated cost developments.

3.2 Action Design Research Approach

We initiated an ADR project [22] to derive theoretically and empirically grounded design principles (DPs). The paradigm underlying our approach involves developing DPs through prototyping an IT meta-artifact [22]. This artifact serves as a general solution continuously instantiated and tested through organizational interventions, guided by the assumptions, expectations, and knowledge of participating members [22]. The approach is particularly suitable, since an "in-depth understanding of the artifact-context relationship" [22, p. 53] is established due to the repeated intervention with the ADR project participants in the building, intervention, and evaluation (BIE) design cycles. Participants include domain experts from different domains across procurement, production, quality, sales and aftersales, research and development and compliance, and the research team. To ensure that the design knowledge is developed in an empirical manner, it will be triangulated out of insights from several scientific methods, that are considered for the interrelated stages and underlying principles [22] and outlined subsequently for the different ADR stages.

Stage 1: To ensure theory-ingrained and practice inspired design principles we first identified and conceptualized the research opportunity, formulated the initial research question, and casted the design problem as an instance of a class of design problems as outlined in the introduction. We further identified contributing theoretical bases and prior technology advances by means of a structured literature review using the method by Webster and Watson (2002) [41]. We performed iterative requirements engineering workshops [42] and thereby aimed at deriving expert stories for an adequate AI solution to the use case. As of now, we conducted 30 workshops with seven different stakeholder groups consisting of two to ten people. This has led to over 135 expert stories of 30 experts. Furthermore, we identified kernel theories and justificatory knowledge from relevant literature by means of search strings containing keywords related to human-AI GDM ((human-ai OR team-ai OR human-machine OR AI OR artificial intelligence OR ML OR machine learning OR hybrid intelligence) AND (teaming OR team OR teams OR collaboration OR coordination OR teammates OR team*mates)) and organizational knowledge creation (knowledge creation OR SECI OR knowledge conversion OR knowledge sharing OR knowledge OR organizational learning OR decision OR decision*making). We performed an abstract based search and identified 69 articles in the AIS Electronic Library, 1,331 articles in the EbscoHost, and 707 articles in the ProQuest database that resulted in a final pool of 1,041 initial peer-reviewed articles, after checking for doubles. We checked initial hits for our inclusion criteria, i.e., the articles must suggest prescriptions about team-AI collaboration for knowledge-driven GDM and/or provide design requirements and/or solutions and performed a forward and backward search to account for drawbacks of the abstract based search and identified 19 relevant scientific articles. This knowledge base was extended by deriving design requirements and/or solutions from the emerging body of literature that addresses robo-advisory. We considered the search string ((robo-advisor OR robo advisor OR robo-advisors OR robo-advisors OR robo-advisory OR robo advisory) AND (meta-requirement OR design principle OR design decision) AND (knowledge creation OR SECI OR knowledge conversion OR knowledge sharing OR knowledge OR organizational learning OR decision OR decision*making OR information) for an abstract based search mode for non-peer-reviewed articles and identified 151 articles in the AIS Electronic Library, 30 in the EbscoHost, and 7 articles in the ProQuest database that resulted in a final pool of 181 initial articles after checking for doubles. After identifying 20 relevant articles we performed a forward and backward search, and additionally accounted for the earlier but more established and related literature on the digitalization and automation of financial advice and investment management, which resulted in 18 additional relevant scientific articles.

Stage 2: For the initial design of the IT meta-artifact, i.e., the customization and execution of the first BIE design cycle, we refined and adjusted the expert stories during the iterative requirements engineering workshops by collectively reviewing and informally evaluating relevant specifics (e.g., interface, process, database, models, etc.) of the IT meta-artifact.

Stage 3: Expert stories were then contextualized with identified kernel theories and justificatory knowledge, by the research team in accordance with the scheme suggested by Shirley et al. (2020). Thereby information related to conditions of material aspects, actions and user characteristics or implementation settings [43] were incorporated. Thus, the initial set of MRs and DPs were informally derived and subsequently evaluated by stakeholder groups within the iterative workshops.

Stage 4: Finally, learning results were formulated and abstracted as final prototype and DPs. These generalized outcomes and insights will be reported towards the ADR project members and are disseminated within the scientific community in this paper. We derived an initial set of MRs and DPs that were validated within iterative requirement elicitation workshops. We structured each MR, that comprises the fundamental patterns of interaction required for continuous dialogue between tacit and explicit knowledge and further derived the related DPs, that benefit the facilitation of the patterns along the design domain (DD) concerning socialization and externalization.

4   Meta-requirements and Design-Principles

4.1   Design Domain I: Socialization

Figure 2 illustrates the complexity of socialization processes between team members (S1) and between team members and the RA (S2). Socialization involves individuals' sharing of learning and thinking processes through observation, imitation, and practice, thereby transferring tacit knowledge to create new tacit knowledge. These processes require self-organized creation and interaction in a field, the establishment of mutual trust, and the sharing of experiences [3, 4], which constitute our MR for the first DD.

MR I: Collaboration and Self-organizing Team. Members creating organizational knowledge interact in a field that defines the domain and context in which perspectives are exchanged. According to Nonaka (1994) principles of self-organization need to be established to allow key members to meet and interact [4]. Organizational GDM usually involves domain experts from different departments who participate in the decision-making process to solve complex problems [35]. Here expertise location, i.e., the awareness of knowledge specialization among team members, facilitates members to leverage knowledge among the members for solving a task. Expertise location is recognized to be an antecedent to knowledge creation [44] and proven to improve team performance [e.g., 45]. Platform solutions like RA may enable an extensive user interaction, authentication, and management design [e.g., 46] that handles user profiles, roles, groups and permissions. Thus, IS systems and applications may facilitate the communication of specific user attributes and thereby facilitate expertise allocation and verification. Core members and key individuals [4] that are associated with a specific expertise may additionally be represented with certain roles.

DP I: For the RA designer to allow for collaboration and self-organization between the team members in the context of team-AI knowledge creation, the RA designer should employ member- and role-specific contents to be generated and reviewed and involve user profiles that provide information on users' expertise and roles as well as information on RA's ML-components, to facilitate the location and assessment of expertise between the decision-makers and the RA.

MR II: Mutual Trust. The sharing of useful tacit knowledge depends on the existence of mutual trust among members [4, 47]. Consequently, solutions in RA design must prioritize fostering human interpersonal trust and shaping positive human perceptions toward an RA.

Past research on RAs was able to link trust requirements and mechanisms [38] as one of the main drivers of investment decisions, adoption of RAs [48, 49], and reliance on RAs [50]. Existing RA research has further explored trust-building mechanisms, including the use of anthropomorphic cues and social presence [51]. However, this prevalent research stream cautions against different anthropomorphic design efforts due to their ambivalent effects [52] and contradictory findings about the role of anthropomorphism. The need for context-specific optimal levels of anthropomorphic cues in RA appearance and communication impedes a generalizable conclusion related to our DPs. Moreover, we identified competence-based trust to be relevant for both, interpersonal trust perceptions [47, 53] (S1) and RA trust perceptions [38] (S2).

DP II: For the RA designer to achieve the sharing of valuable tacit knowledge among decision-makers in the context of team-AI knowledge creation, employ trust-enhancing mechanisms that involve information towards the competence of team members (i.e., human decision makers and the RA), as conveying competence contributes to enhanced trust perceptions.

MR III: Shared Experiences. Tacit knowledge involves different elements that can be of utter importance to organizational decision-making.

While cognitive elements of tacit knowledge capture an individual's perspectives that include "schemata, paradigms, beliefs, and viewpoints" [4, p. 16], technical elements include the individual's "concrete know-how, crafts, and skills" [4, p. 16]. Implementing the exchange of tacit knowledge proves challenging for organizations, given its deep connection to action and the difficulty in transferring it between individuals when abstracted from specific contexts and experiences [4, 15]. As this knowledge is strongly intertwined with an individual's past experiences, this knowledge is hard to explicate and articulate to others—it's simply best to show others "how it is done" and to create high quality experiences. High quality experiences may be reached in relation to different dimensions, as highlighted in management literature [5] and outlined in the following with regard to literature on team-AI collaboration [5]:

From an experience-based perspective, the perceived *novelty* level of an encounter in the decision-making process has different effects on knowledge creation and is therefore advised to be carefully balanced [5, 8, 11]. In this vein, an illustrative example in the team-AI collaboration research demonstrates the effect of updates that improve the predictive performance but diminish the team's confidence, due to reduced comparability with prior experience [30].

The *success or failure* of an experience constitutes another dimension that affects knowledge creation [5]. Mixed research findings on different conditions facilitating team members' knowledge creation based on successful or failure experiences indicate that members' interpretation and anticipation of success perceptions play a crucial role in knowledge creation. It is to be noted that the perception of success in terms of using RAs is not only shaped by the outcome and the effectiveness of a decision [18], but also by the performance of successful process, the ease of navigation [18] the perceived ease of use, the perceived usefulness, and the perceived convenience [54].

Ambiguous experiences may be characterized by forms like unclear input output relations. These experiences can negatively influence knowledge creation processes, e.g., due to difficulties in interpretation or understanding efforts [5]. Negative effects of outcome, data and process ambiguity in recommendation contexts may be prevented by expectation conformity [18, 55] and by the provision of explanation towards the use of data, as this promotes decision-makers' perceptions of transparency [36].

Since knowledge creation may occur before, during and after any experience, the temporal dimension related to *timing and pace* of experience may predetermine the quality of the experience as well [5]. In the RA context timing further relates to the requirement of a reasonable relationship between the required effort to use the RA and the accuracy of attained goals [36]. Pace considerations may be predetermined related to regulatory requirements [38] (e.g., product monitoring and reporting obligations).

Mixed findings towards the benefit for experience *heterogeneity* stress the need for contextualized design efforts that allow for high or low levels of heterogeneity [5]. The GDM setting allows to mitigate knowledge imbalance, which may be realized in targeted RA design that involves members with different knowledge levels within a specific decision process [56].

DP III: For the RA designer to allow for a high-quality experience among decision-makers in the context of team-AI knowledge creation, carefully balance and employ the exemplified dimensions of experiences involving the dimensions of novelty, success, ambiguity, timing, and place, as well as heterogeneity, because the sharing of high quality experiences enhances access to tacit knowledge.

4.2 Design Domain II: Externalization

The conversion of tacit knowledge into explicit knowledge requires the associated processes to take place between the experts and the RA (E2, E3) and in isolation (E1, E4). The processes are triggered by rounds of meaningful dialogue, reflection, and the use of metaphors or analogies [3, 4], which constitute our MR for the second DD.

MR IV: Dialogue. Meaningful dialogue can take the form of communication that is temporary and multifaceted, consensus-oriented, face-to-face, and that facilitates to express ideas freely and openly [4]. In the context of RAs, synchronous interactive dialogue, towards knowledge conversion directions of E1-2, may be facilitated digitally by online meeting sessions, or commentary boxes, protocols and notification functions [e.g., 31]. RA research emphasizes the necessity for a certain degree of controllability over dialogues and the behavior of the RA [36, 57]. Digitally guiding the dialogue, with facilitators that may be core members and key individuals in the organizational GDM context allows for targeted decision processes and dialogues towards E1-3 [25]. Additionally, the relevance of easy-to-understand and transparent dialogue among members has been identified as a key design requirement for RAs [36]. This may be particularly supported through the targeted design of conversational interfaces [e.g., 50] including design solutions towards navigation [36, 55]. Knowledge conversion directions towards E3 may be further supported by design solutions that facilitate the development of human mental models of AI, such as explainable AI [58].

DP IV: For the RA designer to stimulate meaningful dialogue among decision-makers in the context of team-AI knowledge creation, employ context and task-specific, ease to understand, explained, transparent and controllable communication techniques, involving a session function and a protocol that promote a-/synchronous interaction in digital/ face-to-face settings and involving consensus-efficient GDM processes so that meaningful dialogue is performed, documented and accessible.

MR V: Reflection. Reflecting while experiencing facilitates the conversion of tacit to explicit knowledge and refers to all conversion directions E1–E4. Thus, the inclusion of reflection-in-action in the context of RAs may be realized by easing the understanding of retrieved information throughout the robo-advised GDM process [18]. Targeted feedback and experimental learning environment design represent a way to promote informed knowledge creation [59]. Similarly, degrees of error tolerance in the process [36] and educational solutions are suggested in the RA context [38].

DP V: For the RA designer to allow team members' reflection in organizational knowledge creation process, the RA designer should employ feedback mechanisms involving both human and RA feedback to promote knowledge-level checks and knowledge-level improvements, as these facilitate prudent decision-making.

MR VI: Metaphor and Analogy. Members of the GDM process may transform hard to communicate tacit knowledge into explicit knowledge "by linking contradictory things and ideas through metaphor; then, by resolving these contradictions through analogy; and, finally, by crystallizing the created concepts and embodying them in a model." [60, p. 168]. The formation and application of metaphors and analogies are promoted by the flexible acquisition and interpretation of data through interfaces [61]. Their design and structural consistency is addressed in RA research [36]as well and represents a lever for knowledge creation towards the conversion directions E1–E3.

DP VI: For the RA designer to allow for the team members to apply metaphor and analogy in the context of team-AI knowledge creation, the RA designer should employ interface design solutions that give members autonomy over their experiences, as these help team members to develop mental models which support knowledge creation.

5   Conclusion and Future Work

We explore a solution for the design of team-AI collaboration that promotes knowledge creation for organizational GDM. In our ADR project we scrutinized the role of RAs as knowledge artifact that provides support and contributes to knowledge conversion processes. The prototype, crafted for a practical business case at the Porsche AG, showcases the effectiveness and value of utilizing RAs, especially in decision-making scenarios that lack perfectly matched expert knowledge. It is designed to foster cooperation between AI, human experts, and company levels as an imperative capability for economic decision-making problems and nurture the long-term evolution of knowledge creation. Limitations to be considered concern the lack of validation of the prototyping results presented in other business settings, industries, and cultures. Moreover, due to the study's conceptual focus on the theory-ingrained and practice-inspired MRs and DPs, the instantiation and the execution of the design decisions are not reported in this study. Lastly, the study centers on reporting design knowledge pertaining to socialization and externalization. However, we expect to partially mitigate the aforementioned limitations in our future research on the long-term deployment of the RA and by extending the MRs and DPs and addressing the instantiated design decisions for all design domains. In conclusion, with this empirical study we hope to enrich the discussions and research on team-AI collaboration for knowledge creation.

References

1. Alavi, M., Leidner, D.E.: Review: knowledge management and knowledge management systems. MIS Q. **25**, 107–136 (2001)
2. Grant, R.M.: Toward a knowledge-based theory of the firm. Strat. Mgmt. J. **17**, 109–122 (1996)
3. Nonaka, I., von Krogh, G.: Tacit knowledge and knowledge conversion. Organ. Sci. **20**, 635–652 (2009)
4. Nonaka, I.: A dynamic theory of organizational knowledge creation. Organ. Sci. **5**, 14–37 (1994)
5. Argote, L., Lee, S., Park, J.: Organizational learning processes and outcomes: major findings and future research directions. Manag. Sci. **67**, 5399–5429 (2021)
6. Huber, G.P.: Organizational learning: the contributing processes and the literatures. Organ. Sci. **2**, 88–115 (1991)
7. Kogut, B., Zander, U.: What firms do? Coordination, identity, and learning. Organ. Sci. **7**, 502–518 (1996)
8. March, J.G.: Exploration and exploitation in organizational learning. Organ. Sci. **2**, 71–87 (1991)
9. Zercher, D., Jussupow, E., Heinzl, A.: When AI joins the team: a literature review on intragroup processes and their effect on team performance in team-AI collaboration. In: ECIS 2023 Proceedings (2023)
10. Seeber, I., et al.: Machines as teammates: a collaboration research agenda. In: HICCS, vol. 57 (2018)
11. Sturm, T., et al.: Coordinating human and machine learning for effective organization learning. MIS Q. **45**, 1581–1602 (2021)
12. Anthony, C., Bechky, B.A., Fayard, A.-L.: "Collaborating" with AI: taking a system view to explore the future of work. Organ. Sci. **34**, 1672–1694 (2023)
13. Cabitza, F., Campagner, A., Simone, C.: The need to move away from agential-AI. Int. J. Hum. Comput. **155**, 102696 (2021)
14. Brynjolfsson, E., Mitchell, T.: What can machine learning do? Workforce implications. Science **358**, 1530–1534 (2017)
15. Argote, L., Miron-Spektor, E.: Organizational learning: from experience to knowledge. Organ. Sci. **22**, 1123–1137 (2011)
16. Tertilt, M., Scholz, P.: To advise, or not to advise— how robo-advisors evaluate the risk preferences of private investors. JWM **21**, 70–84 (2018)
17. Sironi, P.: FinTech Innovation. Wiley, West Sussex (2016)
18. Jung, D., Erdfelder, E., Glaser, F.: Nudged to win: designing robo-advisory to overcome decision inertia. In: ICIS 2018 Proceedings (2018)

19. Namyslo, N.M., Jung, D.: Towards designing robo-advisory to promote consensus-efficient group decision-making in new types of economic scenarios. In: ECIS 2023 Proceedings (2023)
20. Cichocki, A., Kuleshov, A.P.: Future trends for human-AI collaboration. Comput. Intell. Neurosci. 1–21 (2021)
21. Rai, A., Constantinides, P., Sarker, S.: Next-generation digital platforms: toward human–AI hybrids. MIS Q. **43**, iii–ix (2019)
22. Sein, M.K., Henfridsson, O., Purao, S., Rossi, M., Lindgren, R.: Action design research. MIS Q. **35**, 37–56 (2011)
23. Lesjak, D., Natek, S.: Knowledge management systems and tacit knowledge. IJIL **29**, 166 (2021)
24. Phang, C., Kankanhalli, A., Sabherwal, R.: Usability and sociability in online communities. JAIS **10**, 721–747 (2009)
25. Yi, J.: Externalization of tacit knowledge in online environments. IJEL **5** (2006)
26. Fügener, A., Grahl, J., Gupta, A., Ketter, W.: Will humans-in-the-loop become borgs? Merits and pitfalls of working with AI. MIS Q. **45**, 1527–1556 (2021)
27. Lyons, J.B., Sycara, K., Lewis, M., Capiola, A.: Human-autonomy teaming: definitions, debates, and directions. Front. Psychol. **12** (2021)
28. McNeese, N.J., Demir, M., Cooke, N.J., Myers, C.: Teaming with a synthetic teammate. Hum. Factors **60**, 262–273 (2018)
29. Agrawal, A., Gans, J., Goldfarb, A.: How AI will change the way we make decisions. HBR **26**, 1–5 (2017)
30. Bansal, G., Nushi, B., Kamar, E., Weld, D.S., Lasecki, W.S., Horvitz, E.: Updates in human-AI teams: understanding and addressing the performance/compatibility tradeoff. In: AAAI, vol. 33, pp. 2429–2437 (2019)
31. Metcalf, L., Askay, D.A., Rosenberg, L.B.: Keeping humans in the loop: pooling knowledge through artificial swarm intelligence to improve business decision making. Calif. Manage. Rev. **61**, 84–109 (2019)
32. Fügener, A., Grahl, J., Gupta, A., Ketter, W.: Cognitive challenges in human-artificial intelligence collaboration. ISR **33**, 678–696 (2019)
33. Jussupow, E., Spohrer, K., Heinzl, A., Gawlitza, J.: Augmenting medical diagnosis decisions? An investigation into physicians' decision-making process with artificial intelligence. ISR **32**, 713–735 (2021)
34. Wang, J.F.: An Affordance Perspective of RAs 2.0: Theorizing the New Generation of Recommendation Agents (2021)
35. Cao, G., Duan, Y., Edwards, J.S., Dwivedi, Y.K.: Understanding managers' attitudes and behavioral intentions towards using artificial intelligence for organizational decision-making. Technovation **106** (2021)
36. Jung, D., Dorner, V.: Decision inertia and arousal: using NeuroIS to analyze bio-physiological correlates of decision inertia in a dual-choice paradigm. In: Davis, F.D., Riedl, R., vom Brocke, J., Léger, P.-M., Randolph, A.B. (eds.) Information Systems and Neuroscience. LNISO, vol. 25, pp. 159–166. Springer, Cham (2018). https://doi.org/10.1007/978-3-319-67431-5_18
37. Kobets, V., Petrov, O., Koval, S.: Sustainable robo-advisor bot and investment advice-taking behavior. In: Maślankowski, J., Marcinkowski, B., Rupino da Cunha, P. (eds.) Digital Transformation, pp. 15–35. Springer, Cham (2022). https://doi.org/10.1007/978-3-031-23012-7_2
38. Torno, A., Bähnsch, S., Dreyer, M.: Taming the next wolf of wall street–design principles for ethical robo-advice. In: PACIS 2022 Proceedings (2022)
39. Rico-Pérez, H., Arenas-Parra, M., Quiroga-García, R.: Scientific Development of Robo-Advisor: A Bibliometric Analysis (2022)

40. Namyslo, N.M., Jung, D., Rieker, T.: The use of robo-advisory and AI in reliability analysis for field measure decision-making. In: VDI, pp. 257–270 (2023)
41. Webster, J., Watson, R.T.: Analyzing the past to prepare for the future: writing a literature review. MIS Q. **26**, xiii–xxiii (2002)
42. Paetsch, F., Eberlein, A., Maurer, F.: Requirements engineering and agile software development. In: Proceedings of the IEEE WETICE (2003)
43. Shirley, G., Kruse, C.L., Stefan, S.: Research perspectives: the anatomy of a design principle. AIS **21**, 1622–1652 (2020)
44. Kanawattanachai, Y.: The impact of knowledge coordination on virtual team performance over time. MIS Q. **31**, 783 (2007)
45. Faraj, S., Sproull, L.: Coordinating expertise in software development teams. Manage. Sci. **46**, 1554–1568 (2000)
46. Wu, M., Gao, Q.: Understanding the acceptance of robo-advisors. In: HCI, pp. 262–277 (2021)
47. Levin, D.Z., Cross, R.: The strength of weak ties you can trust. Manag. Sci. **50**, 1477–1490 (2004)
48. Nourallah, M.: One size does not fit all: young retail investors' initial trust in financial robo-advisors. J. Bus. Res. **156**, 113470 (2023)
49. Ruf, C., Back, A., Weidenfeld, H.A.: Designing Tablet Banking Apps for High-Net-Worth Individuals (2015)
50. Hildebrand, C., Bergner, A.: Conversational robo advisors as surrogates of trust. J. Acad. Mark. Sci. **49**, 659–676 (2021)
51. Deng, B., Chau, M.: Anthropomorphized financial robo-advisors and investment advice-taking behavior. In: Proceedings of the AMCIS, vol. 4 (2021)
52. Zhang, G., Chong, L., Kotovsky, K., Cagan, J.: Trust in an AI versus a human teammate. CHB **139**, 107536 (2023)
53. Harris-Watson, A.M., Larson, L.E., Lauharatanahirun, N., DeChurch, L.A., Contractor, N.S.: Social perception in human-AI teams. CHB **145**, 107765 (2023)
54. Sabir, A.A., Ahmad, I., Ahmad, H., Rafiq, M., Khan, M.A., Noreen, N.: Consumer acceptance and adoption of AI robo-advisors in fintech industry. Mathematics **11**, 1311 (2023)
55. Ruf, C., Back, A., Bergmann, R., Schlegel, M.: Elicitation of requirements for the design of mobile financial advisory services. In: HICCS (2015)
56. Gomez, C., Unberath, M., Huang, C.-M.: Mitigating knowledge imbalance in AI-advised decision-making through collaborative user involvement. Int. J. Hum. Comput. **172** (2023)
57. Nussbaumer, P., Matter, I., Schwabe, G.: "Enforced" vs. "casual" transparency. ACM Trans. Manage. Inf. Syst. **3**, 1–19 (2012)
58. Westphal, M., Vössing, M., Satzger, G., Yom-Tov, G.B., Rafaeli, A.: Decision control and explanations in human-AI collaboration. CHB **144** (2023)
59. Heinrich, P., Schwabe, G.: Facilitating informed decision-making in financial service encounters. Bus. Inf. Syst. Eng. **60**, 317–329 (2018)
60. Nonaka, I.: The knowledge-creating company. HRB **85**(7/8), 162–171 (2007)
61. Huang, K.-Y., Güney, S.: Toward a framework of web 2.0-driven organizational learning. CAIS **31** (2012)

Designing for Banking Resilience: A DeFi E-Learning Solution

Christian Zeiß[(✉)] [iD], Lisa Straub [iD], Viktoria Hahn [iD], Konstanze Lang [iD],
Myriam Schaschek [iD], Christoph Tomitza [iD], and Axel Winkelmann [iD]

University of Würzburg, 97070 Würzburg, Germany
`christian.zeiss@uni-wuerzburg.de`

Abstract. Not resilient enough? Is this the reason why banks are losing their power dominance? With the rise of the decentralized financial ecosystem, traditional players in the financial industry have lost their supremacy. The current knowledge level about decentralized finance and the crypto ecosystem within banks is insufficient to face the competition. Dedicated e-learning platforms for bank employees can offer a way forward. But pure knowledge transfer concepts are not suitable to cope with change. Our research addresses these issues and examines the design of an e-learning platform for decentralized finance to strengthen organizational bank resilience. This research paper combines the SECI framework for organizational knowledge creation with an acknowledged e-learning approach. We deploy a design science research method focused on steady evaluation. Using this approach, literature research, sets of expert interviews, workshops, and focus groups were performed. With these data sources, a specific e-learning framework and platform are developed and evaluated. In the last step, two focus groups performing real-world tasks evaluate the results and the instantiated platform. In total, we performed a four-phase multi-step method with numerous consecutive evaluations.

Keywords: DSR · DeFi · E-Learning · Bank · Resilience

1 Motivation and Problem Definition

With the rise of blockchain technology, the financial ecosystem is changing dramatically [19]. Based on a crypto technology approach, a new decentralized financial (DeFi) ecosystem was installed where the old-fashioned players no longer enjoy the monopolistic positions and even be rationalized away [11, 40]. For the financial industry, this situation leads to a massive loss of power and control, reduced capital in custody, customer churn, and declining relevance in the financial ecosystem [11]. Thus, the organizational resilience of banks is crucial. In order to be able to defend their role, traditional financial institutes must be strengthened and regain their resilience to withstand current and future changes better [28]. The banking industry and financial markets are essential for promoting resilience as they are vital to modern societies and significantly contribute to economic growth [27, 28]. But what can they do to achieve this?

© The Author(s), under exclusive license to Springer Nature Switzerland AG 2024
M. Mandviwalla et al. (Eds.): DESRIST 2024, LNCS 14621, pp. 325–338, 2024.
https://doi.org/10.1007/978-3-031-61175-9_22

Our research focuses on organizational resilience, the ability of a company to adapt to adverse conditions and to emerge from difficult situations as a stronger and more resourceful entity [51]. It offers a way to remain stable under high pressure and in the face of change [14, 15]. Implementing innovative digital technologies also enables resilience and sustainability by improving flexibility, avoiding the emergence of risks, reducing the damaging effects of disruptions, and challenging complacency in businesses [27]. In order to ensure an organization's resilience, it is essential to have a broad and diverse knowledge base [16]. Banks must broaden their expertise and skills on DeFi to participate in the market [19]. In the banking sector, blockchain ability and knowledge are essential success factors for gaining resilience [28]. Organizational resilience for financial institutes emphasizes the role of banking employees, as they compose a considerable part of the knowledge base [13, 16]. People are fundamental to future resilience and must develop adaptive skills that help them adjust to and embrace existing and impending change. The current situation for bank employees to learn about crypto assets and expand their knowledge base is satisfactory, as ample opportunities are available. E-learning, a tool for knowledge management [55], is used on the customer side in banking as well for banking employees [18, 24].

Nevertheless, most of these e-learning possibilities are unsuitable for the various levels of employee expertise, and they do not interact as well with exchange possibilities for enhancing resilience [10, 53]. Given the dynamic development, finding reliable sources of DeFi knowledge is difficult, so the experts are still in the learning process and generally lack long-term experience [10]. As the need for a fast learning and knowledge process arises and banks are also often widely dispersed, an e-learning approach seems beneficial [50]. While explicit knowledge can be easily formalized and processed as it is available in the form of data, specifications, or documents, tacit knowledge is considered personal and challenging to present because it is, for example, the individual's objective view, primarily stored in behavior, attitudes, routines, actions, ideals or even feelings [7, 32]. Both sources of knowledge are beneficial in the area of resilience. Banks must establish appropriate information systems to expand existing knowledge bases. This leads us to our research question:

RQ: *How to design a DeFi e-learning platform for banking professionals to strengthen bank resilience?*

Guided by this research question, we conceptualize and develop a DeFi e-learning platform for the banking industry. First, we describe input knowledge and concepts - especially the role of DeFi in the financial ecosystem and knowledge management in organizations (Sect. 2). Next, we introduce the iterative build-evaluate design science research approach [44] as our methodology (Sect. 3). Moreover, we present our DeFi e-learning Framework for banks and our artifact - the CryptoCompass e-learning platform (Sect. 4) as well as the results of the mixed-methods evaluation (Sect. 5). Section 6 discusses our research, concluding with limitations and future research (Sect. 7).

2   Foundations and Theoretical Background

Transformation in the Banking Sector. CeFi, or centralized finance, refers to the traditional financial system in which transactions require an intermediary [11, 19]. This intermediary is usually present in the form of a bank as the central authority [35]. This offers the advantage that the financial system is considered stable, secure, and trustworthy due to its strong regulation [35]. As a result of the global economic and financial crisis, the emergence of blockchain and decentralized finance (DeFi) led to a profound change in the financial sector [11, 19]. DeFi represents an alternative to traditional banking that does not require an intermediary and offers more control and clarity [34, 38]. DeFi uses decentralized blockchain, a disruptive technology that can change the financial and banking industry by simplifying, accelerating, and ensuring transparency in many traditional banking services [38]. In contrast to traditional financial products, such as stocks, deposit accounts, or funds, crypto assets are based on the blockchain and open up new perspectives for banks and customers [34, 47]. Crypto assets enable the tokenization of virtual or physical assets. Fungible and non-fungible tokens (NFTs) differ in their divisibility and replaceability [9, 40]. Payment, utility, and asset tokens are unique tokens by their characteristics [39]. Financial institutes are losing relevance in the monetary system. They are trying to find new business models in this DeFi crypto market by securing licenses to trade or hold crypto assets. For regulation, the EU introduced the Markets in Crypto Assets (MiCA) Regulation in June 2023 [17, 19]. The aim is to ensure financial stability and market integrity, support innovation, and promote Distributed Ledger Technology. MiCA supersedes existing national regulations for DeFi and thus creates a uniform legal framework for providers and users [17].

Organizational Knowledge Creation. Knowledge is essential in creating a long-term competitive advantage for organizations [7, 30], so they need to streamline their resources and enhance internal expertise to ensure sustainability. Knowledge Management in organizations is crucial, as they generate expertise and skill through interactions with suppliers and customers, facilitating assimilation within [13, 42]. Combining external, explicit knowledge with unique internal can create new and exclusive expertness for organizations [56]. Knowledge creation mechanisms' effectiveness directly impacts the bank's human capital quality, positively affecting their structural and customer base [42]. Well-trained, educated, and skilled employees can better respond to customer inquiries and ensure providing satisfactory services [6]. The decisive factor is that companies can only create knowledge with the participation of individuals [10]. Employees are fundamental to developing knowledge, while organizations need to take action to articulate and disseminate the results in a targeted way [30]. On the one hand, organizational knowledge creation refers to the continuous process of providing and expanding the knowledge created by individuals and, on the other hand, to its synthesis and integration into the company's knowledge system [52]. This requires the establishment of appropriate structures within organizations.

Theoretical and empirical research focuses on various aspects and frameworks of knowledge management [12, 23, 29, 33, 52, 54]. One of the prominent approaches is the theory of dynamical organizational knowledge creation [30], which IS researcher are widely employing. The theoretical approach highlights the knowledge creation process as a spiral that ensures the dynamic further development of the knowledge base [30, 32]. From that, a customized SECI framework deals with the four phases of socialization, externalization, combination, and internalization resulting from the interplay of tacit and explicit knowledge [30, 32, 52]. In our subsequent research, we use the SECI framework

[30] as a base because, in contrast to other presented theories and frameworks, it deals explicitly with knowledge generation in organizations, corresponding to our problem of creating organizational resilience through knowledge enhancement.

E-learning is a valuable tool for knowledge management and can revolutionize how a workforce acquires the skills and knowledge necessary to adapt to change [55]. The focus is on learning as a cognitive process for retaining technology-enabled knowledge. Many organizations are beginning to realize that e-learning and its frameworks can be a powerful asset for knowledge management within the company [1, 2, 5, 21, 25, 49, 55]. In contrast to the further presented approaches, Aparicio et al. [4] developed an e-learning framework based on literature and comprehensively examined the components of systems. The focus is on the dimensions of people, technology, and services [4]. Its uniqueness stems from its lack of domain and its focus on technology as well as people, which aligns well with our organizational and IS perspective in this paper. Unlike the SECI framework [32], the focus is not primarily on the knowledge generation process but on the ecosystem and the interaction of the components of e-learning environments.

3 Research Design

We follow the design science research approach by Sonnenberg & vom Brocke [44], commonly used in IS research [22, 45], to design a DeFi e-learning platform to strengthen resilience. As seen in Fig. 1, each of the four activity phases (Identify problem, design, construct, and use) is followed by an evaluation phase in which the result of the previous stage is assessed [44]. A notable aspect of this method [44] is the evaluation before as well as after the instantiation of the artifact, known as ex-ante and ex-post evaluation. In the design phase (first half of the process), we elaborate on our DeFi e-learning framework. Afterward, this derived framework forms the basis for the subsequent development of the artifact, an e-learning platform known as the CryptoCompass. Accordingly, we instantiate the final artifact in the construction and use phase.

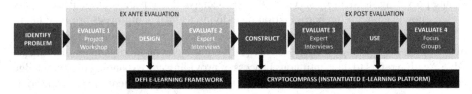

Fig. 1. Iterative Design Science Research approach by Sonnenberg & vom Brocke [44].

3.1 Activity Phases and Their Subsequent Assessments

For the phase **Identify Problem,** we conducted a structured literature review on DeFi. We evaluated our results in a workshop with practitioners and scientists. These results are the foundation for our *Introduction* Chapter, which briefly outlines the problem and the solution space. In the second phase, we focus on the **Design** of the DeFi e-learning framework as groundwork for the solution of the stated problem [44] evaluated through crypto and banking experts (n = 6). For that, our research team conducted in-depth semi-structured interviews and discussed the elements of the DeFi e-learning framework with the specialists. We instantiate a first draft of the CryptoCompass platform within the **Construction** phase [44]. The results achieved so far serve as decisive indicators for the prototype. Building on the previous results, particularly the framework, we derive the principal elements and the basic structure for the e-learning platform. Expert interviews evaluate this step (n = 4). Using the thinking-aloud method [43], users solved given tasks for exploring and learning on CryptoCompass. The refinement of the artifact incorporates the valuable insights generated through this process (Sect. 4.2). In addition, the research team analyzed several educational platforms in the crypto space for their technical implementation, such as Udemy[1] and BISON Academy[2]. Further, as the last activity phase, we **Use** our CryptoCompass artifact in an organizational setting with real people, system, and task [44]. The research team performed two methodically structured focus groups for this evaluation (n = 9).

3.2 Final Evaluation and Conclusion of the Research Process

To close the research process, **Evaluation 4** initiates a systematic evaluation based on a mixed-method approach [8] of our CryptoCompass platform to obtain a validated artifact instance in a naturalistic setting and demonstrate proof of its usefulness [44]. We have enriched our focus group of banking professionals with experts in e-learning design specific to the banking sector. This combination ensures in-depth knowledge and high-quality insights by intensive discussions about the platform through their heterogeneous perspectives. The participants worked with our CryptoCompass platform a few weeks in advance to familiarize themselves with the system and to be able to perform real tasks in a real setting, i.e., with the real system. At the start of the focus group evaluation, we presented the design process of CryptoCompass and highlighted the platform's features. As the participants were already familiar with the platform, the short introduction as an initial warm-up ensured that all participants had the same level of knowledge. The evaluation procedure comprised a quantitative survey and a qualitative open feedback discussion. With the quantitative evaluation part, the focus group participants responded to questions in a survey on a 5-point Likert scale. The statements were created based on the evaluation criteria [44] and presented in Sect. 5 of our paper. The participants' qualitative feedback and the consolidation of the results follow this procedure.

4 Design and Construction

Our research led to the development of a DeFi e-learning framework (Sect. 4.1), which we used to instantiate the CryptoCompass e-learning platform (Sect. 4.2) as our artifact.

---

[1] https://www.udemy.com.

[2] https://bisonapp.com/academy.

4.1 DeFi E-Learning Framework

Based on the dynamic organizational knowledge creation theory, we combine the SECI framework of Nonaka and Takeuchi [32] with the E-learning Framework by Aparicio et al. [4], both mentioned in the research background. While Aparicio's approach ensures the implementation of the central elements of e-learning platforms, SECI focuses on a knowledge spiral and iterative knowledge development within the organization [32]. Given the highly dynamic developments in the crypto asset environment as well as the lack of explicit and tacit knowledge in the banking sector, we see a combination as expedient. Figure 2 shows the final version of our framework, evaluated with practical insights from six experts (I1–I6). The following explanation details its components.

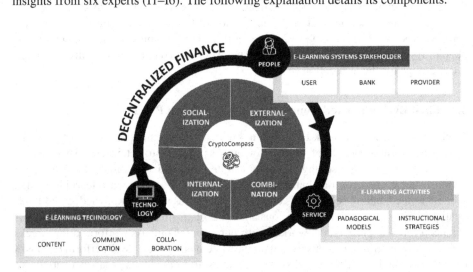

Fig. 2. DeFi E-Learning Framework for Banks.

Transferred Core Elements of E-Learning Framework:

(1) People. The stakeholders of an e-learning platform are crucial. Identifying and addressing the proper user group as well as examining personas [10, 26] and different experience levels are important (I2, I4, I5, I6). Further, the platform needs an infrastructure provider and content provider [4]. An external service provider may provide platform infrastructure or content for one or many banks. In contrast, one bank or a consortium can govern their platform infrastructure or content.

(2) Technology. The platform should publish content with a mix of multiple media types [3] and modularized content elements (I5). It must offer collaborative opportunities for reports from practice (I6) or asking an expert in video calls (I4, I6). A feasible knowledge assessment (I5) is necessary to determine the user's level of expertise [36, 37]. Integrating forums or social networks should enable user exchange [46] as part of communication and collaboration.

(3) Service. For enabling knowledge absorption, users' technical barriers and blockchain aversion must break down [48]. The focus must be on the benefit of the banking employees so they can see practical usefulness (I5, I6). The platform needs a reward system and additional information about news and fact checks (I2, I5). Users can participate, with flexibility in time and location, on the DeFi e-learning offer [4]. There is potential in developing a course with interactive (I3, I5) and gamified elements [36, 37, 41]. Further, it seems essential to foster the implementation of communities of practice (I6), as people share best approaches and collaborate with regular exchange [20].

Transferred Core Elements of the SECI Framework:
(1) Socialization. Central aspects are the exchange of experiences and observation [32]. Accordingly, it is about implicit knowledge. The physical and virtual environments are relevant in this context, as socialization does not take place exclusively on the e-learning platform but also in the direct working environment. The platform should, therefore, act as a supporting component and provide suitable elements that motivate bank employees to share their personal experiences and knowledge with others [10, 24]. This approach involves creating informal discussion groups for in-depth understanding to promote social interaction and tacit knowledge exchange (I2, I6). Discussion areas and virtual meetings tailored to the various roles of bank employees (e.g., IT specialists, consultants) are suitable for this purpose (I2, I5, I6). Nonaka and his co-authors consider socialization the most critical phase, as it addresses hidden or previously unextracted knowledge [7, 31]. Our results also show that tacit knowledge is critical to DeFi knowledge (I1, I3, I5).

(2) Externalization. To establish sustainable knowledge management, converting tacit knowledge into explicit knowledge is essential [32]. Opportunities should be created to encourage people to document their experiences in articles, best practice reports, myth-busters, and guidelines published on the platform and made available to others (I2, I4, I5). In doing so, we advise ensuring that third parties can understand the information without having experienced the observations or dialogues in socialization [10, 28].

(3) Combination. The focus is on explicit knowledge collected, organized, and synthesized [32]. Combining new knowledge with existing knowledge is promising, as well as incorporating information from outside the organization, such as legal requirements or market trends (I2, I3). We recommend transforming the resulting knowledge into targeted learning modules that provide a structured learning path (I3, I4) and modules that ensure a structured learning route (I3, I4). Our research indicates a need to establish different programs tailored to the varied knowledge levels of employees and their specific work areas [10, 26].

(4) Internalization. Conversion of explicit knowledge into practical skills and tacit knowledge [32]. The banks need to foster the learning-by-doing mindset in using crypto assets [10]. For this as motivation and incentive, they should provide reports from practice, tailored guides, and checklists for using the newly generated knowledge in daily work [10, 20]. Further, there is the need for simulations, e.g., how the use of various crypto assets changes users' portfolios (I2).

In order to provide practical as well as theoretical value, the core elements of the presented DeFi e-learning framework for banks were incorporated into the development of an e-learning platform.

4.2 CryptoCompass Platform

CryptoCompass is an e-learning platform developed for DeFi education. It aims to provide banking professionals with a comprehensive understanding of the crypto landscape, regardless of their prior knowledge. The following section presents the core elements of CryptoCompass as our artifact (Fig. 3).

Fig. 3. Course Overview on CryptoCompass.

The current version of our CryptoCompass aims to meet the expectations of bank employees in the German banking industry as key *e-learning system stakeholders* of the platform. Accordingly, the interface of the artifact is German. We host the CryptoCompass platform as a third-party instance (service provider) and enable bank employees to access the system. Our research project team conceptualizes the relevant content of the platform for the banking sector and implements it as a service.

Considering bank employees' different levels of knowledge about cryptocurrencies, the CryptoCompass contains integrated personas and a flexible structure to enable individual learning paths that adapt to the user's experience. These personas cater to different needs based on studies performed in this Construct phase. In addition, with the division into *beginner, advanced, and expert* levels, we take up a commonly known categorization in e-learning. As mentioned before, the exceptional aspect of the CryptoCompass platform is its flexibility and modularity. Unlike traditional educational structures, the learning path has no prescribed or fixed sequence. Learners can curate their educational journey based on their preferences, interests, and learning objectives. This addresses the *combination* phase by the SECI framework, as merging explicit knowledge from courses and content. The freedom allows individuals to create their personalized roadmap, selecting and arranging learning materials to suit their unique pace and depth of understanding. We derive this from our framework's *e-learning activities*. The introductory course covers basics like blockchain technology and DeFi, while the intermediate level delves into various crypto assets, regulatory frameworks, societal impact, and diverse services. The expert course is for mastering complex financial instruments related to crypto assets, mainly focusing on custody fundamentals and regulatory intricacies.

Per our framework element *technology*, the platform integrates interactive and gami-fication elements, such as quizzes and animated videos. These appealing functions facil-itate active learning and keep the learning process entertaining. Quizzes and learning queries provide immediate feedback, and supporting video sequences simplify com-plex concepts. The gamified components, including rewards and milestones for course completions, serve as motivational tools, incentivizing users to actively engage with the learning material [55]. Further, we implemented *socialization* initial zoom sessions on the first experiences with DeFi or crypto assets for beginners. CryptoCompass features practical use and offers reports, checklists, and guidelines for integrating DeFi into daily work. This addresses the *knowledge spiral* that we based our concept on due to the dynamic theory of organizational knowledge creation. For *externalization* and *inter-nalization*, we require experienced users to convert their tacit knowledge into explicit documented knowledge. Additionally, we encourage CryptoCompass users to learn by doing. Dynamic elements, live-tickers and newsfeeds are integrated into the platform to ensure a continuous flow of learning and a permanent return to the e-learning platform.

5 Final Evaluation

We perform a mixed-methods approach for the concluding evaluation (Phase **Evaluation 4**). The quantitative evaluation aimed to determine whether our artifact suits the problem space and justifies the design. We based the criteria for the evaluation on Sonnenberg & vom Brocke [44], who list applicability of the artifact, generality, efficiency, impact on the environment of the artifact and the user, and internal and external consistency as evaluation criteria.

Quantitative Feedback. As part of the final evaluation, we asked the experts to dis-cuss and reflect on the evaluation criteria developed [44] and to compare the website with similar websites that offer comparable services or information. We invited them to discuss their experiences. Our study confirms that banking employees and e-learning experts find CryptoCompass applicable, with an agreement score of approximately 90%. It is essential to note the impact of CryptoCompass and the underlying framework on the environment and users, as our results show a high agreement of 85%. Further, the partic-ipants also confirmed the proposed solution's generality and efficiency (70%). Finally, it is crucial to maintain both internal and external consistency on the platform.

Qualitative Feedback. Afterwards, we invited the participants to discuss their experi-ences and impressions they noticed during use. Also, to compare CryptoCompass with similar websites that offer similar services or information. Based on these insights, we evaluate the structure and user-friendliness of the website as well as receive possible recommendations for improvement.

In the following, we summarize only the key elements the participants discussed in detail in the interviews. The focus group noted that the key elements of our platform, which demonstrates different content through various media, including text, pictures, videos, and audio, are practical (F1, F2). This aligns with the *technology* field in our framework (Sect. 4.1) derived by integrating the approach from Aparicio et al. [4]. The integration of interactive elements such as quizzes motivated the users and was rated positively by the experts (F1). They also found the content, which we elaborated and demonstrated in alignment with our framework prototypically, easy to understand and appreciated the transparent presentation of scientific content generation and well-structured content display design (F2). The entry-level test allowed the experts to find the course that best complements their existing knowledge (F2). We recognized positive feedback on the beginner, advanced, and expert user level (F1, F2).

Finally, the experts also addressed possible suggestions for improvement. Banks face diverse challenges that require strategic approaches to handle user concerns effectively. These relate, for example, to possible misinformation and misadvise that could result from operating our platform (F2). We integrate scientific sources and expert opinions into our platform to control this uncertainty. For the bank's employees to identify more with the platform and illustrate the corporate as well as practical relevance, we assume adding interviews with supervisors from the institute using the platform (F1, F2). This will make the content more reliable for the users. Moreover, the experts mentioned the extension of the content coverage on the platform, e.g., digital securities (F1). This should be made available in the future as it could be particularly interesting for attracting new users to our platform and providing existing stakeholders with comprehensive training in digital assets. Besides, due to the different levels of knowledge of the users, we suggest creating a platform that can meet users' needs regardless of their status of experience in the field of DeFi. The aim is to work out the personas more intensively and develop even more fine-grained modularity of the learning plan (F1, F2). There has also emerged a desire to promote social exchange between specialist users in the banking industry (e.g., bank advisors and IT specialists) (F2).

Overall, the participants from the area of bank employees mentioned clearly that there is no comparable approach to date and that introducing such a platform in their company seems sensible.

6 Discussion

Our research work shows an opportunity to strengthen banks' organizational resilience through the expansion of their knowledge base [16] (Fig. 4). The combination of the e-learning framework [4] and SECI framework ensures sustainable knowledge creation and learning for the whole organization with a platform. The elaborated e-learning framework for crypto assets in banking and our platform address the knowledge of individual bank employees and the integration into the banking organization. Our approach enhances the organizational resilience of banks by targeting adaptation, coping, and anticipation.

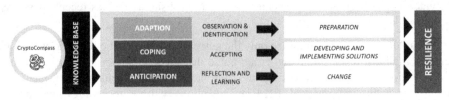

Fig. 4. Knowledge Base As Key Driver For Organizational Resilience By Duchek [16].

What became apparent during the discussions in the focus groups is that providers could be higher-level authorities such as the European Central Bank, banking associations, individual banks, or external service providers in the banking sector (F2). Hosting does not necessarily have to be delivered by a third-party provider or bank. However, it is essential to clarify who is responsible for the content in both conceptualization and execution. An external service provider may supply content for one or many banks, while one or a consortium can govern their content themselves. It is essential to weigh up the advantages and disadvantages of each case. With an overarching concept, banks could benefit from external interaction and expand their in-house knowledge base. As there has been a need for more experts and high-quality knowledge in the DeFi sector so far, such an approach could quickly provide a more extensive knowledge base.

7 Conclusion

In this research paper, we investigated the design of a DeFi e-learning platform for bank institutes to strengthen organizational resilience. We utilized the SECI framework and dynamic knowledge generation theory as a foundation for our research, as well as the e-learning framework of Aparicio et al. [4]. With a Design Science Research approach by Sonnenberg & vom Brocke [44], we derived a DeFi e-learning framework. The main elements are, on the one hand, the stakeholder, the underlying technology, and e-learning activities, and on the other, the socialization, externalization, combination, and internalization to ensure a dynamic spiral of knowledge. As an artifact, we instantiated the CryptoCompass e-learning platform adjusted for a pioneering German bank. In the last phase, we enrolled CryptoCompass in an organizational environment and evaluated the final platform with experts in banking and e-learning.

Limitations and Further Research. As with most studies, our research has limitations due to its methodology. Furthermore, the results apply to German banks, as we cooperated with a practice partner to gain profound knowledge and expert access. In order to examine a generalization of the results, an extension of the research project to an extended group of experts and an enlargement to other nationalities is being sought. It also makes sense to substantiate the results further and develop an empirical study with statistical data collection and measurements to substantiate the framework's validity. Accordingly, acceptance studies are of interest as further research. Another approach would be to analyze the impact on the quality of banking advice for digital assets using the developed framework and platform and to identify further factors that influence the advisory outcome. This would also enable drawing conclusions about the developed framework and expanding research concerning the current limitations. In the case of providing such a platform as a third-party provider, we see the need to continue research in IT security and data protection for the framework and platform. This is particularly important as our target group is financial institutions and banking professionals, where high safety measures must be guaranteed.

Implications. Our solution differs from other approaches by focusing specifically on building knowledge in the DeFi area to deliberately address financial institutions' resilience and prepare them for future streams from the crypto area. Our research extends the existing knowledge bases in Design Science, organizational resilience, knowledge management in banking, as well as crypto assets and DeFi in financial institutions. In the area of practical implications, we offer an initial approach to close the knowledge gaps concerning crypto assets in financial institutes in order to strengthen banks. Our results contribute to the IS research field and address the substantial developments in the financial sector that have arisen from blockchain technology.

Acknowledgements. This work has been developed in the project InKryBa and is partly funded by the DZ-Bank-Stiftung under grant number FRFMM-788/2022. The authors are responsible for the content of this publication.

References

1. Abbas, Z., Umer, M., Odeh, M., McClatchey, R., Ali, A., Farooq, A.: A semantic grid-based e-learning framework (self). In: CCGrid 2005, vol. 1, pp. 11–18. IEEE (2005)
2. Alhawiti, M.M., Abdelhamid, Y.: A personalized e-learning framework. J. Educ. e-Learn. Res. **4**(1), 15–21 (2017)
3. Alomari, H.W., Ramasamy, V., Kiper, J.D., Potvin, G.: A user interface (ui) and user experience (ux) evaluation framework for cyberlearning environments in computer science and software engineering education. Heliyon **6**, e03917 (2020)
4. Aparicio, M., Bação, F., Oliveira, T.: An e-learning theoretical framework. J. Educ. Technol. Syst. **19**(1), 292–307 (2016)
5. Bodea, C.N., Mogoş, R.I., Dascălu, M.I., Purnuş, A., Ciobotar, N.G.: Simulationbased e-learning framework for entrepreneurship education and training. Amfiteatru Econ. J. **17**(38), 10–24 (2015)
6. Bontis, N.: Assessing knowledge assets: a review of the models used to measure intellectual capital. Int. J. Manag. Rev. **3**(1), 41–60 (2001)
7. Bratianu, C., Orzea, I.: Organizational knowledge creation. Manag. Mark. **5**(3), 41 (2010)
8. Bryman, A.: Integrating quantitative and qualitative research: how is it done? Qual. Res. **6**(1), 97–113 (2006)
9. Chalmers, D., Fisch, C., Matthews, R., Quinn, W., Recker, J.: Beyond the bubble: Will nfts and digital proof of ownership empower creative industry entrepreneurs? J. Bus. Ventur. Insights **17**, e00309 (2022)
10. Chang, V., Baudier, P., Zhang, H., Xu, Q., Zhang, J., Arami, M.: How blockchain can impact financial services – the overview, challenges and recommendations from expert interviewees. Technol. Forecast. Soc. Chang. **158**, 120166 (2020)
11. Chen, Y., Bellavitis, C.: Blockchain disruption and decentralized finance: the rise of decentralized business models. J. Bus. Ventur. Insights **13**, e00151 (2020)
12. Choo, C.: The knowing organization: How organizations use information to construct meaning, create knowledge and make decisions. Int. J. Inf. Manage. **16**, 329–340 (1996)
13. Cohen, W.M., Levinthal, D.A.: Absorptive capacity: a new perspective on learning and innovation. Adm. Sci. Q. **35**(1), 128–152 (1990)
14. Cooper, C.L., Liu, Y., Tarba, S.Y.: Resilience, HRM practices and impact on organizational performance and employee well-being: International journal of human resource management 2015 special issue (2014)
15. Coutu, D.L.: How resilience works. Harv. Bus. Rev. **80**(5), 46–56 (2002)
16. Duchek, S.: Organizational resilience: a capability-based conceptualization. Bus. Res. **13**, 215–246 (2020)

17. Ferreira, A., Sandner, P.: Eu search for regulatory answers to crypto assets and their place in the financial markets' infrastructure. Comput. Law Secur. Rev. **43**, 105632 (2021)

18. Garfield, M.: Proposing a knowledge management system (KMS) architecture to promote knowledge sharing among employees. In: ECIS 2014, pp. 1–13 (2014)

19. Gramlich, V., Guggenberger, T., Principato, M., Schellinger, B., Urbach, N.: A multivocal literature review of decentralized finance: current knowledge and future research avenues. Electron. Markets **33**(11) (2023)

20. Hund, A., Holotiuk, F., Wagner, H.T., Beimborn, D.: Knowledge management in the digital era: how digital innovation labs facilitate knowledge recombination. In: ECIS 2019 (2019)

21. Khan, B.H.: A framework for e-learning. LTI Magazine (2001)

22. Klinker, K., Wiesche, M., Krcmar, H.: Digital transformation in health care: augmented reality for hands-free service innovation. Inf. Syst. Front. **22**, 1419–1431 (2020)

23. Leonard, D.: Wellsprings of knowledge: building and sustaining the sources of innovation. J. Organ. Beh. **17**, 197–199 (1996)

24. Li, F., Lu, H., Hou, M., Cui, K., Darbandi, M.: Customer satisfaction with bank services: the role of cloud services, security, e-learning and service quality. Tech. Soc. **64**, 101487 (2021)

25. Mccombs, B.L., Vakili, D.: A learner-centered framework for e-learning. Teach. Coll. Rec. **107**(8), 1582–1600 (2005)

26. Miaskiewicz, T., Kozar, K.A.: Personas and user-centered design: how can personas benefit product design processes? Des. Stud. **32**(5), 417–430 (2011)

27. Min, H.: Blockchain technology for enhancing supply chain resilience. Bus. Horiz. **62**(1), 35–45 (2019)

28. Mishra, R., Singh, R.K., Kumar, S., Mangla, S.K., Kumar, V.: Critical success factors of blockchain technology adoption for sustainable and resilient operations in the banking industry during an uncertain business environment. Electron. Commer. Res. 1–35 (2023)

29. Misra, D., Hariharan, R., Khaneja, M.: E-knowledge management framework for government organizations. Inf. Syst. Manag. **20**(2), 38–48 (2003)

30. Nonaka, I.: A dynamic theory of organizational knowledge creation. Organ. Sci. **5**(1), 14–37 (1994)

31. Nonaka, I., Takeuchi, H.: Organizational knowledge creation. Creative Manage. 64–82 (2001)

32. Nonaka, I., Toyama, R., Konno, N.: Seci, ba and leadership: a unified model of dynamic knowledge creation. Long Range Plan. **33**(1), 5–34 (2000)

33. Petrash, G.: Dow's journey to a knowledge value management culture. Eur. Manag. J. **14**(4), 365–373 (1996)

34. Piñeiro-Chousa, J., López-Cabarcos, M.Á., Sevic, A., González-López, I.: A preliminary assessment of the performance of defi cryptocurrencies in relation to other financial assets, volatility, and user-generated content. Technol. Forecast. Soc. Chang. **181**, 121740 (2022)

35. Qin, K., Zhou, L., Afonin, Y., Lazzaretti, L., Gervais, A.: Cefi vs. defi – comparing centralized to decentralized finance. arXiv:2106.08157v2 (2021)

36. Rowland, C.A.: The effect of testing versus restudy on retention: a meta-analytic review of the testing effect. Psychol. Bull. **140**(6), 1432 (2014)

37. Sanchez, D.R., Langer, M., Kaur, R.: Gamification in the classroom: examining the impact of gamified quizzes on student learning. Comput. Educ. **144**, 103666 (2020)

38. Schär, F.: Decentralized finance: on blockchain-and smart contract-based financial markets. FRB of St. Louis Review, pp. 153–174 (2021)

39. Schwiderowski, J., Pedersen, A.B., Beck, R.: Crypto tokens and token systems. Inf. Syst. Front. **26**, 319–332 (2023)

40. Schwiderowski, J., Pedersen, A.B., Jensen, J.K., Beck, R.: Value creation and capture in decentralized finance markets: non-fungible tokens as a class of digital assets. Electron. Markets **33**(45) (2023)

41. Seaborn, K., Fels, D.I.: Gamification in theory and action: a survey. Int. J. Hum. Comput. Stud. **74**, 14–31 (2015)
42. Shih, K.H., Chang, C.J., Lin, B.: Assessing knowledge creation and intellectual capital in banking industry. J. Intellect. Cap. **11**(1), 74–89 (2010)
43. van Someren, M.W., Barnard, Y.F., Sandberg, J.J.: The Think Aloud Method: A Practical Guide to Modelling Cognitive Processes. Academic Press, London (1994)
44. Sonnenberg, C., vom Brocke, J.: Evaluations in the science of the artificial – reconsidering the build-evaluate pattern in design science research. In: Peffers, K., Rothenberger, M., Kuechler, B. (eds.) DESRIST 2012. LNCS, vol. 7286, pp. 381–397. Springer, Heidelberg (2012). https://doi.org/10.1007/978-3-642-29863-9_28
45. Sturm, B., Sunyaev, A.: Design principles for systematic search systems: a holistic synthesis of a rigorous multi-cycle design science research journey. Bus. Inf. Syst. Eng. **61**(1), 91–111 (2019)
46. Sun, Z., Lin, C.H., Wu, M., Zhou, J., Luo, L.: A tale of two communication tools: discussion-forum and mobile instant-messaging apps in collaborative learning. Br. J. Edu. Technol. **49**(2), 248–261 (2018)
47. Thakor, A.V.: Fintech and banking: what do we know? J. Finan. Intermediation **41**, 100833 (2020)
48. Upadhyay, N.: Demystifying blockchain: a critical analysis of challenges, applications and opportunities. Int. J. Inf. Manage. **54**, 102120 (2020)
49. Vandenhouten, C., Gallagher-Lepak, S., Reilly, J., Ralston-Berg, P.: Collaboration in e-learning: a study using the flexible e-learning framework. Online Learn. **18**(3), 1–14 (2014)
50. Vaughan, K., MacVicar, A.: Employees' pre-implementation attitudes and perceptions to e-learning: a banking case study analysis. J. Eur. Ind. Train. **28**(5), 400–413 (2004)
51. Vogus, T.J., Sutcliffe, K.M.: Organizational resilience: towards a theory and research agenda. In: 2007 IEEE ICMC, Montréal, pp. 3418–3422. IEEE (2007)
52. Von Krogh, G., Nonaka, I., Rechsteiner, L.: Leadership in organizational knowledge creation: a review and framework. J. Manage. Stud. **49**(1), 240–277 (2012)
53. Voskobojnikov, A., Wiese, O., Koushki, M.M., Roth, V., Beznosov, K.: The u in crypto stands for usable: an empirical study of user experience with mobile cryptocurrency wallets, pp. 1–14. ACM (2021)
54. Wiig, K.M.: Knowledge Management Foundations: Thinking About Thinking-How People and Organizations Represent, Create, and Use Knowledge. Schema Press, Limited (1994)
55. Wild, R.H., Griggs, K.A., Downing, T.: A framework for e-learning as a tool for knowledge management. Ind. Manag. Data Syst. **102**(7), 371–380 (2002)
56. Zack, M.H.: Developing a knowledge strategy. Calif. Manage. Rev. **41**(3), 125–145 (1999)

Emerging Topics in DSR

Design Principles for Collaborative Generative AI Systems in Software Development

Johannes Chen[✉][iD] and Jan Zacharias[iD]

Chair of Information Systems and Information Management,
Goethe University Frankfurt, Frankfurt, Germany
`jchen@wiwi.uni-frankfurt.de`

Abstract. Generative artificial intelligence (GAI) has the potential to transform software development practices with prior research indicating significant overall enhancements in developers' productivity. However, there exists a lack of design knowledge for organization-specific GAI systems to assist software development. To bridge this research gap, we derive a design framework for collaborative GAI systems in software development following design science research. Specifically, we conducted eight interviews with practitioners and reviewed extant literature to formulate design requirements and design principles. In our analysis of the literature and our qualitative data, we identify problems surrounding usability, data privacy, hallucination and transparency. To address these problems, we propose GAI system designs that enable user-centricity, data protection, quality control and communication. Our findings contribute valuable design knowledge to the field of generative AI and organizational software development practices.

Keywords: Generative Artificial Intelligence · Large Language Models · Programming Assistant · Software Development · Design Science Research

1 Introduction

Since the launch of OpenAI's chatbot ChatGPT, generative artificial intelligence (AI), and in particular, large language models (LLM)[1], have gained increased attention from the public [7]. Generative AI (GAI) has the potential to fully transform the labor market. Recent research from OpenAI suggests that GAI could affect at least 10% of tasks from approximately 80% of the U.S. workforce, and at least 50% of tasks from 19% of workers. Interestingly, OpenAI finds the

---

[1] LLMs represent a type of GAI models specifically designed to understand, generate, and engage with human language [39]. While the majority of GAI systems that we refer to throughout our paper are based on LLMs, we will use the term GAI for consistency.

M. Mandviwalla et al. (Eds.): DESRIST 2024, LNCS 14621, pp. 341–354, 2024.
https://doi.org/10.1007/978-3-031-61175-9_23

strongest impact on programming tasks [13]. Indeed, developers in all organizations could be on the verge of a significant paradigm shift. Prior research from Microsoft and GitHub has demonstrated that their GAI-based programming assistant Copilot can significantly increase the productivity of software developers [28]. Programming assistants such as Copilot can aid developers in various ways, ranging from routine tasks like synthesizing new code, optimizing existing code, debugging, and even handling documentation [15]. From an organizational perspective, this workflow enhancement could reduce costs as the AI frees up developers' time in conceptualizing code and also aids in error correction.

To fully capitalize on the promised productivity gains of GAI, a prevailing organizational challenge is that a complex model alone is not sufficient for most users. In order to enable software developers to effectively integrate GAI into their workflow, the underlying model must be embedded in a comprehensive system, including relevant databases, a technical infrastructure and an intuitive user interface [2,15]. While most currently established programming assistant systems are general-purpose tools, there is a growing importance of domain- and organization-specific systems. These systems offer tailored solutions fine-tuned to the specific needs and challenges of various use cases and organizations [15]. For instance, a GAI-based programming assistant designed for the gaming industry could understand and generate code, specific to game development platforms. In contrast, an assistant designed for the cybersecurity field might be adept at identifying and suggesting fixes for security vulnerabilities.

However, designing domain- and organization-specific GAI-based programming assistants presents numerous challenges. Organizations must not only tailor these systems to their internal requirements and users but also ensure user-friendliness, effectiveness and data protection [24,29]. In response to these challenges, we build upon design science research (DSR) [18] to formulate design principles for collaborative GAI systems in software development, following the call for research by Feuerriegel et al. [15] and a host of other DSR projects (e.g., [8,38]). The main motivation of our research is to provide organizations with the knowledge to effectively harness the potential of GAI systems, ultimately enhancing their software development processes. Our paper proposes a design framework intended to guide the development and implementation of GAI systems across diverse organizational settings. Our design principles are specifically intended for organizations that aim to implement organization-specific GAI systems, providing a detailed framework that addresses the unique challenges and opportunities within their specific organizational context. To achieve this goal, we reviewed prior literature and conducted eight interviews with practitioners in the field of software development, identifying collaboration issues between GAI systems and users. Subsequently, we developed a design framework consisting of design requirements and design principles. By doing so, we make important contributions to both research and practice. On the one hand, we contribute to ongoing research on generative AI and design science research with design knowledge to instantiate a generative AI system for software development. On the other hand, practitioners can utilize the design knowledge to instantiate their own organization-specific GAI system.

The remainder of our paper is as follows. In Sect. 2, we summarize relevant background literature on generative AI and programming assistants. Section 3 describes our methodology based on DSR and gives an overview of our interviewees. Section 4 presents results of our design framework. Section 5 concludes our paper with a discussion of our findings.

2   Background

2.1   Generative Artificial Intelligence

Generative AI represents a category of AI capable of generating content in various forms, such as text, images, audio, video, and more [34,35]. Unlike discriminative AI, which focuses on modeling relationships between input features and target labels to learn effective decision boundaries [37], GAI aims to infer high-dimensional distributions based on input data [2]. While discriminative AI, as used in tasks like image classification or spam detection, deals with specific predictions, GAI goes one step further by creating new instances based on the learned patterns in the data [2].

GAI has found widespread attention and adoption in the form of chatbot Chat-GPT. The success of this adoption can be attributed not only to the underlying GAI model but also to the user-friendly system built around it, including the intuitive user interface and seamless web-based access [22]. Against this background, Feuerriegel et al. [15] differentiate three different layers in their conceptual model of GAI: the model-, system-, and application layer. First, the model layer refers to the engine of each GAI system: the machine learning architecture—usually a deep neural network [17]—responsible for generating data instances. Second, the system layer comprises the entire infrastructure needed to operate and support the model's functionality. This includes not only the GAI model(s), but also the integration in an organization's technological ecosystem, data processing, and user interface. Finally, the application layer represents the practical use case addressed by the GAI system. Thus, this layer translates technically oriented GAI systems into socio-technical systems that tackle organizational problems.

To engage with GAI systems, users employ a technique called prompting, allowing interactions through natural language [2]. This method enables users to leverage zero-, one-, and few-shot learning. Zero-shot learning involves prompts without specific examples, while one-shot learning improves GAI outputs by providing one example, and few-shot learning involves inputting multiple examples [10].

2.2   Programming Assistants

Software development is a multifaceted process encompassing numerous tasks, such as requirements engineering, conceptualization, coding, verification, and documentation [6]. There have been several proposals on how programming assistants could contribute to software development processes in the past. For instance, to provide guidance in the various stages of software development, Ruhe [32] proposed a paradigm for software engineering decision support systems (SEDSS). SEDSS primarily works by suggesting, evaluating and prioritizing solution alternatives [32]. Additionally, Huff and Lesser [20] introduced a paradigm for plan-based intelligent assistants to support software development processes. This paradigm comprises a sequence of actions, the monitoring of the development process, a context for goals and an assessment of alternatives [20].

Recent advances in deep learning, particularly in the development of GAI, represent a pivotal moment in the capabilities of programming assistants. GAI, with its capacity to process and generate human-like text and code, has opened up new possibilities to assist developers in more sophisticated and context-aware ways. Unlike traditional rule-based systems, GAI can understand the requirements and context of a software development task and generate entire blocks of code [27].

One prominent example of a GAI-based programming assistant is GitHub Copilot. Copilot offers real-time suggestions, proposing a line of code or entire code blocks, for example [9]. By analyzing the context of existing code, it provides suggestions that are contextually relevant to a developer's ongoing task. In addition to pre-trained GAI assistants designed for general use, there is an increasing number of organizations that develop specialized GAI-based programming assistants using their own proprietary code base [24]. This trend underscores the increasing demand for more customized solutions.

3   Methodology

We follow the design science approach of Kuechler and Vaishnavi to formulate design principles for collaborative GAI systems, intended for utilization in software development [23]. In the field of DSR, design principles encompass the capabilities of an artifact to meet its design requirements, providing guidance for both researchers and practitioners throughout the design process [3,25]. To formulate design principles, Kuechler and Vaishnavi [23] propose an awareness of problem and a suggestion phase. During the awareness of problem phase, researchers can conduct literature reviews and interviews with practitioners to identify the problems within the domain that need to be addressed. In the suggestion phase, researchers derive design requirements based on the identified problems to formulate design principles, which are grounded in the existing literature and the expertise of the interviewed practitioners.

To gain a comprehensive understanding of practical needs, we conducted semi-structured interviews with eight practitioners, who work in different roles within the software development field (see Table 1). Conducting interviews and analyzing its content for insights is particularly suited for studying emerging topics [1], such as our endeavor to generate design knowledge for GAI systems in software development.

In our interviews, we followed a semi-structured protocol. We asked practitioners about their organization's utilization of GAI systems (if applicable),

Table 1. Details of interviewed practitioners

ID	Job	Years of professional coding experience
I1	Sales Consultant	10
I2	IT Consultant	5
I3	Software Engineer	10
I4	Machine Learning Engineer	2
I5	Backend Developer	5
I6	Software Engineer	4.5
I7	Senior Manager	20
I8	Software Engineer	2

their perceived challenges associated with the effective use of GAI systems, and solicit improvement suggestions, among other questionnaire items.

For the qualitative analysis of our interview sample, we created recordings and transcripts to investigate general themes of the interviews via conventional content analysis [19]. Conventional content analysis is particularly suited for explorative analyses of qualitative data, i.e., the development of new insights without having pre-conceived ideas in mind [19]. We engaged in coding transcripts and interpreting codes independently to capture problems and suggestions. Subsequently, we discussed our results until we reached a consensus within the team. Following an iterative process, we repeated this process until we found satisfactory convergence in the interpretations of problems and suggestions. This approach allowed us to systematically derive our design framework.

4   Design Framework for Collaborative Generative AI Systems in Software Development

4.1   Awareness of Problem

While the introduction of GAI systems in software development promises productivity gains [28], there are several problems associated with current GAI systems. Drawing from our review of the literature and interviews, we identify four major problem areas, including usability issues, data privacy issues, hallucination, and insufficient transparency (see Fig. 1). We will describe these problems in more detail in the following.

Usability Issues. GAI tools such as ChatGPT can carry out a wide variety of tasks even in software development alone, ranging from writing code for Python scripts to producing tests in Java programming language. However, there are still some people hesitant to adopt such tools due to usability issues. Specifically, several interviewees expressed their concern that the introduction of GAI systems may interfere with their workflow (I2, I3, I5, I7) as highlighted by I7 and I3.

"It is very important that the introduction of LLMs does not interrupt your workflow. Instead, they should support you." (I7)

"I am not sure to what extent an autocomplete or a quasi suggestion when typing helps or just distracts at this point." (I3)

On the one hand, some GAI systems such as ChatGPT require users to switch between different applications when they use it together with an integrated development environment (IDE). On the other hand, other systems, such as GitHub Copilot, are only integrated into specific IDEs. Additionally, in a comprehensive survey of software developers, Liang et al. [24] discovered that 26% of the developers face challenges in controlling the programming assistant to generate code they deem as useful, 23% find the code suggestions distracting, and 22% find it difficult to express their requirements to the tool through natural language. Overall, these factors hinder the effective use of the system (P1).

Data Privacy Issues. A significant organizational concern highlighted by multiple interviewees is that sensitive information in their code, utilized within a GAI system, may raise data privacy issues (I1, I2, I3, I4, I6, I8). When organizations use GAI systems based on models from a third-party API, the sensitive code could be exposed to the third-party provider. Thus, sensitive data such as IP addresses, login credentials or certain characteristics of individuals could leak to other people (I1, I2, I3). For instance, when sensitive code is included in a few-shot learning task as part of a prompt, there is a risk that it could be repurposed as training data. This scenario potentially poses a threat to the privacy of individuals whose data is integrated into the training set, as it could lead to the inadvertent replication of their information among users from other organizations. This issue is best highlighted by the following quote from interviewee I1:

"[...] Where I have to be careful, will customer data be lost, in the worst case sensitive data? Or am I just leaking company knowledge to the outside world? I think that is a very big challenge from a company's point of view." (I1)

Thus, it is crucial to mitigate risks related to data privacy (P2).

Hallucination. GAI systems providing code suggestions are highly dependent on their training data. The data is often based on public code repositories such as GitHub or user responses based on websites such as StackOverflow [39]. Over time, however, many libraries will be updated or completely new ones will be created. In this case, the syntax or functionality of certain methods may be changed or new methods may be introduced. Because GAI relies on probablistic algorithms to generate the most probable outputs, they will not necessarily output the correct response [15]. As users continue to rely on outdated data (I1, I4, I7), the answers provided by GAI systems may therefore not yield the most effective solution, or worse, may be inaccurate.

"An LLM can spit out incredible amounts of code incredibly quickly, and the big question is, is that code correct? Keywords here are code quality and clean code." (I3)

Thus, a fundamental challenge with GAI systems' outputs is that they are prone to hallucinations, i.e., they may produce incorrect outputs (P3) (I2, I3, I4, I5, I6, I8) [2,15].

Insufficient Transparency. Due to the black box nature of AI, it is hard for users to understand how GAI systems arrive at certain suggestions [15,30]. In the case of software development, this characteristic can become problematic, especially when users have to explain to other stakeholders, such as colleagues or auditors, why they wrote certain code through the help of GAI systems. For instance, when deciding between two different methods, explaining the preference for one method may become necessary. Moreover, software development extends beyond the mere creation of code, requiring comprehensive documentation to meet organizational needs, and adhere to regulatory requirements (I2, I7). This becomes particularly crucial in highly sensitive domains like banking or healthcare, where the code is subject to the scrutiny of auditors to comply with regulations, as highlighted by I7.

> "And what is also important is that these tools can generate documentation for you. Software development consists not only of code, but also documentation, e.g., in the regulatory area of a bank." (I7)

Thus, a lack of transparency for users as well as other stakeholders, such as organization and regulators, is an important problem to address (P4).

4.2   Suggestion

To address the identified problem (P) areas, we suggest a design framework consisting of design requirements (DR) and design principles (DP). Based on our literature review and interviews with practitioners, we derive the following four design requirements: user-centricity, data protection, quality control and communication. Based on these design requirements, we formulate eleven design principles, which we outline in more detail in the following (see Fig. 1).

User-Centricity. To assist users in their day-to-day workflow and boost system adoption, GAI systems should be user-centric (DR1). Putting the users into the center ensures that they are more likely to adopt and use the system [26]. While autocomplete, as used by most current programming assistants, is helpful, it is limited in addressing specific needs of individual developers. A user interface that allows conversational prompting is essential, as it enables developers to communicate their unique requirements and discuss alternative solutions more effectively [31], enhancing the overall utility of the programming assistant (DP1).

> "An explicit prompt to generate something specific at a certain point, be it user stories, text, review, or anything else, is more helpful than starting to type my function in the editor and suddenly getting random suggestions which, as we know from LLMs, sometimes don't even match and then end up being more of a distraction." (I3)

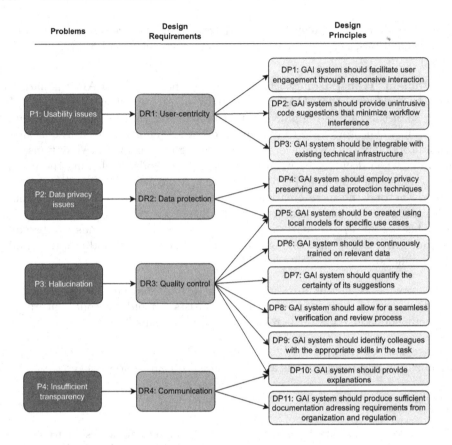

Fig. 1. Overview of problems, design requirements and design principles

To avoid any workflow interference, personalizing the system to each individual user can further reduce frictions between user and system. Specifically, learning the programming behavior of the user and suggesting code only when the system deems it necessary, the system may ensure optimized support for each user over time (DP2). Moreover, as each team within an organization is likely to use a different set of tools, GAI systems should be integrated into the existing technical infrastructure, e.g., IDEs, version control systems or database management systems (DP3) (I1, I3, I4, I5). This integration allows complementaries to exist between the different tools and may potentially improve user experience.

Data Protection. To deal with data privacy issues surrounding the use of GAI systems, data protection measures should be employed (DR2). Consequently, GAI systems should employ privacy preserving techniques to ensure that sensitive information does not leak to users from other organizations (DP4). Examples include differential privacy [33], which refers to adding controlled noise to the sensitive training data ensuring that the model does not encode any sensitive information [33,36], or anonymization of sensitive data [29]. When accessing

APIs from third-party providers, users should manage their own infrastructure, utilizing local models on private servers to ensure data protection (DP5) (I2). This approach aims to prevent the exposure of prompts containing sensitive code to a greater user base.

> "If I don't run this tool on an internal server, I have a lot of difficulties with security and data integrity." (I2)

Ultimately, these measures could potentially address many organizational concerns regarding the use of sensitive code, but also data protection regulations, such as the General Data Protection Regulation (GDPR) of the European Union [14].

Quality Control. Following the fundamental problem of hallucinations (P3), GAI systems used in software development should employ several strategies to ensure overall quality (DR3). Specifically, to enable specificity in the systems' outputs and reduce hallucinations, the system should be based on local model(s) that are fine-tuned to specific use cases (DP5) (I5, I6).

> "[...] I don't think there should be a general language model or you shouldn't use something like that, but something really customized instead." (I5)

> "We will most likely have multiple minor models that are strictly focused on one single thing." (I6)

For instance, a GAI system used for software development in Python should also be fine-tuned to Python-related data. Relatedly, recent literature suggests that GAI systems could incorporate real-time information retrieval to recognize, e.g., updated and novel libraries [15]. To capitalize on this information, GAI systems should be continuously trained on relevant data (DP6) [15]. Furthermore, organizations should establish additional quality control mechanisms, such as periodic model fine-tuning on the newest available training data, to ensure correctness and relevance of model outputs. Prior literature has shown the benefits of incorporating a certainty score to guide decision-makers in comparing their own knowledge with the AI's output [16]. Transferring this feature to our context, GAI systems should highlight outputs with low certainty, allowing users to find areas that may require further scrutiny (DP7). In general, several interviewees find that the system should enable user verification and review processes to ensure correct code (I2, I3, I5, I6, I7, I8) (DP8). This need is highlighted by I3.

> "Topics, such as the four eyes principle in code reviews to ensure code quality will continue to be a factor. You can still argue about whether the four eyes are the two eyes of the developer or the two eyes of an LLM." (I3)

Furthermore, GAI systems can act as matchmaker, fostering collaboration between differently skilled developers: When developers realize that they do not have the necessary expertise to write certain code on their own, but recognize that the GAI system's suggestions are incorrect, the system may compare the code in question with the organization-specific code repository in order to identify colleagues who have worked on similar code or have expertise in the relevant domain (DP9) (I5).

Communication. To improve collaboration with users and other stakeholders from the organization and regulation, GAI systems should incorporate functionalities to enhance communication with these groups of people (DR4). Specifically, GAI systems should explain why certain code and documentation suggestions were made. Here, the field of explainable AI can offer guidance, as it offers methods to create explanations on what factors affected the AI's output [4,5]. GAI systems that are able to explain why they suggest certain outputs could improve people's overall understanding of the system and potentially increase trust (DP10) [15]. To effectively communicate with various stakeholders and provide a clear understanding of the software, developers need to produce documentation that encompasses a broad spectrum of information. For example, this documentation may include details on what the code does, the underlying rationale for that code, and how it aligns with the overall objectives and compliance standards of the organization. To achieve this goal, developers could provide GAI systems with the respective texts containing documentation requirements from organization and regulation. The system should then be able to generate the required documentation (DP11) (I2, I7). The overarching objective is to minimize developers' effort in creating code documentation by ensuring that the generated documentation is not only comprehensive but also requires minimal, if any, adjustments by the developer.

5   Discussion and Conclusion

In our work, we reviewed prior literature and conducted interviews with eight practitioners to formulate design requirements and design principles for collaborative GAI systems in software development. We identified issues surrounding usability, data privacy, hallucination and transparency of existing GAI system designs. To address these problems proactively, we propose to focus on design measures regarding user-centricity, data protection, quality control and communication.

Our findings show that there are multiple problems hindering the effective adoption and use of GAI systems in software development. Importantly, all practitioners mentioned problems related to output errors. Thus, quality control measures seem to be mandatory for the introduction of GAI systems in organizations, which emphasizes the need to create local models. Otherwise, these continuing errors may lead to users becoming averse towards GAI systems' output [12]. Moreover, we can draw parallels to concepts of the technology acceptance model (TAM) [11]. The TAM proposes that the adoption of new, disruptive technologies is influenced by factors such as ease of use and perceived usefulness. In the case of GAI systems, the former may be affected if programming assistants are not seamlessly integrated into developers' workflows and applications, while the latter may be affected if developers perceive the programming assistants as unreliable in their specific use case. Thus, a "one-size-fits-all" approach may not be sufficient for the introduction of GAI systems in every organization, as general-purpose systems do not address use case-specific and organizational demands. To increase the adoption rate, a customized approach is key. Here, our design principles can provide guidance into which capabilities of GAI systems are necessary.

Our work makes important contributions to practice. Based on our literature review and interviews with practitioners, we provide design knowledge on GAI systems for organizations. Organizations that aim to fully reap the benefits of GAI systems in their software development practices can instantiate our design framework. By employing our framework, organizations could obtain greater control over data protection and quality control measures. This control is crucial in addressing regulatory demands [14].

We also make important contributions to research. Using a literature review and qualitative data allowed us to empirically identify problems and make suggestions to address them. Thus, we contribute with prescriptive design knowledge in the form of design requirements and design principles, specifically tailored to GAI systems in software development. Notably, novel design knowledge, such as design principles, constitutes the primary theoretical contribution of design science research [3]. Additionally, we extend the literature on the adoption of GAI systems by presenting prevalent problems from a theoretical and practical perspective, and suggestions on how to address these issues.

Despite our contributions, we acknowledge several limitations of our study. First, our design principles, although derived from a comprehensive review of literature and insights from practitioner interviews, lack empirical evaluation in real-world settings. Future work could connect to our study and empirically evaluate our design framework [21]. Second, our interview sample of eight practitioners may not represent all possible perspectives and experiences of the worldwide software development community, warranting future research. Third, we did not instantiate an artifact based on our design framework. Future research could develop and evaluate a prototype for an organization-specific GAI-based programming assistant, guided by our proposed design principles, to provide practical validation of our theoretical findings.

We address the timely topic of generative AI systems for software development. An important insight that we derived from our interviews is that GAI systems should not be merely viewed as technical artifacts but as socio-technical systems that foster collaboration among software developers. In complex scenarios, this collaboration may encourage deep engagement between software developers with diverse skill sets. A GAI system, equipped with knowledge about an organization's distribution of expertise, could enhance this collaboration by connecting the right employees at the right time. Finally, we advice organizations to make sure that implementing GAI systems does not cause software developers to lose important skills over time. On the one hand, organizations should utilize these new technologies effectively, on the other hand, they should avoid overreliance and ensure that employees keep their skill set up to date.

References

1. Alshenqeeti, H.: Interviewing as a data collection method: a critical review. English Linguist. Res. **3**(1), 39–45 (2014)
2. Banh, L., Strobel, G.: Generative artificial intelligence. Electron. Mark. **33**(1), 1–17 (2023)
3. Baskerville, R., Baiyere, A., Gregor, S., Hevner, A., Rossi, M.: Design science research contributions: finding a balance between artifact and theory. J. Assoc. Inf. Syst. **19**(5), 358–376 (2018)
4. Bauer, K., Hinz, O., van der Aalst, W., Weinhardt, C.: Expl (AI) n it to me-explainable AI and information systems research (2021)
5. Bauer, K., von Zahn, M., Hinz, O.: Expl (AI) ned: the impact of explainable artificial intelligence on users' information processing. Inf. Syst. Res. **34**(4), 1582–1602 (2023)
6. Britto, R., Wohlin, C., Mendes, E.: An extended global software engineering taxonomy. J. Softw. Eng. Res. Dev. **4**, 1–24 (2016)
7. Cao, Y., Li, S., Liu, Y., Yan, Z., Dai, Y., Yu, P.S., Sun, L.: A comprehensive survey of AI-generated content (AIGC): a history of generative AI from GAN to ChatGPT. arXiv preprint arXiv:2303.04226 (2023)
8. Chen, J., et al.: Designing expert-augmented clinical decision support systems to predict mortality risk in ICUs. KI-Künstliche Intelligenz 1–10 (2023)
9. Dakhel, A.M., Majdinasab, V., Nikanjam, A., Khomh, F., Desmarais, M.C., Jiang, Z.M.J.: Github copilot AI pair programmer: asset or liability? J. Syst. Softw. **203**, 111734 (2023)
10. Dang, H., Mecke, L., Lehmann, F., Goller, S., Buschek, D.: How to prompt? Opportunities and challenges of zero-and few-shot learning for human-AI interaction in creative applications of generative models. arXiv preprint arXiv:2209.01390 (2022)
11. Davis, F.D.: Perceived usefulness, perceived ease of use, and user acceptance of information technology. MIS Q. **13**(3), 319–340 (1989)
12. Dietvorst, B.J., Simmons, J.P., Massey, C.: Algorithm aversion: people erroneously avoid algorithms after seeing them err. J. Exp. Psychol. Gen. **144**(1), 114–126 (2015)
13. Eloundou, T., Manning, S., Mishkin, P., Rock, D.: GPTs are GPTs: an early look at the labor market impact potential of large language models. arXiv preprint arXiv:2303.10130 (2023)
14. EU: Regulation EU 2016/679 of the european parliament and of the council of 27 april 2016, article 22. Official Journal of the European Union L 119 **59** (2016)
15. Feuerriegel, S., Hartmann, J., Janiesch, C., Zschech, P.: Generative AI. Bus. Inf. Syst. Eng. **66**(1), 111–126 (2023)
16. Fügener, A., Grahl, J., Gupta, A., Ketter, W.: Will humans-in-the-loop become borgs? Merits and pitfalls of working with AI. MIS Q. **45**(3), 1527–1556 (2021)
17. Hadi, M.U., et al.: A survey on large language models: applications, challenges, limitations, and practical usage. Authorea Preprints (2023)
18. Hevner, A.R., March, S.T., Park, J., Ram, S.: Design science in information systems research. MIS Q. **28**(1), 75–105 (2004)

19. Hsieh, H.F., Shannon, S.E.: Three approaches to qualitative content analysis. Qual. Health Res. **15**(9), 1277–1288 (2005)
20. Huff, K.E., Lesser, V.R.: A plan-based intelligent assistant that supports the software development. In: Proceedings of the Third ACM SIGSOFT/SIGPLAN Software Engineering Symposium on Practical Software Development Environments, pp. 97–106 (1988)
21. Iivari, J., Rotvit Perlt Hansen, M., Haj-Bolouri, A.: A proposal for minimum reusability evaluation of design principles. Eur. J. Inf. Syst. **30**(3), 286–303 (2021)
22. Jo, H., Bang, Y.: Analyzing chatgpt adoption drivers with the toek framework. Sci. Rep. **13**(1), 22606 (2023)
23. Kuechler, B., Vaishnavi, V.: On theory development in design science research: anatomy of a research project. Eur. J. Inf. Syst. **17**(5), 489–504 (2008)
24. Liang, J.T., Yang, C., Myers, B.A.: A large-scale survey on the usability of AI programming assistants: successes and challenges. In: 2024 IEEE/ACM 46th International Conference on Software Engineering (ICSE), pp. 605–617. IEEE Computer Society (2023)
25. Meth, H., Mueller, B., Maedche, A.: Designing a requirement mining system. J. Assoc. Inf. Syst. **16**(9), 799–837 (2015)
26. Myers, B.A., Ko, A.J., LaToza, T.D., Yoon, Y.: Programmers are users too: human-centered methods for improving programming tools. Computer **49**(7), 44–52 (2016)
27. Nguyen-Duc, A., et al.: Generative artificial intelligence for software engineering–a research agenda. arXiv preprint arXiv:2310.18648 (2023)
28. Peng, S., Kalliamvakou, E., Cihon, P., Demirer, M.: The impact of AI on developer productivity: evidence from GitHub Copilot. arXiv preprint arXiv:2302.06590 (2023)
29. Plant, R., Giuffrida, V., Gkatzia, D.: You are what you write: preserving privacy in the era of large language models. arXiv preprint arXiv:2204.09391 (2022)
30. Rai, A.: Explainable AI: from black box to glass box. J. Acad. Mark. Sci. **48**, 137–141 (2020)
31. Ross, S.I., Martinez, F., Houde, S., Muller, M., Weisz, J.D.: The programmer's assistant: Conversational interaction with a large language model for software development. In: Proceedings of the 28th International Conference on Intelligent User Interfaces, pp. 491–514 (2023)
32. Ruhe, G.: Software engineering decision support-a new paradigm for learning software organizations. In: Henninger, S., Maurer, F. (eds.) LSO 2002. LNCS, vol. 2640, pp. 104–113. Springer, Heidelberg (2002). https://doi.org/10.1007/978-3-540-40052-3_10
33. Shi, W., Cui, A., Li, E., Jia, R., Yu, Z.: Selective differential privacy for language modeling. arXiv preprint arXiv:2108.12944 (2021)
34. Susarla, A., Gopal, R., Thatcher, J.B., Sarker, S.: The Janus effect of generative AI: charting the path for responsible conduct of scholarly activities in information systems. Inf. Syst. Res. **34**(2), 399–408 (2023)
35. Wessel, M., Adam, M., Benlian, A., Thies, F.: Generative AI and its transformative value for digital platforms. J. Manag. Inf. Syst. (2023)
36. Winograd, A.: Loose-lipped large language models spill your secrets: the privacy implications of large language models. Harvard J. Law Technol. **36**(2) (2023)
37. Xu, Y., Gong, M., Chen, J., Liu, T., Zhang, K., Batmanghelich, K.: Generative-discriminative complementary learning. In: Proceedings of the AAAI Conference on Artificial Intelligence, vol. 34, pp. 6526–6533 (2020)

38. Zacharias, J., von Zahn, M., Chen, J., Hinz, O.: Designing a feature selection method based on explainable artificial intelligence. Electron. Mark. **32**(4), 2159–2184 (2022)
39. Zhao, W.X., et al.: A survey of large language models. arXiv preprint arXiv:2303.18223 (2023)

Designing a Reference Architecture for Collaborative Condition Monitoring Data Spaces: Design Requirements and Views

Philipp Hagenhoff[1,2]($\boxtimes$) , Steffen Biehs[1] , Frederik Möller[1,3] ,
and Boris Otto[1,2]

[1] Fraunhofer Institute for Software and Systems Engineering ISST, 44147 Dortmund, Germany
{philipp.hagenhoff,steffen.biehs,boris.otto}@isst.fraunhofer.de
[2] TU Dortmund University, 44227 Dortmund, Germany
[3] TU Braunschweig University, 38106 Braunschweig, Germany
frederik.moeller@tu-braunschweig.de

Abstract. Industry 4.0 and the industrial digital transformation drastically reshape manufacturing and maintenance processes. Managing maintenance costs increasingly prompts companies to employ data-based services such as condition monitoring for optimization. Utilizing these novel services requires companies to share data with others for maximum impact. Data spaces for collaborative condition monitoring have emerged as digital artifacts supporting data sharing across companies to enhance the reliability and efficiency of machinery. However, the concept is still being transferred into practice, and we aim to supplement it by reporting on a Design Science Research (DSR) study extracting a set of design requirements for a reference architecture. As a first step, we present necessary functionalities and their distribution to corresponding components. These serve as the foundation for the further development of a reference architecture.

Keywords: Collaborative Condition Monitoring · Data Space · Reference Architecture · Systematic Literature Review · Expert Interviews

1 Introduction

The industrial landscape is undergoing a profound digital transformation that is revolutionizing the way manufacturing and maintenance processes operate [1]. Condition monitoring (CM) of machinery has emerged to ensure uninterrupted production and, consequently, to avoid high economic risks and damages, especially for companies that produce high quantities and operate on tight profit margins [2]. To minimize such risks and damages, the German working group "Plattform Industrie 4.0" has developed a concept for the cross-company sharing of operational data in a Collaborative Condition Monitoring (CCM) data space [3, 4]. Operational data, such as *time series data* obtained from temperature measurements, are shared multilaterally among factory operators, machine suppliers, and component suppliers to establish a robust data foundation for analyzing existing or potentially emerging machine or component issues [4].

© The Author(s), under exclusive license to Springer Nature Switzerland AG 2024
M. Mandviwalla et al. (Eds.): DESRIST 2024, LNCS 14621, pp. 355–369, 2024.
https://doi.org/10.1007/978-3-031-61175-9_24

Although concepts are already discussed extensively [3, 4], practical implementation remains pending. This delay can be attributed to the lack of interoperability, established standards for multi-party computation, and a deficit in understanding the required functionalities and components for such data spaces [5]. However, to leverage these services, manufacturing companies, which are usually more 'traditional' than highly digitized, require a more sophisticated set of digital capabilities [6].

Reference architectures (RA) are a particularly useful type of design artifact with the potential to close this gap through cumulating abstract design knowledge depicting relationships between functionalities and components of a system [7]. Subsequently, this type of design artifact (i.e., a model [8]) is beneficial in accumulating existing design knowledge and producing an extensible artifact supporting the design of CCM data spaces. According to Patton et al. [9 p. 684], "[r]eference architectures provide guidance to conduct repeatable and reproducible studies designed to solve a particular class of problems. In this way, it serves as a 'reference' for the specific architectures that organizations can implement to solve their problems unique to their operating environment."

Existing reference architectures for CCM data spaces exhibit limitations. Ghita et al. [10] propose a hybrid twin architecture, Redeker et al. [11] introduce a digital twin platform for Industry 4.0, and Farahani and Monsefi's [5] present a federated learning approach. These frameworks often center on specific scenarios and do not explore CCM functionalities comprehensively. Consequently, there is a discernible need for a systematic reference architecture characterized by full traceability, given the incomplete coverage of holistic CCM aspects in existing frameworks.

The paper aims to address the limitations of existing architectural frameworks in the realm of CCM data spaces by designing a systematic reference architecture. For this, we employ the 4 + 1 architectural view [12] as *justificatory knowledge* [13] since it provides valuable perspectives (logical view, physical view, development view, process view, and scenarios) and allows specific architectural elements to be highlighted in a particular view catering to different target audiences while interconnecting each perspective. In this stage of the DSR process, we focus on the *logical* and *physical* views of CCM data spaces as they delineate the structural organization and implementation details essential for understanding data flow, storage, and processing within the system architecture. Because of the above, we pursue the following research question (RQ): *How to design the logical and physical view of a CCM data space RA?*

To answer the RQ, we first provide an overview of the relevant research background about CCM and data spaces. Subsequently, we outline the research design and present the results. Finally, we summarize the findings, discuss the contributions and limitations of our research, and suggest possible further research.

2   Research Context

2.1   Collaborative Condition Monitoring

Since about half of all operating costs in most processing and production operations are due to maintenance, companies strive to reduce associated costs through CM [14]. CM generally establishes the present condition of a machine or a plant under investigation by regularly monitoring defined parameters [15]. These signals may encompass vibrations, acoustic emissions, or temperature variations [16]. In addition to the mere measurement of parameters, there is also the detection of potential faults and the systematic identification and description of long-term developments in the form of forecasts [17]. Various methods are employed, such as online or offline monitoring. The former involves a continuously operating and permanently installed monitoring system, whereas the latter conducts intermittent measurements typically using portable measurement systems [16]. CM thus enables companies to identify and fix potential machine problems before they escalate, reducing unexpected downtime and maintenance costs [18].

To enhance the value of CM, companies can share information, leveraging the principles of Industry 4.0 and the growing interconnectivity between companies [19]. In CCM, information regarding the condition of machines and components is shared not in the traditional bilateral manner but rather in a multilateral approach [3, 20]. Typical stakeholders, such as a factory operator, a machinery supplier, or a component supplier, are distributed across the entire value chain. The main objectives include increasing plant availability on the one hand and enhancing the machines and their integrated components on the other [21]. Collaborative information sharing not only benefits individual companies but fosters an environment for industry-wide advancements [22]. This shared knowledge can lead to the standardization of best practices, the development of more reliable components, and the innovation of maintenance strategies. It encourages a collective learning process that can significantly enhance the efficiency and effectiveness of the maintenance processes across various industries [23]. One way to share essential data in a standardized manner on a multilateral basis is through data spaces [24].

2.2 Data Spaces

Sharing data is usually confined to fulfilling contractual obligations or complying with regulations [25, 26]. Among the most prominent reasons for this is the lack of clear value of data sharing or the fear of data misappropriation (e.g., [27]). The data space concept emerged as a novel technological infrastructure that dedicatedly upholds data sovereignty while providing a 'space' for shared innovation based on data [25].

Data spaces generally are grounded in four design principles [28]. First, data sharing within data spaces should uphold *data sovereignty*. This is technically realized by implementing rules for data use by formulating and implementing usage control policies [29]. Second, it is essential to minimize *entry barriers* for new participants within the data space. Upon entry, participants have the option to assume primary roles such as data producer, data provider, data consumer, and/or data owner. Additional roles within the data space pertain to the verification of participants' correct identities, as well as the provision of requisite applications [30]. Third, data spaces are *decentralized soft infrastructure* and rely on interoperable, decentralized IT platforms built on API standards. Users exercise control over data flow through advanced mechanisms of identity and consent management [28]. In practice, established data spaces such as *Catena-X* [31] demonstrate that through combined forces and shared marketplaces, data can be shared more easily, quickly, and cost-effectively than through traditional means.

3   Design Science Research Approach

The study pursues a design-oriented approach, reporting on a DSR study that designed an RA as the design artifact. In particular, DSR is useful in solving specific organizational problems (i.e., the creation of CCM data spaces) and aims to solve them methodologically [32]. In this context, we employ the framework developed by Hevner [33], which consists of *three cycles* (see Fig. 1).

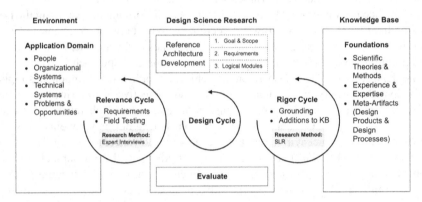

Fig. 1. DSR Process based on [33] as applied in the study.

The *relevance cycle* connects the environment (comprising the application domain, individuals, organizational and technical systems, as well as prevailing problems and opportunities) with the activities of design-oriented research [33]. This cycle defines practical requirements for the artifact to ensure its utility. Collecting design requirements from practice was done through qualitative interviews with six experts from industry and applied research (see Table 1). In selecting the experts, they needed to encompass various perspectives of a CCM data space. Hence, we selected interview partners based on various stakeholder roles. Each interview was conducted utilizing a semi-structured guide that comprised two distinct sections. First, we inquired about general aspects concerning the requirements for CCM data spaces, encompassing topics like the potential benefits and risks involved, technological barriers to entry, and overall technical prerequisites. Additionally, we inquired about the required functionalities within the CCM data space. The second part focused on validating existing requirements and functionalities from literature and initially designed artifacts. Individual adjustments were made based on the experts' knowledge. Thus, the research keeps structure and comparability but still leaves enough flexibility to adapt to ad hoc interview situations [34].

Table 1. Overview of Expert Interviews

Experts	Duration (h)	Experts	Duration (h)
Machine Supplier (I1)	01:02	Data Space Expert (I4)	01:05
Component Supplier (I2)	00:57	Industry4.0 Expert (I5)	01:02
Factory Operator (I3)	00:55	Industry4.0 Expert (I6)	00:59

The *rigor cycle* links design-oriented research activities with the knowledge base, which encompasses scientific theories, methods, experience, expertise, and existing artifacts and processes of the application domain [33]. To identify those, we conducted a systematic literature review (SLR). We identified Scopus and AISel as relevant databases and utilized a combination of the keywords "Collaborative Condition Monitoring" and "Data Spaces" in the search string to gather relevant requirements. The title, abstract, and keyword search in both databases yielded 75 articles from AISeL and 153 articles from Scopus. After filtering the articles based on thematic suitability, excluding redundant and inaccessible articles, and conducting forward and backward searches, our search narrowed down to 35 articles.

The *design cycle* connects artifact creation with evaluation. Within this cycle, we utilize the method by Reidt et al. [35] to develop and evaluate the CCM data space RA. Complementing the DSR framework with this finer-detailed and tailored RA design method allows us to stay true to DSR but account for the specifics of RA design. For instance, while several methods for developing RA exist [36, 37], this approach allows for considering individual enterprise requirements. The method combines an inductive approach, which infers commonalities of an overarching system from existing subsystems and literature (see rigor cycle), with a deductive approach influenced by standards and objectives to guide the creation of the RA (see relevance cycle). Designing the RA consists of three steps. First **(1)**, the RA's goal, scope, and representation method are chosen (see Sect. 4.1). Second **(2)**, design requirements from the SLR and the expert interviews within the rigor and relevance cycle are generalized (see Sect. 4.1). Third **(3)**, developing and allocating logical modules based on collected requirements, where each module aims for a logical, independent function within the system (see Sect. 4.2). In addition to module formation, it is crucial to allocate these to the corresponding components (see Sect. 4.3). Overall, this approach ensures that the developed solution exhibits high practical relevance since many of the requirements directly result from the needs of the examined industrial companies. Also, this approach fulfills the required empirical foundation emphasized by Galster and Avgeriou [38]. The evaluation of the developed artifacts was carried out iteratively by querying the experts (see Table 1) during interviews to determine whether the collected requirements were currently addressed in the design artifact. If this was not the case, the reference architecture (RA) was expanded and subsequently reassessed with the experts.

4   Reference Architecture

4.1   Goals and Requirements

We draw from Kruchten's [12] concept of views as *justificatory knowledge* [13]. This enables us to systematically investigate architectural elements and tailor them specifically to the needs of potential users. We extracted specific design requirements from both the SLR and the interviews. These design requirements were then categorized into *functional* (F) and *non-functional* (N-F) requirements. Functional requirements specify what a system must do, while non-functional requirements define how well it performs its functions [39]. Table 2 displays the conclusive list of requirements. A total of 29 functional and ten non-functional requirements for a CCM data space were identified from the literature and expert interviews. The functional requirements are comprehensively outlined as modules in the synthesis in Sect. 4.2. The following section will cover the non-functional requirements to provide a comprehensive understanding of the broader system constraints and parameters that inform architectural design decisions.

The non-functional design requirements for a CCM data space encompass several critical aspects. Firstly, ensuring *data space security* (R_{30}) is paramount to maintaining data confidentiality, integrity, and availability. The *track & trace* (R_{31}) capability allows for a comprehensive audit trail, which is essential for accountability and troubleshooting. *Data space scalability* (R_{32}) ensures the system's adaptability to changing demands without compromising performance. The flexibility to deploy across various cloud models falls under the requirement for *integrating* various deployment models (R_{33}). Minimizing financial and operational costs associated with data transactions is targeted by reducing *transaction costs requirement* (R_{34}). *Real-time data processing* (R_{35}) is integral, enabling immediate insights and decision-making in response to changing conditions. The ability to seamlessly incorporate data from diverse sources characterizes the integration of *multiple data sources requirement* (R_{36}).

Plug & play (R_{37}) eases integrating new components and participants without extensive manual configuration, promoting interoperability. *Increase in productivity* (R_{38}) enhances operational efficiency through streamlined processes and optimized resource utilization. The fundamental requirement is that the CCM data space is *reliable* (R_{39}), ensuring data availability and consistent operation without unexpected downtime.

4.2 Designing the Logical View

The logical view describes the functionalities and services available to participants in the CCM data space. Thus, the end user is presented with the logical architecture, enabling them to identify the expected services. Functional requirements extracted from literature and practice (see Sect. 4.1) are consolidated into logical units, forming a module to generate this view. Similar requirements and modules are grouped based on logical considerations. This process is repeated until modules are aggregated in a way that allows them to represent individual work packages or technical units from a highly generic technical perspective [12]. A module can inherently encompass any number of requirements and aims to form a logically self-contained unit. The uniqueness of these modules stems from the fact that they each represent core functionalities fulfilling the validated requirements from Sect. 4.1. Consequently, these modules can be identified in almost any CCM data space. Figure 2 provides the overall overview of the identified modules. The logical view of the CCM data space comprises a total of seven modules.

The first module encompasses various elements for the *configuration* (M_1) of the necessary CCM Data space components. The goal of the module is to ensure the foundations for processing and exchanging data by configuring necessary components (based on R_1, R_5, R_9, R_{16}). This includes the configuration of key sensors (F_1), e.g., to define update rates or trigger mechanisms. It is also necessary to configure the data space participant's connector for data transmission (F_2). Among other things, this involves the linking of corresponding endpoints for the negotiation of data usage conditions. In addition, integration with the ERP system (F_3) is required so reports and resulting work orders can be integrated into the system. To capture and manage operational data throughout its lifecycle, Digital Twins are necessary (F₄). Each data space participant must initially configure it within the data space.

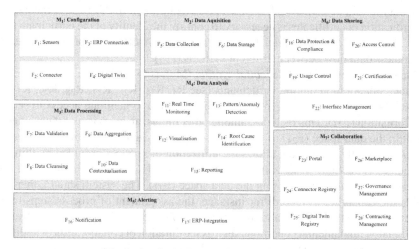

Fig. 2. Logical View of the CCM Data Space

The second module, *data acquisition* (M₂), was developed based on requirements R₆, R₁₄, and R₃₆. The system must be capable of collecting data accurately (F₅) and storing it securely (F₆). The determination of which data to store is defined in the preceding module M₁.

The system should also be capable of *processing* (M₃) data in various ways (see R₈, R₁₀, R₃₉). Initially, data intended for analysis needs to be validated for its quality (F₇). This is crucial to ensure the accuracy of the analysis. If the data quality is not high, potential data cleansing is required (see R₃) to remove any errors or inconsistencies in the data (F₈). Finally, data from a time series can be aggregated (F₉) and contextualized with the help of meta-information (F₁₀) (see R₇, R₁₀).

For advanced *data analysis* (M₄), real-time data observation detects potential issues at the earliest possible stage (F₁₁). In addition to data visualization for a clearer understanding of the data (F₁₂), two key elements take center stage. On one hand, the data is examined for possible patterns or anomalies (F₁₃), and on the other hand, the system is intended to support root cause analysis in case of incidents (F₁₄). Lastly, the module should also encompass the creation of reports (F₁₅) with the results from F₁₃ and F₁₄. The necessity of data analysis is particularly evident in requirements R₁₁, R₁₂, R₁₃, R₁₅, R₁₈.

If an incident occurs, it is important to *alert* (M₅) the involved participants of the data space (see R₁₇, R₂₀). Using a notification (F₁₆), the report created in F₁₅ is to be forwarded (see R₂₅). Additionally, the report should be integrated into the ERP system along with any existing work order (F₁₇).

When it comes to exchanging operational data with other participants, *data sharing* (M₆) should be secure and controlled by the data spaces participants (see R₂, R₁₉, R₂₁, R₂₂, R₂₃, R₃₀). This includes not only encrypting the data but also checking internal compliance regulations (F_{18}). Moreover, the establishment of a comprehensive repository for usage terms is essential, providing participants with a resource for individualized customization (F_{19}). Furthermore, access to the data needs to be controlled to determine which data should be distributed to which participant (F_{20}). In this regard, the issuance and verification of certificates is necessary to confirm the identity of the participant (F_{21}). Lastly, in this context, the administration of necessary interfaces is provided to ensure the seamless data flow between different systems (F_{22}).

The goal of the final module, *collaboration* (M_7), is to clarify and simplify the fundamental collaboration among participants (see R_4, R_{24}, R_{26}, R_{27}, R_{28}, R_{29}, R_{33}). To achieve this, a central portal is intended to be available to facilitate access to services and information (F_{23}). This includes, among other things, an overview of the connectors present in the data space (F_{24}) as well as the employed digital twins of the participants (F_{25}). Additionally, the system allows the utilization of services provided by third parties, such as validation, visualization, or data analysis (F_{26}). Another component is the definition of responsibilities within the data space (F_{27}). The system should, therefore, provide the capability to record, for instance, the assignment of process steps to participants to prevent misunderstandings and thus facilitate an efficient and effective data space. Finally, fundamental conditions such as the duration of collaboration or additional agreements related to business models are to be contractually documented (F_{28}).

4.3 Physical View

The physical view addresses the system topology, distribution, and communication of various components [12]. It provides a perspective for system architects responsible for planning the distribution of the system across different hardware components and network connections [40]. The modules or functions are distributed among the actors and systems in the CCM data space, considering non-functional requirements.

For the CCM data space, these pose specific requirements concerning scalability (R_{32}), reliability (R_{39}), security (R_{30}), and the quick and straightforward application of services (R_{37}). During this phase, the identification and incorporation of appropriate technologies are conducted. In this context, cloud computing, with its capabilities to host customizable storage and computing services, provide multiple data centers to secure data, pursue robust cybersecurity services, and offer Software-as-a-Service, represents a viable technology for the CCM data space [41]. Although cloud computing can address data-centric solutions, storage, processing capacity, and service creation/management challenges, it faces difficulties meeting the service requirements of time-sensitive IoT applications [42]. Due to the critical nature of real-time data processing in the CCM data space (R_{35}), relying solely on cloud computing proves to be insufficient. Edge/Fog Computing provides computational resources on the network edge, enabling device-level intelligence that optimizes computing, storage, and communication resources, addressing the deficiencies of cloud computing. Combining edge with cloud computing leads to lower latencies needed for data processing and enables more efficient distribution of computational tasks, enhancing overall system responsiveness and performance [43].

When combining edge and cloud computing, the architecture is typically divided into three layers [45]: The *cloud layer*, which is the uppermost tier consisting of centralized cloud computing resources; the *edge/fog layer*, an intermediate tier situated between the

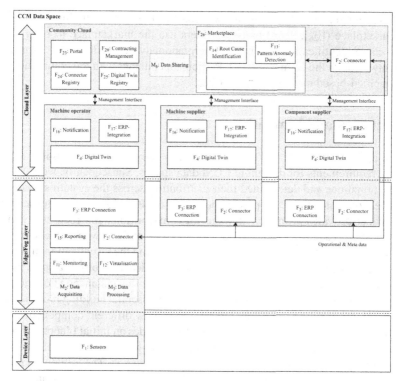

Fig. 3. Physical View of the CCM Data Space

cloud and end-point device layers enabling the deployment of computational resources closer to the data source or end-users, reducing latency and improving real-time processing capabilities; and lastly, the *device layer*, which represents the lowest tier encompassing the physical devices that interact directly with users or the environment. Utilizing the three-tier architecture enables the fulfillment of non-functional requirements for the CCM data space. The modules and functions identified in Sect. 4.2 can be distributed across the presented layers. The comprehensive overview of the physical view of the CCM data space is depicted in Fig. 3.

For the CCM data space RA, the *device layer* includes physical devices, specifically sensors (F_1), with the factory operator being the sole interface to this layer. Above is the *edge/fog layer*, serving as an intermediary between the cloud and devices. It includes functions such as data acquisition (M_2), data processing (M_3), real-time monitoring (F_{11}), visualization (F_{12}), reporting (F_{15}), ERP system connection (F_3), and a connector (F_2) for data sharing. All participants in the data space have connectors and ERP system connections on this layer. The *cloud layer*, the topmost, is divided into lower and upper sections. The lower section represents participants with private and public clouds, featuring functions like notification (F_{16}), ERP system integration (F_{17}), and digital twin (F_4). The digital twin is crucial for the overall functionality of the data space, containing digital images of components and the entire machine. The upper section is the community cloud, hosting collaborative functions such as a portal (F_{23}), contracting management

(F_{28}), connector registry (F_{24}), digital twin registry (F_{25}), data sharing module (M_6), and a marketplace (F_{26}). Third-party providers use the marketplace to offer services like root cause identification (F_{14}) and pattern/anomaly detection (F_{13}), ensuring data sovereignty through the connector (F_2). Participants interact with the community cloud through a cloud-based management interface.

5   Conclusion and Limitations

Based on existing literature and expert interviews, we identified functional and non-functional requirements for designing CCM data spaces. Subsequently, we derived relevant functionalities and determined their distribution across the system's components with the help of an iterative DSR process designing the RA's logical and physical views.

This paper provides primarily **managerial contributions** and focuses on empowering CCM data space participants to design an efficient framework depending on the individual use case. Due to the listing of requirements and the visualization of the developed logical and physical view, the paper also offers **scientific contributions.** First and foremost, our research provides a conceptual framework that enhances a holistic view of the system's structure and functionality. It depicts the essential building blocks and their interconnections, enabling a clear understanding of how different components interact within the CCM data space. In particular, the RA provides an initial blueprint for application in various domains. One example is the upcoming initiative "Manufacturing-X", which is supported by German industry, politics, and research. The initiative's goal is to span an interoperable data space that enables collaborative digital innovation for *greater resilience, sustainability*, and *competitive strength* [20]. Furthermore, researchers can utilize our blueprint as a foundation for additional investigations, thereby fostering dialogue and collaboration toward advancing design science research in information systems and technology.

Our research is subject to **limitations**. Although we tried to conduct our research as objectively as possible, we cannot completely eliminate subjective influences. While our research provides valuable insights, readers should interpret the results with an awareness of the inherent limitations. The scientific process is iterative, and each study contributes to ongoing conversations within the academic community.

Future research concentrates on refining identified components of the RA, enhancing its applicability and effectiveness in diverse contexts. This involves exploring additional use cases, evaluating the architecture's performance, and gathering feedback from practitioners to enhance its effectiveness and usability further. In our case, research findings will be used to develop a proof of concept within the ongoing "Manufacturing-X" initiative to enhance applicability in the field. By addressing these aspects, research can continue to contribute to the advancement of CCM data spaces.

Disclosure of Interests. The authors have no competing interests to declare that are relevant to the content of this article.

Appendix

Table 2. Overview of Extracted Design Requirements

ID	Requirement	Type	Source
R_1	Selection and connection of required sensors	F	[44]
R_2	Data access control	F	[45]
R_3	Cleansing of low-quality data	F	I2, I3, I4
R_4	Overview of deployed digital twins within the data space	F	I3, I5
R_5	Digital representation of the factory and machines	F	[11]
R_6	Collection of operational data	F	[46]
R_7	Aggregation of operational data	F	[47]
R_8	Validation of data for quality	F	[48]
R_9	Establishment of data-sharing mechanisms	F	[49]
R_{10}	Contextualization of operational data to the environment	F	I2, I3
R_{11}	Mapping of patterns to errors and maintenance	F	[50]
R_{12}	Monitoring of machines and components	F	[51]
R_{13}	Regular generation of reports on machine/component status	F	I2
R_{14}	Storage of operational data	F	[49]
R_{15}	Visualization of plant status	F	[47]
R_{16}	Configuration of threshold values for data analysis	F	[52]
R_{17}	Notification of stakeholders in case of malfunctions	F	I3, I4
R_{18}	Root cause analysis of errors	F	[53]
R_{19}	Specification of data usage conditions	F	[26]
R_{20}	Connection and integration with the ERP system	F	I2, I3
R_{21}	Certification of involved partners	F	[54]
R_{22}	Review of legal and organizational compliance	F	I2, I3
R_{23}	Management of interfaces for data exchange	F	I1, I2, I3
R_{24}	Access to services from third-party providers	F	I2, I3
R_{25}	Forwarding of reports to the ERP system	F	I1
R_{26}	Overview of participants in the data space	F	I3, I6
R_{27}	Definition of responsibilities in the CCM process	F	I5, I6
R_{28}	Negotiation and management of data space agreements	F	I1, I3, I6
R_{29}	Dashboard for managing the data space	F	[55]
R_{30}	Data space security	N-F	[56]
R_{31}	Track & trace	N-F	[55]
R_{32}	Data space scalability	N-F	[57]

(continued)

Table 2. (*continued*)

ID	Requirement	Type	Source
R_{33}	Integration of various deployment models	N-F	I1
R_{34}	Reduction of transaction costs	N-F	I5
R_{35}	Real-Time data processing	N-F	[58]
R_{36}	Integration of multiple data sources	N-F	[59]
R_{37}	Plug & play	N-F	I2, I3, I4
R_{38}	Increase in productivity	N-F	[60]
R_{39}	Data space reliability	N-F	I1, I2, I3, I4

References

1. Shang, Z., Zhang, L.: The sustainable digitalization in the manufacturing industry: A bibliometric analysis and research trend. Mob. Inf. Syst. (2022). https://doi.org/10.1155/2022/1451705

2. Lee, W.J., Wu, H., Yun, H., Kim, H., Jun, M.B., Sutherland, J.W.: Predictive maintenance of machine tool systems using artificial intelligence techniques applied to machine condition data. Procedia CIRP (2019). https://doi.org/10.1016/j.procir.2018.12.019

3. Federal Ministry for Economic Affairs and Energy (BMWi): Collaborative data-driven business models. Collaborative Condition Monitoring - How cross-company collaboration can generate added value (2020). https://www.plattform-i40.de/IP/Redaktion/EN/Downloads/Publikation/collaborative-data-driven-business-models.pdf. Accessed 21 Nov 2023

4. Federal Ministry for Economic Affairs and Climate Action (BMWK): Multilateral data sharing in industry. Concept using "Collaborative Condition Monitoring" as a basis for new business models (2022). https://www.plattform-i40.de/IP/Redaktion/EN/Downloads/Publikation/Multilateral_Data_Sharing.html. Accessed 21 Nov 2023

5. Farahani, B., Monsefi, A.K.: Smart and collaborative industrial IoT: A federated learning and data space approach. Digit. Commun. Netw. (2023). https://doi.org/10.1016/j.dcan.2023.01.022

6. Azkan, C., Iggena, L., Gür, I., Möller, F., Otto, B.: A taxonomy for data-driven services in manufacturing industries. In: PACIS 2020 Proceedings, vol. 184 (2020)

7. Legner, C., Pentek, T., Otto, B.: Accumulating design knowledge with reference models: Insights from 12 years' research into data management. J. Assoc. Inf. Syst. (2020). https://doi.org/10.17705/1jais.00618

8. March, S., Smith, G.: Design and natural science research on information technology. Decis. Support. Syst. (1995). https://doi.org/10.1016/0167-9236(94)00041-2

9. Patton, J., Moreland, J.: Reference architecture: An integration and interoperability-driven framework. In: Verma, D. (ed.) Systems Engineering for the Digital Age. Practitioner Perspectives, pp. 683–696. Wiley, Hoboken (2024)

10. Ghita, M., Siham, B., Hicham, M., Amine, M.: HT-TPP: A hybrid twin architecture for thermal power plant collaborative condition monitoring. Energies (2022). https://doi.org/10.3390/en15155383

11. Redeker, M., Weskamp, J.N., Rossl, B., Pethig, F.: Towards a digital twin platform for Industrie 4.0. In: 2021 4th IEEE International Conference on Industrial Cyber-Physical Systems (ICPS). 2021 4th IEEE International Conference on Industrial Cyber-Physical Systems (ICPS), Victoria, BC, Canada, 10.05.2021 - 12.05.2021, pp. 39–46. IEEE (2021). https://doi.org/10.1109/ICPS49255.2021.9468204

12. Kruchten, P.B.: The 4+1 view model of architecture. IEEE Softw. (1995). https://doi.org/10.1109/52.469759
13. Jones, D., Gregor, S.: The anatomy of a design theory. JAIS (2007). https://doi.org/10.17705/1jais.00129
14. de Silva, C.W. (ed.): Vibration Monitoring, Testing, and Instrumentation. Mechanical Engineering Series. CRC Press, Boca Raton, London, New York (2007)
15. Starr, A., Rao, B.: Condition Monitoring and Diagnostic Engineering Management, 1st edn. Elsevier professional, s.l. (2001)
16. Nithin, S.K., Hemanth, K., Shamanth, V., Shrinivas Mahale, R., Sharath, P.C., Patil, A.: Importance of condition monitoring in mechanical domain. Mater. Today Proc. (2022). https://doi.org/10.1016/j.matpr.2021.08.299
17. Kolerus, J., Becker, E.: Condition Monitoring und Instandhaltungsmanagement, 1st edn. expert verlag, Tübingen (2022)
18. Rao, B.K.N. (ed.): Profitable Condition Monitoring. Kluwer Academic Publishers, Dordrecht, Boston (1993)
19. Grand View Research: Machine Condition Monitoring Market Size, Share & Trends Analysis Report By Monitoring Technique, By Component, By Product Type, By Application, By Architecture Type, By Plant Type, By End-use Industry, And Segment Forecasts, 2023 – 2030 (2022). https://www.grandviewresearch.com/industry-analysis/machine-condition-monitoring-market-report. Accessed 20 Nov 2023
20. Federal Ministry for Economic Affairs and Climate Action (BMWK): White Paper on Manufacturing-X. Key points for the implementation of Manufacturing-X in the goods-producing sector to secure Germany's position as a competitive location for industry (2022). https://www.plattform-i40.de/IP/Redaktion/EN/Downloads/Publikation/Manufacturing-X_long.html. Accessed 20 Nov 2023
21. IDSA: Data Space Radar. Faster IDS breakthroughs are within range (2022). https://internationaldataspaces.org/adopt/data-space-radar/. Accessed 23 Oct 2023
22. Cao, Q., Giustozzi, F., Zanni-Merk, C., de Bertrand Beuvron, F., Reich, C.: Smart condition monitoring for industry 4.0 manufacturing processes: An ontology-based approach. Cybern. Syst. (2019). https://doi.org/10.1080/01969722.2019.1565118
23. Goasduff, L.: Data Sharing Is a Business Necessity to Accelerate Digital Business (2021). https://www.gartner.com/smarterwithgartner/data-sharing-is-a-business-necessity-to-accelerate-digital-business. Accessed 21 Nov 2023
24. Hedeler, C., et al.: Pay-as-you-go mapping selection in dataspaces. In: Sellis, T., Miller, R.J., Kementsietsidis, A., Velegrakis, Y. (eds.) Proceedings of the 2011 ACM SIGMOD International Conference on Management of data, pp. 1279–1282. ACM, New York (2011). https://doi.org/10.1145/1989323.1989476
25. Otto, B., ten Hompel, M., Wrobel, S.: Designing Data Spaces. Springer, Cham (2022)
26. Opriel, S., Möller, F., Burkhardt, U., Otto, B.: Requirements for usage control based exchange of sensitive data in automotive supply chains. In: Bui, T. (ed.) (2021). https://doi.org/10.24251/HICSS.2021.051
27. Jussen, I., Möller, F., Schweihoff, J., Gieß, A., Giussani, G., Otto, B.: Issues in inter-organizational data sharing: Findings from practice and research challenges. Data Knowl. Eng. (2024). https://doi.org/10.1016/j.datak.2024.102280
28. Nagel, L., Lycklama, D.: Design Principles for Data Spaces - Position Paper. International Data Spaces Association, Berlin (2021)
29. Hutterer, A., Krumay, B.: The adoption of data spaces: drivers toward federated data sharing. In: Hawaii International Conference on System Sciences (HICSS) (2024)
30. Pettenpohl, H., Spiekermann, M., Both, J.R.: International data spaces in a nutshell. In: Otto, B., ten Hompel, M., Wrobel, S. (eds.) Designing Data Spaces, pp. 29–40. Springer, Cham (2022). https://doi.org/10.1007/978-3-030-93975-5_3

31. Catena-X Automotive Network e.V.: Catena-X. Your Automotive Network. https://catena-x. net/en/. Accessed 10 Jan 2024
32. Simon, H.A.: The Sciences of the Artificial, 3rd edn. MIT Press, Cambridge (1996)
33. Hevner, A.: A three cycle view of design science research. Scand. J. Inf. Syst. **19** (2007)
34. Mayring, P.: Qualitative content analysis: theoretical background and procedures. In: Bikner-Ahsbahs, A., Knipping, C., Presmeg, N. (eds.) Approaches to Qualitative Research in Mathematics Education. Advances in Mathematics Education, pp. 365–380. Springer, Dordrecht (2015). https://doi.org/10.1007/978-94-017-9181-6_13
35. Reidt, A., Duchon, M., Krcmar, H.: Erstellung einer Referenzarchitektur anhand von individuellen Unternehmensanforderungen. In: Bullinger-Hoffman, A.C. (ed.) S-CPS: Ressourcen-Cockpit für Sozio-Cyber-Physische Systeme, vol. 1, pp. 23–42. aw&I - Wissenschaft und Praxis, Chemnitz (2017)
36. Cloutier, R., Muller, G., Verma, D., Nilchiani, R., Hole, E., Bone, M.: The concept of reference architectures. Syst. Eng. (2009). https://doi.org/10.1002/sys.20129
37. Nakagawa, E.Y., Guessi, M., Maldonado, J.C., Feitosa, D., Oquendo, F.: Consolidating a process for the design, representation, and evaluation of reference architectures. In: 2014 IEEE/IFIP Conference on Software Architecture, pp. 143–152. IEEE (2014). https://doi.org/10.1109/WICSA.2014.25
38. Galster, M., Avgeriou, P.: Empirically-grounded reference architectures. In: Crnkovic, I., Stafford, J.A., Petriu, D., Happe, J., Inverardi, P. (eds.) Proceedings of the Joint ACM SIGSOFT Conference, pp. 153–158. ACM, New York (2011). https://doi.org/10.1145/2000259. 2000285
39. Davis, A.M.: Software requirements. Analysis and specification. Prentice-Hall, Englewood Cliffs (1990)
40. Reidt, A.: Referenzarchitektur eines integrierten Informationssystems zur Unterstützung der Instandhaltung. Universitätsbibliothek der TU München, München (2019)
41. Mell, P.M., Grance, T.: The NIST definition of cloud computing, Gaithersburg, MD (2011)
42. Firouzi, F., Farahani, B., Marinšek, A.: The convergence and interplay of edge, fog, and cloud in the AI-driven Internet of Things (IoT). Inf. Syst. (2022). https://doi.org/10.1016/j.is.2021. 101840
43. Firouzi, F., Farahani, B., Panahi, E., Barzegari, M.: Task offloading for edge-fog-cloud interplay in the healthcare internet of things (IoT). In: 2021 IEEE International Conference on Omni-Layer Intelligent Systems (COINS), pp. 1–8 (2021). https://doi.org/10.1109/COINS5 1742.2021.9524098
44. Azouzi, R., Guillot, M.: On-line prediction of surface finish and dimensional deviation in turning using neural network based sensor fusion. Int. J. Mach. Tools Manuf (1997). https:// doi.org/10.1016/S0890-6955(97)00013-8
45. Braud, A., Fromentoux, G., Radier, B., Le Grand, O.: The road to european digital sovereignty with gaia-X and IDSA. IEEE Network (2021). https://doi.org/10.1109/MNET.2021.9387709
46. Zürcher, P., Badr, S., Knüppel, S., Sugiyama, H.: Data-driven approach toward long-term equipment condition assessment in sterile drug product manufacturing. ACS Omega (2022). https://doi.org/10.1021/acsomega.2c04182
47. Grimmelius, H.T., Meiler, P.P., Maas, H., Bonnier, B., Grevink, J.S., van Kuilenburg, R.F.: Three state-of-the-art methods for condition monitoring. IEEE Trans. Ind. Electron. (1999). https://doi.org/10.1109/41.753780
48. Wang, L., Gao, R.X. (eds.): Condition Monitoring and Control for Intelligent Manufacturing. SpringerLink Bücher. Springer, London (2006)
49. Balogh, Z., Gatial, E., Barbosa, J., Leitão, P., Matejka, T.: Reference architecture for a collaborative predictive platform for smart maintenance in manufacturing. In: 2018 IEEE 22nd International Conference on Intelligent Engineering Systems (INES), pp. 299–304 (2018). https://doi.org/10.1109/INES.2018.8523969

50. Han, Y., Song, Y.H.: Condition monitoring techniques for electrical equipment-a literature survey. IEEE Trans. Power Delivery (2003). https://doi.org/10.1109/TPWRD.2002.801425
51. Byrne, G., Dornfeld, D., Inasaki, I., Ketteler, G., König, W., Teti, R.: Tool condition monitoring (TCM) — the status of research and industrial application. CIRP Ann. (1995). https://doi.org/10.1016/S0007-8506(07)60503-4
52. Wang, W.: A model to determine the optimal critical level and the monitoring intervals in condition-based maintenance. Int. J. Prod. Res. (2000). https://doi.org/10.1080/002075400188933
53. Mohanraj, T., Shankar, S., Rajasekar, R., Sakthivel, N.R., Pramanik, A.: Tool condition monitoring techniques in milling process — a review. J. Market. Res. (2020). https://doi.org/10.1016/j.jmrt.2019.10.031
54. Nesheim, D.A., Bernsmed, K., Zernichow, B., Rødseth, Ø., Meland, P.H.: Secure, Trustworthy and Efficient Information Exchange -Enabling Added Value through The Maritime Data Space and Public Key Infrastructure (2021)
55. Demeter: Demeter - Empowering Farmers (2020). https://h2020-demeter.eu. Accessed 20 Nov 2023
56. Wei, S., Zhihua, H., Zikai, W., Zheng, Y., Wei, D.: A method and application for constructing a authentic data space. In: 2019 IEEE International Conference on Internet of Things and Intelligence System (IoTaIS), pp. 218–224 (2019). https://doi.org/10.1109/IoTaIS47347.2019.8980430
57. Arellanes, D., Lau, K.-K.: Decentralized data flows in algebraic service compositions for the scalability of IoT systems. In: 2019 IEEE 5th World Forum on Internet of Things (WF-IoT), pp. 668–673 (2019). https://doi.org/10.1109/WF-IoT.2019.8767238
58. Curry, E., Derguech, W., Hasan, S., Kouroupetroglou, C., ul Hassan, U.: A real-time linked dataspace for the internet of things: Enabling "pay-as-you-go" data management in smart environments. Future Gener. Comput. Syst. (2019). https://doi.org/10.1016/j.future.2018.07.019
59. Franklin, M., Halevy, A., Maier, D.: From databases to dataspaces. SIGMOD Rec. (2005). https://doi.org/10.1145/1107499.1107502
60. Obdenbusch, M.: Reference architecture for cloud-based condition monitoring using the example of packaging machines. Dissertation, Rheinisch-Westfälische Technische Hochschule Aachen; Apprimus Verlag (2017)

Navigating Risks in the Crypto Landscape–A Taxonomy of Risk-Related Aspects of Crypto Assets

Jenny Jakobs[1]([✉]) [iD], Jan Muntermann[1] [iD], and Robert Nickerson[2] [iD]

[1] Augsburg University, Universitaetsstr. 2, 86156 Augsburg, Germany
jenny.jakobs@uni-a.de
[2] San Francisco State University, San Francisco, CA 94132, USA

Abstract. Based on a review of existing literature and an analysis of existing crypto assets, we develop and evaluate a taxonomy of risk-relevant aspects of crypto assets. Despite their rapid expansion and growing acceptance, they have demonstrated significant risks, as illustrated by major incidents in the past years. Additionally, the high volatility and frequent security violations within the crypto asset market further underscore the need for this taxonomy. It can provide a framework for navigating and mitigating risks in this dynamic landscape. Within this context, the taxonomy serves as an artifact, containing constructs in the form of dimensions and characteristics relevant to the risk of crypto assets. It encompasses 11 distinct dimensions that cover various aspects of their design. To evaluate our taxonomy and demonstrate its applicability in classifying real-world objects, we conducted a clustering analysis using actual crypto assets, which resulted in three archetypes. These findings are relevant for various stakeholders including researchers and investors by enhancing the understanding of risks in the blockchain systems.

Keywords: Crypto Asset · Blockchain · Taxonomy Development · Classification · Cryptocurrency

1 Introduction

Since their inception in 2008, blockchain-based crypto assets and related DeFi (decentralized finance) services have surged in popularity. Their core appeal lies in their decentralized structure, which enables peer-to-peer transactions bypassing the traditional banking system. Unlike traditional assets, crypto assets are not tied to a tangible asset or a company, instead their value is determined entirely by the market's perception [1]. Lacking a consensus valuation framework, speculative investors rushing into crypto assets drive up prices, leading to all time-highs in several crypto assets in 2021 [1, 2]. However, the subsequent "crypto-winter", characterized by a decline of up to 65% in market values demonstrated the extreme volatility and risk inherent in these markets [2]. Such volatility not only erodes investor confidence but also poses significant challenges to the broader acceptance of crypto assets. The collapse of UST, a prominent stablecoin, further highlighted these vulnerabilities, underscoring the need for enhanced stability and transparency in these markets. Initially aimed to serve as a new peer-to-peer cash system, UST's failure to maintain its peg triggered a chain reaction. This ultimately resulted in the collapse of both UST and its associated crypto asset LUNA [3]. In addition to these prominent cases, there also exist a multitude of other problems regarding crypto assets, including fraud and cybersecurity incidents [4–6]. However, a secure market environment is crucial for their continued success.

This work contributes to understanding the risks associated with crypto assets by developing a DSR (design science research) artifact in the form of a taxonomy [7]. This taxonomy classifies various risk factors, offering insights to market participants about potential risks within these markets. Given the complex nature of crypto assets, accurately assessing and evaluating them is challenging. To date a deep understanding of their features is still lacking among many stakeholders. This work aims to bridge this knowledge gap, providing a clear framework of risk relevant features of crypto assets. The taxonomy not only aids researchers in creating targeted decision support systems but also helps regulators identify critical regulatory features and investors assess investment risks more effectively.

Although previous studies have introduced various related taxonomies within the cryptocurrency space, none have specifically addressed the risk-related characteristics of crypto assets [8–10]. We are therefore the first to develop a taxonomy of risk-relevant aspects of crypto assets. Our work develops a taxonomy by extracting and integrating information from existing taxonomies. Composing extant knowledge from existing projects offers a richer perspective as solutions to real-world problems often benefit from multiple perspectives over time [11]. By classifying and structuring crypto assets, the taxonomy provides new insights into their functioning. Additionally, by evaluating the taxonomy through a clustering approach and identifying several archetypes, we illustrate the feasibility of our understanding, deepening the nature of crypto assets. By adding to this scarce research stream, our work also creates a basis for further empirical research. The remainder of the paper is organized in the following way: Sect. 2 describes related literature. Section 3 deals with the taxonomy building process. The results are presented in Sect. 4 and evaluated in Sect. 5. Section 6 contains the conclusion and a discussion of implications and limitations of this taxonomy.

2 Literature

In 2008, the first blockchain-based crypto asset, the Bitcoin was created as a trustless transaction processing based on the blockchain technology, which allows the creation of crypto assets by enabling decentralized transactions [12]. There is no uniform definition of crypto assets to date. We therefore adhere to previous literature and jurisdictions and define crypto assets as digital representation of value, capable of being stored and transferred electronically through the use of distributed ledger technology (DLT) or comparable technology [13].

Initially, following their creation, crypto assets were native to their blockchains with Bitcoin emerging as the first of its kind, defining a new asset class that operated within its own unique ecosystem [14, 15]. The evolution into the second generation of blockchain technology expanded its capabilities to include smart contracts and decentralized applications (dApps) [14]. Smart contracts enable automated transactions upon the fulfillment of specified conditions. In the context of crypto assets, they perform various functions, including acting as custodian for these assets [16]. Crypto assets can be native to the settlement layer, like Bitcoin on its blockchain, or issued on an asset layer above the settlement layer. Tokens can be fungible, meaning they are interchangeable, or non-fungible (NFTs), which are unique and not interchangeable [16]. Fungible tokens can be further distinguished according to their purpose. Utility tokens are assets with non-financial purposes that intend to provide access to a service or application based on DLT usually within a blockchain ecosystem [13, 17]. Asset-referenced tokens, or stablecoins, are intended to maintain a stable value by having their value tied to external assets. Assets can also be classified as payment tokens, which are specifically designed to be used as a medium of exchange and possess qualities that should resemble traditional money [13].

To date, an ever-growing research stream analyzes the phenomenon of crypto assets, but most DeFi literature has found to be very positive with challenges and risk if at all, only briefly discussed [18]. Among the various research streams, one investigates the pricing inefficiencies of crypto assets, i.e. when market prices do not accurately reflect the true underlying values. A particular study uncovered a negative relationship between volatility and pricing inefficiencies [6]. Further research analyzes if crypto assets inherit price bubbles, with findings indicating the presence of price bubble periods in Bitcoin [19]. While there is debate on the means and content to regulate crypto asset markets, there exists consensus on the need of regulation to counteract risk. Existing regulation ranges from a total ban of crypto asset trading in some countries to accepting crypto assets as legal tender in others [19, 20]. Besides generating government revenues, restricting illicit activities and achieving price stability is the main goal of regulation [21]. Yet, risk assessment of crypto assets is complicated by their economic and technological complexity. For financial institutions and regulators dealing with crypto assets, an evaluation of these aspects is required [22].

Further research has uncovered additional risks tied to crypto assets. For example, there is evidence that fraud on a crypto asset exchange caused a spike in Bitcoin value [4]. Similarly, the presumed stability offered by stablecoins has been questioned, indicating that their steadiness should not be taken for granted [23]. Cybersecurity incidents are another threat common to crypto assets. Investors rely on cryptographic mechanisms including the consensus protocol of the blockchain to safeguard against cybercrimes. Consensus protocols are used to verify transactions on the blockchain. A widely adopted mechanism is the proof-of-work (PoW) protocol which carries the risk of 51% attacks. In such scenarios, miners can rewrite the blockchain if they control more than half of the networks computing capability. While possible for all blockchains with PoW protocols, one study finds that smaller crypto assets are more susceptible to these attacks due to the lower threshold of computing power required to dominate their networks [5].

Prior research has also developed taxonomies in the context of crypto asset. One study developed a taxonomy of blockchain applications, finding over 20 technical characteristics connected to blockchain application areas [24]. A different taxonomy is centered around the economy of asset tokenization services [25]. Some authors have concentrated more specifically on digital assets themselves, such as taxonomies describing dimensions and characteristics of initial coin offerings [8, 26]. Another work describes a taxonomy of crypto token systems, noting that many characteristics resemble digital and physical token systems though some are distinct to the crypto token system, like wrapping [27].

The existing body of literature highlights the vulnerabilities associated with crypto assets, yet no existing taxonomy concentrates on risk-relevant features of crypto assets. We add to an understanding of how these assets function in relation to their potential weaknesses by proposing a taxonomy of their risk-related aspects.

3   Research Design and Method

Design Science Research (DSR) helps providing insights into designing artifacts, including models or concepts [28]. Building on the DSR paradigm, the development of taxonomies and their underlying constructs has received considerable attention in the DSR research community in recent years. Constructs represent the basic vocabulary used to describe a phenomenon, which can subsequently be combined into a model [29]. Taxonomies can be perceived as artifacts in the type of models. Following its development, the usefulness of the artifact is evaluated, a process that enables the generalization of knowledge [28, 29]. Researchers also utilize taxonomies to examine and explore connections among concepts [30]. Thus, taxonomies enable the organization of extant knowledge in a structured manner. The taxonomy in this work is developed based on an established methodology [7, 30].

The first phase includes describing the object of analysis, intended purpose, and target user groups. Objects of analysis in this work are existing crypto assets. The purpose of this taxonomy is to provide all stakeholders with a toolbox to differentiate crypto assets in terms of their risk relevant characteristics. Target users encompass researchers, investors, or regulators of crypto assets. We derive the meta-characteristic from the purpose of the taxonomy and define it as "risk relevant characteristics of crypto assets".

Next, objective, and subjective ending conditions of the taxonomy are defined. The iterative taxonomy building process ends when all specified ending conditions are met [30]. Objective ending conditions are fulfilled when the taxonomy meets the formal definition of being one. These conditions are met when the dimensions have mutually exclusive and exhaustive characteristics, all objects are evaluated, and the final iteration has no changes or additions in dimensions or characteristics. Additionally, subjective ending conditions, which concern the utility of the taxonomy, are satisfied when the taxonomy is explanatory, extendible, comprehensive, robust and concise [30]. The last phase contains the evaluation of the taxonomy through a clustering which aims at improving the classification of crypto assets based on their relevant aspects [7].

The iterative design process of a taxonomy consists of either empirical-to-conceptual iterations or conceptual-to-empirical iterations. Empirical-to-conceptual iterations start with the identification of a group of objects for classification. These objects are then grouped based on their shared characteristics, all of which must logically follow from the meta-characteristic. Conceptual-to-empirical iterations are deductive and start by conceptualizing dimensions before evaluating objects. This approach relies on extant literature, the researcher's existing knowledge and individual judgement [30].

The first iteration follows a conceptual-to-empirical approach by identifying existing taxonomies of crypto assets. We expanded our knowledge base by identifying existing taxonomies in the field of blockchain through a systematic literature review [31]. More specifically, we utilized the following search string: "taxonom*" and "crypto*" or "blockchain*" or "crypto asset*" or "Defi" or "decentralized finance" or "ICO" or "token" or "non fungible token*". The search string was applied to the title or abstract on different scientific databases, namely ScienceDirect, Business Source Premier, Association for Information Systems eLibrary and Emerald Insight. We excluded publications which were not published in English, white papers, commentaries or similar articles and research-in-progress papers. This led to an initial sample of seven relevant papers. We then performed a forward and backward search to identify further relevant paper and added four additional papers. In total, we analyzed 11 papers in the first iteration, as seen in Table 1.

Table 1. Research topics and related papers.

Category	Papers
Blockchain	Labazova et al. (2019)
ICO	Lipusch et al. (2019), Lausen (2019), Fridgen et al. (2018)
Crypto Assets	Ankenbrand et al. (2020), Oliveira et al. (2018), Hartwich et al. (2023), Schwiderowski et al. (2023)
DeFi	Kölbel et al. (2022), Ballandies et al. (2022), Tasca and Tessone (2019)

Nine dimensions resulted from this literature analysis. The first dimension 'Redeemable' was adapted from [32]. The second dimension 'Spendable' was adapted from [9, 27]. Both dimensions each have the characteristics 'Yes' and 'No'. The dimension 'Implementation Level' with the characteristics 'Native', 'Non-Native' and the dimension 'Chain' with the characteristics 'New Chain, New Code', 'New Chain, Forked Code', 'Forked Chain, New Code', 'Forked Chain, Forked Code' were transferred from [9]. This is followed by 'Consensus' which was derived from [15, 24]. The level transparency of the source code which can either be an 'Open-Source Codebase' or 'Closed Source Codebase' is described by the dimensions 'Code Transparency', derived from [15]. Crypto assets can either be anonymous ('Yes') or non-anonymous ('No'), leading to the creation of the dimension 'Anonymity', taken from [24]. Also, crypto assets can inherit different measures of 'Governance', which include the characteristics 'Voting Rights', transferred from [8, 26] and 'Backed by Legal Entity' adapted from [26, 32]. The 'Ownership' of crypto assets can be either 'Decentralized' or 'Centralized' [8]. Other dimensions, such as the fungibility and consequently uniqueness, were not incorporated as they were not considered to have a clear and immediate impact on the risk of an asset. Since the necessary ending conditions for completing the taxonomy development were not met, we conducted an additional iteration.

The second iteration follows an empirical-to-conceptual approach. Here, we focused on the analysis of real crypto assets. These were identified using the crypto data platform

CoinGecko [2]. We analyzed the top 10 cryptocurrencies and the top 10 NFTs according to their 24-h market volume. After identifying these crypto assets, we conducted an internet search and analyzed the respective documentations for further information. Based on this information, we identified the dimensions 'Liquidity' and 'Volatility' with the respective characteristics 'Low' and 'High'. Further, characteristics of existing dimensions were added and adapted. We identified the two characteristics 'Security Audit' and 'Developers are known' in the governance dimension. We also identified the two characteristics 'Existing Chain, new Code' and 'Existing Chain, forked Code' that we added to the dimension 'Chain'. The characteristics from the dimension 'Anonymity' were replaced with more refined characteristics, namely 'Unlinkable', 'Recipient Anonymity', 'Sender Anonymity', 'Hidden Transaction Values', 'Metadata Unlinkability', 'Multiple' and 'None' [33]. Since the necessary ending conditions for completing the taxonomy development were not met, an additional iteration was performed.

In iteration 3, we could neither extract any further information from the literature review, nor was there any information from the sample of existing crypto assets that would suggest modifying the developed dimensions and characteristics. We thus conclude the taxonomy building process. The taxonomy is evaluated using the ending conditions proposed by the methodology [30]. All objective ending conditions are satisfied. Each subjective ending conditions is assessed individually. The taxonomy is concise, as its range of dimensions allows for meaningful categorization without being overwhelming. Its robustness has been tested by discussing the taxonomy with two independent researchers and confirmed to be effective in distinguishing between the objects of interest and describing the selected crypto assets regarding their risk-related aspects. Additionally, the taxonomy is extensible, as new features can be added when new types of crypto assets emerge.

4   Findings

The final taxonomy is outlined in Table 2 and the dimensions are outlined subsequently:

Redeemable: Redeemable crypto assets can be exchanged for a specific asset or value, including fiat currencies. Their value hinges on the underlying asset, making them vulnerable to its market fluctuations [16].

Spendable: Non-spendable crypto assets cannot be transferred or used in transactions [9]. They can either be non-spendable by design or result from technical issues like lost private keys, freezing of assets due to regulatory actions, or smart contract restrictions. These crypto assets remain in the blockchain wallet but are effectively locked and unusable for transactions or trading. Crypto assets can also become non-spendable through a process known as "burning", which can be implemented into the respective smart contract. This involves permanently removing an asset from circulation by transferring it to a burn address from which retrieval is impossible, thereby reducing the supply of the asset [9].

Implementation Level: Crypto assets can either be native to the blockchain ledger, thereby qualifying as native assets, or they can be non-native, issued on top of the protocol through smart contracts. Non-native tokens rely on smart contracts, which might contain bugs or vulnerabilities, thus exposing them to potential hacking risks [34].

Table 2. Taxonomy of risk-related features of crypto assets.

Dimensions	Characteristics					
Redeemable	Yes			No		
Spendable	Yes			No		
Implemen-tation Level	Native			Non-Native		
Chain	New Chain, New Code	New Chain, Forked Code	New Chain, Forked Code	Forked Chain, New Code	Existing Chain, New Code	Existing Chain, Forked Code
Consensus	PoW	PoS	PoA	PBF	Hybrid	Other
Code Transparency	Open-Source Codebase			Closed Source Codebase		
Anonymity	Unlink-able	Recipient Anonymity	Sender Anonym-ity	Hidden Transaction Values	Metadata Unlinkable	Multiple None
Governance	Voting Rights	Backed by legal Entity	Developers are known	Security Audits	Multiple	None
Ownership	Decentralized			Centralized		
Liquidity	Low			High		
Volatility	Low			High		

Chain: The blockchain represents the lowest layer in the DeFi architecture, significantly influencing the design and characteristics of crypto assets built upon this base layer. This includes tokens developed on new blockchains, as well as those created on existing chains or forked chains, employing either new or forked code [9]. Non-native assets that are designed on a new, forked, or existing chain add complexity, leading to a multi-layered ecosystem where the stability of the new asset is contingent upon the underlying blockchain infrastructure. Consequently, events affecting the base system directly influence the behavior and security of these new assets [27].

Consensus: The consensus algorithm is a core component in blockchain networks as it ensures that all transactions are accurately verified and agreed upon by a decentralized network of nodes thus ensuring the reliability of the system [35]. Besides largely determining the performance of blockchain, the choice of consensus mechanism also affects the security level of crypto assets. One widely used consensus mechanism is Proof of Work (PoW), which requires miners to solve complex cryptographic puzzles to validate transactions and create new blocks. It requires a lot of computational effort and large investments which lead to a centralization of mining power. This increases the risk of a 51% attack which is possible if (a group of) miners gain more than half the computing capability of the network [15]. Proof of Stake (PoS) is another consensus mechanism which relies on validators or provers to validate transactions and create new blocks based on the number of assets they own. Users possessing a significant share of the wealth of the system are typically trusted as validators since they are perceived as more likely to submit reliable verification information [15]. Permissioned blockchains require different consensus mechanisms since access to permissioned blockchains is restricted and users have different rights within the network. Similar to the PoS algorithm, the Proof of Authority (PoA) consensus mechanism relies on validators to verify transactions, but the validators are pre-selected, trusted entities, leading to a more centralized system [15]. The Practical Byzantine fault tolerance (PBFT) is particularly significant in permissioned blockchains and aims at providing consensus even when some nodes are malicious or unreliable [24]. There also exist hybrid consensus mechanisms that e.g., combine PoW and PoS and other, less widely utilized consensus algorithms such as Proof of Burn (PoB).

Code Transparency: Another important technological feature is the transparency of the underlying code. The security of the asset is enhanced when the codebase is regularly updated by development teams having expertise in identifying and mitigating security risks. The codebase can either be open source or closed source, a characteristic that determines the transparency of the source code. Open-source code has the advantage of a broader community engagement, leading to larger growth, faster adoption, and continuous development. Its community-driven approach enables the identification of bugs and security issues due to its diverse group of contributors [15]. In contrast, when the codebase is closed, the identification and resolution of security risks solely depends on the expertise of the selected development team [15].

Anonymity Level: The anonymity features of crypto assets have frequently been associated with illicit activities. However, increased anonymity introduces additional risks, such as making fraudulent activities more difficult to detect and prosecute. This can also hinder the implementation of regulatory oversight, posing risks to both the financial system at large and individual investors [36]. The characteristic of unlinkability, exemplified by stealth addresses, conceals the identity of recipients, making it impossible to ascertain, weather two transactions were sent to the same user. Furthermore, crypto assets can also have the characteristic of recipient anonymity, which implies the impossibility of linking a transaction to a recipient and vice versa. Sender anonymity is another characteristic, describing that transactions cannot be traced back to the originator. Hidden transaction values are another factor affecting anonymity by hiding the amount transferred. Metadata unlinkability refers to the inability to associate transaction-related metadata, such as IP addresses, with specific transactions or wallet addresses. Some crypto assets also display multiple or none of those anonymity characteristics [33].

Governance: Holders of crypto assets with voting rights can impact the decision-making of the project [26]. They distribute the decision-making power among a wider group, reducing the risk of centralized control [37]. Investor confidence can be increased when a crypto asset is supported by a formal legal structure, such as a limited liability company (LLC). This arrangement not only provides a clearer framework but also ensures that the entity can be held responsible for its actions [26]. The presence of identifiable developers behind a project is likely to increase trust among users and investors. Additionally, security audits of a crypto asset are likely to influence its governance by uncovering security flaws, increasing transparency, and enhancing trust among stakeholders by verifying the security of the asset. Crypto assets can also contain multiple or none of those characteristics.

Ownership Allocation: The level of decentralization depends on the allocation of ownership of an asset [27]. Centralized ownership implies more power to individuals which is contrary to the core belief of all crypto assets. We define the ownership to be centralized, when the five largest owners of a given crypto assets hold more than 30% of the asset.

Liquidity: High liquidity of an assets increases the ability of market participants to easily buy or sell the asset [18]. Low liquidity can increase price volatility as small market movements can have a disproportionate impact on the price. We approximate liquidity by volume, as volume is positively related to liquidity [38]. To quantify liquidity in this work, we define a crypto asset to be liquid when the 24-h trading volume exceeds 5 million USD.

Volatility: High price volatility implies large price swings which have been found to worsen price inefficiencies in some crypto assets [6]. To quantify this dimension, we define a certain crypto asset to be volatile, when prices swing more than 30% in five months.

5   Evaluation

The taxonomy was assessed through a clustering approach applied to a sample of crypto assets. Using existing objects to evaluate a taxonomy enhances its comprehensiveness, demonstrating the feasibility of classifying a sample of objects within the applied domain [30]. We utilized the sample of existing crypto assets collected during the taxonomy development [2]. For these twenty crypto assets, information regarding their dimensions and characteristics was collected. Some data, such as 24-h trading volume and historical prices are provided in the data collected from CoinGecko in January 2024. Information on the ownership structure is collected using Opensea and Etherscan [39, 40]. The remaining data is collected using the publicly available documentation of each crypto asset and a web search. A cluster analysis of the crypto assets was conducted using Python 3.12.0 with the SciPy package [41]. We conducted a hierarchical clustering analysis due to the categorical nature of the data. Distances between clusters were computed using Wards linkage since it produces interpretable and compact clusters [42].

The cluster dendrogram presented in Fig. 1 reveals three principal clusters that correspond to distinct categories of crypto assets, facilitating the identification of three archetypes. The first archetype which contains the first cluster describes asset-referenced tokens. Members of this cluster are identifiable by their redeemability, implementation on an existing chain utilizing either new or forked code and are distinguished by their high liquidity and low volatility. Moving on to the middle cluster, which was labeled native tokens, we observe that these tokens, featuring either new or forked codebases, predominantly exhibit high liquidity and volatility. Consensus mechanisms in this cluster vary,

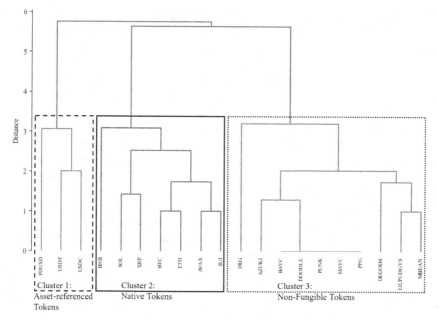

Fig. 1. Hierarchical cluster dendrogram of crypto assets.

with most underlying blockchains employing either PoS or a hybrid consensus mechanism. They are non-redeemable, spendable, implemented open source and mainly have no anonymity features and multiple governance features. Ownership is mostly decentralized. Finally, the third cluster, identified by the label NFTs contains non-fungible tokens. These are non-native, spendable, generally non-redeemable and are developed on existing blockchains through new code using a PoS consensus mechanism. The code for these tokens is mostly transparent, lacking in anonymity features, yet they incorporate multiple governance features with ownership predominantly decentralized. Most of these tokens are characterized by low liquidity and high volatility. These results effectively outline the ability of the taxonomy in systematically classifying specific crypto assets by their unique risk-related characteristics.

6 Discussion

Guided by the question of what risks can be observed in crypto assets, we developed a taxonomy that shows risk-related characteristics of crypto assets build upon the DSR research paradigm. The taxonomy developed in this work can be seen as artifact that describes constructs in form of a model, specifically in the domain of crypto assets. By defining constructs in this domain, it establishes a basis for subsequent research, especially empirical research projects [7, 30]. It is based on an iterative development methodology incorporating both a literature review and an analysis of existing crypto assets, resulting in eleven distinct dimensions along with their respective characteristics. Each dimension possesses explanatory power, as it allows to explain certain aspects of the domain of interest [7, 30]. To further evaluate the taxonomy, we classified 20 crypto assets using a clustering approach, which resulted in the identification of three archetypes. This clustering demonstrates the applicability of the taxonomy to existing objects.

One distinction among crypto assets is their redeemability. Crypto assets, especially payment tokens that are redeemable are often claimed to be directly exchangeable into fiat currencies. When crypto assets cannot fulfill this claim, investors face increased risk [43]. Another key distinction of crypto assets is whether they are spendable. Crypto assets can become non-spendable due to different reasons, one including being frozen by their issuer rendering them inaccessible for their holders. This has happened in previous instances, such as the case of Tether, where over 1 million USD worth of assets were frozen upon the request of an unspecified law enforcement agency [44]. This is a critical point of consideration as it contrasts with the alleged decentralized nature of crypto assets as control by such a central authority should not be possible.

The implementation of a crypto asset as either native asset or non-native asset that is created on the second layer also influences their risk. Smart contracts can be exploited or contain bugs leading to sales without payment being received, such as the case of CryptoPunks [45]. Next, the chain also influences risk as events on the underlying system can impact the subsequent one. For instance, price shocks in Ether were shown to be related to the number of NFT wallets based on Ethereum [46]. This is related to the consensus mechanism implemented in the underlying chain which also influences the crypto assets issued on top. Different consensus mechanisms have different issues and risks, such as the PoW consensus mechanism which is susceptible to 51% attacks. The source code of a crypto asset can either be open or closed source. Besides being transparent, an open source code allows for continuous risk mitigation by multiple contributors and it can hinder the code having hidden, malicious functions [15].

The anonymity of some crypto assets contributes to their misuse by criminals. However, when they become traceable and display less anonymity features, some risks can be mitigated [36]. The display of governance characteristics has shown to mitigate risks inherent to crypto assets [47]. Proper governance can ensure the protection against cyberattacks, e.g., by mitigating bugs in the code through regular security audits. Governance through governance tokens, which grant voting rights to token holders proportional to their ownership, is intended to be decentralized. However, studies have shown that in practice, governance often remains centralized, mainly dominated by protocol insiders and developers [43]. When a particular asset is predominantly held by a small group of major investors, it has shown to influence the market. Research suggests that large investors have been capitalizing on price declines thereby affecting smaller holders [48]. The last two dimensions of this taxonomy, liquidity and volatility also significantly influence the risk. Low liquidity can impact prices through market movements that have a disproportionate impact on the price. Research has also shown that volatile crypto assets impact price efficiency [6].

Further research building upon our findings could address the limitations identified in this study. The sample of twenty crypto assets may not capture the full spectrum of the market. Including crypto assets from various categories could broaden the understanding. Using more diverse research materials covering different aspects would improve the cluster analysis. Additionally, since the crypto asset market continues to evolve rapidly, certain aspects of their design that will emerge in the future are not covered in this work. However, due to the extendable nature of the taxonomy new characteristics can be added as they arise. Moreover, this taxonomy only includes features that are objectively measurable and accessible through public information. Excluding certain, not quantifiable features was necessary to allow an evaluation of the taxonomy using real-world crypto assets. Certain risk-relevant characteristics of crypto assets, such as the quality of the code, the developers' experience or social trust in the network are not easily quantifiable. They are therefore excluded as they also cannot be used by future empirical research. Future work can pursue projects that explain certain characteristics of this taxonomy in more depth, e.g., how exactly the code transparency of a specific crypto asset adds to its security.

The purpose of this paper is to contribute to a better understanding of differences in crypto assets that go beyond their basic characteristics. Different groups of stakeholders can use it as a basis to evaluate risk-relevant characteristics of crypto-assets. First, investors could base their investment decision regarding different crypto assets on our classification scheme. It can also support regulatory authorities involved in creating supervision of crypto assets. Researchers may use the characteristics of this taxonomy as constructs that help explain the reasons that lead to the materialization of risks in crypto assets. Future research can also use risk factors derived from this taxonomy as a basis for a decision support system.

Disclosure of Interests. The authors have no competing interests to declare that are relevant to the content of this article.

References

1. Corbet, S., Lucey, B., Urquhart, A., Yarovaya, L.: Cryptocurrencies as a financial asset: a systematic analysis. Int. Rev. Financ. Anal. **62**, 182–199 (2019). https://doi.org/10.1016/j.irfa.2018.09.003
2. CoinGecko: CoinGecko (2024). https://www.coingecko.com. Accessed 20 Jan 2024
3. Briola, A., Vidal-Tomás, D., Wang, Y., Aste, T.: Anatomy of a Stablecoin's failure: the terra-luna case. Finan. Res. Lett. **51**, 103358 (2023). https://doi.org/10.1016/j.frl.2022.103358
4. Gandal, N., Hamrick, J.T., Moore, T., Oberman, T.: Price manipulation in the bitcoin ecosystem. J. Monet. Econ. **95**, 86–96 (2018). https://doi.org/10.1016/j.jmoneco.2017.12.004
5. Aponte-Novoa, F.A., Orozco, A.L.S., Villanueva-Polanco, R., Wightman, P.: The 51% attack on blockchains: a mining behavior study. IEEE Access **9**, 140549–140564 (2021). https://doi.org/10.1109/ACCESS.2021.3119291
6. Sensoy, A.: The inefficiency of bitcoin revisited: a high-frequency analysis with alternative currencies. Finan. Res. Lett. **28**, 68–73 (2019). https://doi.org/10.1016/j.frl.2018.04.002
7. Kundisch, D., et al.: An Update for Taxonomy Designers. Bus. Inf. Syst. Eng. **64**, 421–439 (2022). https://doi.org/10.1007/s12599-021-00723-x
8. Lausen, J.: Regulating initial coin offerings? A taxonomy of crypto-assets. In: Proceedings of the 27th European Conference on Information Systems (ECIS). Stockholm & Uppsala, Sweden (2019)
9. Oliveira, L., Zavolokina, L., Bauer, I., Schwabe, G.: To Token or not to token: tools for understanding blockchain tokens. In: Proceedings of the 26th European Conference on Information Systems (ECIS) (2018)

10. Hartwich, E., Ollig, P., Fridgen, G., Rieger, A.: Probably something: a multi-layer taxonomy of non-fungible tokens. Internet Res. **34**, 216–238 (2023). https://doi.org/10.1108/INTR-08-2022-0666

11. vom Brocke, J., Winter, R., Hevner, A., Maedche, A.: Special issue editorial –accumulation and evolution of design knowledge in design science research: a journey through time and space. J. Assoc. Inf. Syst. **21**, 520–544 (2020). https://doi.org/10.17705/1jais.00611

12. Nakamoto, S.: Bitcoin. A peer-to-peer electronic cash system (2008). https://bitcoin.org/en/bitcoin-paper, last accessed 2024/07/01

13. European Commission: Proposal for a Regulation of the European Parliament and of the Council on Markets in Crypto-assets, and amending Directive (EU) 2019/1937 (MiCA) (2020). https://eurlex.europa.eu/legal-content/EN/TXT/?uri=CELEX%3A52020PC0593. Accessed 01 July 2024

14. Xu, M., Chen, X., Kou, G.: A systematic review of blockchain. Financial Innovation **5**, 1–14 (2019). https://doi.org/10.1186/s40854-019-0147-z

15. Tasca, P., Tessone, C.J.: A taxonomy of blockchain technologies: principles of identification and classification. Ledger, **4** (2019). https://doi.org/10.5195/ledger.2019.140

16. Schär, F.: Decentralized finance: on blockchain- and smart contract-based financial markets. federal reserve bank of st. louis review, second quarter, vol. 103, pp. 153–174 (2021). https://doi.org/10.20955/r.103.153-74

17. Di Angelo, M., Salzer, G.: Identification of token contracts on Ethereum: standard compliance and beyond. Int. J. Data Sci. Anal. **16**(3), 333–352 (2023). https://doi.org/10.1007/s41060-021-00281-1

18. Ozili, P.K.: Decentralized finance research and developments around the world. J. Bank. Financ. Technol. **6**, 117–133 (2022). https://doi.org/10.1007/s42786-022-00044-x

19. Corbet, S., Lucey, B., Yarovaya, L.: Datestamping the bitcoin and Ethereum bubbles. Financ. Res. Lett. **26**, 81–88 (2018). https://doi.org/10.1016/j.frl.2017.12.006

20. Alvarez, F., Argente, D., van Patten, D.: Are cryptocurrencies currencies? Bitcoin as legal tender in El Salvador. Science, **382**, eadd2844 (2023). https://doi.org/10.1126/science.add2844

21. Chokor, A., Alfieri, E.: Long and short-term impacts of regulation in the cryptocurrency market. Q. Rev. Econ. Finan. **81**, 157–173 (2021). https://doi.org/10.1016/j.qref.2021.05.005

22. Hermans, L., Ianiro, A., Kochanska, U., Törmälehto, V.-M., van der Kraaij, A., Simón, J.M.V.: Decrypting financial stability risks in crypto-asset markets. Financ. Stab. Rev. **1** (2022)

23. Grobys, K., Junttila, J., Kolari, J.W., Sapkota, N.: On the stability of stablecoins. J. Empir. Financ. **64**, 207–223 (2021). https://doi.org/10.1016/j.jempfin.2021.09.002

24. Labazova, O., Dehling, T., Sunyaev, A.: From hype to reality: a taxonomy of blockchain applications. In: Proceedings of the 52nd Annual Hawaii International Conference on System Sciences (HICSS 2019), pp. 4555–4564. Maui, Hawaii (2019)

25. Kölbel, T., Lamberty, R., Sterk, F., Weinhardt, C.: Spotlight on DeFi centerpieces: towards an economic perspective on asset tokenization services PACIS. In: 2022 Proceedings (2022)

26. Fridgen, G., Regner, F., Schweizer André, Urbach, N.: Don't slip on the initial coin offering (ICO): a taxonomy for a blockchain-enabled form of crowdfunding. In: Proceedings of the 26th European Conference on Information Systems (ECIS) (2018)

27. Schwiderowski, J., Pedersen, A.B., Beck, R.: Crypto tokens and token systems. Inf. Syst. Front. **26**, 319–332 (2023). https://doi.org/10.1007/s10796-023-10382-w

28. March, S.T., Smith, G.F.: Design and natural science research on information technology. Decis. Support. Syst. **15**, 251–266 (1995). https://doi.org/10.1016/0167-9236(94)00041-2

29. Hevner, M.: Park, ram: design science in information systems research. MIS Q. **28**, 75–105 (2004). https://doi.org/10.2307/25148625

30. Nickerson, R.C., Varshney, U., Muntermann, J.: A method for taxonomy development and its application in information systems. Eur. J. Inf. Syst. **22**, 336–359 (2013). https://doi.org/10.1057/ejis.2012.26

31. Webster, J., Watson, R.T.: Analyzing the past to prepare for the future: writing a literature review. MIS Q. **26**, xiii–xxiii (2002)

32. Ankenbrand, T., Bieri, D., Cortivo, R., Hoehener, J., Hardjono, T.: Proposal for a comprehensive (Crypto) asset taxonomy. In: 2020 Crypto Valley Conference on Blockchain Technology (CVCBT), pp. 16–26 (2020). https://doi.org/10.1109/CVCBT50464.2020.00006

33. Amarasinghe, N., Boyen, X., McKague, M.: A survey of anonymity of cryptocurrencies. In: Proceedings of the Australasian Computer Science Week Multiconference, pp. 1–10. New York, USA (2019). https://doi.org/10.1145/3290688.3290693

34. Gramlich, V., Guggenberger, T., Principato, M., Schellinger, B., Urbach, N.: A multivocal literature review of decentralized finance: current knowledge and future research avenues. Electron. Markets **33**, 11 (2023). https://doi.org/10.1007/s12525-023-00637-4

35. Ballandies, M.C., Dapp, M.M., Pournaras, E.: Decrypting distributed ledger design-taxonomy, classification and blockchain community evaluation. Clust. Comput. **25**, 1817–1838 (2022). https://doi.org/10.1007/s10586-021-03256-w

36. Kher, R., Terjesen, S., Liu, C.: Blockchain, bitcoin, and ICOs: a review and research agenda. Small Bus. Econ. **56**, 1699–1720 (2021). https://doi.org/10.1007/s11187-019-00286-y

37. Dotan, M., Yaish, A., Yin, H.-C., Tsytkin, E., Zohar, A.: The vulnerable nature of decentralized governance in DeFi. In: Proceedings of the 2023 Workshop on Decentralized Finance and Security, pp. 25–31 (2023). https://doi.org/10.1145/3605768.3623539

38. Holden, C.W.: The empirical analysis of liquidity. Found. Trends Financ. **8**, 263–365 (2014). https://doi.org/10.1561/0500000044

39. OpenSea: OpenSea (2023). https://opensea.io/. Accessed 17 Jan 2024

40. Etherscan: Etherscan (2023). https://etherscan.io/. Accessed 17 Jan 2024

41. Virtanen, P., Gommers, R., Oliphant, T.E., Haberland, M., Reddy, T., et al.: SciPy 1.0: fundamental algorithms for scientific computing in python. Nat. Methods **17**, 261–272 (2020). https://doi.org/10.1038/s41592-019-0686-2

42. Murtagh, F., Legendre, P.: Ward's hierarchical agglomerative clustering method: which algorithms implement ward's criterion? J. Classif. **31**, 274–295 (2014). https://doi.org/10.1007/s00357-014-9161-z

43. Auer, R., Haslhofer, B., Kitzler, S., Saggese, P., Victor, F.: The technology of decentralized finance (DeFi). In: Bank for International Settlements (ed.) BIS Working Papers, vol. 1066 (2023)

44. PYMNTS: Stablecoin Issuer Tether Freezes $1M in USDT (2022). https://www.pymnts.com/cryptocurrency/2022/stablecoin-issuer-tether-freezes-1m-in-usdt/. Accessed 28 Jan 2024

45. MyCrypto: NFT Smart Contract Bugs and Exploits (2021). https://blog.mycrypto.com/nft-smart-contract-bugs-exploits. Accessed 30 Jan 2024

46. Ante, L.: The non-fungible token (NFT) market and its relationship with bitcoin and ethereum. FinTech **1**, 216–224 (2022). https:-//doi.org/10.2139/ssrn.3861106

47. Liu, Y., Lu, Q., Zhu, L., Paik, H.-Y., Staples, M.: A systematic literature review on blockchain governance. J. Syst. Softw. **197**, 111576 (2023). https://doi.org/10.1016/j.jss.2022.111576

48. Cornelli, G., Doerr, S., Frost, J., Leonardo, G.: Crypto shocks and retail losses. BIS Bull. **69** (2023). Accessed 20 Jan 2024

Augmenting Frontline Service Employee Onboarding via Hybrid Intelligence: Examining the Effects of Different Degrees of Human-GenAI Interaction

Philipp Reinhard[1]([✉]) [ID], Nicolas Neis[2] [ID], Lisa Kolb[3] [ID], Dennis Wischer[4] [ID], Mahei Manhai Li[1] [ID], Axel Winkelmann[2] [ID], Frank Teuteberg[4] [ID], Ulrike Lechner[3] [ID], and Jan Marco Leimeister[1] [ID]

[1] University of Kassel, Pfannkuchstr. 1, 34121 Kassel, Germany
{philipp.reinhard,mahei.li,leimeister}@uni-kassel.de
[2] University of Würzburg, 97070 Würzburg, Germany
{nicolas.neis,axel.winkelmann}@uni-wuerzburg.de
[3] University of the Bundeswehr Munich, 85579 Neubiberg, Germany
{lisa.kolb,ulrike.lechner}@unibw.de
[4] University of Osnabrück, 49074 Osnabrück, Germany
dennis.wischer@caballito.io, frank.teuteberg@uni-osnabrueck.de

Abstract. High turnover rates within help desks, caused by excessive workloads, make the efficient onboarding of novices a persistent and recurring challenge. Generative artificial intelligence (GenAI) possesses the potential to augment novice frontline service employees (FSE) during their onboarding phase. However, there is a lack of knowledge on how to design the interaction of FSE and GenAI. Thus, following design science research (DSR), we propose a conversational agent - called co-agent - that leverages the capabilities of large language models and the concept of hybrid intelligence to augment novice FSE. To examine the interaction between novices and GenAI given various task difficulties, we derive and instantiate two hybrid intelligence meta-designs - a *supporter* that provides recommendations and a *collaborator* that allows for prompting the coagent. The results from an online experiment with 75 laypeople show that novices interact with GenAI more frequently and show a higher engagement, especially in difficult tasks. Overall, we uncover a paradox: Despite an increased interaction and a greater time investment, FSEs experience a lower perceived workload with a GenAI-based *collaborator*. From that, we derive implications for designing employee-facing co-agents in customer services.

Keywords: Generative AI · Hybrid Intelligence · Customer Service

1 Introduction

Onboarding new employees in customer service poses a recurring challenge, especially given the high turnover rate of up to 70% for new hires in customer support [48]. Furthermore, the situation is complicated by the high time-to-performance of new call center

© The Author(s), under exclusive license to Springer Nature Switzerland AG 2024
M. Mandviwalla et al. (Eds.): DESRIST 2024, LNCS 14621, pp. 384–397, 2024.
https://doi.org/10.1007/978-3-031-61175-9_26

agents which make up more than six months on average [3] due to the high workload initially experienced by novices. The new FSE in customer service help desks are typically tasked with problem-solving shortly after their initial formal training. Generally, they handle a spectrum of customer issues ranging from simple customer inquiries to more intricate issues and situations that surpass the agent's capacity, necessitating escalation to an expert. Simple inquiries may often be resolved through referencing FAQs. On the other hand, the resolution of more technical queries typically involves consulting detailed descriptions in ticket documentation or exploring discussions in online forums. After the formal training, novices can handle most support requests they have learned during their first weeks, all without direct customer interaction. However, when faced with unfamiliar issues, novices often spend considerable time resolving them, must escalate cases to dedicated experts, and are under great pressure [56].

To reduce novices' workload while preventing longer upfront training and deteriorating performance, leveraging artificial intelligence (AI) to support novices during real-time customer interactions is recommended [54]. Such an AI-assisted approach can address the limitations of traditional upfront training, potentially reducing resignation rates and improving job satisfaction. While research already aimed at providing initial insights about the impact and potentials of AI coaches [22, 36] and assistants [21], we observe a lack of research on the application and design of employee-facing AI-based co-agents and co-pilots [62] to augment novices' problem-solving skills and experiences during their customer conversations. The current challenge involves analyzing the extent of collaboration between humans and AI in human-AI hybrids [17]. To investigate the degree of interaction between novices and AI across diverse task complexities, we establish two hybrid intelligence meta-designs: (1) a *supporter* offering advice and (2) a *collaborator* enabling prompting the co-agent. Through an online experiment involving 75 laypeople, we analyze the impact of these interaction levels and the effect of task difficulty on interaction with AI, task performance, and workload. Hence, we aim to address the following research question: *How does the degree of interaction with emerging GenAI systems influence the workload of novice frontline service employees?*

2 Foundation

Despite the widespread use of AI and primarily conversational agents in customer service, numerous challenges remain (e.g., [2, 41]). AI can reduce costs and streamline processes, but personalized service, as demanded by customers, can only be provided to a limited extent [31]. This leads to a trade-off for companies between service efficiency and quality [2]. The remedy is a combination in which humans perform personal customer interaction, but AI augments them in problem-solving. Combining humans and AI creates a socio-technological ensemble that can serve customers' needs [13, 49]. This hybrid intelligence can achieve complex goals with better results than individual intelligence [12]. AI system developers must coordinate the novice's interaction with the AI to maximize synergies in hybrid intelligence [13]. The AI-based co-agent we introduce in this paper intervenes in an ongoing interaction between humans and supports novices. The intervention should be designed so that the FSE is not interrupted but receives support in solving the problem [39, 58]. The aim is a synergetic integration of humans and

AI with a reduced human workload [49]. The hybrid approach facilitates the generation of new knowledge in challenging domains. This enables the FSEs to learn from the AI, and the knowledge of experienced experts can be provided to novices without the need for extensive onboarding [13, 61].

The evolving landscape of frontline service, shaped significantly by emerging intelligent technologies, is a central area of investigation across numerous studies [11, 34, 55]. In particular, AI-driven approaches, such as the regulation of collaborative AI [30] or AI-assisted interpersonal emotion regulation [26], demonstrate research in this area. Beyond the purely technical perspective of using AI-based augmentation, human collaboration with technologies like AI [50] is also an evolving area of research. Whether investigating service quality [8], the effects on user compliance [2], or specifying the role of AI bots in teams [4, 6], the focus is on human-machine interaction. Other IS scholars are investigating the combination of the intelligence of machines and humans through hybrid intelligence [49, 61]. This involves specifying areas of application [15], determining requirements [56], and deriving design principles [14]. Research in hybrid intelligence combines humans and AI and focuses on fundamental aspects, such as factors influencing cooperation between humans and AI [25, 35]. The use of AI does not only have positive effects; depending on previous experience, but divergent effects on performance can also be observed [64]. In addition, several studies have found a negative effect of AI enhancements on users' mental workload [7, 57]. Due to its invasive properties, the interaction between humans and AI can lead to stressful situations. The study extends previous research on the design principles of hybrid intelligence systems and focuses on collaboration via prompts. It sheds light on the optimal collaboration between humans and AI and emphasizes the impact on human workload in the context of hybrid intelligence.

3 Research Approach

A design-oriented approach [23] is chosen to conduct an experimental study on the impact of different degrees of human-AI interaction. Hevner et al. (2008) [27] serve as the general work foundation. To identify the relationship between the degree of human-AI interaction and the mental workload, we follow the method proposed by Kuechler and Vaishnavi (2008) [33], shown in Fig. 1.

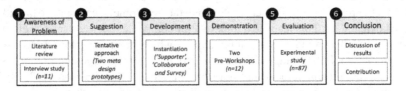

Fig. 1. Research Design (cf. [33])

The study's needs, goals, stakeholders, and requirements [37] are identified through a literature review on hybrid intelligence and a previous study on AI augmentation, human-AI interaction, and the FSE journey [51]. Semi-structured interviews are conducted to deepen the findings and identify further aspects. In the suggestion phase, a precise picture of our research design is created within the ISDT framework [42]. The development phase involves designing and implementing two prototypes based on GenAI for an online experiment on human-AI interaction in customer service [18]. We demonstrate and test the prototypes at two workshops to gather input from the field of IT support and improve the high-fidelity prototypes. Afterward, we analyze the impact of two types of human-AI hybrids (*supporter* and *collaborator*) and their influence on the workload of an FSE in an experimental study with n = 75 participants. Additionally, a survey is conducted to gather insights into participants' perceptions of the GenAI tool [32]. The final operationalization phase, including findings, contributions, limitations, and further research, encompassing the study results [24].

4 Designing a Co-Agent for Novice Frontline Service Employees

4.1 Awareness

The study utilized semi-structured interviews with support staff and experts to comprehend the needs and challenges faced by practitioners in customer service activities [37]. Along with different FSE routines (e.g., assign, transfer, locate, adapt, generate, retain) derived from technical support theory [9, 47], we elaborated on how AI can overcome persistent challenges. We interviewed 11 experts and analyzed the qualitative data through content coding [38] and found several ways to integrate generative AI into support routines in a human-centered way. The interviews showed that generative AI can be used in different ways to process customer requests. Expert 3 explained: "*[...] [that] the tickets [are] not always [...] helpful in the search because they're too long or poorly documented.*" The literature states that the greatest potential lies in decision support and human-AI collaboration [51]. In this way, FSEs retain control of the customer conversation but are accompanied by an AI-based co-agent. This interaction between the FSE and the AI is intended to maximize effectiveness while reducing workload when solving complex tasks [10]. In particular, when a human interacts with a generative AI, increased productivity and an improvement in overall task performance can be observed [43]. Expert 7 describes the following scenario: "*I took some sample tickets [...] and simply changed the ticket description [...]. And then an email was sent directly to the customer [...]. Even though I can't technically assess whether everything in there is correct, I thought it sounded very good*". We have, therefore, identified the problem that the FSE may only receive support from the GenAI to the extent that the FSE must actively process the task to ensure that the response to the customer is correct.

4.2 Suggestion

Our study proposes two GenAI-based co-agents to enhance the FSE onboarding process. We focus on two problem-solving routines, locating and adapting, that require high cognitive effort during customer interactions [9]. This approach is shown in Fig. 2 using the IS design theory (ISDT) approach to connect meta-design, meta-requirements, and constructs in an inner and outer model for our study [42]. For the meta-design, we distinguish between two degrees of interaction: *supporter* and *collaborator*. The *supporter* provides recommendations with minimal interaction, while the *collaborator* enables the FSE to prompt the GenAI-based system.

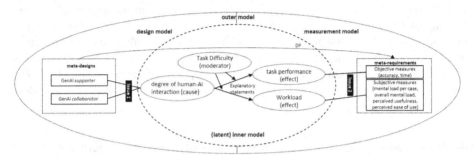

Fig. 2. Research design in the ISDT framework based on [42]

The meta-requirements are based on literature and interview results clustered according to key elements. These key elements are integrated into the experiment using a survey to measure the construct's usefulness, ease of use, and mental load (subjective measurements), as well as task time, the accuracy of correctly solved cases, and interaction counts with the GenAI-based support systems based on participants' responses during the experiment (objective measurements). The core relation (inner model) we analyze through the experiment is the influence of the degree of human-AI interaction (cause) on FSEs' mental workload and task performance (effect). *Task difficulty* acts as a moderator with three difficulty levels. Based on this ISDT research model design, we propose a design principle [14], that guides this study: *To augment novice FSE's problem-solving capabilities in real-time customer interactions with various degrees of difficulty, a higher degree of human-GenAI interaction should be enabled because of the complementary strengths of humans and AI in the form of hybrid intelligence.*

4.3 Development

Next, we developed two different prototypes as instantiations of our meta-designs. Participants interact with the prototypes via a web-based chatbot interface developed with the frontend framework Gradio. The prototypes include a GenAI-based customer bot with a specified customer request and a solution reference. Above that, the prototypes are extended with a "listening" and advice-giving GenAI bot - the co-agent. Additionally, both instantiations contain a search engine based on GPT embeddings. Additionally, we built a backend with a knowledge base and a database to log usage data and messages from the participants and the LLM-generated responses for the customer and the co-agent. We used publicly available data from a mobile provider and generated a data set linked with the co-agent and search engine.

We used two prototypes to reflect the different degrees of interaction between humans and AI. Co-agent one serves as a *supporter* and co-agent two as a *collaborator*, allowing the FSE to interact with the agent for deeper insights or extra information, as shown in

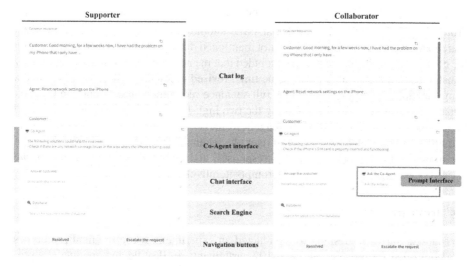

Fig. 3. Side-by-side Comparison of Prototypes with Treatment

Fig. 3. Both co-agent prototypes utilize a state-of-the-art LLM-based architecture [65] with an LLM [46] coupled with a retrieval augmented generation (RAG) system that was instantiated based on LlamaIndex- a framework for connecting GPT models to special knowledge bases and for developing chatbots. The RAG system was tested with a RAGAS evaluation framework [16]. The results ($faithfulness = 0.796$, $answer - relevancy = 0.840$, $context - precision = 0.658$, $context - recall = 0.784$) confirm the efficiency of the conversational agent and show that the co-agent provides reliable results and addresses user needs. For this purpose, we performed excessive prompt engineering. Participants receive a simulated customer request message and have to answer the same questions in the experiment. The tasks are randomly ordered with three levels of difficulty within the three customer requests that participants have to complete. Two cases can be directly solved by the FSE, while the third requires to *escalate* to a second-level agent. The customer request with *low difficulty* was extracted from a FAQ. The customer request with *high difficulty* is based on a forum post and requires more effort to find the correct solution. During the experiment, participants can use the "solved" and "escalate" buttons at the bottom of the interface. They can move on to the next case when they "solved" the customer's request. If the request seems unsolvable, they can "escalate" and move on to the next task.

4.4 Demonstration

Initially, we developed a low-fidelity prototype as a clickable mockup of the coagent [52]. We demonstrated the experimental study in front of 12 workshop participants, including help desk managers and FSEs. Then, we divided the participants into two focus groups. Each focus group was asked to discuss the general use cases for a co-agent in their organization, the potential for augmenting the onboarding phase, the augmentation interface and user experience, and additional configuration levels. In conclusion, the participants argued for a high potential of the presented use cases within the low-fidelity prototype. The participants stated that FSEs should still have direct access to ticket search engines to add specific details not mentioned during the conversation. Regarding the co-agent's interface, the group concluded that the recommendations should be easily transferred to the chat and, at the same time, revised efficiently. Thus, we integrated a copy function, the co-agent provides full-sentence recommendations, and the text box remains interactive. After instantiating the two high-fidelity prototypes, we introduced the co-agents in a second workshop again to the same group of IT support managers and FSEs and conducted a user test. Given the feedback from the experts regarding the performance, the structure of the AI responses, and the database records format, we revised our design and adjusted our prompts iteratively.

4.5 Evaluation

To evaluate our meta-designs we conducted an experiment, using the final prototypes in a controlled setting. We recruited 102 participants on Prolific and conducted a pre-experiment survey consisting of 13 questions to collect the participants' background, expertise, and AI experience. The participants were randomly assigned to the *supporter* and *collaborator* conditions. We assessed their perceived mental load after each task. Participants completed a post-survey after the experiment, rating their perceptions on a 7-point scale (1 = "do not agree at all" and 7 = "fully agree") on task fulfillment, co-agent perception, AI acceptance, trust, confidence, and workload [1]. We carefully cleaned participants' records to ensure data integrity. We removed 27 participants, leaving a final number of n = 75 after verifying the experiment and attention test completion (*supporter* = 42, *collaborator* = 33). Our participant group reflects a broad age range with an average age of 48 years and is almost equally split between males (40%) and females (60%). We conducted an initial correlation analysis between the demographic characteristics and the subjective and objective measurements, which revealed no anomalies that required further investigation.

In the next step, we calculate the mean of different constructs (latent variables) consisting of different items (manifest variables). The constructs are examined through descriptive statistics and frequency analysis [19]. For the final analysis of the ISDT framework, we use linear regression to gain insights into the relationship between the degree of human-AI interaction and mental workload.

Table 1. Perceived usefulness and perceived ease of use

	'Supporter'				'Collaborator'			
	Min	Max	Mean	Std. Deviation	Min	Max	Mean	Std. Deviation
Perceived Usefulness	4	7	5.506	.746	4	6	5.520	.604
Perceived Ease of Use	3	7	5.796	.737	5	7	5.868	.605

Perceived Ease of Use and Perceived Usefulness. We analyzed the perception of ease of use and usefulness ($\alpha = .903(ease\ of\ use)$, $\alpha = .789\ (usefulness)$). To generate questions on ease of use, we referred to the sources [5, 59], and for usefulness, we considered [29, 59]. Our findings, presented in Table 1, highlight the differences between the two levels of interaction degree. We observed a slight increase in the mean value for the *collaborator* condition. This could be attributed to the additional interaction with the co-agent, which allowed participants to better understand the system's functionalities and share an additional response with the customer.

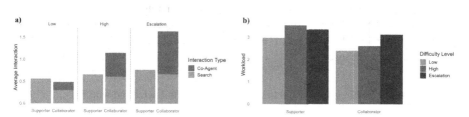

Fig. 4. a) Average interaction with co-agent and search by condition and by task difficulty; b) Average workload by condition and task difficulty

Task Performance. In both conditions, the results revealed that the accuracy of solving the tasks remains comparatively low and decreases with increased task difficulty, as expected. For instance, under the *supporter* scenario, the average accuracy for resolving less complex, FAQ-based tasks stands at 92.68%, while accuracy plummets to 31.43% for cases necessitating escalation to an expert. Hence, accuracy was mainly influenced by the quality of the underlying data source, with distinct outcomes observed between FAQ-based and forum-based information. Specifically, when the generative co-agent utilized FAQ data, a high level of accuracy was achieved, underscoring the reliability of structured and well-curated content in supporting decision-making processes. To compare task performance, we developed a measure consisting of accuracy and time for each case by normalizing the values. That way, we found that despite showing a slightly lower accuracy, the *collaborator* enables a slightly improved overall task performance (*supporter* = 1.191, *collaborator* = 1.305). Although our regression analysis did not reveal any significant results, we can conclude that the treatment does not adversely affect performance. Instead, task performance is slightly improved.

Interaction Between FSE and AI. By comparing *collaborator* and *collaborator* conditions, we observed notable differences in interaction dynamics between FSE and the provided tools. Overall, the *collaborator* condition showed an increase of 65.76% in terms of interactions on average, involving both search activities and communication with the co-agent. This uptick was particularly pronounced in more complex and unsolvable cases (Fig. 4a), indicating that collaboration intensifies when challenges escalate. Our design promoted a higher degree of engagement and interaction with the generative AI-based co-agent, suggesting a strategic shift towards more collaborative problem-solving approaches. Interestingly, the search engine usage was almost as frequent in the *collaborator* scenario as it was in the *supporter* case.

Workload. Despite higher time investment and interaction count, participants in the *collaborator* condition reported a lower mental load per case while maintaining performance levels (Fig. 4b), indicating that interaction with the co-agent contributes to a reduced workload. This mental load measure was collected at the end of each task. On average, the meta-design *collaborator* reduced the perceived mental load by 0.58 points. In a regression analysis assessing the impact of the *collaborator* condition on workload, the condition was associated with a reduction in reported workload ($\beta = -0.575, SE = 0.220, t = -2.612, p = 0.00965$). However, we could not find any moderating effects of task difficulty. Furthermore, these findings imply that AI collaboration could positively affect employee retention, potentially reducing turnover rates. Results from the post-survey confirm these insights. As Table 2 shows, the subjective measures reveal that the overall mean perceived workload ($\alpha = .555(overall\ workload)$) is lower in the case of the *collaborator* condition.

Table 2. Perceived mental load per task and overall perceived workload

	'Supporter'				'Collaborator'			
	Min	Max	Mean	Std. Deviation	Min	Max	Mean	Std. Deviation
Mental load per case and user	1	6	3.310	1.137	1	5	2.707	1.304
Overall mental load	1	7	3.857	1.601	1	6	3.606	1.223

5 Discussion

In light of these results, we can summarize an *interaction effort paradox* as an unexpected finding: Despite having significantly more interaction with the search engine and the co-agent overall, mental load is significantly lower in the case of the *collaborator* condition with the ability to prompt the co-agent. Thereby, we contradict prior research in human-AI collaboration that highlights the mental effort of interacting with digital technology - such as artificial agents or co-bots [7, 57]. In that case, information systems not only benefit human users but cause techno-stress or, more specifically, techno-overload [7]. However, based on our results, we argue that engaging with a co-agent through prompts is more likely to alleviate FSE's task demands than to impose mental effort. The paradox can, therefore, be viewed from a perspective of cognitive offloading [53]. Similar results were found when tracking several objects [60] or in human-AI collaboration in industrial tasks [20]. According to our study, cognitive offloading should be further examined as critical in highly demanding real-time customer interactions at the service frontline. An additional explanation could be that the natural language-based recommendations with the co-agent reduce information overload when compared with the full knowledge base articles from the database [44]. In conclusion, research and practice are urged to examine the positive consequences of AI collaborators in challenging service tasks [28].

In further detail, the results regarding the perceived utility of the co-agent demonstrate great satisfaction with the co-agent. As illustrated by the high average values for perceived usefulness and ease of use illustrate that, the co-agent is likely to be accepted at the workplace of novice FSE. However, the difference between *supporter* and *collaborator* is only marginal. Thus, there are unanswered questions on improving the prompt interface's utility in the second condition. For instance, prompt examples and templates could be provided to stimulate the usage of the co-agent as shown in related work [63]. It remains unclear how novice FSE can effectively prompt RAG-based GenAI tools. A comparison of the provided search engine and the prompt interface is required. Regarding the impact of the *collaborator* on task performance, we found no significant evidence for increased productivity regardless of the difficulty of customer issues. The non-detection of an influence on performance could be due to the study design and task selection, mainly the ease and unsolvability of the low-difficulty task and escalation task. However, we observed no significant results despite assuming a potential influence on the task with a high difficulty level. Our findings indicate that accuracy primarily depends on the task difficulty and the quality of the underlying data source used in the solution material. Utilizing FAQ data resulted in high accuracy, highlighting the reliability of well-structured content for decision-making and the efficiency of GenAI-based conversational agents. Given our design of experimental conditions, the *collaborator* resulted in an intensified overall interaction of the FSE with the given co-agent and search engine. Hence, the co-agent is perceived as a helpful collaborator. Interestingly, the search engine was nearly used as often as in the case of the *supporter*. Thus, further analysis of the usage patterns, the quality of search engine results, and the coagent response are required. Despite the higher overall interaction, we observed a lower perceived workload within the *collaborator* condition. As a key challenge for companies in the customer support sector refers to retaining their employees in the long term to minimize onboarding efforts and reduce costs [48], reducing the workload is the first step towards increasing attractiveness and thus reducing the churn rate. From that perspective, our results show the potential of GenAI for help desks to improve workplace conditions.

This study contributes to both service science and DSR literature by extending frontline service research through the implementation of AI augmentation [26, 36] and studying the different meta-designs of human-GenAI interaction [40]. Our empirical insights shed light on how AI can positively impact novices' perceived workload during initial customer interaction, achieved through a GPT4-based co-agent. Furthermore, we showcased the utilization of emerging GPT-based bots as simulated customers in service triads [11, 45]. Through effective and iterative prompt engineering, we paved the way for promising DSR research on AI augmentation in frontline service triads. Adapting the perspective of outer and inner models according to [42], our approach illustrates the integration of experimental and design-oriented research. To this end, our experiment instantiation including the corresponding data analysis pipeline could be generalized into a method and architecture which other researchers can draw on to conduct experiments in other related domains. This study's practical contributions lie in guiding the design of AI-based co-pilots and co-agents for frontline services and offering design decisions to improve employees' workplaces. Workplaces could be further improved by also introducing and studying the effects of co-pilots in other functions within a company such as the sales department.

Given the functionality of the GenAI-based co-agent and the simulated customer bot, our empirical design study has certain limitations and leaves room for further research. First, due to the generative nature of LLMs, the co-agent does not generate invariable recommendations despite prompt engineering, configuring the temperature, and connecting the co-agent to the database. Thus, further research should evaluate the co-agent's responses to allow for the analysis of issues such as overreliance. However, by testing the RAG system we ensured that the co-agent provides accurate responses. Similarly, the customer bot implies variations. Thus, our results are restricted by the uncontrollable nature of AI. Furthermore, broadening the scope of the study to include a wider range of tasks would provide a more thorough perspective on the co-agent's performance in various contexts. Investigating the efficiency of the co-agent in comparison to the search engine, as well as the prompts and queries formulated by the users, is essential for interpreting the quality of interaction. Lastly, contrasting situations involving the co-agent with those without it will show the influence and benefit of incorporating conversational AI into FSE routines. Thus, the paper allows for numerous avenues of future research. DSR researchers could examine various designs to reach more beneficial degrees of human-AI interaction - for example, by designing mechanisms to stimulate prompting or providing example prompts and templates. After enlarging the sample size, subsequent research could prioritize text-mining techniques for a more comprehensive analysis of the transcripts of customer interactions.

6 Conclusion

Our results show that the design of GenAI-based and employee-facing co-agents and co-pilots in customer service represents a pressing and challenging problem. Based on a practice and theory-driven DSR approach, we developed a "whispering" co-agent based on generative AI. Apart from minor design nuances discussed with IT support FSEs and managers, the paper emphasizes a broader dimension of designing human-GenAI interaction by realizing hybrid intelligence meta-designs. Through an experimental online setup with two distinct conditions, we evaluated two meta-designs for GenAI-driven employee augmentation: a supportive co-agent offering unidirectional decision support and a collaborative co-agent facilitating interaction via. The analysis of more than 300 customer interactions reveals that increased interaction with GenAI-based co-agents can improve FSE's workload during real-time customer service interactions.

Acknowledgments. This research is partly funded by the German Federal Ministry of Education and Research (BMBF) and supervised by PTKA (Project HISS - 02K18D060). Additionally, this work has been developed in the project Hyko and is partly funded by the Bavarian Ministry of Economic Affairs, Regional Development and Energy enabled by the European Regional Development Fund (ERDF) under grant number 1.2-StMWK-F.4-UFR-002. The authors are responsible for the content of this publication.

References

1. Herm, L.V.: Impact of explainable AI on cognitive load: insights from an empirical study. In: ECIS 2023. Research Papers, vol. 269 (2023)
2. Adam, M., Wessel, M., Benlian, A.: AI-based chatbots in customer service and their effects on user compliance. Electron. Mark. **31**(2), 427–445 (2021)
3. Attri, R.K.: Accelerated Proficiency for Accelerated Times: A Review of Key Concepts and Methods to Speed Up Performance. Speed To Proficiency Research (2020)
4. Bao, Y., Cheng, X., de Vreede, T., de Vreede, G.J.: Investigating the relationship between AI and trust in human-AI collaboration. In: HICSS, pp. 607–616 (2021)
5. Benbasat, I., Wang, W.: Trust in and adoption of online recommendation agents. J. Assoc. Inf. Syst. **6**(3), 4 (2005)
6. Bittner, E.A.C., Oeste-Reiß, S., Leimeister, J.M.: Where is the bot in our team? Toward a taxonomy of design option combinations for conversational agents in collaborative work. In: HICSS (2019)
7. Carissoli, C., Negri, L., Bassi, M., Storm, F.A., Delle Fave, A.: Mental workload and human-robot interaction in collaborative tasks: a scoping review. Int. J. Hum. Comput. Interact. 1–20 (2023)
8. Chen, Q., Gong, Y., Lu, Y., Tang, J.: Classifying and measuring the service quality of AI chatbot in frontline service. J. Bus. Res. **145**, 552–568 (2022)
9. Das, A.: Knowledge and productivity in technical support work. Manage. Sci. **49**(4), 416–431 (2003)
10. Davenport, T., Guha, A., Grewal, D., Bressgott, T.: How artificial intelligence will change the future of marketing. J. Acad. Mark. Sci. **48**, 24–42 (2020)
11. De Keyser, A., Köcher, S., Alkire, L., Verbeeck, C., Kandampully, J.: Frontline service technology infusion: conceptual archetypes and future research directions. J. Serv. Manage. **30**(1), 156–183 (2019)
12. Dellermann, D., Calma, A., Lipusch, N., Weber, T., Weigel, S., Ebel, P.: The future of human-AI collaboration: a taxonomy of design knowledge for hybrid intelligence systems. In: HICSS (2019)
13. Dellermann, D., Ebel, P., Söllner, M., Leimeister, J.M.: Hybrid intelligence. Bus. Inf. Syst. Eng. **61**, 637–643 (2019)
14. Dellermann, D., Lipusch, N., Ebel, P., Leimeister, J.M.: Design principles for a hybrid intelligence decision support system for business model validation. Electron. Mark. **29**, 423–441 (2019)
15. Ebel, P., Söllner, M., Leimeister, J.M., Crowston, K., de Vreede, G.J.: Hybrid intelligence in business networks. Electron. Mark. **31**, 313–318 (2021)
16. Es, S., James, J., Espinosa-Anke, L., Schockaert, S.: Ragas: automated evaluation of retrieval augmented generation. arXiv preprint arXiv:2309.15217 (2023)
17. Fabri, L., Haäkel, B., Oberla¨nder, A.M., Rieg, M., Stohr, A.: Disentangling HumanAI hybrids. Bus. Inf. Syst. Eng. **65**, 1–19 (2023)
18. Fink, L.: Why and how online experiments can benefit information systems research. J. Assoc. Inf. Syst. **23**(6), 1333–1346 (2022)
19. Fisher, M.J., Marshall, A.P.: Understanding descriptive statistics. Aust. Crit. Care **22**(2), 93–97 (2009)
20. Fournier, E., et al.: The impacts of human-cobot collaboration on perceived cognitive load and usability during an industrial task: an exploratory experiment. IISE Trans. Occup. Ergon. Hum. Factors **10**(2), 83–90 (2022)
21. Freire, S.K., Panicker, S.S., Ruiz-Arenas, S., Rusa´k, Z., Niforatos, E.: A cognitive assistant for operators: Ai-powered knowledge sharing on complex systems. IEEE Pervasive Comput. **22**(1), 50–58 (2022)

22. Graßmann, C., Schermuly, C.C.: Coaching with artificial intelligence: concepts and capabilities. Hum. Resour. Dev. Rev. **20**(1), 106–126 (2021)
23. Gregor, S., Hevner, A.R.: Positioning and presenting design science research for maximum impact. MIS Q. **37**, 337–355 (2013)
24. Gregor, S., Jones, D., et al.: The anatomy of a design theory. Assoc. Inf. Syst. (2007)
25. Hemmer, P., Schemmer, M., Vössing, M., Kühl, N.: Human-AI complementarity in hybrid intelligence systems: a structured literature review. In: PACIS (2021)
26. Henkel, A.P., Bromuri, S., Iren, D., Urovi, V.: Half human, half machine – augmenting service employees with AI for interpersonal emotion regulation. J. Serv. Manag. **31**(2), 247–265 (2020)
27. Hevner, A.R., March, S.T., Park, J., Ram, S.: Design science in information systems research. Manage. Inf. Syst. Q. **28**(1), 6 (2008)
28. Hollender, N., Hofmann, C., Deneke, M., Schmitz, B.: Integrating cognitive load theory and concepts of human–computer interaction. Comput. Hum. Behav. **26**(6), 1278–1288 (2010)
29. Hone, K.S., Graham, R.: Towards a tool for the subjective assessment of speech system interfaces (SASSI). Nat. Lang. Eng. **6**(3–4), 287–303 (2000)
30. Huang, M.H., Rust, R.T.: A framework for collaborative artificial intelligence in marketing. J. Retail. **98**(2), 209–223 (2022)
31. Khan, S., Iqbal, M.: AI-powered customer service: does it optimize customer experience? In: ICRITO, pp. 590–594. IEEE (2020)
32. Krosnick, J.A.: Questionnaire Design. The Palgrave Handbook of Survey Research, pp. 439–455 (2018)
33. Kuechler, B., Vaishnavi, V.: On theory development in design science research: anatomy of a research project. EJIS **17**(5), 489–504 (2008)
34. Larivi'ere, B., et al.: "Service encounter 2.0": an investigation into the roles of technology, employees and customers. J. Bus. Res. **79**, 238–246 (2017)
35. Li, M.M., Reinhard, P., Peters, C., Oeste-Reiss, S., Leimeister, J.M.: A value cocreation perspective on data labeling in hybrid intelligence systems: a design study. Inf. Syst. **120**, 102311 (2024)
36. Luo, X., Qin, M.S., Fang, Z., Qu, Z.: Artificial intelligence coaches for sales agents: caveats and solutions. J. Mark. **85**(2), 14–32 (2021)
37. Maedche, A., Gregor, S., Morana, S., Feine, J.: Conceptualization of the problem space in design science research. In: Tulu, B., Djamasbi, S., Leroy, G. (eds.) DESRIST 2019. LNCS, vol. 11491, pp. 18–31. Springer, Cham (2019). https://doi.org/10.1007/978-3-030-19504-5_2
38. Mayring, P.: Qualitative Inhaltsanalyse: Grundlagen und Techniken. Beltz (2022)
39. McFarlane, D.C., Latorella, K.A.: The scope and importance of human interruption in human-computer interaction design. Hum. Comput. Interact. **17**(1), 1–61 (2002)
40. Murray, A., Rhymer, J., Sirmon, D.G.: Humans and technology: forms of conjoined agency in organizations. Acad. Manag. Rev. **46**(3), 552–571 (2021)
41. Nicolescu, L., Tudorache, M.T.: Human-computer interaction in customer service: the experience with AI chatbots—a systematic literature review. Electronics **11**(10), 1579 (2022)
42. Niehaves, B., Ortbach, K.: The inner and the outer model in explanatory design theory: the case of designing electronic feedback systems. EJIS **25**, 303–316 (2016)
43. Noy, S., Zhang, W.: Experimental evidence on the productivity effects of generative artificial intelligence. Science **381**, 187–192 (2023)
44. Ocón Palma, M.D.C., Seeger, A.-M., Heinzl, A.: Mitigating information overload in e-commerce interactions with conversational agents. In: Davis, F.D., Riedl, R., vom Brocke, J., Léger, P.-M., Randolph, A., Fischer, T. (eds.) Information Systems and Neuroscience. LNISO, vol. 32, pp. 221–228. Springer, Cham (2020). https://doi.org/10.1007/978-3-030-28144-1_24

45. Odekerken-Schro¨der, G., Mennens, K., Steins, M., Mahr, D.: The service triad: an empirical study of service robots, customers and frontline employees. J. Serv. Manage. **33**(2), 246–292 (2021)
46. OpenAI: GPT-4 Technical Report. arXiv preprint arXiv:2303.08774 (2023)
47. Pentland, B.T.: Organizing moves in software support hot lines. Adm. Sci. Q. **37**, 527–548 (1992)
48. Pierre, X., Tremblay, D.G.: Levels of involvement and retention of agents in call centres: improving well-being of employees for better socioeconomic performance. J. Manage. Policy Pract. **12**(5), 53–71 (2011)
49. Poser, M., Wiethof, C., Banerjee, D., Shankar Subramanian, V., Paucar, R., Bittner, E.A.: Let's team up with AI! toward a hybrid intelligence system for online customer service. In: Drechsler, A., Gerber, A., Hevner, A. (eds.) DESRIST 2022, vol. 13229, pp. 142–153. Springer, Cham (2022). https://doi.org/10.1007/978-3-031-06516-3_11
50. Raisamo, R., Rakkolainen, I., Majaranta, P., Salminen, K., Rantala, J., Farooq, A.: Human augmentation: past, present and future. Int. J. Hum. Comput. Stud. **131**, 131–143 (2019)
51. Reinhard, P., Li, M., Peters, C., Leimeister, J.M.: Generative AI in customer support services: a framework for augmenting the routines of frontline service employees. In: HICSS (2024)
52. Reinhard, P., Wischer, D., Verlande, L., Neis, N., Li, M.: Towards designing an ai-based conversational agent for on-the-job training of customer support novices. In: DESRIST (2023)
53. Risko, E.F., Gilbert, S.J.: Cognitive offloading. Trends Cogn. Sci. **20**(9), 676–688 (2016)
54. Ritz, E., Fabio, D., Elshan, E., Rietsche, R.: Artificial socialization? How artificial intelligence applications can shape a new era of employee onboarding practices. In: HICSS (2023)
55. Robinson, S., et al.: Frontline encounters of the AI kind: an evolved service encounter framework. J. Bus. Res. **116**, 366–376 (2020)
56. Schmidt, S.L., Li, M., Peter, C.: Requirements for an it support system based on hybrid intelligence. In: HICSS (2022)
57. Sun, Y., Li, S., Yu, L.: The dark sides of AI personal assistant: effects of service failure on user continuance intention. Electron. Mark. **32**(1), 17–39 (2022)
58. van Turnhout, K., Terken, J., Bakx, I., Eggen, B.: Identifying the intended addressee in mixed human-human and human-computer interaction from non-verbal features. In: ICMI, pp. 175–182 (2005)
59. Venkatesh, V., Morris, M.G., Davis, G.B., Davis, F.D.: User acceptance of information technology: toward a unified view. MIS Q. **27**, 425–478 (2003)
60. Wahn, B., Schmitz, L., Gerster, F.N., Weiss, M.: Offloading under cognitive load: Humans are willing to offload parts of an attentionally demanding task to an algorithm. PLoS ONE **18**(5), e0286102 (2023)
61. Wiethof, C., Bittner, E.A.: Toward a hybrid intelligence system in customer service: collaborative learning of human and AI. In: ECIS (2022)
62. Wiethof, C., Poser, M., Bittner, E.A.C.: Design and evaluation of an employeefacing conversational agent in online customer service. In: PACIS (2022)
63. Zamfirescu-Pereira, J., Wong, R.Y., Hartmann, B.: Why Johnny can't prompt: how non-AI experts try (and fail) to design LLM prompts. In: CHI, pp. 1–21 (2023)
64. Zhang, G., Raina, A., Cagan, J., McComb, C.: A cautionary tale about the impact of AI on human design teams. Des. Stud. **72**, 100990 (2021)
65. Zhao, W.X ., et al.: A survey of large language models. arXiv preprint arXiv:2303.18223 (2023)

Designing a Large Language Model Based Open Data Assistant for Effective Use

Till Carlo Schelhorn[1]([envelope]), Ulrich Gnewuch[2], and Alexander Maedche[1]

[1] Institute of Information Systems and Marketing (IISM), Karlsruhe Institute of Technology (KIT), Karlsruhe, Germany
{till.schelhorn,alexander.maedche}@kit.edu
[2] University of Passau, Passau, Germany
ulrich.gnewuch@uni-passau.de

Abstract. Open data is widely recognized for its potential positive impact on society and economy. However, many open data sets remain underutilized because users, such as civil servants and citizens, lack the necessary technical and analytical skills. Additionally, existing open data portals often fall short of providing user-friendly access to data. Although conversational agents equipped with Large Language Models have emerged as a promising solution to address these challenges, it is unclear how to design Large Language Model based open data assistants that allow users to formulate their information needs in natural language and ultimately use open data effectively. To address this gap, we undertake a Design Science Research project guided by the theory of effective use. In this first cycle of the project, we present meta-requirements and propose initial design principles on how to design a Large Language Model based open data assistant for effective use. Subsequently, we instantiate our principles in a prototype and evaluate it in a focus group with experts from a medium-sized German city. Our results contribute design knowledge in the form of design principles for open data assistants and inform future design cycles of our Design Science Research project.

Keywords: Open Data · Conversational Agents · Large Language Models · Theory of Effective Use · Design Science Research

1 Introduction

"Everyone has the right to [...] seek, receive and impart information" [34, Art. 19]. Freedom of information is recognized as a fundamental right in democratic states. Therefore, legislative frameworks have been established in many countries to speed up the opening of data to the general public, e.g. in the EU [8] or the US [25]. These open data initiatives are motivated by the objective of increasing openness and transparency, enabling participation in the democratic process, and thus strengthening democracy [22]. Beyond its positive impact on society, open data can also benefit the economy by laying the foundation for innovative digital services and the development of new business models [29]. The European Commission estimates that open data could boost the European economy by €40 billion annually [7].

M. Mandviwalla et al. (Eds.): DESRIST 2024, LNCS 14621, pp. 398–411, 2024.
https://doi.org/10.1007/978-3-031-61175-9_27

Open data is typically published on open data portals on different levels, e.g. on the level of cities, municipalities, states, or state unions such as the EU [22]. As an example, the open data portal of the EU contains over 1,600,000 data sets [9]. Yet, open data is not limited to government data but includes all data "that can be used, studied, and modified without restriction" [24, p. 1]. In order to leverage the potential of open data, it must also be used. Open data usage refers to "the activity that a person or an organization conducts to view, understand, analyze, visualize or in other ways use a dataset that has been provided to the public" [44, p. 429].

Although the benefits of open data are widely acknowledged, various challenges impede users from using and leveraging its potential [1, 5, 26, 43]. First, the user base of open data portals is diverse, encompassing citizens, journalists, activists, researchers, employees of private companies, and civil servants [32]. This diversity results in a wide range of skill sets and domain knowledge among users. Thus, many users lack the technical and analytical skills or the domain knowledge required to effectively utilize open data portals [38]. Second, amplifying these issues, open data portals often have complex user interfaces with challenging navigation structures and inadequate search capabilities, hindering the identification of relevant datasets [26]. Consequently, many datasets available on open data portals remain unused by the public [27]. Nevertheless, there is a demand for public information captured by open data. Public offices increasingly receive requests for public information leading civil servants to retrieve relevant open data [11]. However, this creates additional workload and leads to a bottleneck. For example, FragDenStaat, a German website facilitating citizens' requests for public information, reports an average response time of 43 days for these requests [10].

Amidst these challenges, conversational agents (CAs) emerge as a potential solution providing accessible interfaces through natural language [23]. According to the theory of effective use [3], transparent interaction is a key dimension for effectively using Information Systems (IS). Indeed, Ruoff et al. [30] demonstrate that conversational interfaces can significantly enhance the effective use of IS, particularly in the context of dashboards, by achieving heightened levels of transparent interaction. Moreover, Burton-Jones and Grange [3] identify representational fidelity, and informed action as additional dimensions influencing the efficiency and effectiveness of IS usage.

In addition, prototypes of "open data assistants" have been introduced in literature to facilitate access and utilization of open data [13, 18, 37]. The ascent of Large Language Models (LLMs) has further expanded possibilities, as their extensive capabilities in natural language comprehension can be leveraged to create powerful CAs [39]. Recent literature has showcased the potential of LLMs for reasoning and solving complex tasks through self-generated chain-of-thought [40]. Additionally, attention has been given to enhancing LLMs' capabilities for answering domain-specific questions by utilizing various external knowledge sources [21]. This effort extends to structured data through the generation and execution of SQL queries [16, 28]. These advancements demonstrate promise for the development of open data assistants that not only assist users in understanding the data but also provide insight into how answers to their questions are generated. However, there is limited research on the application of LLM-powered CAs for open data. This raises the following research question: *How to design an LLM-based open data assistant for effective use?*

To address this question, our research follows the Design Science Research (DSR) paradigm proposed by Hevner et al. [12]. DSR aims to solve a real-world problem by suggesting an innovative solution. We conduct our DSR project in a real-world environment in cooperation with a medium-sized German city that already runs an Open Data portal and is faced with the challenges introduced above. Thus, from a stakeholder perspective we include both civil servants and citizens. This paper encompasses the first design cycle of our larger DSR project. Our research is grounded in the theory of effective use (TEU) as kernel theory [3]. Guided by interviews, focus groups, and a review of existing literature on the barriers of open data, we identify several meta-requirements for an LLM-based open data assistant. In response to these requirements, we formulate three initial design principles to guide the implementation of our artifact. The artifact, along with its underlying design principles, undergoes evaluation in a focus group comprising civil servants from our partner city. Through this, we successfully demonstrate how an LLM-based open data assistant can support the utilization of open data portals by users with varying technical and analytical skills. This contribution extends design knowledge in the form of design principles for open data assistants, providing actionable guidance for the creation of such assistants and offering valuable insights for future design cycles.

2 Foundations and Related Work

2.1 Conversational Agents and Large Language Models

Conversational User Interfaces (CUIs) enable users to interact with IS in written or spoken natural language [23]. "Conversational" refers to all types of spoken interaction supporting the use of spontaneous language and often displaying human-like characteristics [23]. Research on CUIs has a long history with ELIZA being the first chatbot developed in the 1960s [41]. Since then there has been a large interest in research on CUIs in the form of chatbots and CAs in different contexts [6]. Recent literature has investigated the influence of CAs on effective use in the context of dashboards showing that CAs can complement traditional graphical user interfaces [30].

Large Language Models (LLMs) have rapidly reshaped the landscape of natural language processing (NLP) and CAs [39]. The self-attention mechanism of the underlying transformer architecture enables the models to capture and understand the relationship between different words of an input sequence [35]. ChatGPT made LLMs available to the general public and became the fastest growing consumer application in history [14]. Since then, LLMs have shown remarkable capabilities in code generation tasks, such as generating SQL queries, showcasing their versatility beyond conventional language understanding [28].

To address challenges like hallucinations, research has extended LLM functionality with Retrieval-Augmented Generation (RAG) integrating the models with external knowledge sources and enabling them to answer domain-specific questions [21]. Additionally, the explicit prompting of chain-of-thought has emerged as a strategy to guide LLMs in solving complex tasks [40]. These developments have facilitated the implementation of LLM-powered agents with extensive capabilities consisting of a reasoning engine and access to different external tools and knowledge bases [17, 42].

2.2 Theory of Effective Use

To achieve maximum benefits from IS, they need to be used effectively [3]. Burton-Jones and Grange define effective use as "using a system in a way that helps attain the goals for using the system" [3, p. 633]. They define a hierarchy of three dimensions that influence the effective and efficient use of IS: (1) transparent interaction, (2) representational fidelity, and (3) informed action [3]. Each dimension is a requirement for the higher-level dimension. A user needs to be able to transparently interact with an IS to obtain a faithful representation of the underlying domain (representational fidelity) in order to be able to take an informed action [3]. Transparent interaction is defined as "accessing the system's representations unimpeded by its surface and physical structures" [3, p. 642]. The surface structure refers to the user interface of the IS and the physical structure to devices in the physical world that are used to interact with the IS (e.g. mouse and keyboard).

Burton-Jones and Grange state two major types of actions to improve effective use: adaption and learning. Adaption is "any action a user takes to improve (1) a system's representation of the domain of interest; or (2) his or her access to them" [3, p. 644]. They further define learning actions as "any action a user takes to learn (1) the system (its representations, or its surface or physical structure); (2) the domain it represents; (3) the extent to which it faithfully represents the domain (i.e., its fidelity); or (4) how to leverage representations obtained from the system" [3, p. 644].

2.3 Related Work

Several conversational assistants for open data have been proposed in the literature, including for the city of Aragon [13], Austria [18], and Shanghai [37]. However, del Hoyo-Alonso et al. [13] conclude that traditional intent-based CAs can assist users interacting with open data, but require extensive implementation effort to satisfy all possible user questions. They suggest extending the capabilities of open data assistants with LLMs. Yet, they also raise concerns regarding the generation of hallucinations by these models and stress the need to ensure the validity of the information provided to the user [13]. In addition, initial practical solutions are also offered: ZurichGPT, an LLM-based agent for exploring open data of the city of Zurich, was published recently [4]. They focus on providing the sources of retrieved information with the generated answer. However, they also explicitly state that users should always check information on the official website of the city [4].

Nevertheless, current research rapidly develops the capabilities of LLMs further. The explicit prompting of chain-of-thought [40] and provisioning of external knowledge [21] enables the development of LLM-powered agents with extensive problem-solving capabilities [17, 42]. These could answer questions more reliably and even answer questions regarding complex tasks. For example, Bran et al. developed a chemistry agent by augmenting an LLM with chemistry tools enabling it to automate several chemistry-related tasks [2]. However, limited research exists on theory-guided design for LLM-based agents. Additionally, the works on open data assistants we found either excluded users from their evaluation or the assistants lacked LLM capabilities. We therefore argue that there is limited knowledge of what design principles should guide the development of

LLM-based agents. We address this gap using a DSR approach to design and evaluate an LLM-based open data assistant for effective use in a real-world environment.

3 Methodology

Our research is guided by the DSR paradigm [12] and follows the DSR method described by Kuechler and Vaishnavi [19]. This paper encompasses the first design cycle of our DSR project. To understand the challenges faced with open data we undertook an initial literature review, conducted two focus groups with citizens, and interviewed civil servants responsible for the open data portals of five different German cities. Based on the identified issues related to the use of open data we derived meta-requirements and proposed three design principles. Our research is grounded in the TEU as the kernel theory [3]. To complement this, we draw prescriptive knowledge from existing literature. Specifically, Ruoff et al. [30] propose the adaption of dashboards with conversational interfaces achieving higher levels of transparent interaction leading to enhanced efficiency and effectiveness. Furthermore, we rely on existing knowledge on the creation of LLM-based agents [17, 42] and providing them with access to external knowledge sources [21]. We instantiated our design principles in a prototype, an LLM-based open data assistant, and equipped it with access to open data from our partner city. The city is a medium-sized city in the south of Germany. It inhabits around 250.000 people and employs over 4.000 people in its city administration. Furthermore, in 2020 the city started a large smart city project sponsored by the German Federal Ministry for Housing, Urban Development and Building. This showcases its commitment to innovation and technological advancements, making it a promising candidate for collaboration on our DSR project.

Venable et al. [36] suggest multiple formative and summative evaluation episodes for DSR. In our first cycle, we undertook a formative and qualitative evaluation to evaluate our artifact. This evaluation occurred within an expert focus group comprised of eight civil servants (ranging from 28 to 57 years old, with 2 females and 6 males). The participants are all stakeholders in the open data portal of the city with diverse technical skills and domain knowledge. They serve various roles, either as active users of the portal or as contributors to its development and content.

Moving forward, our research plan includes another design cycle informed by the insights gained from the initial evaluation. This iterative process aims to refine both the design principles and the implemented artifact. In the subsequent evaluation, we intend to conduct a summative quantitative evaluation episode to shed light on the impact of our refined design principles on the effective use of our open data assistant.

4 Designing the LLM-Based Open Data Assistant

4.1 Awareness of Problem

In the upcoming section, we will address the issues identified in existing literature on open data usage, as well as insights obtained from our focus groups with citizens and interviews with civil servants. Our approach involves aligning the findings from literature with the statements gathered during the focus groups and interviews. Subsequently, we derive three meta-requirements informed by our kernel theory TEU (see Sect. 2.2).

First of all, open data portals serve various users with a wide range of different skill sets [32]. Many lack the technical and analytical skills or the domain knowledge to effectively use open data [38]. Furthermore, open data portals often come with poor usability and do not "take the user's perspective into account" [15, p. 256]. The participants of our focus groups criticized the insufficient search capabilities of open data portals and struggled to identify "what data is available and where to find it". This issue is reinforced by the large amount of heterogeneous open data initiatives and portals available [1]. Additionally, open data portals often contain raw data and information is fragmented across different files [43]. The participants found that "downloading and analyzing CSV files is not feasible" for them. Even though some data was presented with visualizations and reports, finding relevant information was still challenging for the participants due to multiple layers of menus and sub-menus. Lastly, poor (meta-) data quality further impedes users trying to find relevant information [31]. The participants of our focus group complained about the "confusing and inconsistent labeling of data" that makes the identification of relevant information unnecessarily difficult. Our findings were confirmed through the conducted interviews. According to insights gathered from civil servants, open data portals primarily serve as a resource for city internal sources. Despite the availability of visualizations and reporting tools on numerous open data portals, these features often go underutilized due to their perceived complexity. Consequently, many users, encompassing citizens, researchers, and journalists, prefer to directly request information from the respective departments within the city.

To derive meta-requirements (MRs) for a system solving these identified issues we draw existing knowledge from the theory of effective use (TEU) [3]. To effectively use an IS, the user must have unimpeded access to the system's representations [3]. We showed that users of open portals often struggle to identify relevant data and extract information thus not being able to interact transparently with the system. One approach to improve the transparent interaction is to adapt the system's surface structure (e.g. its user interface) [3]. Natural language can be used to interact more naturally with open data portals independent of the user's skills and the interface of the portal [30]. Therefore, we propose our first MR:

MR1: The system should allow users to ask questions about and interact with open data using natural language to help them achieve higher levels of transparent interaction.

The second level in the hierarchy of TEU is representational fidelity, the extent to which a user can obtain a faithful representation of the underlying domain by the system [3]. Learning the fidelity of the system's representation is one way to improve this. Enabling the user to comprehend how the system concludes its answer enables them to recognize if the system faithfully represents the underlying domain, e.g. gives a correct answer. Therefore, when obtaining an answer from the system based on open data, being presented with the steps of how the system came up with this answer helps the user to achieve higher levels of representational fidelity. We propose our second MR:

MR2: The system should augment its responses with information about its internal reasoning process to help users achieve higher levels of representational fidelity.

The final dimension of TEU is the informed action the user performs based on the information obtained through the system's representations [3]. Users accessing open data usually have some information needs they want to satisfy. This information is then used to make data-driven decisions, may it be in their private or professional life. Providing false information would hinder the user from taking such an informed action. Therefore, we propose our third MR as follows:

MR3: The system should avoid provisioning responses that contain false or fabricated information in order to enable users to take informed action.

4.2 Suggestion

To address these MRs we formulate three initial DPs. We draw from existing prescriptive knowledge regarding the design of CAs for effective use and LLM-based agents. To enable the user to use natural language when interacting with the assistant (MR1) requires a CA [30]. Serving a large number of different requests by users not knowing the domain-specific terminology the CA should have extensive language comprehension capabilities. Del Hoyo-Alonso et al. [13] therefore suggest providing the assistant with an LLM-powered agent. Thus, to address our first MR we formulate our first DP:

DP1: Provide the open data assistant with an LLM-based agent to increase its language comprehension and generation capabilities.

Enabling the user to understand the internal reasoning process of the assistant is supposed to achieve higher levels of representational fidelity (MR2). LLM-powered agents generate a sequence of actions. Based on the observation resulting from the previous action the agent decides which action to take next until it solves their task. This sequence of actions is often called chain-of-thought [40]. Providing the user with this chain-of-thought could enable them to understand the agent's reasoning process. We therefore address our second MR by formulating the following DP:

DP2: Enable the open data assistant to present the chain-of-thought the conversational agent generates to increase transparency of the system for the user. To reduce hallucinations and provisioning of false answers (MR3) by LLMs, RAG proved as a viable strategy [21]. Providing the LLM-based agent with access to data available on the open data portal and explicitly prompting it to base its answer on this data achieves this. Therefore, we formulate our last DP:

DP3: Provide the open data assistant with the capabilities to access available open data and restrict it to only use this data for generating responses.

4.3 Development

As the next step of our design process, we instantiated the design principles in a prototype to evaluate the proposed design. We developed an LLM-based open data assistant using two high-level Python frameworks: Langchain [20] for the implementation of the LLM agent and Streamlit [33] for the web-based interface of the application. As LLM we relied on the OpenAI API using the GPT-3.5 Turbo foundational model. Figure 1 shows the architecture of our prototype system.

The prototype offers a CA that enables the user to chat with the open data assistant through natural language (DP1). The users' input is forwarded to the Langchain agent

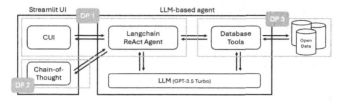

Fig. 1. Overview of the schematic architecture of our prototypical implementation

running in the back. We followed the ReAct approach [42] for the design of the agent. It is equipped with access to an SQL database comprising 42 diverse datasets sourced from the open data portal of our partner city (DP3). Four different tools enable the agent to interact with the database: (1) retrieving the five most relevant datasets for the users' input, (2) querying the SQL schema for a specific dataset, (3) assessing the syntactical and semantic correctness of a provided SQL query, and (4) executing a SQL query and retrieving the resulting data. Upon receiving user input, the agent dynamically selects the appropriate tool and input. Subsequently, based on the observed response from the chosen tool, the agent determines whether to provide an answer directly or invoke another tool. This chain-of-thought (tool, input, and observation) is transparently displayed in the Streamlit UI throughout the interaction (DP2). Upon completion of the sequence of actions, the UI provides a comprehensive display of executed SQL queries and relevant tables employed during the process. This ensures transparency and traceability of the agent's decision-making process. Figure 2 shows the web-based Streamlit UI with an exemplary user question.

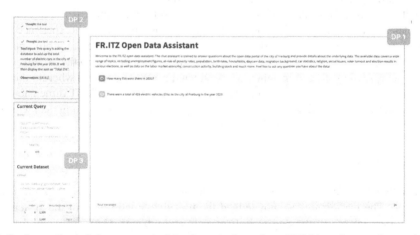

Fig. 2. Screenshot of the prototypical implementation of our LLM-based open data assistant answering an exemplary user question

The UI features a chat window that provides a brief description of the open data assistant. Upon sending a message, the agent's reasoning process is revealed on the left, showcasing the chain of thought. Further details about specific actions can be accessed by expanding the individual thoughts, revealing natural language descriptions and the observed return values. When data is queried from the knowledge base, both the query and results are presented below. The complete dataset is also visible, with an option for the user to expand the table view for more in-depth examination.

5   Evaluation

5.1   Method

In collaboration with eight experts from our partner city, we organized a focus group to evaluate our prototype and conduct a SWOT analysis. The expert group comprised individuals from various departments, namely (1) two IT department employees responsible for developing the city's open data portal, (2) two employees from different specialized city administration departments, and (3) four employees from the statistics department, tasked with providing reports and addressing data-specific inquiries from both internal city departments and external requests. These participants, being stakeholders of the open data portal, represent diverse perspectives and skill levels.

Our primary objective was to gather feedback from both technical and nontechnical users of the open data portal. The IT department, characterized by high technical proficiency, primarily focuses on data provisioning through the portal. Contrarily, the specialized departments represent the data consumer side, possessing significant domain knowledge but limited technical and analytical capabilities. Acting as intermediaries, the statistics department combines technical and analytical skills with domain knowledge, preparing reports, data, and responses for various city administration departments and external entities, including citizens, journalists, and researchers.

Following a brief introduction, we presented our prototype to the experts, showcasing examples and explaining distinct design features. Subsequently, each expert accessed the system from their respective devices, enabling them to explore the prototype. We then gathered feedback in a discussion to understand their opinions on the prototype. To further analyze the gathered insights, we conducted a SWOT analysis wherein the participants documented their comments, later categorized into the SWOT dimensions. In the next section, we will discuss the results of this evaluation, highlighting the identified strengths, weaknesses, opportunities, and threats.

5.2   Results

The results of our focus group evaluation indicate an overall positive reception of our prototype. The participants acknowledged the usefulness and utility of the system for both the internal use of the city's civil servants and citizens. However, there are still some issues where data is misinterpreted by the open data assistant. Nevertheless, the experts in our focus group praised our approach and gave valuable feedback on further improvements.

Strengths. The experts liked the robust natural language understanding of the prototype. The system demonstrated a capacity to accurately comprehend and interpret queries, even when questions were imprecise or contained erroneous terminology. One participant emphasized this point, stating, "knowing the exact keyword that is used for the relevant dataset is typically necessary for finding specific data", but not with our system. The system's capability to allow users to articulate their information needs in natural language was highlighted, particularly for non-technical users. A participant noted that many of their colleagues are unaccustomed to handling data and found that "formulating a question in natural language eases the access to the data." Furthermore, commendation was given to the system's rapid accessibility of information. A participant remarked that under normal circumstances, it would take several minutes to locate the correct dataset and subsequently analyze the data for the required information. However, they identified our system "as definitely the fastest way to extract information." Lastly, participants expressed appreciation for the transparent display of the chain-of-thought. This feature was acknowledged for aiding the understanding of the data utilized in generating responses, making it simple to determine the correctness of dataset usage and the accuracy of data queries.

Weaknesses. Despite the notable strengths observed in our system, the expert identified several weaknesses, particularly in the prototype's occasional misinterpretation of data. Instances were noted where the agent erroneously presented values from incorrect columns or aggregated columns when such computation was unnecessary. Consequently, these misinterpretations led to incorrect answers, posing a potential challenge to the system's reliability. While displaying the chain-of-thought enables users to verify the relevance of queried data the participants expressed their concerns. Firstly, they highlighted the practicality issue, as most users may not undertake the time-consuming task of double-checking every response. Moreover, participants expressed worries about the potential harm to the assistant's credibility and the decline in user trust. One participant emphasized the current perception of the system as more of an "expert tool," primarily due to the display of executed SQL queries and data tables. Despite acknowledging the transparency inherent in this design principle, participants desired a more direct approach to displaying the chain-of-thought. A suggestion was made to "supply the relevant actions for retrieving the information directly with the answer through natural language," enhancing the user's understanding of the system's decision-making process. Furthermore, experts articulated the need for additional information about the data. For instance, inquiring about the number of employees might not encompass civil servants, self-employed individuals, and marginal employees in the count of socially insured people. Supplying such context was considered essential to assist users in verifying agent's responses, particularly for users lacking domain-specific knowledge. Lastly, concerns were raised regarding the sustainability of utilizing OpenAI's language model, encompassing environmental impact, future operational costs, and the security of users' data.

Opportunities. Amidst these identified weaknesses, experts highlighted valuable opportunities to enhance the prototype. First and foremost, they recommended incorporating a broader range of open data sources from the city into the assistant. One participant suggested, "Enriching the answers with background information and metadata" as a means to mitigate data misinterpretation by both the agent and the user, consequently reducing the potential for misinformation. Another proposed enhancement involves the inclusion of existing analyses and reports conducted by civil servants.

This addition could not only improve the agent's overall performance but also contribute to decreased query times, particularly when data is already preprocessed and evaluated. Furthermore, experts advised simplifying the technical aspects of the explanation of the chain-of-thought. This is seen as a means to enhance system accessibility, particularly for non-technical users, thereby making the system accessible to a broader audience. The final suggestion put forth was exploring on-premise open-source LLMs as a potential alternative to the OpenAI models. While this could reduce dependence on OpenAI, it could also decrease system performance. These opportunities present avenues for refining the prototype and addressing its identified shortcomings.

Threats. The experts also named their concerns about potential threats to our system. The primary concern expressed by the participants centered around the system providing inaccurate answers. One participant emphasized the difficulty in detecting misinterpretations of data by the system, noting that "supplying incomplete or false information could be very harmful to users." Consequently, the participants agreed that it is crucial to prioritize the evaluation of erroneous results in the future to prevent the spread of false information. In addition to this, participants recommended enabling users to more easily detect false answers by simplifying the presentation of reasoning steps and underlying data. This approach is seen as essential in enhancing the system's transparency and facilitating user verification of responses. Furthermore, the dependence on OpenAI, previously identified as a weakness, was acknowledged as a potential threat. Concerns were raised about the variability in model performance and the associated costs of maintaining the service, which could pose obstacles to the sustained effectiveness of our system.

6 Discussion and Conclusion

This paper presents the first design cycle of our Design Science Research project, dedicated to the design of a Large Language Model based open data assistant for effective use. Based on interviews, focus groups, and a literature review we derived meta-requirements and subsequently proposed three design principles grounded in the theory of effective use. We instantiated the principles in a prototype and evaluated the artifact in a focus group consisting of eight civil servants from a medium-sized German city. The overall feedback was very positive underscoring the potential of open data assistants. This research contributes design knowledge in the form of three design principles and an artifact. Our results provide valuable insights for future research on the design of Large Language Model based open data assistants for effective use. Moreover, our work offers practical guidance for open data providers and city administrations seeking to enhance data accessibility.

It is crucial to acknowledge limitations of our study. This includes the small sample size and the absence of a quantitative evaluation, both of which constrain the generalizability and comprehensive understanding of the prototype's impact on effective use of open data. While recognizing these limitations, we believe that this initial design cycle lays a robust foundation for subsequent iterations. Our study has shown promising avenues for future research, such as enhancing the transparent representation of the system's reasoning process and advancing the interaction between the user and the assistant to support human-AI collaboration. Adapting the assistant to varying user skill levels and facilitating mutual learning between users and the assistant could be an interesting avenue for future research. Additionally, the development and evaluation of additional DPs, supported by empirical evidence, would contribute further to the knowledge base in this domain.

References

1. Attard, J., Orlandi, F., Scerri, S., Auer, S.: A systematic review of open government data initiatives. Gov. Inf. Q. **32**(4), 399–418 (2015). https://doi.org/10.1016/j.giq.2015.07.006
2. Bran, A.M., Cox, S., Schilter, O., Baldassari, C., White, A.D., Schwaller, P.: ChemCrow: augmenting large-language models with chemistry tools, October 2023. https://doi.org/10.48550/arXiv.2304.05376
3. Burton-Jones, A., Grange, C.: From use to effective use: a representation theory perspective. Inf. Syst. Res. **24**(3), 632–658 (2013). https://doi.org/10.1287/isre.1120.0444
4. Christian Stocker: Ask ZüriCityGPT anything about the government and administration of the City of Zurich, June 2023. https://www.liip.ch/en/blog/askzuricitygpt-anything-about-the-government-of-the-city-of-zurich
5. Conradie, P., Choenni, S.: On the barriers for local government releasing open data. Gov. Inf. Q. **31**, 10–17 (2014). https://doi.org/10.1016/j.giq.2014.01.003
6. Diederich, S., Brendel, A., Morana, S., Kolbe, L.: On the design of and interaction with conversational agents: an organizing and assessing review of human computer interaction research. J. Assoc. Inf. Syst. (2022). https://doi.org/10.17705/1jais.00724
7. European Commission: Riding the wave How Europe can gain from the rising tide of scientific data Final report of the High Level Expert Group on Scientific Data. European Commission, January 2010
8. European Parliament: Directive (EU) 2019/1024 of the European Parliament and of the Council of 20 June 2019 on open data and the re-use of public sector information (recast), June 2019. http://data.europa.eu/eli/dir/2019/1024/oj/eng
9. European Union: The official portal for European data. https://data.europa.eu/en
10. Frauenhofer DPS: FragDenStaat Analytics. https://publicanalytics.fokus.fraunhofer.de/fragdenstaat/dashboard
11. German Federal Ministry of the Interior and Community: Informationsfreiheitsgesetz. https://www.bmi.bund.de/DE/themen/moderne-verwaltung/opengovernment/informationsfreiheitsgesetz/informationsfreiheitsgesetz-artikel.html
12. Hevner, A.R., March, S.T., Park, J., Ram, S.: Design science in information systems research. MIS Q. **28**(1), 75–105 (2004). https://doi.org/10.2307/25148625
13. del Hoyo-Alonso, R., Rodrigalvarez-Chamarro, V., Vea-Murgía, J., Zubizarreta, I., Moyano-Collado, J.: Aragón open data assistant, lesson learned of an intelligent assistant for open data access. In: Følstad, A., et al. (eds.) Chatbot Research and Design. CONVERSATIONS 2023. LNCS, vol. 14524, pp. 42–57. Springer, Cham (2024). https://doi.org/10.1007/978-3-031-54975-5_3
14. Hu, K., Hu, K.: ChatGPT sets record for fastest-growing user base - analyst note. Reuters, February 2023. https://www.reuters.com/technology/chatgpt-setsrecord-fastest-growing-user-base-analyst-note-2023-02-01/
15. Janssen, M., Charalabidis, Y., Zuiderwijk, A.: Benefits, adoption barriers and myths of open data and open government. Inf. Syst. Manag. **29**(4), 258–268 (2012). https://doi.org/10.1080/10580530.2012.716740

16. Jiang, J., Zhou, K., Dong, Z., Ye, K., Zhao, W.X., Wen, J.R.: StructGPT: a general framework for large language model to reason over structured data, October 2023. https://doi.org/10.48550/arXiv.2305.09645

17. Karpas, E., et al.: MRKL systems: a modular, neuro-symbolic architecture that combines large language models, external knowledge sources and discrete reasoning, May 2022. https://doi.org/10.48550/arXiv.2205.00445

18. Keyner, S., Savenkov, V., Vakulenko, S.: Open data Chatbot. In: Hitzler, P., et al. (eds.) The Semantic Web: ESWC 2019 Satellite Events. ESWC 2019. LNCS, vol. 11762, pp. 111–115. Springer, Cham (2019). https://doi.org/10.1007/978-3-030-32327-1_22

19. Kuechler, W., Vaishnavi, V.: On theory development in design science research: anatomy of a research project. EJIS **17**, 489–504 (2008)

20. LangChain Inc: LangChain Docs. https://python.langchain.com/docs

21. Lewis, P., et al.: Retrieval-augmented generation for knowledge-intensive NLP tasks. In: Advances in Neural Information Processing Systems, vol. 33, pp. 9459–9474 (2020)

22. Lourenco, R.P.: An analysis of open government portals: a perspective of transparency for accountability. Gov. Inf. Q. **32**(3), 323–332 (2015). https://doi.org/10.1016/j.giq.2015.05.006

23. McTear, M., Callejas, Z., Griol, D.: The Conversational Interface. Springer, Cham (2016). https://doi.org/10.1007/978-3-319-32967-3

24. Murray-Rust, P.: Open Data in Science. Nature Precedings, p. 1, January 2008. https://doi.org/10.1038/npre.2008.1526.1, publisher: Nature Publishing Group

25. Orszag, P.: Open Government Directive (2009). http://www.whitehouse.gov/open/documents/opengovernment-directive

26. Purwanto, A., Zuiderwijk, A., Janssen, M.: Citizen engagement with open government data: a systematic literature review of drivers and inhibitors. Int. J. Electron. Gov. Res. **16**(3), 1–25 (2020). https://doi.org/10.4018/IJEGR.2020070101

27. Quarati, A., De Martino, M.: Open government data usage: a brief overview. In: Proceedings of the 23rd International Database Applications & Engineering Symposium. pp. 1–8. IDEAS '19, June 2019. https://doi.org/10.1145/3331076.3331115

28. Rajkumar, N., Li, R., Bahdanau, D.: Evaluating the Text-to-SQL Capabilities of Large Language Models, March 2022. https://doi.org/10.48550/arXiv.2204.00498

29. Ruijer, E., Grimmelikhuijsen, S., Meijer, A.: Open data for democracy: developinga theoretical framework for open data use. Gov. Inf. Q. **34**(1), 45–52 (2017). https://doi.org/10.1016/j.giq.2017.01.001

30. Ruoff, M., Gnewuch, U., Maedche, A., Scheibehenne, B.: Designing conversational dashboards for effective use in crisis response. J. Assoc. Inf. Syst. **24**(6), 1500–1526 (2023). https://doi.org/10.17705/1jais.00801

31. Sadiq, S., Indulska, M.: Open data: quality over quantity. Int. J. Inf. Manag. **37**(3), 150–154 (2017). https://doi.org/10.1016/j.ijinfomgt.2017.01.003

32. Safarov, I., Meijer, A., Grimmelikhuijsen, S.: Utilization of open government data: a systematic literature review of types, conditions, effects and users. Inf. Polity **22**, 1–24 (2017). https://doi.org/10.3233/IP-160012

33. Streamlit Inc.: Streamlit Docs. https://docs.streamlit.io/

34. United Nations General Assembly: Universal Declaration of Human Rights (1948). https://www.un.org/en/about-us/universal-declaration-of-human-rights

35. Vaswani, A., et al.: Attention is all you need. In: Advances in Neural Information Processing Systems, vol. 30. Curran Associates, Inc. (2017)

36. Venable, J., Pries-Heje, J., Baskerville, R.: FEDS: a framework for evaluation in design science research. Eur. J. Inf. Syst. **25**(1), 77–89 (2016). https://doi.org/10.1057/ejis.2014.36

37. Wang, D., Richards, D., Bilgin, A.A., Chen, C.: Implementation of a conversational virtual assistant for open government data portal: effects on citizens. J. Inf. Sci. (2023).https://doi.org/10.1177/01655515221151140, publisher:SAGEPublicationsLtd

38. Weerakkody, V., Irani, Z., Kapoor, K., Sivarajah, U., Dwivedi, Y.K.: Open data and its usability: an empirical view from the Citizen's perspective. Inf. Syst. Front. **19**(2), 285–300 (2017). https://doi.org/10.1007/s10796-0169679-1
39. Wei, J., et al.: Emergent Abilities of Large Language Models, October 2022. https://doi.org/10.48550/arXiv.2206.07682
40. Wei, J., et al.: Chain-of-thought prompting elicits reasoning in large language models. Adv. Neural. Inf. Process. Syst. **35**, 24824–24837 (2022)
41. Weizenbaum, J.: ELIZA—a computer program for the study of natural language communication between man and machine. Commun. ACM **9**(1), 36–45 (1966). https://doi.org/10.1145/365153.365168
42. Yao, S., et al.: ReAct: Synergizing Reasoning and Acting in Language Models, March 2023. https://doi.org/10.48550/arXiv.2210.03629
43. Zuiderwijk, A., Janssen, M., Choenni, S., Meijer, R., Sheikh Alibaks, R.: Socio technical impediments of open data. Electron. J. eGov. **10**, 156–172 (2012)
44. Zuiderwijk, A., Janssen, M., Dwivedi, Y.K.: Acceptance and use predictors of open data technologies: drawing upon the unified theory of acceptance and use of technology. Gov. Inf. Q. **32**(4), 429–440 (2015). https://doi.org/10.1016/j.giq.2015.09.005

Theorizing the Lean Startup Approach: Towards Well-Grounded Design Principles

Katharina Sielski and Christoph Seckler[(✉)] [iD]

ESCP Business School, Berlin, Germany
`cseckler@escp.eu`

Abstract. The lean startup approach and its principles are increasingly gaining relevance in entrepreneurial theory and practice. At the same time, key principles such as 'pivoting' and the 'build-measure-learn cycle' remain under-theorized. This hurts the clarity of these concepts, and it hinders more effective use of them in practice. We tackle both issues in this article. First, we draw on action regulation theory to theorize the practice concepts of 'pivoting,' as well as of the 'build-measure-learn cycle.' Subsequently, we build on this theorizing to develop theoretically grounded design principles. This article contributes to literature in two ways. First, theorizing the lean startup principles improves the clarity of the focal concepts and helps to understand why, for whom, and when they work. Second, the developed design principles contribute to the increasing body of design knowledge which provides scientifically grounded guidance for entrepreneurs and entrepreneurship educators.

Keywords: Entrepreneurship · Lean Startup · Design Principles

1 Introduction

An increasingly relevant entrepreneurial approach for practice and education is the lean startup approach (e.g., [1–3]). The idea of the lean startup approach is to engage in short, iterative, hypothesis-driven learning cycles to explore and validate business ideas [4]. Two of the key principles of the lean startup approach are 'pivoting' and 'build-measure-learn cycle' [4]. Pivoting is a structured course correction designed to test new, fundamental hypotheses about a startup's strategy [1]. The 'build-measure-learn cycle' describes the phases of developing hypotheses, testing them, and developing novel knowledge. Both principles have originally been developed in entrepreneurship practice, yet they have also been widely adopted by entrepreneurship educators [5].

While lean startup principles have gained considerable traction, both the concept of 'pivoting' and the concept of the 'build-measure-learn' cycle remain under-theorized (e.g., [1–3]). This under-theorization misses at least two opportunities. First, it misses the opportunity to clarify some of the central concepts of the lean startup approach. Both pivoting and the build-measure-learn cycle have been criticized to be vague [2]. Second, the lack of theoretical foundation of these practice principles makes it difficult to develop well-grounded design knowledge [6, 7].

© The Author(s), under exclusive license to Springer Nature Switzerland AG 2024
M. Mandviwalla et al. (Eds.): DESRIST 2024, LNCS 14621, pp. 412–423, 2024.
https://doi.org/10.1007/978-3-031-61175-9_28

In this article, we tackle these issues in two steps. First, we theorize both lean startup principles by drawing on action regulation theory (ART). ART is a well-established cognitive theory in applied psychology [8]. ART describes and explains action, that is, goal directed behavior. It depicts action to follow a certain action sequence and explains how these phases are regulated on different cognitive levels. ART has been prominently applied to study entrepreneurial phenomena and to design entrepreneurship trainings [9–11]. After theorizing the lean startup approach based on ART, we formulate theoretically grounded design principles. Design principles are a form of instrumental knowledge which may guide action [6, 12, 13].

Overall, this study contributes to literature and entrepreneurial practice. First, it contributes to the emerging literature on lean startup principles (e.g., [1–3]) by conceptualizing pivoting and the build-measure-learn cycle from an ART perspective. The theoretical clarification of these principles will facilitate the accumulation of knowledge on these principles in the future [14]. Second, by theorizing about pivoting we outline novel antecedent conditions, moderators, and consequences of pivoting. Particularly, we explain why pivoting may have both positive, as well as negative performance consequences, and how pivoting is influenced by both the mental model of the entrepreneur, as well as the entrepreneur's metacognitive abilities. Third, our study contributes to the increasing body of design knowledge in entrepreneurship [6, 7]. This is by developing theory-based design principles which may guide entrepreneurs and entrepreneurship educators in the future [16].

2 The Lean Startup Principles

We lay the basis for our subsequent theorization about the lean startup principles by briefly outlining the original description of the key principles as documented mostly in the seminal book 'The Lean Startup' [4]. Please note that 'The Lean Startup' is oriented towards a practice audience which also entails a practice language. Nevertheless, we describe the lean startup principles as closely as possible to the original writing to transport its main ideas which will subsequently be theorized by drawing on action regulation theory [8].

2.1 Build-Measure-Learn Cycle

A first key principle that Ries [4] describes is the 'build-measure-learn' cycle. The build-measure-learn principle is about the continuous and repeated process of business plan development through customer feedback [4]. The build-measure-learn principle is important in the lean startup approach because it allows to develop and validate a business model through quick iterative learning cycles. Quick iterations through the product development cycle enables startups to react early to problems and adapt to customers' needs accordingly. Ries [4] claims that this reduces the creation of undesired products and services. The iterative learning cycle consists of three phases: (1) The build phase, (2) the measure phase and (3) the learn phase.

First, in the *build* phase entrepreneurs are asked to formulate key hypotheses for their emerging business [4]. In this context, a hypothesis is described as an unverified implicit or explicit assumption about a part of a startup's business [4]. In practice, this means to systematically make hypotheses about a startup's vision and its business model. The purpose of a vision is to provide clear guidance for a business to achieve goals. While a vision, in the lean startup approach functions as overarching guidance, the derived strategy makes a vision actionable [4]. Such an actionable plan is called business plan or model. Eventually, the business plan consists of hypotheses that are guided by a startup's vision [4]. Once hypotheses have been formulated, they are translated into a 'minimum viable products' (MVPs). An MVP enables entrepreneurs to go through the build-measure-learn cycle with a 'minimum amount of effort' and resources [4: 96]. Hence, an MVP lacks many features as its only purpose is to test fundamental hypotheses quickly.

Second, after the build phase, the *measure* phase follows. The measure phase is about checking the truth of the hypotheses and the overall progress of the business model development. In Ries' [4] description the measurement phase is linked to what he calls innovation accounting. Innovation accounting is a method that measures and provides objective evidence on the progress made in developing the business [4]. An example for innovation accounting is the 'cohort analysis' for product development [4: 123–124]. For example, this analytical technique enables entrepreneurs to test assumptions about customers' behavior at different sales stages. Thereby, entrepreneurs can use collected customer data to adequately measure user behavior and reveal weaknesses of their sales process [4]. Innovation accounting is an important part in the measure phase for two reasons. First, the quantitative feedback approach enables startups to objectively keep track on the progress made. Second, timely feedback data allows entrepreneurs to disclose and measure contingencies as well as problems early on [4].

Third, after the measure phase follows the *learn* phase. The learn phase is a process of reflecting the hypotheses vis-à-vis the collected evidence to adapt the course of action. Ries [4] is referring here to the principle of validated learning. He describes validated learning as a process of efficient progress in product development through valuable learnings from customer feedback in experiments [4: 46]. He describes that validated learning is achieved through positive improvements in a startup's core metrics [4]. As an example, for validated learning, Ries refers to Blank's approach of 'customer development' [4]. Customer development is about customer interaction and co-creation during product development [4]. Thereby, entrepreneurs learn what customers desire and integrate the learnings into product development. Hence, productivity is not measured in terms of built product features but with respect of how much validated learning has been generated [4]. Validated learning plays an important role because it constitutes the value-adding process within the lean startup approach. Through validated learning startups move away from good guesses to external validation for their business models based on feedback-based data [4].

2.2 Pivoting

A second core lean startup principle which Ries [4] describes is pivoting. Pivoting is a structured course correction of a startup's vision and its related strategy [4]. In the lean startup approach, a pivot can happen after every iteration in the build-measure-learn cycle. He describes that, in practice, a pivot is a radical change to test new fundamental hypotheses on a startup's business model [4]. One example for pivoting is the 'customer segment pivot' [4: 169]. The 'customer segment pivot' is about a shift in the target customer segment with constant product functionalities [4].

According to Ries [4] pivoting is an essential part of the lean startup approach for two main reasons. First, a major strategy change can prevent a startup to get stuck with a strategy that is not able to generate substantial business growth in the future [4]. Second, pivoting can lead to validated learning. Thus, a pivot enables startups to turn towards relevant business opportunities that have not been considered before [4].

Pivoting involves two main steps: (1) Signal identification and (2) new hypothesis creation. First, Ries advises that startups need to pay attention to the signals that indicate a need for a pivot [4]. Startups need to pivot if further adaptations of business model hypotheses do not lead to an improvement of baseline metrics. Thus, a startup does not make sufficient progress as the effectiveness of minimal viable product (MVP) experiments decreases [4]. Ries encourages startups to owe up to a strategy pivot, if necessary, to avoid further insufficiencies [4]. Second, startups are advised to create a new hypothesis. In practice, startups make significant changes to one or more dimensions in their business model [4]. Afterwards, the new hypothesis is tested against customer feedback. Through a repeated performance of pivots, startups get more efficient. Hence, the time to build an MVP and test new hypotheses gets reduced [4].

3   Action Regulation Theory

To properly theorize the lean startup principles, it is essential to introduce the core tenets of Action Regulation Theory (ART). ART elucidates how individuals regulate their actions to achieve their goals [8]. Three fundamental tenets of ART include: (1) the sequence of action regulation, (2) the hierarchical structure of action regulation, and (3) the concept of mental models. We consider ART particularly well-suited for theorizing about both pivoting and the build-measure-learn cycle. The sequence of action regulation facilitates an understanding of the build-measure-learn cycle, while the hierarchical levels of action regulation, as well as the idea of mental models provide insights into pivoting. We delve into these core tenets in greater detail in the following section.

3.1   Sequences of Action Regulation

ART proposes a comprehensive analysis of every action through five phases: (1) Goal development, (2) orientation, (3) plan generation and decision, (4) execution-monitoring, and (5) feedback processing [8].

First, the action sequence initiates with *goal development*, involving the creation of a cognitive representation of a future state [17]. Goals function as mental reference points for comparing actions, guiding them toward goal achievement based on feedback [18]. ART identifies critical parameters for goal development, including goal difficulty, specificity, connectedness, orientation (long-term or short-term), valence, and whether goals are process or end-state oriented [8].

Second, orientation is the process of action regulation based on stimuli from the environment [8]. Upon detecting signals, individuals begin searching for action-relevant information in both their memory and the external environment [18]. Essential for goal achievement, orientation enables individuals to detect signals and effectively map information [18]. This phase is influenced by the characteristics of the signal and the prior knowledge of the actor [8].

Third is the sequence of plan generation and decision. Plan generation is the development of cognitive representations of behavioral steps to achieve a goal [8]. Metaphorically speaking, plans are the bridge between goals and behavior. Plans are important because they enable individuals to translate their goals and intentions into goal directed behaviors [8, 19]. Four important characteristics of plans are their detailedness, their problem inclusiveness, their hierarchization, and their time range [8].

Fourth, Execution-monitoring is the process of checking the progress of an action with reference to the plans and goals [8]. Execution-monitoring is essential as it allows individuals to change plans for discrepancies between the actual state and desired results. Key parameters in execution monitoring are: (1) Flexibility, (2) speed, (3) sharing and coordination, and (4) overlapping [9].

Fifth, during feedback processing, individuals receive external information as feedback about their actions [8]. Depending on feedback's deviation from goals, actions might be adapted [8]. Feedback serves as a point of reference towards the level of goal achievement [20]. Through feedback individuals learn what plans are useful to achieve a desired goal [8]. Essential elements of feedback are: (1) Locus or source of feedback, (2) timing, (3) articulation, (4) value, (5) self-concept, and (6) feedback search rate [8].

3.2 Hierarchical Structure of Action Regulation

According to ART, actions are regulated hierarchically on various levels. Most relevant for our study are the following three levels: (1) 'level of flexible action patterns', (2) 'intellectual level', and (3) 'heuristic level' [8]. While ART suggests that there is a hierarchical structure in action regulation, it also suggests that both a top-down as well as bottom-up mental processing regulate actions [18, 21].

First, the level of flexible action regulates actions based on flexible learnt action schemata [8]. Think of the flexible action patterns that people use while driving a car. Action schemata are 'patterns of thought or behavior' that organize information categories and relations between them [8]. Action schemata are readily available in memory and triggered by environmental signals [22].

Second, at the intellectual level individuals consciously make complex analyses of situations to develop and select plans and goals for actions [8]. Hence, action regulation on the intellectual level consumes more cognitive resources and is more complex. Due to an increased complexity, execution and monitoring of such plans is slow and more controlled. However, repetition can lead to automatization and a shift from the intellectual level to lower levels of the hierarchy [8]. Respective feedback processing at this stage deals with the analysis of new information intake [18].

Third, at the heuristic level, actions are regulated and steered by meta-cognitive templates or heuristics. Every individual has general heuristics that consciously guide all action regulation processes. Particularly, in complex situations, heuristics provide action guidance and a point of reference to identify logical inconsistencies between actual actions and expected results. How a problem is handled depends on the heuristics that are available to individuals [8].

3.3 Mental Models

The mental model is also called 'Operative Image System' in ART [8]. A mental model is a long-term memory to store knowledge for each sequence of action regulation [23]. Mental models play a key role in ART for two main reasons. First, mental models guide actions to attain goals [8]. Second, depending on the quality of mental models, performance can increase or decrease. For example, better knowledge and understanding of signals as well as of tasks enables one to derive at more effective plans, strategies, goals, and feedback processing [8, 24].

4 Theorizing Lean Startup Principles

4.1 Theorizing Pivoting

Building on ART, we suggest the theoretical model of pivoting illustrated in Fig. 1. From an ART perspective, we suggest that pivoting can be conceptualized as a cognitive mechanism. Furthermore, we suggest that pivoting may lead to both positive performance effects, as well as negative effects. We suggest that the performance effect crucially depends on the quality of the mental model of the entrepreneur. Finally, we suggest that the likelihood of pivoting depends on the meta-cognitive abilities – metacognition - of the entrepreneurs. In the following, we explain our theoretical model of pivoting in more detail.

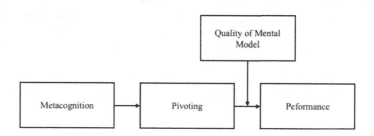

Fig. 1. An Action Regulation Theory Model of Pivoting

Drawing on ART helps to conceptualize pivoting. Pivoting in the lean startup describes a learning process triggered by some kind of error, failure or rejected hypothesis [4]. Such learning from errors, failure, or rejected hypothesis plays a key role in ART. In ART, pivoting can be conceptualized as a cognitive process of re-intellectualization of routinized action to change goals and plans and related behaviors [8]. Frese and Zapf claim that routinized 'lower-level actions can lead to changes in goals at higher levels when it turns out that one cannot pursue them adequately' [8]. Consequently, a shift from lower levels of action regulation to higher, intellectual levels of action regulation takes place [8, 21]. At the intellectual level, cognitive analysis of the goal failure situation takes place. Consequently, individuals develop and select new goals and related plans to change behavior [8]. Thus, from an ART perspective pivoting can be defined as follows:

Definition: Pivoting is a cognitive process of re-intellectualizing routinized action resulting in a change in goals and plans and related behaviors.

Moreover, we suggest that pivoting may be a double-edged sword regarding entrepreneurial performance. Campbell define performance as to be 'goal-relevant actions that are under the control of the individual' [24]. On the one hand, pivoting may have positive effect on performance because more adequate goals are set, and better plans may be adapted. But on the other hand, ART suggests that pivoting may also have a negative effect on performance. First, it may be uncertain whether the newly set goals, plans, and behavior are beneficial. Second, pivoting demands a certain number of cognitive capacities which leaves less capacity for other phases such as executing, and feedback which are relevant to adequate behavior [8]. Third, repeated pivoting entails a higher number of related plans. The more plans created the more cognitive capacity is demanded [8]. The more cognitive capacity used, the less detailed plans can be created which may decrease performance. Taken together, we suggest that pivoting may be related to both positive and negative to performance of entrepreneurs.

Proposition 1a: Pivoting is positively related to performance.

Proposition 1b: Pivoting is negatively related to performance.

Drawing on ART, we propose that the impact of pivoting on performance is contingent on the entrepreneur's mental model quality, defined as the availability of knowledge, schemata, and understanding for action [8]. We argue that a positive relationship exists between pivoting and performance when the quality of mental models is high. This is because the ability to adapt plans relies on a thorough understanding of discrepancies between action and goal states. A high-quality mental model enhances the conscious perception and reflection on these discrepancies facilitating the development of plans to achieve new goals [25]. Conversely, we suggest a negative relationship between pivoting and performance when the quality of mental models is low [8]. In this context, a lack of adequate knowledge and understanding impairs the recognition and reflection upon inconsistencies between action and goal states [8]. Without the ability to reflect on these inconsistencies, the formulation of behavioral steps and plans to achieve goals does not occur.

Proposition 2: The relationship between pivoting and performance is moderated by the quality of the mental model. For a high quality of the mental model, the relationship between pivoting and performance is expected to be positive. For a low quality of the mental model, the relationship between pivoting and performance is expected to be negative.

Drawing on ART, an entrepreneur's metacognitive ability, or metacognition, is a key antecedent condition influencing engagement in pivoting. Metacognition, defined as the ability to regulate one's cognitive processes is crucial for observing thoughts, decisions, and actions during goal-directed activities [8, 20]. Strong metacognition enables the identification of discrepancies between intended and actual outcomes, allowing individuals to recognize and evaluate deviations. This awareness triggers a metacognitive evaluation, facilitating the reassessment and re-intellectualization of current goals and plans based on ongoing feedback. Therefore, we propose that higher levels of metacognition increase the likelihood of engaging in pivoting.

Proposition 3: Metacognition is positively related to pivoting.

4.2 Theorizing the Build-Measure-Learn Cycle

The 'build-measure-learn cycle' can be theorized by drawing on the action sequence from ART. Figure 2 illustrate how the phases the build-measure-learn cycle correspond to the sequences of action. In the following, we build on the insights on the action sequence to conceptualize the different phases of the build-measure-learn cycle and to outline crucial parameters that need to be considered in each of these phases.

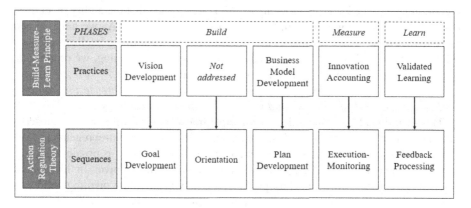

Fig. 2. The Build-Measure-Learn Cycle from an Action Regulation Theory Perspective

First, the *build phase* as described by Ries crucially depends on the development of a vision. Drawing on the ideas of goal development from ART allows to clarify what vision development entails and what critical parameters are. From an ART perspective a vision can be conceptualized as a cognitive representation of long-term desires [8]. Also drawing on ART we suggest that in developing the vision the crucial parameters are the vision difficulty, the vision specificity, and its hierarchization [8].

Second, drawing on ART also allows to better conceptualize the *measure phase* in the lean startup. The measure phase in the lean startup is related to the execution-monitoring sequence in ART. Taking both, execution and monitoring together, the measure phase can be defined as the process of plan execution with continuous monitoring of actions in reference to expected goals.

Third, the *learn phase* can be conceptualized as the feedback processing sequence in ART. From an ART perspective, the principle of validated learning can be defined as the process of receiving external information as feedback about one's action in reference to the degree of goal achievement [8]. Thereby, the evaluation of hypothesis-related metrics towards hypothesis validation corresponds to the degree of goal achievement in action regulation.

5 Towards Lean Startup Design Principles

The theorizing of pivoting and the build-measure-learn cycle allows us now to propose theoretically grounded design principles [6, 13]. Design principles are a form of instrumental knowledge which helps to guide action. While explanatory knowledge on the lean startup principles helps to understand them, design principles prescribe what to do to achieve a goal [6, 13]. Although a multitude of design principles can be inferred based on the theoretical grounding, we present in the following three exemplary inferred design principles and discuss how they contribute to the lean startup approach.

First, we propose a design principle related to pivoting as an essential tenet of the lean startup approach. More specifically, we suggest a design principle relevant to entrepreneurship education. Drawing on ART, we suggest that the ability of students to pivot may increase with the students' metacognitive abilities. As we have argued, improved abilities to reflect on one's own cognition will enhance the re-intellectualization of one's actions to change goals and plans. Building on this reasoning, we propose the following design principle for entrepreneurship educators:

Design Principle 1: If entrepreneurship educators want to increase the ability of pivoting of their students, they should work on the students' metacognition.

This theoretically grounded design principle transcends existing practice prescriptions in the lean startup approach [4]. For example, Ries advises entrepreneurs to learn from their mistakes and be able to see signals for pivoting as early as possible [4]. Yet, the lean startup approach is silent on how to improve the ability to pivot. In this context, we offer entrepreneurship educators guidance on how to facilitate pivoting. And how they can improve their awareness that pivoting proves necessary. As pivoting is seen as to be an important process particularly in earlier stages of the lean startup approach, we provide insights into how to improve the likelihood pivoting of students.

Second, we suggest that the developed visions or goals of the entrepreneurs should satisfy three design requirements: adequate level of difficulty, specificity, hierarchization. Drawing on ART, suggest that these three characteristics are crucial for effective learning of entrepreneurs [8]. Therefore, we propose the following design principle:

Design Principle 2: To learn effectively from their actions, entrepreneurs need to form a vision with an adequate level of difficulty, specificity, hierarchization.

With this design principle, we extend the body of design knowledge on vision development [4]. Ries advises entrepreneurs to develop an overarching vision that guides startups during business plan development [4]. Although Ries provides helpful real-case examples for goal development, he does not outline how entrepreneurs can design effective visions. Our design principles can provide three more generally valid parameters to guide entrepreneurs for the design of adequate goals. A practical principle of the lean startup is that the vision needs to be designed 'strong' and 'huge' to create a thriving business [4]. Yet, Ries does not specifically define what strong and huge goals are and how they are developed. Based on our design principles, we outline that vision should be particularly attentive to the vision difficulty, as well as the vision specificity. Consequently, we can offer more specific guidance related to design requirements for the vision.

A third design principle that we suggest is related to the design requirements related to the plans needed to realize set goals. Drawing on ART suggests that crucial design requirements for plans are that they have the right level of detailedness, problem inclusiveness, and a hierarchization [8]. Therefore, we propose the following design principle:

Design Principle 3: If entrepreneurs want to effectively implement their visions, they should develop plans with right level of detailedness, problem inclusiveness and hierarchization.

With this design principles, we contribute to the design knowledge on how effective plans should be developed. The proposed design principles transcend existing guidance of business plan development provided by the lean startup. For example, Ries recommends entrepreneurs to develop simplified business plans based on MVPs that include only the number of features needed to generate customer feedback [4]. However, we argue that entrepreneurs should vary detailedness of plans depending on the complexity of a situation. Specifying the conditions for detailed plans enables entrepreneurs to act more purposeful. Another example suggested by Ries is A/B testing for business plan development [4]. For A/B testing entrepreneurs need to create MVPs with distinctive features to be able to find the best solution [4]. In this context, we reveal some negative consequences of backup plans that have not been outlined before. With additional information on the downside of backup plans, we deepen knowledge about backup plans' cognitive and action-related impact that entrepreneurs need to consider.

6 Conclusion

While the lean startup approach has gained considerable traction in both theory and in practice, its key principles have remained under-theorized. We have drawn on ART to theorize both principles. Based on this theoretical grounding, we have formulated design principles which may guide entrepreneurs' action in the future. In the following, we explain both the theoretical and the practical contributions of the article.

First, this article contributes to lean startup literature (e.g., [1–3]) in three keyways. Firstly, we offer grounded conceptualizations for key lean startup concepts, specifically pivoting and the build-measure-learn cycle phases, drawing on ART. Pivoting is defined as a cognitive process involving re-intellectualization of goals and plans and related actions. Contrary to Ries' primarily behavioral definition, our approach emphasizes cognitive mechanisms and the resulting changes in course of action [4]. Secondly, we extend conceptualizations to the build-measure-learn cycle phases, outlining associated cognitive processes and parameters. This improved clarity on core constructs and processes aids scholars in fostering mutual understanding and communication about the lean startup approach [14].

Second, by leveraging ART, our understanding of pivoting improves in three key aspects (e.g., [1–3]). First, we challenge the assumption that pivoting always leads to positive outcomes, proposing scenarios where negative performance results are plausible.

Second, we introduce the novel idea that the impact of pivoting on performance is moderated by the entrepreneur's quality of mental models, a factor overlooked in lean startup literature. Third, we emphasize the significance of metacognition in the pivoting process, contending that stronger self-reflection enhances the likelihood of entrepreneurial pivots. Future research should further empirically test these propositions.

Third, the exemplary proposed design principles provide theoretically well-grounded guidance for entrepreneurs. They aid entrepreneurs in enhancing their actions, particularly under uncertain conditions. Drawing from lean startup examples, these principles offer detailed insights into implementing actions across various entrepreneurial contexts [26]. By considering our design principles, entrepreneurs gain valuable guidance, not only outlining key parameters for goal achievement but also suggesting ways to improve and influence their actions for desired outcomes. These principles serve as practical tools guiding entrepreneurs in venture creation. Additionally, they offer guidance for effective entrepreneurship education, emphasizing the importance of metacognition and students' mental model development. Furthermore, the design principles are applicable in action theoretical trainings on the lean startup approach, aligning with research-derived principles [11].

However, it is important to acknowledge that the applicability of these design principles may vary depending on contextual factors such as industry dynamics and organizational maturity. Future research should explore these nuances to provide tailored guidance for specific contexts, thereby enhancing the practical utility of the principles. Addressing these concerns will foster a more nuanced understanding of how design principles operate in real-world settings, ultimately advancing their application and impact.

References

1. Hampel, C.E., Tracey, P., Weber, K.: The art of the pivot: how new ventures manage identification relationships with stakeholders as they change direction. Acad. Manag. J. **63**(2), 440–471 (2020). https://doi.org/10.5465/amj.2017.0460
2. Ghezzi, A.: Digital startups and the adoption and implementation of lean startup approaches: effectuation, bricolage and opportunity creation in practice. Technol. Forecast. Soc. Change (2019). https://doi.org/10.1016/j.techfore.2018.09.017
3. Grimes, M.G.: The pivot: how founders respond to feedback through idea and identity work. Acad. Manag. J. (2018)
4. Ries, E.: The Lean Startup by Eric Ries. The Starta (2016). https://doi.org/23
5. Ones, D., Anderson, N., Viswesvaran, C., Sinangil, H., Zacher, H., et al.: Action Regulation Theory: Foundations, Current Knowledge and Future Directions. The SAGE Handbook of Industrial, Work & Organizational Psychology (2017). https://doi.org/10.4135/9781473914957.n7
6. Berglund, H., Dimov, D., Wennberg, K.: Beyond bridging rigor and relevance: the three-body problem in entrepreneurship J. Bus. Ventur. Insights (2018). https://doi.org/10.1016/j.jbvi.2018.02.001
7. Romme, A.G.L., Reymen, I.M.: Entrepreneurship at the interface of design and science: toward an inclusive framework. J. Bus. Ventur. Insights **10**, e00094 (2018)
8. Frese, M., Zapf, D.: Action as the Core of Work Psychology: A German Approach. Handbook of Industrial and Organizational Psychology, vol. 4 (2nd Ed.) (1994)

9. Frese, M.: Toward a psychology of entrepreneurship - an action theory perspective. Found. Trends Entrep. (2009). https://doi.org/10.1561/0300000028
10. Campos, F., et al.: Teaching personal initiative beats traditional training in boosting small business in West Africa. Science **357**(6357), 1287–1290 (2017)
11. Glaub, M.E., Frese, M., Fischer, S., Hoppe, M.: Increasing personal initiative in small business managers or owners leads to entrepreneurial success: a theory-based controlled randomized field intervention for evidence-based management. Acad. Manag. Learn. Educ. **13**(3) (2014). https://doi.org/10.5465/amle.2013.0234
12. Seckler, C., Mauer, R., vom Brocke, J.: Design science in entrepreneurship: conceptual foundations and guiding principles. J. Bus. Ventur. Des. (2021). https://doi.org/10.1016/j.jbvd.2022.100004
13. van Aken, J.E.: Management research based on the paradigm of the design sciences: the quest for field-tested and grounded technological rules. J. Manag. Stud. (2004).https://doi.org/10.1111/j.1467-6486.2004.00430.x
14. Suddaby, R.: Editor's comments: construct clarity in theories of management and organization. Acad. Manag. Rev. (2010).https://doi.org/10.5465/AMR.2010.51141319
15. Dimov, D.: Toward a design science of entrepreneurship Models of start-up thinking and action: theoretical, empirical and pedagogical approaches: Emerald Group Publishing Limited (2016)
16. Veenman, M.V.J., van Hout-Wolters, B.H.A.M., Afflerbach, P.: Metacognition and learning: conceptual and methodological considerations. Metacognition Learn. (2006). https://doi.org/10.1007/s11409-006-6893-0
17. Austin, J.T., Vancouver, J.B.: Goal constructs in psychology: structure, process, and content. Psychol. Bull. **120**(3) (1996). https://doi.org/10.1037/0033-2909.120.3.338
18. Zacher, H., Hacker, W., Frese, M.: Action regulation across the adult lifespan (ARAL): a metatheory of work and aging. Work, Aging and Retirement (2016). https://doi.org/10.1093/workar/waw015
19. Gollwitzer, P.M.: Implementation intentions: strong effects of simple plans. Am. Psychol. **54**(7) (1999). https://doi.org/10.1037/0003-066X.54.7.493
20. Keith, N., Frese, M.: Self-regulation in error management training: emotion control and metacognition as mediators of performance effects. J. Appl. Psychol. (2005)
21. Hacker, W.: Action regulation theory: a practical tool for the design of modern work processes? Eur. J. Work Organ. Psychol. **12**(2) (2003). https://doi.org/10.1080/13594320344000075
22. Hacker, W.: Action regulation theory and occupational psychology: review of German empirical research since 1987. Ger. J. Psychol. **18**(2) (1994)
23. Hacker, W., Sachse, P.: Allgemeine Arbeitspsychologie. Allgmeine Arbeitspsychologie (2013). https://elibrary.hogrefe.com/book/99.110005/9783840925405
24. Campbell, J.P., McCloy, R.A., Oppler, S.H., Sager, C.E.: A theory of performance. Personnel Selection In Organizations (1993)
25. Dörner, D., Schaub, H.: Errors in planning and decision-making and the nature of human information processing. Appl. Psychol. **43**(4) (1994). https://doi.org/10.1111/j.1464-0597.1994.tb00839.x
26. Bamberger, P.: Beyond contextualization: using context theories to narrow the micro-macro gap in management research. Acad. Manag. J. (2008). https://doi.org/10.5465/AMJ.2008.34789630

Meta-requirements for LLM-Based Knowledge Exploration Tools in Information Systems Research

Jonas Sjöström[1,2(✉)] and Stefan Cronholm[1]

[1] Borås University, Borås, Sweden
Jonas.sjostrom@hb.se
[2] Halmstad University, Halmstad, Sweden

Abstract. The problem we address in this paper is that the potential impact of Large Language Models (LLMs) on the research practice in information systems is not well understood. The focus has been on how LLMs could support literature review processes. Therefore, this paper aims to advance knowledge on how Large Language Models (LLMs) could support knowledge exploration through literature reviews. The knowledge contribution consists of meta-requirements that inform the design of LLM-based tools assisting knowledge exploration. The meta-requirements are theoretically justified by scrutinizing established IS literature review methodologies, reported challenges of LLMs and design process experiences. Furthermore, we introduce an LLM supported literature review process model that maps the relationships between the meta-requirements and specific phases of the process model. This work contributes to the field by providing a foundation for designing transparent, controllable, and resource-efficient tools for knowledge exploration, and supporting the rigor of knowledge exploration in information systems research.

Keywords: LLM · meta-requirements · literature review · knowledge exploration

1 Introduction

Large language models (LLMs) are a cutting-edge form of artificial intelligence (AI) that possess the ability to interpret natural language as well as generate natural language responses [3, 34, 39]. They are built on advanced deep-learning techniques and have demonstrated remarkable efficacy in a multitude of applications, such as natural language processing, machine translation, and text generation. Furthermore, LLMs have garnered widespread acclaim due to their ability to generate coherent and contextually relevant responses, as exemplified by the renowned ChatGPT system, which has captivated considerable audiences since its inception in November 2022. Within two months, ChatGPT had surpassed 100 million active users [44].

The advent of LLMs has the potential to disrupt multiple domains of practice, including research practice. There is a growing interest in their use in research workflows

M. Mandviwalla et al. (Eds.): DESRIST 2024, LNCS 14621, pp. 424–439, 2024.
https://doi.org/10.1007/978-3-031-61175-9_29

[42]. The potential impact of LLMs on research is significant because they offer new ways to approach problems related to natural language processing and understanding. For example, LLMs can be used to analyze large amounts of unstructured data [44], e.g., social media posts, customer reviews or transcripts of interviews, and extract insights from this data.

Our literature review has uncovered that the potential impact of LLMs on research practice – in information systems and beyond – is not yet well understood. While there have been promising results in various applications, there are challenges and limitations to consider. First, there is a need to reflect on how to best use tools for knowledge exploration, as well as epistemological concerns related to tool use in research [5, 28, 32, 37]. This is especially valid in the case of qualitative research, aiming for a heuristic process of deep understanding of various phenomena. Austin et al. [1] conducted a qualitative analysis to better understand how valuable LLMs can be as assistive tools. They conclude that human supervision of LLMs is needed when synthesizing complex applications. The use of LLMs may counteract the fundamental idea of qualitative analysis, i.e., a human reading of text striving for deep understanding through a hermeneutic process.

Second, LLMs require large amounts of data to learn from, which can be a challenge for smaller organizations or those with limited resources [e.g., 26]. Additionally, the complexity of LLMs can make them difficult to understand and interpret, which could limit their adoption in some contexts. However, solutions are emerging to use LLMs for dedicated, small-scale applications [17]. That is, new application areas and related research opportunities are emerging, given the ongoing adaptation of LLMs for different contexts of use.

Third, LLMs' potential to be used as research tools has been overshadowed by fears of how this technology can be misused [34]. Scholars have reported that LLMs could threaten scholarship and collaborative research [ibid.]. On the contrary, there are opinions such as that AI creates opportunities in terms of efficiency and efficacy [38].

We recognize that LLMs can be helpful in different stages of research approaches. However, the overall purpose of this paper is to advance knowledge on how LLMs could support knowledge exploration through literature reviews. We define knowledge exploration as an iterative process of searching and synthesizing knowledge [25, 35]. In this view, knowledge exploration is an LLM-based alternative to conventional literature reviews, which typically involve crucial decisions such as: setting boundaries, identifying relevant literature, and structuring and synthesizing the review [43].

The need to develop knowledge exploration tools supporting literature reviews has been discussed by several scholars. For example, it has been discussed as a means to improve rigor [2]. As expressed by Dobrkovic et al. [6]: "keyword-based literature searches result in large collections of documents beyond humans' ability to process or the extensive use of filters to narrow the search output risks omitting relevant works.". While Dobrkovic et al. propose a collaborative approach to managing the amount of literature, this paper proposes LLMs as an alternative approach to exploring the knowledge base.

One area of interest is using LLMs as an alternative or a complementing approach to existing traditional literature reviews – through their potential to rapidly provide insights from a vast number of research publications [7]. However, given the characteristics of

LLMs (e.g., their reliability and accuracy), additional research is needed to better understand how to design LLM-based applications to support rigorous knowledge exploration. The advent of LLMs requires a renewal of the use of tools in design science research (DSR) [28, 37]. In order to advance knowledge on how LLMs could support knowledge exploration through literature reviews, we have suggested meta-requirements. A meta-requirement is generically described as "the class of goals to which the theory applies" [41, p. 43]. Gregor and Jones [12, p. 325] clarify the meta-aspect of the term 'meta-requirement' by stating that "These theory requirements are meta-requirements; they are not the requirements for one instance of a system, as would be the case if there was a need to build a single system in industry". In our case, it means that the suggested meta-requirements should be considered when developing other instances of knowledge exploration tools. We posit the following research question: *What meta-requirements should govern the design of LLM-based knowledge exploration tools to support researchers in exploring the knowledge base?*

In the next section, we describe the research method. Then, we present the theoretical justification of the meta-requirements and our experiences from artefact design. Finally, we present a concluding discussion.

2   Research Approach

While our ambition in this paper is to articulate meta-requirements for knowledge exploration tools, we adopted a DSR approach [15, 16]. The meta-requirements are grounded in insights from the literature review and experiences from developing a knowledge exploration tool. Our research approach involved the following research activities: theoretically justify meta-requirements (see Sect. 3), exemplify and reflect on the meta-requirements based on the design of a knowledge exploration tool (Sect. 4), concluding our research contributions (see Sect. 5).

To theoretically justify the meta-requirements, we analyzed literature regarding a) IS literature review methods, b) tool support for literature reviews and c) generic challenges regarding LLMs. In the second step, the meta-requirements identified through the theoretical justification were evaluated by the designers when constructing and testing the knowledge exploration tool. Cronholm and Goldkuhl (2003) refer to this type of evaluation as "goal-based evaluation as such" and state that it is appropriate in the early stages of software development and that the evaluation results could be used for redesign and succeeding evaluations with real users. During the evaluation, we used a scenario, which included identifying DSR tensions regarding different views on ontological and epistemological positions. We characterize our evaluation as an informed argument, defined by Hevner et al. [16, p. 86] as follows: "Use information from the knowledge base (e.g., relevant research) to build a convincing argument for the artifact's utility". This means the suggested meta-requirements are based on insights from existing theory and scenarios-based experiences. Our epistemological foundation comes from multi-grounded theory [11], i.e., that knowledge claims should be justified by theory, empirical data, as well as the consistency between abstracted concepts.

The development of the knowledge exploration tool also serves as a proof-of-concept [30], illustrating the feasibility of implementing a software tool based on the theoretically justified meta-requirements, LLM challenges and design experiences. Through these research activities, we contribute with (i) a set of meta-requirements and a process model for knowledge exploration, i.e., abstracted knowledge to support others in the design of knowledge exploration tools, and (ii) experiences from the design and construction of a tool following the meta-requirements, within the identified process of knowledge exploration. The process includes *incremental model training, exploration and result interpretation*, and *concluding knowledge exploration*.

3   Theoretically Justified Meta-requirements

The purpose of this section is to theoretically justify an LLM-based knowledge exploration process and meta-requirements supporting the development of knowledge exploration tools. The LLM knowledge exploration process and identification of meta-requirements have been based on a) well-known IS literature research review methods, b) an examination of existing tool support for literature reviews and c) generic challenges regarding LLMs.

3.1   IS Literature Research Methods

To reconstruct a knowledge exploration process and identify meta-requirements, we have analyzed four well-known IS literature research methods: "A Guide to Conducting a Standalone Systematic Literature Review" [31], "Standing on the Shoulders of Giants: Challenges and Recommendations of Literature Search in Information Systems Research" [40], "Achieving Rigor in Literature Reviews" [2] and "Analyzing the Past to Prepare the Future" [43]. See Table 1 (Confer each publication for detailed descriptions).

All the methods advocate for a systematic, rigorous approach to literature reviews that begins with precise planning, involves meticulous search and selection of literature, demands critical appraisal and detailed analysis, and results in a structured and insightful write-up. Each stage builds upon the previous, promoting a comprehensive, transparent, and methodical examination of the existing body of literature. Based on the analysis of both similarities and dissimilarities between the four methods, we have identified four generic steps which correspond to basic meta-requirements:

First, *Planning*: This involves the initial setup where the purpose of the literature review is defined. It sets the foundation for the entire process by establishing clear objectives, research questions, and protocols that guide the scope and direction of the review. This planning stage is critical for aligning the review with the desired outcomes and ensuring it remains focused and relevant.

Second, *Search and Selection*: A rigorous search strategy is employed to gather literature from various databases and sources. This stage is methodical, often utilizing specific keywords, inclusion and exclusion criteria, and timeframes to filter the literature effectively. The selection process is equally thorough, with studies being chosen based on their relevance to the research question and their contribution to the topic at hand. This ensures that the literature compiled is pertinent and comprehensive.

Third, *Critical Appraisal and Detailed Analysis*: Once relevant studies are selected, they undergo a quality appraisal to evaluate the robustness of the research methodology,

428   J. Sjöström and S. Cronholm

Table 1. Steps in IS Literature Review Methods.

Literature review method	Steps
A Guide to Conducting a Standalone Systematic Literature Review [31]	Eight-step guide: Identify the purpose, draft protocol and train the team, apply practical screen, Search for literature, Extract data, appraise quality, synthesize studies, and Write the review
Standing on the Shoulders of Giants: Challenges and Recommendations of Literature Search in Information Systems Research [40]	Literature search, literature selection and literature synthesizing
Achieving Rigor in Literature Reviews [2]	Extraction of relevant literature, organization and preparation for analysis, coding and Analysis, and write-up and preparation
Analyzing the Past to Prepare the Future [43]	Identifying relevant literature, structuring the review, tone and tense, theoretical development, evaluating your theory, and creating your discussion and conclusion

the validity of the findings, and the relevance to the research questions. Data extraction involves pulling out necessary details from the studies for analysis. The analysis itself is a deep dive into the data, using techniques like coding to identify patterns, themes, and gaps in the research. This synthesis aims to integrate findings from individual studies into a cohesive understanding of the research topic.

Fourth, *Structured Write-Up*: The final write-up of the literature review is where the researcher presents the synthesized information. The structure of the review typically includes an introduction that outlines the purpose and scope, a methodology section that details the search and appraisal strategies, a results section that presents the findings from the literature, and a discussion that interprets these findings in the context of the research questions. The conclusion then summarizes the key insights and identifies implications for future research, practice, or policy.

The four phases described above have guided our search for meta-requirements governing the design of LLM-based knowledge exploration tools. An LLM-based tool should support a complete literature review workflow, enabling researchers to search, select, synthesize, and conclude with robust reporting features for transparency and reproducibility.

MR-1: Fine-tuning based on publication data. The tool support should facilitate an easy way to combine existing tools for literature search and download with fine-tuning of the LLM, i.e., go from a set of identified research publications to a fine-tuned LLM. In addition, the tool should be able to keep track of and make use of extensive publication metadata.

MR-2 Synthesizing the literature. The tool should support the researcher in describing, summarizing and conceptualizing the knowledge base.

MR-3 Concluding the literature review. The tool should support the researcher in crafting the final written version of the knowledge exploration process, e.g., by features to export results and exploration process logs.

Meta-requirements 2 and 3 imply that LLM needs sufficient baseline training to achieve sufficiently sophisticated analytical capabilities, and interpretation and expression of results in natural language.

3.2 Tool Support for Knowledge Exploration

One difference between the literature review method suggested by Bandara et al. [2] and the other three methods presented above is that Bandara et al.'s method explicitly addresses digital tools to support the literature review process. Tools are broadly categorized into *databases and citation analysis* tools, *reference management* tools, and *qualitative data* analysis tools [2]. The first category includes tools to search, e.g., Google Scholar, Web of Science, and Scopus. The second category includes tools to manage literature metadata and full texts, e.g., Mendeley, Zotero, BibDesk, and EndNote. Tools in the third category, such as NVivo and Atlas TI, facilitate analysis, annotations, and coding of text. Typically, there are features to simplify the transition between these tools, e.g., exporting found citations from Google Scholar into Zotero.

The literature review methods presented here [2, 31, 40, 43] promote rigor and transparency in the literature review process. Simply put, as a researcher you are expected to account for the steps taken in your research and justify choices that may impact your results (such as using certain keywords and inclusion criteria in the literature review). Here, we find a contrast to the use of LLMs, which tend to make the knowledge exploration process opaque rather than transparent. Further, any new tool introduced in the research practice should easily connect with the existing infrastructure. For example, augmenting LLMs with domain-specific tools such as database utilities can facilitate easier and more precise access to specialized knowledge [18]. Consequentially, we see a need to highlight rigor and transparency issues in the design of LLM-based knowledge exploration systems, leading to the following MRs:

MR-4 Maintaining research control. Maintaining control of the research process requires LLM to support transparency that provides an understanding of the various steps of knowledge exploration. The knowledge exploration tool should provide transparency, context, and explanations for the results it presents. For increased rigor, the system should keep logs of prompts as well as the contextual factors related to each query and response.

The use of LLMs potentially disrupts the traditional literature review process. Therefore, we proceed in the next section with an overview of challenges associated with LLM tools for knowledge exploration.

3.3 Generic LLM Challenges

We conducted a literature review to identify generic LLM challenges that could be used as meta-requirements for designing a knowledge exploration tool to support researchers exploring the knowledge base. We followed the method suggested by vom Brocke et al. [40]. We searched publications on Google Scholars using the keywords "Evaluation of Large Language Models" and "Goals of Large Language Models". Our literature review resulted in a vast number of challenges regarding the design and use of LLMs. In order to limit the result to a manageable number of articles, we selected well-cited articles [3, 4, 7, 19, 42]. We recognize that our literature review does not correspond to a complete literature research. However, we identified that expanding the literature selection did not offer noticeably new insights regarding challenges. Instead, further articles repeated what had already been mentioned in the well-cited articles. Therefore, the identified challenges were considered sufficient to articulate meta-requirements for LLM-based knowledge exploration tools. We synthesized the challenges into four abstract categories: training, prompting, result interpretation, and feasibility.

Training. Scholars report that training an LLM is challenging [13, 21, 27]. The size of modern pre-training datasets renders it impractical for any individual to thoroughly read or conduct quality assessments on the encompassed documents [19]. Training consists of two aspects: 1) The training required to promote general conversational and analytic capabilities. We call this the *baseline training*. 2) The training is required to respond to queries about a specific discourse (i.e., the research discourse we want to explore). We call this the *fine-tuning*. Fine-tuning is often regarded as training based on human feedback, meaning that the model learns from its mistakes and improves performance over time [3, 4]. Moreover, fine-tuning allows LLMs to adapt to specific tasks by adjusting their parameters, making them suitable for sentiment analysis, text generation, or document similarity tasks. Also, open-access peer-reviewed articles offer valuable insights into the latest findings and advancements in the field [20]. On top of supporting MR-1 (*Fine-tuning based on publication data*), the training challenge leads us to articulate another meta-requirement:

MR-5 Interoperability and data management. To facilitate fine-tuning, the tool should be able to interconnect with existing research software applications, e.g., *databases and citation analysis tools* and *reference management tools*.

Prompting. Prompt engineering is the systematic manipulation of prompts to improve outputs, and researchers should be transparent about both their prompt engineering procedures and the final prompts used in the research [42]. Skillful prompt engineering is necessary for the high performance of LLM:s [3]. For example, careful prompting enables LLMs to generate more coherent and contextually relevant responses, making them suitable for interactive and conversational applications (ibid.). Furthermore, variations of the prompt syntax, often occurring in ways unintuitive to humans, can result in dramatic output changes, and slight modifications of the benchmark prompt or evaluation protocol can give drastically different results [19]. Recently, the concept of prompt template engineering has emerged. Prompt template engineering is the process of creating a prompting function that results in the most effective task performance [23]. A prompt template can take a manual or automated approach to create prompts of the desired shape. Manually created prompts involve improvements by self-analysis, while automated prompts can either be discrete (e.g., prompt mining, prompt generation, prompt scoring) or continuous (described directly in the embedding space of the underlying LLM) [23].

MR-6: Exploration Clarity. The tool should support the researcher in directing queries towards a well-defined discourse (i.e., a selected subset of the literature). E.g., by prompting templates and a UI to select a subset of literature to query. The tool should include citations to the literature used to render its results.

MR-7: Documenting and re-using queries. The system should keep a record of executed prompts and queries. There should be an option to specify which subset of documents to query in order to increase the transparency of publication sources underlying LLM outputs and allow queries to be re-executed after further fine-tuning.

Result Interpretation. The problem of false information (known as "hallucinations") is discussed by several scholars [3, 7]. A "hallucination" is a generated text that is fluent and natural but unfaithful to the source content (intrinsic) and/or under-determined (extrinsic) [19]. It is well-known that LLM software often "hallucinates" and cannot reliably answer a question accurately [10, 24, 46]. Hallucinations make LLMs rather unsuitable for repeatable tasks in which any AI tool is supposed to excel. However, some efforts have been taken to minimize hallucination. For instance, there is research suggesting the use of fact-checking systems [10], token-level hallucination detection [24], and methods for learning hallucination detection in neural networks [46].

Despite technological improvements to counteract hallucinations, there are still epistemological unclarities concerning LLM use. Following [8], AI can be used for *automation* of processes or *augmentation* of human practice. For instance, recently, Google Gemini has been used to do automated meta-analysis of a vast amount of research publications. The results of such large-scale automation initiatives are difficult to validate; thus, the epistemological value of LLM output and consequential knowledge claims is unclear. We assert that both automation and augmentation of AI need to be governed by principles of interpretive research [22], e.g., the principle of suspicion, and to account in detail for the knowledge exploration process.

This LLM challenge further justifies MR-4 (*Maintaining research control*). It stresses that LLM-based exploration tools need to further embrace eXplainable AI capabilities in general, governed by the need for researchers to be able to assess the origin and–ultimately–the truthfulness of content generated by the LLM.

Performance and Feasibility. Several studies have evaluated the performance and feasibility of LLMs [3, 4, 45]. Individuals increasingly use LLMs due to outstanding performance in handling different applications such as general natural language tasks and domain-specific ones [19]. Moreover, the authors argue that performance should be evaluated regarding natural language processing, robustness, ethics, biases and trustworthiness. The authors also state that LLMs evaluation datasets could be used to test and compare the performance of different language models on various tasks. Inference latencies remain high because of low parallelizability and large memory footprints [19]. One reason is that limited context lengths are a barrier for handling long inputs well to facilitate applications like novel or textbook writing or summarizing.

Furthermore, performance increases through larger computer budgets but at a decreasing rate if the model or dataset size is fixed, reflecting a power law with diminishing returns. Fine-tuning entire LLMs requires the same amount of memory as pre-training, rendering it infeasible for many practitioners. When adapting an LLM via full-model fine-tuning, an individual copy of the model must be stored (consuming data storage) and loaded (expanding memory allocation) for each task [19]. There is ongoing progress in optimizing LLMs with fewer parameters to achieve capabilities similar to less resource-efficient models [e.g., 17].

MR-8: Promoting resource efficiency. The system needs to be resource-efficient enough to be usable for researchers using their ordinary computer resources, either by running it locally or accessing the system as a cloud service at a reasonable cost.

3.4 Concluding the Theoretical Justification

We can conclude that there is a lack of explicit meta-requirements supporting the design of knowledge exploration tools based on LLMs. When we compare the literature review methods presented in Sect. 3.1 to the meta-requirements derived from the generic LLM challenges presented in Sect. 3.2, it is evident that conventional literature review processes will be affected by LLMs. That is, LLMs may play a role in searching the literature, selecting relevant literature, synthesizing the literature, and concluding the literature review. Therefore, we outline a new knowledge exploration process (Fig. 1) that complements the literature review methods presented in Sect. 3.1. The knowledge exploration process is depicted as a sequential process. However, we realize that there are several moves back and forth between the four phases.

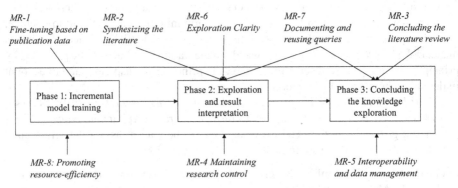

Fig. 1. Meta-requirements in the knowledge exploration process

We conclude the theoretically grounded meta-requirements by explaining them in relation to the phases in Fig. 1.

First, while incrementally extracting literature to train the system, there is a need to search for literature and retrieve metadata as well as full-text documents. Thus, the knowledge exploration tool needs support fine-tuning the LLM based on the selection/import of publication metadata and full-text documents. In order to facilitate features to implement MR-1, the tool needs support for interoperability and data management (MR-5). The researcher should be supported in selecting publications for ingestion by the LLM as well as an update of related publication metadata taking place in the background.

Second is the exploration and result interpretation phase, which is associated with most meta-requirements. This phase includes support for synthesizing the literature by providing queries (including prompts to the LLM) and getting responses (MR-2). These responses should be presented to allow the researcher to interpret them, i.e., by presenting a rich contextual view of the situation, including transparency about source publications in the LLM response (MR-6). MR-7 posits that queries should be documented, allowing for a 're-run' of queries whenever the model is further fine-tuned.

Third, in concluding the literature knowledge exploration, there are two sets of data that should be available: LLM-generated results and a detailed log that can be used to rigorously account for the knowledge exploration process (MR-3).

The whole process concerns the maintenance of research control (MR-4). It is based on the fact that the tool is resource-efficiently implemented to be used without unreasonable costs or waiting times (MR-8). We suggest that the cost and response times for tools in conventional literature review constitute a suitable benchmark.

The process of LLM-based knowledge exploration, as outlined here, is characterized by iterative work and incremental fine-tuning of the LLM. The process builds on continuous knowledge exploration through repeated queries and additional fine-tuning. Once the researcher finds that the fine-tuning is satisfactory, the queries can be asked a final time to render the desired analytical results from the literature. In contrast, conventional literature reviews require more human work when adding new literature the further along the coding process has progressed.

Ngwenyama and Rowe [29] raise the exciting question, "Should We Collaborate with AI to Conduct Literature Reviews?". They report that automatic literature reviews may compromise quality because interpreting data or drawing scientific conclusions cannot be automated because machines cannot perform these tasks correctly. Although AI can speed up literature reviews, it means that epistemic beliefs and values are challenged. Epistemological beliefs generally refer to the ideas of how it is possible to get information about a subject and how valid that information is [9]. In our case, it translates to trust in the results of the knowledge exploration process and how it is supported by transparency and explainability. In addition, the lack of transparency affects delegation and control of knowledge creation, curation and consumption [36]. Therefore, an overall perspective we adopt is that literature reviews should be cautiously conducted. However, our view is that AI could *assist humans* in specific phases of the literature review process such as "exploration and result interpretation" and "concluding the knowledge exploration".

4 Experiences from Artifact Design

In this section, we present the design of 'Knowledge Explorer' (KeX) – a prototype software we designed to illustrate and reflect further about the theoretically grounded meta-requirements. We report on experiences from the design process. These experiences serve to exemplify and reflect about the theoretically justified meta-requirements.

We structure our presentation based on Fig. 2. Section 4.1 explains the design foundations based on meta-requirements relating to all phases of knowledge exploration. Sections 4.2–4.4 explore each phase of knowledge exploration, and how meta-requirements related to the design process.

4.1 Foundations (MR-5 and MR-8)

In addressing the meta-requirement MR-8 for resource efficiency, we strategically opted for open-source solutions. This choice was driven by the dual goals of cost reduction and maintaining control over the system design. Our search led us to the Mistral 7B-instruct LLM—rooted in the Llama2 framework—and the open-source initiative, PrivateGPT, both meeting our criteria of efficiency and local deployment.

The Mistral 7B-instruct model [17] is preliminarily trained for interaction, delivering performance on par with ChatGPT3.5. This established a foundation for subsequent fine-tuning using scientific publications, thereby aligning with the meta-requirements for model training (MR-1, see Sect. 4.2).

We integrated the software with the reference management tool Zotero. The integration not only adhered to MR-5, promoting interoperability, but also streamlined the import of metadata and full-text, directly addressing MR-8.

Despite these advancements, interoperability challenges persist, particularly concerning the ingestion of metadata and full-text documents. Crossref [14] is a comprehensive but insufficient database for publication metadata. We overcame this through bespoke Python scripts that scraped web data, allowing for the import datasets as illustrated in Table 2. The datasets included DESRIST proceedings papers, selected 'DSR canon' publications, and all volumes from the journals Information Systems Education Journal (ISEDJ) and Journal of Information Systems Education (JISE). Nonetheless, this workaround, while effective, highlights the pressing need for a universally accepted standard for publication data to simplify such integrations.

Table 2. Imported datasets

Dataset	Articles	Techniques employed
DESRIST papers 2009–2023	528	Scraping of bibtex data from SpringerLink as well as ACM web pages (the proceedings shifted published in the time period). ACM scraping complicated due to protection against bot downloads from web site. Resulted in Zotero metadata as well as full-text downloads (through library subscription)
JISE (all volumes)	973	Scraping of journal web page. Resulted in Zotero metadata as well as full-text downloads (through library subscription)
ISEDJ (all volumes)	1040	Scraping of journal web page. Tweak of the script to scrape the JISE web page. Resulted in Zotero metadata as well as full-text downloads (through library subscription)
DSR Canon	51	Manual selection and download of 'DSR canon', i.e., seminal DSR articles selected by the authors. Metadata manually added to Zotero

All automatically imported datasets required a 'quality control' due to missing metadata, e.g., missing authors, abstracts, or issue/volume numbers. The curation work took several days in total.

4.2 Incremental Model Training (MR-1, MR-4, and MR-6)

Compliant with MR-1, we initiated incremental model training. PrivateGPT enables the absorption of new knowledge by processing PDF documents. This capability allows us to tailor the tool for specific discursive domains, as shown in Table 2.

A notable concern is the potential loss of informational fidelity during LLM model training. To address this and maintain researcher control (MR-4) and exploration clarity (MR-6), our system architecture incorporates mechanisms that preserve the lineage between text segments ingested by the LLM and their source publications. Illustrated in Fig. 2, the LLM_doc table encapsulates this relationship, mapping chunks of text to corresponding metadata entries from the source literature. This structure not only enhances our ability to trace the LLM's outputs back to the original publications but also enriches the training process with a transparent data layer.

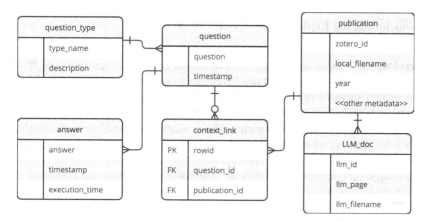

Fig. 2. E/R model for publication mapping and question/answer logging

Our implementation therefore introduces an innovation in LLM training methodologies by augmenting the standard process with a transparent, traceable framework. The implementation of solutions to identify source text based on LLM output is not trivial. Our design solution manages to correctly produce citations in some cases, but more work is required in this area to satisfyingly identify source publications for LLM output. Our advancement parallels the transparency-centric features found in emerging applications like the Consensus app, which is built atop the OpenAI GPT platform.

4.3 Exploration and Result Interpretation (MR-2, MR-6, and MR-7)

Our GUI development included a selection feature for querying subsets of data, enabling targeted inquiries to the LLM within specific segments of the literature. A cross-comparative query function was added, permitting parallel questioning of the LLM across different literature segments, thereby aiding in the structured examination of diverse research discourses. For example, this allows us to dissect the concept of 'evaluation' or 'artifact' across various DSR genres [33].

Also, we integrated a feature that enriches queries with predefined prompts, which applies default prompts to each query to elicit a particular style or level of response from the LLM. The efficacy and characteristics of such prompts are an ongoing research focus, likely influenced by the specific LLM deployed (e.g., Mistral 7B–Instruct vs. GPT-4).

Although the logging (MR-4) and re-querying (MR-7) mechanisms were not fully operational in the initial prototype, the underlying database architecture is in place, as illustrated in Fig. 2. The prototype's event-handling system is designed for future integration with database connectivity, which will complete the logging and re-querying functionalities.

To mitigate the LLM's tendency for 'hallucinations,' we configured the system with a temperature setting of 0. Furthermore, by increasing the token limit to 1024, we enabled the LLM to handle a larger influx of input tokens and generate extensive output, maintaining efficiency with a fine-tuned dataset of approximately 1000 publications (MR-8).

4.4 Concluding the Exploration (MR-3, MR-7)

The current prototype does not encompass features dedicated to the final stage of knowledge exploration – those associated with documentation and exportation of findings. These include logging (MR-7) and the development of custom features to facilitate the transfer of text to word processing software (MR-3). Technologically, exporting text to targets such as LaTeX, Google Docs, or Microsoft Word is straightforward, courtesy of several readily available libraries. The primary challenge lies in the conceptual domain—determining what data should be exported to best support researchers during the write-up phase of knowledge exploration.

Our design process has identified two essential types of data that a custom export feature should integrate to bolster the knowledge exploration narrative. First, a log that captures the knowledge exploration journey, assisting researchers in meticulously documenting the evolution of their inquiry. Second, the substantive content derived from the knowledge exploration, such as comparative analyses of concepts across literature subsets, including the examination of their similarities and differences.

5   Concluding Discussion

In concluding this research, we underscore our contributions in the form of meta-requirements for the design of LLM-based knowledge exploration tools. The paper has outlined eight meta-requirements that address various aspects of the knowledge exploration process, drawing from rigorous theoretical grounding and practical design experiences. These MRs serve as a foundational framework for future design and research in the field, ensuring that the development of knowledge exploration tools remains structured, transparent, and aligned with scholarly rigor. We have also illustrated these meta-requirements and their relationships through a knowledge exploration process model.

The MRs have been related to the various stages of the knowledge exploration process, from the initial planning and fine-tuning of the LLM to the concluding write-up stages. They offer a systematic approach to harnessing the potential of LLMs while maintaining control over the research process, ensuring the clarity of exploration, and documenting the query and response mechanisms to support repeatability and transparency.

The proposed MRs are not only a theoretical contribution but have also been the basis for the design of the 'Knowledge Explorer' prototype. This instantiation and the design process journey have provided insights into the practicality of the MRs, highlighting areas for improvement and generating practical examples of design implications of the meta-requirements.

Furthermore, the paper contributes to the ongoing discourse on the methodological implications of LLMs in information systems research (and beyond). It suggests that while LLMs introduce innovative capabilities for literature synthesis and knowledge discovery, their integration into the research process requires careful consideration of transparency, control, and resource efficiency. As future research, we suggest a complementing empirical evaluation involving studies of researchers using the tool.

References

1. Austin, J., et al.: Program synthesis with large language models. ArXiv Prepr. Arxiv:210807732 (2021)
2. Bandara, W., et al.: Achieving rigor in literature reviews: insights from qualitative data analysis and tool-support (2015)
3. Chang, Y., et al.: A survey on evaluation of large language models. ArXiv Prepr. Arxiv:230703109. (2023)
4. Chen, M., et al.: Evaluating large language models trained on code. ArXiv Prepr. Arxiv:210703374 (2021)
5. Davidson, J., Paulus, T., Jackson, K.: Speculating on the future of digital tools for qualitative research. Qualit. Inq. **22**(7), 606–610 (2016). https://doi.org/10.1177/1077800415622505
6. Dobrkovic, A., Döppner, D.A., Iacob, M.-E., van Hillegersberg, J.: Collaborative literature search system: an intelligence amplification method for systematic literature search. In: Chatterjee, S., Dutta, K., Sundarraj, R.P. (eds.) DESRIST 2018. LNCS, vol. 10844, pp. 169–183. Springer, Cham (2018). https://doi.org/10.1007/978-3-319-91800-6_12
7. Dwivedi, Y.K., et al.: Opinion paper: "so what if ChatGPT wrote it?" multidisciplinary perspectives on opportunities, challenges and implications of generative conversational AI for research, practice and policy. Int. J. Inf. Manag. **71**, 102642 (2023). https://doi.org/10.1016/j.ijinfomgt.2023.102642
8. Enholm, I.M., et al.: Artificial intelligence and business value: a literature review. Inf. Syst. Front. **24**(5), 1709–1734 (2022). https://doi.org/10.1007/s10796-021-10186-w
9. Fieser, J., Dowden, B.: Epistemic Value (2011). https://iep.utm.edu/epistemic-value/
10. Galitsky, B.A.: Truth-o-meter: collaborating with llm in fighting its hallucinations (2023)
11. Goldkuhl, G., Lind, M.: A multi-grounded design research process. In: Winter, R., Zhao, J.L., Aier, S. (eds.) Global Perspectives on Design Science Research, pp. 45–60. Springer, Heidelberg (2010). https://doi.org/10.1007/978-3-642-13335-0_4
12. Gregor, S., Jones, D.: The anatomy of a design theory. J. Assoc. Inf. Syst. **8**(5), 312–335 (2007)

13. Hadi, M.U. et al.: A survey on large language models: Applications, challenges, limitations, and practical usage. Authorea Preprint (2023)
14. Hendricks, G., et al.: Crossref: the sustainable source of community-owned scholarly metadata. Quant. Sci. Stud. **1**(1), 414–427 (2020)
15. Hevner, A.R.: A three cycle view of design science research. Scand. J. Inf. Syst. **19**(2), 87–92 (2007)
16. Hevner, A.R., et al.: Design science in information systems research. Mis Q. **28**(1), 75–105 (2004)
17. Jiang, A.Q., et al.: Mistral 7B. ArXiv Prepr. Arxiv:231006825 (2023)
18. Jin, Q., et al.: Genegpt: augmenting large language models with domain tools for improved access to biomedical information. ArXiv (2023)
19. Kaddour, J. et al.: Challenges and applications of large language models. ArXiv Prepr. ArXiv230710169. (2023)
20. Kamnis, S.: Generative pre-trained transformers (GPT) for surface engineering. Surf. Coat. Technol. **466**, 129680 (2023)
21. Kasneci, E., et al.: ChatGPT for good? on opportunities and challenges of large language models for education. Learn. Individ. Differ. **103**, 102274 (2023)
22. Klein, H.K., Myers, M.D.: A set of principles for conducting and evaluating interpretive field studies in information systems. MIS Q. **23**(1), 67–94 (1999)
23. Liu, P., et al.: Pre-train, prompt, and predict: a systematic survey of prompting methods in natural language processing. ACM Comput. Surv. **55**(9), 1–35 (2023)
24. Liu, T. et al.: A token-level reference-free hallucination detection benchmark for free-form text generation. ArXiv Prepr. Arxiv:210408704. (2021)
25. Liu, W.: Knowledge exploitation, knowledge exploration, and competency trap. Knowl. Process. Manag. **13**(3), 144–161 (2006)
26. Martin, L., et al.: CamemBERT: a tasty French language model. ArXiv Prepr. Arxiv:191103894 (2019)
27. Meyer, J.G., et al.: ChatGPT and large language models in academia: opportunities and challenges. BioData Min. **16**(1), 20 (2023)
28. Morana, S., et al.: Tool support for design science research—towards a software ecosystem: a report from a DESRIST 2017 workshop. Commun. Assoc. Inf. Syst. **43**(1), 17 (2018)
29. Ngwenyama, O., Rowe, F.: Should we collaborate with AI to conduct literature reviews? changing epistemic values in a flattening world. J. Assoc. Inf. Syst. **25**(1), 122–136 (2024)
30. Nunamaker, J.F., Jr., Briggs, R.O.: Toward a broader vision for Information Systems. ACM Trans. Manag. Inf. Syst. TMIS. **2**(4), 20 (2011)
31. Okoli, C.: A guide to conducting a standalone systematic literature review. Commun. AIS. **37** (2015)
32. Paulus, T.M., et al.: Digital tools for qualitative research: disruptions and entanglements. Qual. Inq. **23**, 10 (2017). https://doi.org/10.1177/1077800417731080
33. Peffers, K., et al.: Design science research genres: introduction to the special issue on exemplars and criteria for applicable design science research. Eur. J. Inf. Syst. **27**(2), 129–139 (2018). https://doi.org/10.1080/0960085X.2018.1458066
34. Rossi, S., et al.: Augmenting research methods with foundation models and generative AI (2024)
35. Santoro, G., Usai, A.: Knowledge exploration and ICT knowledge exploitation through human resource management: a study of Italian firms. Manag. Res. Rev. **41**(6), 701–715 (2018)
36. Schwartz, D., Te'eni, D.: AI for knowledge creation, curation, and consumption in context. J. Assoc. Inf. Syst. **25**(1), 37–47 (2024)
37. Sjöström, J.: DeProX: a design process exploration tool. In: Maedche, A., vom Brocke, J., Hevner, A. (eds.) DESRIST 2017. LNCS, vol. 10243, pp. 447–451. Springer, Cham (2017). https://doi.org/10.1007/978-3-319-59144-5_29

38. Tripp, A., et al.: Sample-efficient optimization in the latent space of deep generative models via weighted retraining. Adv. Neural. Inf. Process. Syst. **33**, 11259–11272 (2020)
39. Valmeekam, K., et al.: Large Language Models Still Can't Plan (A Benchmark for LLMs on Planning and Reasoning about Change). ArXiv Prepr. Arxiv:220610498 (2022)
40. Vom Brocke, J., et al.: Standing on the shoulders of giants: challenges and recommendations of literature search in information systems research. Commun. Assoc. Inf. Syst. **37**(1), 9 (2015)
41. Walls, J.G., et al.: Building an information systems design theory for vigilant EIS. Inf. Syst. Res. **3**(1), 36–59 (1992)
42. Watkins, R.: Guidance for researchers and peer-reviewers on the ethical use of Large Language Models (LLMs) in scientific research workflows. AI Ethics 1–6 (2023)
43. Webster, J., Watson, R.T.: Analyzing the past to prepare for the future: Writing a literature review. MIS Q. xiii—-xxiii (2002)
44. Wu, T., et al.: A brief overview of ChatGPT: the history, status quo and potential future development. IEEECAA J. Autom. Sin. **10**(5), 1122–1136 (2023)
45. Xu, F.F., et al.: A systematic evaluation of large language models of code. In: Proceedings of the 6th ACM SIGPLAN International Symposium on Machine Programming, pp. 1–10 (2022)
46. Zhou, C. et al.: Detecting hallucinated content in conditional neural sequence generation. ArXiv Prepr. Arxiv:201102593 (2020)

Beyond E-Commerce: A Design Science Study into Crafting a Model for Customer-Centric M-Commerce

Christoph Tomitza$^{(\boxtimes)}$ ⓘ, Sebastian Spies ⓘ, Ulvi Ibrahimli ⓘ, Christian Zeiß ⓘ,
Lisa Straub ⓘ, and Axel Winkelmann ⓘ

University of Würzburg, 97070 Würzburg, Germany
christoph.tomitza@uni-wuerzburg.de

Abstract. The integration of mobile devices and applications has fueled the global growth of M-Commerce. Understanding customer needs has been critical in designing mobile information systems (IS) and remaining resilient against technological threats through upcoming market changes. We use customer focus theory and customer-centric IS framework to shape the theoretical-conceptual framework. Employing design science research (DSR) methodology, we synthesize the findings of a structured literature review with interviews and construct a set of design requirements and design principles. This forms the groundwork for crafting a model-based guideline for designing customer-centric M-Commerce. The model provides structured guidance on approaching the design of a customer-centric M-Commerce solution. The developed design artifact helps online retailers understand the key elements and considerations involved in creating an effective mobile commerce solution.

Keywords: Mobile Commerce · Customer-centric · Design Science Research

1 Introduction

In the realm of Information Systems (IS) scholarship, understanding the end-user requirements has been the cornerstone of designing well-functioning web-based systems, such as electronic commerce (E-Commerce) websites [4]. In this domain addressing such dynamic user needs with the help of design tools is instrumental in customer relationship management (CRM). As E-Commerce expands within the corporate landscape, mobile commerce (M-Commerce) emerges as a prominent and swiftly growing subset of this paradigm, propelled by the widespread adoption of smartphones and mobile applications [56]. The global growth of M-Commerce generates economic value while introducing new challenges. These include, for example, the necessity to align content with the comparatively confined screen dimensions of mobile hardware [21, 48], adapt to the lower computing power of the smartphone processors, and the scarcity of high-performance wireless mobile networks [52]. The academic literature on E-Commerce involves intense discussions on various issues of M-Commerce such as framework evaluation [43], user satisfaction [54], usability [18], and interface design [2]. Some also

M. Mandviwalla et al. (Eds.): DESRIST 2024, LNCS 14621, pp. 440–454, 2024.
https://doi.org/10.1007/978-3-031-61175-9_30

address the customer-centricity issues in E-Commerce. Karn et al. [25], for instance, address the cold-start and data sparsity problems of current recommender systems (RS). Albert et al. [4] construct a model to guide the design, content management, tracking, and user experience on online shopping platforms. Yet, those and similar models are hardly directly applicable to mobile online shops and the literature lacks user-oriented reference models that can directly be utilized by online retailers to design their mobile appearance. This gap poses challenges for companies seeking to extend CRM into the mobile context, implement personalization, and design user-friendly interfaces. Hence, we pose the following research question (RQ).

RQ: *How can companies develop a customer-centric mobile commerce design from a conceptual point of view to enhance customer experience?*

To address this question, we introduce a model rooted in design science research (DSR) to guide the development of M-Commerce channels. Our focus centers on crafting an initial conceptual model aimed at providing established E-Commerce retailers with structured guidance to fortify their resilience against emerging competitors in the mobile online retail sector. Through our model-based guidelines, companies can tailor M-Commerce platforms to prioritize customer needs, thereby adapting to dynamic market conditions. Notably, our work aims to bridge a gap by presenting a design model specifically tailored for mobile online stores, integrating practical insights and theoretical underpinnings. The contribution of this paper is threefold: It contributes to design science research (DSR) by developing a model for an unexplored commerce area. Given that electronic and mobile commerce systems serve as both information systems and marketing channels [19], our work also contributes to scholarly discussions in these domains.

The paper unfolds as follows: The introduction is followed by a conceptualization of M-Commerce. Next, design requirements are elucidated and later summarized in four design principles. We structure these design principles into a model for practical application and subject it to two evaluation phases. We conclude with insights gleaned from the process, addressing research limitations and implications.

2 Research Background

2.1 Conceptualization of Mobile Commerce

M-Commerce refers to transactions initiated on portable mobile devices - such as smartphones and tablets - in the context of online commerce [40, 51]. Data is transferred from the end devices via the wireless mobile networks [21, 23]. This allows customers to access and purchase the products offered by online retailers from any location and at any time [14, 23]. The compact design and the technological features - e.g., due to the intuitive operation via touch-sensitive displays - form the basis for designing an appealing transaction experience for mobile online stores [53]. In addition, the development of new transmission technologies facilitates the integration of M-Commerce into consumers' everyday lives [52]. Against this background, websites that are designed for mobile content can be seen as a resource- and cost-efficient entry point into the mobile environment from a developer's perspective [5]. Native applications (apps), for instance, are similar in their visual design to the browser-based websites but must be downloaded and installed by the user from an app store [38, 47]. Due to this direct integration into the respective operating system, however, apps offer the possibility of incorporating the hardware and software functionalities combined by the respective end device - e.g., for the provision of augmented reality (AR) content, the transmission of push notifications and the integration of location-based services - into the customer journey [3, 39]. Some of these can also be used temporarily without connecting to a mobile network [47]. There are further distinctions between E-Commerce and M-Commerce, which are summarized in Table 1.

Table 1. Distinction between E-Commerce and M-Commerce

Categories	E-Commerce	M-Commerce
Location [21, 23]	Dependent use (LAN and WLAN)	Independent use (WLAN and mobile network)
Display [21, 36, 48]	Desktop view	Mobile view (smaller screen)
Operation [53]	Mouse and keyboard	Touch-based
Computing power [5, 52]	Standard computer processor	Compressed processor
Interaction [3, 52]	Contact via the website and e-mail	Extended accessibility through notifications at any time
Functions [3, 39, 42]	Standard	Sensor-based extensions
Access [38, 47]	Through browser	Through browser or application

Hence, it can be concluded that mobile online retail offers another layer of centralization around the customer. Yet, it is under-researched how mobile webshops should be designed so that the virtual shopping environment is optimally tailored to customers' needs. Specifically, the literature lacks guidelines on the design of IS-enabled solutions for mobile retailing to enable mobile customer centricity.

2.2 Customer-Centric IS and Customer Focus Theory

The advent of digital environments, where customers openly share knowledge and experiences [50], necessitates a scholarly rethinking of customer-centric business paradigms. At the heart of this notion is the understanding that customers possess unique needs and preferences that they alone can articulate. Liang and Tanniru's [33] customer-centric IS framework underscores the customer's pivotal role as the kernel and driving force behind the system. In this framework, customer profiles are meticulously analyzed to discern needs and inform information requirements, often through the customization of products or services. These tailored offerings, in turn, dictate how business processes are configured - be it through design, assembly, or adaptation. Enabling such configuration necessitates an IS architecture capable of dynamic user profiling. This intricate interplay is evident in web-based systems like M-Commerce, which offer opportunities for service-enabled processes (e.g., service-oriented architecture) to enhance product bundling [33]. Yet designing customer-centric web-based systems, with their multi-tier

IS structure, deviates from traditional life cycles [4]. The existing M-Commerce solutions pose additional requirements on companies to adopt navigation of user-centric design principles for mobile shops to maximize profitability [46].

Acknowledging the interdisciplinary nature of our design artifact, we integrate customer focus theory from the intersection of IS and marketing literature, where the concept of the customer is more mature. Lohan et al. [35] delineate subconstructs of customer focus theory. Engineering customer requirements (1) is a challenging task, yet a robust understanding of customer needs is essential in designing a user-oriented system architecture. Collecting and utilizing customer information (2) in the design process is equally important, as customer data may reveal latent needs impacting design orientation [10]. Lastly, the improvement of customer relationships (3) is also an essential part of the construct since system improvements are achieved through customers being an integral part of IS development because they enable the system to drive its value [6, 30, 33].

The amalgamation of customer focus theory [35] and user-centric IS framework [33] forms the conceptual basis of our model for customer-centric M-Commerce design. Such recombination allows us to address the cascading set such design issues regarding customer-centricity. For instance, prioritizing customer requirements holds paramount importance in the design of any IS [33], a principle that becomes particularly salient within the realm of M-Commerce due to the dynamic nature of customer preferences toward mobile systems [35]. Moreover, in the mobile context, online retailers have enhanced channels for processing customer data, such as user accounts within mobile apps, compared to the desktop version, facilitating personalized content delivery. These aspects also resonate with the products or services component of Liang and Tanniru's [33] IS framework.

3 Research Methodology

The DSR approach of Kuechler and Vaishnavi [29] forms the central framework for developing our domain-specific knowledge and artifacts. This combines the theories of the behavioral sciences, which are mostly guided by organizational and human characteristics, with the innovative and problem-centered solutions that result from the design sciences [15]. Figure 1 illustrates the conducted steps.

Fig. 1. Design science procedure according to Kuechler and Vaishnavi [29]

Our research approach began by analyzing the existing literature on the problem space. A structured literature review according to vom Brocke et al. [8] was carried out. We perform the literature search with search strings containing synonyms of e-commerce to gain a broad overview of existing publications. We focus on qualitative high-ranked journals (vhb ranking A+, A, and B) and databases and obtain $n = 439$ results after our keyword search. Conducting the steps of the literature review we assess $n = 50$ publications as highly relevant according to our further steps of designing the model of an optimized M-Commerce design. The resulting findings were used to develop a guideline-based interview procedure, according to Bell et al. [7], to obtain additional information regarding the possibilities of designing a mobile presence to supplement the theory-based findings with the experiences of domain experts from online retailers. We conducted $n = 12$ interviews (I1 - I12) with domain experts. Our interview questions were aimed at first obtaining information about the person's and company's experience in the field of M-Commerce. Next, we explicitly addressed the interviewee experience already gathered on design aspects of M-Commerce to gain as many practical insights as possible to expand the theory of the literature. Given the sequential nature of the qualitative research, we analyzed the information obtained based on the qualitative content analysis method applied by Mayring [37]. Within internal workshops, the input knowledge from the theory from Sect. 2.2, the results from the literature analysis, and the interview insights were processed and design requirements were developed. These were then converted into design principles and contextualized in a model. To evaluate our artifact, $n = 2$ focus groups and $n = 2$ expert interviews were conducted, and their estimation of the model was also collected quantitatively. Furthermore, the interviewees from the initial phase were addressed with the finished model and were able to provide quantitative feedback.

4 Designing Model-Based Guidelines for Customer-Centric M-Commerce

4.1 Design Requirements

Building upon the DSR literature discussed earlier, we initially identified eleven design requirements (DR) that serve as essential qualities for our M-Commerce design model as an artifact. The synthesis of the theories, a structured literature review, and multiple rounds of expert interviews are analyzed to derive design requirements.

DR1: Reach Customers on Emotional Level. Integrating high-quality visual components such as images, animations, videos, and AR content is pivotal in designing a mobile solution [3, 17, 48, 55] (I1, I3, I5, I6, I9–I11). This approach accommodates the emotion-driven needs of customers by providing adequate and comprehensible product presentations [32, 41] (I1, I3, I8, I10, I11).

DR2: Provide Relevant Information. Highlighting relevant facts, including product descriptions and transaction terms and conditions, positively influences rational customer decision-making [23, 41] (I9). Providing clear usage instructions has been shown to enhance this positive effect further [48] (I2, I5, I8–I10, I12).

DR3: Customize M-Commerce Content. Implementing content customization based on collaborative buyer behavior and personal engagement enhances customer experience [12] (I3, I5, I6, I8–I12). Such personalization of content is perceived as value-enhancing [9, 31].

DR4: Minimize Content and Process Complexity. Graphical and textual presentations should be concise and tailored to mobile devices to enhance customer focus [3, 17] (I1, I7–I9). Simplifying the transaction process by providing intuitive page navigation, clear product categories, effective filter mechanisms, and an optimized search mechanism reduces obstacles and facilitates customer exploration [20, 39].

DR5: Streamline the Check-Out Process. By shortening the input forms, it is advisable to request only relevant information for completing the transaction and shipping of the products (I8, I9). Reducing the abandonment risk involves using essential or value-adding elements only [20] (I5, I6, I9–I12). Integrating various payment options and payment service providers (I3, I10, I11) and their express check-outs (I3, I5, I7, I9–I11) positively shape the customer experience.

DR6: Align User-navigation Concept to Mobile Environment. Optimizing the user navigation to a mobile environment can be achieved by ensuring clear graphical contrast ratios (I5, I6, I11, I12). In addition, the mobile solution should be geared towards the one-handed condition (I8, I10, I12) - using click, swipe, and zoom gestures [44].

DR7: Minimize Loading Times. The media to be displayed should be reduced in number and visual size and, if necessary, adapted to a compressing file format (I1, I4–I6, I8–I12) or should be hidden (I9, I10). Speed advantages can also be achieved by revising the scripts integrated into the source code (I1, I3, I4, I6, I7, I8), providing the content via a performance network infrastructure (I3, I6, I8, I10, I12), and technological approaches (I3, I6, I8, I9, I10, I12).

DR8: Offer Customer Support and Complementary Services. Specific content or topic pages can answer customer questions and provide informative content (I4, I5, I10). Personal contact channels (I4, I6), automated dialog systems (I4, I6, I8), and self-service solutions (I5, I6, I8) strengthen the corporate customer focus efforts [16, 26] (I1, I4, I5, I10, I11). Complementary services such as virtual fitting rooms [57] capture additional value in the mobile context [58]. These services can be integrated across pre-sales, sales, and after-sales phases of the customer journey.

DR9: Transmit Customer Relationship to Mobile Context. Establishing the existing customer relationship in the mobile context requires integrating payment service providers in the check-out process [59], showcasing product reviews from past buyers [13, 27] (I1, I3, I11, I12), and transparently presenting the company's data protection guidelines [34] (I2, I5, I6, I8). It also pays off to integrate third-party data protection seals [24] (I1, I3, I4, I6–I9, I11), such that it highlights the legitimacy of the service offerings. The additional guarantees, the offer of purchase on account (I5, I6, I8, I10, I12), and the proactive disclosure of any fees and (shipping) service providers (I10, I12) have a positive effect on customer trust.

DR10: Create a Cross-channel Customer Experience. In addition to the strictly content-related issues, Harmonizing the basic structure on both desktop and mobile devices is essential to enable a seamless cross-channel experience for customers [3, 52] (I6, I10, I11).

DR11: Develop the Mobile Solution Continuously. Adapting the mobile solution to evolving customer requirements and technological frameworks is crucial for maintaining resilience against dynamic technological developments (I1, I4, I5).

4.2 Design Principles

The DRs outlined above lay the groundwork for developing a set of design principles (DPs). These encapsulate the essential requirements for crafting a customer-centric M-Commerce design and provide a structured overview for its design and development.

DP1: Presentation of Content. In E-Commerce, where interactions between customers and sellers occur solely through the online shop interface, the appearance of the interface plays a critical role in forming customers' first impressions and trust in the company [36]. It's crucial to incorporate both rational (DR2) and emotional (DR1) content to engage users effectively [12, 32, 48]. Additionally, personalization features can enhance the customer experience by tailoring the website to individual preferences [9, 31]. Graphic content, if included, should be optimized for high resolution on mobile devices [3].

DP2: Handling of the Interface. The architecture of mobile devices in M-Commerce differs significantly from that of desktop-based E-Commerce platforms, resulting in distinct touch-based operating options [1]. Gestures like swiping replace traditional mouse and keyboard inputs, necessitating intuitive interface design [17, 39] (I1, I2, I8). To enhance usability, complexity should be minimized (DR4), the checkout process streamlined (DR5), and user navigation optimized for the mobile environment (DR6). Furthermore, reducing loading times is essential due to limited computing resources and mobile network connectivity (DR7), facilitating seamless user interaction in a mobile context.

DP3: Integration of Services. Mobile devices enable customers to make purchases any-time and anywhere, allowing shops and information to be accessible at all times. This constant accessibility presents new opportunities for service applications and adver-tising measures, as customers can be targeted differently throughout various shopping phases. Mobile applications equipped with sensors and cameras further enhance service efficiency and customer value. Integrating services throughout pre-sales, sales, and after-sales stages (DR8) addresses consumer concerns (I3–I6, I8, I10) and enhances customer engagement. This approach not only provides added value and assistance to customers but also proactively reduces potential costs for online retailers. Hence, personalized, automated, and content-based services should be prioritized (I1–I6, I8–I12).

DP4: Perception by Customers. Customers judge websites based on appearance, brand identity, and overall user experience. While desktop-based online shops have already established brand identities and received customer ratings, transitioning this relation-ship to the mobile context is crucial (DR9). Mobile solutions must positively influence customer perception by instilling user confidence (I1–I3, I5, I6, I8, I10, I12), delivering a seamless cross-channel experience (DR10), and continu-ously evolving the offered web application (DR11). By prioritizing these aspects, companies can enhance custom-er focus and loyalty in the mobile shopping environment.

4.3 Model for Customer-Centric M-Commerce Design

When synthesizing the theoretical insights with the inputs from interviews and the developed DPs, we discovered dependencies across the different DPs and DRs. Furthermore, there exists some prioritization for companies to reach a customer-centric M-Commerce design. To solve these dependencies, we derive a model from our resulting DPs to illuminate important points and gain more insights for the E-Commerce companies to develop their M-Commerce design. The representation of the principles in our model is oriented toward the construction of a house, which requires a stable foundation formed by meaningful content. Figure 2 provides the final model. In M-Commerce, care must be taken to ensure that the content in the mobile version of the shop addresses the user's emotional and rational needs, as is the case in classic desktop versions. Another point here is a personalized presentation of the content and use of the new possibilities of mobile shopping. This forms the foundation for the design of a customer-centric M-Commerce solution.

Next, it is important to note that mobile devices have a different form of handling; they cannot be controlled using a mouse or keyboard but often rely on swipe functions. To enable handling of the mobile shop or app, it must be designed user-friendly, the check-out process must be optimized, and operation must be made easier. It is also desirable to optimize page loading times to create a shopping experience, especially in mobile, flexible shopping.

Another point is the integration of services in a mobile context. Services can be integrated into the various phases of customer contact. On the one hand, these can be free or chargeable and support the customer directly with questions or problems or offer them additive services for new possibilities in different phases of the shopping process. The mobile app area, in particular, enables completely new possibilities, as the shop is available to the customer at all times and can be used by them in various daily situations.

The last part of the model comprises the customer's perception. Here, it is important to maintain the existing relationship with the customer and to be able to transfer this from the desktop environment to the mobile context and thus maintain trust here, too. Furthermore, the corporate identity must also be ensured in the mobile context. It is also important to create added value for the customer across all channels and thus create a customer experience. Finally, continuous further development is necessary to be able to utilize new technologies in a mobile context.

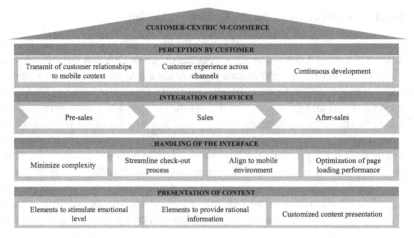

Fig. 2. Model for a customer-centric M-Commerce design

4.4 Evaluation

To ensure a rigorous evaluation of our model, we put the model under examination in two phases. We started our evaluation with the first phase, a quantitative approach, and sent a survey to all our interview participants from the awareness of the problem phase. Our questionnaire used open and closed questions to gain as much insights as possible. The closed questions are based on the second ex ante evaluation criteria according to Sonneberg and vom Brocke [45] and used seven items Likert Scales. We asked questions about the content quality of the model, for example, the understandability, clarity, simplicity, completeness, and level of detail. A number of $n = 7$ interviewees answered our request, and we got a first insight into the quality of our result (EA1–EA7). Overall, we achieved an approval rating of 6.5 and 6.8 for the individual questions, with the lowest scores achieved for understandability and the highest for level of detail. The open questions aimed to optimize the graphic design, content adjustments, and supplementary aspects. The main result of the qualitative evaluation is that the model contains aspects that are also important for a customer-centric E-Commerce design, and the structure of the model should illustrate these elements.

Only limited insights were gained from the first evaluation phase, so we decided to extend the evaluation. Further steps were taken to evaluate the model to gain more in-depth insights. Firstly, the model was evaluated in two expert interviews (EI1 and EI2) with $n = 2$ managers of online retail companies to evaluate our artifact from a broad angle. This was followed by two focus groups. In the first focus group (FG1), $n = 2$ academic experts from the field of digital marketing and e-commerce were confronted with our artifact. Later, we conducted a second targeted focus group (FG2) interview consisting of $n = 4$ people with expertise in e-commerce and online marketing to evaluate our artifact more profoundly from the perspective of practical robustness. The qualitative evaluation showed that points such as the company's orientation (EI1, FG2) and technical (EI1, EI2) as well as legal (EI2) aspects are important to the participants. The first quantitative survey from phase one and the qualitative surveys from phase two show that the participants see the model as limited to M-Commerce and would apply it to E-Commerce. In the second phase, after the interviews and focus groups, we involved all participants to complete a quantitative survey, again using the second evaluation criteria from Sonneberg and vom Brocke [45]. The final ratings of the quantitative survey of the participants in the qualitative study fluctuate between 5.75 and 6.5, with simplicity and consistency showing the lowest results. In contrast, the clarity and understandability of the model received the highest scores.

5 Discussion and Implications

Our model provides a comprehensive overview of aspects that are necessary to construct a customer-centric M-Commerce design. The presented artifact makes a novel contribution to the scholarly discussion on customer-centric IS [4, 28, 33, 50], by providing a model-based guideline on how to design customer-centric M-Commerce shop. The model also provides innovative insights into crafting a holistic corporate M-Commerce presence based on a company's existing ECommerce to enable a resilient market presence for the growing change from desktop-based shopping to mobile shopping [11]. The multiple expert interview rounds, as well as focus group interviews, helped to shape the final model output and generate design knowledge in the M-Commerce context. The model focuses on the design of an M-Commerce presence but contains different aspects that are also important for a successful E-Commerce presence (EA4, EI1, FG2). Because of the differences between the two areas, for example, the display size or the different data transfer time via mobile networks, we focus on a model, especially for M-Commerce, and exclude the view of E-Commerce generally to support companies by developing their mobile shopping environment. The use of mobile devices enables new services in the field of shopping apps and can create new competitive advantages [46] (EI1). However, interviewees stated that the development of an app is usually not worthwhile or is not considered due to a lack of human capital and high costs (I1–I3, I8, I10, I12). Nevertheless, a switch to mobile applications appears inevitable (FG2). In this respect, incumbent companies - to maintain their market share - are forced by new market entrants to develop new technologies like intelligent chatbots for shopping support based on generative artificial intelligence (genAI) or the device integrated sensors (EI1, FG2). However, it is important to analyze the spillover effects for customers of innovative services in mobile shopping that are not included in normal desktop-based shopping to prevent damage to the customer relationship. Our model illuminates the three service components where a company can include new services to support customers and capture value. Integration of the newest digital technologies like genAI-powered chatbots in those areas may cause reputation loss due to overconfidence in the output of text-based services since the output is not always accurate [49]. Here decision support models [28] may help to reshape the AI-customer interplay [22] in the context of mobile retailing.

Our model for customer-centric M-Commerce design provides online retailers with a foundation for strategic and operational decisions. It is a scientific starting point for creating and improving a mobile web shop. It serves to provide an overview of the aspects that need to be considered when operating M-Commerce. This provides the opportunity to improve the customer experience efficiently and thus increase product sales. In addition, the artifact can provide an argumentation baseline for necessary steps to the strategic management of the respective company. As a result, recommendable approaches and the associated correlations can be clarified and supported against the background of potential investments. The structured guidelines are also intended to relieve the burden on the human resources involved in designing a mobile online shop.

Based on our DSR procedure according to Kuechler and Vaishnavi [29], we developed an artifact in the instance of a model. This is specifically generated towards the M-Commerce domain but can be generalized. We used customer focus theory and user-centric IS as foundational groundwork upon which we developed the requirements and principles. The study contributes to the theoretical understanding by delineating the requirements and principles involved in designing an information system (e.g., mobile systems) that is subject to constant change and improvement. Our model bridges the gap in existing research and offers valuable guidance for crafting such solutions. Yet, our study primarily focuses on conceptualizing a model comprising distinct aspects. The practical application of each aspect warrants further investigation, particularly within a suitable M-Commerce testing and validation environment for initial implementation. Moving forward, we encourage future research to construct a framework for real-world application settings for each aspect of our model, followed by empirical validation. This approach will bolster the validity of the conceptual model and ensure its effectiveness in actual M-Commerce scenarios.

6 Conclusion

The integration of smartphones and the widespread use of mobile applications have fueled the global growth of M-Commerce, generating economic value while also introducing new challenges. By leveraging existing practical insights and theoretical research our model provides a structured overview of the factors that online retailers need to consider to design their mobile solutions around the customer needs. Employing DSR methodology, using the synthesis of a structured literature review and multiple rounds of expert interviews as our knowledge base, we construct a set of design requirements. The outlined design principles encompass aspects such as the presentation of content, handling of the interface, integration of services, and perception by customers of the mobile solution. Each of these addresses specific challenges and opportunities inherent in the M-Commerce environment, aiming to enhance customer focus and experience. Furthermore, the design principles distilled from the requirements offer practical guidelines for M-Commerce developers and retailers to follow. From the presentation of content to the handling of the interface, integration of services, and perception by customers, these principles underscore the importance of customer-centric design and seamless functionality across different devices and channels. Our study has limitations, firstly because the results of the interviews relate exclusively to German E-Commerce companies. Secondly, the practical influence on the research results is limited by a small number of interviews and evaluation participants but the theoretical foundation is based on high-ranked literature to ensure a qualitative result. Further points need to be analyzed in depth in the individual aspects and their effect on the customers; only then can we develop a complete model. By organizing insights into a model, businesses and developers gain structured guidance on how to approach the design of a customer-centric M-Commerce solution. The model provides a systematic framework that helps stakeholders understand the key elements and considerations involved in creating an effective mobile commerce solution.

Acknowledgement. This work has been developed in the project Hyko and is partly funded by the Bavarian Ministry of Economic Affairs, Regional Development and Energy enabled by the European Regional Development Fund (ERDF) under grant number 1.2-StMWK-F.4-UFR-002. The authors are responsible for the content of this publication.

References

1. Adepu, S., Adler, R.F.: A comparison of performance and preference on mobile devices vs. desktop computers. In: 2016 IEEE 7th Annual Ubiquitous Computing, Electronics & Mobile Communication Conference (UEMCON), pp. 1–7 (2016)
2. Ahmad, Z., Ibrahim, R.: Mobile commerce (m-commerce) interface design: a review of literature. J. Comput. Eng **19**, 66–70 (2017)
3. Al-Nabhani, K., Wilson, A., McLean, G.: Examining consumers' continuous usage of multichannel retailers' mobile applications. Psychol. Mark. **39**(1), 168–195 (2022)
4. Albert, T.C., Goes, P.B., Gupta, A.: Gist: a model for design and management of content and interactivity of customer-centric web sites. MIS Q. 161–182 (2004)
5. Baek, T.H., Yoo, C.Y.: Branded app usability: conceptualization, measurement, and prediction of consumer loyalty. J. Advert. **47**(1), 70–82 (2018)
6. Balka, E.: Broadening discussion about participatory design: a reply to kyng. Scand. J. Inf. Syst. **22**(1), 7 (2010)
7. Bell, E., Bryman, A., Harley, B.: Business Research Methods. Oxford University Press, Glasgow (2022)
8. Brocke, J.V., Simons, A., Niehaves, B., Niehaves, B., Reimer, K., Plattfaut, R., Cleven, A.: Reconstructing the giant: on the importance of rigour in documenting the literature search process. In: ECIS 2009 Proceedings, pp. 2206–2217. Verona (2009)
9. Choi, J., Lee, H.J., Kim, Y.C.: The influence of social presence on customer intention to reuse online recommender systems: the roles of personalization and product type. Int. J. Electron. Commer. **16**(1), 129–154 (2011)
10. Coltman, T.: Why build a customer relationship management capability? J. Strateg. Inf. Syst. **16**(3), 301–320 (2007)
11. Costa, J., Castro, R.: Smes must go online—e-commerce as an escape hatch for resilience and survivability. J. Theor. Appl. Electron. Commer. Res. **16**(7), 3043–3062 (2021)
12. Frey, R.M., Xu, R., Ammendola, C., Moling, O., Giglio, G., Ilic, A.: Mobile recommendations based on interest prediction from consumer's installed apps–insights from a large-scale field study. Inf. Syst. **71**, 152–163 (2017)
13. Furner, C.P., Zinko, R.A.: The influence of information overload on the development of trust and purchase intention based on online product reviews in a mobile vs. web environment: an empirical investigation. EM **27**, 211–224 (2017)
14. Heinze, J., Matt, C.: Reducing the service deficit in m-commerce: how servicetechnology fit can support digital sales of complex products. Int. J. Electron. Commer. **22**(3), 386–418 (2018)
15. Hevner, A.R., March, S.T., Park, J., Ram, S., Ram, S.: Research essay design science in information. MIS Q. **28**(1), 75–105 (2004)

16. Ho, S.Y.: The effects of location personalization on individuals' intention to use mobile services. Decis. Support Syst. **53**(4), 802–812 (2012)

17. Hoehle, H., Aloysius, J.A., Goodarzi, S., Venkatesh, V.: A nomological network of customers' privacy perceptions: linking artifact design to shopping efficiency. Eur. J. Inf. Syst. **28**(1), 91–113 (2019)

18. Hoehle, H., Venkatesh, V.: Mobile application usability. MIS Q. **39**(2), 435–472 (2015)

19. Hong, W., Tam, K.Y., Yim, C.K.B.: E-service environment: impacts of web interface characteristics on consumers' online shopping behavior. In: E-Service: New Directions in Theory and Practice, pp. 108–128. Routledge (2016)

20. Huang, G.H., Korfiatis, N., Chang, C.T.: Mobile shopping cart abandonment: the roles of conflicts, ambivalence, and hesitation. J. Bus. Res. **85**, 165–174 (2018)

21. Huang, L., Lu, X., Ba, S.: An empirical study of the cross-channel effects between web and mobile shopping channels. Inf. Manag. **53**(2), 265–278 (2016)

22. Huang, M.H., Rust, R.T.: Express: the caring machine: feeling AI for customer care. J. Mark. 00222429231224748 (2023)

23. Hubert, M., Blut, M., Brock, C., Backhaus, C., Eberhardt, T.: Acceptance of smartphone-based mobile shopping: mobile benefits, customer characteristics, perceived risks, and the impact of application context. Psychol. Mark. **34**(2), 175–194 (2017)

24. James, T.L., Ziegelmayer, J.L., Schuler Scott, A., Fox, G.: A multiple-motive heuristic-systematic model for examining how users process android data and service access notifications. ACM SIGMIS Datab. DATABASE Adv. Inf. Syst. **52**(1), 91–122 (2021)

25. Karn, A.L., et al.: Customer centric hybrid recommendation system for e-commerce applications by integrating hybrid sentiment analysis. Electron. Commer. Res. **23**(1), 279–314 (2023)

26. Keith, M.J., Babb, J.S., Lowry, P.B., Furner, C.P., Abdullat, A.: The role of mobilecomputing self-efficacy in consumer information disclosure. Inf. Syst. J. **25**(6), 637–667 (2015)

27. Khansa, L., Zobel, C.W., Goicochea, G.: Creating a taxonomy for mobile commerce innovations using social network and cluster analyses. Int. J. Electron. Commer. **16**(4), 19–52 (2012)

28. Kreuzer, T., Röglinger, M., Rupprecht, L.: Customer-centric prioritization of process improvement projects. Decis. Support Syst. **133**, 113286 (2020)

29. Kuechler, W., Vaishnavi, V.: A framework for theory development in design science research: multiple perspectives. J. Assoc. Inf. Syst. **13**(6), 3 (2012)

30. Kyng, M.: Bridging the gap between politics and techniques: on the next practices of participatory design. SJIS **22**(1), 5 (2010)

31. Lee, D., Gopal, A., Park, S.H.: Different but equal? a field experiment on the impact of recommendation systems on mobile and personal computer channels in retail. Inf. Syst. Res. **31**(3), 892–912 (2020)

32. Li, M., Tan, C.H., Teo, H.H., Wei, K.K.: Effects of product learning aids on the breadth and depth of recall. Decis. Support Syst. **53**(4), 793–801 (2012)

33. Liang, T.P., Tanniru, M.: Customer-centric information systems. J. Manag. Inf. Syst. **23**(3), 9–15 (2006)

34. Liu, B., Pavlou, P.A., Cheng, X.: Achieving a balance between privacy protection and data collection: a field experimental examination of a theory-driven information technology solution. Inf. Syst. Res. **33**(1), 203–223 (2022)

35. Lohan, G., Conboy, K., Lang, M.: Examining customer focus in it project management: findings from irish and norwegian case studies. Scand. J. Inf. Syst. **23**(2), 2 (2011)

36. Lucas, G.A., Lunardi, G.L., Dolci, D.B.: From e-commerce to m-commerce: an analysis of the user's experience with different access platforms. Electron. Commer. Res. Appl. **58**, 101240 (2023)

37. Mayring, P.: Qualitative inhaltsanalyse: Grundlagen und techniken. Dt. StudienVerlag (1997)
38. McLean, G., Al-Nabhani, K., Marriott, H.: 'regrettable-escapism' the negative effects of mobile app use: a retail perspective. Psychol. Mark. **39**(1), 150–167 (2022)
39. McLean, G., Al-Nabhani, K., Wilson, A.: Developing a mobile applications customer experience model (mace)-implications for retailers. J. Bus. Res. **85**, 325–336 (2018)
40. Omonedo, P., Bocij, P.: E-commerce versus m-commerce: where is the dividing line. Int. J. Social Behav. Educ. Bus. Ind. Eng. **8**(11), 3610–3615 (2014)
41. Ono, A., Nakamura, A., Okuno, A., Sumikawa, M.: Consumer motivations in browsing online stores with mobile devices. Int. J. Electron. Commer. **16**(4), 153–178 (2012)
42. Racat, M., Plotkina, D.: Sensory-enabling technology in m-commerce: the effect of haptic stimulation on consumer purchasing behavior. Int. J. Electron. Commer. **27**(3), 354–384 (2023)
43. Sharma, S., Gutiérrez, J.A.: An evaluation framework for viable business models for m-commerce in the information technology sector. EM **20**, 33–52 (2010)
44. Shi, S.W., Kalyanam, K.: Touchable apps: exploring the usage of touch features and their impact on engagement. J. Interact. Mark. **44**(1), 43–59 (2018)
45. Sonnenberg, C., vom Brocke, J.: Evaluations in the science of the artificial – reconsidering the build-evaluate pattern in design science research. In: Peffers, K., Rothenberger, M., Kuechler, B. (eds.) DESRIST 2012. LNCS, vol. 7286, pp. 381–397. Springer, Heidelberg (2012). https://doi.org/10.1007/978-3-642-29863-9_28
46. Stocchi, L., Pourazad, N., Michaelidou, N., Tanusondjaja, A., Harrigan, P.: Marketing research on mobile apps: past, present and future. J. Acad. Mark. Sci. 1–31 (2021)
47. Tandel, S., Jamadar, A.: Impact of progressive web apps on web app development. Int. J. Innov. Res. Sci. Eng. Technol. **7**(9), 9439–9444 (2018)
48. Thongpapanl, N., Ashraf, A.R., Lapa, L., Venkatesh, V.: Differential effects of customers' regulatory fit on trust, perceived value, and m-commerce use among developing and developed countries. J. Int. Mark. **26**(3), 22–44 (2018)
49. Tomitza, C., Myriam, S., Straub, L., Winkelmann, A.: What is the minimum to trust AI?—a requirement analysis for (generative) AI-based texts. In: Wirtschaftsinformatik 2023 Proceedings, vol. 35 (2023)
50. Wagner, C., Majchrzak, A.: Enabling customer-centricity using wikis and the wiki way. J. Manag. Inf. Syst. **23**(3), 17–43 (2006)
51. Wagner, G., Schramm-Klein, H., Steinmann, S.: Online retailing across e-channels and e-channel touchpoints: empirical studies of consumer behavior in the multichannel e-commerce environment. J. Bus. Res. **107**, 256–270 (2020)
52. Wang, N., Shen, X.L., Sun, Y.: Transition of electronic word-of-mouth services from web to mobile context: a trust transfer perspective. Decis. Support Syst. **54**(3), 1394–1403 (2013)
53. Wang, R.J.H., Malthouse, E.C., Krishnamurthi, L.: On the go: how mobile shopping affects customer purchase behavior. J. Retail. **91**(2), 217–234 (2015)
54. Wang, Y.S., Liao, Y.W.: The conceptualization and measurement of m-commerce user satisfaction. Comput. Hum. Behav. **23**(1), 381–398 (2007)
55. Wen, C., Wang, N., Fang, J., Huang, M.: An integrated model of continued mcommerce applications usage. J. Comput. Inf. Syst. **63**(3), 632–647 (2023)
56. Xu, K., Chan, J., Ghose, A., Han, S.P.: Battle of the channels: the impact of tablets on digital commerce. Manag. Sci. **63**(5), 1469–1492 (2017)
57. Yang, S., Xiong, G.: Try it on! contingency effects of virtual fitting rooms. J. Manag. Inf. Syst. **36**(3), 789–822 (2019)

58. Zhang, K., Wang, J., Zhang, J., Wang, Y., Zeng, Y.: Exploring the impact of location-based augmented reality on tourists' spatial behavior, experience, and intention through a field experiment. Tour. Manag. **102**, 104886 (2024)
59. Zhou, T., Lu, Y., Wang, B.: Examining online consumers' initial trust building from an elaboration likelihood model perspective. Inf. Syst. Front. **18**, 265–275 (2016)

Author Index

M. Mandviwalla et al. (Eds.): DESRIST 2024, LNCS 14621, pp. 455–456, 2024.
https://doi.org/10.1007/978-3-031-61175-9

Printed in the United States
by Baker & Taylor Publisher Services